CW01574726

KEVIN GRANT

RENEGADE WESTERNS SIGNATURE EDITION

CLARK HODGKISS

RENEGADE WESTERNS
MOVIES THAT SHOT DOWN FRONTIER MYTHS

First edition published by FAB Press, June 2018

FAB Press Ltd.
2 Farleigh
Ramsden Road
Godalming
Surrey
GU7 1QE
England, U.K.

www.fabpress.com

Text copyright © 2018 Kevin Grant and Clark Hodgkiss.
Foreword copyright © 2018 Edward Buscombe.
The moral rights of the authors have been asserted.

Layout and Design by Harvey Fenton,
with thanks to Francis Brewster for production assistance.

This Volume copyright © FAB Press Ltd, 2018.

World Rights Reserved.

No part of this book may be reproduced or transmitted in any form or by any means, electronic or mechanical, including photocopying, recording, or by any information storage and retrieval system, without the prior written permission of the Publisher.

Copyright of illustrations reproduced in these pages is the property of the production or distribution companies concerned. These illustrations are reproduced here in the spirit of publicity, and whilst every effort has been made to trace the copyright owners, the authors and publishers apologise for any omissions and will undertake to make any appropriate changes in future editions of this book if necessary.
Acknowledgements are due to the following companies:
ABC Pictures Corporation, Aglaia Cinematografica, ALCO Productions, Allied Artists, Alta-Light, American Releasing Corporation, Associated Film Releasing Corporation, Atlantida Films S.A., Avco-Embassy, Bellotti Film, BFI, Bryna Company, Carousel Productions, Cedic, Cesareo Gonzalez S.A., Chevron, Cinecom Corporation, Cinema Center Films, Cinerama Releasing (UK) Ltd., Columbia Pictures, Columbia-Warner Distributors, Criterion Film Distribution, Cross City Films, C.V. Whitney Pictures, CWF, DEAR International, Entertainment Film Distributors, Europa Corp., Evenstar Films, Film4, Filmax, First Artists, Globe Enterprises, Gold Film, Gramercy Pictures, Hanway Films, HBO Films, Hecht-Lancaster, HOWCO, ICA Projects, Jack H. Harris Enterprises, Jaffilms, Inc., Lea Productions, Lionsgate, Loew's Inc., Majestic Films International, Malpaso Company, Manson Distributing Corporation, Medusa Distribuzione, Mercurio Films S.A., Metro-Goldwyn-Mayer, Miramax Films, The Mirisch Corporation, Motion Picture Investors, Mundial Films S.A., National General Pictures, National Student Film Corporation, New Zealand Film Commission, Orion Pictures Corporation, Pando Company, Pandora Film, Paramount, Partisan Productions, Pathé America, Pax Enterprises, PiC Distribuzione, Rachel Gardner Films, Regia Films, Republic Pictures, Ring Film Verleih, RKO Radio Films, Saban Films, Scimitar Films, Screen Guild Productions, See Saw Films, Seven Arts Productions, Stanley Kramer Productions, Suevia Films, TIG Productions, Titanus Distribuzione, Twentieth Century-Fox, United Artists, Universal, Warner Bros., Waypoint Entertainment, The Weinstein Company, YLK Distribution.

Front cover illustration: Cover design adapted from the original US one-sheet poster for **The Outlaw Josey Wales**.

Back cover illustrations, top, left to right: **The Searchers**, **The Wild Bunch**, **The Hateful Eight**.

Frontispiece illustration: Adapted from the original Italian theatrical release poster for **Hud**.

A CIP catalogue record for this book is available from the British Library.

hardcover:
ISBN 978 1 903254 92 9

paperback:
ISBN 978 1 903254 93 6

Printed in India

A FAB PRESS PUBLICATION

Renegade Westerns

Movies That Shot Down Frontier Myths

Kevin Grant & Clark Hodgkiss

Acknowledgements

A word from the authors

We would like to thank Edward Buscombe, Bo Hopkins and L.Q. Jones for taking the time and trouble to contribute.

We are grateful to Ray Ramos, Rob Word and Tom Betts for helping to arrange the interviews.

Simon Gelten and Phil Hardcastle provided useful advice and encouragement in the early stages.

Thanks also to Julian Grainger, Kevin Lyons, Alex Marlow-Mann and Matt Blake, for combined moral support, and Harvey Fenton, for his sound judgement and Ford-like mastery of the visual medium.

Dedications

Kevin Grant's dedication

For my mother, Diana, and for Lucy, Elliott and Melody, back at the ranch.

Clark Hodgkiss's dedication

For my family for their unwavering support and for Leon, number one son and dearest friend.

Contents

Artwork adapted from a Polish poster for *Tell Them Willie Boy Is Here*.

Foreword by Edward Buscombe

Looked at from the viewpoint of the needs of the film industry, the western was for many years almost the perfect product. At a time when Hollywood made most of its money from its domestic market, the western had a dependable appeal, offering to Americans a largely flattering portrait of their history and the myths which sustained their society. The western format was immediately recognisable; audiences needed little in the way of explanation for the character types and situations which the genre set in motion. It quickly built up a reservoir of actors, extras and stuntmen who could embody the western style, plus a repertoire of sets and costumes, and within easy reach of Los Angeles were dozens of suitable locations and landscapes. Most importantly, there was a dependable pool of writers, publishing mostly in pulp magazines and in the more upmarket slicks, who churned out formulaic narratives in large numbers. American cinema spent the early years of the twentieth century sorting out exactly which parts of the corpus of western history and culture were most usable in the movies, after which the production line could be relied upon to deliver what the public expected.

And yet, from the beginning, there were always films which went against the grain. For example, most of the early film comedians (notably Chaplin, Keaton, Laurel and Hardy) made at least one film set in the West in which the main joke was the absence of the supposedly essential and manly grit and courage required in a western hero.

Not only were there these "anti-westerns"; it's essential to the working of the industrial model which Hollywood pursued that each example of the product must be at once like all the others (delivering the same satisfactions to the audience), and yet different. Those who don't like westerns are prone to remark that if you've seen one, you've seen 'em all. But this simply cannot be true. All genres work on the principle of combining similarity and difference. Each film, no matter how much it may seem stereotyped, has to offer something fresh to the audience. Hollywood did not grow rich by expecting its patrons to see the same film over and over again (as later breeds of cinephiles liked to do). People demanded novelty equally with familiarity: the same character (westerns specialised right from the start with series based on a single character, such as Broncho Billy or Cheyenne Harry) in a different setting, or a different character in a familiar setting.

At the same time as being remarkably well adapted to producing an endless series of variations on a dependably similar format, the western proved in later years capable of shifts not merely in details but in the fundamental paradigms. Not only was the development of the western determined by the economic imperative of endless similarity and difference, as a means of pleasing the audience; the genre also showed itself capable of responding to shifts in the society which engendered it and which it served. The western, like other forms of cinema, was not just an industrial product; it was also a social one. As the authors of this volume demonstrate, from the Fifties film-makers began to reconfigure the character of the hero. Whereas before he had been the apotheosis of strong, silent manhood, confident of his role and his ability to discharge his duties, now the hero appeared increasingly troubled, full of doubt, and suspicious of the society which he served. This society was in turn presented as frequently corrupt and venal. At the same time, though to a lesser extent, the western's traditional conception of the role of non-whites and of women was subjected to revaluation.

above: Henry Fonda (right) and Leigh Whipper in **The Ox-Bow Incident**.

from left: Ben Johnson, Warren Oates, William Holden and Ernest Borgnine in **The Wild Bunch**.

This process has generally been known as revisionism. It may be said to have achieved its most developed form in westerns such as *The Wild Bunch*, in which the anti-heroes eventually discover a kind of honour among thieves, but one which offers only nihilistic self-sacrifice, while the society which they reject has virtually no redeeming features whatsoever.

This evolution of the traditional western is examined by the authors of this book in a series of extremely perceptive and stylishly written short essays dealing with nearly a hundred significant films produced over the past half-century. They carefully trace the many shifts in the genre during its artistically most productive period. These shifts are then subtly related to changes in the wider society. Reading films as an expression of their times is always a risky thing to do, since it is all too easy to make glib connections which can be neither proved nor disproved. But the present authors are careful not to overstate their case. The connections they make are both intelligent and convincing.

This is an enjoyable book to read. Half-forgotten films are brought to life with fresh insights, and cumulatively the book builds into a history of the ways in which the western film, while managing to remain still recognisable as the genre first formed a hundred years ago, mutated into a form capable of adapting to the social and cultural shifts of the wider society.

Renegade Westerns is a book that can be dipped into, perhaps in advance of viewing a specific film, but also read progressively as an account of Hollywood's greatest genre. The views of individual films are sometimes provocative, but offer persuasive commentaries, often accompanied with helpful details of the film's process of production. If the western film itself appears now a threatened species, studies of this rich and varied form are clearly in a healthy state.

~ Edward Buscombe is the editor of The BFI Companion to the Western. *His books as author include* Injuns! Native Americans in the Movies *and* Cinema Today.

Jeffrey Hunter and Natalie Wood in **The Searchers**.

Introduction

One of the earliest, if not the first, film genres to firmly take root, the western has demonstrated considerable flexibility and diversity over the course of its existence. Yet still, to a considerable extent, it is regarded as a monolithic form, its creed, like the mindset of its characters, somehow fixed – as unyielding to outside influences and pressures as the primitive landscape against which its quasi-mythical stories unfold.

The purpose of this book is to refute this, to show that the western never has been solely a haven for hidebound traditionalists preaching moral absolutism or sanctifying westward expansion. It is a malleable form that has moved with the times, adapting to audience moods and social pressures, accommodating artists of all sensibilities and political persuasions. For Richard Slotkin, "The mythic space of the genre should be thought of as a field for ideological play which is attractive precisely because a wide range of beliefs and agendas can be entertained there."[1] That the western has served as a tool for forging and reinforcing a sense of national identity among Americans, as well as projecting that vision abroad, is inarguable; the immense popularity of *The Iron Horse* (1924), *The Plainsman* (1936) and other early epics saw patriotism seared into the genre's flanks like a brand. Just as its archetypes and iconography have been deployed to support the dominant ideology, however, so they have been ranged against it. Many westerns, with all the trappings in place, have pushed against the confines of jingoistic pride that once limited – at least in theory – the genre's freedom of expression. By challenging the assumptions behind American exceptionalism and denying the legitimacy of Manifest Destiny, they have highlighted the contradictions in the national self-image that have always attended fictional stories and popular histories of the frontier.[2] (In European-made westerns, of course, the genre was shorn of its strictly American character and reabsorbed into the wider body of mythic narratives from which it had sprung in the first place.)

David Lusted is correct to point out that, to meet the demands of a genre, "All westerns must to some extent revise."[3] But the process of chipping away at the monolith, of deflating the air of triumphalism, began in earnest in the genre's middle years. "After 1950," writes Michael Coyne, "the western's principal theme veered from the glory of the pioneer achievement to its awful cost... A nation confronted with new complexities at all levels of postwar society could not find easy reassurance in celebratory narratives of the prewar type."[4] While plenty of traditional westerns continued to be produced – particularly for television, where they practically monopolised the schedules – a significant proportion turned a sharply critical eye on the historical events and personages that made up the majority of plots and to this day profoundly influence attitudes about America. This was an unexpected development in more ways than one. As John H. Lenihan points out: "In a decade disparaged for its unquestioning complacency regarding social problems, it is striking that a genre designed for mass appeal exhibited such a critical perspective."[5]

Disparate film-makers realised that audiences were thirsting for adult stories and rounded characters; they also recognised the western's capacity, largely untapped at that point, to accommodate alternative viewpoints – indeed, to provide a form of camouflage, given what Slotkin calls its "identification with the heroic fable of American progress". The western became a vehicle for examining the consequences of actions it had previously depicted so blithely. The West was not won cleanly, nor was it virgin land. The motives of the conquerors were not necessarily pure, and had disastrous consequences for the area's existing inhabitants. Violence, even when unavoidable, was shown to have a corrupting effect on its perpetrators and, by extension, on the society that condoned and benefited from it. At the same time, the genre became what Coyne terms "a vital medium for reflecting and articulating crucial issues of modern American society",[6] from Cold War anxiety to political pressure for the promotion of civil rights – both Native American and African American – as well as recognition of the historical wrongs committed against racial others. The pacification of the frontier assumed a far from glorious impression once the perspective was altered to represent the losers in the settlement, rather than the winners. In this light, the old biases and stereotypes that had nourished the western for so long seemed, to many, both unsupportable and unpalatable.

The rate of revisionism accelerated exponentially in the Sixties and Seventies, even as commercial interest in the genre declined. Indeed, these developments were complementary; for the western to survive in a sceptical age, it was practically forced to adapt. A schism developed: John Wayne and the old guard, trotting out broadly traditional westerns such as *The War Wagon* (1967) and *The Good Guys and the Bad Guys* (1969), offset by iconoclasts and antiheroes who disowned the folklore and falsehoods that, in their opinion, had given the nation a distorted image of its past. This was in tandem with divisions in society over social and political issues. The most contentious of these, of course, was the Vietnam War, the

repercussions of which can be perceived in the revival of the cavalry-Indian plot as an allegorical framework. Other westerns, channelling popular discontent, particularly among the young, advocated dropping out of mainstream society and living on the margins, or retreating to nature. The latter resumed its traditional association with indigenous peoples, whose culture now became idealised, elevated above that of modern America; accordingly, screen Indians radiated what the Cherokee actor Wes Studi wryly called "the connected-to-the-earth, mystical-stewards-of-nature thing".[7]

The radical notion of renouncing frontier mythology and rejecting the status quo was augmented by an enhanced awareness of physical realism, in everything from costumes to sets, and an overhaul of the depiction of violence – a response in large part to the turbulence of the times, which so distressed the White House that in 1968 President Johnson established a National Commission on the Causes and Prevention of Violence. (Back in Hollywood, lessons were also learnt from the box-office killings made by the more wantonly sadistic Italian westerns.) Where violence had always been integral to the western and, of course, inseparable from the actual settling of the West, film-makers from Sam Peckinpah to Clint Eastwood issued explicit reminders of just what a bloody, ghastly business it was – especially after the relaxation and eventual abandonment of the Production Code – and how America remains in its thrall.

"I learnt something that day. Apache women cried over their sons. Apache men had a sense of fair play."

There had been sympathetic or at least balanced portrayals of Native Americans as early as the silent period.[8] Helen Hunt Jackson's hugely popular 1884 novel, *Ramona*, with its pro-Indian subtext, had been filmed four times by the mid-Thirties, and John Ford exercised his liberal principles with his considered adaptation of *Fort Apache* (1948), the film that, according to J. Hoberman, "revised the western with notions of racial tolerance"[9]. It wasn't until the Fifties, however, in the wake of moral lessons learnt in the Second World War and amid a wider effort by Hollywood to address racial inequality, that a sustained effort was made to rescue 'savages' from perpetual ignominy. In *Broken Arrow*, *Devil's Doorway* (both 1950), *The Battle at Apache Pass* (1952), *Sitting Bull* (1954), *White Feather* (1955) and several others, Indians were not simply bloodthirsty demons; they were rational people with peaceful intentions and legitimate grievances, people with whom Anglo-Americans could do business. (This did not extend to recalcitrant 'hostiles' – the 'bad' Indians juxtaposed against the 'good' ones even in many otherwise progressive westerns.)

These were films marked by "[a] liberalism that favours negotiation, co-existence and mutual respect… tolerance and integration".[10] Moreover, white attitudes and actions were just as culpable in the conflict as the 'backwardness' of the Indians. And while the narrative prerequisite of virulent individuals – maverick military officers, avaricious prospectors or land grabbers, crooked agents and traders – tended to deflect criticism away from government policies or national preconceptions, this remained implicit: racism is endemic in these films, and not just among the military (see social attitudes towards miscegenation, below); promises over land rights are routinely reneged upon; treaties habitually broken, all by representatives of Washington's will.

Progressivism had its limits, however. For many critics writing subsequently, the films' good efforts in depicting Indians as human beings rather than wild beasts are undermined by their advocacy of the reservation system, usually framed as the only viable

top: from left: Jeff Chandler, Debra Paget and James Stewart in **Broken Arrow**.

alternative to extinction (Ulysses S. Grant famously espoused this view in the White House), and the broader policy of assimilation. (Another bugbear was the casting of white actors in virtually every sympathetic Indian role, while Native performers generally played villains.) 'Good' Indians only merit that status if they are willing to compromise their racial identities, to adopt the ways of the white man, a theme broached in *Broken Arrow*, *Apache* (1954), *Walk the Proud Land* (1956) and many others. In other words, Hollywood could afford to be high-minded towards an enemy that had already been defeated, absorbed into a system they ultimately had little option other than to accept, preferably with the stoicism befitting the 'noble savage' stereotype.

Miscegenation, the most controversial issue in Indian westerns, received mixed treatment in revisionist films. While some – *Broken Arrow* conspicuously – adhered to convention, cutting short relationships between white men and Indian maidens (it was usually that way round) by killing off the women, others condemned the underlying social attitudes, in particular the stigma attached to white females exposed to Indian captivity: *The Searchers* (1956), *Trooper Hook* (1957), *The Tin Star* (1957), *Two Rode Together* (1961) and *The Stalking Moon* (1968). (This criticism was in no way redundant: as late as 1968, as many as 72 per cent of Americans in a Gallup poll remained opposed to interracial marriage.) The cautious optimism of the early pro-Indian films faded as the Fifties drew to a close, and the promise of racial harmony in these western fictions diminished; the genre projected instead what Angela Aleiss calls "a discord of two incompatible cultures",[11] mirroring, deliberately or otherwise, the increasingly bitter struggle over civil rights in the nation at large.

If we follow Douglas Pye's assertion that, "The western, and particularly the western involving Indians, has always been in some sense 'about' imperialism," this leads naturally – via a detour into revolution-racked Mexico, with American 'advisers' intervening among insurgents and despots – to Indian-themed films of the counterculture period. (As Steve Neale has written, there is a danger, if postwar Indian films are really 'about' the oppression of other races, that Indians themselves become reduced, in critical discussions, to the status of ciphers, as if their own concerns are not as pressing or relevant as, say, those of African-Americans, in liberal films from the civil rights era, or Vietnamese peasants.[12]) The likes of *Tell Them Willie Boy Is Here* (1969), *Little Big Man*, *Soldier Blue*, *A Man Called Horse* (all 1970) and *Billy Jack* (1971) no doubt resonated with opponents of US involvement in Vietnam. At the same time, they reflected the admiration felt by young Americans for indigenous cultures as a 'pure' alternative to what many saw as the materialistic, morally bankrupt mainstream.[13] "The view of the Indian in the revisionist western," writes Michael Valdez Moses, "is often less an image of the historical Native American of the 19th century than of the countercultural rebel of the Sixties who drops out of white bourgeois society in order to find his roots, get his head together, and live free."[14]

As elsewhere in popular cinema, the mood in these westerns was firmly anti-establishment. Assimilationism was a tarnished notion in this context. As John H. Lenihan puts it, by the late Sixties, "The integrationist concept [of *Broken Arrow* et al] is no longer attractive given the degeneracy of white society."[15] This line of thinking was picked up by 1990's *Dances with Wolves*, in many ways an anachronistic work, which nevertheless captured the popular mood to such an extent that it earned the genre its first Oscar for Best Picture since *Cimarron* in 1931.[16] Kevin Costner's film self-consciously projected the concerns espoused by his liberal forebears, as well as those of Native American interest groups and environmentalists. It also abided by the unwritten rule that Indian stories, if they are to reach the widest possible audience, are best told by a sympathetic white interpreter.

When the western grappled with racial tensions of a different nature by positioning black characters in prominent narrative roles, it demonstrated what George Lipsitz calls "genre anxiety"[17], disputing the hegemony of white protagonists in popular histories and reconstructions of the period. (An earlier cycle of all-black westerns, part of the 'race films' phenomenon that ran from the Teens to the Forties, had tried something similar, but was produced exclusively for African-American audiences.[18]) Belatedly acknowledging the African-American presence in the Old West, where an estimated one in four working cowboys was black, via Ford's landmark *Sergeant Rutledge* (1960), Hollywood released a number of films offering major parts to black actors such as Sidney Poitier, Sammy Davis Jr. and Jim Brown. In some cases – *Rio Conchos* (1964), *Duel at Diablo*, *The Professionals* (both 1966), featuring *Rutledge* star Woody Strode – the characters' colour was more or less irrelevant. Of course, against a backdrop of devastating race riots, it was inevitable there was at least a degree of racial antagonism in Sixties westerns – *Invitation to a Gunfighter* (1964), *Major Dundee* (1965), the sardonic *The Scalphunters* (1968). It would have been strange, perhaps even irresponsible, had the issue been ignored. This only became a dominant theme, however, in films from the blaxploitation era. Of these, Poitier's *Buck and the Preacher* (1972) was the most assured; *The Legend of Nigger Charley* (1972) and *The Soul of Nigger Charley* (1973) the most forthright, foreshadowing *Django Unchained* (2012) in their focus on aggressively self-determined, itinerant former slaves turned racial avengers. While the first *Nigger Charley* achieved commercial success, it was not enough to be considered a breakthrough, and none of these films secured crossover critical support. (The only 'black' western to buck this trend was Mel Brooks' brilliant burlesque *Blazing Saddles* in 1974. The casting of Cleavon Little as a mock-sheriff served to ridicule racist attitudes while subverting the reputation of frontier heroes – and that of the blaxploitation variant – for unadulterated masculinity.) Despite occasional efforts to reinsert African-Americans into the history books – *Glory* (1989), *Posse* (1993) – the black western as a subset in its own right remains, regrettably, a footnote in genre history.

"Never seen a woman who was more of a man. She thinks like one, acts like one, and sometimes makes me feel like I'm not."

The liberalisation of attitudes towards Native Americans in the Fifties was not matched by an enhancement in the status of women, although there were significant advances. *Westward the Women* (1951), albeit anchored by a rugged male protagonist, gave females a physical presence beyond the decorative or perfunctory. The female leads in *Cattle Queen* (1951), *Rancho Notorious* (1952), *Johnny Guitar* (1954), *The Maverick Queen* (1956) and *Forty Guns* (1957) were powerful, even emasculating figures. As Nicholas Christopher has written of the femmes fatales of film noir, "Their dress runs a tight gamut, always between the twin poles of sexuality and power".[19] Beginning with *The Furies* (1950), Barbara Stanwyck became a bona fide genre icon, launching a one-woman range war on chauvinistic opinions regarding 'ladylike' behaviour and the function of women in the genre. B-movie westerns such as *Two-Gun Lady* (1955), *Gunslinger* (1956) and *The Dalton Girls* (1957) proposed women in roles previously reserved for men, often to campy or titillating effect. There were a handful of biopics, *Calamity Jane* (1953) being the most famous, with Doris Day grasping the reins with characteristic gusto in the title role, alternating between masculine and feminine attire at will and proceeding more or less on *her* terms, not those of a man. In most cases, however, the push for gender equality was not sustained: "The woman [ultimately] relinquishes her desire to be active and independent, ceding power to the hero and accepting secondary status."[20]

With the exception of novelty items and star vehicles – Jane Fonda in *Cat Ballou* (1965), Doris Day in *The Ballad of Josie* (1967), *Hannie Caulder* (1971), with Raquel Welch – women were excluded from leading roles in later westerns, although the impact of the feminist movement can perhaps be gauged from the prevalence of proactive, self-reliant female characters in a chain of revisionist films, from the proud, unbowed prostitutes in *The Ballad of Cable Hogue*, *Monte Walsh* (both 1970), *Doc* and *McCabe & Mrs. Miller* (both 1971), to Verna Bloom's sexually autonomous rancher in *The Hired Hand* (1971). The trend for female-centred films enjoyed a minor resurgence in the Nineties and onwards, although *Bad Girls* (1994), a kind of *Young Guns* meets *Thelma and Louise*, the Sharon Stone vehicle *The Quick and the Dead* (1995), *Gang of Roses* (2003), cast with black urban music stars, and *Bandidas* (2006), with Salma Hayek and Penélope Cruz, were too busy mining the seam of western clichés to seize the genre for feminist ends. *The Ballad of Little Jo* (1993) came closer, denouncing gender inequality and negative stereotyping in the guise of a (fact-based) cross-dressing fantasy. Not uncoincidentally, it was the only one of these films written and directed by a woman, much as *Meek's Cutoff* (2011), an austere re-creation of historical events with a marked feminine bias, benefited from having a woman at the helm.

"That's right. I've killed women and children. I've killed just about everything that walks or crawled at one time or another."

And what of the white male protagonist? The postwar Hollywood western traced what R. Philip Loy refers to as "the descent of the hero".[21] Like his counterparts in film noir and melodrama, the westerner became a compromised figure, both in his own actions and attitudes – surely only villains were subject to such rages as consumed James Stewart in his Anthony Mann films, or displayed such pathologically vicious racism as John Wayne in *The Searchers* – and in his relations with a society that seemed increasingly unworthy of his efforts. As film became fascinated by psychoanalysis, even the supposedly uncomplicated and self-assured westerner came under scrutiny. He now openly voiced fears (*High Noon* [1952], *At Gunpoint* [1955], *The Fastest Gun Alive* [1956]) or became an object of fear himself (notably in the town-taming western: *Man with the Gun* [1955]; *Warlock* [1959]; *Lawman* [1971]; *High Plains Drifter* [1973]). He displayed neuroses (*Winchester '73* [1950], *Johnny Guitar*) and, on occasion, a psychotic

bent better suited to his antagonists. Douglas Pye, talking about the westerns of Anthony Mann, hit upon a central motif of the era: "The hero and villain [are] constructed as versions of each other… the hero has to confront and destroy these figures from his past, a process of both disavowal and… self-destruction."[22] From Ethan Edwards stalking his Comanche alter ego in *The Searchers*, to the sheriff destroying the embodiment of his own outlaw propensities in *Pat Garrett and Billy the Kid* (1973), this idea framed the drama in a powerful sequence of westerns, and not only those of an openly revisionist persuasion (see the Budd Boetticher-Randolph Scott series, for example).

Many critics bemoaned, even resented, this tendency; condemning what he called 'the superwestern', André Bazin asserted that western heroes belonged in saddles, not on analysts' couches.[23] What the 'adult' western demonstrated, however, was how stale the standard formula had become in comparison with the moral complexities of film noir (indeed, many westerns demonstrated a distinctly noir-like sensibility – see appendix 1) and the uncertainties engendered by the Cold War. The westerner was remoulded accordingly. His nature kept pace with the evolution of acting styles, the relaxation of moral standards and a contagious disillusionment, so that, by the dawn of the Seventies, audiences were offered cynics, mercenaries (especially in European imports), rapists (in the comic western *Waterhole #3* [1967]), inveterate killers (*The Wild Bunch* [1969]) and misfits (*Little Big Man*) in place of the square-jawed, straight-shooting heroes of old. The western, once the most unequivocal of genres, had become a complicated proposition for a complicated world.

One theme that flows through almost all tributaries of the revisionist western is the alienation of the hero. To an extent it was always so: tasked with carrying out society's dirty work, he was thereafter unclean, "unwanted and unnecessary" in the new social order he has helped to establish.[24] From the Fifties onwards, however, he became ever more isolated from settlers and citizens – the Chosen People of the new Promised Land for whose Manifest Destiny he has bloodied his hands and whose integrity had been called into doubt as early as *Stagecoach* (1939) and *The Ox-Bow Incident* (1943). *High Noon* was a watershed, the most prominent and influential of a raft of Fifties films that emphasised the disparity between the bravery and rectitude of their protagonists and the spinelessness and moral failings of mainstream society in a paranoid, persecutory America. "The hero maintains his status, as demanded by his code. He acts heroically, but clearly he is dissatisfied with the whole process of trying to do right, of trying to protect people who won't help themselves."[25]

Using the western, the American genre nonpareil, to criticise the state of the nation at the peak of McCarthyism was undoubtedly bold (if in some cases incidental or even opportunistic), yet it chimed with a growing sense of unease among influential public figures. Within two years of *High Noon's* release, the commentator Alistair Cooke discerned widespread anti-McCarthyism – "an impulse of moral revulsion" against the threats and tactics issued by the Senator's staff and in his name. Cooke communicated this in the same month – June, 1954 – of journalist Edward R. Murrow's celebrated anti-McCarthy broadcast on national television.[26] That society is too weak to defend itself from predators is a given in the western; what was new was the feeling that heroic efforts on its behalf were in vain.

This sense of estrangement was never stronger than in films that captured the death throes of the frontier, with the concomitant devaluation of ideals associated with its settlement. In *The Man Who Shot Liberty Valance*, *Ride the High Country* and *Lonely Are the Brave* (all 1962), "Society is clearly adjudged at fault for marginalising [the protagonists]: it cannot accommodate them gracefully, it does not value their experience, it condemns their brand of individualism as outmoded."[27] The elegiac tone of these twilight westerns shaded into bitterness in the likes of *The Misfits* (1961) and *Hud* (1963), in which the modern West mocked the spirit of the old; *Death*

above: from left: Marilyn Monroe, Clark Gable and Montgomery Clift in **The Misfits**.

of a Gunfighter and *Tom Horn* (1980), with their archaic antiheroes betrayed by civic corruption and corporate ruthlessness; and *Monte Walsh*, in which ageing cowboys and wranglers faced the threat of extinction posed by "the mighty forces of modernisation".**28** Cowboying itself lost its romantic lustre; it was depicted as the last word in drudgery in *Will Penny* (1967), *Wild Rovers* (1971) and *The Culpepper Cattle Co.* (1972).

"If there was a death blow to the western genre," writes David A. Cook, "it was delivered by the political violence of 1968, Vietnam and Watergate, after which the heroic utopian mythology of the American West became impossible to sustain."**29** For Jack Nachbar, writing in 1974, "The fragmenting of the genre… illustrates some disturbing truths about the mood of the people in contemporary America… the movies' unified myth of the West [has] run up against the social and political nightmares of the Sixties and Seventies and that heretofore solid vision has exploded into pieces."**30** In this climate, attacks on societal racism (*Hombre* [1967]), cowardice (*Welcome to Hard Times* [1967]) and hypocrisy (*The Wild Bunch*, *A Gunfight* [1971], *Pat Garrett and Billy the Kid*) sounded ever louder. Revisionist film-makers, much like the title character of *Buffalo Bill and the Indians, or Sitting Bull's History Lesson* (1976), claimed "a better sense o' history" than that of the western's pioneers. In many cases, they wanted to redress the balance after decades of hagiographic portraits; in others, they simply tailored the facts to an ideological agenda of their own. Historical personalities, far from being exemplars of virtues that America liked to claim as its own – fortitude, incorruptibility – or Hobsbawm-esque social bandits, became maverick avengers (Wyatt Earp in *Hour of the Gun* [1967]), scapegoats for greed, venality and other plagues on the modern body politic (Earp again, in *Doc*), sociopaths (William Bonney in *Dirty Little Billy* [1972]; Jesse James in *The Great Northfield Minnesota Raid* [1972] and *The Assassination of Jesse James by the Coward Robert Ford* [2007]) or contemptuous blowhards (Custer in *Little Big Man*; Cody in *Buffalo Bill and the Indians*). And the most infamous example of New Hollywood hubris, Michael Cimino's *Heaven's Gate* (1980), interpreted the Johnson County War as the oppression of ethnic minorities by the nation's economic elite.

The failure of *Heaven's Gate* did not sound the last post for the western; audience tastes were drifting elsewhere in any case. A smattering of straightforward westerns in the Eighties seemed to signal an artistic and cultural retreat – or perhaps they were inevitable, with a cowboy president in the White House – yet it took another deeply personal, self-consciously revisionist production, *Dances with Wolves*, to spark the genre back into life, commercially and critically. Some of the best-received westerns since – *Unforgiven* (1992), *Geronimo: An American Legend* (1993), *The Ballad of Little Jo*, *Dead Man* (1995), *The Assassination of Jesse James by the Coward Robert Ford*, *The Homesman* (2014), not to mention the television series *Deadwood* (2004-6) – have continued to interrogate and dismantle the myths upon which their predecessors meditated. That films of this ilk have held their own alongside broadly traditional westerns such as *Open Range* (2003), *Appaloosa* (2008), remakes of *3:10 to Yuma* (2007) and *True Grit* (2010) – Quentin Tarantino's patchworks *Django Unchained* and *The Hateful Eight* (2015) fall somewhere in the middle – says much about the tenacity of a genre that was first pronounced dead even before the advent of sound. It also confirms that the ambiguities in the American national character, embodied in the popular imagination by the westerner and first exposed to scrutiny more than half a century ago, remain unresolved. **KG**

footnotes

1 *Gunfighter Nation: The Myth of the Frontier in Twentieth-Century America* (University of Oklahoma Press, 1998).
2 Manifest Destiny – a concept devised by Democratic Party mouthpiece John L. O'Sullivan in 1845 – was a mindset widespread in the mid-19th century that the expansion of the United States was ordained by Providence: "The Europeans and their descendants... were the dominant race and therefore responsible for the Indians – along with their lands, their forests and their mineral wealth" (Dee Brown, *Bury My Heart at Wounded Knee*, Vintage, 1991).
3 *The Western* (Pearson, 2003).
4 Michael Coyne, *The Crowded Prairie: American National Identity in the Hollywood Western* (I.B. Tauris, 1996).
5 'Westbound', in *Wanted Dead or Alive: the American West in Popular Culture* (Richard Aquila, ed, University of Illinois Press, 1998).
6 Ibid.
7 Interview with Wes Studi by Walter Chaw, Film Freak Central.
8 See, for example, Edward Buscombe, *'Injuns!' Native Americans in the Movies* (Reaktion Books, 2006).
9 *An Army of Phantoms: American Movies and the Making of the Cold War* (The New Press, 2011).
10 Steve Neale, 'Vanishing Americans', *Back in the Saddle Again* (Edward Buscombe and Roberta E. Pearson, eds, BFI, 1998).
11 *Making the White Man's Indian: Native Americans and Hollywood Movies* (Praeger, 2000).
12 If revisionist theory runs unchecked, says Neale, "[Native Americans] once again come close to disappearance, not just from the films that seem to be about them, but also from postwar America, and from postwar struggles, debates and concerns over racial prejudice, civil rights and America's ethnic make-up" ('Vanishing Americans', *Back in the Saddle Again*).
13 Another spur was the foundation, in 1968, of the radical American Indian Movement, as well as the publication in quick succession of incendiary revisionist histories and political tracts: *The Return of the Vanishing American* (1968), *Custer Died for Your Sins* (1969) and *Bury My Heart at Wounded Knee* (1970).
14 'Savage Nations', in *The Philosophy of the Western* (Jennifer L. McMahon and B. Steve Csaki, eds, University Press of Kentucky, 2010).
15 John H. Lenihan, *Showdown: Confronting Modern America in the Western Film* (University of Illinois Press, 1980).
16 The success among ordinary Americans of *Dances with Wolves'* message that the distinctness of indigenous culture was something worth preserving can be gauged in part from historian Richard M. Abrams' identification of "the idea of America as a 'multicultural' nation" gaining traction in the late Eighties. "In some sectors of the society, *diversity* tended to displace *integration*" (*America Transformed*, Cambridge University Press, 2006).
17 'Genre Anxiety and Racial Representation', in *Refiguring American Film Genres: History and Theory* (Nick Browne, ed, University of California Press, 1998).
18 The mixed-race actor/singer Herb Jeffries, for example, made several musical westerns in the Thirties as the 'Bronze Buckaroo'.
19 *Somewhere in the Night: Film Noir and the American City* (Henry Holt, 1997).
20 Pam Cook, *Screening the Past: Memory and Nostalgia in Cinema* (Routledge, 2004).
21 *Westerns in a Changing America*, 1955-2000 (McFarland, 2004).
22 *The Movie Book of the Western* (Studio Vista, 1996).
23 'The Evolution of the Western', in *What is Cinema? Volume 2* (University of California Press, 2004).
24 David Lusted, *The Western* (Routledge, 2003).
25 Ken Hada, 'The Cost of the Code: Ethical Consequences in High Noon and The Ox-Bow Incident', in *The Philosophy of the Western*.
26 Alistair Cooke, *Reporting America: the Life of the Nation 1946-2004* (Overlook Press, 2012).
27 Michael Coyne, *The Crowded Prairie.*
28 *Monthly Film Bulletin.*
29 *Lost Illusions: American Cinema in the Shadow of Watergate and Vietnam 1970-1979* (University of California Press, 2002).
30 'Riding Shotgun: the Scattered Formula in Contemporary Western Movies', in *Focus on the Western* (Jack Nachbar, ed, Prentice-Hall Inc, 1974).

The Films

Henry Fonda in **The Ox-Bow Incident**.

The
OX-BOW
INCIDENT
starring
HENRY FONDA
Dana ANDREWS
Mary Beth HUGHES
DIRECTED BY
WILLIAM A. WELLMAN
PRODUCED AND WRITTEN FOR THE SCREEN BY
LAMAR TROTTI
20th CENTURY-FOX PICTURE

The Ox-Bow Incident

1943, B/W, 75 mins.

D: William A. Wellman. P: Lamar Trotti (Twentieth Century-Fox). W: Lamar Trotti. Ph: Arthur C. Miller. M: Cyril J. Mockridge. St: Henry Fonda (Gil Carter), Dana Andrews (Donald Martin), Frank Conroy (Major Tetley), Harry Morgan (Art Croft), Anthony Quinn (Juan Martinez/Francisco Morez)

"There are some other good men here... only they don't seem to realise what they're doing. They're the ones I feel sorry for. Cos it'll be over for me in a little while, but they'll have to go on remembering for the rest of their lives."

Solemn, angry clouds gather behind the credits, about to bear witness to a great injustice. Produced as the US's involvement in the Second World War was intensifying, *The Ox-Bow Incident* is a forthright diatribe against the iniquity of lynch law, decrying the human tendency to follow false leaders, create scapegoats and succumb to criminality in the name of protecting society. Noirish in look and theme and dispensing with conventional heroes – despite the noble presence of Henry Fonda – *Ox-Bow* would be the first to usher in a new type of genre product: more cerebral, less celebratory and more realistic in tone than the myth-making movies that had preceded it.[1]

The West had, until then, been a popular draw in literature and cinema, largely because it "provided the perfect symbol for Americans to rally around when confronted by progressive reforms"[2] and external crises. However, amid the turbulence of the war years, when other genre films comprised "uplifting frontier tributes to national unanimity",[3] William A. Wellman offered his countrymen a darker chapter of their past, noticeably lacking in patriotic ardour; its disappointing box office indicates that they were not prepared to digest it.[4]

Entering the frontier town of Bridger's Wells, Gil Carter and Art Croft try to drown their boredom with whisky. The town is tense. Cattle rustling has made serious dents in its economy and the two are initially treated with suspicion merely because they are "different", rootless, even though they have evidently passed through town before. When it's announced that Larry Kincaid, a local rancher, has been shot in the head, the inhabitants' ire is inflamed. As the townsfolk debate in the street, a posse forms. Although some are against the idea, the authoritarian voice of Major Tetley weighs in on the side of the angry majority, seducing the undecided into joining the posse. Reluctantly, Gil and Art join up to deflect continuing suspicion, and when it's revealed that three men have been seen with 600 head of cattle bearing Kincaid's brand, the posse head out to track them down. Finding the three men sleeping wild, they ambush them. A long night ensues as Tetley establishes a kangaroo court and Martin, the captives' young spokesman, proclaims their innocence. Gil and a small group oppose the lynching, pushing instead for a proper trial.

The human psyche was a prominent theme in the novels of Walter Van Tilburg Clark, who would often use the ruggedness of the West as an arena to explore the dark recesses of men's minds and the consequences of their actions. In his 1940 novel of the same name, Art is the narrator and voice of conscience. The film – adapted by Lamar Trotti, author of Wellman's clammy noir western, *Yellow Sky* – conflates the protagonists' personalities so that Gil, whose first actions are to get drunk, provoke a fight and vomit in the street, becomes the most proactive, while Art spends much of his time supporting his fiery-tempered friend in his decisions. (Van Tilburg Clark was also the source for another Wellman western drama, *Track of the Cat* [1954], a figurative account of a man's battle against his demons, symbolised by the titular panther.) As with the locals, these characters are not chimerical. Their actions and reactions are steeped in real human behaviour; this was rare, if not unknown, in a genre predicated largely on escapism.

As the people of Bridger's Wells gather in the dusty street, we are given a lesson in power games during a brilliantly scripted political exchange in which the town's class structure is laid bare. While the majority, the working population, consider Kincaid to be one of their own and want to pursue and lynch his alleged murderers, Davies, the storekeeper, argues that the judge or sheriff

should manage the broiling situation. He represents the lower middle class, having built a small enterprise that serves individuals whose social standing is both below and above his own. Perhaps this central position allows him to see more dispassionately. But Davies is not a rancher and is argued down – a small voice of dissent quickly silenced. With the sheriff absent at the Kincaid ranch, the verbose but ineffectual judge proves unable to resist the general consensus, buckling under the bombast of the self-appointed leader, Tetley, the vengeful ranting of Farnley (Marc Lawrence), Kincaid's best friend, and the humiliating, almost emasculating barracking from Ma (Jane Darwell), the town harridan.

Tetley cuts a mysterious figure. He oozes confidence and is only too happy to exploit the potency of his army uniform, yet no one really knows about his war record. He commands respect, yet it is implied that he has "something to hide"; there are rumours that he was once run out of another town for his involvement with a woman. In his opinion, his status makes him the natural leader. No doubt the tantalising prospect of leading armed men again is a motivating factor but, as the narrative continues, a more sadistic purpose suggests itself. He is also in favour of a posse because he wants to make a man of his son, the introspective and unmasculine Gerald: "I will have no female boys bearing my name," he tells him.

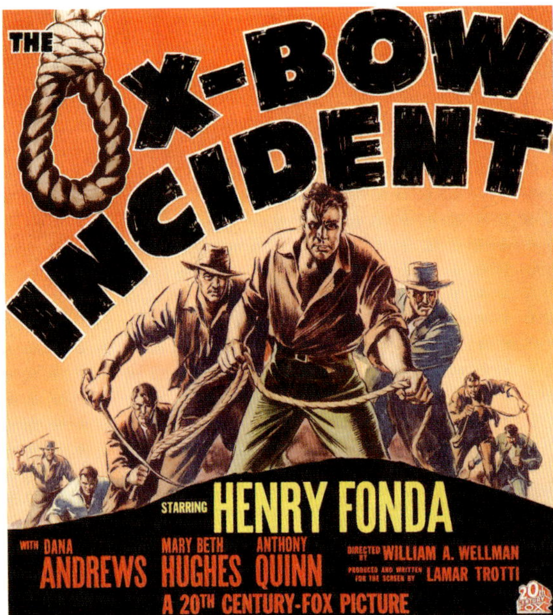

In contrast to the haziness of the Major's past, the background of another member of the posse brings one of the film's major themes into sharp focus. Sparks (Leigh Whipper), an unassuming black man guided by his faith, has encountered peremptory frontier justice before: "I seen my own brother being lynched… even now I wakes up dreaming about it."[5] Whipper, founder of the Negro Actors Guild, lends a soulful dignity to his devoutly Christian character. Looking at life with simplicity, but perhaps traumatised by experience, he has the humanity, and the courage, to add his voice to the brave minority that will eventually oppose the execution.

Tetley continues leading the posse, with overzealous military precision, ever further into the dark heart of the frontier. Soon, obscured by the shadows of black, wizened trees, they see three sleeping men. With the trio defenceless, the Major instructs the posse to creep up on them. This scene would play very differently in more conventional genre products, usually with guns drawn on both sides, yet Wellman's treatment robs the scene of any sense of triumph or heroism, especially when the captives realise the sheer number of men who have ridden against them and the hopelessness of their situation.

It is here that Sparks' tale of intolerance begins to resonate. "We haven't done anything… a hanging? What have we done?" protests Dana Andrews' Donald Martin. It is arguably Andrews' most affecting performance. (He later played another victim of lynch law in the noir-esque *Three Hours to Kill*, in which he survives the ordeal and seeks vengeance on his would-be executioners.) Martin tries in vain to explain that he bought the cattle from Kincaid, but he has no bill of sale. Halva Harvey (played by John Ford's brother, Francis), the oldest of the three, is too "feeble-minded" to help himself or his friends. Their case is not helped when it is revealed that the last man, the Mexican Martinez, has been lying about his ability to speak English, "and ten other languages… but I won't tell anything I don't want to in any of them". His defiance and pathetic escape attempt stoke the posse's indignation like the embers in the campfire. After the chaos, the interrogation and Tetley's sadistic mind games, Martin reconciles himself to the fact he is going to die, asking if he can, at least, write a letter to be delivered to his wife. The atmosphere is a disturbing mixture of jocundity and solemnity, the carnality of Ma's laughter mingling with Sparks' blues-inflected hymn-singing while everyone waits until dawn for the hanging.

The horror of the lynching, in scenes reminiscent of Wellman's earlier western *The Conquerors* (1932), which also portrayed an illegal hanging, smashes home when the sheriff intercepts the posse and informs them that Kincaid is only wounded, and that his actual assailants have already been caught. Every member of the band knows that behind them three men have been murdered, and those for and against the hanging hold a degree of collective responsibility. "God better have mercy on you," the sheriff tells them. "You won't get any from me." Humiliated and discredited, the Major returns to his home followed by his son, who calls his father a "depraved, murderous beast". Gerald's taunts are interrupted by gunshots from inside the house as the Major commits suicide; a look bordering on satisfaction passes across Gerald's face. Meanwhile, in the saloon, the camera tracks along the silent, ashamed faces of the men in the posse as Gil reads from Martin's letter, in a moment of high pathos.

Van Tilburg Clark's stated intention was to create a parable about fascism. It is not clear whether Wellman and Trotti had the same motivation, but their film preserves the metaphor by chronicling the relative ease with which would-be tyrants can corrupt the rule of law, especially at a time of domestic crisis when the masses, possessing little or no faith in the legal system, are prone to lash out at 'enemies' and 'criminals'. As Farnley remarks to the terrified Martin, "The law's slow and careless around here sometimes; we're here to see it speeded up." Art and Gil feel they must become part of the crowd to avoid suspicion, even as the 'justice' meted out becomes increasingly less humane. There are conscientious objectors – Davies, Sparks – but they are overruled, their views sidelined, amid the general uproar. The Major is, perhaps, the most conspicuous symbol. With his military past, his motives and his humanity in question, still he manages, through demagoguery and force of personality, to lead men to commit an appalling act. It is tempting, with hindsight, to view his lonely suicide, as he sees that he has been defeated, as a foretaste of the end of Nazi terror. (The Major's death, serving as punishment for his actions, was an important factor in securing Production Code Administration script approval.)

However, in revisionist terms, the film explored a theme that had rarely been confronted with such rigour: that of mob rule. For Jon Tuska, *Ox-Bow* is a "serious social commentary on the folly of lynch law in the West... an examination of injustice precisely where justice was the most touted".[6] When first released, such a liberal, unromantic western would certainly have jarred with lovers of Wild West folklore – one need only compare it with Owen Wister's oft-filmed *The Virginian*, one of the sacred texts of the genre, in which the protagonist is morally exonerated after supervising the hanging of a group of rustlers, including his best friend. Yet it stands as one of the most important westerns of its era, signalling the introspective turn the genre was to take in the postwar years, and remains one of American cinema's most powerful achievements.

The heart-rending final scene is directed in masterly style: as he reads Martin's letter, much of Fonda's face is shaded to allow a chink of emotional detachment, the actor's warm, clear tones linking the posse's actions at the Ox-Bow with other injustices in the world. As Martin writes: "A man just naturally can't take the law into his own hands and hang people without hurting everybody in the world, 'cause then he's not just breaking one law but all laws. What is anybody's conscience except a little piece of the conscience of all men that ever lived?" **CH**

above: Henry Fonda with Dana Andrews (left) as the doomed Donald Martin.

footnotes

1 Noir scholar James Ursini brackets *Ox-Bow* with other "early example[s] of the Fox cycle of social realist noirs" such as *House on 92nd Street*, *Call Northside 777* and *Crossfire* (*Film Noir: The Encyclopedia*; Overlook Duckworth, 2010).

2 Richard Aquila, *Wanted Dead or Alive: The American West in Popular Culture* (University of Illinois Press, 1996).

3 John H. Lenihan, *Showdown: Confronting Modern America in the Western Film* (University of Illinois Press, 1980).

4 Having bought the property from a producer who had envisaged it, bizarrely, as a vehicle for Mae West, Wellman had trouble convincing any studio to finance it, this being a period when morale-boosting themes were the order of the day. His agreement with Darryl F. Zanuck at Twentieth Century-Fox stipulated that Wellman would make two commercial films in return: *Thunder Birds* (1942), a tribute to the US Air Force, and the heroic Joel McCrea western *Buffalo Bill* (1944).

5 Henry Fonda himself witnessed an example of vigilante justice when he was about 13 or 14, in his home town of Omaha, Nebraska. A young black man had been accused of rape, arrested and put in the temporary jail in the courthouse. An angry, armed crowd gathered, and the man was dragged from the jail. "A great huzzah went up when they saw the poor fellow," Fonda says. "They took him, strung him up to the end of a lamp-post, hung him, and while his feet were still dancing in the air, they riddled his body with bullets. It was the most horrendous sight I'd ever seen. Then they cut down the body, tied it to an auto, and dragged it through the streets of Omaha" (as told to Howard Teichmann in *Fonda: My Life*, EP Dutton, 1984).

6 *The Filming of the West* (Doubleday, 1976).

I Shot Jesse James

1949, B/W, 81 mins.

D: Samuel Fuller. P: Carl K. Hittleman (Lippert Productions). W: Samuel Fuller. Ph: Ernest Miller. M: Albert Glasser. St: John Ireland (Bob Ford), Preston Foster (John Kelley), Barbara Britton (Cynthy Waters), Reed Hadley (Jesse James), J. Edward Bromberg (Harry Kane)

"When I killed Jess I had a cause – if you turn against me, I got no reason."

Originating in Samuel Fuller's desire to analyse the mindset of an assassin, *I Shot Jesse James* is one of the earliest anti-westerns. The film's exclamatory title signals its unusual perspective, but even so it was a bold move by the director – especially as this was his feature debut – to evoke the famous outlaw only to sideline him in favour of Bob Ford, the "dirty little coward" who shot Jesse in the back. Not for 60 years would Ford, the black sheep of frontier folklore, meet the glare of the cinematic spotlight again, in the form of Casey Affleck's skin-crawling performance in *The Assassination of Jesse James by the Coward Robert Ford*.

Although it opens with a botched bank robbery, staged in the manner of a gangster movie, during which Jesse saves the wounded Bob's life, *I Shot Jesse James* is a psychodrama as much as a western, with Ford – hotheaded, paranoid, insecure, ever so slightly dense – supplanting Jesse at the centre of the narrative. Jesse is portrayed in a complimentary light, extending a fraternal hand to his associate and nursing him back to health under his own roof.[1] (Is it more than brotherly love? A homoerotic bond is insinuated, notably during a scene in which Jesse first invites Bob to scrub his back as he bathes, then gifts him a fancy new pistol. This could, of course, imply a death wish on Jesse's part, but taking into account Fuller's ambiguous motivation – "My story was based on one quote from Oscar Wilde: "Each man kills the thing he loves" – it gives Bob's final line in the film, "I loved him," an unexpected resonance.[2])

In Fuller's rendering of the tale, Bob's betrayal of his illustrious friend is not motivated principally by venality but by his adoration of Cynthy, an itinerant actress. Bob hopes the amnesty promised for Jesse's death or capture will convince Cynthy to marry him, but she is horrified at what he has done; whatever love she once felt for him calcifies into a mixture of fear and pity. Bob becomes subject to popular opprobrium and the occasional challenge by wannabe gunmen; like the born losers of film noir, he bears an increasingly haunted, hunted expression, the burden of repressed guilt (and, perhaps, shame, if his feelings for Jesse *were* more than fraternal) evident in John Ireland's slightly stooping demeanour. His fortunes improve, materially at least, when he strikes it rich in a silver town, but Bob's jealousy of Cynthy's relationship with lawman John Kelley, stirred up by the vengeful Frank James, is destined to consume him.

Fuller's script is largely fanciful (the real Bob Ford never cited a woman among his reasons for going against Jesse; he was much younger than he appears here, and the date of his death was almost 10 years later), but verisimilitude is not the point. The director is concerned less with *how* events transpired than *why*; hence his decision to frame familiar material as an unflattering but intriguing character study. It is difficult to imagine an established star accepting the central role; nor does it seem likely the production, made by the penny-pinching Lippert Pictures, could have afforded

one. Ireland, however, a steady supporting player who had previously squared up to John Wayne in *Red River* (1948), is equal to the task. Brimming with black bile, Bob never seeks sympathy; merely the understanding that is destined to elude him. He is the first in a long line of Fuller outsiders – a man engulfed in a mental fog, continually nonplussed by others' responses to his actions: "I tried to get a groping, not half-witted, but not too mentally alert type of a man," said Fuller.[3]

Besides anticipating the psychological westerns of the Fifties, the film demonstrates a surprising level of self-awareness – musing, in a modest way, on myth and spectacle. Bob, misguided as ever, hopes to salvage his reputation by re-creating his killing of Jesse on stage as a "special added attraction" – or "freak" as Cynthy would have it – during her show. (The real Ford capitalised on his notoriety in much the same way.) But he is unable to pull the trigger; the real shooting is superimposed over the action, as if Jesse really were the "ghost" Bob imagines is haunting him. (Bob does earn a modicum of redemption later on, when he prevents another man from being shot in the back.) This is followed by an encounter in a saloon between Bob and a wandering troubadour, who sings a popular ballad about Jesse's betrayal unaware that the villain of the piece is in attendance. Bob reveals his identity and forces the singer to continue, but his motives – misplaced vanity? Masochism? – are unclear.

Where the western is associated with wide shots and landscape, Fuller gives us close-ups and interiors. Although budgetary pressures and scheduling issues may have forced his hand to an extent, this seems primarily to have been an artistic choice, the director eliding genre conventions. Likewise, the frequent resort to front-page newspaper inserts as both punctuation and exposition reflects both B-movie dynamics and Fuller's background in popular journalism. The close shots are particularly effective in scenes involving Bob and Cynthy, the camera relentlessly scrutinising the shifting emotions on their faces, Bob's paranoia mounting as Cynthy's anxiety prevents her from explaining how she really feels. He fills in the gaps, imagining the worst, leading to a showdown with Kelley – shot at night, with Bob all but swallowed up by the darkness – in which, once again, Fuller's staging wrong-foots audience expectations. **KG**

"Not too mentally alert": John Ireland (right) as the abject Bob Ford.

footnotes

1 Although the outlaw is presented benignly here, Fuller deplored the historical Jesse, calling him "one of the most despicable, ruthless, falsely publicized characters in the American western folklore… a true bastard… In case we ever meet after I die, I will hit him as soon as I see him." Interview with Sam Fuller by Stig Bjorkman (1965), reprinted in *Samuel Fuller: Interviews* (University Press of Mississippi, 2012).

2 "Robert Lippert… didn't catch that," Fuller said of Ford's final line, and its possible implications. "He just thought it was a kind of Damon-Pythias relationship, and he let it remain." Interview with Sam Fuller by Eric Sherman and Martin Rubin (1968), reprinted in *Samuel Fuller: Interviews*.

3 Interview with Sam Fuller by Eric Sherman and Martin Rubin.

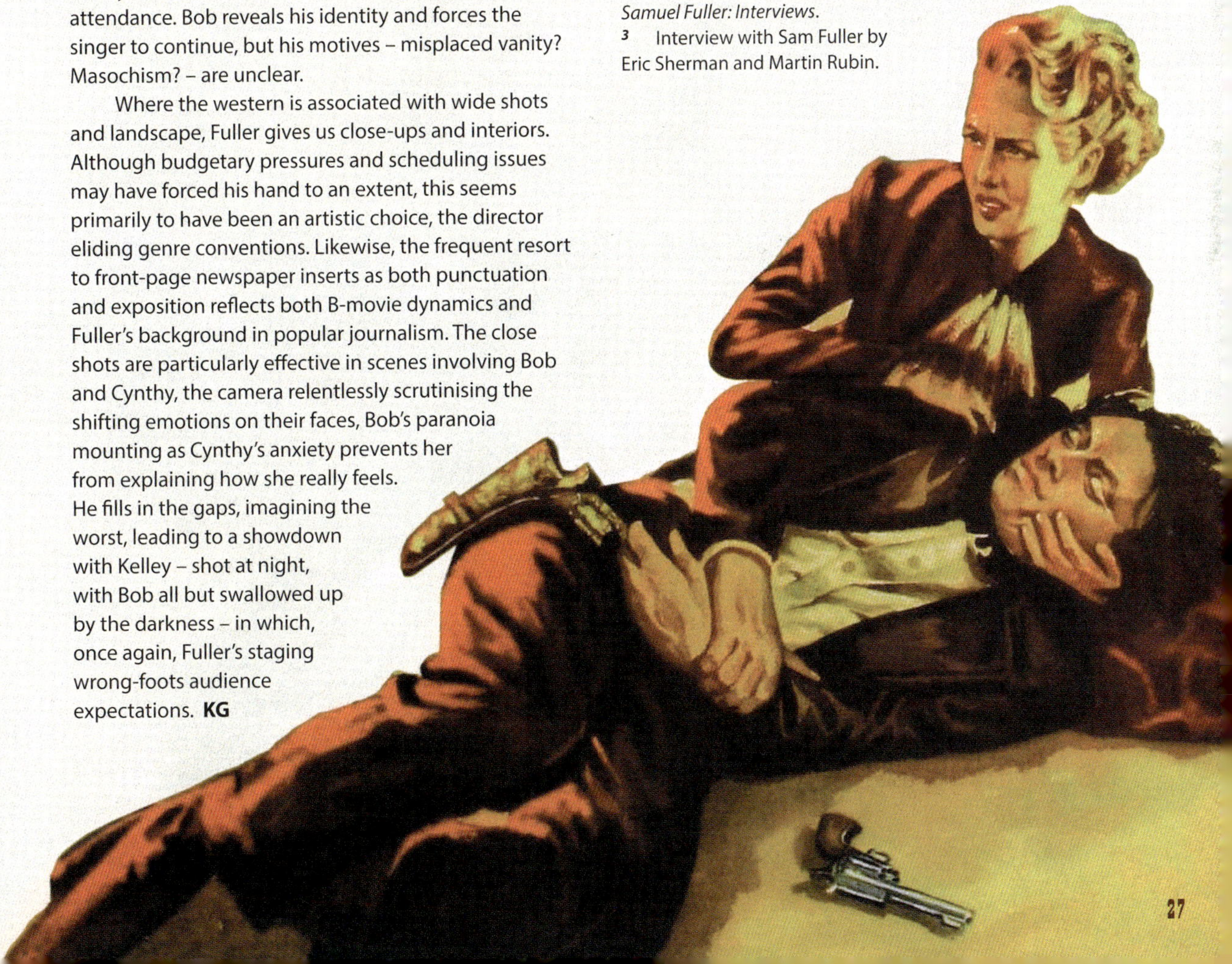

Broken Arrow

1950, Colour, 93 mins.

D: Delmer Daves. P: Julian Blaustein (Twentieth Century-Fox). W: Michael Blankfort [front for Albert Maltz]. Ph: Ernest Palmer. M: Hugo Friedhofer. St: James Stewart (Tom Jeffords), Jeff Chandler (Cochise), Debra Paget (Sonseeahray), Basil Ruysdael (General Howard), Will Geer (Ben Slade)

"Maybe one day you will kill me, or I will kill you. But we will not spit on each other."

Celebrated, disparaged, analysed exhaustively, *Broken Arrow* is one of the most divisive westerns ever made. By setting out to depict Indians with respect – to humanise the 'alien' – it was lauded by as many liberals for its progressivism as it was criticised by others who felt it didn't go far enough. Either way, it was the most popular western of 1950, its takings buoyed by the top billing of James Stewart, and was the first link in a chain of major pro-Indian westerns that would eventually lead to the critical and commercial phenomenon of *Dances with Wolves*.

Not that *Broken Arrow* – or Anthony Mann's equally revisionist, but ultimately bleaker, *Devil's Doorway*, released the same year – occurred in a vacuum.[1] With a mind to the principles so many had recently fought and died for, Hollywood had already begun making conscientious efforts to speak out against racial and ethnic persecution – of Jews, for example, in *Crossfire* (1947), which demonstrated the limits of progressive thinking by substituting anti-Semitism for homophobia, the focus of its source novel; Mexican migrants in Mann's *Border Incident* (1949); African-Americans in Fox's *Pinky* (1949). More specifically, Native American rights were the subject of much political wrangling at the time of *Broken Arrow's* production and release. Conservatives in Congress favoured the 'termination' of federal responsibility for Indian affairs – ending their special legal status, which recognised the sovereignty of tribes and exempted them from certain statutes, among other provisions, and therefore accelerating their 'assimilation' into mainstream society, while liberals made the case for maintaining the reservation system as "a form of benevolent paternalism", in Edward Buscombe's words.[2] The argument in favour of reservations, which would in theory ensure the preservation of tribal cultural identity, is a central thrust of the narrative, as Buscombe makes clear. (The idea of reaching out to an enemy in the spirit of peaceful co-existence had particular resonance in a Cold War context.[3])

Other westerns, meanwhile, had anticipated *Broken Arrow's* peaceful overtures towards the old enemy. This was increasingly evident in the war years, when national unity was of paramount importance and antagonistic storylines fell out of favour: "A national campaign to purge the land of its Indian inhabitants smacked of fascist genocide," as Angela Aleiss put it.[4] Accordingly, a new tolerance was evident in such high-profile productions as *They Died with Their Boots On* (1941) and *Buffalo Bill* (1944). *Broken Arrow* also took its lead, in part, from John Ford's *Fort Apache*, in which it is the Custer figure, played by Henry Fonda, whose pig-headedness and overt racism ignite conflict with Cochise (Miguel Inclán) and his followers, who are presented sympathetically.[5] And Cochise, played in *Broken Arrow* by Jeff Chandler, subsequently became the standard-bearer for Hollywood's liberal reappraisal of the Indian Wars and, by implication, of the status in society of contemporary Native Americans and other minority groups.[6]

Adapted by Albert Maltz – a blacklistee who relinquished screen credit to his friend Michael Blankfort – from Elliott Arnold's ground-breaking 1947 novel *Blood Brother*, *Broken Arrow* telescopes the perilous peace process between whites and Apaches into the friendship that develops between two men of reason and vision: ex-Army scout Tom Jeffords and Chiricahua chief Cochise. Maltz was insistent that his adaptation was as attentive to veracity as the novel itself, although it omits or elides much of the conflict's historical context for the sake of even-handedness (and, perhaps, to spare its audience some unpalatable home truths about the consequences of Manifest Destiny – after all, this was 20 years before *Little Big Man* and *Soldier Blue*), to the ire of the film's most trenchant critics.[7] Jeffords' opening narration informs us: "What I have to tell happened exactly as you'll see it. The only change will be that when the Apaches speak, they will speak in our language." This was quite a departure – no previous western had deemed a disclaimer necessary. Again, this well-intended gesture has fallen foul of detractors, for whom the language issue signals assimiliationism. While clichés remain in the cadence and content of their speeches, however, 'Anglicising' the Apaches' dialogue allowed the Indians to speak in flowing sentences rather than heap big halting chunks. Producer Julian Blaustein boasted, not unreasonably: "We have treated [the Indians] as people, not savages, have tried to show that the only real 'heavies' are ignorance, misunderstanding and intolerance. In short, none of our Indians say 'Ugh!'"[8]

Balance is key to the film-makers' strategy. The tension between whites and Apaches – and by extension between all indigenous peoples and white Americans – pivots on "the actions of bad people on both sides".[9] Jeffords reminds the blinkered bigots in Tucson, on the front line of the fight, that it was the actions of whites, not Apaches, that ignited the conflict. He even goes so far as to question the right of white America to encroach on tribal land, to expand its dominion, an attitude that almost gets him lynched by his own people ("Maybe you've forgotten which side you're on") in one of the film's most remarkable scenes. (Stewart plays Jeffords as a man easily riled, the veteran of many a violent encounter with Apaches and therefore an unlikely peacemaker – if *he* can make the leap of faith, the film told post-war audiences, then so can they.) In the Apache camp, meanwhile, Cochise, who is as pragmatic as he is philosophical about the need for compromise if his people are to survive ("If a big wind comes, a tree must bend, or be lifted out by its roots"), is contrasted with Geronimo (Jay Silverheels), whose bellicosity and recalcitrance are presented in accordance with fictional western tradition but in defiance of historical facts. (Hollywood continued to demonise Geronimo – or else to neuter him – in a number of productions before amends were made in Walter Hill's laudatory 1993 biopic.)

Jeffords and Cochise make it their mission to repair the mistrust between the races, as best they can, while troublemakers – Geronimo's breakaway band; an Army colonel; a vengeful rancher spoiling for a fight – do their worst to wreck the heroes' efforts. Jeffords, as the narrator and focal point of the film, forms a bridge between the cultures, initiating and pursuing treaty negotiations, which survive such breaches as an attack on a stagecoach by some of Geronimo's warriors. This scene culminates in a significant retort to genre stereotyping, when Jeffords rides to the rescue with braves sent by Cochise: "Apaches protecting Americans – and I lived to see it," remarks the driver in astonishment. (Elsewhere it is made clear that scalping is not an Apache custom – this practice is only carried out in the film by whites.) Jeffords furthers the cause by immersing himself in Apache lore and marrying Sonseeahray, an Indian maiden in the mould of Pocahontas. Their romantic encounters in a bucolic lakeside setting invoke the dream of an integrationist Utopia, but their relationship is inevitably cut short by bullets. Hollywood's horror of miscegenation meant that happy endings for mixed-race couples (even if, as here, the actors were both white) were rare; even 40 years after *Broken Arrow*, *Dances with Wolves* sidestepped the issue by having Kevin Costner's Sioux-adopted cavalryman fall for a captive white woman, rather than an Indian.

Chandler's charismatic, Oscar-nominated performance as Cochise, a paradigm of dignity, strength, magnanimity and wisdom, has proved problematic for many commentators, chiefly because Chandler, as the 'good' Indian, is white beneath his make-up, while Silverheels, the 'bad', is of Native blood. For Richard Slotkin, this means "the racism that the film banishes on one level returns on another. We can trust the Indians and make peace with them because they are 'just like us'; but to demonstrate that 'truth' we have to transform them into whites and expel or suppress the ethnic Indian from the picture."[10] This is a valid argument, and relates back to the disservice done to Geronimo's memory by his presentation as a warmongering renegade. It is difficult, however, if not impossible, to imagine a major studio at that time casting an Indian actor – and Silverheels is as apposite an example as any – in such a prominent role as Cochise occupies here. For all its progressive instincts, *Broken Arrow* guides its audience relatively cautiously towards a more enlightened treatment of the western's traditional bête noire; the fact remains there were no Indian actors of sufficient experience (and box-office calibre) to stand toe-to-toe with James Stewart. If *Broken Arrow* does reflect racist attitudes it is indirectly and, in my view, inadvertently. I feel the same can be said about its retention of a white perspective in the person of Jeffords – *Devil's Doorway*, which centres on a Shoshone protagonist, is unquestionably the bolder film, but even there the character is played by a white actor.

Any art form that purports to be a faithful re-enactment of historical events makes a rod for its own back should it fail to justify its claims. *Broken Arrow* is culpable in that sense in a number of ways. In addition to the points mentioned above, the treaty brokered by Jeffords and signed by Cochise and the American government – and 'sealed', the film would have it, by the death of Sonseeahray – did not solve the dispute between the cultures, and Washington was to renege on the agreement after Cochise's death in 1874. In terms of its narrative, *Broken Arrow* does not look that far ahead. It asserts that peace is possible if mutual respect can be achieved and misunderstandings made good. Its outlook is optimistic, commensurate with its lushly photographed landscapes and warm Technicolor palette (again, the contrast with the starkly monochromatic *Devil's Doorway* is marked). If approached as a product of mid-20th century liberal idealism, as a passionate plea for "desegregation, civil rights and equal rights" in law, it makes a lot more sense – and is far more stimulating – than if its assertions of accuracy regarding the Apache wars of the 19th century are taken at face value.[11] Moreover, it was, and remains, a significant chapter in the maturity of the western; director Delmer Daves, whose attitude towards Native Americans took shape when he lived briefly with Navajo and Hopi tribes as a teenager, would follow the path himself with *The Last Wagon* (1956) and his script for *White Feather* (1955), while expressing less sympathy than may be expected for the warring Modocs of *Drum Beat* (1954).[12] **KG**

footnotes

1 *Devil's Doorway*, produced at MGM, was actually completed before *Broken Arrow*, but the studio, apprehensive about the reception such a comparatively radical western might receive, opted to hold it back until Daves's film – made for Twentieth Century Fox – had tested the commercial waters.

2 *'Injuns!' Native Americans in the Movies* (Reaktion Books, 2006).

3 For discussions of this angle at greater length, see Peter Biskind, *Seeing Is Believing* (Bloomsbury, 2001) and Steve Neale, 'Vanishing Americans: Racial and Ethnic Issues in the Interpretation and Context of Post-war "Pro-Indian" Westerns' (*Back in the Saddle Again*, British Film Institute, 1998). Neale also notes the "remarkable and ironic coincidence" in the attitudes of liberals and conservatives towards the issue of assimilation.

4 Angela Aleiss, *Making the White Man's Indian: Native Americans and Hollywood Movies* (Praeger, 2005).

5 Many silent-era westerns – shorts and features – were well disposed towards Indians, and it was not uncommon to see Native characters in central, heroic roles. Far from advocating assimilationism, a number of these films stressed (some even relished) the incompatibility of the races, with nostalgic stories often treating Indian homelands as a kind of lost Eden, Indians themselves as untainted and white society as a kind of 'contaminant' (see Angela Aleiss, *Making the White Man's Indian: Native Americans and Hollywood Movies*). *Fort Apache's* positive attitude towards Indians, meanwhile, contrasts sharply with the tone of the story it was based on. *Massacre*, by James Warner Bellah, reeks of unreconstructed prejudice; Ford biographer Joseph McBride judges Bellah's works "virtually unreadable today [for] their racist invective against Indians" (*Searching for John Ford*, Faber and Faber, 2003).

6 Chandler reprised the role in two further films: *The Battle at Apache Pass* (1952) – based on historical events that took place before those depicted in *Broken Arrow* – and *Taza, Son of Cochise* (1954). Proving he was no one-trick pony, Chandler also played a virulently racist martinet in the intelligent cavalry western *Two Flags West* (1950) and a Jeffords-like mediator in *The Great Sioux Uprising* (1953).

7 Frank Manchel attacks the film and its makers for, in his view, distorting the historical record, in his essay 'Cultural Confusion' (see Peter C. Rollins, *Hollywood's Indian: The Portrayal of the Native American in Film*, University Press of Kentucky, 1999).

8 *Los Angeles Times*, 21 May, 1950.

9 Buscombe, *'Injuns!' Native Americans in the Movies.*

10 Richard Slotkin, *Gunfighter Nation: The Myth of the Frontier in Twentieth Century America* (University of Oklahoma Press, 1998).

11 Steve Neale, 'Vanishing Americans: Racial and Ethnic Issues in the Interpretation and Context of Post-war "Pro-Indian" Westerns'.

12 *Broken Arrow's* popularity eventually led to a television series of the same name, which ran from 1956-8 and starred John Lupton as Jeffords and Michael Ansara as Cochise.

Devil's Doorway

1950, B/W, 84 mins.

D: Anthony Mann. P: Nicholas Nayfack (Metro-Goldwyn-Mayer).
W: Guy Trosper. Ph: John Alton. M: Daniele Amfitheatrof.
St: Robert Taylor (Lance Poole), Louis Calhern (Verne Coolan),
Paula Raymond (Orrie Masters), Marshall Thompson
(Rod MacDougall), James Mitchell (Red Rock)

"It's hard to explain how an Indian feels about the earth. It's the pumping of our blood... If we lose it now, we might as well all be dead."

Made before, but released a few months after, the better known *Broken Arrow*, Anthony Mann's *Devil's Doorway* can retrospectively be credited with opening the debate about Native American rights – in terms of their status as genre archetypes, as historical subjects in a wider sense and, more problematically, as metaphors for other ethnic minorities.[1] It marked an important development in the maturing of the genre in the Fifties and is the most emphatic of all the major films that attempted to expose, rather than evade or even celebrate, the iniquities committed in the name of Manifest Destiny. It is also the most pessimistic about the prospects of racial equality in the Land of the Free.

It is far from simplistic, however. Its hero, Lance Poole, is a multifaceted character, well written (by Guy Trosper) and played with straight-backed conviction by Robert Taylor – an unusual choice, for sure, but an actor with a proud bearing bespeaking nobility, dignity, and also stubbornness. (Given the support for *Devil's Doorway* expressed by the Communist *Daily Worker*, J. Hoberman suggests a more appropriate lead may have been John Garfield.[2]) Poole is a Shoshone Indian, but we see him first in a Union Army uniform as he returns home from distinguished service in the Civil War, where he earned a Congressional Medal of Honor. An integrationist (it is significant that he has Anglicised his tribal moniker, Broken Lance), he is sanguine about the nation's future – "The country is growing up" – foreseeing a new era of racial harmony. (His ailing father's gloomier prognosis – "Our people are doomed. The white man knows great hate for us" – proves more prescient.) Production of *Devil's Doorway* dovetailed with the struggle by demobbed black, Asian and, of course, Native American soldiers to advance their status in society following service in the Second World War, only to be denied the full benefits of the GI Bill, as well as access to new 'egalitarian' housing developments, by persistent de facto racial segregation. Their problems reflect those of Poole, whose arrival home to the town of Medicine Bow, which abuts Sweet Meadows, his tribe's ancestral land, is when his real fight begins.

It is when he experiences the extent of bigotry among local whites – mobilised by the smug lawyer Coolan, who uses statutes and speeches to stoke the flames of intolerance – and realises the implications of the new Homestead Act, which denies Indians the rights enjoyed by white settlers hungry for Shoshone land, that Poole's other side is revealed.[3] He becomes hardheaded, unbending; at times he seems almost to be willing a conflict to erupt. And he's not immune to prejudice himself, as with his reaction on discovering the lawyer he wants to petition the government is a young woman, Orrie Masters, played soberly by Paula Raymond. (Poole's reaction underlines the novelty of the situation; few westerns of this period – reflecting frontier history, no doubt – placed a woman in such a potentially influential position, even if, as expected, her endeavours come to nought.) Ultimately, Poole exhibits the same intransigence associated with conservative cattle ranchers in traditional westerns when faced with encroachment – in this case by sheep farmers, familiar underdogs in range-war plots, here spurred on by Coolan – on the territory Poole views as sacred.

Poole's tragedy is that he is eventually forced by society's prejudice to become that cliché of dime-novel legend and westerns of yore: a bellicose figure attacking wagon trains, obstructing 'progress', sheltering pathetic Shoshone 'renegades' and defying white paternal authority (Orrie having informed Poole that the Indians are considered wards of the government, not citizens in their own right). But the paradox of his position is underscored by his decision, during the climactic assault on his ranch, to twin his tribal headband with the uniform in which he served 'his' country – in part, with unexpressed but inescapable irony, for the liberty of a different racial underclass. Duly adorned, he goes out to face a cavalry troop, his former comrades-in-arms, sent not to break a siege but to press it home – another cliché inverted.

Robert Taylor (left) with Chief John Big Tree.

The ending elevates Poole to a higher moral/heroic plane, displaying what Jim Kitses terms a "dark exaltation" in his suicidal demise – "an action that celebrates the uncompromising quality of Mann's characters".[4] (Style mirrors content – Mann, working again with his DP of choice, John Alton, often deploys the dark arts of film noir to bolster the bleakness of his message: a savage fight in a bar, where Poole is accosted by a racist thug, is shot from disorientating angles, intercut with close-ups of leering faces, lit from below, while a storm rages on the soundtrack; later, in a tight two-shot, Poole's profile is obscured by shadow as he rejects Orrie's plea for compromise.) Poole's cry for justice, taken up by Orrie and declaimed with increasing vehemence by the script, falls on deaf ears, attuned only to the clamour among whites for new laws that will favour their ends while keeping the Indians – or any other undesirables – in check.

Despite its significance, Mann's first western remains one of his least known, along with *The Furies*, a similarly transitional work with even stronger ties to film noir, and *The Last Frontier*, this film's thematic blood brother. In the last-named, Victor Mature's rough-hewn mountain man wavers between the freedom of the backwoods and the trappings, in all senses, of civilisation, encoded in that case as the army. There, the hero chooses assimilation; here, it is never a realistic prospect – nor is it a desired one. **KG**

footnotes

1 For a stimulating study of this topic, see Steve Neale, 'Vanishing Americans: Racial and Ethnic Issues in the Interpretation and Context of Post-war "Pro-Indian" Westerns' (*Back in the Saddle Again*, British Film Institute, 1998).

2 *An Army of Phantoms: American Movies and the Making of the Cold War* (The New Press, 2011).

3 As Richard Slotkin wrote, the Homestead Act does not seem to refer to any specific statute, but may have been a reference to similar laws that have "historically legitimised and enforced regimes of racial exclusion and oppression". He cites Jews in Europe, blacks in pre-Civil War America, and "the dispossession of Japanese-Americans from their farms and businesses in California" during the Second World War (*Gunfighter Nation: The Myth of the Frontier in Twentieth-Century America*, University of Oklahoma Press, 1998).

4 Angela Aleiss, *Making the White Man's Indian: Native Americans and Hollywood Movies* (Praeger, 2005).

The Furies

1950, B/W, 109 mins.

D: Anthony Mann. P: Hal B. Wallis (Wallis-Hazen Inc). W: Charles Schnee. Ph: Victor Milner. M: Franz Waxman.
St: Barbara Stanwyck (Vance Jeffords), Wendell Corey (Rip Darrow), Walter Huston (T.C. Jeffords), Judith Anderson (Flo Burnett), Gilbert Roland (Juan Herrera)

"You're like a filly that never had a rope on her."

The most baroque of Anthony Mann's films after *The Black Book* (1949), *The Furies* accelerated his segue from noir to western via dynastic melodrama, and saw Barbara Stanwyck lasso her persona to a genre overwhelmingly masculine in orientation. The story brings to the surface those "mythic patterns" the director discerned in the narrative conventions and typical characters of the western.[1] Adapted from a Niven Busch novel that fuses Greek tragedy with neo-Freudian psychology, it imbues its female lead with a powerful Electra complex and casts her, figuratively, as one of the vengeful deities alluded to in the title.[2] This is also the name of the ranch Vance stands to inherit from her father, the autocratic T.C. Jeffords, who receives deference from just about everybody except for his daughter – "I never let him beat me," she purrs proudly. Their love-hate relationship, more suited to lovers than father and daughter, breaks down over her choice of prospective husband, T.C.'s courtship of a gold-digging widow and his execution of her best friend, Juan – a "squatter", in T.C.'s terms, on ancestral land swallowed up by the Furies. (T.C. also has a son. Were this a routine treatment of a common western plot, he would be the one defying paternal authority. He is a milquetoast, however, who leaves the fighting to his ballsier sister.)

Although it opens with a testimonial to T.C. and pioneers of his ilk, it is his daughter who drives the action – the first female protagonist to really crack the whip in a major American western, barring a handful of heavily embellished biopics.[3] It is sustained, moreover, by the agency of forceful women – from Vance's late mother, whose bedchamber T.C. maintains like a shrine, to Flo, his inamorata, played by Judith Anderson in a performance dripping with sweet-tasting poison. The early scenes establish Vance's power over her father, whether sitting with her boots up on his desk or greeting him in one of her mother's frocks – a deed that is highly suggestive of her desire to supersede the latter in his affections.[4] Intimations of incestuous attraction underlie their semi-comic sparring, as well as Vance's jealous ire when Flo turns T.C.'s head and begins undermining his daughter's position on the ranch. The cold war between the women escalates from passive-aggressive exchanges, played with impeccable poise on both their parts, to one of those shocking eruptions of violence that became a hallmark of Mann's work, when Vance throws a pair of scissors into her rival's face. The battle for control of the Furies then takes a convoluted, and not especially thrilling, course: this is a territorial dispute decided not by land raiding but by bear raiding, with Vance buying up T.C.'s bad debts with the aid of the gambler Rip Darrow, her father's sworn enemy and her own object of desire.

Stanwyck's portrayal is both compelling and complex – "one of the most multi-faceted she ever attempted".[5] Hauteur turns to tearful frustration when she is spurned and humiliated by Rip, the only man, aside from Juan, for whom she lowers her defences. Vance's struggle with pride and her passion for a man so like her (and, significantly, like her father) in personality and temperament represents the star's finest work in a genre that often found her torn in this way, eliciting sympathy for a character who never actively seeks it. Notwithstanding excellent work by Anderson and a bravura valedictory display by Walter Huston, *The Furies* is Stanwyck's film. Even so, it is not quite Vance's. As Jeanine Basinger points out, the focus vacillates from her to the bullish T.C., the kind of man who takes umbrage at a wild bull being nicknamed "the king of the Furies" and proceeds to wrestle it into submission, thus reclaiming his crown. The patriarch was clearly more agreeable to Mann, given what Basinger calls the director's "general lack of interest in a female protagonist".[6] (It hardly seems coincidental that T.C., a cattle baron very much in the imperious mould of Jackson McCanles from Busch's *Duel in the Sun*, bears a marked resemblance to the similarly intransigent Alec Waggoman and Dock Tobin, from Mann's *The Man from Laramie* and *Man of the West* respectively.) This uncertainty saps a certain amount of tension from the drama; with two such hubristic figures competing for attention, as well as for control of the ranch, the narrative struggles to do both justice. The irrepressible Stanwyck secures a narrow victory for Vance.

With its fatale-like fulcrum and the cruel interplay of its principals, the film is strongly redolent of noir – Mann's formative genre and Stanwyck's spiritual home. The dualistic nature of the opposing pairs – T.C. and Rip, Vance and Flo – contributes a "discomforting and fascinating tension that can be found in many a film noir".[7] There are few scenic shots, while many key scenes take place at night. Victor Milner's Oscar-nominated photography stresses shadows and silhouettes, while Mann utilises settings and props – claustrophobic interiors; mirrors; inhospitable terrain; louring skies – as psychological shorthand. At times, he achieves a perfect fusion of styles, as when Vance takes her anguish into the outback, where her problems seem as insurmountable as the cliff face atop which Juan and his family reside. This is the site of the film's one genuine action set piece – a nocturnal shootout between the Herreras above and T.C.'s gunmen below that anticipates the precipitous confrontations Mann staged with such aplomb in *Winchester '73* and *The Naked Spur*.

Vance's relationships with her father and Rip have the same destructive potential as the fatal attraction between Pearl and Lewt in *Duel in the Sun*, as well as the noxious pairings characteristic of noir. Yet for all the animosity and bloodshed that result from Vance and T.C.'s mutual intractability, amends are made and compromises struck for the unconvincing finale. With Vance brought to heel by the masterful Rip and seemingly keen to assume the obedient role so often allotted female characters, the spotlight returns to T.C. He accepts his defeat at his daughter's hands with a good grace that is scarcely credible, given his bloodcurdling threats against her; that the scene works at all testifies to Huston's ornery charm and the character's place in Mann's affections as a bastion of self-determination and male virility – the kind that has been challenged and displaced by Vance. The reconciliation is cut short, however, by another of the Furies: Juan's vengeful mother (played as a banshee by Blanche Yurka) reasserts the decisive role of women in this most idiosyncratic of Fifties westerns. **KG**

footnotes

1 Jim Kitses, *Horizons West* (BFI, 2007).

2 Doubtless Mann was also drawn to the novel's resemblance to *King Lear*. Making a western version of Shakespeare's tragedy was one of the director's longstanding ambitions. He incorporated some of its key themes into *The Man from Laramie* and *Man of the West*, and announced a more direct transposition shortly before his death, in 1967.

3 Stanwyck, for example, gave a typically gutsy performance in the title role of 1935's *Annie Oakley*.

4 Huston and Stanwyck's fond relationship on the set informed their more intimate scenes together. "[Walter] came into the house and gave me a lusty kiss," remembered Stanwyck. "The director said, 'You're playing father and daughter you know,' and Walter said, 'Leave me alone! I'm enjoying it. I'll play it my own way!'" Quoted in *Barbara Stanwyck* by Al DiOrio (Coward-McCann Inc, 1983).

5 Dan Callahan, *Barbara Stanwyck – The Miracle Woman* (University Press of Mississippi, 2012).

6 Jeanine Basinger, *Anthony Mann* (Wesleyan University Press, 2007).

7 Mary Lea Brady and Kevin Stoehr, *Ride, Boldly, Ride* (University of California Press, 2012).

Paramount présente
Une production
HAL WALLIS
LES FURIES
BARBARA
STANWYCK
WENDELL
COREY
WALTER
HUSTON
"Les Furies," c'est le domaine de la violence et de la passion...
avec JUDITH
ANDERSON
GILBERT
ROLAND
THOMAS
GOMEZ
BEULAH
BONDI
Réalisation de
ANTHONY MANN
Scénario de Charles Schnee
d'après le roman de Niven Busch
C'est un Film Paramount
Films Paramount
Imp. A. KARCHER . PARIS

The Gunfighter

1950, B/W, 84 mins.

D: Henry King.
P: Nunnally Johnson (Twentieth Century-Fox).
W: William Bowers, William Sellers, Andre de Toth (story).
Ph: Arthur Miller. M: Alfred Newman.
St: Gregory Peck (Jimmie Ringo), Helen Westcott (Peggy Walsh), Millard Mitchell (Marshal Mark Strett), Jean Parker (Molly), Karl Malden (Mac)

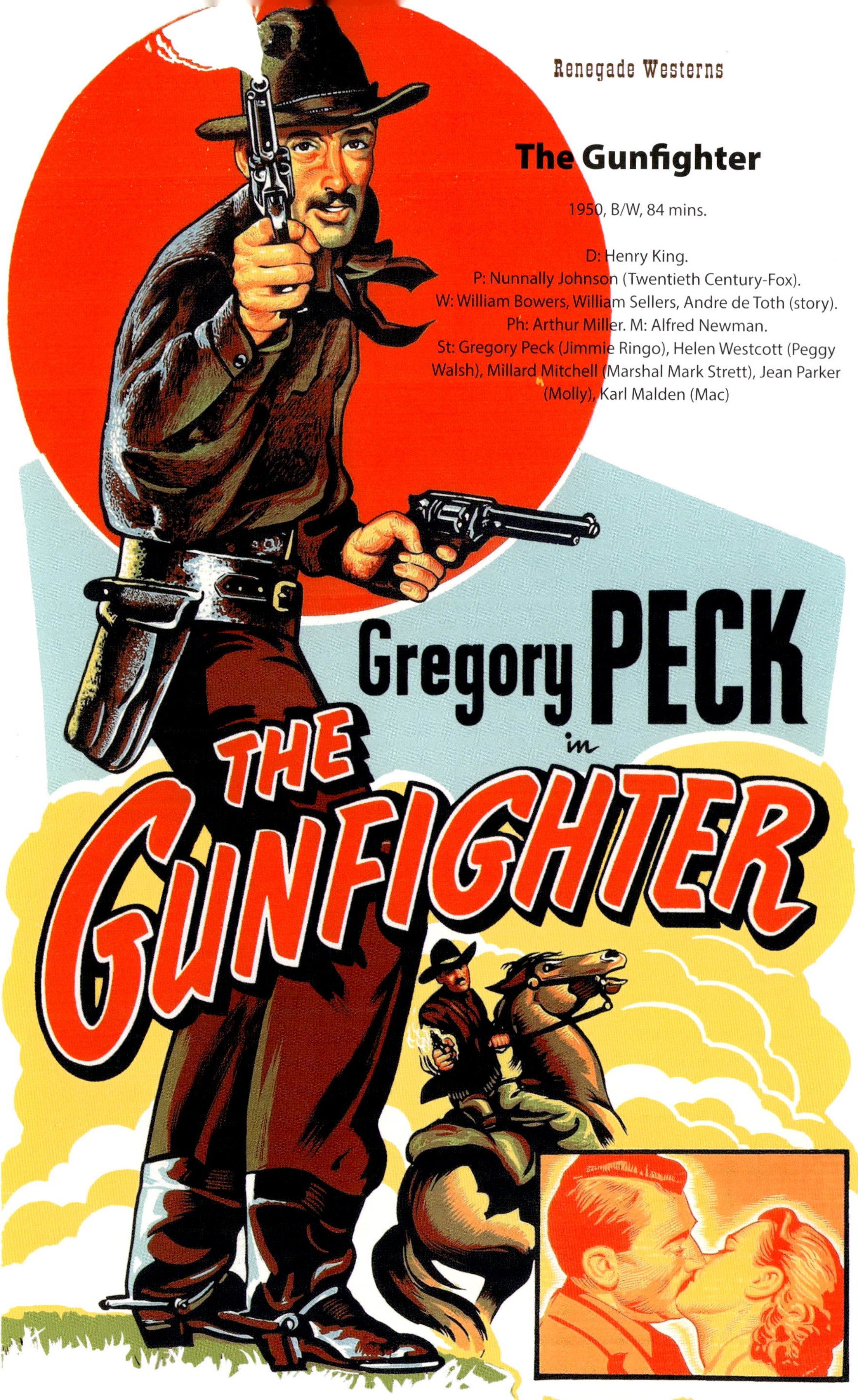

"He's not wild any more. Just sorry."

From an embryonic story by prolific writer/director Andre de Toth, with a leanly plotted script predating the similarly themed *Shane* and informing the structure of *High Noon*, *The Gunfighter* deserves its status as a landmark western.[1] It was the first major film of its kind to "begin to dismantle the popular myths of the West", as producer Nunnally Johnson stated – to depict gun violence as a sordid business, something that can so damage a man psychologically that any journey to redemption is likely to reach a dead end. (In this sense, it is reminiscent of film noir.) Johnson also remarked that audiences "brought up with Jesse James were probably put off by the relatively realistic depiction of [title character] Ringo".[2] Indeed, it faired comparatively poorly at the box office, although many critics praised it for being more contemplative than preceding westerns; moreover, its bitter tone paved the way for the introspective westerns that so marked the Fifties.[3]

Jimmie Ringo, a gunman with too many notches on his barrel, is forced to shoot down Eddy (Richard Jaeckel), yet another saloon upstart, and seeks refuge in Cayenne. He has history there: Peggy, Ringo's estranged wife and the mother of his son, is the local schoolteacher; marshal Mark Strett is a former colleague-in-crime; the barman, Mac, is an old friend from another town. Aware that Eddy's three brothers are making their way to Cayenne to avenge his death, Ringo stations himself in the saloon, hoping that someone can persuade Peggy to speak to him. While the clocks tick and Ringo anxiously paces the room, another threat looms as Hunt Bromley (Skip Homeier), a snot-nosed local with designs on Peggy, decides that this could be an opportune time to make a name for himself.

Like vultures, the constituents of the town circle the saloon waiting for something to happen – a killing, something synonymous with the name Jimmie Ringo. The film denounces society's role in the creation of the gunfighter legend – an increasingly shabby myth in which the title character is depicted as a man constantly on the run or cornered, spooked by his own shadow. The idea of Ringo being akin to a trapped animal, as well as a prisoner of his reputation, is reinforced by the way he sits in the bar in Cayenne, keeping the walls behind him as protection, hinting at the wariness that goes with his profession, occasionally pacing the floor, snapping at those gawping outside to move away. It is a mode of behaviour that has been forced on him by necessity: "He lives according to a discipline of watchfulness, preparedness and restraint – the marks of his professionalism and signs of his isolation."[4] Meanwhile, Mac sniffs an opportunity to drum up extra business, asking permission to commemorate this special day.

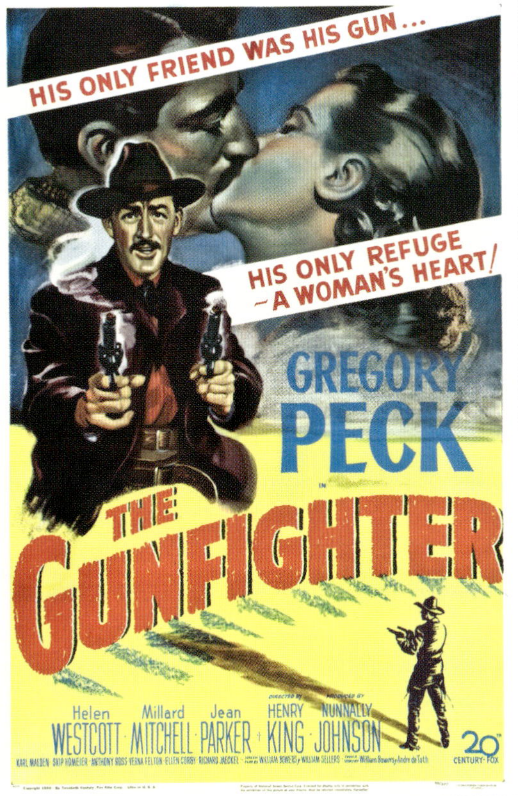

Gregory Peck's performance is unusually revealing for an actor who gives little away in terms of emotion. He is equally strong when Ringo is fretful, hoping that the love of his life will speak to him, and self-assured, brushing away obnoxious braggarts like Bromley – "If I didn't have something else on my mind, I'd slap you cross-eyed"; or, most touchingly, correcting the behaviour of the son he meets for the first time. Over the course of the film, the allure of the gunfighter is drained away to expose the real human being. Despite his love for Peggy and desire to start a new life with her and their son, there is a fatalism to Ringo, a weariness that Peck rarely brought to other roles. As Strett says to Peggy, "[He is] a little older, a little tireder, not as cocky as he used to be."

As part of the demythologising process, Peck and the director were meticulous in choosing Ringo's less than flamboyant attire. "We wanted this fellow to… dress in a motley collection of clothes like the people in the daguerreotypes of the early West," said Peck. "I put on a handlebar moustache and a funny-looking corduroy coat. They gave me a soup-bowl haircut, a 15-center, not at all romantic-looking." The studio brass did not appreciate their efforts. Fox president Spyros Skouras was reputedly enraged at Peck's unromantic appearance; Darryl F. Zanuck also feared the box office would suffer as a result: "This man [Peck] has a young following," he is reported to have said. "That moustache, I'm afraid, is going to kill it."[5]

Millard Mitchell provides ironclad support as the marshal. He performs a balancing act, interceding with Peggy on his old friend's behalf while placating a sorority of upstanding gossips, outraged that such a bad egg as Ringo has camped in their town. The film's drollest scene sees these women, led by Mrs. August Pennyfeather (Verna Felton), confronting the marshal and Ringo, unaware of the latter's identity, and offering their solutions for dealing with the outlaw. When Ringo reveals himself, their disgust and fear spill forth. The marshal, once a member of the same gang, has managed to live down his past and now has the only thing that Ringo craves: acceptance within civilised society, for what that is worth.

As in *Shane*, one of the films it arguably influenced, *The Gunfighter* examines its protagonist's damaged psyche and finds his humanity battered but basically intact. Ringo confronts Jerry Marlow, a grieving father armed with a shotgun who believes that the outlaw killed his son. Ringo refutes the allegation. "You're crazy thinking if I killed someone, I wouldn't remember it." This echoes his riposte to the marshal, who is surprised that Ringo knows precisely how many men he's killed. "You keep count?" remarks Street. "Don't ask dumb questions," is Ringo's terse response. Both Shane and Ringo are ersatz role models:

the former to a child who wants him to replace his father; the latter to a boy unaware of who this man really is. Both men, of course, have too much blood on their hands for domestic harmony to be a realistic option.

As Eddy's brothers make their way to Cayenne, King ramps up the tension, ticking clocks counting down the remaining hour or so of Ringo's life. He steals edgy sideways glances at the saloon's timepieces, and many of the conversations are filmed in looming close-ups. Pendulums swing back and forth between him and Peggy as her negative responses continue to frustrate him. It makes for a tightly paced portrait of a man scrabbling for redemption, the desperate chance to reconcile a family unit. Ringo tries to avoid violence, strives to become faceless and to set a positive example for his son in the all-too-brief moment they have together. The film's "noirish, deterministic take on its hero", however, never relents: "While Ringo wants to change and make a fresh start, the world will simply not let him."[6]

The script by William Bowers and William Sellers must have impressed Carl Foreman, since many of *The Gunfighter's* motifs emerge in *High Noon*, which emulates and, due in great part to Gary Cooper's haunted performance, surpasses the dramatic tension derived from a real-time drama bound for bloodshed.[7] The inhabitants of both towns want their gunmen to go away, even though Will Kane and Jimmie Ringo represent opposing sides of the law. Both Hadleyville and Cayenne are relatively civilised and the presence of a lone gunman carries the unwanted scent of the West's bloody past. The motivation of each man is self-validation: Ringo's to make amends to his family and be accepted within society; Will Kane's to prove he won't run away from anything. In contrast, though, it is the lawman (Kane) who knows he must resort to the gun as a solution, while it's the criminal (Ringo) who is willing to renounce violence. And in each case, women prove pivotal to the plot. Both Kane's spouse (Grace Kelly) in *High Noon* and Peggy are persuaded to stand by their men by women who have their own history with the heroes. Ageing good-time girl Molly in *The Gunfighter* and entrepreneur Helen Ramirez (Katy Jurado) in *High Noon* are given more influential roles and afforded more respect than the usual disposable female sex interests that peppered the genre.

Immortalised in the lyrics of Bob Dylan's *Brownville Girl*, Ringo's demise – shot in the back by the cowardly Bromley – is as inevitable as it is wasteful, the empty promise that he'll see his son again the following year echoing through his final breath. What makes this ending so extraordinary is that Ringo, at the close of his own futile quest for repentance, does not urge his assassin to mend his ways; nor does he express forgiveness. Instead, he curses him, insisting that Bromley be given credit for gunning him down in a fair fight, ensuring the boy will take his place as the target for every fame-hungry punk with a gun and condemning him to the same kind of lonely lifestyle. The drama thus culminates in tragedy, but Ringo at least achieves a posthumous reconciliation with the woman he loved. Whether he has earned acceptance by the community is less certain, as is the merit of society's embrace. **CH**

above: Gregory Peck with Skip Homeier (right) as the odious Hunt Bromley.

footnotes

1 As a young script analyst, Roger Corman did some uncredited polishing on an early version of the screenplay, as recounted in his memoir, *How I Made a Hundred Movies in Hollywood and Never Lost a Dime.*

2 De Toth based his protagonist on historical gunman Johnny Ringo, who earned renown as a cultured but vicious killer and was reputedly involved in the gunfight at the O.K. Corral in Tombstone in 1881. He is believed to have been shot down by a braggart who served as the model for this film's Hunt Bromley.

3 Henry King felt *The Gunfighter* was the best of the six films he made with Gregory Peck: "It was a serious, adult western, but I was not aware that I was starting a trend… I directed the film because I thought the story contained a great deal of truth" (Interview with Gene D. Phillips in *American Classic Screen*, 1981).

4 Richard Slotkin, *Gunfighter Nation: The Myth of the Frontier in Twentieth Century America* (University of Oklahoma Press, 1998).

5 Quoted in *Gregory Peck: A Charmed Life* by Lynn Haney (Robson Books, 2003).

6 David Meuel, *The Noir Western* (McFarland, 2015).

7 Cooper was the first choice of de Toth and William Bowers for the role of Ringo in *The Gunfighter.*

Winchester '73

1950, B/W, 92 mins.

D: Anthony Mann. P: Aaron Rosenberg (Universal-International). W: Robert L. Richards, Borden Chase, Stuart N. Lake (story). Ph: William Daniels. M: Joseph Gershenson. St: James Stewart (Lin McAdam), Shelley Winters (Lola Manners), Dan Duryea (Waco Johnnie Dean), Stephen McNally (Dutch Henry Brown), Millard Mitchell (High Spade)

"That's too much gun for a man to have just for... shootin' rabbits."
"Or for shootin' men in the back."

In 1950, the western was poised between the comparative moral certitude of the pre-war years and the anxieties articulated by film noir in the Forties. Few artists, certainly among those regularly associated with westerns (and noir, in his case), managed the transition as dexterously as Anthony Mann. The first of his collaborations with James Stewart straddles the divide itself, and was Mann's own favourite among his westerns. Indian attacks, bank robberies and references to real people and events provide a patina of familiarity, but Stewart's highly strung performance – "I liked the idea of a man who was *driven*"[1] – propels the film into uncomfortable psychological terrain, alternating knightly virtue with emotional instability as he pursues a relentless vendetta against his brother, the man who killed their father. Typically for Mann, there is no way for the hero to ride around the fatal confrontation; here, as elsewhere, he is impelled by primal instincts, his mania matching or even exceeding that of his opponent. Ultimately, his 'victory', conventional in narrative terms, is akin to a defeat. He is made to bear a terrible burden that can only – despite the token consolatory presence of a heroine – exacerbate his alienation from the civilized world.

Having inherited the project from Fritz Lang, partly at Stewart's suggestion, Mann brought in Borden Chase to rewrite the original script, initiating another rewarding creative partnership. The doubling motif, twinning the hero with a corrupt or evil alter ego, usually with an arduous trek or quest as a backdrop, is typical of Chase (*Red River*, Mann's *Bend of the River* and *The Far Country*, *Vera Cruz*, *Backlash*, *Night Passage* [1957]). In Mann's hands, the theme became a means to force his protagonists to face themselves – their capacity for violence, their psychoses, their past deeds and place in the world. Mann and Stewart (and Gary Cooper, in the stormy *Man of the West*) would refine the idea in later films, but in essence it is here, together with all the sub-themes and character types (and several of the actors: Jay C. Flippen, John McIntire, Millard Mitchell) that unify the Mann-Stewart cycle.

The episodic plot follows the prized rifle ("one of a thousand") as it passes from one character to another, determining the destiny of all who possess it: first Lin McAdam, who wins it in a shooting contest in Dodge

City against his hated brother, Dutch Henry Brown, who then steals it; it is subsequently acquired, in each case fleetingly, by a cagey gunrunner and the Indian chief he supplies,[2] a cowardly ex-outlaw, the sneering desperado Waco Johnnie Dean, and finally Dutch Henry again. Not until the closing moments does McAdam reclaim it, by which time it has become a poisoned chalice.

These 'chapters' are "united through the dominant metaphor of the gun",[3] as are the recurring characters that provide continuity. Shelley Winters' long-suffering saloon girl, for example, first seen being bundled out of Dodge City at the behest of local prudes in a gesture towards *Stagecoach*, vies with the Winchester for the status of lust object. In a development that would no doubt draw fire from feminists, she is passed around like the rifle itself, only less tenderly, from her no-good lover to Waco Johnnie Dean. (Female leads often seemed surplus to requirements in Mann's westerns. Even Winters was nonplussed by her role: "I don't know what the hell I was doing in that picture. I always figured that there were all these guys running around trying to get their hands on this goddam rifle who should've been trying to get their hands on me. But that doesn't make for a good western, I guess. In the end, nobody remembers me being in it."[4]) She has her sights set firmly on McAdam, however; even their flirting employs guns and bullets as sexual innuendos. Accepting the loan of his pistol during a siege by Indians, she tells him she "understands about the last one"; when the threat has passed, she wants to keep the bullet anyway – implicitly, as a substitute for McAdam's seed, just as his valour and proficiency with weapons function as conventional demonstrations of virility. If that seems retrogressive for a film regarded as a watershed, the deployment of Indians for cheap laughs or as target practice for whites – Rock Hudson's stereotypically bloodthirsty war chief leads his braves in an almost comically naive frontal assault – feels like a hangover from a different era entirely. Better could justifiably have been expected of Mann and Stewart, director and star respectively of the same year's groundbreaking *Devil's Doorway* and *Broken Arrow*.

James Stewart looking out for Shelley Winters (*above*), and manhandling Dan Duryea (*top right*).

More pleasing is Will Geer's interpretation of Wyatt Earp in the opening sequence. In place of the stern moral arbiter of *My Darling Clementine* (1946), the foursquare hero of *Gunfight at the O.K. Corral* (1957) or the unscrupulous figure played by Harris Yulin in *Doc*, Geer gives us a wry, folksy patriarch of advanced years whose easy-going demeanour belies the rigour with which he upholds the law; even McAdam, a tough customer by any standards, becomes sheepish when he learns Earp's identity.[5] Besides demonstrating his authority, the marshal's no-guns rule in Dodge City defers the showdown between the brothers: in one of the most powerful displays of the almost psychopathic urges to which Mann's central characters were prone, McAdam and Dutch Henry spot each other in the saloon and instinctively reach for their empty holsters, quivering with mutual animosity. It must have been startling for filmgoers to see James Stewart behaving this way; this was the genial star of films such as *Destry Rides Again* (1939), source of an in-joke when Dutch Henry mockingly orders McAdam a glass of milk, Destry's preferred tipple. Moreover, as Jeanine Basinger has pointed out, the 'shootout' "forces a viewer to re-evaluate the ritual… Stripped of the violent glory of the gunfight, the 'reach-and-draw' scene is laid bare as a psychotic event."[6]

Although they would clearly have shot each other there and then, given the chance, it somehow would not do for the primary antagonists of this or any other Anthony Mann western – his key works, at any rate – to settle their differences the Owen Wister way: at ten paces on main street. Given the primitive state to which they are reduced when the red mist descends, the natural world is their rightful arena, and Mann sets the final duel between McAdam and his brother in a craggy outcrop; the terrain "finally seems to be an inner landscape, the unnatural world of a disturbed mind".[7] Wedged between rocks, pinned down by rifle fire, bullets ricocheting inches from their faces, they taunt each other until McAdam fires the fatal shot. Stewart's simple gesture of slowly lowering his head, filmed from behind, conveys relief and remorse, both at the killing itself and, possibly, the fact that his quest is at an end (as his sidekick High Spade had suggested to him earlier, "You're beginning to like it"). Actions always spoke louder than words in Mann's films, and Stewart's posture at the end eloquently defines violence, even if morally justifiable, as both psychologically damaging and physically draining.

Winchester '73 helped steer the western hero, via a series of situations culled from innumerable prior stories, into a new era of self-doubt and emotional honesty. The pain of the process is reflected in Stewart's performance. The star's eagerness to redefine his image was evident in the dedication he brought to the role. "I practised not just firing the gun, but learning how to hold it in such a way that it looked like the most natural thing in the world for me to walk down the street with a rifle in my hand," he said.[8] Mann was duly impressed, and the five westerns they made together in as many years retain a combined significance as great as any in the genre. **KG**

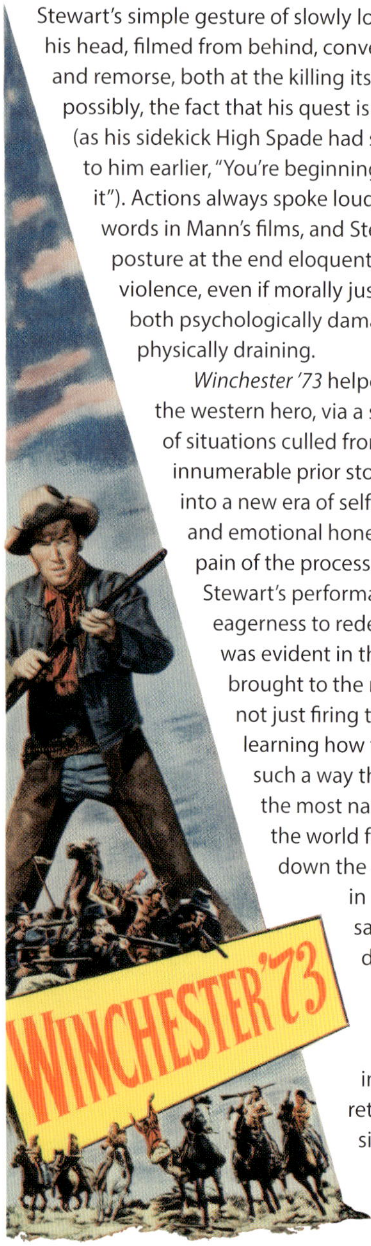

footnotes

1 Quoted in *Jimmy Stewart: The Truth Behind the Legend* by Michael Munn (Robson Books, 2005).

2 Selling guns to 'hostiles' had particularly negative connotations in the early years of the Red Scare. As John H. Lenihan has noted, plots about keeping 'superweapons' out of the clutches of America's enemies in films such as *Colt .45* (1950) and *Springfield Rifle* (1952) can be seen as a reflection of atom-age anxiety about Russia's nuclear programme.

3 Jeanine Basinger, *Anthony Mann* (Wesleyan University Press, 2007).

4 *Jimmy Stewart: The Truth Behind the Legend.*

5 *Winchester '73* was based on a story by Stuart N. Lake, a confidant of Earp's, author of his first major – now generally discredited – biography, and the source of many Earp-related movies and TV series, including *My Darling Clementine.* Geer's winning performance notwithstanding, Earp was barely into his 30s during his tenure as a peace officer in Dodge City, and never rose above the rank of assistant marshal, despite his later claims to have held the top job.

6 Jeanine Basinger, *Anthony Mann.*

7 Jim Kitses, *Horizons West* (BFI Publishing, 2007).

8 *Jimmy Stewart: The Truth Behind the Legend.*

Westward the Women

1951, B/W, 116 mins.

D: William A. Wellman. P: Dore Schary (Metro-Goldwyn-Mayer). W: Charles Schnee, Frank Capra (story). Ph: William Mellor. M: Jeff Alexander. St: Robert Taylor (Buck Wyatt), Denise Darcel (Fifi Danon), John McIntire (Roy Whitman), Hope Emerson (Patience Hawley), Julie Bishop (Laurie Smith)

"I'll make men out of your women... By the time we get to that valley, you'll know the women who are left are fit stock."

Following in the dusty wagon tracks of *Red River* (co-scripted by Charles Schnee) and *Wagon Master* (1950), via a distinctly idiosyncratic route, *Westward the Women* puts a distaff spin on one of the western's oldest formats. So unusual was this endeavour, certainly for its era, that the film cannot sustain its proto-feminist intentions – its progressive urges, like the gains made by its female charges in terms of gender stereotyping, are ultimately kept in check by a combination of endemic conservatism and male anxiety vis-à-vis the fairer sex. ("There are only two things that scare me," announces Robert Taylor early on, "and a good woman is both of them.") Summarising *Westward's* duality, Peter William Evans says that it "reaffirms Fifties American attitudes towards sex and gender... Nevertheless, the film also succeeds, in a genre traditionally concerned with male desire, in representing the more heroic, less 'feminine' forms of female desire."[1]

The script views women in both a traditional light – as prospective wives for a community of miners in Roy Whitman's California valley; as the "roots", in his words, that will transform the desert into a garden – and as pioneers in their own right. One hundred and fifty of them sign up for the hardships of a 2,000-mile trek from Chicago to Whitman's promised land. The journey becomes tougher still when most of the male crew desert, leaving the women at the mercy of the elements, the rugged terrain and the equally unyielding trail guide, Buck Wyatt, an unashamed misogynist whose cajoling and carping help forge those women who survive the ordeal – and many don't – into a hardy and effective unit.[2] (Scenes in which they handle guns, wrangle mules, repair wagons and tackle other tasks traditionally associated with men could almost be a metaphor for women's 'encroachment' on the male terrain of heavy industrial factories during the Second World War.) Their growth as characters, or at least their development beyond the bounds of archetype, is in a sense matched by that of Buck: the experience erodes his misogyny to the extent that he acquires a fiancée of his own in the form of dance-hall girl Fifi Danon, the feistiest and earthiest of the women in his entourage.

The film's coup is not merely to pass the buck, as it were, from the trail guide and his right-hand men to the women who comprise their precious 'cargo', but to do so in an entirely plausible manner. The plot may boil down to 'a woman's gotta do what a man's gotta do', but the novelty value of, say, the similarly inclined *The Guns of Fort Petticoat* (1957) is not the issue here. William A. Wellman's no-nonsense direction keeps events grounded in dirt and sweat (the absence of lens filters aids the film's exceptionally stark photographic style), with random breaks for tragic mishaps – a mother accidentally shoots her young son dead; a wagon is swept away in a flash flood – and a fatal encounter with Indians.[3]

In the film's most poignant scene, Wellman shows only the aftermath of the attack, with the names of the dead called out as if inscribed on a monument. The absence of music here and elsewhere – only the titles and the closing moments are scored – contributes to the naturalistic and largely unsentimental tone.

Another of the film's strengths is that, unlike other female characters given central roles in westerns, the women are not intended to be exceptional. These are not formidable Barbara Stanwyck types; nor do they bear any resemblance to the femmes fatales, spunky outlaws or maverick queens of the gender-bending westerns made later in the decade. These are ordinary women – widows, school teachers – mostly rather plain, who rise to the challenge posed by an arduous expedition without abandoning what the script insists are 'typical' feminine virtues: compassion for a pregnant comrade, for example, or the importance of keeping up appearances. (Buck, chided by Fifi for his grimy complexion, is bemused by the efforts the women go to, even in the dust and heat of the desert, to stay as clean as possible. When they are finally within spitting distance of their destination, they refuse to move further until he supplies them with material with which to fashion new attire. He meekly accedes.)

The pleasing spectacle of women rising above their allotted social/gender/genre roles and behaving in a more 'masculine' fashion, as when two of them resolve their bickering with a full-blooded fistfight – no slapping, scratching or hair-pulling – is balanced by an undertow of unease about what this means for men, what 'damage' it may do to the 'natural' gender order. While it is refreshing that a woman is allowed to be the 'aggressor' in a putative relationship, for instance, the romance between Buck and Fifi feels imposed on the narrative, the pace of it forced, as if to underline the threat posed to masculine supremacy. (In defence of this, Buck resorts to verbal and physical abuse to 'tame' her; reassuringly, for male viewers sharing Buck's mindset, she melts into his arms after he slaps her, his primitive methods "a reminder to a woman of her weakness and subordination to male authority".[4]) It is when the guide is led astray from the path of macho individualism – when his command is undermined – that disaster strikes. His dalliance with Fifi, for example, causes Buck to neglect the wagons before the Indian attack. This points to a sub-theme in which, as in *Red River* and the psychological westerns of the Fifties, the hero's competence and judgement are called into question. Like Tom Dunson, Buck's iron discipline drives his men away; and during the storm that claims another two lives, he gets recklessly drunk with the diminutive Japanese cook, Ito – his comic-relief sidekick and, broadly, this film's equivalent of *Red River's* Matt Garth, the hero's 'sensitive' alter ego and nagging voice of reason.

The theme of imperilled masculinity is reinforced when Buck – now symbolically clean-shaven – takes his place among the husbands-to-be in Whitman's valley at the climax. Having won their battle of wills with Buck and triumphed over adversity, the women flaunt their newly empowered status when the imposing Patience, their de facto spokeswoman, informs the miners: "Don't think you're going to do the choosing." There are no complaints from the men, whose sense of self-respect is less pronounced than that of their newly acquired brides. It is the culmination of Wellman's efforts to heroise his female protagonists, who are often filmed from ennobling low angles, rather than merely objectify them. (If anybody is objectified, it is Robert Taylor; Fifi's flattering references to Buck's "beautiful face" allude to the actor's Hollywood sobriquet: 'the man with the perfect profile'.) In the context, given how unusual this outcome was for a western of this (or any) period, the concomitant neutering of the male hero – of all the male characters – seems a fair price to pay. **KG**

footnotes

1 Peter William Evans, 'Feminising the Wilderness' in *The Movie Book of the Western* (Studio Vista, 1996).

2 Wellman warned his actresses that the shoot – locations were filmed in Utah's Canyonlands and the California desert – would be gruelling, and urged any faint hearts to quit before it began. Buck gives a similar speech near the beginning of the film (Frank T. Thomson, *William A. Wellman*, Scarecrow Press, 1983).

3 The rigours of the would-be brides' overland odyssey reflect the testimony recorded in the *Covered Wagon Women* series of memoirs. En route from Ohio to Oregon in May 1851, 19-year-old Harriet Talcott Buckingham notes "one of the most terrifine storms I ever witnessed. The heavens seemed to be opened. The rain fell in torrents. The lightning was most vivid. We were obliged to move as soon as possible for fear of being overflown. Our cattle was skatered miles around us... I had often heard of the Platt[e] river storms & we realized it beyond the most vivid descriptions." (*Covered Wagon Women: Diaries and Letters from the Western Trails, 1851, Volume 3*, edited by Kenneth L. Holmes, University of Nebraska Press, 1996).

4 Peter William Evans, 'Feminising the Wilderness', *The Movie Book of the Western.* This section of the film preserves the essence of Frank Capra's original story, which he described as being like "*The Taming of the Shrew*. It was about one strong-willed woman who had to have her way and the man had to finally knock her down. Then she finally learned her lesson." (Quoted in Thompson, *William A. Wellman*).

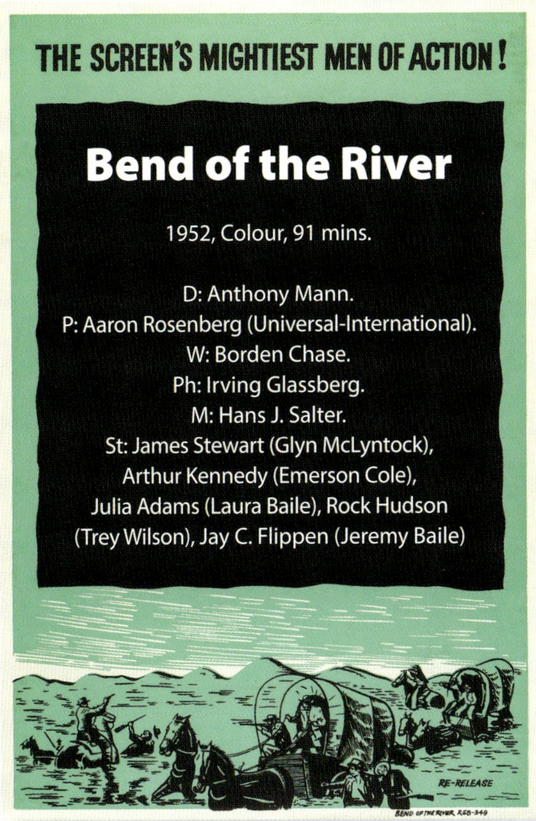

"That kind can't change. When an apple's rotten, there's nothing you can do except throw it away or it will spoil the whole barrel."

The second Mann-Stewart western ploughs heavily furrowed territory – the struggles of hardy settlers – while tracing its protagonist's psychological development. Based very loosely on a novel by Bill Gulick, Borden Chase's script exercises once again his fascination with the duality of man, the potential for change – for better and for worse. *Bend of the River* enlarges on this theme, wrapping subsidiary characters, even an entire town, in its embrace. As Jeanine Basinger has summarised, the film itself expresses a dual nature, changing course like the raging river where much of its defining action takes place.

Stewart's character, Glyn McLyntock, at first appears more stable than the vengeful Lin McAdam of *Winchester '73*. Instead of seeking retribution, he's looking to put down roots, escorting a wagon train of pioneers from Missouri to the Oregon Territory. It's rough country, scenic but unyielding. As McLyntock scouts an easier route for the wagons, Mann throws in a jarring zip pan to reveal Emerson Cole, his head in a noose, about to be hanged. The rapidity of the camera movement creates a visual bond between the two men – almost, but not quite, blurring their identities. This is cemented when McLyntock frees Cole, and reinforced by their near-identical reactions when each learns the other's name and realises they share the same murderous background as Kansas-Missouri border raiders. All Mann's heroes underwent trials, crises, before they could redeem themselves, and this encounter in the wild has an almost providential quality: "It is as though, in seeking to evade not only the mountain but his own past, Glyn conjures up the image of that past."[1] McLyntock has covered up his criminal deeds, like the rope scar around his neck that testifies to his own previous run-in with a lynch mob, but Cole's arrival (and eventual betrayal) forces him to challenge his demons – a painful but purifying process.

Cole is comfortable with who he is, and recognises that McLyntock is anything but. (Arthur Kennedy's astute performance is the equal of his turns for Mann in *The Man from Laramie* and for Fritz Lang in *Rancho Notorious*.) He pinpoints his new friend's motivation for joining the settlers: McLyntock, as he admits, is running away from the man he once was; Cole warns him he won't be able to outrun that man forever. "The irony is that he has, of course, already caught up with him,"[2] for Cole embodies all his old instincts (they demonstrate these together when they snake out into the woods to kill an Indian raiding party), and shares the same history. Cole is not evil, but neither is he repentant. He knows he will never be accepted by the kind of community the settlers hope to establish, and may be speaking from experience when he warns McLyntock not to harbour false hopes: "They won't let you change… [when] they find out you're the Glyn McLyntock that used to raid along the Missouri border [they'll] kick you out." The stark moralising of the settlers' patriarch, Jeremy, adds weight to Cole's words.

As ever, Mann is in his element, quite literally, when dramatising the physical and mental agonies of his characters against an imposing backdrop of natural obstacles (the film was shot, in ravishing Technicolor, more or less where it is set, along the Columbia River, the Snake River and in the Cascade Mountains). Footage of wagons rumbling over rock-strewn riverbeds or

above: from left: Julia Adams, Arthur Kennedy and James Stewart.

struggling through mountain passes celebrates man's tenacity; comparisons with *Red River* (co-scripted by Charles Schnee), are unavoidable. But the scenes set in the bustling town of Portland, from where the settlers continue their journey via steamer, have an equally vital thematic function. Welcomed heartily on their first visit, Jeremy and McLyntock receive an altogether different reception when they return months later to chase up a shipment of supplies: gold has been discovered nearby, and Portland has been transformed. It is now a boom town in moral decline. Greed is the new ethos – the supplies have been requisitioned, their value having soared in line with the demand from mining camps, and McLyntock has to shoot his way out, aided by Cole, now a saloon enforcer, and Trey Wilson, a suave gambler. (As in many westerns, farming is viewed as a benign use of nature's gifts, while mining for gold is both despoliation and the catalyst for destructive desires.)

On the arduous trek back to the homestead, both Cole and McLyntock revert to their 'natural', pre-civilised state: the former when he and his cronies hijack the supplies, intending to sell them to miners for a profit; McLyntock when he lets his demons loose, using the environment as a screen – blending with it – to attack his enemies. The correlation of Mann's protagonists with the natural world was never clearer, and the sequence culminates in McLyntock symbolically slaying his old self, drowning Cole after a tussle in the Snake River. Stewart is more restrained than he was in *Winchester '73*, but when he does allow McLyntock's mask to slip, the effect is never less than convincing – the scene in which he attacks Fifties stalwart Jack Lambert with a knife, eyes burning with murderous intent, is justly famous for its intensity.

Bend of the River's shortcomings are both generic – perfunctory romantic entanglements; female character as male hero's conscience – and specific. Both Trey Wilson and Laura, Jeremy's eldest daughter, have a dramatic potential that is never realised; he is tempted by the glitter of gold, she by the decadence of Portland, but they are cut adrift once the narrative zeroes in on McLyntock's clash with Cole. In addition, Stepin Fetchit's comedic-negro shtick is likely to grate or offend modern audiences. But as a synthesis of Mann's preoccupations, and those of Borden Chase, the film is immensely satisfying. The protagonist with something to hide harks back to the director's films noir, and the easy rapport between Stewart and Kennedy makes the rupture between them all the more affecting. The outcome is unusually clear-cut: McLyntock emerges from his river ordeal exhausted but cleansed, baptised into the settlers' community. Jeremy's acceptance that 'rotten apples' *can* change comes off as pat, but Stewart's rounded performance validates the sentiment. None of Mann's other western heroes was able (or permitted) to overcome his crises – both internal and external – so completely. **KG**

footnotes

1 Douglas Pye, "The Collapse of Fantasy: Masculinity in the Westerns of Anthony Mann" (*The Movie Book of the Western*, Cassell, 1997).

2 Jeanine Basinger, *Anthony Mann* (Wesleyan University Press, 2007).

High Noon

1952, B/W, 85 mins.

D: Fred Zinnemann. P: Stanley Kramer Productions Inc. W: Carl Foreman. Ph: Floyd Crosby. M: Dimitri Tiomkin. St: Gary Cooper (Will Kane), Grace Kelly (Amy Fowler Kane), Katy Jurado (Helen Ramirez), Lloyd Bridges (Harvey Pell), Thomas Mitchell (Jonas Henderson)

"They're making me run; I've never run from anyone before."

Both a distillation of the western and a refutation of some of its most cherished tropes, *High Noon* has become a repository for the anxieties and agendas of competing interest groups. At first glance Fred Zinnemann's sole venture in the genre seems as conventional as they come, albeit more brilliantly realised than most. Break the surface, however, and ripples of meaning emerge: some that reflect its creators' stated intentions, others that stretch beyond and even contradict them. It is clear why the film has provoked so much argument, so many reinterpretations, since its release.

Zinnemann once said, "To me it's about conscience as against compromise: how far can one follow one's conscience before having to compromise."[1] A hero makes a stand, overcoming his own fear, the cowardice and even hostility of sections of the community he is striving to protect, and the opposition of his pacifist wife; she ultimately relents, conceding the moral high ground to her husband. But he also stated, "We wanted to see whether we could take the rigid classic form of the western and give it new meaning." The director was unaware that screenwriter Carl Foreman was writing, in part, about his own experiences as a former Communist at the height of the Red Scare. Subpoenaed by the House Committee on Un-American Activities (HUAC), Foreman was classed as an "un-cooperative witness" when he refused to implicate other 'fellow travellers'; he took himself off to England before *High Noon* was finished, knowing he would be blacklisted for his non-cooperation. (Unlike the central character in his script, Foreman was not alone in his troubles: the careers of the film's cinematographer, Floyd

Motion Picture Association of America, at the expense of one of their own. (These pressures are represented in the film by faceless financiers from "up north" looking to invest in the town, and also by the Miller gang, who could even be the former's minions, depending how far one is willing to run with the analogy.) In short, Foreman saw the film as a parable about "the death of Hollywood". Following Foreman's lead, the citizens represent what one critic has called "civic complacency", a concept that can and has been seized upon by ideological opposites: to those on the political left, it is moral cowardice, allowing McCarthyism to operate unchecked; to the right, it stands for lack of vigilance against anti-American influences – in other words, people like Foreman.[2]

In the eye of the storm stands Marshal Will Kane, perhaps *the* iconic fictional western lawman. Like Shane, Kane is a paradigmatic genre hero – "the man of superior knowledge, courage and capability"[3] – stripped to his essence; at one point he all but says, "A man's gotta do…". But a paradigm is the plaything of interpretation. Given the production's Cold War context, Kane is also, for some commentators, a stand-in for America as global policeman, imploring his fellow citizens – analogues for the United Nations – to back him in his fight – the Korean War –

Crosby, and actors Lloyd Bridges, Virginia Farmer and Howland Chamberlain were also affected by the boycotts.)

Foreman said that "Hadleyville" was a variation on "Hollywood", supporting his intention to criticise the majority's abandonment of HUAC-branded undesirables and the submission to external pressures by the filmmaking community, spearheaded by powerful organisations like the Screen Guilds and the

against the Miller gang – external communist aggression. After all, Kane has bailed them out before, albeit as part of a posse, when he sent Frank Miller up for murder, just as America's involvement had proved instrumental in the Second World War. Kane's new wife, Amy, a Quaker and pacifist, is the isolationist in this scenario. So Kane the rugged individualist is forced to go it alone, forsaken by spineless friends and a wife who values her principles ahead of his, thus enshrining the western hero's code of self-reliance. (The first of *High Noon's* subversive acts is to undermine its protagonist's independence: we first see him at his wedding, being absorbed by the community, until it suits them to spurn him, and being tamed by a woman, or so it seems. The man of violence in western narratives habitually stands apart from these enervating forces; Kane's predicament would have been unthinkable for Shane, for example.) Equally, however, his pleas for support have been attacked for weakening the lone-hero archetype and for advocating something like collectivism, prompting John Wayne and Howard Hawks to fashion *Rio Bravo* (1959) as a belated riposte.

Amplifying the ambiguity of the situation is the anti-populist thrust of the plot. (The casting of Gary Cooper, Frank Capra's man of the people in *Mr. Deeds Goes to Town* and *Meet John Doe*, adds a delicious coating of irony that would have been lacking had producer Stanley Kramer's first choice, Gregory Peck, played the role.) Kane exemplifies traditional heroic virtues, but the film questions whether the beneficiaries of his actions are worth the trouble. "Nothing that happens here is really important," the judge tells him shortly before departing, urging the marshal to save his own skin and leave the town to its fate. Kane's quest for deputies sees the initial impression of a tightly knit, neighbourly community begin to unwind. Some are fearful for their lives and families – one man volunteers, but backs down when he realises he won't be part of a posse. He, like Will's friend Sam (Henry [Harry] Morgan), who forces his wife to lie about his whereabouts when Will comes calling, will probably feel shame for the rest of his life. But there are other elements in town that either have grudges against Kane (Harvey, his upstart deputy) or consider his efficiency and probity in enforcing the law to be bad for business.

For the denizens of the saloon (the town's social strata are neatly delineated), Frank Miller and his associates were confederates, not to mention good customers; they greet Frank's brother, Ben, like an old friend when he takes time off from his vigil at the railway station to pay them a visit. But for the town burghers, those who imagine Hadleyville to be in line for investment by industrialists, it is self-interest or, to put it more favourably, their own version of civic responsibility that motivates them to cut Will adrift and to entreat him, in turn, to take his problems elsewhere. They don't take his point that he is fighting for their survival as well as

his own. Perhaps they are right – although one woman does remind her peers of what an intimidating place the town was in Miller's day, there is no indication that his gang would sack the town in the event of Will leaving; this is not *High Plains Drifter*, one of *High Noon's* many progeny. (See also: *Silver Lode*, a Red Scare western that impudently names its villain 'McCarty'; *At Gunpoint* [1955], *A Lawless Street* [1955] and *A Man Alone*; *Man from Del Rio* [1956]; and several films in which a town tamer is betrayed by his employers, notably *Warlock*, *Death of a Gunfighter* and *Tom Horn*.)

Kane's decision to stand his ground arises from a web of personal and professional motives: pride, self-respect, a sense of duty. It is that last quality that, shockingly for the time, proves to be misplaced; a wasted effort. Frank Miller's pardon is the catalyst for the crisis. Kane directs his frustration at this decision at the lawmakers "up north" – whence those mysterious capitalist forces are apparently poised to transform Hadleyville's fortunes. Could they have sent Miller to clear their path, fearing intervention from the upstanding and officious Kane? (It is a notion that Sergio Leone entertained in *Once Upon a Time in the West* [1968], in which his villain, not uncoincidentally named Frank, does the dirty work for a railroad magnate.) Kane's mentor, a broken-down, cynical ex-lawman played by Lon Chaney Jr., castigates the criminal justice system, the job itself and, by extension, those it purports to serve: "You risk your skin catching killers and the juries turn them loose so they can come back and shoot at you again. If you're honest you're poor your whole life, and in the end you wind up dying all alone on some dirty street. For what? For nothing. For a tin star." It could almost be a portrait of Harry Callahan at retirement. (The film's most famous image, of course, is Kane's own badge of office lying in the dust, where he has dropped it – Callahan was more emphatic, throwing his shield into a reservoir.) *High Noon's* damning indictment of both Kane's ungrateful constituents and the complacency of the legal system continues to provoke indignation across the political spectrum.

One can almost forget that beneath these layers lies a marvellous western. Relentlessly taut, it is a lesson in pacing, progressing almost in real time, and was the prototype for a run of prestigious, town-bound suspense westerns during the Fifties (*3:10 to Yuma*, *Last Train from Gun Hill*). Zinnemann and Floyd Crosby conduct a masterclass, too, in black-and-white photography and staging in depth, in how to communicate a message formally: take its acclaimed crane shot, one of the most devastatingly effective in film history, when the rapidly ascending camera isolates Kane against a backdrop of empty streets; the point-of-view shot as the marshal enters the church, hostile faces turned towards him from the pews; the montage of faces – citizens' and clocks' – in the final desperate minutes before the train whistle shatters the tension; the townsfolk scurrying out of their hiding places once the gunfight is over, the high-angle shot heightening their resemblance to insects.

High Noon meets the demands of a traditional western, but it does so on its own terms. This is evident in Gary Cooper's subtly anguished performance, in the worry lines etched on his face, subverting the stereotype of the stoical hero. And it is there in the film's far-sighted portrayal of a woman in an influential position. I am not speaking of Grace Kelly's starchy Amy, despite her famous *volte-face* in killing one of the villains on her husband's behalf. Rather, it is Katy Jurado's Mexican entrepreneur, Helen Ramirez, who stands out as the most perceptive and self-assured character in the film, challenging the status (and avoiding the fate) generally accorded Latino women in more conservative westerns – especially when they are contrasted against prim blondes such as Amy. Helen's past affairs with both Frank Miller and Kane add a frisson to the men's impending showdown, but it is her individuality that is refreshing – she is prosperous and beneficent, obviously resented and snubbed by many locals (she implies the town is racist), and is clearly the dominant partner in her current relationship, with the immature Harvey. Her plain speaking ("What kind of woman are you? How can you leave him like this?") eventually has an effect on Amy, while her disdain for the hypocritical townsfolk she leaves behind at the end, and for their malleable values, foreshadows that of her character in *Pat Garrett and Billy the Kid*, the formidable wife of Slim Pickens' sheriff who tries to dissuade him from clearing out a nest of outlaws: "This town is not worth it." **KG**

footnotes

1 Interview with Fred Zinnemann by Arthur Nolletti Jr. in *The Films of Fred Zinnemann: Critical Perspectives* (State University of New York, 1999).

2 Foreman found support from an unexpected quarter during filming when Gary Cooper, who had been forthright in his anti-communist views, stood four-square beside the writer. Foreman's son Jonathan said: "Hollywood has never been noted as a place for courage… And great friends of [my father's] suddenly abandoned him. People crossed the street just to get away. Of course, other people turned out to be loyal… When people like [producer] Stanley Kramer said, 'Look at this. You have got to leave, it will ruin this film,' Cooper said, 'If he goes, I go.'" (Quoted in Michael Freedland, *Witch-Hunt in Hollywood: McCarthy's War on Tinseltown*, JR Books, 2009).

3 Richard Slotkin, *Gunfighter Nation: The Myth of the Frontier in Twentieth Century America* (University of Oklahoma Press, 1998).

Rancho Notorious

1952, Colour, 89 mins.

D: Fritz Lang. P: Howard Welsch (Fidelity Pictures Inc).
W: Daniel Taradash, Silvia Richards (story). Ph: Hal Mohr. M: Emil Newman.
St: Marlene Dietrich (Altar Keane), Arthur Kennedy (Vern Haskell),
Mel Ferrer (Frenchy Fairmont), Gloria Henry (Beth Forbes),
William Frawley (Baldy Gunder)

"Sometimes cold like ice, sometimes burning like the Sun – a pipe dream in blue jeans or in a birthday dress."

After his self-imposed exile from Nazi Germany, Fritz Lang found his calling within the US studio system, crafting a number of idiosyncratic genre movies. The best of these were characterised by claustrophobic set design, sexually voracious female leads, men obsessed – with the women in question, with revenge or with both – and the deconstruction of gender roles. Whereas his previous westerns, *The Return of Frank James* (1940) and *Western Union* (1941), were rather pedestrian affairs, *Rancho Notorious*, a galloping gumbo of Langian obsessions and wry touches, clearly engaged his interest.[1] While paying lip service to audience expectations, it's also a genre hall of mirrors, distorting accepted tropes, drawing on noir sensibilities and employing a sensual brand of imagery that is rare for the western.

The corny theme tune, which is heard repeatedly throughout the running time, does not bode well; a mawkish cowboy ballad with pretensions as a Greek chorus, it explains motivation and informs us of the plot. A cloying opening scene introduces us to Vern Haskell and his fiancée, Beth, discussing their future. The mood shifts when Vern goes to round up cattle, leaving his prim sweetheart behind, and Beth is cornered by the libidinous outlaw Kinch (Lloyd Gough). "She was spared nothing," Vern is told, and he takes a vow of revenge. His only clue to the killer's whereabouts is a phrase, "Chuck-a-Luck", uttered by Kinch's dying partner, back-shot by his accomplice during their escape. After months of searching, Vern finally locates the Chuck-a-Luck ranch, presided over by the charismatic Altar Keane, a former saloon girl who offers sanctuary to hardened outlaws – in exchange for ten per cent of their ill-gotten earnings. As Vern tries to uncover the identity of his fiancé's murderer, the ranch becomes an arena of intrigue, passion and retribution.

At face value, it's a conventional tale of "hate, murder and revenge", to quote the ballad, but even a cursory glance will reveal its Langian, subversive qualities. To accentuate Vern's increasing obsessiveness, Lang's stylistic touches reflect his artistic and cultural background. Scenes set in the studio-shot "canyon", with its lush painted backdrop and angular rock formations, betray not merely budgetary constraints but also a large debt to expressionism, adding an almost surrealistic quality to the visuals. The use of skewed angles in the prison scenes when Vern springs Frenchy, Altar's gunfighter lover, to help him gain access to Chuck-a-Luck, mark a further departure from genre customs and illustrate, in true noir style, Vern's distorted mindset.

Lang makes flamboyant use of Technicolor, notably during the extended flashbacks that introduce the legend of Altar Keane, one of the genre's most formidable heroines. The sensual colour palette eroticises Marlene Dietrich's image. Both a sultry, sassy saloon girl and a 'Venus' straight from the pages of Sacher-Masoch, her presence and strength of character add an element of gender transgression; in this sense, *Rancho Notorious* pre-empted *Johnny Guitar* as a radical distortion of genre motifs. During our first encounter with Altar, rich scarlet and azure dance on the screen in a fun saloon "race" in which a number of inebriated punters pose as horses, hurdling chairs and tables, with Altar and her fellow damsels astride their backs. This physical role reversal – saloon gals riding their punters like steeds – is both brazen and amusing. In another flashback, Altar tells her exploitative employer where to put his job and slaps away an over-amorous customer while throatily singing 'Gypsy Davey'. When Vern arrives at the ranch with Frenchy, Altar is bent over a work bench, clad in masculine cowboy garb – hitherto she has been seen in a series of kaleidoscopic frocks. "Hello, boss," says Frenchy pointedly, implying the dynamics in their relationship are very much in her favour.

At Chuck-a-Luck, Altar has been transformed from a source of sexual objectification to surrogate alpha male. The men who hide there give up their money and surrender their macho authority. Vern catches Altar's eye and a dangerous attraction brews. Their dialogue is rife with innuendos: "When you see a fenced range, do you always try to climb over?"; "I always see if the gate's open first." She thus has two men vying for her affections, with Frenchy transformed from tough guy to jealous lover. (To reinforce the feminisation theme, the name of Mel Ferrer's character is the same as that of Dietrich's famously ballsy saloon girl in *Destry Rides Again*.) The sexual politics are further complicated when, on the canyon set, Altar sits on a rock and talks down to Vern, who reclines wistfully on the floor in a feminised manner.

Lang claimed that this film was the father of the adult western, overlooking a number of challenging examples that had been made beforehand. Nevertheless, there is a pervasive unwholesomeness absent from most of its contemporaries. The moral disintegration of Arthur Kennedy's amiable hero makes him difficult, for much of the time, to distinguish from the rogues' gallery of bad eggs at Chuck-a-Luck. It is a typically Langian development – "The director's most revealing characters… all believe, as Lang did about himself,

above: Altar Keane (Marlene Dietrich) leads her saloon girls in a spot of gender role reversal.

that they have been martyred by fate," writes Patrick McGilligan, comparing Vern to the protagonists of *M*, *The Big Heat* and *Scarlet Street*.[2] The fitful bursts of violence are ferocious: a fistfight in a barber's is particularly brutal and, while Kinch's assault on Beth occurs offscreen, a close-up of her dead hand, shaped grotesquely into a claw, signifies the brutality of the struggle.

Having initiated the narrative, Vern's desire for revenge fizzles out. A perfunctory shootout – Vern and Frenchy on one side; the rest of the resident outlaws on the other – results in Kinch's death, but the event is overshadowed by Altar's demise. It confirms her place, and that of the magisterial Dietrich, at the heart of the drama. The star's relationship with Lang was fraught, and some commentators have complained that this blunted Dietrich's powers. On the contrary, her aloofness bolsters her portrayal; Altar is both commanding and emotionally pained, adding a classically tragic dimension to the character. Dietrich stole the limelight, but this was still Lang's party. Didactic and forthright as ever, he put sexual politics and gender dynamics at the centre of a standard revenge plot, resulting in one of the earliest examples of transgression in the western. **CH**

footnotes

1 According to Lang biographer Patrick McGilligan, *Rancho Notorious* was one of only two original screen stories that Lang developed from scratch during his time in Hollywood, the other being *Hangmen Also Die*.

2 *Fritz Lang: The Nature of the Beast* (Faber, 1997).

Metro-Goldwyn-Mayer PRESENTA
JAMES STEWART
JANET LEIGH
ROBERT RYAN
RALPH MEEKER
LO SPERONE NUDO
MILLARD MITCHELL
TECHNICOLOR
SAM ROLFE
HAROLD JACK BLOOM
ANTHONY MANN
WILLIAM H. WRIGHT
(THE NAKED SPUR)

The Naked Spur

1953, Colour, 91 mins.

D: Anthony Mann. P: William H. Wright (Metro-Goldwyn-Mayer). W: Sam Rolfe, Harold Jack Bloom. Ph: William Mellor. M: Bronislau Kaper. St: James Stewart (Howard Kemp), Janet Leigh (Lina Patch), Robert Ryan (Ben Vandergroat), Ralph Meeker (Roy Anderson), Millard Mitchell (Jesse Tate)

"Choosing a way to die, what's the difference? Choosing a way to live, that's the hard part."

Anthony Mann and James Stewart's third genre foray is conspicuously savage, yet is probably the former's least complex, the story stripped down to a power play in which five desperate characters traverse the director's merciless natural domain. Jim Kitses observed that, "Mann's heroes are driven by a vengeance they must inflict upon themselves for having once been human, trusting and therefore vulnerable."[1] In *The Naked Spur*, Stewart's Howard Kemp epitomises this figure, taking up a violent lifestyle having been abandoned by the woman he loved, unable to hope or even care. Yet despite his near-demented actions, it is because he was once a member of a civilisation that is missing so ominously from the narrative that his humanity, however scarred, finally affords him redemption. Transcending their work on the previous year's *Bend of the River*, here director and star subverted notions of the heroic westerner almost beyond recognition.

Entering the foothills of the Rockies, Kemp, gun in hand, comes across Jesse Tate, a down-at-heel prospector. Kemp explains that he is searching for Ben Vandergroat, a criminal wanted for murder. Allowing Tate to presume he is a sheriff, Kemp offers him $20 if he can find a new trail. Soon, a rockslide stops their progress, set off by Vandergroat on top of a cliff. Kemp and Tate encounter an ex-army lieutenant, Roy Anderson, who offers his help to capture the outlaw. Kemp checks the soldier's credentials, which note that Anderson received a dishonourable discharge. Nevertheless, together they apprehend the cackling outlaw, along with Lina, the daughter of Vandergroat's late accomplice. Unhinged but cunning, Vandergroat exposes that Kemp is not a lawman but simply an opportunistic bounty hunter, and conflict arises upon the revelation that Kemp has concealed the fact of a $5,000 reward. Both Anderson and Tate want in and, after a near fatal standoff, join Kemp in escorting the prisoner back to custody and the gallows. Vandergroat exploits the mistrust and rapacity among his captors as well as their attraction to Lina, who, despite her reluctance, kowtows to the older man by helping him distract his enemies.

Unlike the majority of Mann westerns, there are no interiors, towns or trains to position the movie in an American West on the verge of being tamed. Even the Native American drama *Devil's Doorway* has Robert Taylor's Shoshone Indian attempting (but failing) to assimilate into mainstream Wyoming society. *The Naked Spur* has nothing anchoring its players to a home life. Instead, they are forced into a fateful game in an inhospitable wilderness. From the painterly opening composition of the Rockies interrupted by the jagged star of Stewart's spur, the film is laden with reminders of the precariousness of the characters' existence in this terrain. Kemp's attempt at scaling the cliff face to capture Vandergroat is brutally curtailed when he slips back, the rope burning his hands. Mann switches from an idyllic, almost pastoral view of the high country to an Indian brave monitoring the progress of the group, indicating imminent danger. Kemp takes a bullet in the leg in the ensuing fight, causing debilitating pain and night terrors. Mann was an antecedent of Sam Peckinpah in his cinema of physicality, linking the bodily and mental hardships of his characters with the topography of the landscape and the power of the elements. Few characters in Fifties cinema would endure as much agony and loss as those directed by Mann and portrayed by Stewart.

The screenplay skilfully sifts in more clues to Kemp's motivation. Initially he seems callous, even cruel. In the lead-up to the Indian attack, the group realise that Anderson's actions have brought about the situation. Kemp tells Anderson to ride ahead of them, as a target, responding coldly ("You're losing time") to the lieutenant's protests. During the battle with the Blackfeet, however, Kemp instinctively protects Lina and is compelled to save Vandergroat's life. Stewart's performance exudes a real sense of a man driven to perform atrocious and dehumanising acts to achieve a wretched outcome. As in most American westerns, bounty hunting is viewed as a dirty game. Kemp's incentive, however, is not greed – he wants to return to society by buying back his land; his fiancée sold the deed, and left Kemp for another man, while he was in the army. Vandergroat represents his best chance to earn the money; the outlaw feigns disappointment that a man like Kemp could stoop so low. Typically for Mann, with his strong affinity for film noir, 'hero' and 'villain' reside on the same plane, if only temporarily: "The moral distance from the venal motives of the ostensibly heroic Kemp to the smiling treachery of Vandergroat is a short one."[2]

While many of Kemp's actions border on psychotic, it is Vandergroat whose mental state is truly unstable. Robert Ryan's performance is looser than usual, but no less convincing. Sporting an uncharacteristic mop-top hairstyle, he is a grinning bully who can change from flippancy to premeditated nastiness in a moment. His dealings with Lina are disturbing. While the full extent of their relationship is never made explicit, Vandergroat's refrain that he is 'taking care' of her suggests more than a degree of exploitation, especially given his willingness to use her womanly charms to distract Kemp, a man he implies is a sexual predator. This further destabilises the group dynamic and seems to align Kemp with Anderson, who alludes to a liaison with a Blackfeet squaw as the catalyst for their belligerency. Tate asks him pointedly, "Was she willing?" It was, of course, commonplace for westerns to regard Native American men as sexually threatening, but the insinuation that a white man – a military one at that – would rape an Indian woman was highly unusual.

The Oscar-nominated screenplay is one of the most uncompromising of the decade. The tension between the characters is never allowed to relax. Even a hiatus from the trek, to find respite in a cave, juxtaposes a tender moment between Kemp and Lina with a standoff between Kemp and Anderson, and ends with an escape attempt by Vandergroat. One could look at the five unwanted souls of the story as a squabbling, feral family, establishing a thematic link with the director's *Winchester '73*, *The Man from Laramie* and *Man of the West*. With Tate, the most sympathetic character, as a rather doddery grandpa, Kemp, the angriest, as the father trying to hold the fractious clan together, and Anderson, Vandergroat and Lina as siblings, the inter-relationships on display could almost have been culled from the pages of a gothic novel, replete with mistrust, betrayals and violent death.

In the virtuoso finale, greed leads Kemp's assistants to their deaths. The devilish Vandergroat tempts Tate away from Kemp, then murders him in cold blood, shooting gleefully at the dead man's boots, manically flaunting his true colours. Mann's artistry is in full effect. He favoured vertical arrangements of figures, and here he locates Vandergroat and Lina on top of a cliff, adding a dynamic punch with a quick camera tilt from the rapids up to villain and girl. Anderson fires at Vandergroat from a mesa below while Kemp scales the cliff face from the rear using the titular spur. Anderson shoots Vandergroat but, in battling to retrieve the precious corpse from the rapids, he is swept away by the torrent and his own avarice.

Kemp and Lina are the sole survivors, their tentative romance in the balance as Kemp scrambles to recover Vandergroat's body from the river. His inner rage proves stronger than the elements, but as he drags the body, still stooped over with the pain inflicted by his ordeal – his posture almost a manifestation of his distorted psyche – Lina tells him that she will marry him. Kemp does not understand. "Why?" he asks. "I'm taking him back… I'm gonna sell him for money." But he has experienced an epiphany – the realisation of the immoral, ignoble act he is committing – and breaks down. Lina has offered him a chance for redemption. The only way he can cleanse his soul is by burying the dead man and all he represents. Stewart thus signals his character's rebirth, finally standing tall and straight. **CH**

footnotes

1 *Horizons West* (BFI, 2007).

2 Alain Silver, *Film Noir: The Encyclopedia* (fourth edition; Overlook Duckworth, 2010).

Apache

1954, Colour, 87 mins.

D: Robert Aldrich. P: Harold Hecht (Hecht-Lancaster Productions). W: James R. Webb. Ph: Ernest Laszlo. M: David Raksin.
St: Burt Lancaster (Massai), Jean Peters (Nalinle), John McIntire (Al Sieber), Charles Bronson (Hondo),
John Dehner (Weddle), Monte Blue (Geronimo)

"If an Apache cannot live in his home mountains like his fathers before him, he is already dead."

If Robert Aldrich's first western lacks the punch of his signature works, the director's vision was not at fault. From a position of sympathy with Native American concerns – one shared by his star, Burt Lancaster – Aldrich posits the historical figure of Massai, maverick Apache, explicitly as a guerrilla warrior – a terrorist, in modern parlance. Refusing to surrender peacefully alongside Geronimo, he escapes from the train conveying captive braves to Florida and walks hundreds of miles back to Apache (now Anglo-American) territory, from where he carries out hit-and-run raids on Army units and installations. (But not the indiscriminate killings attributed to the real Massai. Aldrich would have to wait until the Seventies, when censorship had abated and sensitivities altered, to depict the gruesome realities of Apache attacks and military reprisals in *Ulzana's Raid*.)

Telling the story from the perspective of such a 'renegade' was a typically provocative manoeuvre by Aldrich, whose roster of 'heroes' went on to include mercenaries (*Vera Cruz*), an amoral private detective (*Kiss Me Deadly* [1955]) and war criminals (*The Dirty Dozen* [1967]). The director intended to cap the story with Massai's murder by soldiers at the moment he abandons his campaign, alerted by the cries of his newborn child, fusing individual tragedy with an indictment of racial intolerance and the conduct of the Indian Wars. "I felt [Massai] could not possibly be re-accepted or survive, for progress had passed him by," said Aldrich. "I respected his audacity, courage and dedication, but the world no longer had a place for his kind."[1]

Aldrich's preferred conclusion took revisionism too far for the liking of United Artists and the film's producers, Harold Hecht and Lancaster himself, despite the latter's initial support for his director. Killing off Lancaster would "take $1 million off the gross", worried United Artists joint chief Arthur Krim, and the studio insisted that Aldrich shoot what would be, from its point of view (i.e. that of the dominant culture), an upbeat, assimilationist alternative, in which Massai "survives to live a farmer's productive, emasculated existence".[2] UA's 'positive' ending "made a joke out of the whole film", complained Aldrich.[3] As Angela Aleiss explains, "*Apache* thus advocated the loss of Indian identity to achieve peaceful coexistence."[4]

Apache was Aldrich's first major film, and Lancaster was the perfect man to pitch it to. A supporter of the Hollywood Ten, an opponent of McCarthyism and, in the following decade, a campaigner for Martin Luther King and civil rights, the star was, according to film producer Max Youngstein, "one of the most sensitive men to the race issue I've ever met". For Lancaster, *Apache* was "meant by all involved to make a broader statement on the injustice of racism".[5] Moreover, it was a showcase for his crowd-pleasing athleticism and Olympian physique – he

spends much of the film bare-chested, running or fighting, leaping from trains or from rock to rock like a mountain lion, low camera angles enhancing his stature. The combination of topicality and Lancaster's marquee appeal made *Apache* the top box-office western of 1954. Tone was clearly a more relevant factor in its performance than verisimilitude. Audiences were accustomed to white actors impersonating Native Americans – which undeniably helped sell the integrationist message of films like *Apache* – and, unlike certain critics at the time and many cultural commentators reflecting on the practice today, they didn't baulk at the notion. Films of this nature simply would not have been made, or at least distributed so widely, without a star of sufficient magnitude at the centre.[6]

Yet Massai is not an obvious candidate for "peaceful coexistence", even if one discounts the depredations that earned him notoriety in real life, but are scaled down here. "It is a bold person who will dare to say that a wilder savage ever lived than an Apache Indian. And in this respect no Apache can rival Massai," wrote Frederic Remington in 1898.[7] His nobility is fiercer than that of Jeff Chandler's statesmanlike Cochise in *Broken Arrow*, for example; he is closer in spirit to that film's Geronimo (a far cry from the despondent figure glimpsed briefly at the start here) – that is, a slave to racial and individual pride. Not the sort of man, in short, suitable for – or desiring of – integration. His brief visit to bustling St. Louis, where he is nonplussed by the crowds, the traffic and the trappings of affluence, jostled, mocked and chased by the locals, is a disconcerting experience, reinforcing his sense of alienation.

His cunning and tenacity make him an admirable adversary and his integrity is beyond question, yet his truculence, paranoia (however justifiable, as the St. Louis scenes prove) and emotional rigidity paint him as a perennial outsider: "Every white man, every Indian, is my enemy. I cannot kill them all and someday they will kill me."[8] He is also chauvinistic: he sneers at the ways of the whites and the pacified tribes who have adopted them – like the Cherokee farmer he encounters on his cross-country trek, who counsels him to plant corn, a symbol of compliance on the one hand, survival on the other; and for much of the film he treats Nalinle (Jean Peters, blue-eyed like Lancaster), the woman he has kidnapped from her treacherous father's side, little better than a dog. (According to most accounts, the real Massai killed her mother before spiriting the girl away.)[9]

It is a credit to Aldrich, Lancaster and scriptwriter James R. Webb (*Vera Cruz*, *The Big Country* [1958], *Cheyenne Autumn*) that Massai is permitted to be so 'difficult', so hostile, and that his viewpoint is unmediated by a white counterpart. Nalinle, too, rises above stock status. Her stereotypically 'feminine' unswerving devotion, which is difficult to comprehend when Massai is subjecting her to physical abuse, combines with her 'masculine' hardiness to find a way to his heart. They make a home in the wilderness, plant corn like the whites and the Cherokees, and Nalinle becomes pregnant. But when army scout Al Sieber and the soldiers close in, it is the heroine who, most unusually in a western, urges her man not to swallow his pride and surrender, but to "die the warrior's death you've always wanted", and which he had been denied by Sieber in the film's opening scene. What Aldrich called "the inevitability of his death" seems certain, but at the studio's insistence a compromise was reached: Massai lives, he and his family having established a place for themselves away from both the reservation and the world of the whites. Yet there is a note of regret in Sieber's closing address that with this peaceful resolution, which still amounts to the vanquishing of a noble foe, something vital has been lost: "This is the only war we had. And we ain't likely to find another." **KG**

footnotes

1 Interview with Robert Aldrich by George Addison, 1962, reprinted in *Robert Aldrich: Interviews* (University Press of Mississippi, 2003).

2 Kate Buford, *Burt Lancaster: An American Life* (Aurum Press, 2008).

3 Interview with Robert Aldrich by Ian Cameron and Mike Shivas, 1963, reprinted in *Robert Aldrich: Interviews*.

4 Angela Aleiss, *Making the White Man's Indian* (Greenwood, 2005).

5 Kate Buford, *Burt Lancaster: An American Life*.

6 Outside the western genre, Lancaster played the title role in *Jim Thorpe: All-American* (1951), the mixed-race Native American athlete who won two Olympic golds at the 1912 Games only to be stripped of them on a technicality a year later.

7 'Massai's Crooked Trail', *Harper's New Monthly Magazine*, January 1898.

8 The real Massai was more accommodating in his younger days, even serving as an army scout against his own people, circa 1880. In the film, the principal Apache scout, played by Charles Bronson, is a figure of contempt.

9 Aldrich saw no need to apologise for Indian attitudes towards women. Here, it is even the source of wry humour, as when Massai expresses amazement that the Cherokee farmer fetches his own water despite having a woman around – "Some of the white man's ways are hard," acknowledges the other.

OSTATNIA WALKA APACZA
BARWNY FILM PRODUKCJI AMERYKAŃSKIEJ
REŻYSERIA:
ROBERT ALDRICH
WYKONAWCY:
BURT LANCASTER
JEAN PETERS I INNI
PRODUKCJA: UNITED ARTISTS
FANGOR

The Far Country

1954, Colour, 97 mins.

D: Anthony Mann. P: Aaron Rosenberg (Universal-International). W: Borden Chase. Ph: William Daniels. M: Joseph Gershenson. St: James Stewart (Jeff Webster), Ruth Roman (Ronda Castle), Corinne Calvet (Renée Vallon), Walter Brennan (Ben Tatum), John McIntire (Gannon)

"I don't need other people. I don't need help. I can take care of me."

The most transparent of their films together, *The Far Country* contains, with *Bend of the River*, the most satisfying character arc of any Mann/Stewart western. The psychological divisions that threaten to destabilise Stewart's protagonists in the other films in the series are given a different focus here. Rather than projecting his flaws onto a separate character – his thematic twin – as in *Winchester '73* or *Bend of the River*, or disclosing his capacity for elemental brutality, Borden Chase's script shows Stewart's misanthropic loner the error of his ways via the altruism of others, the kind of selfless behaviour viewed with suspicion by a man whose mantra is "nobody ever did anything for nothing". The denouement may be predictable (the entire film has the quality of a fable), but the journey, taking in spectacular vistas of the Athabasca Glacier and the Canadian Rockies, is plotted with Mann's customary precision and undertaken by Stewart with authentic grit and conviction.

If one metaphor – no man is an island – explains the moral of the story, then landscape, as so often in the western, and never more forcefully than in Mann's works, performs the same function for the hero. "Mentally and emotionally, [Stewart's character] always lives in the far country, that… distant world that is as cold and remote as he is."*1*

Although he travels with an older companion, Ben, garrulous and sociable where his partner is taciturn and detached, Jeff Webster is the epitome – the nadir in some ways – of the genre's self-reliant individualists. An outsider by choice and, the script implies, by dint of bitter experience, he neither accepts nor offers favours, can barely even comprehend the concept of reciprocity if it isn't on a business basis. He operates on the margins of society in the same way that he skirts around the law, driving a herd north to cash in on the Klondike gold rush with a ruthlessness to rival that of *Red River's* Tom Dunson. We learn that he killed two drovers – potential quitters – on the trail from Montana. Their comrades call it murder; he calls it rough justice. Waylaid in the border town of Skagway by a Roy Bean figure, the corrupt, perversely genial Judge Gannon, Jeff contrives to 'steal' back his requisitioned herd, covering his tracks by signing on with the entrepreneurial Ronda Castle as an escort to the remote mining camp of Dawson. Here the people are honest and amicable, the opposite of the hard-nosed, venal opportunists of Skagway. When Gannon and his gunmen move in, branching out into claim-jumping and murder, counting Ben among their victims, Jeff, wounded and chastened, is forced to abandon his every-man-for-himself mentality, which has come to seem irrational as well as ignoble.

DISTRIBUZIONE
Universal International
TECHNICOLOR
JAMES
STEWART
CORINNE CALVET
RUTH ROMAN
TERRA LONTANA
WALTER BRENNAN • JOHN Mc INTIRE • JAY C. FLIPPEN
SCENEGGIATURA BORDEN CHASE REGIA DI ANTHONY MANN PRODUZIONE AARON ROSENBERG

DAWSON
SKAGWAY
Filmed in the Great Canadian Northwest!
THE FAR

Jeff's callousness undermines his position as protagonist at two points in particular. On the journey to Dawson, he insists on taking his cattle through a valley – a longer route, but with grazing opportunities – and leaves Ronda and her team to take a short cut across a glacier, between two mountains. When an avalanche strikes them – which Jeff had predicted, but only after the others had left – he initially refuses to help. Even Ben is horrified at his friend's cold-bloodedness. Later, when the people of Dawson ask him to pin on the marshal's badge, he is "not interested" – neither in the job, nor in their predicament. When Gannon and his minions move in, the miners are forced to appoint the grizzled Rube (Jay C. Flippen), brave but powerless, to 'protect' them. Jeff spurns not just his civic duty, but also his moral responsiblity, flunking a test that most heroes of the classical western were required to pass. (The issue became cloudier in films influenced by *High Noon*, where the community often failed to measure up to the hero, not the other way round.) Only by taking a stand, however belatedly, can Jeff earn his redemption and fulfil his allotted function.

The notion of counterparts was vital to the structure of Mann/Chase westerns. Here, the idea is both varied and extended. The glacial expanse that forms the gateway to Dawson equates with Jeff's mental terrain, while in person he is paralleled not by the villain – Gannon is far more personable, an oddly happy-go-lucky tyrant – but by Ruth Roman's ambiguous Ronda, perhaps the most strong-willed female character in Mann's canon of westerns. She is similarly mistrustful by nature, strictly quid pro quo; inevitably, sexual sparks fly between them, although both are characteristically hesitant to commit. They are indifferent to the effect of their dealings on the "awful nice folks" of Dawson. Jeff sells Ronda his cattle when she outbids the locals, even though their need is greater; moreover, they blame her, as much as Gannon, for the corruption in Skagway. Their fears are realised when Ronda opens a saloon in their midst and allies with Gannon, who proceeds to fleece the miners. The rapacious ethos that governs Skagway seeps into Dawson like a poison, mirroring the discoloration of Portland in *Bend of the River* when gold fever strikes. Ronda's downfall comes when she betrays her instincts and rushes to Jeff's aid in the climactic shoot-out: "[Her] death represents the death of Stewart's non-social self," opines Jeanine Basinger.

Ronda is offset by the kind-hearted, boyish Renée, who drip-feeds Jeff the milk of human kindness. (Renée: "What kind of world would it be if everybody was…" Jeff: "Like me?") She and Ben, and Rube to a lesser extent, rotate the role of Jeff's nagging conscience between them. When it eventually has the desired effect, Jeff acts through a combination of revenge for Ben and resignation that his chosen path has proved to be a dead end. Where Stewart finishes most of his Mann westerns in a state of emotional exhaustion, here his lone wolf appears sheepish, saddened. *The Far Country* is a relatively minor piece, but its principal theme is consonant with Mann's classics; even here, he denies his protagonist the luxury of self-assurance. **KG**

footnotes

1 Jeanine Basinger, *Anthony Mann* (Wesleyan University Press, 2007).

COUNTRY

Johnny Guitar

1954, Colour, 110 mins.

D: Nicholas Ray. P: Nicholas Ray (Republic Pictures). W: Philip Yordan, Roy Chanslor. Ph: Harry Stradling. M: Victor Young. St: Joan Crawford (Vienna), Sterling Hayden (Johnny Logan/Johnny Guitar), Mercedes McCambridge (Emma Small), Scott Brady (the Dancin' Kid), Ward Bond (John McIvers)

"A posse isn't people. I've ridden with 'em, and I've ridden against 'em. A posse is an animal that moves like one and thinks like one."

Even the most seemingly liberal-minded of Fifties westerns could not escape the gravitational pull of the genre's innate conservatism entirely. *Johnny Guitar* is no exception. A feminist western with a misogynist streak, an anti-McCarthyite screed (at least in theory) that condemns one level of prejudice while supporting another, it is almost as neurotic as its characters. Traditional gender roles are realigned, even merged in the case of Vienna, Joan Crawford's hero/heroine, and yet the screenplay rolls out the hoariest of western clichés: an infamous gunfighter fleeing his past; a gang with a secret hideout (behind a waterfall, no less) who are given 24 hours to get out of town; cattle ranchers protesting the opening up of the West to "dirt farmers… squatters". As V.F. Perkins writes, it has the "serious themes [and] weighty style" of an A-western, but also the "blood-and-thunder melodrama" of a simple crowd-pleaser.[1] Many reviewers at the time were bemused by this concoction, with Britain's *Monthly Film Bulletin* marking "the general effect of fascinating, portentous lunacy". Somehow, beneath the dreamlike lustre of Nicholas Ray's direction and the seductive patina of Trucolor, the contradictions are made to cohere. It manages to be both rugged in the traditional sense and thrillingly seditious – the work of a romantic and a rebel.

The film's political subtext – the paranoia of the established order, its persecution of Crawford's independent entrepreneur

Johnny Guitar

and her nonconformist acolytes – evaded serious attention at the time, although with hindsight it seems as glaring as the prime colours that are such a key part of Ray's *mise-en-scène*. Ray himself promoted this interpretation in later years ("Vienna also mirrored reality. Under fire from McCarthy, she refused to inform"), as did credited screenwriter Philip Yordan.[2] In his critical appraisal of the director, Bernard Eisenschitz remarks, "This mistrust of the mob and the silent majority, the distinct bias towards the outsider, was not new in Ray's work."[3] It is evident in *They Live By Night* (1948) and *Knock on Any Door* (1949), in *Rebel Without a Cause* and another western, *Run for Cover* (both 1955), in which James Cagney and John Derek are prejudged and almost killed by a trigger-happy posse. The significance of the theme here – and it relates not just to Vienna, but to the 'outlaws' as well, actually free-living miners made desperate by the intolerance of society – arises from male lead Sterling Hayden's cooperation with the House Un-American Affairs Committee. (Whether Ray did likewise remains a matter of conjecture.) The actor deeply regretted his testimony, and it is tempting to believe that he (and possibly Ray) approached the production as a form of penitence. Hayden's title character, certainly, for all his introspection and relative ineffectiveness, is squarely on the side of the minority.[4]

This is not primarily the story of Johnny Guitar, however. Joan Crawford saw to that as much as Ray did. She owned the screen rights to Roy Chanslor's pulp novel and was effectively the producer. (By all accounts she made everybody's lives a misery on set, not least Ray's, with whom she entered into an unhappy affair; her antipathy towards Mercedes McCambridge, younger and more popular with the crew, has passed into legend.[5]) She was also a fading screen luminary determined to reclaim the limelight, and ordered the script rewritten to move her character from the sidelines to centre stage, radically altering the film's gender perspective in the process. "I want to play the man," she told Philip Yordan. "I want to shoot it out in the end with Mercedes McCambridge, and instead of me playing with myself in a corner, let Sterling play with himself in the corner and I'll do the shoot-out."[6]

Vienna's self-confidence and composure under pressure mark her as the film's true protagonist, much more so than the female leads of comparable westerns such as *Rancho Notorious*, *The Maverick Queen*, *The Oklahoma Woman* and *Forty Guns*, who are in each case paired with an authoritative male counterpart. "Never seen a woman who was more of a man," says one of Vienna's male croupiers. "She thinks like one, acts like one, and sometimes makes me feel like I'm not." (The similarities between Vienna and Crawford's eponymous heroine in *Mildred Pierce* [1945], another woman who throws off the shackles of male authority, are easy to discern.) Johnny, haunted gunman and

above: The lynch mob loses patience with Joan Crawford; Mercedes McCambridge looks on.

Vienna's old flame, becomes merely her satellite, summoned to her aid in an unnamed corner of Arizona where her isolated saloon, built on land craved by railroad and ranchers alike, is effectively under siege from cattle barons led nominally by the reactionary McIvers, played by Ward Bond. (Yordan liked the idea of casting the arch-Republican actor as an "extreme fascist". A similar trick was played on him in Republic's subsequent *A Man Alone*.)

In a reflection of Vienna's dominant position vis-à-vis Johnny, McIvers surrenders the role of antagonist to McCambridge's Emma Small, a fire-breathing, sexually repressed she-devil who contorts local fears about immigration and criminal deviancy into a moral crusade, impelling McIvers and his followers to act against the "railroad tramp" they accuse of harbouring local black sheep the Dancin' Kid and his friends: "You all think she's some fine lady and that doing nothing makes you fine gentlemen. Well she ain't! And you're not!" Emma's loathing of Vienna stems, in part, from jealousy of the latter's on-off romance with the Kid, who also has eyes for Emma, and partly, it has often been speculated, from sublimated Sapphic desire for Vienna herself. The Kid "makes her feel like a woman, and that frightens her", observes Vienna, but Emma's obsession with her rival – she stares fixedly at her in almost all their scenes together – allied with her hoydenish demeanour and vindictiveness, mark her, in Hollywood terms, as a classic closeted lesbian – a "predatory butch", as Judith Halberstam puts it.[7] (McCambridge came to regret being typecast as similar figures, "the worst harridans, the most hard-bitten women": a masculine cowgirl put out by Elizabeth Taylor's presence in *Giant* [1956]; a leering biker who orchestrates Janet Leigh's torment in *Touch of Evil* [1958]; a sadistic prison warden in Jesus Franco's *99 Women* [1969]).

For Jennifer Peterson, "Using Emma as a sexually caricatured figure who must shoulder the blame for all society's ills merely reproduces the [male-oriented]

power structure Ray thinks he is critiquing."[8] That may be so, but the allotment of primary roles in a western to women – one of them a glorified saloon girl, of all things – still represented a subversive act, one that remains worth savouring. The intensity of the leading ladies' characterisations creates a balanced, although hardly nuanced, view of female wiles and virtues, as filtered through the imagination of the film's male writers and director and refracted through generic conventions. As much as Ray looks down on Emma, he looks up to Vienna – often literally, filming her from a reverent low angle in her saloon domain. She enjoys unusual latitude for a female character, changing roles as readily as she changes attire: steely and gun-toting in tight-fitting black trousers; feminine in frocks (in an especially striking scene, she confronts her accusers wearing a virginal white gown, symbolic of innocence, while their black and white garb expresses their morality). She is sexually liberated (she has clearly tangoed with the Dancin' Kid, as well as with Johnny) and even maternal: attempting to shield Turkey, the youngest member of the Kid's bunch, from the ire of the mob, she tells him "save yourself" when he is browbeaten into naming her as their accomplice in a robbery they have been provoked into carrying out. It is the film's most damning indictment of McCarthyite methods. Emma connives to have them both strung up regardless of Turkey's 'confession'; only Johnny's timely intervention frees Vienna, and the pair seek refuge with the Kid in his hilltop lair, with Emma and the posse in pursuit.

The diminished status of the eponymous hero – indeed, the marginalisation of all the men in the plot – could be said to reflect emasculation anxiety among post-war American males, a collective anguish about female empowerment. Johnny's substitution of guitar for pistol, of pseudonym for a surname laden with notoriety, signals both a repudiation of violence and a damaged psyche, a common impairment for the protagonists of Fifties westerns and of film noir – rewarding artistic terrain for Ray. Equally predictably, Johnny remains "gun crazy", given the opportunity, although his psychosis is addressed only fleetingly. (The guitar, incidentally, receives equally scant attention.) Vienna's – and Crawford's – agenda dominates, further signifying a shift in the balance of power between genders. Just as Crawford's mission to

above: From left, at the bar: Ben Cooper, Joan Crawford, Sterling Hayden, Royal Dano. Foreground, from left: Frank Marlowe, Ward Bond (centre), Mercedes McCambridge, Scott Brady.

reassert her authority as a star informed her performance, Hayden, mired in guilt over his HUAC testimony and facing marital breakdown to boot, brought to his role the "air of having lost all his illusions… [a] dreamy detachment".[9] Johnny spends the early stages commenting sardonically on the action like a genuine troubadour, while Vienna propels the plot and calls the shots in their rekindled relationship. Their dialogue abounds with regrets and recriminations. At times they are like star-crossed lovers in a contemporary romance; at others like enemies negotiating an armistice.

Eventually, after Emma burns down Vienna's saloon in an act of pure spite, McCambridge's face alight with malicious glee, Johnny becomes the man of action we have been expecting, and the film, like many another post-war melodrama, begins to rein in its free-spirited heroine. She emerges from her carapace, confessing to longing for Johnny as much as he has yearned for her, and it looks as if she will be tamed – and gender order set to rights – in much the same way as in *Mildred Pierce*. Yet the jealous sparring between Johnny and the Kid, in an odd little domestic interlude, hardly restores their masculinity. And then, audaciously, the men are demoted once more while Vienna and Emma settle their account: Emma impulsively shooting the Kid in the forehead before rushing at Vienna like one of the Furies; McIvers and his followers shrinking from the fray as Vienna slays the wicked witch and reunites with Johnny. As equal partners, one presumes.

The all-female showdown, charged with what Philip French called "a strong whiff of erotic perversity", seals Ray's achievement in re-enacting the rituals of the western while disturbing its equilibrium, much as the blasting of dynamite interrupts Sterling Hayden's serene ride through Arizonan hills in the opening scene. As a political allegory, whether intentional or incidental, *Johnny Guitar* measures up to the most progressive and enduring westerns of the decade, but this hard edge is blunted by a fairy-tale quality: Harry Stradling's sumptuous colours; Ray's lush landscape shots; the grotto-like interior of Vienna's mountain-side saloon, its rear wall formed of red rock. (Given the shelter it provides for Vienna's male dependents, her establishment is also something of a womb.) But its most celebrated aspect is undoubtedly its female bias, however inconsistent, embodied in the spellbinding performances of Crawford, magnetic and Medusa-like, and McCambridge, who enjoys moments of almost delirious malevolence. The feud between these distaff gunfighters (and displaced lesbians?) continues to endear the film to connoisseurs of camp entertainment; more significantly, in terms of cinema history, it constituted an insurrection against western conventions, the like of which has yet to be repeated. **KG**

footnotes

1 'Johnny Guitar', in *The Movie Book of the Western* (Ian Cameron and Douglas Pye, eds, Cassell, 1996).

2 The authorship of *Johnny Guitar* continues to exercise debate. Yordan is the only writer credited, although some sources – notably Patrick McGilligan – suggest he merely "massaged" the script, working with Roy Chanslor's first draft adapted from his own novel. The name of blacklisted writer Ben Maddow has also been thrown into the mix; Maddow had worked incognito on several scripts carrying Yordan's name in the Fifties (see McGilligan, *Nicholas Ray: The Glorious Failure of an American Director*, HarperCollins, 2001; and *Backstory 2: Interviews with Screenwriters of the 1940s and 1950s*, University of California Press, 1997).

3 *Nicholas Ray: An American Journey* (Faber, 1996).

4 Robert Mitchum and Jeff Chandler were the other notable actors considered for the title role before Hayden.

5 *Joan Crawford: The Essential Biography* by Lawrence J. Quirk and William Schoell (University Press of Kentucky, 2002).

6 McGilligan, *Backstory 2: Interviews with Screenwriters of the 1940s and 1950s*.

7 *Female Masculinity* (Duke University Press, 1998).

8 'The Competing Tunes of Johnny Guitar', reprinted in *The Western Reader* (Jim Kitses and Gregg Rickman, eds, Limelight Editions, 1998).

9 Bernard Eisenschitz, *Nicholas Ray: An American Journey.*

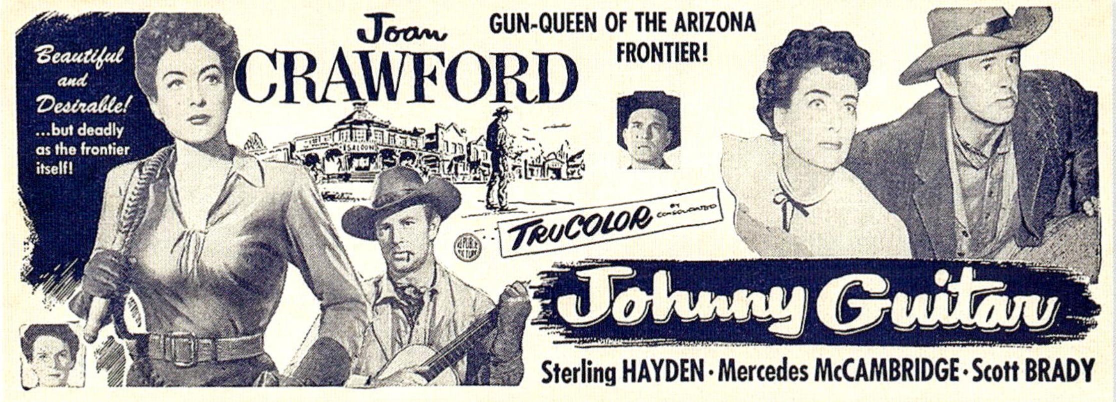

Silver Lode

1954, Colour, 80 mins.

D: Allan Dwan. P: Benedict Bogeaus (Pinecrest Productions). W: Karen DeWolf. Ph: John Alton. M: Louis Forbes. St: John Payne (Dan Ballard), Lizabeth Scott (Rose Evans), Dan Duryea (Fred McCarty), Dolores Moran (Dolly), Emile Meyer (Sheriff Woolley)

"Dan sure don't act innocent."
"How do we know what he used to do?"

The shadow of *High Noon* looms over *Silver Lode*, obscuring one of the most pugnacious criticisms of McCarthyism produced in the Fifties. Allan Dwan's succinct, suspenseful B-movie mirrors the plot and themes of its illustrious predecessor but, made outside the studio system by an independent producer, it cuts to the point with less ambiguity and was received with far less fuss or fanfare. Properly considered a companion piece to *High Noon*, rather than a rip-off, it invokes also Fritz Lang's *Fury* (1936), *The Ox-Bow Incident* and the film noir *The Sound of Fury* (1950) with its damning portrayal of model American citizens behaving like a lynch mob.

This story of a man fighting for his life and freedom begins, fittingly, on Independence Day, a celebration of liberty. In Silver Lode, the wedding of Dan Ballard and local dignitary's daughter Rose is interrupted by a stranger, provocatively named McCarty, who claims to be a US marshal and says Ballard is wanted for back-shooting McCarty's brother during a poker game and making off with $20,000. Rather than refuting the charges outright, Ballard keeps his counsel and, with McCarty missing no opportunity to inflame opinions, becomes guilty by suspicion. Tongues wag and doubts creep in; Ballard has only lived in Silver Lode for two years, and little is known about his past. The town's moral guardians withdraw their invitation to Ballard to judge a children's speechmaking contest ("Some of the mothers… under the circumstances"), and are horrified when he appears to have the support of good-time girl Dolly (a vivid portrayal by Dolores Moran, wife of producer Benedict Bogeaus), his old flame. Even Rose comes to distrust him, albeit fleetingly, as Ballard, who admits to her that he did indeed shoot McCarty's brother, but in self-defence, asks the judge for a two-hour stay of extradition (the deadline being another nod in the direction of *High Noon*) for the chance to clear his name and expose McCarty and his deputies as bogus.

While Dan Duryea's demagogic villain instigates Ballard's persecution for his own ends – revenge for his brother, in part, plus the chance to get his hands on that $20,000 – the real focus of the film's moral ire is the community of Silver Lode itself. The locals seem friendly and welcoming, inviting McCarty and his men to take part in their 4th of July picnic when they first appear, and initially they rally round Ballard, marching behind him in a solemn procession of support. But, as in *High Noon*, propriety rules; they don't want anything to spoil their neat and tidy town, to sully its reputation, even if it means throwing Ballard, their adopted son, to the wolves. Worse, they join the hunting pack.

Even when they side with Ballard, the townsfolk are hardly an unequivocally positive force – some even profess their willingness to kill McCarty (whom they believe to be a federal marshal, someone they ought, in theory, to respect) on Ballard's behalf, prompting McCarty, with no little irony but with good cause, to bleat to the sheriff about "mob law". It comes as less of a shock, therefore, when they eventually turn on Ballard, prompted in large measure by McCarty's rhetoric, by Ballard's reluctance to speak in his own defence – pleading the Fifth, as it were – and his increasingly rash actions, as when, at his lowest point, with the sheriff's murder pinned on him as well, he is forced to hold his neighbours at gunpoint, playing into McCarty's hands. He acts guilty, and that is enough for the majority of the locals.

John Payne is well cast as a man not quite as upstanding as he first appears. The actor made his name in musicals and was the leading man of Christmas perennial *Miracle on 34th Street* (1947), but made a Dick Powell-like shift in his forties towards hard-boiled parts in westerns and film noirs. His character here endures a noir-esque nightmare – a previous violent act reverberates around him, forcing him into increasingly incriminating situations – in broad, Technicolor daylight. (The handsome photography is by noir veteran

John Alton. One superb, jittery tracking shot in particular, which keeps pace with Ballard as he evades his pursuers, slipping through the streets and crouching for cover, would grace any showreel.) Ballard's predicament is neatly plotted by writer Karen DeWolf (like director Dwan, a versatile old-stager; she honed her skills on 'Blondie' comedies – not exactly the resumé of a potential radical); each development – save the "act of God" that seals McCarty's downfall[1] – seems plausible, as do the characters' reactions. With McCarty's near-namesake at his apogee at the time of its release, the message of *Silver Lode* is plain: injustice on this scale could happen anywhere in America, and even the most high-minded of Americans – perhaps they most of all – can fall prey to the herd instinct, prepared to sacrifice the rights of the individual to preserve the collective self-image. **KG**

footnotes

[1] David Meuel interprets this turn of events – when McCarty's bullet deflects off the church bell and kills him instead of Ballard – as a metaphor for the self-defeating methods employed by the inquisitors of the House Un-American Affairs Committee (*The Noir Western*, McFarland, 2015).

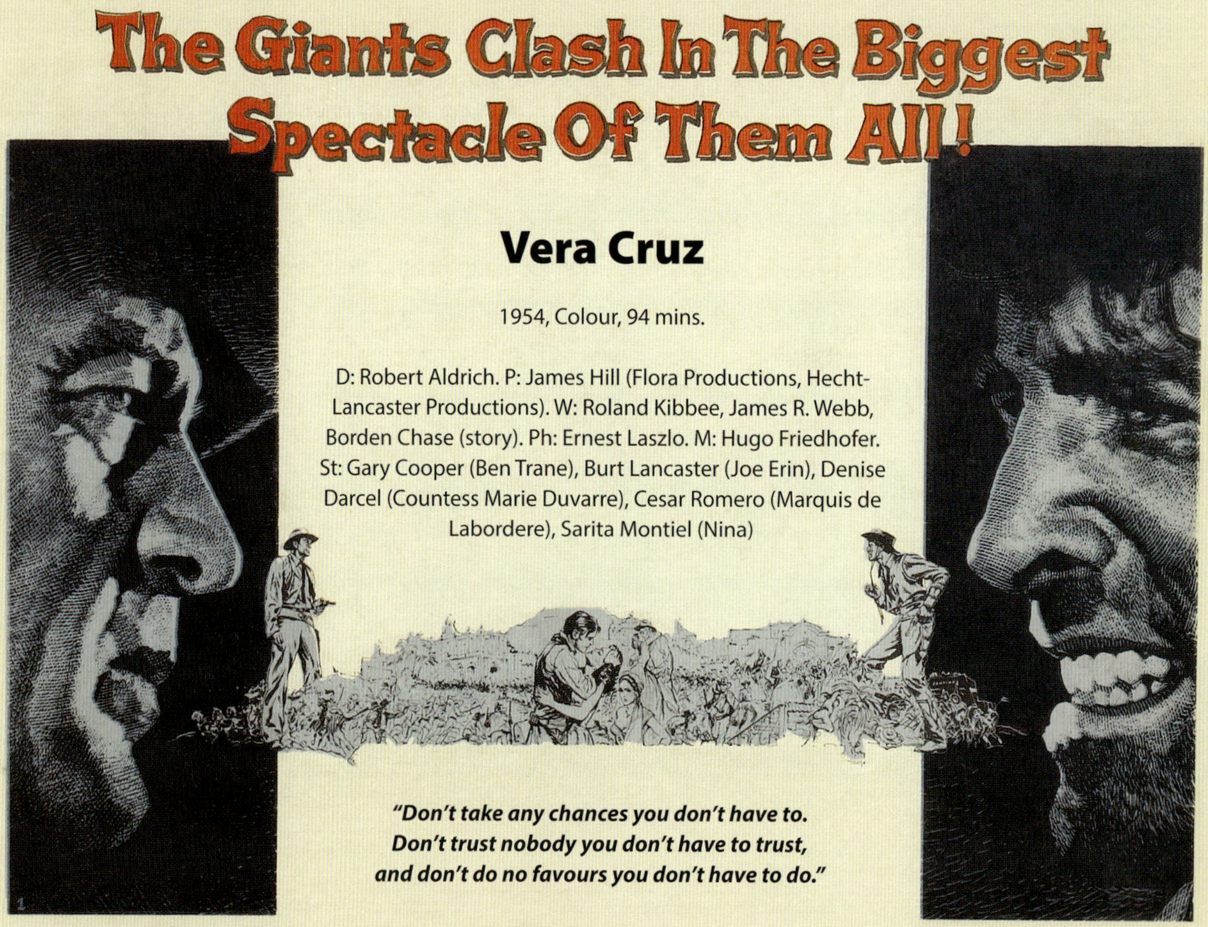

Vera Cruz

1954, Colour, 94 mins.

D: Robert Aldrich. P: James Hill (Flora Productions, Hecht-Lancaster Productions). W: Roland Kibbee, James R. Webb, Borden Chase (story). Ph: Ernest Laszlo. M: Hugo Friedhofer. St: Gary Cooper (Ben Trane), Burt Lancaster (Joe Erin), Denise Darcel (Countess Marie Duvarre), Cesar Romero (Marquis de Labordere), Sarita Montiel (Nina)

"Don't take any chances you don't have to. Don't trust nobody you don't have to trust, and don't do no favours you don't have to do."

A key transitional title in the evolution of the western, *Vera Cruz* was "one of the very first… to dispense with the Manichean moralism that had underpinned the genre for so long"[1]. Based, like many of the Fifties' most enduring westerns, on a story by Borden Chase, it contributed greatly to the ascent of the anti-hero, and prefigured the 'professional' westerns of the Sixties with its between-the-lines commentary on American adventurism in the Third World – referring to *The Wild Bunch*, its most illustrious descendent, director Robert Aldrich said: "I think we did it before, with *Vera Cruz*."[2] And with its pungent humour, its focus on venality, scheming and counter-scheming, it was a conspicuous influence on European westerns, particularly those directed by Sergio Leone and others set during the Mexican Revolution, most of which pitched ambiguous, avaricious foreign fortune-hunters into the conflict. Film historians Paul Buhle and Dave Wagner went so far as to state, "The Eurowestern was made possible by… Robert Aldrich, if not exclusively then more than any other filmmaker."[3] They were not far off the mark.

Aldrich's film is set in Mexico during an earlier upheaval, the Juarista rebellion against the Emperor Maximilian, not long after the American Civil War.[4] The director summarised it as the tale of "a hero and an anti-hero, with the hero surviving only after choosing a rightful battle and destroying the anti-hero, whom he admired in spite of their disparate credos".[5] For much of the film we are led to believe that both protagonists are anti-heroic, as American adventurers Ben Trane, a bankrupt ex-Confederate officer, and Joe Erin, a ruthless freebooter, form a wary alliance with each other, and with the forces of Maximilian, to escort the Countess Marie Duvarre to Vera Cruz. Yet their real goal is a strongbox full of gold, secreted in the countess's coach, and it is the contest for this fortune that gradually reveals the distinction between them. ("He likes people, and you can never count on a man like that," says Erin of Trane.) The countess herself, however, has designs on the gold, and attempts to enchant Joe in a plot to secure it. Completing the picture, and doing some conspiring of their own, are the emperor's acolyte, the suave and canny Marquis Henri de Labordere, and the Juaristas, the only ones for whom the treasure represents more than just material gain.

A web of deceit is thus spun: Trane and Erin against each other, and together against their employers; Maximilian and the Marquis against the Americans; the Marquis, wise to her plans, against the Countess; the Countess against the Americans; Nina, a closet

Juarista, against the Americans; Erin's men, fleetingly, against their leader… The higher purpose embodied by the rebels, while not exactly an afterthought, doesn't occupy the director's attention to the same extent as all this skulduggery (to the chagrin of contemporary critics, of which more below), and the script is peppered with humorous double-edged dialogue and cynical exchanges. We may be in Mexico, but we are a long way from *Viva Zapata!* (1952). One of Burt Lancaster's lines in particular, "No such thing as an innocent man," would resound ever louder as the genre entered the Sixties, when the seeds sown by Aldrich in films such as *Vera Cruz* and *The Last Sunset* (1961) produced a bumper harvest in Hollywood and beyond – the aforementioned Sergio Leone was a noted admirer of the Aldrich style, particularly the emotionally loaded showdowns in this film and *The Last Sunset*.[6]

In the main, the contrasts between the film's sets of characters are drawn according to genre conventions: the Americans, at least Erin and his gang of cut-throats, are rugged and unrefined, a far cry from the stuffy sophistication of the Emperor and his entourage on the one hand – displayed to comic effect in a lavish banquet scene at the imperial residence – and the modesty and earnestness of the rebels on the other. Trane is the odd man out, cultured and sober without being supercilious; he has a sense of honour, dormant as it may be, that ultimately marks him as the hero, despite his dalliance with Erin. (And despite the fact that his motive for being in Mexico is to restore his plantation to working order – he has therefore profited from slave labour in the past, although nothing is made of this in the film. Trane is treated as a gallant freedom fighter, albeit a disillusioned one, in the romantic, lopsided manner typical of most post-Civil War westerns. Certainly, the Juaristas' cry of *libertad* is designed to appeal to him in particular.)

The trek to Vera Cruz – across sumptuous Mexican locations and landmarks, including some spectacular shots of the pyramids at Teotihuacan[7] – culminates in the inevitable reckoning between Erin and Trane. The mutual respect between these unlikely accomplices – established in a breezy opening sequence in which they steal each other's horses – proves unsustainable for a number of reasons, chiefly because their values are at odds. Erin, in a vigorous portrayal by Lancaster, is all dash, duplicity and insincere grin; he mocks Trane for having a "soft spot" – towards injured horses, children, and – this is what really drives a wedge between them – the Juaristas. Trane's nobility, by contrast, although battered by his troubles back home, remains intact. Gary Cooper's aura of integrity (something that intimidated Lancaster, according to Aldrich, even though the former was the film's co-producer) makes some of Trane's mercenary dialogue ring less than true – "Money. Is that worth risking you life for?" he is asked. "It comes closer than anything I know."

In his essay *Social Class and the Western as Male Melodrama*, David Lusted sees the rift that opens between the lead characters as symptomatic of class divisions, with Erin the rough proletarian and Trane his social superior. If this seems a stretch, far more convincing is the status commonly allotted to them of surrogate father and son. The dynamic of older/younger protagonists at cross-purposes was typical for the period, in melodramas (peaking, perhaps, with 1955's *Rebel Without a Cause*) as well as westerns such as *Broken Lance* (1954), *Run for Cover* (1955), *The Left Handed Gun*, and most of those written by Borden

above: Burt Lancaster (left) and Gary Cooper (right).

Chase, from *Red River* (1948) onwards. Here, while the gap in ages between the leads is not especially pronounced – Cooper was 53, Lancaster 41 – their respective screen images, as well as their characters' mindsets and body language, even their modes of dress (Trane classic, neutral; Erin more flamboyant), mark them as products of different generations. It is difficult not to read in Trane's anguished face as he kneels by Erin's corpse a kind of displaced paternal anguish at what he has been forced to do.

Vera Cruz was as profitable as it was influential, reaping $9m from a $1.5m budget (some sources adjust the figures to $11m and $3m respectively), making it one of the most successful westerns of the decade. Many critics, however, felt that its amoral tone debased the genre, and resented its depiction of conniving gringos descending on Mexico like jackals. (The potential of this device as a metaphor for America's foreign policy would be exploited more fully in the following decade.) Bosley Crowther of the *New York Times* wrote, "The whole picture appears to be designed as a mere exhibition of how wicked and vicious men can be." (He must have been particularly appalled by Erin's gang, a fine coterie of Fifties heavies including Ernest Borgnine, Jack Elam and Charles Bronson, the kind of men who fight with broken bottles and threaten children.) Clearly, the public responded more favourably to the changes Aldrich had wrought and were fascinated "to see just how dirty, how like the enemy an American hero can become and still remain an American hero".[8] What we see in *Vera Cruz* – a process that has come to seem a reflection of America's travails in Cold War splinter conflicts, culminating in Vietnam – is heroism itself being redefined. **KG**

footnotes

1 Julian Petley, *The BFI Companion to the Western* (British Film Institute, 1988).

2 Interview with Robert Aldrich by Harry Ringel (1974), reprinted in *Robert Aldrich: Interviews* (University Press of Mississippi, 2004).

3 *Hide in Plain Sight: The Hollywood Blacklistees in Film and Television 1950-2002* (Palgrave Macmillan, 2004).

4 For Richard Slotkin, "The post-Civil War setting is a convention which signals a parallel between the theme of the movie and the concerns of post-World War America": that is, armed struggles being waged in parts of the Third World and their possible consequences for American strategic interests (*Gunfighter Nation: The Myth of the Frontier in Twentieth Century America,* University of Oklahoma Press, 1998).

5 Interview with Robert Aldrich by George Addison (1962) reprinted in *Robert Aldrich: Interviews*.

6 Aldrich was not such a fan of Leone's. The Italian was in charge of the second unit on Aldrich's *Sodom and Gomorrah* (1962), based near Marrakech: "He was supposed to start shooting at ten in the morning," recalled Aldrich. "When I arrived at 10.30 he hadn't gotten a first shot. Eleven o'clock, still no shot. Noon still no shot. At half past noon, he took off two hours for lunch... I asked him what was going on. He said, 'I just got a great shot.' 'When?' I asked. 'About a half-hour ago,' he said. So I told him, 'Great. You're fired.'" Interview with Robert Aldrich by Patrick Brion, Michel Mahéo, Dominique Rabourin and Noel Simsolo (1983), reprinted in *Robert Aldrich: Interviews*.

7 Cinematographer Ernest Laszlo shot *Vera Cruz* in the new Superscope process; its distinctly grainy results heighten the film's resemblance to many of the European westerns that followed, which had a similar texture courtesy of the Italian Techniscope system.

8 Richard Slotkin, *Gunfighter Nation: The Myth of the Frontier in Twentieth Century America*.

above: Cooper and Lancaster with Cesar Romero as the conniving Marquis.

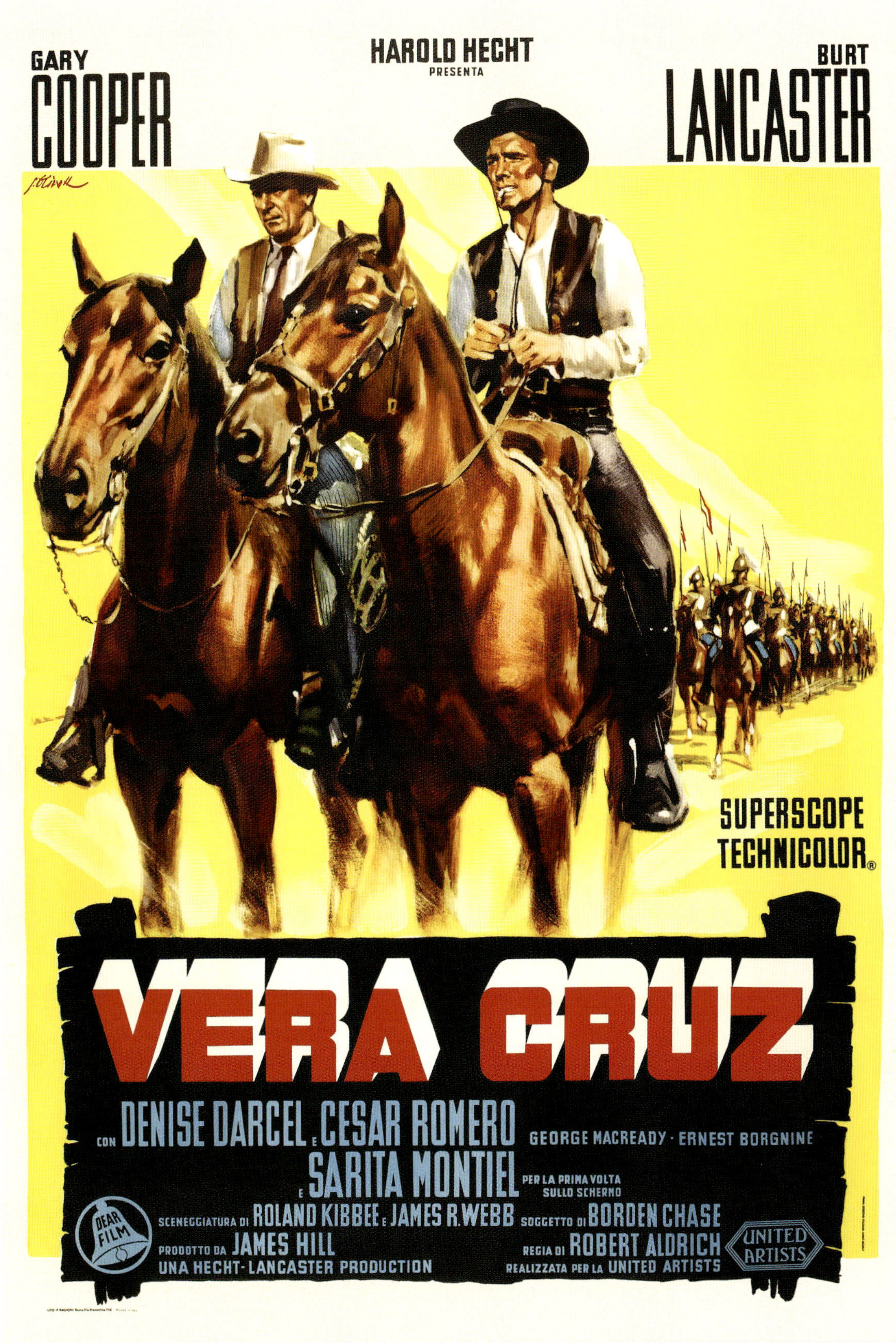
GARY
COOPER
HAROLD HECHT
PRESENTA
BURT
LANCASTER
SUPERSCOPE
TECHNICOLOR®
VERA CRUZ
CON DENISE DARCEL E CESAR ROMERO
GEORGE MACREADY · ERNEST BORGNINE
E SARITA MONTIEL
PER LA PRIMA VOLTA SULLO SCHERMO
SCENEGGIATURA DI ROLAND KIBBEE E JAMES R. WEBB
SOGGETTO DI BORDEN CHASE
PRODOTTO DA JAMES HILL
REGIA DI ROBERT ALDRICH
UNA HECHT-LANCASTER PRODUCTION
REALIZZATA PER LA UNITED ARTISTS
DEAR FILM
UNITED ARTISTS

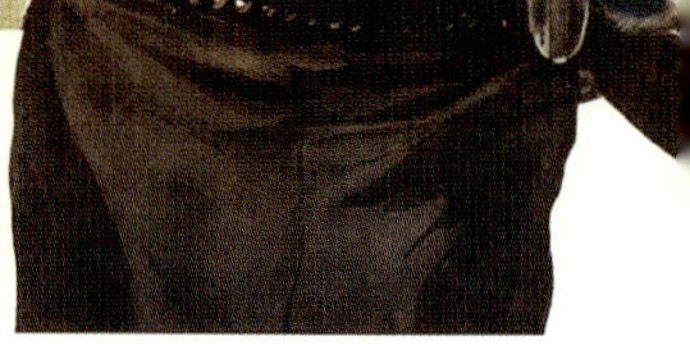

A Man Alone

1955, Colour, 96 mins.

D: Ray Milland. P: Herbert J. Yates (Republic Pictures).
W: John Tucker Battle, Mort Briskin (story). Ph: Lionel Lindon. M: Victor Young.
St: Ray Milland (Wes Steele), Mary Murphy (Nadine Corrigan), Ward Bond (Gil Corrigan), Raymond Burr (Stanley), Arthur Space (Dr. Mason)

"Right unfriendly town you live in..."

Made at the midpoint of a decade in which America's domestic agenda was distorted, if not determined, by Cold War insecurities, *A Man Alone's* thematic concerns echo those of *High Noon* and *Johnny Guitar*. It joins a string of westerns and other popular films contentiously identified, at the time or in retrospect, as anti-McCarthyite and/or displaced social commentaries. Moreover, with its persecuted protagonist, urban setting and claustrophobic, shadowy compositions in cellars, side streets and back rooms, it evokes the visual dynamics of film noir – a more congenial context for director/star, Ray Milland, and lead villain, Raymond Burr. Milland's direction is patchy (this was his first attempt), his own performance perfunctory when measured against actors such as Gregory Peck and Glenn Ford in comparable roles (see *The Gunfighter* and *The Fastest Gun Alive* [1956], respectively). Nevertheless, for a 'routine' Republic programmer, the film's dystopian outlook is unusually strong, contesting the perception of the West – indeed, America itself – as a land of liberty and limitless opportunity.

The grandeur of the West is obscured in the opening scenes by a dust storm, through which Milland's hard-bitten gunfighter, Wes Steele, struggles on foot after shooting his lame horse. He discovers a stagecoach, the passengers massacred, their possessions ransacked and scattered. Taking one of the horses to the nearest town,

Mesa, he shoots and wounds a gun-wielding figure – actually the acting sheriff – in the dusty darkness and becomes the object of a manhunt. When his identity is discovered, his reputation makes him the ideal scapegoat for the stagecoach killings and the murder of a respected citizen – secretly a criminal confederate – by the banker, Stanley, and his hired gunman Clayton (Lee Van Cleef). "He couldn't have come at a better time," crows Stanley, who inflames public opinion with sanctimonious speeches and encourages the formation of a lynch mob.

Milland spends the first act hiding in shadows, confined into corners like the victim-heroes of film noir. (Although shot in Republic's Trucolor system, most of the film resembles an ode to noir, notably a scene where Steele confronts Stanley in the church: in an ironic two-shot, the innocent party, Steele, is cloaked in shadow, while his

nefarious opponent has a candlelit glow.) The star often had a self-satisfied air, but this is the harassed Milland of *Ministry of Fear* (1944) or *The Big Clock* (1948), his urbane demeanour – somewhat incongruous in a western – rattled. He has no dialogue until he is discovered, sheltering in a cellar, by Nadine, the daughter of sheriff Gil Corrigan, with whom she lives in the house above. Conveniently for Steele, Corrigan is stricken with yellow fever, which enables Steele to bond with Nadine, rebut the accusations against him and show his humane side by helping tend her father. The romance develops implausibly smoothly, the script's attempts to equate their predicaments unconvincing. Steele airs the common grievance of the reluctant gunfighter: "Fellas come along trying to prove that you're not as good as they are. Pretty soon it gets out of hand and you find you've got to shoot to live"; while Nadine's yearning to escape her domineering father is symbolised by the hope chest she keeps buried in the cellar. Her scenes with Corrigan enter the domain of melodrama, with suppressed filial resentment challenging patriarchal authority, her cause bolstered when she discovers he is on Stanley's payroll.

The casting of Ward Bond, one of Hollywood's most outspoken conservatives, as a hypocritical moraliser would have pleased liberals, given his role as attack dog for the Motion Picture Alliance for the Preservation of American Ideals. (Nicholas Ray had employed Bond as a quasi-HUAC thug in the previous year's *Johnny Guitar*.) But Bond handles his 'confession' scene with Murphy with sensitivity, a big man brought low by bitter experience. The dream of prosperity he shared with Nadine's mother has been shattered by the economic reality of life in the "dog eat dog" West, which, in his description, is the antithesis of the Eden envisioned by ignorant Easterners and romanticised in a thousand complacent fantasies.

The image of the West, specifically the communities that have made it their home, is tarnished further when Corrigan is almost strung up by his neighbours for refusing to give up Steele. It is a disturbing example of mob rule that casts average Americans as bloodthirsty hysterics. Steele breaks the spell by exposing Stanley and Clayton, killing the latter in a gunfight. But the superficially tidy resolution, with Steele and Nadine deciding to settle in Mesa, signals not so much the exoneration of the citizens as an acknowledgement that corruption, intolerance and injustice are endemic. Corrigan's assertion that "this is a rotten town" seems to presage a star-in-the-dust moment, a disgusted departure *à la* Gary Cooper in *High Noon* or Dana Andrews in *Three Hours to Kill*; but, as Steele says, "Who knows if this place is any worse than the next one I hit?" **KG**

55-462 MAN WITH THE GUN
A MAN WHO LIVED and BREATHED VIOLENCE!
WARNING
Wearing of Guns or other Weapons in Town is Banned
CHECK ALL HARDWARE AT THE MARSHAL'S OFFICE
olators will be Shot
SIGNED
CLINT TOLLINGER
SAMUEL GOLDWYN, JR. presents
ROBERT MITCHUM as
MAN WITH THE GUN
Co-starring JAN STERLING
with KAREN SHARPE · HENRY HULL · EMILE MEYER · JOHN LUPTON
BARBARA LAWRENCE · TED DE CORSIA · LEO GORDON · JAMES WESTERFIELD
Story and Screenplay by N.B. STONE, JR. & RICHARD WILSON · Produced by SAMUEL GOLDWYN, JR. · Directed by RICHARD WILSON · Released thru UNITED ARTISTS
MAN WITH THE GUN 55-462

Man with the Gun

1955, B/W, 84 mins.

D: Richard Wilson. P: Samuel Goldwyn Jr. (Formosa Productions Inc). W: N.B. Stone Jr., Richard Wilson. Ph: Lee Garmes. M: Alex North. St: Robert Mitchum (Clint Tollinger), Jan Sterling (Nelly Bain), Karen Sharpe (Stella Atkins), Henry Hull (Marshal Lee Sims), Emile Meyer (Saul Atkins)

"He always dresses in grey. Black would fit his profession better."

Sheridan is the kind of beleaguered town that became an increasingly common backdrop in westerns of the Fifties, a place where brutal incidents like the one that opens this film – a gunman shooting dead a boy's pet dog when it yaps at him too insistently – "ain't even news" any more. The plot that unfolds there is similarly paradigmatic: caught in the crossfire of a feud of their own creating, the locals take a predictably hypocritical stance when the town tamer they have hired to root out a tyrannical rancher and his minions proves too ruthlessly adept for their liking – and for business. By the same token, Robert Mitchum's eponymous anti-hero, the man in the eye of the storm, now seems archetypal of the morally ambiguous, psychologically suspect protagonist who has come to symbolise westerns of that decade.

The Gunfighter and *High Noon* are the obvious reference points here. Mitchum's Clint Tollinger rides into Sheridan with a fearsome reputation and an estranged wife living there incognito. Sworn in by the timid marshal, Tollinger brooks no interference as he sets about freeing the town from the grip of the covetous land baron Holman, employing a combination of arbitrary edicts (the banning of firearms evokes Wyatt Earp) and brute force, burning down Holman's saloon in a destructive rage in the process. When the town council begins bleating about his methods

top right: Jan Sterling (left) rushes to the aid of Robert Mitchum.
above: Mitchum's authority is challenged by Leo Gordon (right), a prolific Fifties heavy.

(specifically, of course, their repercussions for the local economy), Tollinger's wife, Nelly, who has never come to terms with his vocation, could almost be quoting from the script of *High Noon*: "[You're] a target right to the end. Standing in front of people who won't stand in back of you."

The point about men of principle and courage betrayed by civic complacency and self-interest – with its implications for America's preparedness and willingness to face its obligations in the Cold War – was hammered home in westerns throughout the Fifties. The year 1955 alone saw the appearance of *Wichita*, *At Gunpoint*, *Top Gun* and *A Lawless Street*; *Man from Del Rio* (1956) featured Anthony Quinn's racial outcast in the central role ("He's good enough to do your killing for you, but it's got to be on the other side of the street"); while the more complex *Warlock* capped the cycle at the end of the decade. Director Richard Wilson approached the theme from a different angle in the ambitious but meandering *Invitation to a Gunfighter* (1964), with Yul Brynner cast shrewdly as a cultured Creole hitman who turns on his venal, implicitly racist paymasters.

Man with the Gun stands out from many of its contemporaries for the pall it casts over its nominal hero, who forges a connection with film noir that is reinforced by Lee Garmes' crisp monochrome photography and Wilson's intelligent use of the frame. In one early scene, as the town councillors gather in a barn to debate Tollinger's employment, he stands at the rear, undetected, almost completely obscured by shadows. (Yul Brynner occupies a similar shaded position at significant points in *Invitation to a Gunfighter*.) Mitchum was on a run of black-hearted roles – he'd just made *Track of the Cat* (1954) and *The Night of the Hunter* (1955) – and locates the menace beneath his character's conventionally taciturn exterior. Tollinger has similarities with *The Gunfighter's* Jimmie Ringo (he also has a child he has not seen for years, only Tollinger's daughter turns out to have died) and with *High Noon's* Will Kane, but is neither a tragic figure like Ringo nor a sacrificial lamb like Kane. Nelly makes some pat observations about her husband's inhumanity, but there is a real sense that Tollinger takes pleasure in killing – on two occasions he goads opponents into drawing on him – or at least derives a level of satisfaction that can't be squared with his purportedly heroic status.

Nonetheless, Tollinger's rigour is preferable to the "weak and shifting values" of those sections of Sheridan's micro-society who view their tainted saviour with distaste.[1] Nelly, who oversees the town's saloon girls, is also something of an undesirable – one puritanical lady suggests Tollinger turn his talents to evicting Nelly and her employees – but her role is underwritten, her position subservient to that of her husband. Wilson grants them a last-minute reconciliation in an optimistic ending that feels meretricious in the light of Tollinger's dark deeds. **KG**

footnotes

[1] John H. Lenihan, *Showdown: Confronting Modern America in the Western Film* (University of Illinois Press, 1980).

The Last Hunt

1956, Colour, 103 mins.

D: Richard Brooks. P: Dore Schary (Metro Goldwyn-Mayer). W: Richard Brooks. Ph: Russell Harlan. M: Daniele Amfitheatrof. St: Robert Taylor (Charley Gilson), Stewart Granger (Sandy McKenzie), Lloyd Nolan (Woodfoot), Debra Paget (Indian girl), Russ Tamblyn (Jimmy),

"Killing's like… the only real proof you're alive."

If Richard Brooks' indignant western failed to dislodge William F. Cody and men of his ilk from the pantheon of American folk heroes, it was not for want of trying. Buffalo hunters and their bloody trade are exposed as instruments in the oppression of the plains Indians and the eradication of their independent way of life.[1] Charley Gilson – a cousin of *The Searchers'* Ethan Edwards ("Killin' buffalo's as good as killin' Indians") – remembers with pride General Sheridan rewarding hunters with medals for their contribution to the elimination of native peoples as a threat to white hegemony. Sheridan's famous dictum – "Let them kill, skin and sell until the buffalo is exterminated, as it is the only way to bring lasting peace and allow civilisation to advance" – encapsulates the same racist conception of natives that Charley holds in his heart: Indians "ain't even human", no better than beasts. It is a notion that his partner, the veteran hunter Sandy McKenzie, has come to view as shameful – a stain on his own character as well as that of the nation.

What is really shameful is that it is Charley, not Sandy, who appears to be more consonant with public opinion; effectively, as John Ford did with *The Searchers*, Brooks holds up a mirror to his audience, confronting them with the unsightly aspects of the heroic mythology upon which the western was founded. The bulk of the drama takes place in the great outdoors, with Sheridan's 'civilisation' represented by "an ugly, muddy town with grimy, bigoted people [which] stands out conspicuously against the beauty of the landscape".[2] Charley's racist views, like his infatuation with killing, may be symptomatic of mental fragility (we are deep in psychological western territory); equally, however, they are rife in the white community. An old Indian is kept shackled in the street; the young half-breed Jimmy, subsequently employed by Sandy, is beaten for offering the captive a drink. Sandy's contrary attitude – rooted partly in remorse over the misery his actions have visited on the Indians, however indirectly – is heretical in this milieu; it later embroils him in a drunken fight with some loutish hunters whose line of thinking – if they think at all – is closer to that of Charley.

The Last Hunt's standpoint on bigotry hardly made it anomalous among postwar westerns. It *was* unusual in projecting an environmental message – the bucolic charm of the scenery is besmirched by evidence of the buffalo hunters' grisly business: "an endless desolation of bones and skulls and rotting hooves"[3] – and in acknowledging the importance of buffalo to the plains tribes, not only in terms of food, but touching on their wider significance and spiritual value: "They mean life for Indians, so they made a religion of 'em."[4] It is not difficult to see the buffalo as surrogates for Native Americans themselves, with the campaign against the herds a metaphor for the suppression of the tribes – a displaced military offensive. Charley speaks of bison as if they were enemy combatants; much like Indians, they must be exterminated if white men are to progress. (He uses this argument to convince the jaded Sandy, whose cattle have been destroyed in a buffalo stampede, to join him in one final hunt.) Sandy's barroom diatribe against the injustice of the hunting trade recalls Tom Jeffords disputing the legitimacy of Manifest Destiny in *Broken Arrow*, and invites a similarly violent response – for 'buffalo lover' read 'Injun lover'. Considering the warning issued early on by Woodfoot, a grizzled, whisky-soaked buffalo-skinner, about the threat to the creature's very existence as a result of the 'offensive', the parallel extends further still. We see few Indians on screen; in the most poignant scene, set on a barren reservation, the pathetic natives have already eaten their dogs and horses and, the agent says, will surely starve unless the army sends them supplies.

Aside from Jimmy, a racial misfit, the only major Indian character is an unnamed girl (played, almost inevitably, by Debra Paget[5]) – the last survivor, along with a small child, of a raiding party executed by Charley when they try to steal his ponies. Charley's contempt for everything Native American doesn't prevent him from claiming the girl as his concubine, while the mutual affection that blossoms between her and the courteous Sandy – one of the script's relatively few concessions to romantic tradition – contributes to Charley's increasingly paranoid behaviour as well as his isolation from his companions.

This is especially evident in two telling scenes. In the first, he slaughters dozens of buffalo with undisguised exhilaration, pausing only to cool his rifle with water, while Sandy shoots sparingly and reluctantly. (The numbing horror of this scene is all too real: Brooks was given permission to film licensed hunters on their annual cull of buffalo herds in Dakota's Custer State Park. Stewart Granger felt the director "seemed to revel in taking close shots of maggots crawling out of the corpses… or of the skinning and butchering of the stinking animals".[6] These graphic details do not appear in the film.)

The hunters drift further apart when they spy a rare white buffalo; while Sandy looks enchanted, Charley shoots it without hesitation. The girl is horrified: these animals are "big medicine" to her people, and tantamount to sacred – "You take away our food; now you kill our religion." Charley's only concern is the premium its hide will fetch on the market, and he spitefully denies a request from an Indian friend of Jimmy's to trade for it. Instead, he agrees to fight the newcomer – for the "pure pleasure" it would give him to kill an Indian – and mortally wounds his opponent. The fate of the precious hide finally fractures the partners' relationship.

Like shell-shocked veterans from film noir, Charley and Sandy have been scarred by their wartime experiences. But where Sandy is weary of killing, Charley has become desensitised. "Killin', fightin', war – that's the natural order of things," he says; his bigotry, meanwhile, may be the result of nurture as much as nature, given the demonisation of Indians by white society. Sandy pities him, implying that he is not fully in control of his actions ("You're a special case – I've never seen a gun wear a man before"), and it is to Robert Taylor's credit that the character merits at least a degree of sympathy. This was not a commercially popular film – the ageing MGM poster boy scored far bigger hits in the Fifties with glossy period pieces such as *Quo Vadis* (1951) and *Ivanhoe* (1952) – but it offered him the most rewarding role of his middle years, a period in which he strove successfully to broaden his range, from the autocratic trail boss in *Westward the Women* to the corrupt detective in *Rogue Cop* (1954). Granger is fine in a less demanding role, holding the moral centre while Taylor skirts the periphery.

By reframing the conquest of the frontier as an ecological as well as a human tragedy and issuing a call to arms against racism, *The Last Hunt* demonstrated the social consciousness that typified Brooks' work (it was bracketed by *Blackboard Jungle* [1955] and the anti-colonialist

Something of Value [1957]), as well as much of MGM's output under producer Dore Schary. As one of the leading proponents of social realism in postwar American cinema, Schary believed that audiences demanded "pictures of more moment". During his time at RKO he oversaw Edward Dmytryk's film noir *Crossfire* (1947), based on a novel by Brooks, which he hoped would "insulate" people against anti-Semitism. He was also a principal antagonist of the reactionary Motion Picture Alliance for the Preservation of American Ideals – of which Robert Taylor was a founder member – which arose partly in response to the liberal politics he and Brooks transmitted in their movies.

Schary opposed anything that was "tinsel and rose-coloured and cream puff". None of those terms could be applied to *The Last Hunt's* damning account of America's expansionist past, notwithstanding its patina of a polished studio production. The luscious photography mirrors Russell Harlan's spectacular frescoes for Howard Hawks, while the script is incisive, eschewing prolix moralising. Much of the film's power, however, emanates from Taylor, who shoulders such weighty themes as "the low and demoralising influence of a lust for slaughter upon the nature of man" with the discipline of a seasoned contract player.[7] The ending is where his character and Ethan Edwards diverge. Charley has no opportunity for expiation; having stalked Sandy and the girl through the wintry landscape, he dies of hypothermia, shrouded in a frozen-solid buffalo hide, a grim-faced monument to madness, animosity and intolerance. It is a long way indeed from the popular image of Buffalo Bill. **KG**

footnotes

1 Although the film acknowledges the role of Indians themselves in the diminution of buffalo numbers on the Great Plains, as well as competition for grazing land by horse herds, many sources attribute the greatest decline to the accelerated pace of westward expansion by white settlers after the Civil War, the growing export market for meat and hides and the industrial-scale slaughter initiated by the railroad industry. (William F. Cody himself was one of the railroad's most prolific employees, claiming to have killed 4,280 animals on the plains of Kansas in 18 months, thus earning his famous moniker. He later argued in favour of a preservation order on the species.) Estimates vary on the population of bison before the peak killing years; a 1902 survey for the US Department of the Interior put it at around 20,000,000 in 1850, falling to 20,000 in 1885, with fewer than 1,000 recorded in 1895.

2 John H. Lenihan, *Showdown: Confronting Modern America in the Western Film* (University of Illinois Press, 1980).

3 Dee Brown, *Bury My Heart at Wounded Knee* (Holt, Rinehart & Winston, 1970).

4 For many plains tribes, "the buffalo was almost everything. It was food and it was clothing. A dozen cured buffalo hides made a tipi home. Buffalo leather could also make war shields, kettles and even coracle-like boats. The bones in the skull, cracked open with a buffalo hoof, helped tan the hide. Horns were used for drinking cups, and ceremonial dress. Large bones were weapons, small ones awls and needles. Buffalo dung made 'chips' for fires. The Blackfoot extracted no fewer than 88 commodities from the buffalo, excluding food" (Jon E. Lewis, *The Mammoth Book of the West*, Carroll & Graf, 1996).

5 The little-known Anne Bancroft was due to play the part, but suffered an injury in the early stages of production. Paget thus played yet another exotic maiden, which became her speciality in the wake of *Broken Arrow*.

6 Stewart Granger, *Sparks Fly Upward* (Granada, 1981).

7 Bosley Crowther, *The New York Times*, 1 March, 1956.

Reprisal!

1956, Colour, 74 mins.

D: George Sherman. P: Lewis J. Rachmil (Romson Productions, Inc). W: David P. Harmon, Raphael Hayes, David Dortort. Ph: Henry Freulich. M: Mischa Bakaleinikoff. St: Guy Madison (Frank Madden/Neola), Felicia Farr (Catherine Cantrell), Kathryn Grant (Taini), Michael Pate (Bert Shipley), Edward Platt (Neil Shipley)

"It's lonely trying to be something you are not, isn't it?"

In 1950, Arthur Gordon wrote a novel about racial tensions and revenge in the American South, inspired by the murder of four black people by white vigilantes in Monroe, Georgia. Such material would have been too provocative for a straight adaptation, certainly at that time. Instead, it is coded as an Indian-themed B-western, preserving the framework of the story and the motifs of prejudice and injustice while displacing the friction between whites and African-Americans to a mythical, emotionally distancing historical setting. The contemporary resonances, however, remain unmistakable, at least in retrospect, as does the tone of reproach, which plots *Reprisal!* on a line of continuity that runs from *Devil's Doorway* and *Broken Arrow* through to *Run of the Arrow* and beyond.

Like those films, *Reprisal!* considers questions of racial, individual and national identity, of tolerance – or the lack thereof – and the rights of minorities. These would seem to be negligible: the opening scene finds the three Shipley brothers being acquitted of lynching two Indians who had, they claim, trespassed on their land. The fictitious town of Kendall is divided between those with progressive views – the judge, who voices his disgust at the outcome of the trial, which clearly isn't the first such travesty; the land agent's daughter, Catherine Cantrell, the counterpart of *Devil's Doorway's* high-minded Orrie Masters – and the racists and reactionaries who are evidently in the ascendency. The defence attorney expresses his own outrage that the testimony of an Indian eyewitness was even considered admissible, while the judge's liberal pronouncements are greeted with sneers and jibes ("He must be the chief of the tribe").

Into this combustible situation strides Frank Madden, a new rancher who has recently returned to the area. He affects strict neutrality on the racial issue, not from indifference but as a consequence of his ancestry – he looks white but is half Indian, and feels estranged from both sides. He implores his Cherokee grandfather, Matara, not to give away his secret, and shrugs off Taini, an Indian girl who takes a fancy to him, all to suppress and deny his ethnic make-up. Eventually, through the promptings of Catherine and Matara and the machinations of the elder Shipleys, who falsely accuse him of killing their younger brother, he is forced to admit the truth and take a stand.

The pleas of Catherine and Matara, who jointly represent Frank's conscience, could just as well have been addressed to the nation at large. The script makes repeated and pointed reference to the "shame" and "guilt" brought on the community by policies that discriminate so blatantly against ethnic others. As the trial scene makes plain, as far as the majority of those in Kendall are concerned, "savages" don't even have the same right to life as whites, much less equal privileges under the law. Furthermore, the prosperity of the town is juxtaposed against the dilapidation of the Indian village, the better to indict racial segregation.

Frank's own actions speak to the toxic side effects of societal racism. Having seen his tribe dispossessed and his Indian mother killed, he has concealed himself on the fringes of Caucasian society, light-skinned enough to pass as white, in the knowledge that a Native American would be debarred from owning land. (Here is evidence, unaddressed in the film, of Frank's alienation from tribal beliefs; obviously he craves something more tangible than a spiritual bond with nature.) Leaving aside the issue of the actor's ethnicity (a red herring, perhaps, in a story about a half-breed), Guy Madison is a good fit for the role. Never the most effusive of performers, he is guarded and sullen, with a seasoning of self-loathing; fans of his laid-back manner in TV's *The Adventures of Wild Bill Hickok* may have been disappointed. (We can infer the actor's keenness to expand his repertoire from the fact his production company was the driving force behind *Reprisal!*)

From beneath the camouflage of a mid-budget western, *Reprisal!* makes its points with the fervour of a firebrand. Broadening its attack on lynch law when the Shipleys incite public ire against Frank, it comes to resemble *The Ox-Bow Incident*, *Three Hours to Kill* and *Silver Lode* – all films in which a relative outsider is made a scapegoat by a citizenry lacking in moral fibre. Frank is freed thanks to Taini, who lies about spending the night with him on the occasion of Tom Shipley's murder. As the crowd recedes (including Catherine, who proves that bigotry is ingrained when she expresses humiliation at Frank's choice of a "squaw" over her), George Sherman pays tribute to *High Noon* – with Frank left alone in the frame, the camera cranes up to maximise his solitude.

The ending is noteworthy for its bitterness. Taini's bravery, and that of Matara, who is killed while protecting him, resolves Frank to rejoin Indian society: "That part of me that is white I deny." With Catherine in tow (a development that feels entirely perfunctory), he abandons his quest for "security and social status" and rejects the new America as morally inferior to the civilisation it has swept aside.[1] This was a bold statement to make in what was – and what for many remains, at least putatively – the most patriotic of Hollywood genres. **KG**

footnotes

1 John H. Lenihan, *Showdown: Confronting Modern America in the Western Film* (University of Illinois Press, 1980).

LA WARNER BROS. PRESENTA
UN FILM DI C.V. WHITNEY
CON
JOHN WAYNE
IN
DISTRIBUZIONE
DEAR
INTERNATIONAL
WB
SENTIERI SELVAGGI
CON
JEFFREY HUNTER · VERA MILES · WARD BOND · NATALIE WOOD
SCENEGGIATURA DI FRANK S. NUGENT
PRODUTTORE ESECUTIVO MERIAN C. COOPER
PRODUTTORE ASSOCIATO PATRICK FORD
REGIA DI JOHN FORD
TECHNICOLOR
VISTAVISION
PRIMA EDIZIONE ITALIANA 1971
AVVERTENZA
Printed in Italy · by ROTOLITOGRAFICA · G. Racc. Anulare Km. 32,400 · Roma · Tel. 415141

The Searchers

1956, Colour, 119 mins.

D: John Ford. P: Merian C. Cooper (C.V. Whitney Pictures Inc). W: Frank S. Nugent. Ph: Winton C. Hoch. M: Max Steiner. St: John Wayne (Ethan Edwards), Jeffrey Hunter (Martin Pawley), Vera Miles (Laurie Jorgensen), Ward Bond (Captain Reverend Samuel Johnson Clayton), Natalie Wood (Debbie Edwards)

"Seems like [the Indian] never learns there's such a thing as a critter that'll just keep comin' on. So we'll find 'em in the end, I promise you. We'll find 'em. Just as sure as the turnin' of the Earth."

Every great trek saga is ultimately a journey into the self. This is true of *The Searchers* not only where the wandering hero is concerned, but also filmgoers compelled by custom to ride with him. Ethan Edwards' pursuit of the Indians who have ravaged his brother's farm and kidnapped his niece brings into focus the contradictions inherent in the frontier hero, as well as the ambiguities in his relationship with his audience. It becomes, figuratively, an exploration of the character's tormented psyche; it suggests, like many westerns from the Fifties, that the 'heroic' actions demanded of their protagonists can be both brutalising and destabilising. Much of the film's disturbing power derives not merely from Ethan's virulent racism and what this may or may not say about John Wayne, the emblematic western actor, and John Ford, its most iconic director; it is also the fact that the character's function as an intermediary for the viewer is never fully disputed. "By postponing the unmasking of Ethan's hatefulness and by refusing to entirely dispel the suggestion that his hatred of Indians is legitimate grounds for sympathy, Ford prevents the audience from adopting a position of comfortable disdain toward Ethan," says Richard Slotkin. "We retain a sense of kinship with him and may discover that we share (in some degree) Ethan's obsessions."[1]

There are warning signs early on. Ethan arrives at his brother's ranch like a guardian angel, very much in the spirit of Shane, with a similarly glamorous yet dangerous aura. His nieces and nephew worship him, as does his sister-in-law, Martha – their unspoken mutual affection is perhaps the decisive factor in Ethan's subsequent behaviour. But he quickly reveals darker sides to his character: his disdain for his sibling's swarthy adopted son, Martin – "Fella could mistake you for a half-breed" (he is indeed part Cherokee) – indicates Ethan's views on race; and the presence in his saddlebags of a horde of "fresh-minted" Yankee dollars hints that this diehard Confederate ("I don't believe in surrenders") may have spent time as a border raider. As the hunt for the Comanche attackers develops into an obsession, it is not so much Ethan/Wayne's domineering personality that creates a problem for the audience; Martin, after all, counteracts the older man's obduracy. (There are unmistakable echoes here of the dynamic between Wayne and Montgomery Clift in *Red River*.) The issue is rather the explicitly racial nature of Ethan's hatred. As well as actuating psychotic, if largely symbolic, deeds of violence – shooting out the eyes of a dead Comanche brave, condemning his soul to "wander forever between the winds"; frenziedly killing buffalo, to deny them to the Indians – it fuels his murderous intent towards Debbie, the niece stolen as a bride for chief Scar (Henry Brandon) and thus, in Ethan's eyes, contaminated, fit only for a bullet. As he says when they encounter captive white women rescued by the army,

"They ain't white. Not any more. They're *Comanch*." If looks could kill, his gaze, magnified in close-up, would destroy them on the spot.[2]

Rather than supporting or advocating Ethan's stance on this point, as short-sighted critics have been wont to attest, *The Searchers* challenges the audience to reject it, as Martin does – to recognise the insanity of the creed that determines "better dead than red" and assumes the moral and cultural superiority of one race over another. To this end, Ford makes the provocative suggestion that Ethan's racism, rooted in miscegenation anxiety, is deeply entrenched in society. Indeed, it is synonymous with the civilising mission with which he has been entrusted. In one of the film's more shocking scenes, Laurie, Martin's intended, angrily denounces her fiancé's compassion for Debbie, referring to her as "the leavin's of a Comanche buck" and claiming that Martha would have wanted Ethan to kill the girl. (Ethan finds the body of Debbie's sister, Lucy, on the trail.) Laurie represents the homesteaders, an almost sacred breed in westerns, busily sowing the seeds of civilisation while men like Ethan secure the frontier on their behalf. So for her to speak these words is significant. Her outburst gives us pause: what kind of reception will Debbie receive, not only at the Jorgensens', but in the wider community? If the basically wholesome Laurie is driven to distraction by the thought of miscegenation, this bodes ill for Debbie's future. Ford's thoughts on the matter were later the subject of the sour *Two Rode Together* (1961), which dramatises and decries the social rejection of returned captives – of both sexes, in that case. The topic was treated in a number of other westerns – *Trooper Hook* (1957), *The Tin Star* (1957), *The Unforgiven* (1960), *Duel at Diablo* (1966), *The Stalking Moon* (1968) – each time highlighting what John H. Lenihan calls "the hypocrisies and emotional instability of white society".[3] The recurrence of the theme at a time when black-white relations topped the socio-political agenda in America hardly seems like a coincidence, although this was not addressed in the film's contemporary reviews, some of which (*Time*, *Variety*, *The New York Times*) failed to distinguish *The Searchers* from more routine westerns.

As it maps Ethan's increasing derangement over his seven-year quest, *The Searchers* justifies Ford's description of it as "a psychological epic", charting the contours of a mind that has become unbalanced by violence. Ethan continually violates the westerner's heroic code, not just in his determination to murder an innocent girl – his own kin, no less – but in his ruthlessness in general, as when he uses Martin as bait to draw out an assailant, then thinks nothing of shooting the man in the back. Audiences were expected to square this with the image of John Wayne, sculpted across more than 60 previous westerns, as a man who was tough and resolute, but never obsessive and unscrupulous, as he is here (it would have been less of a shock to those who bore in mind Wayne's autocratic performance in *Red River*). They would also have to come to terms with the hazier distinction between protagonists and antagonists at an individual level – a fixation of the Fifties 'adult' western, particularly those directed by Anthony Mann – and the redrawing of moral boundaries in a wider sense, particularly in the context of cavalry-Native American conflict.

Ford is not regarded for his impartiality in this area – as the director of the much-loved Cavalry Trilogy, he remains associated, not entirely unjustly, with the stereotypes of the valiant trooper and the ravaging, wild-eyed Indian of frontier demonology. Here, however, he indicts both sides for 'war crimes'; thus the massacre of innocents at the Edwards ranch is balanced later in the film by the searchers' discovery at the Indians' winter camp of scores of dead Comanche, including women and children, following a Cavalry assault.[4] It is a sight that would become commonplace in revisionist Vietnam-era westerns, but here it signifies Ford's desire to show the West in more complex terms, moving beyond a black and white – or red and white – moral perspective.

above: from left: Jeffrey Hunter, John Wayne and Ward Bond.

The Searchers continues in this vein by positioning Scar – the bad guy, in the conventional sense – as both Ethan's adversary and his "crazy mirror".[5] Scar's loathing of the white eyes is not merely reflexive but, he explains, the consequence of depredations against his family and tribe. (His blue eyes point to another possibility – if he is of mixed race himself, then self-loathing may be a factor in his belligerence.[6]) His viciousness, like that of Ethan, is explained partly as revenge for the murder of loved ones by his racial enemies, represented by the military in general and by Ethan in particular. The director implies their affinity at several points: the way Scar looms over young Debbie during the attack on the ranch prefigures Ethan's menacing motion towards her near the end; a beautifully composed shot in Monument Valley, which has rarely looked more majestic on film, has each riding at the head of a column of riders – Ethan and the posse in the foreground, Scar and his warriors shadowing them on a ridge behind; when the characters first meet, in Scar's village, they use the same words to compliment their command of each other's language; later in this scene, the chief is seen to wear the medal given by Ethan to Debbie at the beginning of the film; and, although

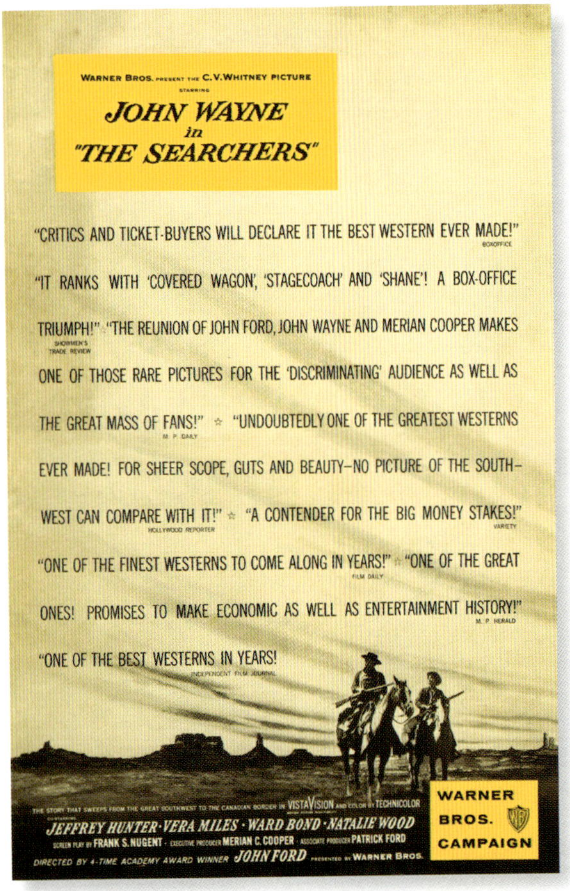

more has been made of this by commentators than was perhaps intended by Ford, Scar's presumed rape of Martha may be an enactment of Ethan's own repressed desire. Ultimately, the status of Ethan, the white man, as 'civilised' hero, and Scar, the Indian, as 'barbaric' villain, is rendered meaningless when the former, denied the pleasure of killing his foe personally, resorts to scalping Scar's corpse, an act of desecration associated almost exclusively with 'savages' and one that shows how seriously his cultural identity has become degraded. "It is because Ethan is closer to Scar than to his own culture that he is so compelling dramatically and the film so challenging," concludes Jim Kitses.[7]

By the same token, Ethan's increasing estrangement from society can be measured in the distance between his behaviour, manner and worldview and that of Martin, whose moral stature grows as the other's declines. (He is complicit, however, in the film's most infamous and poorly judged sequence – the mocking and physical abuse of Look, the unwanted Comanche 'bride' Martin acquires in a trade and dispenses with by kicking down a hill. To make matters worse, hers is among the bodies they find at the Indians' camp. All the film's comic interludes jar; centred principally on Ken Curtis, Ford's son-in-law, and his old acolytes Hank Worden and Ward Bond, they merely indulge the director's weakness for heavy-handed humour and knock the main plot off course.) Being of mixed blood, Martin symbolises an idealised vision of a multi-racial America – a riposte to the anti-miscegenation views expressed by Laurie and the white supremacist Ethan; arguably, he also addresses the fears about racial integration swirling around America at the time, particularly in the Southern states, in the wake of the seismic Brown v Board of Education ruling against racially segregated schooling in May 1954 and in the midst of the ongoing Montgomery Bus Boycott.[8] Martin's emergence as a hero at his companion's expense becomes pronounced when he stands between Debbie and Ethan's gun and is cemented when he dispatches Scar, leaving Ethan to his bloody consolation prize.

The climax is justly famous, and encapsulates the film's complexity. The fact that Ethan spares Debbie, having sworn to kill her, has been interpreted in many ways: as a cop-out by Ford; a sop to family values; a sign that Ethan sees Martha, his great lost love, in Debbie's face. (This is, in fact, what Ethan says to her in the shooting script. Ford changed the scene on location.) The last point is especially persuasive if it is taken in tandem with another suggestion, raised by a number of writers, that Ethan's scalping of Scar is the prelude to his dramatic volte-face. "The act proves cathartic," argues Joseph McBride, respecting Ford's "psychological epic" assertion; having sacrificed himself "on the altar of savagery" (Patrick McGee) by mutilating his 'primitive' alter ego, Ethan is purged of his murderous desires towards the girl he now saves.[9]

This marks his redemption, yet Ethan remains an outcast. When he and Martin return with Debbie to the Jorgensens', Ethan cannot cross the threshold; nor does anybody look back for him. Again like Shane, he knows that his place is in the desert, not the garden. The embodiment of society's id, just as Scar was his, Ethan and his neuroses must be suppressed for the

above: Jeffrey Hunter with Vera Miles as Laurie, whose views are not as wholesome as she looks.

common good: "[His] craziness is shared by the society he represents so well that in the end he must be expelled from it, like a bad dream," notes McBride. (Ford returned to this idea in *The Man Who Shot Liberty Valance*.) While Debbie's homecoming is a 'happy ending' on the surface – we still have Laurie's racist rant ringing in our ears – Ethan's fate illustrates Ford's disenchantment with the myths he had done so much to popularise. The implications of the final shot, with Ethan shut off from civilisation, make it one of the bleakest and most tragic in western history.[10] As David Lusted summarises, "It is as if the door closes not only on the character, but also on the very figure of the romance hero."[11] **KG**

footnotes

1 *Gunfighter Nation: The Myth of the Frontier in Twentieth-Century America* (University of Oklahoma Press, 1998).

2 This scene upsets many observers for the way it apparently reinforces the image of Indian society, and Indians themselves, as less than human; any whites unfortunate enough to be captured are likely to become corrupted or, as with these women, mentally unhinged. (See Michael Hilger, *From Savage to Nobleman*, Scarecrow Press, 1995.) The scene has been submitted as evidence that the film is as prejudiced as its protagonist, even though it ought to be clear by this point just how disturbed Ethan is. Its effect is diminished, moreover, by the image of Debbie, who has retained her senses and her identity and evidently been well treated by the Comanche.

3 *Showdown: Confronting Modern America in the Western Film* (University of Illinois Press, 1980).

4 The script contained a scene after this one in which Ethan upbraided a Custer-like cavalry commander, taking him to task for targeting women and children. Ford felt this suggestion of Ethan's nobility compromised the character's essential ruthlessness, however, and omitted it from the film.

5 Joseph McBride, *Searching for John Ford* (Faber & Faber, 2004).

6 If the intention was to suggest that Scar had a white mother or father, here is an instance where the casting of a white actor as an Indian chief – a common Hollywood practice, of course – supports one of the film's key themes. The German-American Brandon went on to play another chief, the real-life Quanah Parker, in Ford's *Two Rode Together*. Quanah Parker, also a Comanche, was himself mixed race – his mother, Cynthia Ann Parker, who was captured in a Comanche raid at the age of nine, was the same woman who inspired the character of Debbie in *The Searchers*. She was never able to readjust to white society and committed suicide in her mid-forties.

7 *Horizons West* (BFI, 2007).

8 Martin's Cherokee heritage was a detail added by Ford and screenwriter Frank Nugent; in the source novel by Alan LeMay, Martin is white.

9 Patrick McGee, *From Shane to Kill Bill: Rethinking the Western* (Wiley-Blackwell, 2006).

10 The ending was one of several crucial alterations made by Ford during filming. In Nugent's script, Ethan is welcomed back into the family fold along with Debbie. It was also Ford's decision to have Ethan scalp Scar.

11 *The Western* (Routledge, 2003). In his isolation from society and his ambiguous relationship towards it, Ethan became the template for American cinema's most troubled antiheroes, notably Travis Bickle of *Taxi Driver* (1976), whose director, Martin Scorsese, and writer, Paul Schrader, are among *The Searchers'* most vocal champions.

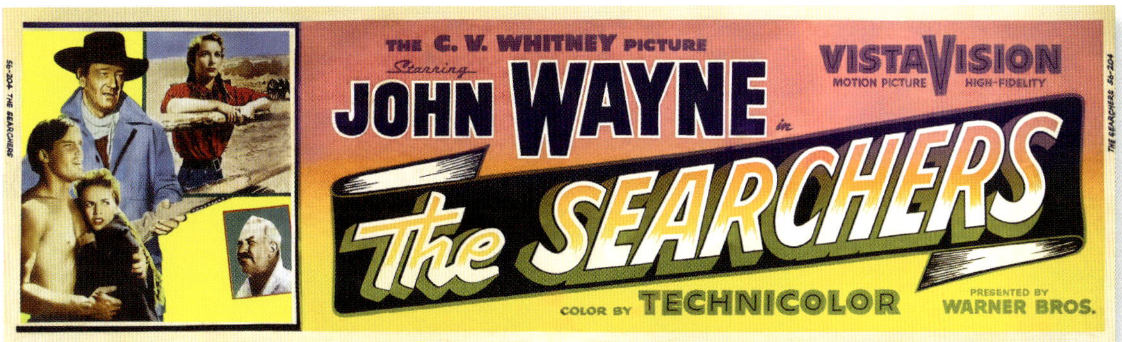

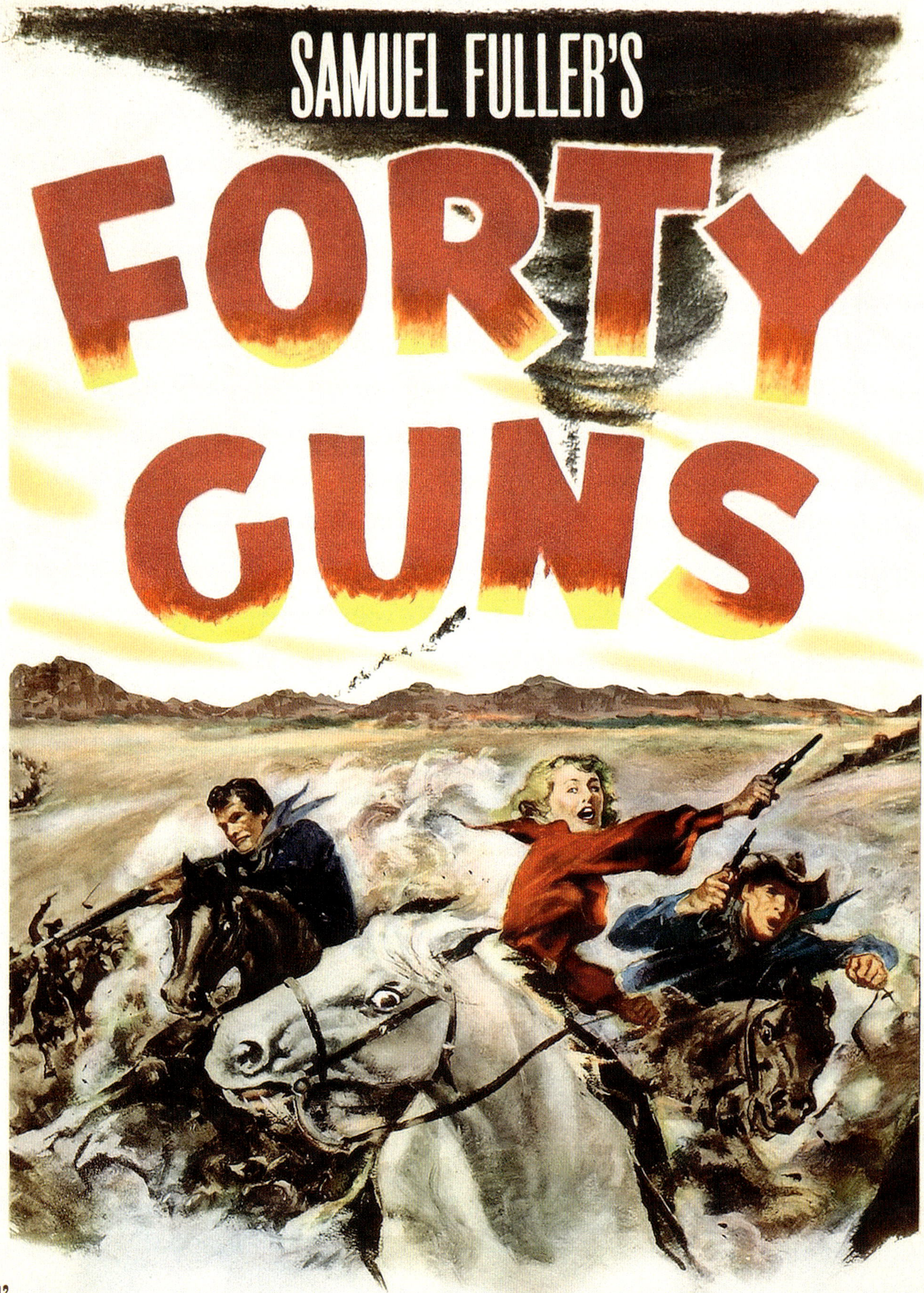
SAMUEL FULLER'S
FORTY
GUNS

Forty Guns

1957, B/W, 80 mins.

D: Samuel Fuller. P: Samuel Fuller (Globe Enterprises Inc). W: Samuel Fuller. Ph: Joseph Biroc. M: Harry Sukman. St: Barbara Stanwyck (Jessica Drummond), Barry Sullivan (Griff Bonnell), Dean Jagger (Ned Logan), John Ericson (Brockie Drummond), Gene Barry (Wes Bonnell)

"What's happened to us is like war – easy to start, hard to stop."

Love was often a battlefield in Samuel Fuller's films, but never so explicitly as in *Forty Guns*. Sex and violence are yoked together in a manner normally reserved for melodramas. Double entendres and visual innuendo propel a story of dangerous passions – centred on the relationship between two formidable characters: gunfighter/lawman Griff Bonnell and land baroness Jessica Drummond – that critiques key western tropes while expanding the genre's stylistic parameters. Many American critics felt the film's tone histrionic, its shifts of mood too brutal, and were put off by Fuller's formal experimentation, from the dynamic editing to the expressive widescreen cinematography. But these same qualities were lapped up by French cineastes (most famously Jean-Luc Godard and Luc Moullet), for whom Fuller was central not just to the renaissance of the western, but also – as a writer-producer-director – to the auteur theory.

The Griff/Jessica romance – rekindling the stars' on-screen relationship from *Cattle Queen of Montana* – progresses precariously along a rocky road strewn with complications, principally the reckless actions of her younger brother, Brockie, the terror of Tombstone. But it is only the trunk of a narrative that branches off in a number of thematic directions, not all of which it pursues. *Forty Guns* pulses with energy and ideas, the strongest and most transgressive being the prominence of a powerful, emasculating female – a "high ridin' woman with a whip" – occupying the kind of role customarily reserved for men.[1] Fuller doesn't have the space to elucidate all of his notions; typically, he elides and condenses, juggling with fragments of themes, such as civic corruption, that would take up entire plots in other westerns. One such tantalising thread has Griff – modelled on Wyatt Earp, complete with two brothers in tow – representing the gunfighter as dying breed. "You shot your way across the map," says Jessica, urging Griff to hang up his gun, or at least to hang it on her bedpost. "This is the last stop – the frontier is finished." Griff realises his era is passing, and tries to dissuade his youngest sibling, Chico (Robert Dix), from following in his footsteps or those of his other brother, Wes, and becoming a "freak" like him. Yet when Chico kills his first man, to save Griff's life, the sense of a threshold being crossed, of innocence evaporating like gunsmoke, is skirted over; previously voluble, Chico is presented in subsequent scenes as calmer, more mature – more like his brothers. His value as a counterpart to the volatile Brockie, displaced from the Fifties school of juvenile delinquent films, is similarly overlooked.

Fuller is at his strongest when sending up the western's phallocentric bearing (as he had, even more daringly, in *I Shot Jesse James*), amplifying and satirising the eroticization of weaponry implicit in genre iconography. In two of the film's most famous episodes, Eve Brent (playing Louvenia, the gunsmith's daughter) is objectified through a rifle barrel (an image filched by Godard for *À bout de souffle*); and Jessica asks to handle Griff's "trademark", his pistol, and is warned, "It might go off in your face." The subplot involving Louvenia's romance with Wes is equally playful. Soon after they meet, Wes remarks how he'd like to "clean her rifle", while their pillow talk revolves around bullets and guns. The correlation of violence and sex extends to two extraordinary scenes. In the first, a tornado is both the spur and a symbolically turbulent backdrop to Griff and Jessica's first tryst, signifying the excitement of their union, almost as if forces greater than themselves are bringing them together, but also the danger that threatens to tear them apart, namely Griff's dispute with her brother.

Significantly, barred shadows fall on their bodies as they shelter in a shack and talk of settling down, painting them as noir-esque prisoners of fate. More disturbing still is the way an intimate encounter at Jessica's ranch is interrupted first by gunfire, when the crooked county sheriff (Dean Jagger), hopelessly in love with Jessica, tries to kill Griff, and then, after she has spurned him, by the sound of his boots knocking against a wall as his body swings from a noose.

Such fluctuations in tone were a hallmark of Fuller's films. *Forty Guns* contains an abundance of them, from the dramatic introduction of Jessica and her titular entourage (who are otherwise an irrelevance) in the opening scene, thundering past Griff and his brothers in their gently swaying buckboard, to the shockingly brief wedding of Louvenia and Wes, who is felled by Brockie's rifle within minutes of the ceremony. Fuller cuts from this busy frame, full of light, bodies, energy and movement, to one of the most hauntingly understated funeral scenes in American cinema: the camera pans slowly past a grieving Louvenia, shot from a low angle, standing beside a hearse on a lonely hillside, to actor/singer Jidge Carroll, zooming in discreetly as he sings the sombre ballad *God Has His Arms Around Me*, before returning to study the widow once more. For a director renowned for his mastery of Sergei Eisenstein's 'kino-fist' aesthetic, it is a remarkably tender portrait of mourning.

Throughout, Fuller proves adept at deflecting expectations. The first confrontation between Griff and a drunken Brockie is set up for a straightforward showdown, but Fuller instead pioneers the 'walkdown' – one of the most famous demonstrations of moral authority in the western. Griff's march towards his

dumbfounded opponent, which culminates in him clubbing Brockie down, illustrates courage and resolve far more effectively than if he had simply shot the boy. By contrast, the ruthlessness that has secured Griff's reputation is stamped home late in the film when he shoots through Jessica to get to Brockie, who had been using her as a shield; the disbelief on Brockie's face as his wounded sister falls away would have been shared by filmgoers accustomed to gallantry from their western heroes, the shock compounded by Griff's curt remark as he walks past – "Get a doctor, she'll live." It would have made a perfect ending.

Unfortunately, Fuller goes on to heal the rift, in a conclusion that compromises the integrity of his female protagonist. Having tried and failed to buy Brockie's freedom before the rash act that leads to his death, Jessica loses both her ranch (another example of Fuller skimming over a significant plot development) and her imperiousness, chasing desperately after Griff who, by preparing to leave, at least remains true to himself.[2] It is not clear whether this positive outcome was pressed on Fuller; it was apparently present in the script he pitched in 1953 to Darryl F. Zanuck at Twentieth Century-Fox, who found the idea of a land baroness "phony", expecting adherence to "social norms" and "generic expectations" in westerns made at his studio. The film was eventually produced by Globe Enterprises, where Fuller enjoyed greater artistic licence, yet he

claimed that Zanuck forced his hand, insisting the heroine survive and rejecting Fuller's plans for a "rough ending".[3] All the same, *Forty Guns* is Fuller's finest western, "his most audacious assault on classical and generic conventions up to this point in his career"[4]; thanks to Joseph Biroc, who also shot Fuller's *Run of the Arrow*, it is also as good an example of CinemaScope and monochrome photography as the genre produced in the Fifties. Its anticlimax is merely a reminder of what those "conventions" entail, and why it was important for Fuller to fight against them. **KG**

footnotes

1 "I love the whole idea of any women on the screen having balls because generally they *do* have balls," Fuller said. "Unfortunately *man's* rule and *man's* beliefs… have made them the inferior sex and subjected them to slavery in a form without any stripes, in a jail without any cells." Interview with Sam Fuller by Donald Ranvaud (1982), reprinted in *Samuel Fuller: Interviews* (University Press of Mississippi, 2012).

2 R. Philip Loy writes: "Those two images [the opening and closing shots, with their opposing impressions of Jessica] tell us much about the conflicted role of women in the United States in 1957" – empowered during the war years, when their labour proved crucial to the nation's economy and consequently its ability to finance the good fight, then forced back into subservience when the men returned from the fray (*Westerns in a Changing America 1955-2000*, McFarland, 2004).

3 Fuller complained after the fact that the positive ending both betrayed his vision of Griff Bonnell as an "executioner… The moment he squeezes that trigger, he's a different man", and was a cliché: "I've seen so many pictures… where the heavy grabs the girl and holds her in front of him, putting the hero in a hell of an embarrassing situation. Always, at the last minute, she pushes him away, and the hero kills him. I don't like that in any western. It doesn't make sense." Interview with Sam Fuller by Eric Sherman and Martin Rubin (1968), reprinted in *Samuel Fuller: Interviews*.

4 Lisa Dombrowski, *The Films of Samuel Fuller: If You Die, I'll Kill You!* (Wesleyan University Press, 2008).

Run of the Arrow

1957, Colour, 85 mins.

D: Samuel Fuller. P: Samuel Fuller (Globe Enterprises, Inc, RKO Teleradio Pictures, Inc). W: Samuel Fuller. Ph: Joseph Biroc. M: Victor Young. St: Rod Steiger (O'Meara), Sarita Montiel (Yellow Moccasin), Brian Keith (Captain Clark), Ralph Meeker (Lt. Driscoll), Jay C. Flippen (Walking Coyote)

"I'll hang before I recognise that flag."

A combustible mixture of the conventional and the confrontational, *Run of the Arrow* demonstrates Samuel Fuller's fascination with conflicts of identity, both cultural and racial. It can be bracketed with *China Gate* (1957), with its biracial heroine, and *The Steel Helmet* (1951) and *The Crimson Kimono* (1959), with their *nisei* characters, but extends the idea by having its hero – an outsider, of course – 'go native', making it one of the earliest revisionist westerns to employ this trope.

The overarching theme is "the paradox of America", to borrow a phrase by Fuller biographer Lisa Dombrowski. The protagonist, O'Meara, is a Confederate diehard of Irish extraction (and variable accent) who resents the authority of the North, refuses to pledge allegiance to the Union and opts to go West, into Indian territory.[1] There, he is embraced by the Sioux – after surviving the ritualistic 'run of the arrow' by outpacing his pursuers, barefoot, across rough terrain – but is soon wrestling with his allegiances when trouble erupts over the location of an army fort on Sioux land. Despite asserting, "I'm not an American," O'Meara cannot commit to killing citizens of the nation, and race, he had earlier so bitterly renounced, not even if they are "damn Yankees". Ultimately, reluctantly, he accepts that his future lies away from the Sioux in the reborn Land of the Free.

RKO's publicity machine trumpeted the film's authenticity and originality, especially regarding its treatment of the Sioux. Fuller similarly played up its groundbreaking denouement – "It was the first American picture where the Indians won" – and its positive reception among tribal peoples: "They liked the movie, because they didn't act like, 'Ugh! Me go. White man speak broken tongue. Red man speak straight tongue.'"[2] Nevertheless, plenty of clichés lurk among the more thoughtful passages. Apart from Walking Coyote, a drunken former scout – played in a black wig by bulldog-faced Jay C. Flippen, surely one of the least convincing 'Native Americans' in screen history – the first Sioux we encounter is Crazy Wolf, who epitomises the dime-novel stereotype of the bloodthirsty savage. The run of the arrow was an invention, and the cavalry-Indian skirmishes, while filmed with Fuller's customary vigour, are rooted firmly in genre iconography. So too, irrespective of historical veracity, is the Sioux method of flaying enemies alive. Just as significantly, O'Meara's disgusted reaction to this practice invites the conclusion – against the film's ethos – that white America's assertion of cultural and moral superiority is justified and that Indians will never be 'civilised'.

Yet in other important respects *Run of the Arrow* is progressive: O'Meara's relationship with the squaw Yellow Moccasin, for all its overtones of Pocahontas-style romantic fantasy, is allowed to blossom free of any moral anxiety over miscegenation; in that sense, Fuller's film shows greater maturity (and courage) than the more celebrated *Broken Arrow*. (One can't help wondering, however, what reception this mixed-race couple will receive back in the 'real' America. At one point, Fuller has one of his characters chastise O'Meara's beloved South – "Free, white and Christian, huh? Burning crosses, hiding under pillow cases and terrorising families..." The civil rights movement was in its infancy when *Run of the*

Arrow was made. Fuller's final challenge – "The end of this story can only be written by you" – was issued to Southerners still bearing a grudge against the North; perhaps we can also read into it a plea for racial tolerance in a broader sense.[3])

As writer-director, Fuller takes narrative shortcuts to quicken the pace as O'Meara's past catches up with him. He is rapidly established as a trusted member of the tribe and given the task of guiding the army engineers. These are led by Clark, a pragmatic, conciliatory figure who compares O'Meara's hatred to a disease (not the only person in the film to do so), and by Driscoll, a bigoted and belligerent cavalry officer – and Meara's old antagonist – who precipitates the crisis with the Sioux.[4] These figures have their counterparts among the Indians: Clark is twinned with chief Blue Buffalo (Charles Bronson), who similarly embodies tolerance, proclaiming the equality of O'Meara's professed Christianity with the Sioux's animistic beliefs; Driscoll by Crazy Wolf, a reckless warmonger like himself.

The subtext of symmetry between races is hardly revolutionary, but it chimes with the rhyming nature of the narrative: as a renegade of sorts, Walking Coyote mirrors O'Meara's misfit status; the run of the arrow is repeated late on, this time with O'Meara the hunter and Crazy Wolf the prey – a reversal of their earlier roles; and the film begins and ends with O'Meara shooting Driscoll with the same bullet, wounding him with the final shot of the Civil War, at Appomattox, then putting an end to his torture at the hands of the vengeful Sioux. O'Meara's actions in these scenes have paradoxical effects – conducting the run demonstrates his commitment to Sioux customs, while the mercy killing identifies him, in the film's ambiguous conclusion, with 'American values'. There may be symmetry between the races, but a sharp distinction remains. **KG**

footnotes

1 Rod Steiger was an unlikely leading man for a western, which is precisely why Fuller cast him: "He was blubbery. I thought he would look ungainly on a horse, and he did. He was perfect for that role; he was a misfit." Interview with Sam Fuller by Eric Sherman and Martin Rubin (1968), reprinted in *Samuel Fuller: Interviews* (University Press of Mississippi, 2012).

2 Interview with Sam Fuller by Stig Bjorkman (1965), reprinted in *Samuel Fuller: Interviews.*

3 Fuller felt that attitudes in the South towards the North had scarcely changed a century on from the Civil War: "I wanted the [Steiger] character… to be the basic root of all the hate that exists now in the South. That's why I liked *Easy Rider* so much. The man with the shotgun is today what Steiger was one hundred years ago." Interview with Sam Fuller by Ian Christie et al (1969), reprinted in *Samuel Fuller: Interviews.*

4 Ralph Meeker, who plays Driscoll, found himself in Steiger's shoes a year after *Run of the Arrow*, living among Indians in the title role of Dorothy M. Johnson's *A Man Called Horse*, adapted for the *Wagon Train* TV series 12 years before Hollywood made it into a feature film.

above: Blue Buffalo (Charles Bronson) seals the relationship of O'Meara (Rod Steiger) and Yellow Moccasin (Sarita Montiel).

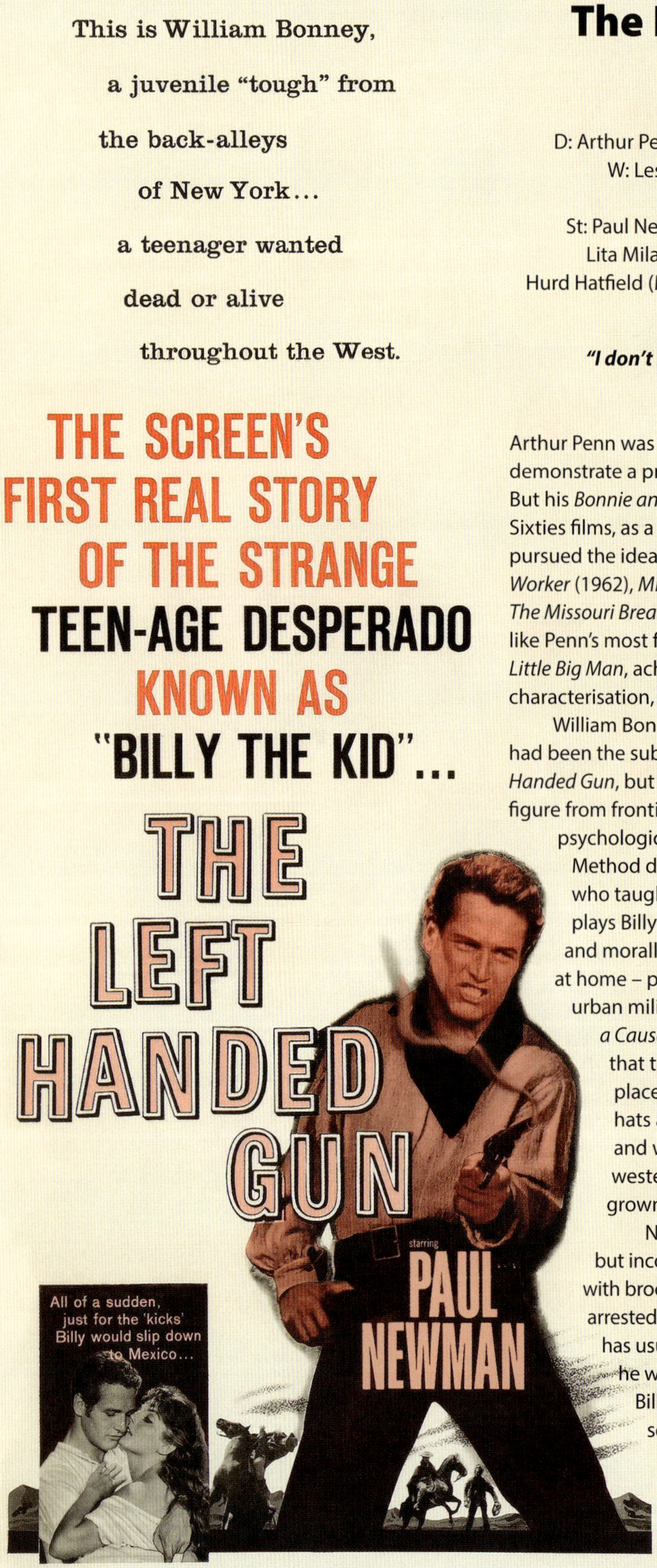

The Left Handed Gun

1958, B/W, 102 mins.

D: Arthur Penn. P: Fred Coe (Haroll Productions Inc).
W: Leslie Stevens. Ph: J. Peverell Marley.
M: Alexander Courage.
St: Paul Newman (Billy the Kid [William Bonney]),
Lita Milan (Celsa), John Dehner (Pat Garrett),
Hurd Hatfield (Moultrie), James Congdon (Charlie Boudre)

"I don't run. I don't hide. I go where I want. I do what I want."

Arthur Penn was hardly the sole Hollywood maverick to demonstrate a predilection for outlaws and social pariahs. But his *Bonnie and Clyde* (1967) stands out, even among Sixties films, as a defining example of the theme, and he pursued the idea, in one form or another, in *The Miracle Worker* (1962), *Mickey One* (1965), *The Chase* (1966) and *The Missouri Breaks*. It began here with his debut, which, like Penn's most fully realised works, *Bonnie and Clyde* and *Little Big Man*, achieves a deft balancing of romanticised characterisation, myth deflation and gut-wrenching realism.

William Bonney, real name probably Henry McCarty, had been the subject of more than 30 films before *The Left Handed Gun*, but this was the first time that he – or any major figure from frontier mythology – had undergone a searching psychological evaluation. It was the perfect stage for Method devotee Paul Newman. Encouraged by Penn, who taught classes at the Actors Studio, Newman plays Billy as an impulsive man-child, emotionally and morally fragile; he would have seemed equally at home – perhaps more so – in the contemporary urban milieus of *Blackboard Jungle* or *Rebel Without a Cause* (both 1955). "I read in a number of books that the West was not this great, clearly defined place where there were all white hats and black hats and that's how you knew who was good and who was bad," said Penn. "I brought to [the western] the street urchin mentality that I'd grown up with."[1]

Newman's bravura performance is exhilarating but inconsistent. Alternating adolescent exuberance with brooding self-absorption, he strongly suggests arrested development, enhanced by the fact that, as has usually been the case with actors playing Billy, he was too old for the role – Newman was 33, Billy just 21 when he died. (This was Newman's second stab at the part, having starred in the 1955 teleplay on which the film was based.) He employs a range of mannerisms and gestures, grinning sheepishly in his more relaxed moments, burying his head in his arms in a mock-maternal embrace to express vulnerability. Newman was relatively inexperienced on the big screen, and occasionally his portrayal feels more like the application of technique, rather than truly instinctual. But there are also irresistible moments of anarchic physicality, as when Billy marches frenziedly with a broom to the sound of a pianola, or indulges in horseplay with his friends. In all cases, the impression is of a young man who can neither adequately articulate nor control his emotions.

Billy is possessed of a childlike righteousness, with little or no concern for consequences. We learn that his first killing was to avenge an insult to his mother, and the pattern repeats itself when he becomes obsessed with punishing the men who have gunned down his employer, cattle rancher John Tunstall (Colin Keith-Johnston), the first in a series of father figures. The murder kick-starts the Lincoln County War, the episode that cemented Billy's notoriety, but Penn, working from a script originated by Gore Vidal but rewritten at the studio's insistence, is not overly concerned with historical veracity (Billy was not actually left handed, for a start).[2] The background to the conflict is brushed over in a single scene, while Billy has just two comrades to face the powers-that-be in Lincoln, rather than the larger force of 'Regulators' who took part in reality. Billy alone is seen to kill the town's sheriff, Brady (Robert Foulk), to strengthen his position as figurehead and underline his recklessness, for which his friends and benefactors are made to pay. Another paternal, protective figure, Alexander McSween (John Dierkes), is burnt alive for shielding Billy after a siege at his house, while his friends Charlie Bowdre and Tom Folliard (James Best) have little option but to follow their charismatic leader to an early grave in the course of his vendetta.

Penn saw Billy as a tragic figure, with a (self)-destructive streak that perhaps could have been checked by a stabilising role model – very much in the mould of the wayward youngsters so common on Fifties screens. ("A left-handed boy who never meant wrong… look on him tenderly," croons the theme song, striking a sentimental note that Penn does well to avoid elsewhere.) Yet each time Billy is presented with a surrogate father, he invariably betrays his faith: Tunstall and McSween implore him fruitlessly to "put away childish things" – revenge for one – and rise above life's provocations; he repays the kindness of Saval, a Mexican gunsmith with whom he once lived, by seducing his wife; most famously, he rejects Pat Garrett's counsel, ultimately forcing him – after a superb, tense scene at Garrett's wedding, where Billy breaks his word to his friend by killing Tunstall's last remaining assassin – into outright opposition. As in most other westerns of the decade with the theme of generational strife, there can only be one outcome. When Garrett, in

a fine performance by John Dehner, kills Billy – finally so overwhelmed with remorse that he faces his pursuer with an empty holster, feigning to draw and effectively committing suicide – he confirms paternal, and thus Establishment, authority.[3] As Michael Coyne puts it, "The older hero's triumph implicitly reasserted the hegemony of the existing power structure."[4]

Penn illustrates Billy's fractured psyche via a passage from Corinthians. Early on, Tunstall enchants Billy with the metaphor "through a glass darkly", explaining it is "the way some people see things… all dark and twisted up". This is essentially how Billy views the world, and Penn provides frequent reminders: as McSween tries to pacify Billy, in a vigil by Tunstall's coffin, the camera catches an upright magnifying glass on the table before him that distorts the background; Billy uses a dusty pane to trace out his plan to ambush sheriff Brady; and, at his lowest ebb, with his friends dead, Billy looks forlornly through a splintered window. The symbolism is unsubtle, but effective; more to the point, it was daring for the genre at the time.

Anticipating *The Man Who Shot Liberty Valance*, *The Left Handed Gun* explores the creation of legend, and takes the process apart. Billy hides out in a shack decorated with his own wanted posters, while Hurd Hatfield plays a character named Moultrie, a would-be Ned Buntline and forerunner of *Unforgiven's* Beauchamp, whose stock-in-trade is "souvenirs of the West". He trails Billy like a combination of disciple and public relations man ("He is no common outlaw"), providing Eastern newspapers with embroidered accounts of Billy's exploits. While Billy is cooling his heels in Lincoln jail, Moultrie presents him with dime novels – *Outlaw King*, *Killer of the West*. In their final encounter, however, late in the film, Billy turns on him. Moultrie's disillusionment pours forth, almost like a spurned lover, in a beautifully played breakdown: "You're not like the books… You don't wear silver studs, you don't stand up to glory… You're not *him*!" Billy has failed to measure up to the myth that Moultrie has been instrumental in creating, and this sense of betrayal drives Moultrie to report Billy's whereabouts to Pat Garrett.

Penn's contribution to the western was sparing – just three films – but substantial. In each case he utilised conventions, but looked at them askance. His influence was considerable. Billy's shooting of ornery deputy Ollinger (Denver Pyle) with a shotgun, for example, is uncommonly graphic for the period, and was almost certainly the first instance of slow-motion violence in an American western. Sam Peckinpah restaged it almost shot for shot, angle for angle (but with extra stage blood) in *Pat Garrett and Billy the Kid*.[5] The grotesque details – Ollinger's boot standing upright, beside his prone corpse; a young girl's amused reaction – would not have looked out of place in the aftermath of the Starbuck massacre that opens Peckinpah's *The Wild Bunch*.

In the Sixties, Penn came to be regarded as an iconoclast. *The Left Handed Gun* is not one of his great works, but it clearly established his credentials as a moderniser, if not yet a master of the medium. "I think that the form of the classical western legend was coming apart then," he said. "We were perfectly happy to go in a new direction provided we didn't diminish what we thought was important, which was the increasing tension and the showdown... But, while doing that, we felt also that we could begin to open up the western into the areas of human psychology which had been there ever since the western was born, but had found relatively few outlets in western movies."[6] **KG**

footnotes

1 Interview with Arthur Penn by Richard Combs, reprinted in *Arthur Penn: Interviews*, ed. Michael Chaiken and Paul Cronin (University Press of Mississippi, 2008). The impression in *The Left Handed Gun* of Billy as a displaced urbanite is apt given that Bonney/McCarty actually hailed from New York City.

2 While Penn had shared some of the studio's reservations about Vidal's script, Newman felt the alterations all but ruined the film. Penn's preferred ending – an elegy for Billy – was replaced with a bland scene involving Garrett and his wife. Vidal, predictably, disowned the film; he eventually revived his script for a respected, but little-seen, made-for television production, *Gore Vidal's Billy the Kid* (1989), starring Val Kilmer.

3 Billy's gesture prefigures that of Kirk Douglas in Robert Aldrich's *The Last Sunset* (1961).

4 Michael Coyne, *The Crowded Prairie: American National Identity in the Hollywood Western* (IB Tauris, 1997).

5 For *Pat Garrett…*, Peckinpah also borrowed the image of Billy surrendering to Garrett with his arms outstretched, Christ-like, although the character was a martyr to a different cause in Peckinpah's lament for lost freedom.

6 Interview with Arthur Penn by Gordon Gow, *Films and Filming*, July 1971.

Man of the West

1958, Colour, 99 mins.

D: Anthony Mann. P: Walter Mirisch (Ashton Productions Inc). W: Reginald Rose. Ph: Ernest Haller. M: Leigh Harline. St: Gary Cooper (Link Jones), Julie London (Billie Ellis), Lee J. Cobb (Dock Tobin), Arthur O'Connell (Sam Beasley), Jack Lord (Coaley)

"Lasso's a ghost town and that's what you are, Dock. A ghost. You've outlived your kind and you've outlived your time."

A synthesis of themes addressed by Anthony Mann in his films with James Stewart, *Man of the West* was the director's ultimate expression of the dichotomy between the increasingly urbanised American male and his antecedent – the tough, almost feral westerner. Mann was lauded for his employment of natural landscapes to reflect the inner conflicts of his protagonists and here, as tonalities shift and conflict develops, the drama is powered by the harsh and changing environment of the American West. Mann signposts each segment of his hero's journey into his past, to lay his ghosts to rest, by exploiting the varying terrain that he passes through, thus confronting "his own 'geography' and implications".[1]

The film was received with indifference in the US – perhaps because audiences weren't prepared to see Gary Cooper perpetrate the kind of violence on display – but European cineastes took kindly to it. Jean-Luc Godard, about to start his own career as a cinematic revisionist, said of Mann's final genre masterpiece, "Each shot … gives one the impression that Anthony Mann is redefining the western. It is, moreover, more than an impression. He does reinvent." As Link Jones descends further into the dark heart of the West, the story reveals its roots in Greek epic poetry, cementing the genre's position in the realm of the mythical.

The relationship between Mann and Stewart, which had produced such a robust body of work in the Fifties, ended with disagreement on the set of *Night Passage* the previous year. (That film was taken over by director James Neilson.) Stewart Granger was initially nominated for the role of Link, but it is hard to imagine him emulating the stateliness of Cooper, as displayed to arresting effect behind the opening credits. To the left of an elegantly composed 'Scope frame, Cooper sits astride his horse with the ruggedness of the West behind him, the film's title filling the opposite half of the screen. It is a simple yet enduring image; underlining Cooper's synonymity with the genre, it is also emblematic of Mann's entire western canon.

In the town of Crosscut, the deceit of this heroic effigy begins to unravel. Link shaves, dons a jacket more suited to a city gent than a cowboy, conceals his pistol and makes for the train station. Before boarding the train, he is questioned about his identity by Crosscut's sheriff, to whom he looks familiar. The lawman drops the name of Dock Tobin, a notorious outlaw, but Link claims ignorance. A sense of threat remains, however, as the sheriff's holster engulfs the foreground of the frame. Link shifts awkwardly in his train seat and is startled as it lurches before its journey. In these early scenes, Cooper subtly plays him as a fish out of water, unused to travelling by any mode other than horseback, civilisation presenting new challenges.

The safety of the carriage, albeit with its mild discomforts, is rudely disrupted when, in a wild, frenzied sequence, outlaws attack the train. Briefly knocked unconscious, Link comes round to find that the money he was carrying to Fort Worth to hire a schoolteacher for his town has been stolen. At least 100 miles from the nearest town, Link has to take responsibility for two fellow passengers: sassy saloon singer Billie, and Sam Beasley, an affable conman. As they set about their trek, Link sheds his tie and jacket, the accoutrements of his civilised persona. Leading them to a lone shack, Link tells his companions that he used to live there. "When you were a boy?" they ask. Link's ominous response, "I don't know what I was," suggests prior experiences that do not chime with the man before them. The contrast between the brilliant sunshine of the exterior and the clammy darkness of the shack is jolting; equally, there is a shocking disparity between the preceding lightness of tone and the psychological torment and physical violence that predominate once they cross the threshold – almost as if they have left the western behind and entered film noir.

Jim Kitses remarks that Mann's villains are "more or less an unbalanced version of the hero", and here the men that the protagonist must confront inside the shack are even further removed from civilisation than those in his other westerns. With the scheming Coaley, oafish Ponch and mute child-man Trout led by the grandiose, psychologically damaged father figure of Dock, Mann portrays an extension of the wandering wilderness 'family' of *The Naked Spur*. Fortunately for Link, the old man enters the confined space of the shack in time to stop his depraved rabble from killing the hero. Now Link's true history is revealed. He is Dock Tobin's nephew and was once, like them, a murderous thief.[2] In an impassioned, rambling soliloquy, Dock explains how he felt when Link ran out on him years before: "I got so mad I could have pushed your guts right out your back," and shows the hold he had over his former charge: "I put a piece of work into you. Every last idea that shot through your head was mine."

Although Dock has illuminated the pitch darkness with lanterns, an atmosphere of menace lingers like mildew on the shack's wooden ceiling. Through meticulous framing and Lee J. Cobb's stalking, manipulative performance, Mann establishes the power relationships in this claustrophobic set-up and leaves us in little doubt about the extent of the brutality Link was once a part of: "God forgive us. We painted their walls in blood." Knowing that their only hope of survival is to assuage Dock's pride, Link tells the old man that he is back to join the outfit. The notion of identities being exposed continues as the gang, with Beasley and Link outside, force Billie to strip to her underwear. It's an unsettling scene, especially since Link has told them she is his woman, but old

customs die hard in Dock's gang and they want things "like they used to be". Clearly, a woman involved with one member is granted no autonomy over her body.

François Truffaut, another darling of the *Nouvelle Vague*, called Mann "the director who is most sensitive to nature". It is hard to disagree, as the characters – augmented by Claude (John Dehner), the most loyal of Dock's cohorts – ride into an unforgiving backdrop of bare rocks and desert towards the town of Lasso, where Dock claims is the biggest bank haul they'll ever find. Their entry to this pitiless place is signalled by the film's most brutal scene. Link takes a rest stop for the wagons as an opportunity to goad Coaley. He questions the latter's manliness, provoking a fight in which both men employ natural objects, branches and rocks, to inflict a savage mutual beating. Close-ups of the two men against harsh rock formations reinforce their savagery. It is a crucial turning point, establishing the duality of the hero's nature, the 'link' he forges between the barbarous past and the pacified frontier where he hopes his future lies.

As Link's demon is unleashed, he forces Coaley to strip, partly in direct revenge for the humiliation of Billie, partly because he knows his opponent is low enough to be hiding loot from a recent train job, and also, perhaps, because Coaley has tried to replace Link in Dock's affections. Mann torches the myth of the western hero by making Cooper – embodiment of that ideal – the aggressor in such a violent and, essentially, sexually degrading scene; he suggests that the frontier itself, such an oppressive environment, has inculcated in men like Link the necessity to commit atrocious acts to establish ascendancy and ensure survival. Conversely, in an act of selflessness that even the character himself could not foresee, Beasley takes a bullet from Coaley's gun, preserving Link's life and, by extension, Billie's best hope of survival. It remains for Dock to affirm his love of Link by cutting down Coaley.

Lasso itself makes a mockery of Dock's vision and his plans. It has become a ghost town, populated only by an elderly Mexican woman. Here, these relics from

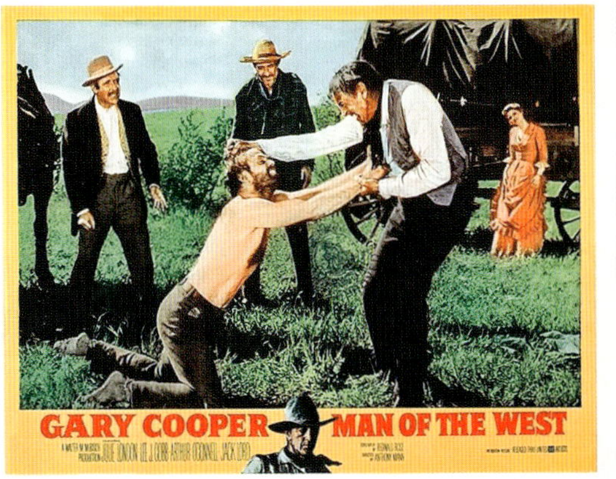

above: Gary Cooper flanked by Royal Dano (left) & Arthur O'Connell (right).
bottom left: Link (Cooper) gives Coaley (Jack Lord) a taste of his own medicine.

the past play out their final act. Link shoots Trout, who runs screaming – the first sound we hear him make – like a wraith towards the desert. The gunfight that follows is one of the director's most refined sequences. Using disorienting angles, Mann positions Link and Claude in separate frames, or in the same shot with their views obscured – a tactic Mann had used before to unite antagonists, notably in *Bend of the River*. The exchange of bullets culminates with Link lying on a porch while Claude lies under its walkway, facing upwards, a symbolically pure widescreen tableau: two men raised and moulded in the image of Dock, a morally corrupted idol.

Mann subtly employs the myths of the ancients to explode the codes of the genre. After Link has finished off Claude, the final scene sees Dock standing on a precipice like a deranged, angered Olympian god, challenging his prodigal son to kill him: "Shoot! Have you lost your taste for it?" Link's triumph over Dock breaks the psychological chains that bind both men to a shared past and an outmoded way of life. It is a summation of one of the most crucial themes in Mann's cinema. Link, his soul cleansed, can return to his small town, his wife and his children. Billie, violated by Dock, in love with Link, must return to the certainty and safety of the urban environments she is used to. Behind them, they leave a desert of phantoms. While the opening credits position Cooper's Link Jones as the titular man of the West, it may be that, in his penultimate western, Mann was bidding farewell to figures such as Dock Tobin – outlaws unable to accept that the new frontier had been conquered, clinging dementedly to the thrilling excitement and boundless possibilities it once offered. **CH**

footnotes

1 Jeanine Basinger, *Anthony Mann* (Wesleyan University Press, 2007).

2 Although he plays the older man here, Cobb was actually 10 years Cooper's junior.

NO NAME ON THE BULLET

No Name on the Bullet

1959, Colour, 77 mins.

D: Jack Arnold. P: Jack Arnold, Howard Christie (Universal-International). W: Gene L. Coon, Howard Amacker (story). Ph: Harold Lipstein. M: Herman Stein.
St: Audie Murphy (John Gant), Charles Drake (Luke Canfield), Joan Evans (Anne Benson), Virginia Grey (Roseanne Fraden), Warren Stevens (Lou Fraden)

"A man's guilt's his own burden. There's nothing he can do about it."

War hero, western icon, country-music songwriter, Audie Murphy embodied all-American integrity and pioneer heroism. His genre characters were a medley of misunderstood outlaws and altruistic good guys whose aim was to better a situation, not just for themselves, but for the entire community. Almost invariably cast as men of honesty, or at least nobility, protectors of the sacred American community, Murphy's image was moulded in the morally clear scenery of the Fifties B-western. It was something of an anomaly, then, that he was offered the lead in Jack Arnold's surprisingly bold low-budget horse opera. Implicitly allegorical, loaded with paranoia and suspicion, *No Name on the Bullet* is one of many Fifties westerns that evokes, deliberately or otherwise, the traumatic experience of McCarthyism.

Black-clad gunman John Gant arrives in the town of Lordsburg and checks in to the town's hotel. Mention of his name causes fear to sweep through town. Gant is usually hired to settle old scores, and anyone with a weight of guilt about their past breaks into a sweat. Gant's tactic is to impel his mark into drawing first, thus ensuring he always kills within the law. The gunman begins a perfunctory but philosophical relationship with the town surgeon, Luke Canfield, who comes to believe that Gant's way of life can be changed. Believing that their business rival, Ben Chaffee, has hired Gant to kill them, mine owners Stricker and Pearce attempt but fail to buy him off. Eventually, Pearce's terror overwhelms him and he shoots himself. When the sheriff confronts Gant and goes for his gun, the latter shoots him in the hand. Fervour grips the town and a vigilante mob confronts Gant on the hotel porch. Unperturbed by their threats, Gant individually names the men who would die at his hand before they could rush him, and the mob disperses. When Gant later survives a fierce gunfight, the sheriff throws away his badge, acknowledging his powerlessness. Gant has now identified his quarry and takes steps to complete his contract.

One might expect that, at a brisk 75 minutes and produced on a conservative budget, the film would have little to distinguish it from other Murphy vehicles. The choice of director, however, suggests a novel approach. By culling techniques and ideas forged in Red Scare science-fiction and horror pictures, Arnold directed one of the more interesting psychological westerns of an already rich decade. Trading in the murky black-and-white cinematography of his earlier films for a vibrant 'Scope frame, Arnold introduces Gant as a McCarthyist hunter, sowing seeds of fear among the townsfolk with his mere presence. As the hotel manager reads out the assassin's name from the register, past wrongdoings, ethical and immoral, come back to haunt the more venerated members of society: "You watch some of our respected citizens now," says the sheriff. Given the prevailing tone of contemporary science-fiction opuses such as Arnold's own *It Came from Outer Space* (1953), it is tempting to see *No Name on the Bullet* as part of a shared, politically charged reaction to the persecution of Communists, sympathisers and other liberals in the late Forties that laid waste to so much of Hollywood's creative talent. In the following decade, a quiet revenge was exacted through the typewriters of those scribes whose lives had been rocked. It seems significant that Gant is first seen wearing a black shirt, with an arrogant bearing, as he rides emotionlessly, ominously, towards a farm house to be greeted by a fearful homestead couple and an unfriendly barking dog. In a reversal of *Shane* (1953), it is clear that Gant is not welcome. Where Shane offered deliverance, this avenging angel is a far more menacing proposition.

Our initial view of Lordsburg itself (named, perhaps, after the destination in *Stagecoach*) is not especially propitious either. The town is framed through a blacksmith's forge, flames in the foreground lending an infernal symbolism. Prominent citizens cast nervous glances in the newcomer's direction as Gant stations himself in the saloon, echoing Jimmie Ringo in *The Gunfighter*. However, while Ringo's nerves crackled beneath his skin, Gant is unfazed and plays a calculated waiting game, drawing out the tension. The game of chess becomes symbolic of Gant's style: a contest of entrapment, requiring the player to think two moves ahead to force an error. The chessboard is the arena for his debates with Canfield.

While the doctor tries in liberal desperation to make the cultured gunman see the folly of his vocation, Gant explains that he is the greater moral arbiter. While Gant eliminates bad eggs for past deeds, the doctor saves lives so that the same men can commit more crimes. The killer's logic centres on retribution and natural punishment.

The McCarthy investigations were great fodder for B-movies in the Fifties, but that did not mean, of course, that every seemingly liberal noir or western of the period came out in favour of the victims. Films such as *High Noon* are more politically ambiguous than a simple reading may suggest. There is an implication here that the men Gant is after are, of course, guilty of something immoral, and that past associations mustn't go unpunished. (As it turns out, his eventual victim is blameworthy only of an aberration.) It is highly debatable, dependent on one's politics, whether those whose lives were ruined by the blacklist were immoral themselves or, indeed, a threat to American democracy. Given Arnold's previous output, it is more likely that the director was inclined towards a critical view of McCarthyism, and the script offered up the chance to re-create the paranoid atmosphere engendered by the witch-hunts. Gant, played in Murphy's impeccably cool, easy style, may be the most charismatic personality here but, once we've spent time with the gallery of upstanding rogues in Lordsburg, we are left wondering, as we are in Arnold's science-fiction films, who the monsters of the piece really are. **CH**

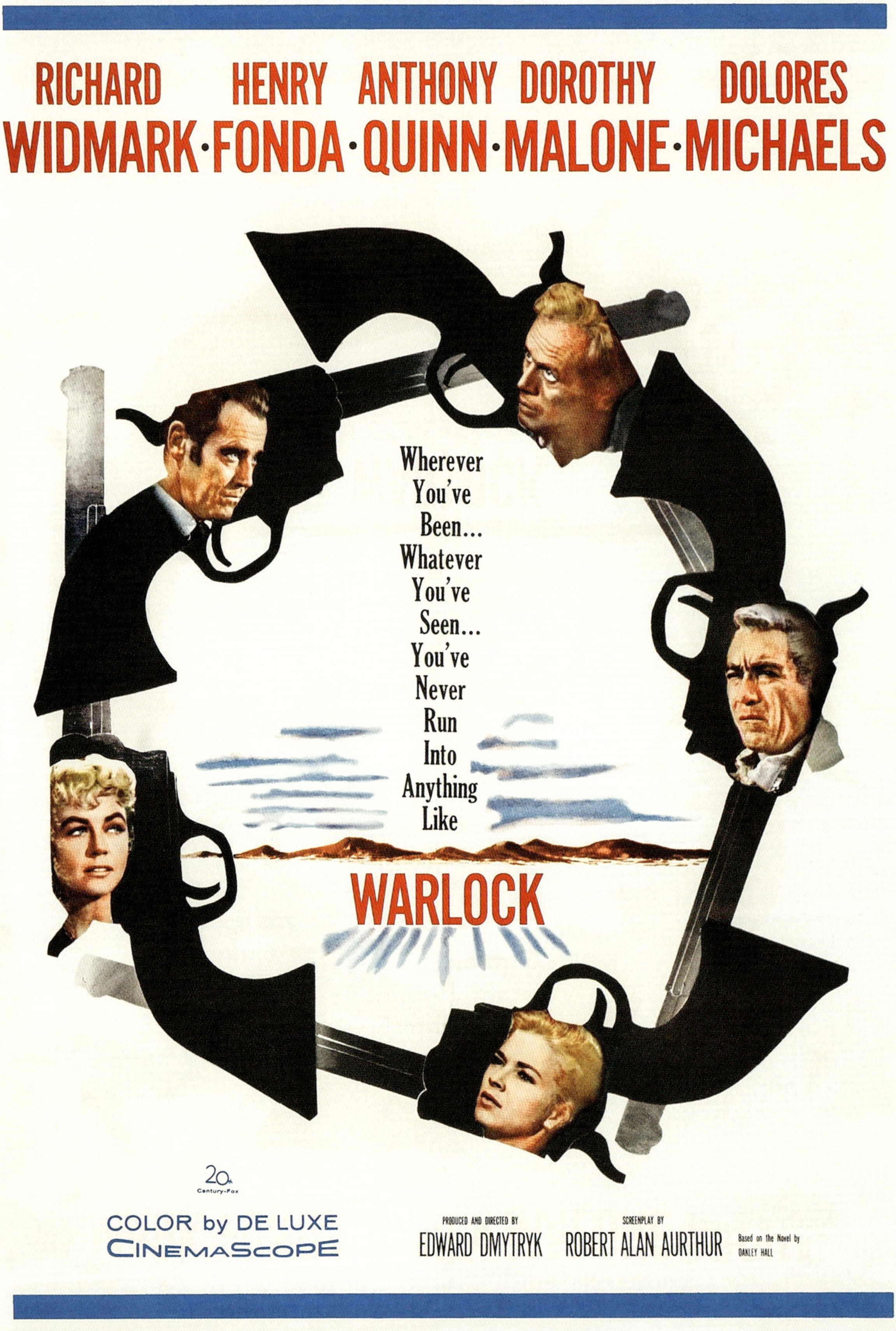

RICHARD WIDMARK · HENRY FONDA · ANTHONY QUINN · DOROTHY MALONE · DOLORES MICHAELS
Wherever You've Been... Whatever You've Seen... You've Never Run Into Anything Like
WARLOCK
20th Century-Fox
COLOR by DE LUXE
CINEMASCOPE
PRODUCED AND DIRECTED BY EDWARD DMYTRYK
SCREENPLAY BY ROBERT ALAN AURTHUR
Based on the Novel by OAKLEY HALL

Warlock

1959, Colour, 121 mins.

D: Edward Dmytryk. P: Edward Dmytryk (Twentieth Century-Fox). W: Robert Alan Aurthur. Ph: Joe MacDonald. M: Leigh Harline. St: Richard Widmark (Johnny Gannon), Henry Fonda (Clay Blaisdell), Anthony Quinn (Tom Morgan), Dorothy Malone (Lily Dollar), Dolores Michaels (Jessie Marlow)

"I come here as your salvation on a very high wage… At first you're pleased, because there's less trouble. Then, a strange thing happens. You begin to feel I'm too powerful, you begin to fear me. Not me, but what I am."

Capping a decade of psychological westerns, *Warlock* subjects genre archetypes – both characters and themes – to a severe examination in the course of a plot that owes as much to melodrama as it does to frontier mythology. Evoking *High Noon*, as well as a slew of films concerned with the alienation of the gunfighter, it has also been deciphered as director Edward Dmytryk's attempt to put his controversial role in the anti-Communist investigations of the era into perspective.

Dmytryk outlined his principal theme as "the civilizing of a frontier area through the gradual and painful imposition of law".[7] Having essayed Wyatt Earp in *My Darling Clementine*, Henry Fonda here plays an ersatz Earp, Clay Blaisdell, in a similarly imperious fashion. Hired by the mining town of Warlock to purge it of a rowdy gang of cowboys from the San Pablo spread, Clay arrives with a reputation for ruthless efficiency and his own Doc Holliday figure, the club-footed Tom Morgan, his companion and guardian angel. Summed up by the disapproving judge as "vigilante… gambler… gunman", Clay is a legendary town tamer (he has already had a dime novel written about him, as has Morgan), somewhat cynical in middle age, concerned as much about his image and his income as he is about dispensing justice. Clay swiftly intimidates the cowboys and their leader, McQuown (Tom Drake), and he and Morgan make a killing by taking over the town saloon – a condition of their agreement. But Clay's mission is compromised when Johnny Gannon, a reformed San Pabloite, takes on the duties of deputy sheriff, and complicated further when Clay falls for a local girl, Jessie. Meanwhile, the arrival in Warlock of Lily Dollar, Morgan's former consort, sheds light on the latter's machinations, past and present, and provokes a series of confrontations in which the tone of the film becomes increasingly overwrought.

Adapted from Oakley Hall's Pulitzer-shortlisted revisionist novel, Robert Alan Aurthur's script offers rich central characters, but sacrifices momentum and narrative clarity in its efforts to accommodate their back stories (those involving Clay, Morgan and Lily are especially byzantine) and to unpick their motivations.

The relationship between Clay and Morgan is far more rewarding dramatically than the conventional romances between Clay and Jessie, and Lily and Gannon. Commonly viewed as homoerotic, it is actually more complicated. Morgan, played a shade too flamboyantly by Anthony Quinn, shadows Clay like a mixture of jealous lover and officious factotum. Dressed in embroidered waistcoats, fastidious and feminised in the way he redecorates their apartments, he is also dangerously neurotic, manipulative and murderous – for years he has engineered a chain of events, including killings, in his determination to keep Clay's reputation intact. It is like a trail of gunpowder, set alight when Lily seeks revenge for another old boyfriend's death at Clay's hands (this too, we learn, was set up by Morgan).

But while Morgan shares Clay's aura vicariously, Clay implicitly enjoys the adulation, and, as one of the West's star attractions, benefits from Morgan's skills as an agent-cum-manager, not to mention back-up gun. (Fonda went on to play another illustrious fictitious gunfighter whose legacy is maintained and stage-managed by a devoted admirer in Tonino Valerii's *My Name Is Nobody* [1973].) Lily's intervention illuminates Morgan's possessiveness towards his friend – "I'll kill anyone who comes between us" – while Clay's decision to settle down and surrender his authority to Gannon stokes Morgan's insecurities. (These are exacerbated by his physical impairment, a manifestation of his fractured emotions; more than once he expresses gratitude that Clay, unlike most people, has never belittled him as a "cripple".) He can't abide the prospect of Clay playing "second fiddle" to anybody; as for hanging up his guns: "If you ain't the marshal, you're

nothing!" Meaning that Morgan, in his own warped estimation, will be less than nothing. The question then becomes not whether Morgan loves Clay in more than a fraternal sense, but whether his infatuation is with the man or with his status – something Morgan has worked surreptitiously to cement.

Gannon, meanwhile, represents another fixture of Fifties westerns – the anxious hero, forged in the films of Anthony Mann. Richard Widmark would have been welcome in Mann's world, with his readiness and ability to portray conflicted characters without resorting to thespian fireworks (of the kind that James Stewart, Mann's regular star, occasionally indulged in). Haunted by his involvement in San Pabloite violence (we see an example of this when he goes to the ranch and is beaten and stabbed in the hand, a reminder of Mann's *The Man from Laramie*), Gannon becomes torn between fidelity to his brother, a firebrand who has remained with McQuown's bunch, and a compulsion to make amends for his own misdeeds. A marginal figure at first, he grows in stature, displaying a quiet but determined sense of duty that makes a clash with Clay, via Morgan, inevitable. Putting public service above personal aims, even when his brother dies at Clay's hands, Gannon's role is a response to the judge's insistence that, "There's something bigger than all men, and that's the law."

Gannon has also been seen as Dmytryk's proxy, a man who has repudiated his past for the sake of principles – although Dmytryk's decision to appease his inquisitors at the height of the Red Scare seems to have been driven as much by pragmatism. Having refused to testify before the House Un-American Activities Committee (HUAC), the former Communist became *persona non grata*, one of the original Hollywood Ten, and was jailed for contempt of Congress. Upon his release, he recanted, citing, among other justifications, what he viewed as the cynicism and double standards of the ideologues he had turned against. (He was also heavily in debt – a major incentive to get back into the studios' good books.) "They said they were fighting for freedom of speech, the commonweal. They weren't. They were protecting freedom of speech for the Communists. They didn't give a good goddamn about freedom of speech."[2] In his persuasive appraisal of *Warlock*, Michael Coyne defines it as Dmytryk's rationalization for cooperating with the HUAC: Clay is his witch-hunter; Gannon his "consensual hero"; the San Pabloites the enemy within. But there are problems with this argument. On one level the film

above: from left: Dorothy Malone, Anthony Quinn and Henry Fonda.

seems to validate the work of the HUAC and Dmytryk's belated denunciation, even demonisation, of his former comrades. Despite an attempt at balance – one member of the Citizens' Committee suggests not all the villains are bad, addressing Clay in the manner of a friendly witness: "There are one or two real trouble makers. If I give you their names..." – the 'communist' contingent, the San Pabloites, are by and large a reprehensible bunch. Following Dmytryk's rationale, it seems only right and decent for Gannon to turn against them.

Yet there is consistent criticism of Clay's position vis-à-vis the law; and the repeated, virulent condemnation of back-shooting as a treacherous, despicable act could be seen as a metaphor for back-stabbing in Hollywood – another form of treachery, in the opinions of many. The script returns time and again to ideas of fairness and justice, seesawing between notionally 'liberal' and 'conservative' modes. One scene in particular encapsulates the confusion: two members of the San Pablo outfit have been arrested for a stagecoach hold-up. A lynch mob gathers outside the jail. It takes Clay, a glorified hired gun, whose appointment and methods circumvent legal procedure, to cow the errant citizens into submission: "Think how being in a lynch mob is as low a thing as a man can do" – restating sentiments Fonda had expressed as a bleeding-heart cowboy in *The Ox-Bow Incident*, in which his co-star here, Anthony Quinn, was one of those executed in error.

Material this volatile profits from a minimum of directorial intervention. Dmytryk obliges, although he does slip the reins for the traumatic showdown between Clay and Morgan. Forced to kill his companion, Clay's torment summons up a storm and, in the film's most famous scene, he carries Morgan's body into the saloon and turns it into a funeral pyre – "a supreme moment of melodramatic excess".[3] When he then has to face Gannon the next day, the effect is deflating. Clay, armed with gold-handled Colts, easily outdraws his rival but, in one of the genre's great non-showdowns, Clay is the one who loses. He throws down his pistols, surrendering the symbols of his authority in a spin on Gary Cooper's gesture at the end of *High Noon*. The mythological hero thus concedes the stage to a more foursquare figure. Fonda's proud bearing as he departs the scene, acknowledging there is no place in society for a man like him once his civilising function has been fulfilled – a maxim of the western – makes this a moving moment. It also provides the film with a closing bracket: in the opening sequence, the San Pabloites had run Warlock's feeble but brave deputy sheriff out of town while the terrified citizens watched from their windows, like their counterparts in *High Noon's* Hadleyville. Clay, at least, exits with dignity intact. **KG**

footnotes

[1] Edward Dmytryk, *It's a Hell of a Life, But Not a Bad Living* (NY Times Books, 1978).

[2] Quoted in the *Los Angeles Times*, 28 January 1996.

[3] David Lusted, *The Western* (Longman, 2003).

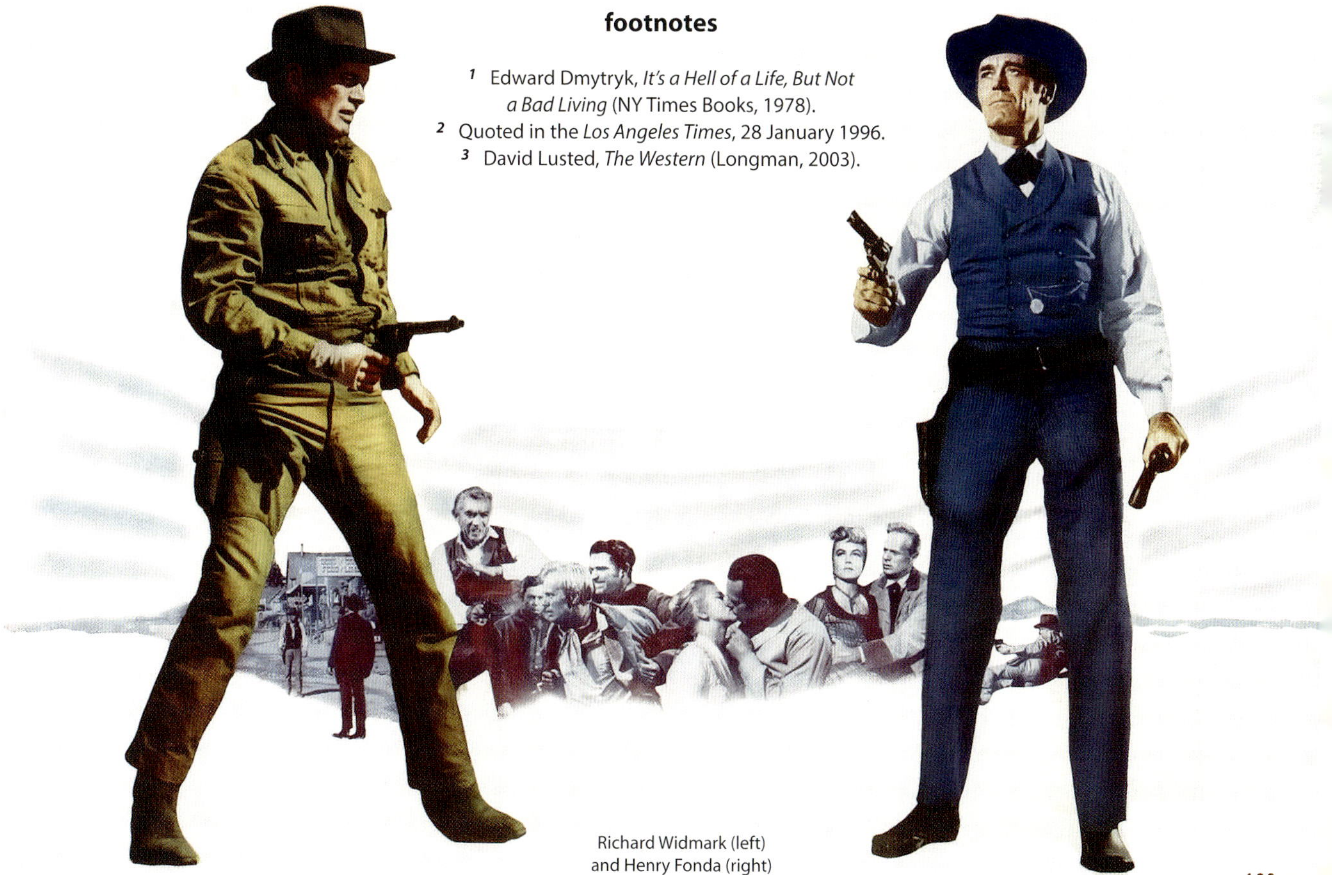

Richard Widmark (left)
and Henry Fonda (right)

Sergeant Rutledge

1960, Colour, 111 mins.

D: John Ford. P: Willis Goldbeck, Patrick Ford (Warner Bros). W: James Warner Bellah, Willis Goldbeck. Ph: Bert Glennon. M: Howard Jackson.
St: Jeffrey Hunter (Lt. Tom Cantrell), Constance Towers (Mary Beecher), Billie Burke (Cordelia Fosgate), Woody Strode (Sgt Braxton Rutledge), Juano Hernandez (Sgt. Skidmore).

"It was all right for Mr. Lincoln to say we were free, but that ain't so. Not yet. Maybe some day, but not yet."

From the inflammatory image of a black hand clamped over a terrified white woman's mouth ("It was as though he'd sprung up from the earth… from a nightmare") to the equation of 'guilt' with 'Negro' by the sneering prosecutor, John Ford's courtroom drama-cum-social critique puts the community's – read America's – ingrained prejudices on trial, challenging audiences to confront and disown their own racist preconceptions. Ford's methods may be different, but the intention recalls *The Searchers* and would recur in *Two Rode Together* and *Cheyenne Autumn*. As Joseph McBride says, in his twilight years, "Ford deliberately sought… to rectify some oversights and imbalances in his work, finding stories about groups that he usually had relegated to supporting status – blacks, Indians and women [in *7 Women*] – and giving them the starring roles."[1]

This is true up to a point. In *Sergeant Rutledge*, as in most westerns that have taken up the cause of ethnic minorities, it is white liberals who make the case for the defence – quite literally here, since Rutledge, accused of violating (perhaps 'raping' was considered too incendiary a word) and murdering a white girl and her military father, is represented at his court martial by his commanding officer, Lt. Cantrell, and supported by the chief witness, Mary Beecher. Their testimonies, presented mostly in flashback, balance the hostility displayed towards Rutledge by the prosecutor, Captain Shattuck (Carleton Young); the civilians, who bay for the defendant's blood before the trial even begins; the military physician; and, more subtly, by the judge's wife, Cordelia Fosgate, who represents for Ford the kind of prissy, narrow-minded busybody he had been deriding since *Stagecoach*. (Ford uses the petty bickering of the Fosgates as light relief at a number of points; where comedy was concerned, the director's timing was often as deficient as his judgement.)

The elephant in the courtroom is that familiar bugbear, miscegenation. For Rutledge's accusers, the nature of the crime itself seems almost secondary to the 'fact' that the colour boundary, not just the dead girl, has been 'violated'.

As in the similarly themed *To Kill a Mockingbird*, published the same year, much of the drama is concerned with exposing and decrying racial bigotry, particularly the assertion by the hero's accusers that 'degeneracy' is a condition peculiar to blacks. The scene in which Mary is surprised by Rutledge at an isolated railway station on the night of the killings plays upon white fear of black male sexual aggression; the darkness, close-ups and Bert Glennon's noir-laced photography further exploit audience unease. Mary's own fears are allayed when Rutledge protects her from renegade Apaches, but the sequence opens up the debate about racial anxiety by intuiting it is Rutledge who has more reason to be afraid if they are discovered together, "mindful [as he is] of his compromised situation, given the sexual dynamics surrounding white women and black men".[2] He even tries to dissuade Mary (a forerunner of Carroll Baker's similarly charitable Quaker in *Cheyenne Autumn*) from treating his injuries, and desperately resists when Cantrell arrives to arrest him with the remainder of Rutledge's all-black regiment.[3]

Rutledge's apprehension – well founded, as the atmosphere at the trial makes plain – is a damning indictment of societal attitudes, both historical and contemporary. Asked by the sympathetic yet duty-bound Cantrell why he ran from the scene of the crime, Rutledge, without the need to allude to his colour, explains, "Nobody'll believe I never touched her." This accounts for his attempt to escape when opportunity arises during the march back to the fort across Monument Valley, and why he speaks bitterly of the 'fruits' of emancipation. As with many recruits in the actual Ninth Cavalry, Rutledge was once a slave. Despite the gratification he finds in military service, he remains conscious of his lowly status in white America – a position that Woody Strode's fourth-placed billing inadvertently reflected. This apparent slight had more to do with practical considerations: Strode was unknown to the majority of filmgoers; among black actors, only Harry Belafonte and Sidney Poitier had sufficient prestige to sell a major studio production, which is why Warners urged Ford to cast one of them in the lead. The director refused – "They're not tough enough" – much to his credit and Strode's everlasting gratitude.[4]

Regardless of how it was marketed, the film broke new ground for the genre by presenting a black man as protagonist and acknowledging the role of African-Americans in the history of the frontier. It was the first time Ford had allowed 'buffalo soldiers' into his pantheon of cavalry heroes; David Lusted considers it "a crucial stage in the revisionist western, transforming the generic meaning of the cavalry in reimagining roles for black characters".[5] Ford was not one for half measures. As he told the film-maker Bertrand Tavernier in 1966, he felt it important to show Rutledge as "not just a nice black guy, but someone nobler than anybody else in the picture".[6] Much as the script was inspired by an ennobling portrait of black cavalrymen by Frederic Remington, Ford's technique aggrandizes Strode/Rutledge throughout. The character is regularly filmed from low angles against a backdrop of sky or sandstone, looking every inch the "top soldier" of his regiment. In one particularly iconic image, Strode's head and chest are positioned to the right of the frame in medium close-up, like a bronze bust from the heroic age, with the camera tilted upwards so that he appears to be the same height as a butte on the left. As well as providing incontrovertible evidence of Ford's respect for the character, it confirms Rutledge as the embodiment of the idealised 'Captain Buffalo' sung about in the movie's theme song: "Did you ever see a mountain / Come a walking like a man?"

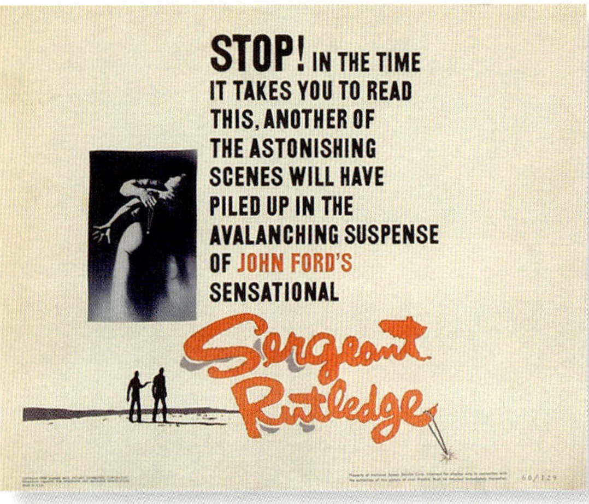

What prevents this from sliding into condescension is Strode's identification with the character and his situation, which endows Rutledge with greater emotional depth than the noble savages of the *Broken Arrow* westerns he in many ways resembles. This was the first time that Strode, a former athlete who had also been a trailblazer for African-Americans in the National Football League, had been granted a central role, and he took the responsibility seriously. Referring to the scene in which Rutledge, having seized the chance to abscond, returns to help his regiment see off an Apache counter-attack in the desert, Strode could scarcely contain his satisfaction: "You have never seen a Negro come off a mountain like John Wayne before. I had the greatest Glory Hallelujah ride across the Pecos River that any black man ever had on the screen. And I did it all myself. I carried the whole black race across that river."[7]

His key scene, however, and the most compelling of all, takes place in the courtroom, when Rutledge, needled by Shattuck's accusation that his change of heart on the trail was merely a way to appease the authorities, responds through tears of anger and pride: "The Ninth Cavalry was my home... the way I was deserting it, I wasn't nothin' but a swamp-runnin' nigger, and I ain't that. I'm a man!" Ford, as was his wont, bullied the inexperienced actor into the right frame of mind for this scene ("He knew how to pluck me like a harp. That old man not only directed me, he split my personality"[8]), but Strode's evincement of self-respect, individual as well as racial, clearly came from the heart. It is perhaps the most explicit instance of character and actor merging, and certainly one of the most emotionally affecting monologues, in any Ford film.

For a western so anxious to rectify the genre's historical denigration, or at best neglect, of one ethnic minority, *Sergeant Rutledge* propagates the same old derogatory stereotype of American Indians. The Apache warriors against whom Rutledge and his regiment demonstrate such gallantry are the faceless, feral phantoms of the crudest dime novels; they really do seem to have "sprung up... from a nightmare". If this smacks of double standards, the film drew additional fire from some quarters for being "counter-revolutionary": in the midst of the civil rights campaign and the Vietnam War, here were "blacks... being recruited on the screen by whites to continue the long genocidal campaign against the Indians".[9] Joseph McBride felt it a "tragic irony" that Rutledge should have to prove his worth as an American citizen by his expertise in killing Indians. Rutledge denies that the Ninth Cavalry are tools of the military establishment: "It ain't the white man's war. We're fighting to make us proud." His words have a hollow ring, however, envisaging an egalitarian future ("Someday...") that must have seemed like a naïve fantasy to those on the front lines of the civil rights movement.

Beneath this flaky layer of Fordian gloss, there is little in the film to encourage Rutledge's optimism. His reprieve is won not by virtue of his testimony or those on his behalf, but by the courtroom confession of the actual culprit – "a *deus ex machina* kind of narrative convenience", complained Ford scholar William Darby, "tacked on to bring the plot to its conclusion".[10] This follows the implication that a black man's life is worth less to the authorities, as represented by Shattuck, than the honour of the recently deceased white boy blamed for the rape by Cantrell – it is the boy's father who breaks down on the stand, in a melodramatic fashion that cheapens the moment: "The way her body moved... she drove me crazy..." (Cantrell resorts to physical force to expedite this admission. Atticus Finch would have blanched.)

It is curious that Ford abandons Rutledge at the point of vindication. The character's reflections on his experience could have made for a powerful and poignant conclusion, but were evidently deemed less important than the rekindling of Mary and Cantrell's romance, as if that were the real meat of the drama. In another abrupt shift in tone, Ford cuts to the canoodling couple as Rutledge and his fellows file past, saluting and grinning inanely. Ford preferred to stress the positive wherever possible, but here it feels decidedly forced. The implications of the sergeant's ordeal are ignored. The military, in which the director placed such faith, remains tainted by racism, as do the society it serves and the legal system. While these matters go unaddressed, the closing shots provide a reminder of Ford's artistic legacy and how far he has travelled: a formation of cavalrymen, outlined against Monument Valley, with the crucial difference that the riders are black. **KG**

footnotes

1 *Searching for John Ford* (Faber & Faber, 2004). The last western Ford planned to make would have continued the trend. *Appointment with Precedence*, or *The Josh Clayton Story*, was to have starred Fred Williamson – like Strode, an athlete turned actor – as a black graduate of West Point who goes on to command a cavalry unit. Woody Strode was lined up in support, with rumours of cameos for John Wayne, James Stewart and Henry Fonda. Even more intriguingly, it could have been Ford's first Italian-financed western, with producers from that country expressing an interest. Of course, nothing came of the plans.

2 Jim Kitses, 'John Ford: Founding Father', in *Horizons West* (BFI, 2007).

3 Ford edited the scene of Mary tending Rutledge's wounds in the early scenes so that she wasn't seen to touch his black skin – a sop to prevailing social attitudes towards interracial relationships.

4 Strode's lowly billing reflected, he felt, his humble place in Hollywood's "caste system".

5 *The Western* (Pearson, 2003).

6 *John Ford: Interviews* (Gerald Peary, ed, University Press of Mississippi, 2001).

7 Quoted in *John Ford*, by Joseph McBride and Michael Wilmington (Da Capo, 1988). In his autobiography, *Goal Dust* (Madison Books, 1990), Strode wrote, "I wasn't the first, but I was one of the first [black actors in Hollywood] to play dignified roles." A fair point where *Rutledge* is concerned, but his career quickly tailed off into stereotypical supporting parts – Ford cast him as John Wayne's factotum (*The Man Who Shot Liberty Valance*), a bloodthirsty Indian (*Two Rode Together*) and a Chinese warrior (*7 Women*). The actor would have to wait until he moved to Italy in the late Sixties for more diverse, if not exactly challenging, roles to come his way. He even got to play a messianic freedom fighter in the powerful *Black Jesus* (1968), based on the life of Congo's Patrice Lumumba.

8 *Goal Dust*.

9 Andrew Sarris, *The John Ford Movie Mystery* (Indiana University Press, 1983).

10 *John Ford's Westerns: A Thematic Analysis* (McFarland, 2006).

Walk Like a Dragon

1960, B/W, 95 mins.

D: James Clavell. P: James Clavell (Paramount Pictures Corp). W: James Clavell, Daniel Mainwaring. Ph: Loyal Griggs. M: Paul Dunlap. St: Jack Lord (Lincoln 'Linc' Bartlett), James Shigeta (Cheng Lu), Nobu McCarthy (Kim Sung), Mel Tormé (the Deacon), Josephine Hutchinson (Ma Bartlett)

"I came because I believed that this was the land of free men." "You're a fool. No land is ever free."

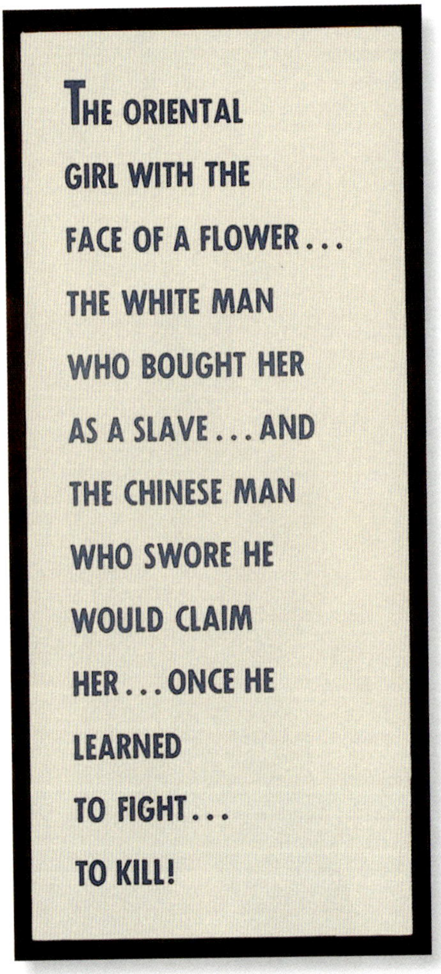

An ambitious western that has slipped through the cracks, *Walk Like a Dragon* attempts to do for Chinese immigrants what a slew of postwar films had done for indigenous Indians: to rehabilitate the image of a traditionally maligned racial minority. This early work from James Clavell – whose fascination for all things Asian would eventually spawn blockbuster novels such as *King Rat* and *Shogun* – could almost have been designed to shame modern Americans about the legacy of racial prejudice in the land of the free, as well as its lingering presence in the early years of the civil rights movement.

Clavell's script describes the limits of racial tolerance in America in the aftermath of the Civil War. Its Anglo protagonist, Linc Bartlett, is fervently anti-slavery, and cites that cause repeatedly to explain his emancipation of Kim Sung, a timid 19-year-old he rescues from a slave market: "We don't buy and sell people here, not any more." (He is still required to pay for her, nevertheless.) Yet segregation and bigotry persist even in the victorious, progressive North. The Chinese have a right to work and run their businesses, but feel compelled to humiliate themselves (speaking pidgin English when addressing whites, for instance, despite being fluent), endure insults and live in separate precincts. America, as represented by Linc's home town of Jericho, may be a melting pot – the ineffective sheriff is Hispanic; Linc's lover has French and Indian blood – but it is simmering with racial tension. This only intensifies when Linc falls for Kim Sung and plans to marry her, sparking the animosity of his neighbours – especially those of a Christian persuasion – and inflaming his rivalry with another Chinese newcomer, Cheng Lu, who has designs on the girl himself.

The rivalry between Linc and Cheng stems as much from their similarities as it does their feelings for Kim Sung. Cheng's resolve to achieve parity with the whites – to "walk tall like a dragon" through Jericho, rather than slink meekly like his countrymen – parallels Linc's desire to "cross the colour line" by marrying Kim Sung. Both are proud, arrogant and prone to hypocrisy. Linc is more liberal-minded than most of the locals, but still regards the Chinese as an inferior race; Cheng abhors his second-class status, yet gives the impression that if he were to win Kim's hand – through payment, if necessary – she would be little more than a domestic drudge.

Neither man qualifies as a hero. Similarly, the villain of the piece is not to be found among the characters; rather, it is society's denigration of minorities and hard line on miscegenation that force the crisis. (David T. Courtwright points out that in California in the late 19th century, there were "15 state anti-miscegenation laws, two of which carried penalties of up to ten years in prison".[1]) Linc and his mother, who takes Kim Sung under her wing, are shunned and scorned by the townsfolk, while Linc's business partners punish him for his dalliance by withholding orders. The girl becomes stranded between customs and cultures, between Linc's efforts to assimilate her into his world – "You would have me white," she cries – and Cheng's insistence that she belongs with her people in Chinatown. The plot manoeuvres the men into a showdown, but ultimately

Clavell abandons western conventions for sobering reality: Kim agrees to go with Cheng, both to preserve the peace and in acknowledgement that America is not ready to give an interracial relationship its blessing – indeed, anti-miscegenation laws were still in existence at the time of production, and were not repealed nationwide until seven years after the film was released.

While Clavell's inexperience as a filmmaker is apparent throughout – a number of scenes are awkwardly blocked; he resorts too readily to emotional manipulation; character motivations can be fuzzy – his sensitivity towards his Chinese subjects brings their experience as racial outcasts into focus like few westerns before or since.[2] (It also ensures they are not merely surrogates for other embattled minorities – an argument frequently made about the tribes in pro-Indian westerns.[3]) He spotlights aspects of their religion, culture and history – the significance of men's braids, for example, in asserting their national identity. Perhaps of greatest value, he gives voice to their frustration and resentment, as expressed by Cheng, as well as the pragmatism and fatalism of other Chinese characters resigned to their subservient position on the fringes of frontier society. **KG**

footnotes

1 *Violent Land: Single Men and Social Disorder from the Frontier to the Inner City* (Harvard University Press, 1996).

2 Although Chinese immigrants flocked to the Western frontier in tens of thousands at the height of the Gold Rush, their experiences have been largely ignored by the genre. Exceptions have included the *Kung Fu* TV series, a short-lived run of Italian-made martial arts westerns (the best being *The Fighting Fists of Shanghai Joe* [1973] and *The Stranger and the Gunfighter* [1974]), *The Ballad of Little Jo* and Walter Hill's miniseries *Broken Trail* (2006), in which Robert Duvall and Thomas Haden Church become custodians of five Chinese women destined for a life of servitude and prostitution.

3 Another comparison with westerns such as *Broken Arrow* and *Apache* might be the casting: in those films, white actors were asked to play Indians; here, the key Chinese characters are played by Hawaiian-born, Japanese-American singer-actor James Shigeta and Canadian-Japanese model-actress Nobu McCarthy. This is less likely to be an example of casual Hollywood racism ('all Orientals look alike') than a belief that, at the time, there were no young Chinese actors of sufficient standing or experience. The film does feature ethnic Chinese performers further down the cast.

The Deadly Companions

1961, Colour, 93 mins.

D: Sam Peckinpah. P: Charles B. FitzSimons (Carousel Productions). W: Albert Sidney Fleischman. Ph: William H. Clothier. M: Marlin Skiles. St: Maureen O'Hara (Kit Tilden), Brian Keith (Yellowleg), Steve Cochran (Billy), Chill Wills (Turkey), Strother Martin (Parson)

"I know somebody who spent five years looking for a man he hated… When he caught up with him, it was the worst day of his life. He'd get his revenge all right, but then he'd lose the one thing he had to live for."

In terms of his overall career, the title of Sam Peckinpah's first feature would prove as prescient as its content; disagreements with his producer – here Charles FitzSimons – as recurrent as any of his cherished motifs. Skirmishing with the 'suits' fuelled a persecution complex that drove Peckinpah, in later years, to bloody-minded bouts of artistic self-sabotage. Straitjacketed by FitzSimons' strict criteria – no script rewrites; limited (if any) direction of leading lady Maureen O'Hara, the producer's sister; crucially, no guarantee of final cut – Peckinpah had little chance to impose his personality on a project that sorely needed strong directorial intervention.

FitzSimons had been nurturing A.S. Fleischman's script, a far-fetched story of revenge, redemption and love against the odds, for three years, and considered it perfect. Peckinpah felt otherwise, referring to it after the fact as "unmanageable", full of "awful bullshit": gimmicks, unconvincing inter-relationships and stilted dialogue. His suggested changes were rejected, however. After all, he was just a hired gun, recommended by male lead Brian Keith, his collaborator on *The Westerner* TV series.[1] (Keith's casting had been assured by his successful pairing with O'Hara in Disney's *The Parent Trap*.)

He and Keith amended some of the material surreptitiously, while Peckinpah's other ally among the key production personnel was the cinematographer, William H. Clothier, whose landscape work graced a great many westerns and is frequently breathtaking here.

So Peckinpah soldiered on with Fleischman's saga of an ex-Yankee soldier, Yellowleg, pursuing a vendetta against Turk, the "drunken Reb" who scalped him on the field at Chickamauga. (Turk is an authentic western grotesque, defined by Jim Kitses as "a gross, shambling barbarian"; he fits the Peckinpah aesthetic perfectly.) After rescuing Turk from a lynch mob, Yellowleg embroils him and his partner, Billy, a brash gunfighter, in a plan to rob the bank in Gila City. On the appointed day, in a contrivance typical of the script, another gang has the same idea. During the mêlée, Yellowleg accidentally shoots a child dead. He insists on accompanying the mother, Kit – widow, saloon girl and social pariah – on a trek through Indian territory to bury the boy alongside his late father's grave in Siringo. (Town gossip has it that Kit was never really married.) Yellowleg's "deadly companions" tag along, sneering and plotting – Billy lusting after Kit, Turk rambling about creating his own fiefdom, 'Freedonia', staffed by slave Indians.

In Siringo, now a ghost town, a reckoning becomes due: as Peckinpah filmed it, Yellowleg kills Billy without breaking stride – "a brutal, realistic act", claimed the director – in the course of advancing on Turk. Partly through Kit's imploring, however, he cannot bring himself to scalp and murder the man he has been hunting, turning him over to the Gila City posse. Yet FitzSimons recut the ending so that Turk appears to shoot his partner in the back, leaving Yellowleg morally unscathed to ride off with Kit.[2]

Although it lacks the piquant flavour of Peckinpah's signature works, many of the ingredients are in place. Yellowleg, whose restless spirit resembles that of Dave Blassingame, the character Keith played in *The Westerner*, is one of the director's traumatised outsiders. A continuation of the damaged protagonists of Fifties psychological westerns, he is a fundamentally decent man warped by his revenge drive. (As more than one writer has observed, it is not difficult to imagine *The Deadly Companions* in the hands of Budd Boetticher and Randolph Scott.) But Fleischman's script presses the point by giving the character's emotional impairment a physical dimension: a bullet embedded near his clavicle affects his aim (hence the wayward shot that fells Kit's son), while the scalping scar on his forehead compels him to keep on his hat at all times. (A detail perhaps lifted from the 1951 Hugo Fregonese western *Apache Drums*.) Kit, in theory, is Yellowleg's counterpart. "What about *my* scars?" she wails, equating the stigma of single motherhood and 'saloon work' (it was still not

permitted to call it prostitution) with Yellowleg's war wounds. Their relationship ricochets between mutual hostility and mutual recognition, with each positioned as the other's redeemer. But it never rings true. O'Hara's cold, self-pitying performance robs her character of vitality (compare the earthy "whores-as-heroines", to borrow Paul Seydor's phrase, in Peckinpah's later *The Ballad of Cable Hogue* [1970] and *Bring Me the Head of Alfredo Garcia* [1974]). As written and played, Kit seems more concerned with proving her son's legitimacy – and thus her own virtue – than she is with his death. She is never seen to work through her grief, and her acceptance, in the course of just a few days, that Yellowleg is a suitable partner despite his (accidental) killing of her son borders on preposterous.

The mission undertaken by Civil War enemies, complete with the threat of Apaches, became the premise of *Major Dundee*, and one of Fleischman's plot devices that irked Peckinpah the most – the transportation of a corpse across hot, hostile terrain – was dealt with much more realistically in *Alfredo Garcia*; there is no hint of putrefaction, no buzzing of hungry flies, in *The Deadly Companions*. Gila City, meanwhile, represents the kind of small-town hypocrisy that was a hallmark not just of Peckinpah's films but also the post-war western in general, spurred by *Stagecoach*. It is the kind of place where the saloon doubles as a church (the bartender covers up a nude portrait ahead of the parson's sermon, much to Billy's disgust), and its self-righteous citizens, quick to judge Kit, prove even quicker to pursue Turk and Billy after the duo mount a second assault on the bank. Their earlier trepidation about entering Apache country doesn't hold the posse back: "You know how people are," says the sheriff. "As long as it's their money, the gates of Hell wouldn't stop them."

Vignettes provide an inchoate sense of Peckinpah's ability to reinvigorate B-movie material, to transform it into something approaching abstract art. The pursuit of a stagecoach by Indians, perhaps the quintessential western motif, is revealed to be a re-enactment of an earlier attack: the 'passengers' are also Indians, some of them wearing plundered dresses, all of them drunk. Careful camera placement and judicious editing maintain the dreamlike uncertainty of the images. And after Yellowleg steals a horse from the raiders that night, one of the perpetrators goes on to stalk the hero and heroine, culminating in a gothic scene inside a cave in which the Apache's presence is revealed by a flash of lightning, enabling Kit to shoot him.

Had his shackles been removed, or at least loosened, would the director have made *The Deadly Companions* more coherent and compelling than it is? Given the presence in the script of themes and characters that he would develop successfully in subsequent films, it is tempting to assume that he would have. As it stands, these pointers to stronger works cannot help but detract from his debut's modest virtues. Like the character of Kit, it remains "a collection of possibilities" (Seydor), a promise awaiting fulfilment. **KG**

top right: The film was retitled for a 1963 re-release.
above: Brian Keith (standing) reins in Chill Wills.

footnotes

1 Coincidentally, the plot of *The Westerner* episode 'Going Home' foreshadowed that of *The Deadly Companions*, complete with a cross-desert trek with corpse in tow.

2 FitzSimons found Peckinpah's ending inexplicable: "How can you have a man shoot another against whom he bears no grudge and then turn around and be unable to kill the man he's hated for years?" It is a fair point, but the script called for Billy and Yellowleg to have a conventional showdown – would it have been any more believable for the hero, who cannot raise his gun arm unaided, to have outdrawn a younger, faster opponent? As it stands, it is Turk's killing of Billy that truly defies logic.

It shouts and sings with life... explodes with love!

CLARK Gable · MARILYN Monroe · MONTGOMERY Clift

The Misfits

1961, B/W, 125 mins.

D: John Huston. P: Frank E. Taylor (Seven Arts Productions). W: Arthur Miller. Ph: Russell Metty. M: Alex North. St: Clark Gable (Gay Langland), Marilyn Monroe (Roslyn Taber), Montgomery Clift (Perce Howland), Thelma Ritter (Isabelle Steers), Eli Wallach (Guido)

"Damn 'em all.
They changed it, changed it all around.
Smeared it all over with blood...
It's like roping a dream now.
I just gotta find another way to be alive."

The psychological, 'adult' westerns of the Fifties gave way to – indeed, paved the way for – a mood of melancholia and loss as the decade turned. Cowboy heroes were no longer ciphers for exploring human foibles; they had become symbolic of the death of freedom, as the West became increasingly modernised and the wheel became the principal mode of transport. Steve Judd and Gil Westrum in *Ride the High Country* found themselves anachronisms in a world of automobiles, uniformed police and unfettered greed, while Jack Burns in *Lonely Are the Brave* attempted to keep the frontier spirit alive in a contemporary milieu, testing his vitality against police cars and helicopters. Only Paul Newman's Hud embraced modernity, and he was a significantly younger and more cynical character, emblematic of the decay of western traditions.

The Misfits represents, perhaps, the most morbid of a group of films depicting the moribund cowboy archetype. While Judd and Westrum find their notion of honour conspicuously lacking in the civilised world and Burns confronts the rule of property law head on, the male characters of John Huston's film – like Hud's father – appear resigned to the erosion of their way of life. Desperate not to work for "wages" but, as Arthur Miller observed of real Nevadan cowboys, "adrift, lacking in purpose and direction", his anti-heroes are engulfed by an overwhelming sadness. This bleakness is occasionally broken by brief romances, mustang hunts and the construction of ever-unfinished houses.

In the divorce hotspot of Reno, newly single Roslyn Taber meets car mechanic Guido and cowboy Gay Langland. Both men spend much of their time drinking in local bars and chasing divorcées. Gay's philosophy – "Just live" – is attractive to Roslyn and, despite Guido's advances and the misgivings of her friend Isabelle, she falls for the rugged cowboy. Taking up residence in the house that Guido once shared with his late wife, Roslyn starts to enjoy the experience of living in the American badlands, while Gay adjusts to domestication and Guido continues to compliment Roslyn for the light she's brought into their lives: "You have a gift for life. The rest of us are just looking for a place to hide." The air of harmony is broken when Gay tells Guido his plan to

capture 15 Nevada mustangs and sell them for profit. (The horses are the misfits of the title, although the tag obviously fits the human protagonists as well – both are a fading breed, as Gay implies in a wistful moment.) Needing a third man to help them, they enlist Perce Howland, an alcoholic rodeo rider just about young and fit enough for the work. With Perce racked by injuries and riding a heavy hangover, the men, accompanied by an anxious Roslyn, drive to the high plains of the desert to locate the horses.

The relationship between Gay and Roslyn is a case of both opposite attraction and acute need. Gay expresses no self-pity at being left by his wife, but still requires feminine warmth and comfort, while Roslyn finds a weathered machismo in Gay that has been lacking in her previous loves. Theirs is a "desperate reaching out of solitary individuals", as Miller's biographer Christopher Bigsby puts it, both trying to matter in somebody else's life.[1] Roslyn is both fascinated and alarmed by the desert isolation and the rawness of life on the frontier. Her reaction to Gay grabbing a rifle to eradicate pests on their land is hysterical and naïve, and this grows to horror when she learns what fate lies in store for the mustangs, which are destined to be sold for dog food. Her attitude, and the insult Gay perceives when she offers to buy the lives of the horses, spurs him to assert his masculinity: "I won't have anyone making my mind up for me." Marilyn Monroe's idolising of Clark Gable – as a child, she would fantasise that he was her real father – adds a poignancy to their scenes together; Gay's treatment of Roslyn does appear somewhat paternal (he compares himself to a chastising father at one point). Monroe's hospitalisation during production, however, due to her drug consumption, tested the patience of all involved, particularly Gable who, at 59 – 24 years Monroe's senior – found it difficult to cope with interminable on-set waiting.

top: from left: Eli Wallach, Thelma Ritter, Clark Gable and Marilyn Monroe.
above: Director John Huston (left) on set with Marilyn Monroe and Arthur Miller.

For his part, Montgomery Clift, hopelessly addicted to pain-killing drugs and out of control at cast parties, was impeccably behaved and professional when it mattered. Of the four principal characters, Perce starts as the most intoxicated by Nevada life, but matures quickly when he realises the wretched position they're in; "I'm beginnin' to smell wages all over you," says Gay disapprovingly when the rodeo rider contemplates a change of lifestyle. Although seemingly attracted to Roslyn, Perce's estranged relationship with his mother is a better indicator of what he requires from female contact, and Roslyn becomes his maternal surrogate. Perce's vulnerability contrasts sharply with Guido's sly, cynical worldview. His initial gentlemanliness towards Roslyn culminates in underhanded stabs at Gay, his best friend, as he tries to steal her affections. His final, pathetic attempt at winning her favours by freeing the horses – "Give me a reason and I'll stop it" – is met with an angry diatribe: "A reason?... Do you have to get something to be human? You could blow up the world and all you'd feel is sorry for yourself."

Aside from Thelma Ritter's Isabelle Steers, who adds a little *joie de vivre* to the depressed demeanour of the four protagonists, the film's other main character is the unforgiving Nevada landscape. The desert scenes were shot in temperatures that often reached 120 degrees Fahrenheit. In spite of the infernal setting, Monroe's omnipresent acting coach, Paula Strasberg, would insist on wearing an all-black outfit. According to Bigsby, "Strasberg's explanation was that she wore the outfit so as to be inconspicuous." Miller, for his part, was not pleased with the film's aesthetic; he had envisaged the characters being framed against the vastness of the desert more often than they actually are. This was to misunderstand Huston's directorial strategy: scene after scene is set in bars, cars, houses, trucks and telephone booths – "images of containment, of figures framed or confined", emphasising the trappings, in a visual as well as a metaphorical sense, of the modern world.[2] Closer to Miller's vision is Roslyn's acerbic verbal attack on the three men, as the trauma of the mustang hunt finally overwhelms her and we see her, in the distance of an infinite wide shot, isolated from her companions: "Killers… Murderers… You can only be happy when you see something die… You're three sweet dead men."

It shouts and sings with life... explodes with love!
Seven Arts Productions presents
CLARK Gable
MARILYN Monroe
MONTGOMERY Clift
in the John Huston production of the Misfits
Co-starring
Thelma Ritter Eli Wallach
Screenplay by Arthur Miller
Produced by Frank E. Taylor
Directed by John Huston
Music by Alex North Released thru United Artists

Decay and death permeate Miller's script, as Roslyn slowly learns that the men she has become involved with live in a limbo state, somewhere between the ideals of a vanishing past and the necessities of daily survival. Gay's attitude to death is one of fearless acceptance: "Dyin's as natural as livin'. The man who's afraid to die is too afraid to live"; and to justify the mustang hunt, "Nothing can live unless something dies." Earlier, Roslyn's frustration at the seeming impossibility of human connection is expressed with more references to mortality: "We're all dying, aren't we? We're not teaching each other what we really know, are we?" Guido is the most morbid of all, dwelling on the passing of his wife and the thousands of lives that would have been ended by his bombing expeditions during the war. While they claim to be free spirits, clinging to a quasi-frontier existence, he and Gay remain entombed within a conservative middle-American community, with all the stifling boredom that entails. The film's disparagement of modern modes of transport, which it shares with *Lonely Are the Brave* and *Hud*, peaks during the mustang hunt, when Guido, the only one of the protagonists closely associated with modern technology, corrals the horses towards Gay and Perce in his twin-propeller aeroplane. The two tired cowboys, meanwhile, pursue and lasso them from the rear of a pick-up in a sad imitation – almost a mockery – of former glories.

The inclusion of Huston's film in a study of western revisionism calls into question the elements needed to make a genre picture. Certainly, the emphasis on male anxiety would suggest Miller was intending the kind of angst-ridden western melodrama that was so prominent in the latter half of the Fifties. The casting of method artists like Clift and Eli Wallach directs the viewer inexorably to this conclusion. Monroe complained that the film was "their movie. It's really about cowboys and the horses. That's all they need. They don't need me at all." Indeed, although Roslyn's role, which was enhanced by Miller during rewrites, is an important one – to stir the consciences of the men in her thrall – *The Misfits* primarily concerns Westerners and their battle with solitude, nature and the waning of their lifestyle, all of which factor into Gay's final duel with the stallion, the rest of the mustangs having been freed by Perce. In this sequence, Gay's virility comes to the fore – proof, after a fashion, that the mythical Westerner was a real man who existed on the fringes of genuine American communities. In a display of scintillating stunt-work, much of it performed by Gable, the grizzled anti-hero is dragged along the salt flats until, through physical strength allied to pride and willpower, he brings the exhausted stallion down, demonstrating a spiritual bond with the creature by comforting it as it falls.

Despite the difficulties brought to the production by the heat, by Monroe's trauma (which was compounded by the breakdown of her marriage to Miller) and by Strasberg's intrusiveness, Huston crafted a film that is both absorbing and affecting. A faint sense of hope rises at the end, with Gay and Roslyn seemingly reconciled by Gay's decision to cut loose the stallion, although the feeling lingers that he and Perce, as representatives of a bygone era, are left, like the audience for conventional westerns, hankering for daring and adventure, unable to face blunt existential fact. Monroe died soon after shooting was completed, leaving behind a cloud of mystique and adulation, while some say it was the tribulation of making *The Misfits* that finally ended Gable's life; too much waiting around on too strenuous a shoot for a man of failing health. However, for every moment he's on the screen, he gives the finest performance of his career. From his drunken wailing when deserted by his children to asserting his manliness in the desert arena, the great star understood what Gay Langland represented: a myth dragged through the dust so many times that it was time to be laid to rest. **CH**

footnotes

1 *Arthur Miller* (Phoenix, 2009).

2 Edward Gallafent, 'Not with a Bang: the End of the West in *Lonely Are the Brave*, *The Misfits* and *Hud*', in *The Movie Book of the Western* (Studio Vista, 1996).

Lonely Are the Brave

1962, B/W, 107 mins.

D: David Miller. P: Edward Lewis (Joel Productions). W: Dalton Trumbo. Ph: Philip Lathrop. M: Jerry Goldsmith. St: Kirk Douglas (John W. 'Jack' Burns), Gena Rowlands (Jerri Bondi), Walter Matthau (Sheriff Johnson), Michael Kane (Paul Bondi), Carroll O'Connor (Hinton)

"Have you ever noticed how many fences there's getting to be? And the signs they got on them: no hunting, no hiking, no admission, no trespassing, private property, closed area, start moving, go away, get lost, drop dead."

John W. 'Jack' Burns asserts his disdain for modern society, in which land once wild and open is now sectioned off by private business, by cutting the wires that protect those interests and trespassing on territory where *all* men were formerly free to roam. Released in 1962, the same year as *Ride the High Country* and *The Man Who Shot Liberty Valance*, two more classic elegies to the dying West and its anachronistic heroes, *Lonely Are the Brave* deposits our cowboy protagonist not in turn-of-the-century twilight but in the headlight glare of the post-Second World War consumer age. It's a key contemporary western and, according to Kirk Douglas, his favourite among his movies: "I love the theme that if you try to be an individual, society will crush you."[1] Burns, notionally a cowhand, has been reduced to herding sheep when the work is available. In his pursuit of a hopelessly romanticised ideal, however, he sets himself up as an increasingly marginalised, even eccentric, figure. His old friend Paul is serving time in the penitentiary for assisting Mexican immigrants to cross the border – just more fences that need cutting and folk that need helping – and Burns, with a view to landing himself in the same jailhouse, engages in a barroom brawl and an assault on a police officer. But Burns has a plan – albeit in his boot, not up his sleeve: with the help of two concealed hacksaw blades, he cuts the cell bars so that he and Paul can break out. Paul, however, has a wife and child and decides to take his sentence manfully – "You grew up on me, didn't you?" remarks Burns ruefully, an implicit admission of his own arrested development. The remainder of the film sees Burns pursued over harsh terrain towards the Mexican border, his cunning and resourcefulness pitched against the modern technology wielded by the lawmen symbolically obliged to rein in the free-ranging cowboy spirit.

It's a film laden with contrasts, not least in Burns' painful realisation of the gulf between Paul's familial obligations and his own quasi-anarchic principles. He expresses these when asked to produce official identification in the police station: "I don't need cards to figure out who I am. I already know." Visual juxtapositions abound, brought into sharp focus by Philip Lathrop's elegant monochrome photography. The classical opening shot of Burns, stetsoned and booted, lying prone in open country, is shattered by the roar of jet planes overhead. Later, he rides his mare, Whiskey, past a mausoleum of mangled motorcars, positioned ironically next to a human graveyard.

As Burns heads up into the high country, his limited perspective of the awesome New Mexico landscape, mirroring his restricted outlook in general, is magnified by the whirlybird's-eye view enjoyed by the police helicopter. (Burns later evens the odds somewhat by forcing it to land with high-precision shots from his rifle.) Most tragically, in the film's heart-rending denouement, the cowboy's mode of transport collides with a contemporary form on a rain-slicked highway. Whiskey, critically wounded, is spared the same fate as Burns, for whom incarceration almost certainly awaits – a fate, one feels, he would consider worse than death.

Complementing Kirk Douglas' exceptional leading performance, which both he and his son Michael regard as the great actor's best work, are an impressive supporting cast. As the sheriff, Walter Matthau can't help but share the audience's admiration for his quarry's guile, while Gena Rowlands invests Paul's wife, Jerri, with both tenderness and frustration, forced to live in the real world while the men around her put their principles first. (Burns all but disregards her criticism as the opinion of a displaced Easterner, yet it's clear from the crackling tension between them that he and Jerri have a legacy of mutual unconsummated passion.) An ursine, bilious George Kennedy, meanwhile, sweats clammy hatred as a sadistic deputy, who bloodies Burns' face for his own entertainment and is later sideswiped in (proportionate) revenge.

According to Douglas, Dalton Trumbo's fluid script, based on a novel by the environmentalist and anarchist Edward Abbey, was so perfect that not one word was changed during filming. Trumbo was blacklisted during the McCarthy years, but saw his career virtually resurrected when Douglas insisted he be given full credit for his screenplay to *Spartacus*. Here, the rebel writer perfectly captures the essence of Abbey's outsider thesis, as Burns finds *his* West fast becoming nothing but acres of barbed-wired land forbidden to unauthorised personnel, and certainly to a vagabond like him. Burns is an obvious descendant of an earlier Douglas character, Dempsey Rae, whose loathing of barbed wire is a

top: Kirk Douglas grapples with a one-armed brawler (Bill Raisch).
above: Douglas with Michael Kane.

prominent theme of the 1955 film *Man Without a Star*. The actor empathised with men like these and their beliefs, saying of *Lonely Are the Brave*: "It happens to be a point of view I love. Out of all the characters [I've played], I love John W. Burns the most. Poor misfit. How hard it is to be an individual. He just wanted to help his friend. He just wanted to be himself. It's very difficult. You have to conform or the forces of society come down on you like a truckload of toilets."[2]

Burns' dismal fate reflects Douglas' pessimistic view of the homogenisation of modern life. Unlike the protagonists of *Ride the High Country* and *Liberty Valance*, Burns is denied his heroic fall, his grand gesture of sacrifice or redemption. As Jerri sums it up, "The world you and Paul live in doesn't exist." Essentially, Burns' cowboy, as well as being indubitably brave, is exposed as a risk-taking dreamer whose individualistic crusade leads to his futile downfall, brutally affirming Jerri's dictum: "Either you go by the rules or you lose." While not exactly condemning the central figure, Trumbo certainly criticises the archetype and leaves it to a woman's plain talking to give voice to painful reality. **CH**

footnotes

1 *The Ragman's Son* (Simon & Schuster, 1988).
2 Ibid.

JAMES STEWART JOHN WAYNE

The Man Who Shot Liberty Valance

1962, B/W, 123 mins.

D: John Ford. P: Willis Goldbeck (John Ford Productions). W: James Warner Bellah, Willis Goldbeck. Ph: William H. Clothier. M: Cyril Mockridge. St: John Wayne (Tom Doniphon), James Stewart (Ransom Stoddard), Vera Miles (Hallie), Lee Marvin (Liberty Valance), Edmond O'Brien (Dutton Peabody)

"This is the West, sir. When the legend becomes fact, print the legend."

John Ford's penultimate western is preoccupied with themes evident in his major works: the forging of civilisation (*My Darling Clementine*); the trauma this may inflict (*The Searchers*); the diversity, ethnic and social, upon which America is built (*Stagecoach*). In particular, it picks up a thread from *Fort Apache*, acknowledging the need for heroes, for legendary deeds, in the collective memory, but weaves it into tragic drama rather than triumphalism. At the same time, it relies heavily on iconic Fordian romanticism to become what Ford biographer Joseph McBride called the director's "artistic summation". It is also his most powerful film. Jim Kitses recognised its analytic design: "The film evidences a post-modern complexity at once nostalgic and critical."[1] The script, which maps community relations as intricately as a George Eliot novel, is the most refined of any Ford western in its reconstruction of the birth of modern American statehood – and the most wistful about the death of the untamed frontier. It also offers an unlikely (and falsely venerated) town tamer in the shape of an attorney at law rather than a professional gunman.

That lawyer is now senator Ransom Stoddard, who returns to the town of Shinbone from his office in Washington for the funeral of old friend Tom Doniphon. Local pressmen demand that Stoddard explain who Doniphon was and, in flashback, the narrative unfurls. Stoddard, a young, idealistic Eastern attorney, is beaten and flogged on arrival in the West by the psychotic Liberty Valance in a stagecoach hijack. Doniphon and his African-American friend, Pompey (Woody Strode), rescue Stoddard from the desert and take him to a restaurant in Shinbone owned by the Ericsons, a Scandinavian couple, and waitressed by Hallie. Indignant and pompous, Stoddard declares that he is going to bring Valance to justice. "If that's what you wanna do, you better start packing a loaded gun," states Doniphon, the epitome of masculine self-reliance. In exchange for bed and board, Stoddard works in the kitchen and then as a waiter, mocked by Valance and his heavies. He then watches impotently as Doniphon and Valance face each other down.

Friendship blossoms between Stoddard and Hallie and, learning that she can neither read nor write, he is inspired to found a schoolroom for the teaching of history, literacy and the Constitution. The newspaper editor, Peabody, offers space in his office for the lawyer to set up practice, attracting the wrath of Valance. Stoddard realises, "When force threatens, talk's no good any more." He is taught how to shoot by Doniphon, who can't resist humiliating him (shades of Valance) by unloading his gun on a paint pot above Stoddard's head. The townsfolk, spurred on by Stoddard's lessons in democracy, gather to elect a local delegate, rejecting Valance's candidature and, with it, the tyranny of the cattlemen. Peabody, drunk on whisky and his own oratory, is beaten to within an inch of his life by the villain and his henchmen, forcing Stoddard to abandon his principles and confront his nemesis on the night-time streets of Shinbone.

Unlike in the majority of Ford's classic westerns, the majestic buttes of Monument Valley – symbolic totems of the durability of his frontier heroes – are conspicuous by their absence. These natural wonders are replaced by soundstage work, by turns realistic and expressionistic, illuminated by low-key lighting and with minimal set dressing. Detractors have occasionally cited such frugal decoration as an indication of penny-pinching or indifference, but early Ford scholar Lindsay Anderson recognised a deeper purpose: "Whether by design or by accident, this lack of visual refinement has an artistic result which is not just negative. The lines of the story emerge clearly… with no decorative distraction."[2] He called *Liberty Valance* "a parable of cinema", comparable to Bertolt Brecht in its attempt to delineate important historical changes. Indeed, looking at the film's main points of action – the restaurant kitchen, Peabody's press office, the schoolroom – Ford's staging comes to resemble a didactic theatre piece. The emphasis on interiors, like the use of studio sets for the major nocturnal scenes – the stagecoach robbery and the gunfight – provides what Douglas Pye calls "a sense of enclosure", compressing the action in a noir-like manner. It also gives *Liberty Valance* the stamp of a B-production or a silent western, especially in combination with William H. Clothier's black and white photography, revealing Ford's intention to get "back to the basic values of moviemaking".[3]

The power of this evolutionary fable is to be found in the words and the performances rather than the extraordinarily photogenic landscapes seen in *The Searchers* or the cavalry pictures. The story is both intimate and epic, rustic and metropolitan. John Wayne's Tom Doniphon – "A contradictory mixture of reactionary values and progressive behaviours"[4] – personifies these dichotomised attributes. With Hallie he is mostly charming and simple; occasionally he is patronising, assuming that she is going to wed him, despite her passivity on the matter, and is building an extension to his modest ranch in anticipation of the nuptials. He is, though, the only man who appears to have any backbone. He handles Valance by an ancient code, both men tied to each other in their acceptance of violence as the only solution. As he tells Stoddard, "Liberty Valance is the toughest man south of the Picketwire – next to me."

Doniphon's relationship with Stoddard is the one most sealed in fate: an unlikely union that will clear the path for statehood and, absurdly, consign the spirit of the West – embodied by Doniphon as much as by Valance – to history. Doniphon both respects and resents this tenderfoot (he calls him "pilgrim", shrewdly gauging the other's character), yet he rescues him, watches over him, then sacrifices himself for the lawyer and what he represents – shooting Valance from the shadows, then retreating there while Stoddard is granted the limelight.

above: James Stewart (foreground) gets the drop on Lee Marvin – or so legend has it.

He assuages the latter's guilt by owning up to the killing and presses him to stand for office, to forge a future that Doniphon can't be a part of but knows must come to pass: "Hallie's you're girl now. You taught her how to read and write, now give her something to read and write about." The rancher's drunken, self-destructive rage after yielding the stage to Stoddard, burning down the love nest he was erecting for Hallie, stands alongside the final scene of *The Searchers* as the most poetically conceived moment in both Ford's canon and Wayne's career.

James Stewart's performance is one of mounting agitation. Stoddard's transformation from meek citizen to gun-wielding avenger takes the actor back to territory mapped out in *Destry Rides Again* and the Anthony Mann series. With Hallie he is initially somewhat condescending (highlighted by her shame in revealing she is illiterate), but he is feminised through circumstance – "What good has reading and writing done you?" asks Hallie. "Look at you. In an apron." Hallie becomes arguably the prime mover in the drama, urging both Stoddard and Doniphon to take decisive action at key moments. Her own pivotal decision – choosing Stoddard over Doniphon – elevates her to a position of influence well beyond the confines of the kitchen and coheres with the romantic union of East and West in prior Ford films, notably *My Darling Clementine*. Her behaviour in the closing scenes, however, when she tenderly places a cactus rose on Doniphon's coffin, suggests her emotional dilemma has never been resolved.

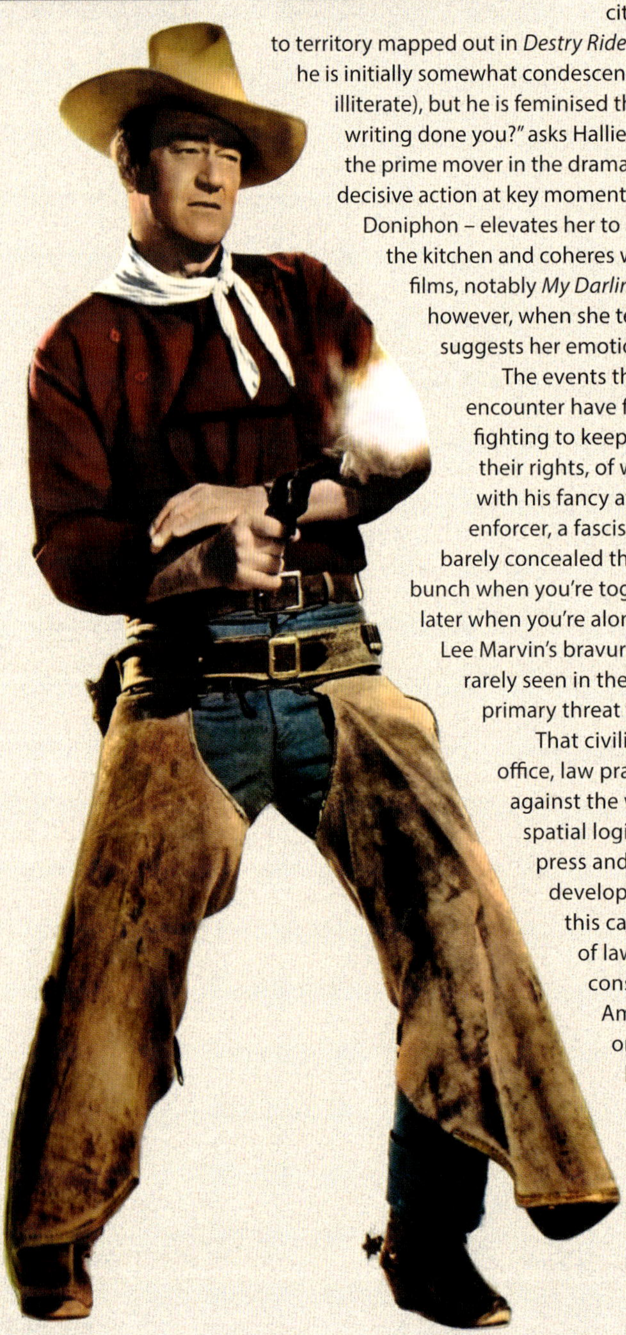

The events that manoeuvre the male leads towards their fateful encounter have fuelled numerous western narratives – cattle barons fighting to keep the range open, small homesteaders agitating for their rights, of which statehood would be a guarantee. Valance, with his fancy attire and silver-topped whip, is the big ranchers' enforcer, a fascistic figure who attempts to cow the populace with barely concealed threats of brutal reprisals: "You sodbusters are a brave bunch when you're together, but don't vote any way now that you'll regret later when you're alone." He is the most Sadean of the director's rogues; Lee Marvin's bravura performance invests him with a level of cruelty rarely seen in the director's films, supplanting Native Americans as the primary threat to Ford's emergent civilisation.[5]

That civilisation is symbolised by the three pillars of press office, law practice and schoolroom, forming a natural bulwark against the whip and the gun. As Kitses states, "The film's spatial logic establishes a relationship between the law, the press and education." Here, the foundation of society is the development of a well-informed, literate community, in this case helmed by Peabody and Stoddard, with a rule of law applicable to all men. In true Fordian style, his constituents are multi-ethnic, representative of modern America, and there is a feeling that Stoddard's lessons on democracy and the Constitution were aimed beyond the classroom. Most significantly, he affords Pompey, a black man, the opportunity to remind us that, "All men are created equal." The position of Pompey is complex. Segregation is clearly in effect in the town – he is refused a drink in the saloon and appears dislocated from the fervour of the election process – but Doniphon treats him largely with fondness.

Given the year *Liberty Valance* was made, this complexity reflects the standing of blacks in US society, as well as in Hollywood, at the time. Ford had received both liberal plaudits and reactionary criticism for choosing Woody Strode to play the idealised black trooper in *Sergeant Rutledge*; he then back-tracked, or so it seemed, by casting the same actor as a rampaging savage in *Two Rode Together*. In the midst of the civil rights campaign, *Liberty Valance* seemed to acknowledge that true racial equality was still a long way off. Anecdotes about on-set attitudes towards Strode suggest that the film-makers themselves may not have been ready for such a day to come.

There is an elegiac quality in Ford's later work that is felt most acutely in *Liberty Valance* – the first of three major westerns released in 1962 that lamented the passing of an individualist-oriented era.[6] "For Ford, *Liberty Valance* represents the true closing of the frontier, both his own mythic frontier and that of the film genre he helped create."[7] It is as if, to paraphrase Jon Tuska, Ford wanted to believe, but couldn't any more.[8] Hence his decision here, contrary to the newspaperman's famous dictum, to print fact rather than legend. "We've had a lot of people who were supposed to be great heroes," he told Peter Bogdanovich, mentioning Custer and Pat Garrett in particular, "and you know damn well they weren't. But it's good for the country to have heroes to look up to… On the other hand, of course, the legend always had some foundation."[9] Stoddard has parlayed his legend into a glittering career, but it is clear at the end that living a lie has destroyed completely the innocence with which he rode into Shinbone. While expressing due praise for Stoddard's brand of nation-builder, armed with books of law, the director finally acknowledges that it is the likes of Doniphon, primitive, marginalised and forgotten, whose grit and guns paved the way. **CH**

footnotes

1 Jim Kitses, *Horizons West* (BFI Publishing, 2007).

2 Lindsay Anderson, *About John Ford* (Plexus, 1989). In Joseph McBride's opinion, "The almost total absence of landscape in *Liberty Valance* is itself a statement of Ford's loss of faith in the ideal of the American frontier; the civilization of Shinbone seems a dead end" (*Searching for John Ford*, Faber & Faber, 2004).

3 Joseph McBride, *Searching for John Ford*. It has been suggested, by Peter Bogdanovich among others, that Ford decided to shoot in black and white partly to disguise the ageing make-up applied to James Stewart and Vera Miles in the framing story.

4 Jim Kitses, *Horizons West*.

5 This was the first time Marvin had worked with Ford and, not being exactly easygoing himself, he claimed to have found the director's legendarily bearish manner inspiring rather than intimidating: "No matter how tough the old bastard was to me I couldn't wait to get to the day's work" (Donald Zec, *Marvin*, Hodder & Stoughton, 1979).

6 *Liberty Valance* was released in April 1962, followed a month later by *Lonely Are the Brave* and in June by *Ride the High Country*.

7 Joseph McBride, *Searching for John Ford*.

8 Jon Tuska, *The Filming of the West* (Doubleday, 1976).

9 Quoted in Peter Bogdanovich, *John Ford* (University of California Press, 1978).

Ride the High Country

1962, Colour, 94 mins.

D: Sam Peckinpah. P: Richard E. Lyons (Metro-Goldwyn-Mayer). W: N.B. Stone Jr. Ph: Lucien Ballard. M: George Bassman. St: Randolph Scott (Gil Westrum), Joel McCrea (Steve Judd), Mariette Hartley (Elsa Knudsen), Ron Starr (Heck Longtree), Edgar Buchanan (Judge Tolliver)

"My father says there's only right and wrong – good and evil, nothing in between. It isn't that simple, is it?"
"No, it isn't. It should be, but it isn't."

In David Weddle's view, Sam Peckinpah in the early Sixties was a man "with one foot in the past and one in the future; his work became the link between the two, embodying what America had been and what it was becoming".[1] *Ride the High Country* illustrates the point. The director's second feature revived prominent themes from Fifties westerns – anachronistic gunmen; the interaction of seasoned westerners and cocky upstarts; the growing estrangement of heroic champions from the society they have served – but his thinking was also in step with contemporary developments in the genre. As in *The Misfits* and *Lonely Are the Brave*, modernisation on the frontier, from automobiles to organised policing, does not represent a bright new dawn; rather, it casts a lengthening shadow over jaded individuals in the twilight of their lives. This was a classic Peckinpah refrain and, like much of his work, *High Country* is both a valediction (not without irony) for a fading breed and a judgement on a world they helped forge only to be spurned by in return.

The stars' synonymity with westerns – Randolph Scott had made more than 60 of them; Joel McCrea, 30 – infused their characters with a degree of gravitas the script alone could not provide. It also gives them a shared history – over and above the reminiscences, typical of Peckinpah, woven into the script – that makes for a powerful contrast between the bonhomie of the early scenes and the vituperative tone that develops later on. Steve Judd and Gil Westrum are town tamers turned old-timers – greying, rheumatic dinosaurs facing extinction at the turn of the 20th century. They reunite when Judd takes the job of escorting a shipment of gold from Coarsegold mining camp, high in the Sierras, down to the bank in bustling Hornitos – the centre of progress, where Judd is quickly made to feel out of place. He trades on his reputation, for those who remember it, for integrity and honour; Westrum embroiders his, posing as the Oregon Kid ("who single-handedly sent the infamous" – and apocryphal – "Omaha Gang to their graves") in a rigged carnival sideshow.

Judd, with his frayed cuffs and fading eyesight, sees this job as a chance to regain self-respect; Westrum, turned cynical with the advancing years,

disparages this aim. "What's that worth on the open market?" he asks rhetorically, and has designs on the gold itself. He enlists his snotty young partner, Heck Longtree, and hopes to persuade his old comrade, by force if necessary, that they deserve the bounty for their years of selfless service. It is another instance of the betrayal theme that was almost a constant in Peckinpah's films, from *The Deadly Companions* onwards: Westrum betrays Judd, and the values he holds dear; in a wider sense, the settled West has abandoned them both, sold them short. This, not malice, is the key to Westrum's motivation.

Along the way the trio are joined by Elsa, a farm girl in flight from her tyrannical father. They escort her to Coarsegold and her fiancé, the swaggering Billy Hammond (James Drury), who has four even scurvier brothers – "dry-gulchin' Southern trash" in the grand Peckinpah tradition. Much of the film from here takes Elsa's perspective: almost gang-raped by the Hammonds on her wedding night – a delirious sequence set in Coarsegold's rowdy house of pleasure – she is rescued by the heroes and led back to her home, where a reckoning with the Hammonds awaits. The journey becomes redemptive and transforming, with Elsa at its heart. Heck discovers nobility, falling for the girl and deserting Westrum for Judd, while the latter learns to bend his "ironbound" code of ethics. (These, Westrum reminds him, cost him the chance to settle down with a woman whom Elsa resembles, pointing to Judd's essential loneliness.) Conversely, it is the easygoing Westrum who becomes inflexible, his determination to steal the gold stiffening even as the amount diminishes. Judd took the job believing $250,000 was as stake; the real total comes to a little over $11,000, marking a depreciation in the value of his services, if not his honour.

top: The film was retitled for its UK release.
above: from left: Joel McCrea, Mariette Hartley and Ron Starr.

This was a deeply personal work for Peckinpah. Given a sympathetic producer and a relatively free hand – both rarities in his career – the director rewrote most of the dialogue in N.B. Stone's serviceable script, giving it that salty twang so characteristic of his best films, and studded the story with autobiographical details. Coarsegold was named after a real settlement Peckinpah had visited in his youth; the wedding ordeal was reportedly inspired by an anecdote his grandparents liked to share. Most significantly, the director turned Joel McCrea's character into a kind of idealised version of his father; Judd's much-quoted line, "All I want is to enter my house justified," was one of Peckinpah senior's sayings, borrowed from the Bible. Peckinpah also made what producer Richard Lyons called "the single most important structural change": in the film it is Judd who dies, not Westrum.[2] This violates the unwritten rule that malefactors should be punished (Westrum instead is redeemed by the death of his friend); hence, "Westrum's survival constitutes the movie's final refutation of the Manichaeism of the western."[3] On another level, it deepens the sense of loss for a time and place in which men like Judd could make a difference – by example, if not always in practice.

Judd's tragedy is that his principles, centred on honesty and the sanctity of contracts, prove to be fatally out of step with those that govern the evolving West.[4] Westrum has adapted more successfully. Coded as the devil on Judd's shoulder (he is attired in red long johns in one scene), he is the tempter in the wilderness, continually reminding his partner of the sacrifices they have made. His efforts to divert Judd from the path of righteousness culminate in an electrically charged confrontation in a glade where, jaws set firmly, the redoubtable old stagers exchange recriminations. It is a high point for both actors: McCrea venting Judd's wounded pride with Old Testament ferocity – an indignant Christ lashing out at Judas, to vary the biblical allusion; Scott's visage hardening with desperate resolve before he dismantles Westrum's sardonic facade with a seemingly throwaway line: "I don't sleep so good any more."

Whenever his characters took up entrenched positions, Peckinpah would shift the sand from beneath their feet, relishing the resultant irony. It is Westrum, for example, who engineers Elsa's release from her marriage vows, forcing the drunken judge in Coarsegold to lie about his credentials, whereas Steve, a respecter of law, would have left her fate up to a miners' court. It is the same with Elsa's father, a religious zealot determined to "keep the dirt away" from his daughter, railing against the iniquity of the wider world while suppressing (implied) incestuous desires. Even so, his warnings prove accurate when it comes to Coarsegold and, especially, the Hammonds, who "erupt… into his [Knudsen's] home like the rebellious instincts he fears", killing him, leaving his body in a praying position, and lying in wait for Judd and company.[5] Yet even the Hammonds cannot be taken for granted. When Judd and Westrum, now back in the fold, challenge them to a straight-up fight in the open, Billy rallies his siblings by evoking "family loyalty". It is a dynamic set piece, Peckinpah filming his heroes from an ennobling low angle as they advance purposefully, like the Wild Bunch, into the field of fire. Editor Frank Santillo uses flash cuts – soon to be a Peckinpah staple, of course – to create a montage of gunfire, grimaces and twisting, tumbling bodies.

above: from left: Joel McCrea, Randolph Scott, Ron Starr and Mariette Hartley.

Traditional yet transitional, *High Country* has been called "the grand finale to the classical western".[6] Peckinpah dextrously holds a number of contrasts in check: Edenic landscapes – shot by Lucien Ballard with an accent on autumnal shades – are offset by the corruption of Hornitos, the squalor of Coarsegold and the oppressive atmosphere of the farmstead; the worldliness of the heroes by the cloistered ignorance of Joshua Knudsen; their poise by the bestial cunning of the Hammonds. The casting carries on the theme of epochs colliding, with McCrea and Scott (who retired after filming) nurturing newcomers Mariette Hartley, sweet yet strong-willed, and Ronald Starr, rather callow in a standard role. Warren Oates and the rest of the Hammonds, for their part, represent Peckinpah's vital vision unleashed; they're like a pack of jackals, squabbling among themselves but united against the world. Oates makes the strongest impression as the simple-minded Henry, toting a raven like a white-trash Barnaby Rudge, holding off his brothers at knifepoint when they attempt to bathe him, shooting manically at chickens on Knudsen's farm. Peckinpah clearly adored these characters, but his respect is reserved for the veterans: Westrum, who rediscovers his sense of loyalty; Judd, a synonym for the mythic West of yesteryear. In retrospect, he represented the last stand of unsullied heroism in a Peckinpah western. Hereafter, as America's traumas intensified and the director's own travails mounted, such a notion would have seemed absurd. **KG**

footnotes

[1] *Sam Peckinpah: If They Move... Kill 'Em* (Faber, 1996).
[2] According to Peckinpah's sister, the famous closing shot of Judd, mortally wounded, looking back at the mountains before falling out of frame, was composed to resemble a photograph of their father.
[3] Terence Butler, *Crucified Heroes: The Films of Sam Peckinpah* (Gordon Fraser, 1979).
[4] McCrea's turn as a weathered Bat Masterson in *The Gunfight at Dodge City* (1959) now seems like a rehearsal for his role in *High Country*. Masterson's moral staunchness similarly sets him at odds with an undeserving society.
[5] Butler, *Crucified Heroes.*
[6] Jim Kitses, *Horizons West* (BFI, 2007).

Peckinpah's Peckerwood

L.Q. Jones Looks Back

A specialist in scraggly villains, native Texan L.Q. Jones often brought an almost feral vitality to his roles. His impressive CV (he was also a writer, producer and director in his time) includes films by the great western directors Budd Boetticher and Anthony Mann, but it is the five movies he made for Sam Peckinpah in which he made the strongest impression.

What put you on course for an acting career?

I was born. It sounds flippant. I don't mean that. In my family you could be a friendly neighbourhood rapist, but to be an actor – terrible, terrible, we couldn't allow that. I don't know… actors are born. You can teach a person technique, some of the niceties of the business, but if you're an actor, you're an actor, and you go from there.

How did Justus McQueen Jr. become L.Q. Jones?

My first picture was *Battle Cry* and the name of the character I played was L.Q. Jones. The studio wanted to change it and, hell, I didn't care as long as the cheques were there.

You worked extensively in television westerns – *Cheyenne, Annie Oakley, Wichita Town, Laramie* – at the tail end of the Fifties. Did you find the process of working on small-screen westerns markedly different from making features?

How the hell do I explain this? The two are the same, movies and television, except in television you don't have too much time to think, which is probably a blessing. To me there is no difference. The only difference is that you have to move quicker. You must be more attuned to what you're doing.

L.Q. Jones (standing far right) with Robert Ryan (standing centre), Strother Martin (standing far left) and the "egg-sucking, chicken-stealing gutter trash" on the trail of The Wild Bunch.

In 1958, you worked with Budd Boetticher, playing Pecos Hill in *Buchanan Rides Alone*. What memories do you have of the film and the director?

He was totally insane, for Chrissakes! I'll just tell you the way he was. I'd never worked for him before. His lady love at the time was Karen Steele. Lovely lady, very talented. They got in an argument – I mean really fierce – and my suite was next to theirs and I could hear it plainly. They were just this side of killing each other [laughs], which was normal for them, for Chrissakes. After about 15 or 20 minutes there was a knock at my door and there she was. She no longer had a room and I tried to get her one, but they were full up. I said, "To hell with it, sleep in my room for Chrissakes," and I slept on the sofa. Well, the next day Budd found out from her that she spent the night with me and I damn near had to kill him to get him to calm down. After about 15 minutes of screaming and threats, we went back to the fun we were having and got on with our business.

I really don't believe that there was anyone in our business, including Peckinpah, who could do more with less money than Budd Boetticher. If you gave him a big budget he'd probably have a heart seizure and not be able to finish it, but he was so good at wringing every little bit of juice out of it. He was marvellous. He did not make cheap westerns; he made tight-budget westerns.

If you look at the stuff he did and the actors that he used, he realised that was the way to get there. John Ford said, "How do you make such good pictures?" and Budd said, "All I do is get a great script and great actors and stay the hell out of the way." He would set things up so that the people he was dealing with realised they were part of the direction of the piece. You did not feel the slightest bit squeamish about suggesting something to Budd. He realised that's the way your crews work better. And he worked that out early about actors and made very good pictures for very tight money.

You had quite a substantial role and spent a lot of screen time with a bona fide western icon, Randolph Scott. What did you gain from this experience?

I guess there was a better human being in the world than Randy, but I'd be damned if I knew who it would be. He was a gentleman. He had more money than God and almost that much talent. He was a joy to be around, to work with. I did two, maybe three pictures with him. Of course I did *Ride the High Country* with him and Joel [McCrea] and they were two of the best men God ever put together. He had a sense of humour. When we started the piece, only Randy and I were working the first week. No other actor showed up. He was getting on a bit in age and he was working his fanny off. We were shooting in Old Tucson. He and I were sitting against one of the adobe structures and Randy was trying to get his breath, because he had been working just constantly in front of the camera. The company had moved off to do some insert shots and they were about three or four blocks away, and along came a little lady with two kids. They must have been about four or five or something like that, and she was dragging them along and they didn't know what the hell they were doing. She spied us and came on the dead run. She was screaming, "Oh my God, I never thought I'd ever get to meet ya! This is one of the greatest pleasures of my life. You're the greatest thing in the business. I've always wanted my children to meet Joel McCrea." At that point Randy collapsed in absolute laughter, signed everything she stuck in front of him and then went back to sleep. That was Randy.

It's one of your few heroic roles. Do you prefer to play a good guy or a bad guy in westerns?

It's always more fun to play the heavy. You can do what you wanna do. You're not saying the crappy line. When I started out they were grooming me for better things.

At Warners I was doing the good guy and the love interest, and that was the most boring time I ever had in the motion picture business. They never let me play a heavy. I complained to Mr. Warner and the executives but they just said, "L.Q., hit your marks, say your line, pick up your cheque and shut up." It got to be where it was tough, and it took almost seven years until I got a heavy role in [TV series] *The Rebel*. I got nominated for an Emmy, and then they wouldn't let me do anything but heavies. But it's more fun for me to do those parts.

You worked with three of the great American directors of westerns: Anthony Mann (*Cimarron*), Budd Boetticher (*Buchanan Rides Alone*) and Sam Peckinpah (*Ride the High Country; Major Dundee; The Wild Bunch; The Ballad of Cable Hogue; Pat Garrett and Billy the Kid*). How would you summarise their different attitudes to the genre? Who do you think was the most radical?

That's hard to answer, because the three that you mentioned were all busy directors, all had good careers. Slightly different in their approach. Sam's forte, and people don't realise it, was his attention to detail. I have never, ever seen anybody like that. I have worked for maybe 300 directors, but no one paid that much attention or was that sincere about it. Many of them say they do, but they don't live up to it. On *The Wild Bunch* he fired our prop master about halfway through the picture because he didn't count the beans on my plate. The long shot and the close-up were maybe five or six weeks in between, but he miscounted the beans and Sam fired him. You're an insane man if you fire your prop master. There goes your picture. But that's what Sam wanted to do. Sam was good at that. He was a better writer than he was a director. He had unusual strength in casting. He had his stock company, but his stars, if you look at them, they would normally be in other types of movies. Chuck Heston [star of *Major Dundee*] almost killed him with a sword because he got so mad at him, and I've never seen Chuck get upset, much less furious. Sam understood what made Chuck the actor that he was. He understood what Bill Holden needed, Richard Harris… the list is endless.

The other two directors were very good, but they had different approaches. Budd was better at tight budgets. Mann was better at getting what was inside of an actor, although Sam was pretty hard to beat at that as well. It's very tough to come up with a definitive answer.

How did you end up in Sam Peckinpah's orbit? How did you get to know him?

Well, I first worked for Sam when he was an assistant, not a director, and he said, "You're great. We're going to work together." I said, "You bet." You hear that all the time. I would guess six months later he called up and we went to work. I think Warren [Oates] and I made the most films for him, so if I tell you Sam was crazy, that kind of explains something about me. I was able to get along with him. We came to terms on *Major Dundee*. Sam's approach to pictures was, on the first day he would get everyone worked up so that nobody would talk to anybody else on the set. The producer wouldn't talk to the director, the director wouldn't talk to the stunt people, the stunt people wouldn't talk to the actors. It was furious. It would go on that way for about three days, and Sam would put it back together with him as the father figure, and everything was fine. But if you notice in his later films, something like *Pat Garrett and Billy the Kid*, you notice how uneven the show is. There are two or three sensational sequences and the rest of it is crap. It's because Sam took it apart but he no longer had the strength to put it back together, so it was every man for himself.

We came to an understanding quickly. On *Dundee* I was petrified of him, I guess, like everybody else. During the river crossing when there's a huge fight going on, they're chasing Warren Oates, Ben Johnson and myself down the river. Finally I heard, "Cut." Sam was talking almost under his breath and I thought, "Oh, someone's in deep caca." We started back. Now, Sam was on a tower that was mounted in the water on railroad rails, so they could move back and forth on the water and cover the fight. He was about 10 or 11 feet above the rest of us. We started back and Sam was saying, "You dirty…" He thought of every expletive in the book. "I'm telling you, you're the sorriest excuses." The three of us! He got worse and he got filthier and he was nearly screaming. When we got to the tower I'd had enough of it, and I stood up on my horse and started climbing the tower. I slung over the railing by the side and grabbed him by the shirt front and said, "Peckinpah, you don't have enough talent to direct me to the men's room." Everything froze, everyone stopped breathing – they wanted to know how far he was going to throw me or whether I was going to leave by limo or bus. We stood there for about 15 or 20 seconds and he said, "Ah, it's just a joke," and off we went, and after that I realised that was the only way you could stay alive with Peckinpah. If you let him get inside your head, he'd kill you; otherwise you kick him on the defence, and I guess I was the only one who knew how to do that.

Did you feel a sense of loyalty towards him in any way?

I'm not saying I disliked him. He was hugely talented, but he was also just hag-ridden with problems. He didn't help himself. Everyone who worked with him was aware of the problems and almost all of us adored the man, because he was great fun to work with if you could stay alive. He was so imaginative. He kept things moving and, by the same token, because he was so imaginative, he could give you things to do. But Sam very seldom told you what to do, because you had to figure it out. He had a stock company. We were used to him and we'd figure out what he wanted, and even though we missed it a couple of times, we at least tried. He appreciated that, but he hated to tell you what to do. The challenge was so great. He scared Strother Martin. He was practically a basket case by the time he got through working with Sam, but Strother did some of the best work he's ever done. Sam was good at that.

I suffered for him as a human being. Sam was so beat upon by his imagination that those of us who really, really liked him almost got as bad as he was trying to straighten him out. It worked a bit at the beginning when he was just drinking, but then he added dope, because it kept him going. If you left Sam alone he'd work 24 hours a day on a picture. So, how long can a human body take that before it starts to pull in here and tuck in there? We tried to help, but most of the time it didn't work because Sam was so out to lunch. You could only help him so much. He was very clever in the way he cast; he relied on a number of people. Then when he started wandering off and he was not using those people, he had a great deal of trouble. It fell on him. We were going to do a bunch of pictures together. He wanted me to produce – of course, with my money. I got rid of that thought right off the bat.

In *Ride the High Country* you played Sylvus Hammond, one of the Hammond brothers, the first of Peckinpah's gangs of "redneck peckerwoods". Sam loved having groups of unsavoury characters to counterbalance his antiheroes. Did you see any differences in style between you and your brothers – especially John Davis Chandler and Warren Oates – and old timers like Randolph Scott and Joel McCrea?

Oh, of course, yeah. We were in the business for a different reason. Randy and Joel got started back in the Twenties and Thirties, when it was a way to make a living when everyone else was starving to death. Each generation of actors picks up the same references but every 15 years or so that all changes, and we brought new things to it. But half the time I stood in absolute awe. These were people I'd only seen on the screen, and here I was face to face with them, trying to stay alive in a sequence or a scene.

Sam Peckinpah (*above, left*) on the set of *Major Dundee* with Charlton Heston and (*opposite, bottom left*) with Richard Harris.

We all came at it from slightly different angles, yet those of us who ended up working round Sam a lot had sort of the same impetus: attention to detail. And that was everything you did – what you ate, what you wore, the way you spoke, the rhythm, how you rode a horse. We learnt from [the older actors], and maybe we taught them a few things. We all kind of approached it in a homogenised way, yet even in that you can stand out. If you watch [our movies] carefully, Warren, Slim [Pickens], Strother, me… we specialised in certain things in the business and, although we seemed to work together a lot, you'll notice that there's always a standout characteristic. There was a difference between Warren and myself or Slim and Strother. We learnt that's the way to make the canopy come alive. Be the same, but be different at the same time. Very difficult to do at times.

Did you spend time with Warren Oates?

Oh yeah. When we were doing *The Wild Bunch* there was only one motel. They called it The Country Club. It had a golf course, if you didn't mind shooting past dead cattle and snakes. That's where Sam was. That's where they were doing the editing. The rest of us were around in private homes. In my house, [stunt coordinator] Archie Butler was in the bedroom closest to the street, number two bedroom was Ben Johnson, Warren Oates was in number three and I was in number four. So we spent a lot of time together and Warren and I became really good friends. We ended up doing six or seven shows together. Oddly enough, in many of those we played brothers. He was having a great deal of trouble at the time with his wife, because she was unhappy that he was spending so much time shooting pictures. She needed someone around the house, for Chrissakes. When he finished shooting in the afternoon, he rented a car or had a chauffeur drive him to the airport, which was about 60 miles away, then he'd catch a plane to a bigger city, then catch a bigger plane to fly to LA to see her. He'd have 10 or so hours and then have to reverse that. He'd make the round trip almost every day when we were on location.

Can you cast your mind back to *Ride the High Country* and the scene where your character is shot point blank by Ron Starr. It's the first time in a Peckinpah film that you see that change of direction with the violence – you're staring at the man who's killed you for what seems an age. Could you give us an idea of what you were all trying to achieve with that scene?

Ron Starr was not a favourite of Sam, but he was a nice kid. He was trying to get along, making a living, but he got on Sam's bad side. Nothing he did pleased Sam. It didn't make any difference. I was trying to work out how to please both of them and get a shot that maybe would help the picture, and finally I worked out the way for me to do it was to be absolutely furious that I'd just been shot, thinking, "How the hell did that happen?" I thought that would make Sam happy. I explained to Ron what we were going to do and he said, "Oh yeah, fine, I'd love to do it," and we did it that way. Can you see in your mind the terrain where we were shooting?

It's very rugged. Where was it shot?

It was filmed here [in Los Angeles] as a matter of fact, because we started out on location and then they pulled the plug without telling Sam. We came down one morning and the buses and the cars were going back to the studio, so we shot that scene in Bronson Canyon. Sam was so pissed. Imagine, we're shooting on the side of a hill. My back is against a big chunk of rock and in front of me are thousands of shards of jagged rock. So, at the very top of the screen, Ron makes his appearance. He sees me, I see him, he shoots me. I'm so stunned that I can't quite conceive it. I'm really pissed off, but it doesn't make any difference, I'm dead. I take a long, long time to fall over on my face down the hill. I slid with my face down in the gravel maybe a foot and a half and Sam said, "Do it again." Do it again? They put stuff on my face for 15 minutes to staunch the flow of blood. We shot that fucking scene six times. My face was absolute hamburger. The sixth take was the same as the first, but Sam had to do it again. When the scene started I weighed 180 pounds. When it was over I weighed 170. I left skin, blood, bone, all the way down the hill, but we finally got it. It worked well for the picture.

There was a saying on that picture, "Take a Hammond to lunch." We were ostracised by the rest of the actors and crew. We were put well away from them, so most of us were pissed when we came to work in the morning because the rest of the crew were having fun and we got the short end of the stick. That was the way Sam did it. And as you pointed out, there's generally always a gang of miscreants rather than one heavy and it all sprang from, "Take a Hammond to lunch."

Let's move on to *Major Dundee*. It seems to be making a comment on divisions within American society – North v South, black v white, working class v ruling class. What are your feelings about the film and what Sam was trying to achieve?

Well, you have to give Sam a bit of a break. That was his first big-budget picture. He had done *The Deadly Companions*, where he had spit for money; not a bad picture, because of the cast. Then we get to *Ride the High Country* where we had an adequate budget, a tight budget. Now, all of a sudden, here's all of this money lying on the table and Sam is not used to that. As long as you are watching your budget you will be careful with the way you shoot, careful to do a scene so that four of you will look like 40. He now had this huge budget; we were using the Mexican cavalry, at least 200 of them. Look what the costs are doing. You're not feeding five actors and 50 crew members; you're feeding 500, because you've got all of these people coming in and 150 in the crew. So while you've got a whole lot more money in your pocket, you're also getting huge bills that you really don't think about. So Sam is thinking, "Wait a minute, I had more freedom when I was doing a cheap picture, for Chrissakes."

I hate to say it, but [producer Jerry] Bresler didn't help him. They weren't out to get Sam, but the producers wanted to impose certain things because they had raised

the money to make the picture; they had put the deal together. Sam didn't give a fig about that. He wanted the picture done the way he saw it, and if it took stomping on your feet as the producer, he didn't hesitate a second. The picture was everything. Bresler didn't realise that and he was fired later by the head of the studio because of this. In the end he came to me and said, "What do I do?" and I said, "Prayer! It's the only thing open to you, because you weren't smart enough to call the people he worked with when he did *Ride the High Country* or *Deadly Companions,* and they would have told you, 'He's going to make a picture. Don't get in his way. Help him.'" Instead they ran around screaming about what a terrible job he was doing.

Now the pressure gets strong. People from the studio show up and they want Sam replaced because he is not following studio rules. The picture's good, really good, but we've got to keep it so that we control it. So Chuck steps up to the plate and, bless his heart, he says, "I want Sam to stay on the picture and to show my good faith I won't take any money for doing the picture." Marvellous! And he says to us – we're all his good friends by now – "They're not really going to do that," and he talks to his agent that night who says, "You're a blithering idiot. They've already called me and taken you up on it." And the rest of us said, "We won't stay either," but they didn't care. All they cared about was Chuck. If you look at the picture, it's so uneven. There are scenes in it that should not be there; the action and the acting are marvellous, and then a bunch of horseshit scenes will follow because they shot them and added them to the picture.

There is one shot – I was watching them do it – when we've escaped. We're the Confederate soldiers. Dundee has caught us and brought us back, we're at the fort before that big scene where everybody is on the ground listening to Chuck. Remember in *The Wild Bunch* where they set fire to the straw that burnt up the scorpion? That's telling you what's going to happen in the picture. Go back to *Dundee* and they cut from us screaming, hollering and beating to two little kids – a boy and a girl, she's about three, he's two and a half. They're dirty, the snot's running out of his nose, their clothes are just terrible, no shoes, and they're looking at something off screen. You begin to hear a noise grow and, if you look carefully at the boy's feet, there's little puffs of dust. All of a sudden there's screaming, and you cut from the faces of these children to Dick Harris, Warren, Ben [Johnson] and myself being dragged along, and we go sweeping by and you go back to the little kids. Absolutely gorgeous images that never made it to the screen because Bresler said, "No, we don't want that type of a picture."

Just to pinpoint one of the scenes in *Dundee*, there's the moment where Warren Oates, who's playing your brother, is condemned to death having tried to escape. You project some strong emotions at that point while remaining silent. Can you share any memories of filming it?

Oh, you bet, because Warren's a hell of an actor and he did a hell of a job. There was this gorgeous waterfall behind us where we shot that. We're all arranged around the rock with the waterfall and lake behind us and Warren is brought in from the other direction. We had hell to get to that place. We were driving across areas that had no roads. We made our own roads. We were doing this for about five or six days, because that's where Sam wanted it. Look at the position – look at what it's telling you. Chuck loved it, Sam loved it. That's one of the great scenes in that picture – and there ain't that many – but everybody is working perfectly and Sam is telling you no matter how pretty the day is, no matter how warm you feel, somebody's ass is in trouble. It happened to be Warren's character. He was saying the same thing as all the rest of us thought but had not been able to bring to fruition. In my particular case there's that, plus the fact we are brothers.

Yes, you look very conflicted. It's a fine scene for the stock company.

Right, I was absolutely deadpan. If that character gives away anything, he's got to go over the top and he's going to get killed, too, from trying to step in. It's a beautifully orchestrated scene, and beautifully shot. Like the kids with the puffs of dust coming up from the ground, Sam will give you a very simple story but he'll catch your attention with things like that.

Go forward to *The Wild Bunch*, remember when the Bunch go to see the Mexican general and Jaime [Sanchez] has shot the girl who has taken up with the general? After that, what happens? It's dark and you hear a chant. You see all of the people who are willing to kill you at the drop of a hat, but you hear a chant and you look up and there's a bunch of old ladies. What the hell are they doing? You can't really tell until they get a little closer and they've got a stretcher and a beautiful lady's body is on it, candle-lit. Lucien [Ballard] was the one who showed Sam what to do, how to shoot it – if you look at it, it's a cinematographer's shot. Sam would listen if he admired what you were. In fact, Lucien told him to stick it up his ass and wouldn't work with him for about three pictures, and finally had to come back because Sam begged him so much. Everybody I knew who worked on Sam's pictures absolutely stood in awe of what he did. You felt so sorry seeing him killing himself. He saw a booger behind every tree. He was fighting unbelievable odds; it was affecting his thought and the more he got into it, the worse he got. He got to where he would not trust producers even for a second, because they'd short-changed him so many times.

Can you confirm that you directed a western in 1964 using your real name, called *The Devil's Bedroom*?

[Laughs] Oh yeah, OK. I try to forget that.

I think it's quite a rare film.

Very rare, thank God! It may well be one of the worst pictures ever made. I think our entire budget for the picture was like $27,000. You spend more than that on paperclips when you're making a picture, for Chrissakes. It was based on a true story. It was with Dick Jones and John Lupton, both of whom were tremendous actors. Alvy Moore is in it, Morgan Woodward. It's so bad. We shot it with household bulbs; the sound is erratic. We got back here and we had not seen any of the rushes. We then finally got a chance to see them and they were all slightly out of focus, so when I tried to add something to the picture to help it, I had to find a photographer who could shoot slightly out of focus, and that's hard to do. I finally found one. That was chosen by a number of movie magazines as one of the 10 best pictures of the year, and that'll tell you something about critics. The out-of-focus shots were so bad, but I finally got to talk to a couple of critics and they said, "Oh no, that's what you *meant* to do." They think that it's so bad, it couldn't be accidental – it had to be done that way to make a point. So I shut up and let them think what they want to think.

You appeared in Ted Post's *Hang 'Em High* with Clint Eastwood, who'd just come back from Italy after westerns with Sergio Leone. What did you and your colleagues think of Europeans making westerns?

Well, they were certainly different, but I don't like them. I don't dislike them; I just don't care for them. But things have got to change. You can't do the same thing all of the time, but we had got used to a particular style and that was not present in what they did. One of the things that broke your back [when shooting westerns] was just getting the dialogue. The sound mike was on the end of an extendable, cranked-out fishing pole that would reach out about eight or 10 feet. You could always spot the soundman, because he had huge bulging muscles from running about, covering you [with the mike] without leaving a shadow on your face. Very tough to do. Very tough for the actors to be heard under a lot of conditions. Now you get the Europeans and there's no lip-synch because they're not saying the words [while shooting], they're just moving their mouths. They can plug in anything they want in the way of dialogue – and rightly so – because the audience has now accepted the fact that there's no lip-synch. That bothered us. We worked our fannies off, you understand? And now all of a sudden no one's paying any attention to it. You had to take what we thought with a grain of salt, because we had to adjust real quickly. I worked in Europe [the western *The Hunting Party* was shot in Spain] and it was pretty hard to do, because you had to act as if you were saying something. It's tough to work in those conditions, but a good actor accommodates, sees what's got to be done. You're not there to be comfortable; you're there to do a job, so you do it the best you can and hope that works.

Did you spend any time with Clint Eastwood? Did you have any idea he was going to be a director of note?

Clint and I worked a lot together on *Rawhide*. I was a regular on that for a couple of years. I knew Clint quite well. Nice man. He was fun to work with, very quiet; still is. Loves what he does. I don't like what he directs, but I'm sure that doesn't give him sleepless nights, for Chrissakes. The best thing he ever did, in my opinion, was *Play Misty for Me*. He did a great job, but I don't like the way he does westerns. But if I'm so goddam smart, how come I ain't rich? It puts me into perspective. Clint was always the thinker, very serious about the business. He trained very carefully with Don Siegel. Sam was working as an assistant to Don when we crossed paths early on. Don was really a good director, but he was given a lot of films to do – and a lot of crap.

He learnt to say, "To hell with you," and dedicate himself to what he was doing, and Clint liked that. Clint's moved himself up into that position and I take my hat off to him. He's done a hell of a job. He's a pleasure to work with.

Let's get on to *The Wild Bunch*. How long did it take to film the opening sequence at Starbuck?

Well, let's see. It took four months to shoot the picture and the robbery took altogether about two weeks. No, it was longer than that. You remember stunts like the man going through the window? That took weeks to plan and set up. Do you know what a hamper is on a motion picture? It's for the laundry – the clothes you're going to use. A very busy picture would have two or three hampers for the laundry; maybe five if it's hideously busy. I think we had maybe 49 hampers with uniforms in them.

Sam learnt very quickly that shooting this picture relied on clothing. That sounds very simple, but how do you do it? You have, say, 45 people and they all get shot, stabbed and blown up, and every time you're doing that you're taking something from the wardrobe. You may have the shot, but what can you clothe your extras in? You've ruined your wardrobe, there's nothing there. Sam went off with the rest of us and left Gordy [Dawson, wardrobe supervisor] in charge and he had a system whereby no matter what he tore up during the day, he could send to the laundry and the seamstress and have it back in the morning. A large amount of the stuff you see in the big fight in *The Wild Bunch* was directed not by Sam but by Gordy Dawson. He was there shooting for months while the rest of us were filming the rest of the picture, and it worked beautifully.

There's no better man than Gordy. I've worked with him on about three or four jobs and he's very talented, very knowledgeable. He helped them make that picture. The wardrobe made the whole thing. He put it together in such a way that Sam could get on with what he had to do while the wardrobe was being redone. It was a brilliant concept, and Sam and Gordy worked it out. You don't hear of things like that. I directed a show where I shot 27 pages with multiple cameras. We did masters, two-shots, approaches, entrances, close-ups, extreme close-ups, over the shoulder and departure shots. Twenty-seven pages in one take. You can't do that! But I did it. Nobody ever talks about it. Nobody really talks about what Peckinpah and Gordy did [with the wardrobe] on The *Wild Bunch*. If you took that away from it, my God, you'd lose half the picture.

What about some of the physical action and the stunts?

Remember the bridge? They started on that about two months before production began. When it came to shooting, I was sitting in a chair by the shore. They had sprung cables across the river and had put a barge along these cables [for the camera], so it went from side to side to get the shots that Sam wanted of this bridge blowing up. That's one of the climaxes of the picture. I was sitting

Claiming the spoils in Starbuck: Jones as T.C., with Strother Martin as Coffer, in *The Wild Bunch*.

there, the barge was right there and I was talking with Sam and [producer] Phil Feldman, both looking at me. And then I looked at them and said, "Incidentally Sam, your bridge just collapsed." "Hahaha! That's funny," and then he looked round and sure enough the damn bridge had collapsed, which meant, three months into the production, we had to start all over again and redo the bridge so we could blow it up later. But I knew Sam. I knew what he was going to do. One of the touches of Sam's direction, and if you watch his pictures again you'll see, is that everyone in the scene is in the action. Normally if you have a scene with five, six or 50 people you'll start with some of them and then see them in the beginning, the middle and the end. Now look at Sam's pictures. You see them at the beginning, you see them at the end and you see them all in between. Everybody is involved in that action and I've never seen a man do that. Even Ford could not do that, but Sam could do it automatically. He added things like that. Then there was his ability to write, so the corrections that were made really worked for the picture, plus his attention to detail. These were the things that made him, but they were also the things that ate him alive when things started going bad.

In *The Wild Bunch* you play T.C., one of the rather unpleasant bounty hunters, alongside Strother Martin as Coffer. There's a slight campiness about you both. Did you bring that to the characters?

That is not accidental. We were looking at what we wanted to do and how we wanted to do it. Look at all the carnage that we followed. There is 10 minutes of nothing but constant action. How do you make a mark and get your character across? And I finally decided, and Strother agreed, yes, a little bit of campiness, but also a little bit of gay. These guys have got something going on between them that you never see but, by God, you can tell that it's there.

The very first day Bill Holden came on the scene in Starbuck, we were shooting Strother and me running out to fight over the bodies. It took us two or three hours to get everything set up, then up rolled a limo and out came Bill. He came over to the camera, over to Sam and they were shaking hands and hugging. Bill was talking to people, and Sam called for a chair and put it next to the camera and we got all that crap out of the way. Sam never told us what to do at all, he just said, "I want you to end up here so the camera can cover you." If you notice when we start to run across the street – three of us, Albert Dekker, Strother and myself – we come out of a building and the camera stays on all of us. But to clear myself, I realised I had to go to my right, which was camera left, and I had to go quite a ways to get to my mark, but the camera stayed with Strother and Albert Dekker – I nearly go out of the shot before I end up at the spot where we're fighting over the boots and the people we killed. We finished the shot and Sam said, "OK. That's a cut," and the instant he said that, Bill jumped up and almost ran to his limousine. Sam said, "What's wrong? What's the matter?" Bill looked back and said, "Sam, is that the way you're going to shoot the rest of the picture?" Sam said, "Yes." Bill said, "I'm going to my room and start studying that fucking script," and he ran off and left us.

There were a lot of stuntmen involved with this film. Were there any standout incidents involving any of them?

Oh, every day. I think we had about 27 stuntmen; normally you have three or four. One thing I'm sure you'll notice if you watch at the beginning, when the fight has really started and all the bullets are flying around, there's a horse that runs into a little girl and stands on top of her. The idiot that was riding the horse was a stuntman; he was so bad that if you mentioned his name on the set you had to put five dollars into a kitty. At the end of the week we probably had about $150 from cursing him. We took it out and the party started Saturday night. Anyway, he was sitting on the damn horse, which was dancing on that girl. Ben Johnson saw this and, being a person of bravery and savvy about horses, realised that the only way you could move it was by lowering your shoulder and running into the horse. Do you know how to ride a horse?

No, never tried it.

Well, the guy who was riding the horse, if he had just released the reins, it would have gotten off the girl instantly, because it can't stand anything on its feet. But Ben saw that, so he slammed into the horse and knocked it off the girl. She was very badly injured; ambulance came and picked her up and took her to a hospital. Now, the girl was an ex-wife of Emilio Fernandez, who had killed a man. He carried a weapon and I've never seen a barrel that long on a six-shooter. It had to be 14 inches. And he used to shoot people with it! They got her in the hospital and Sam, as only Sam would do, he got a bunch of us – Ben, Warren, a couple of guys who could play the guitar – and we went to visit her in the hospital. We raised such a stink playing and singing for her that the nurses had to ask us to leave [laughs].

So we left and Sam wanted a drink, so we stopped. It was now about three o' clock in the afternoon. It was about 12 o'clock at night when we got through drinking, and we were about to go back home through another part of town where the people weren't the nicest in the world. Sam was in the front seat with the chauffeur; Ben and I were in the back seat. Sam wanted to get another beer and I ripped out some of the lining of the roof of the car trying to keep him from going in this slush bar. He got away from me and went in the bar. Ben and I both went in after him. He was already at the bar and ordered a beer. Sam took a swig from it, spat it in the bartender's face and asked him if he'd been pissing in the beer. The fight was on. About five or ten minutes later, Ben and I were fighting for our lives with knives and broken bottles, and we were backed up in the corner with a big table behind us, which has been turned over. We couldn't go any further and it looked like the end of our lives. We looked around and Sam was no longer fucking there. He'd left, got in the car and gone home. Ben and I fought for our lives for about 30 minutes. We barely made it!

Can you understand why people were upset – even shocked – by the level of violence in *The Wild Bunch*?

Of course. We were, too, but once you got to know Sam, you realised that he detested violence and he thought that if he rubbed your nose in it enough, it would get so you would dislike it enough not to become involved in it. The action was intense. We were on the picture for a few months and Jimmy [Jim Sheppard], one of the greatest stuntmen of all time, had made enough money in three days of work to buy a brand new Cadillac convertible, which was very expensive. Sam worked 24 hours straight for three days, so the union took that into account and these guys were getting thousands of dollars per stunt. For a stunt you'd usually get $20,000 for, all of a sudden you're getting $45,000. What's the film he made with Dustin Hoffman?

That's *Straw Dogs*.

Yes, *Straw Dogs*. The rape scene in that film is sickening to watch. Sam was trying to make a case against it and he did it in his own way. A lot of people didn't believe that. I can understand that, but I know what Sam wanted to say, having worked with him for so long and learnt to listen to what he was trying to say. The man was brilliant. It was a shame that he had so many problems. A lot of people have problems and they overcome them. Sam didn't seem able to, or was not interested enough to do so, and it killed him.

As a matter of fact, R.G. Armstrong and I were supposed to be in *Straw Dogs*. It was originally going to be called *Siege at Trencher's Farm*. We were going to go because we could speak with British accents, but Sam decided it was going to be too expensive, so we didn't do it.

Let's move on to *Pat Garrett and Billy the Kid*...

I did the part of Black Harris, and that's the scene where Slim Pickens gets killed. It's a marvellous scene. I wanted to do something else at the time but Sam called me so many times that I said, "OK." I called my agent and told him what I wanted and my agent said, "You're joking. They won't pay that sort of money." And I said, "That's what I want and if they don't give it to me, then screw them." He called me back 30 minutes later and said, "My God, they're paying it." I was making a pile of money. Slim and I went down on the plane together. In this business if someone is making a pile of money like that, they meet you at the airport, put you in a limo, go to wardrobe, drive you out to the location and you change in the limousine. You get there, Sam tells you what to do, you shoot it and then you're in the limo again going back to the airport. So, you've earned all this money, but you did it in the perfect time without any overtime. So Slim and I went down there and I didn't see Sam for more than 10 days. Then he called me and said, "L.Q., they're having some trouble with wardrobe. Will you help Gordy [Dawson]?" I'm making more money than half of the company and I'm working on wardrobe! I love wardrobe and I love Gordy, so I started doing it, but it didn't make any sense. I didn't understand until at the end of two weeks Sam sent the limousine for me. I went out and I got on the set and they told me to wait at the trailer for Sam. Sometimes when you see someone you know, you look at him and you say to yourself, "That person's going to die." That's how I felt when I saw Sam – that he wouldn't be with us the next day. But he was, even though he was so ill that we barely got the sequence that we did with Jimmy [Coburn], Slim, Katy [Jurado] and myself. I'm on the roof fighting it out with Jimmy, and Katy and Slim go down and he's dying by the water.

Did you actually hang around to watch that part of the sequence being filmed?

Oh good God yes! It was the best thing Slim ever did. I was sitting there because I had to. It's a long story but [earlier in my career] I had wanted to direct a picture but couldn't raise enough money [for the script rights]. Later, I got a call from Sam saying, "I need some money".

The memorable death of Sylvus Hammond in *Ride the High Country*.

"What for?" He said, "I've found this fantastic story," and he starts to tell me. And he gets to about three lines in and I finish it for him, because it was the one they had offered me. He had never paid me back and I was there trying to get that money. But anyway, you bet I was there. It was an incredible scene. You recall it was almost dark. They had about 30 minutes to shoot and they took a gamble that they could get it done. And Slim and Katy were so good, and I was there trying to get my money out of Sam, which was not successful, but I was rewarded by watching Slim do the job and he did it marvellously.

There's a line in the film that your character says: "Us old boys oughtn't be doing this to each other." It pretty much sums up the mood of the whole movie.

Yes, I wrote that line and I felt it worked well. Jimmy was so good [in that scene], but that was just a precursor to the beautiful death of Slim at the creek. That for me is the most complete sequence in *Pat Garrett and Billy the Kid* – and they are few and far between – because Slim understood Sam and what he wanted so well.

Have you seen the version that was released in the Eighties based on Peckinpah's edit?

As a matter of fact, I did the voiceover for the trailer. It was a mistake to do it the way he did it. He was indulging himself. Well, I say it was a mistake, that's not all true, because he was being hustled so hard and he was so ill. The picture doesn't work for me, but the casting is marvellous. I remember that Sam was sitting there with Kris Kristofferson. I was talking with them, and they decided that they liked my character so much that he wasn't going to die, which meant we would have had to go back and reshoot about a third of the picture. That thought lasted about five or six hours until half of the studio said, "He's dead! Get on with it!" That was Sam then. He really was in terrible shape.

Going back to just after *The Wild Bunch*, you made *The Ballad of Cable Hogue*, which was very different. Can you describe the shoot and what Peckinpah was like at the time?

Well, everybody talks about *The Wild Bunch,* but for me that is only the third best picture Sam did. The first was *Ride the High Country*, the second was *The Ballad of Cable Hogue*. We did it under the worst conditions possible. The story is about the lack of water, and the night before we started shooting the rain was so heavy it was a wash-out. In the area where we were shooting, water was supposed to be the most expensive thing in the world, but in the morning we went out to the location and as far as the eye could see it was a lake. It may only have been about an inch deep, but water was everywhere. What the hell could we do? The whole idea of the story was gone. So, Sam was not a very happy camper. Jason [Robards], Strother and I just commiserated with our eyes, the crew started filing off and the make-up man, who had worked with Sam for ages, was nice enough to pat him on the shoulder and say, "Don't worry Sam, we'll get you through it." He walked off and Sam called the studio and said, "Put his ass on the bus." He didn't even get to open his make-up kit and he was fired! On that picture he fired somewhere in the neighbourhood of 65-70 per cent of the cast and crew. Sam fired me five times in one day. It got so bad that they kept a limousine on the set all day to take people back to the hotel and then to the airport, and there was another limousine at the airport to transport incoming crew and cast to the hotel and then to the set, so they could be fired the next day.

The first shot of the picture was in the laundry room of the hotel. It had been converted into a soundstage. But it was raining all the time. We started later in the day, at 6.30 in the evening, because it would rain at night and be bone dry by then, but then thunderstorms would start. We were behind, we could not get a shot, and Sam was going insane. In the end, though, we finished. I had gone on to [film] *The McMasters* and Strother had gone home, and Sheila [Clague], the production secretary, called and said, "We need you for a shoot on Saturday afternoon." I said, "I can't do it, because that's our production day and I'm the centre of a scene along with Jack Palance. I can't leave." Sam called me and I told him the same thing. I said, "Well, Sam, you can scream all you like. You can call the producer." I gave him the number and an hour later the producer called and said, "I'll agree to anything as long as you get this idiot off my phone. We'll finish at noon so you can fly over to the shoot."

We flew over – we almost crashed because there was a thunderstorm, but we finally got there. The limo was waiting for me, and in the limo we had wardrobe and a make-up person. We got to the set, Strother was there and Lucien [Ballard] said, "We've got five minutes left, maybe six, that's it, and we're shutting down for the day". Sam really got us there for the party, but he told us what to do for the shot and it was the first sequence of the picture, where we're leaving Jason in the desert to die. It's the part where we've stolen the mule, and we do the shot and Strother screws up. Just one of those things. So we hurry, the light's going, we do it again and Sam says [low voice], "Cut." We're about a block's distance away and you can't hear him, but he is pissed. He starts in on Strother; he calls him every name anyone has ever thought of. It was so bad that it was embarrassing. Sam is screaming at him now, he is so furious. And I said, "Sam, he didn't screw up, I did!" Everything stops. Sam looks at me, he turns back to Strother and says, "You sonofabitch," and starts on him because he let Sam chew on him without blaming me. Strother got it for both reasons. That's Peckinpah.

Let's talk about *The McMasters*. For me, the film's intention is to parallel America at the end of the Sixties with America post-Civil War. What are your thoughts about the film and the message it was trying to put across?

Well, that's it. That's the message you get from it. I thought it was a good script, a hell of a cast and everybody worked their ass off to get it done. Part of it works and part of it doesn't. Brock Peters was marvellous in it. Who was the singer who was in it? Burl Ives. He was fucking marvellous! I asked him so often to sing for me that for years after that, maybe at three o'clock in the morning, maybe at high noon, I'd answer the telephone and it would be Burl Ives on the other end. He wouldn't say a word; he just would sing the songs I requested a thousand times. He did that maybe 10 or 15 times, bless his heart – never said anything, just sang the songs. He was a marvellous man, a hell of an actor. The film was very uneven, though.

It's a good piece, but I would agree with you. It's not consistent.

It's one of those things where I can say, "It's a good film," and not be embarrassed by that.

It's a challenging film. Thematically, it's strong. You're a horrible villain in it.

I'm not very nice. [Laughing]

It has a disturbing scene where you break into Brock Peters' house and humiliate him. Can you recall how Peters felt about filming that particular scene?

Well, Brock and I had known each other for years. He's a very sincere man in what he does. But in that particular instance he may have been expected to do more than the script allowed him to do. Burl is such a strong character and we had a bunch of real terrible people working against him. Brock may not have been quite up to the task, whereas if you had given him another two or three years he would have dominated it. Not that he was weak, I didn't mean that, but he was kind of indecisive in one or two instances where he needed something else and he didn't have it. I felt sorry for him. I tried to help, but it's just one of those things where it isn't quite working right, but you don't know what it takes.

Well, it is an extreme scene. It must have been very difficult.

I was trying to do certain things – some worked and some didn't. The girl [Nancy Kwan] was marvellous. If you watch Ford's pictures, for example, if there's any doubt about what he's telling you with the visuals, he says it. He wants to be sure that you understand what he's talking about. Not many directors do that. In that scene [in *The McMasters*] they were trying to give you the visuals. The visuals of the rape scene in *Straw Dogs* work. You don't have to say anything. We all know how she felt, and how the rapist felt as a matter of fact. But [when watching *The McMasters*] not all of us know how a black person would react with his Indian wife being abused by these terrible people. You have to override any doubt and any problem to get that across, and you may have to vocalise it.

As an actor one could say you're synonymous with the western genre. So what inspired you to write and direct *A Boy and His Dog*, a post-apocalyptic sci-fi movie?

I loved the piece. I read the book one night. At midnight I started reading it and I got about a third of the way through it and I said, "What a shame. This is a marvellous idea but you can't keep it up. It's got to fall." And I got two thirds of the way through and I was saying the same thing, and then I finished it about two o'clock in the morning and I fell on the floor. I was laughing so hard at what it was. And I went in the next morning and told my secretary that this was the picture we were going to make. And [co-star] Alvy Moore read it and never understood what the ending was. We made it that way [like the book], which I'm very proud of. Have you ever seen it?

Yes. It's very quirky, even surreal, but it also has some very stark imagery in it.

It's very unusual; it was so far ahead of its time. I almost went too far with it, but the ending: 25 per cent of people understood what was happening, the look between the boy and the girl; another 25 per cent understood it when they saw the wedding gown; another 25 per cent got it with the dog's last line; another 25 per cent never understood what happened. And that was marvellous as far as I was concerned. That dog was the most talented animal I have ever seen in my life. I've seen the picture 500 times, but every time I watch the dog I see something that I was not aware of. It is the most brilliant performance ever recorded on film by an animal. In fact there was talk of nominating the dog for an Oscar. I would give directions to the dog just by talking to it.

That scene where they're on their way to the drop shaft, and the dog is trying to persuade the boy not to go because he's going to be killed? We did the shot and I said, "Cut, cut, cut." The dog was doing a marvellous job and I said, "Don [Johnson], pick it up a bit, you're dragging," and to the dog, "Tiger, goddammit, you're on the wrong side of the man. I can't see you over there. Get on this side where you belong and would you kindly, when he stops, you stop." Now, I'm talking to the dog and the trainer is reading a magazine a couple of hundred yards away. If you remember when that scene comes, the dog has moved from his right side to his left side. He's limping, so when the boy stops, the dog stops like I told him to. And just before I could say, "Cut," he started limping ahead towards the drop shaft, stopped, still in camera, looked at the drop shaft, turned around to face the kid, limped back to him, looked him in the face, looked over his right shoulder and, to end the scene, moved towards the boy and put his head in his lap. I told Jason Robards, who was in the picture and also one of the best in our business at that time, "If you can act like that and remember your lines, I'll make a star of you." He knew exactly what I was talking about. Later in that scene the dog cried. The dog fucking cried!

Have you seen any of the major new westerns of the past ten years or so – Tarantino's most recent films, for example? What do you think of the state of the genre now?

Well, I tell you what. You can call them westerns, but they're not westerns. You can change their mode of travel from horseback to BMW and use the same language and lines, but they're not westerns. A western is a morality play. Everybody knows what they should do and no-one will do it except the hero. The last person really to do a western like that was Sam. They still try. I'm the only one left who would know how to direct a real western, but I'm too gutless. I wouldn't try it, because we haven't got the people to do it. The best in the business – the guys I worked with, Ben Johnson, Slim Pickens, Strother Martin – they made westerns work. Why? How? I don't really know.

There's something really earthy about those actors.

That's what it is. There's something very special. The tendency is to throw stones at the actors, but that's BS. Stop and look at it. I've done 200 or so pieces in my time. The kids today are lucky if they can do three or four. You can't learn. I don't care how talented you are, you need the chances. Acting is a muscle – you have to use it. You have to exercise it, otherwise it atrophies. The people we have today, while they do a good job, they don't understand. When we made westerns, while it was the stars that drew the crowds, everybody in it had to be working and working right. Today the scripts are written for stars and that's it. They don't have Strothers, they don't have Slims – their contribution was eternal, and you cannot do without it. The pictures they make now, they're not bad, they're just not as good – to me.

Going back to early in your career. In *Buchanan Rides Alone* you have this lovely scene with Randolph Scott where you're riding along sharing sentiments about

Texas. You were born in Beaumont in Texas, your career's taken you all over the world and you now live in LA. Where would say your heart lies?

Probably in my business, because I only lived in other places until I was about 27 and I've been here 60-odd years. It is a business I love. It is unbelievably difficult. People think it's easy; it isn't. But I've been allowed to make a small contribution and I'm just tickled at that. I had no idea after I did *Battle Cry* that I would ever do another picture again, much less a couple of hundred. As you can see my view is somewhat jaundiced. I love the people here and we have our shortcomings but, well, that's us. I've been lucky enough to be in a number of films when there was no going back – everything was up there on the screen, everybody was involved, and that is an unbelievable feeling.

Which of your film-making experiences do you think were the most fulfilling or educational?

Only about 200 of them. Other than that it was kind of slack [laughing]. I know it sounds Pollyanna-ish, but it was my blessing to grow up with a group of people who not only were dedicated to what they were doing, but were equipped to do it and to stay alive on the screen with great actors like Jason Robards. What can you contribute when you're working with people like that? I said, "Wait a minute. I can do whatever I want to do. It doesn't make any difference, because he is so good that he'll do something better and it'll work." So I don't have to worry about stealing scenes – just staying alive in the business, for Chrissakes.

I remember when I used to live in Camarillo, which is about 50 miles outside of LA. I did the first *Gunsmoke* with a large black cast [*The Good Samaritans*, aired 10 March 1969]. It was two hours long, a very special show, and I was the heavy. I did everything – I raped people, killed people, scalped 'em. I even kicked a dog. If you want to be a heavy, try kicking a dog. I was not a very nice person. I worked with some of the best black actors, like Rex Ingram. After it aired, when I was going to work, I got near the studio and the traffic was inching along. I was driving my MG, the top was down. I was hissed and booed, people threw sandwiches at me, donuts, food, for about 15 miles because of that show the night before. Great fun.

That's when you know you've made it.

I hear that. No matter how crappy it was or how terrible we were, people reacted to the shows. At that time you'd either go out to eat, go dancing or go and see a motion picture. You didn't have the things we have today to pass the time. People were dedicated to the movies. At that point in time half the population was going to the movies. We don't do that any more; we have 25 other things to do. We worked at a time when cinema was sorely needed and really welcome and it was done well. It was done with style, with class. There was still some crap, but every now and again you would do *Ride the High Country*, *The McMasters*, or any of those pictures that Sam did. We were part and parcel of a historic time and it will not, I think, visit us again. I was blessed, still am, to be part of it.

Hud

1963, B/W, 112 mins.

D: Martin Ritt. P: Martin Ritt, Irving Ravetch (Dover Productions, Salem Productions). W: Irving Ravetch, Harriet Frank Jr. Ph: James Wong Howe. M: Elmer Bernstein. St: Paul Newman (Hud Bannon), Melvyn Douglas (Homer Bannon), Patricia Neal (Alma), Brandon de Wilde (Lon Bannon), John Ashley (Hermy)

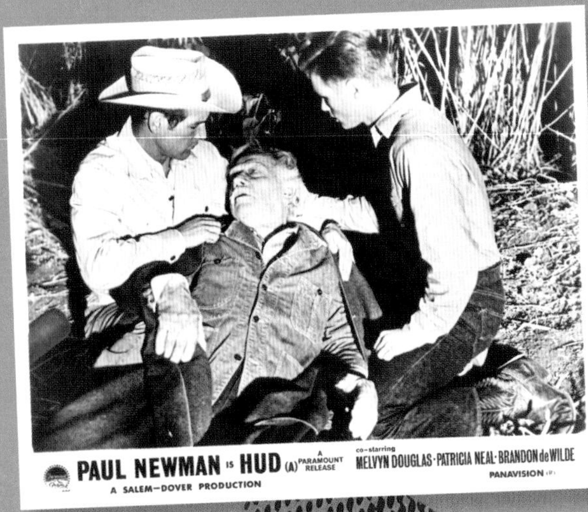

"You don't give a damn about people… You don't value nothing… You don't respect nothing… You live just for yourself, and that makes you not fit to live with."

From the establishing shot of a horse, the westerner's default mode of transport, traversing the landscape in the back of a pick-up truck, *Hud* documents the disjunction between the traditions of the old West (and the western) and the exigencies of the modern world. The rupture is personified on one hand by the title character, who possesses the requisite glamour and bravado of the western individualist but none of his nobility; and on the other by his father, Homer, who, as his name implies, belongs to an age that has passed into legend, the days before mechanisation and materialism transformed the land and the mindset of its inhabitants.

This dynastic struggle, building on the generational conflict of post-*Red River* westerns, takes place on the Bannon ranch, located in a sweltering corner of Texas bleached of all vitality by James Wong Howe's stark monochrome photography. A crisis erupts when foot-and-mouth infects the cattle. Hud's readiness to sell the stock to an unsuspecting buyer, passing on the problem rather than dealing with the consequences, appals his father, who cannot conceal his contempt for Hud's lack of principles and dissolute lifestyle. Hud, in turn, views Homer's compliance with the government's destruction order on the herd as capitulation; his refusal to allow drilling for oil as evidence of mental incompetence. Initiating legal proceedings, Hud plots to seize his birthright: "I want out of this spread what I put into it." Mediating between the combatants are their pragmatic housekeeper, Alma, who bats away Hud's repeated advances (wearily but, one senses, reluctantly), and Hud's impressionable nephew, Lon, in whom the older men invest their hopes for the future of the Bannon brand.[1]

In the person of Hud, Martin Ritt finds a moral vacuum at the heart of the cowboy's macho culture. In Paul Newman's scintillating performance, fully deserving of the Oscar he was only nominated for, Hud greets the world with a cocksure swagger and a sneer.[2]

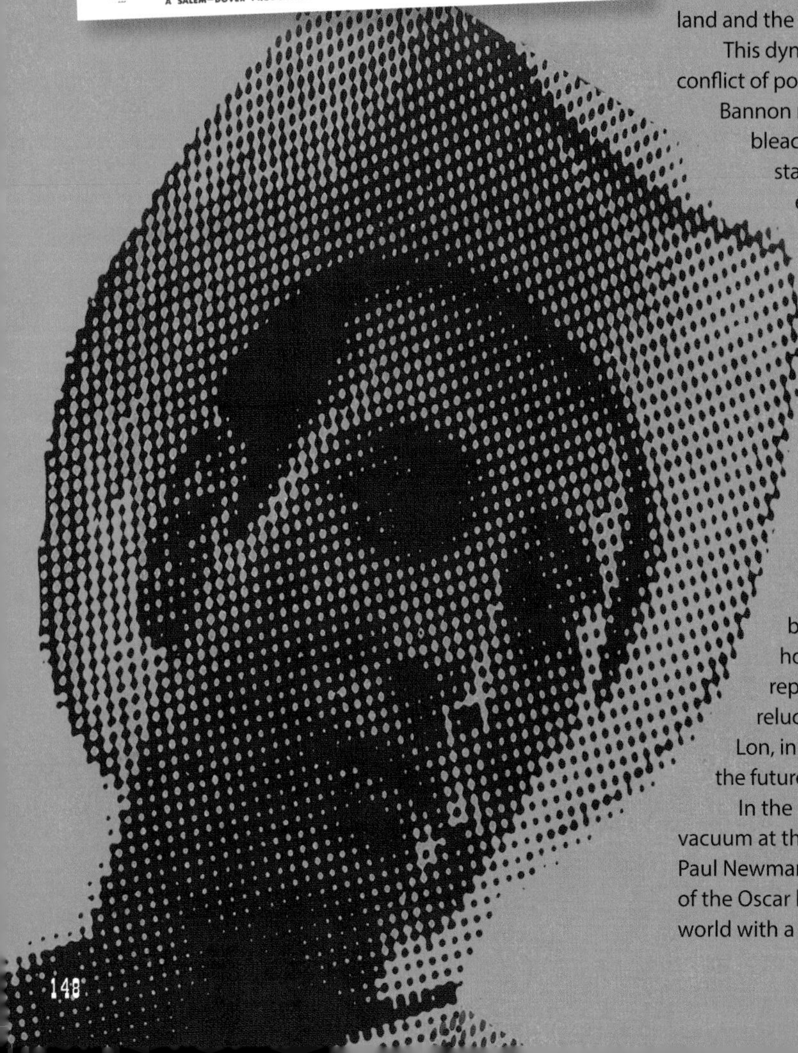

He cares nothing for the land or the legacy of its pioneers – the pride in its settlement that flows in his father's veins. When not stumbling out of bars or married women's bedrooms, he is speeding along in his flashy pink Cadillac, a symbol of narcissism and decadence. (Homer, by contrast, is associated with his beloved Texas longhorns, another dying breed: "I just keep 'em… to remind me how things was.") All the while, Hud undermines his father's fading authority and drip-feeds his nephew caustic observations: "This world is so full of crap, a man's gonna get into it sooner or later whether he's careful or not." His actions and attitude mock the values associated with the nation's founders, much as Ritt's film looks askance at the romantic notions propagated in westerns of yore. (The casting of Brandon de Wilde as Hud's young adherent forces us to consider both the title character and the film as a counterpoint to *Shane*, perhaps the most mythic of all westerns.)

Hud is an outsider in many respects – Ritt often sets him apart from the other members of the Bannon household in group shots, using the Scope frame to emphasise Hud's alienation – but there is also the sense that his outlook is more acceptable in society than the morally inflexible Homer, and the film-makers themselves, would like to believe. "How many honest men you know?" he challenges his father, implying that corruption and self-advancement – "price-fixing, crooked TV shows, inflated expense accounts" – are the (modern) American way. Lon affirms that many in the community share his uncle's sentiments, and it is notable that Hud is welcomed in town like a hero, the ultimate Texan alpha male. As Gabriel Miller writes, "The West of the Sixties is not a place for heroes, but a wasteland where Hud's code of selfishness and materialism prevails."[3] The despairing Homer, for his part, lives in limbo, pining for the days when – as far as he recalls it – there was an emotional bond between a man, the land and his livestock, when fortunes had to be built up by hand, not dug up with machines. John H. Lenihan aligns him with the anachronistic protagonists of *The Misfits*, *Ride the High Country*, *Lonely Are the Brave* and *The Man Who Shot Liberty Valance* – "discards of societal progress", the detritus of a bygone era.[4]

A relatively minor character in Larry McMurtry's source novel, Hud was given the limelight both to disentangle the cowboy archetype from the briars of myth and to capitalise on Newman's facility for creating alluring outsiders. At once roguish and reprehensible, never more so than when he drunkenly attempts to rape Alma, Hud is so ruthless, so heterodox in his behaviour and his views, that studio executives quailed when they read the script: "One of them said, 'When does he get nice?'" recalled producer and co-writer Irving Ravetch. "I said, 'Never.'" Ritt saw his protagonist as a variation on the classic American "shitheel", the

kind of man who usually finds redemption through selflessness or romance; here, he remains true to himself, unrepentant, even though he ends the film alone, his father dead of heart failure, Alma and Lon moved on. The film-makers were horrified, therefore, when audiences, particularly the young, supported Hud, despite or even because of his many blemishes. As with Newman's characters in *Cool Hand Luke* (1967), *Butch Cassidy and the Sundance Kid* (1969) and Ritt's subsequent *Hombre*, Hud's scorn for propriety and the Establishment earned him anti-authoritarian kudos: "The very energy of his defiance sets him apart from the lifeless world around him."[5]

The star was nonplussed: "We thought that the fact that he was basically rotten at the core would be the distinguishable feature. What we didn't realise was that all of the other things overwhelmed that single flaw and he came away a folk hero… He apparently was a part of the American dream."[6] Ritt described Hud's lionisation by young filmgoers as "a terrible experience". "If I'd been near as smart as I thought I was, I would have seen that Haight-Ashbury was right around the corner. The kids were very cynical; they were committed to their own appetites."[7]

The presence of Newman, arguably the most seductive of the screen's great rebels, was thus a double-edged sword. His mixture of bile and braggadocio ("A cross between Richard III and Elvis Presley,"[8] in his biographer's wording), while dangerously attractive, endows the character and the film with an emotional complexity they may have lacked had an actor with a darker disposition or a narrower range been cast in the role. Beneath the brash exterior, behind the sparkling eyes, Newman finds quiet moments to convey flashes of compassion for his ailing father, as well as the suppressed guilt (Hud was driving when his brother, Lon's father, was killed in a car crash years before) that ameliorates, without excusing, Hud's despicable behaviour.

Ritt elicits equally candid performances from the other principals. Melvyn Douglas, slow and purposeful in his movements and delivery, deflects Newman's brashness with an earnest, quiet dignity, quite unlike the domineering patriarchs of earlier ranch-based westerns. Homer's stoicism during the film's most harrowing scene, where the cattle are herded into a purpose-built pit and shot, channels his grief that his way of life is heading for extinction. If Elmer Bernstein's elegiac guitar score befits any of the characters, it is Homer. Patricia Neal's warm-hearted Alma, meanwhile, lightens the tone in the all-male household. Down to earth and uninhibited, Alma has been around the block and encountered more than her share of men like Hud. Although his assault is the catalyst for her departure, she hints with regret that they would probably have got together eventually without the need for what he dismisses as "roughhousing".

The only characterisation that seems less than fully formed is that of Lon, but that is not necessarily a slight on de Wilde, since Lon's innocence is ultimately the crux of the film. In the final reckoning, *Hud* asks which path this low-key character, representing the next generation, will take: whether he will absorb his uncle's ruthlessness or his grandfather's probity. The latter's advice sums up his dilemma: "Little by little the look of the country changes because of the men we admire... You're just going to have to make up your own mind one day about what's right and wrong." **KG**

footnotes

1 In Larry McMurtry's novel, Alma was black. Ritt had dealt with inter-racial relations before (*Edge of the City* [1957]), but in *Hud* he wanted to focus on the title character, without the distraction of a secondary, potentially incendiary theme.
2 *Hud's* three Oscars went to James Wong Howe, Patricia Neal and Melvyn Douglas.
3 *The Films of Martin Ritt: Fanfare for the Common Man* (University Press of Mississippi, 2000).
4 *Showdown: Confronting Modern American in the Western Film* (University of Illinois Press, 1980).
5 Gabriel Miller, *The Films of Martin Ritt: Fanfare for the Common Man.*
6 Quoted in Carlton Jackson, *Picking up the Tab: The Life and Movies of Martin Ritt* (Bowling Green State University Popular Press, 1994).
7 American Film Institute seminar, 1983.
8 Shawn Levy, *Paul Newman: A Life* (Aurum Press, 2010).

from left:
Paul Newman, Melvyn Douglas and Brandon de Wilde

Cheyenne Autumn

1964, Colour, 158 mins. (original version 170 mins.)

D: John Ford. P: Bernard Smith (Ford-Smith Productions). W: James R. Webb. Ph: William Clothier. M: Alex North. St: Richard Widmark (Captain Thomas Archer), Carroll Baker (Deborah Wright), Karl Malden (Captain Wessels), Sal Mineo (Red Shirt), Ricardo Montalban (Little Wolf)

"We are asked to remember much. The white man remembers nothing."

With his body of genre work honouring the progression of European emigrants across the American West, John Ford has often been criticised for projecting propagandist, even racist, attitudes. Much of his filmography glorifies Manifest Destiny and its agents; the working man is lionised in his town tamers, Indian fighters, Irish families and sentimental officers. His Cavalry Trilogy of *Fort Apache* (1948), *She Wore a Yellow Ribbon* (1949) and *Rio Grande* (1950) is an aggregation of the grandiose and the personal that celebrates loyalty, honour, love and community values. Most importantly, everyone stands side by side to repel the Indian hordes threatening land now claimed by the settlers; even the arrogant and foolhardy actions of Henry Fonda's Colonel Thursday in *Fort Apache* are ultimately airbrushed to preserve the good name of the military.

While many have found Ford's sentiments unpalatable, for others they represent the genre at its apex. His westerns are, perhaps more than most, products of their era. It would be near impossible for a contemporary audience to empathise with a town marshal who expresses the same casual racism as Fonda's Wyatt Earp in *My Darling Clementine*. The Indian question was expressed most ambivalently in *The Searchers*, which examined a character at odds with himself, a mind so poisoned by racial hatred that he would consider the murder of a family member who has been captured and adopted by a Native tribe.

On closer inspection, Ford's legacy is more complex. With the American mindset changing rapidly in the early Sixties and film-makers as diverse as Sam Peckinpah and Martin Ritt querying the genre's mythic foundations, Ford's brand of western had fallen out of favour. Ford himself was disenchanted; what Joseph McBride calls the director's "loss of faith in America's future" closely informed the films he was making about its past. After *Two Rode Together* and *The Man Who Shot Liberty Valance*, he voiced the desire to atone for the derogatory treatment of Indians in many of his previous films (as he famously said, "I've killed more Indians than Custer, Beecher and Chivington put together") and persuaded a sceptical Warner Bros. to back an epic drama about the Northern Cheyenne Exodus of 1878-79. The director had been pondering a film on the subject since the early Fifties (the actor Richard Widmark had been amassing material independently), "but the political climate of the blacklist era was not congenial to such a project".[1]

Ironically, the script Ford eventually came to shoot was inspired partly by the blacklisted writer Howard Fast, whose historical novel *The Last Frontier* was an uncredited source, alongside Mari Sandoz's *Cheyenne Autumn*.

With the Cheyenne portrayed ostensibly as refugees, despair and hardship substitute for the humour and dignity associated with Ford's white heroes. The first image of the tribe is that of a collective standing stoically under a searing sun, waiting for a delegation of white dignitaries that never arrives. Running short of food and medicine and unwilling to tolerate further breaches of their treaty, they embark upon a march from the reservation to Yellowstone, their ancestral home. This rejection of assimilationism is voiced by Dull Knife (Gilbert Roland), who spurns the pleas of Deborah, a Quaker teaching English to the Cheyenne children: "The white man's words are lies; it is better our children do not learn them." Appalled at their suffering, Deborah disregards Captain Archer's warnings and takes to the trail with her charges, caring for the sick and attempting to broker peace between Indians and whites. (As William Darby has observed, it is significant that Deborah is never once threatened or mistreated by her tribal hosts, distancing this film's vision of Indians from that of *The Searchers* and *Two Rode Together*.[2]) Hers is the "necessary sympathetic white perspective to mediate and balance with the racism of mainstream America"[3] – an echo of Ford's own views, if he is to be taken at his word.

As a man in an invidious position, Archer is a more nuanced character than Ford's previous cavalry leaders, many of whom were respectful of their Indian foes but never questioned their duty. The war-weary Archer undergoes a (relatively) radical transformation, from battlefield professional to protector and deliverer of the wandering tribe. His 'neutral' voice-over tries but fails to mask his impatience with the way the government deals with the indigenous population. Describing the barely subsisting Indian village at the opening of the film, he comments, "I wish every bigwig in Washington could see this place." Charged with the capture of the Cheyenne, he finds himself gradually awed by their resilience. Ford mirrors Archer's admiration for the Indians by the way he stages the burial of the old chief Tall Tree: "A fair effort to match the funerals [Ford's] cowboys receive… his corpse entombed in a cave behind boulders."[4]

The film doesn't so much document the Cheyenne's flight as convey a general sense of their mistreatment and desperation. It avoids presenting the full horror of their plight; we don't see disease gripping the tribe or members dying from hunger and exhaustion. (That kind of detail would have to wait until the 2007 adaptation of *Bury My Heart at Wounded Knee*.) When Dull Knife leads a breakaway group into Fort Robinson to negotiate with the army, it is the precursor to a symbolic comparison between the atrocious conditions in which they are kept and the internment of the Nazis' enemies in concentration camps. In chilling scenes the Cheyenne, denied food, water or firewood, are locked in bunkers, peering through frosted glass at the murky shadows of guards patrolling outside. Captain Wessels – pointedly of Prussian extraction – is in charge of this operation and, despite professing sympathy for the captives, he is fanatical about obeying orders. The Cheyenne's predicament so outrages Archer that he rides to seek assistance from Secretary of the Interior Carl Schurz (a canny turn by the venerable Edward G. Robinson), who compares the campaign for Cheyenne rights with the battle to liberate African-Americans in the Civil War.

Ford levers in one of his overused drunken Irishmen during the Fort Robinson segment. Doctor O'Carberry (Sean McClory) enters into an ethical debate with Deborah about the Cheyenne's treatment and whether a man of medicine should put duty before ethics. With Archer absent, Deborah reminds O'Carberry about his Hippocratic obligations until, in a moment of moral clarity, the doctor forces command of the fort from a drunken Wessels, interring the latter in his own quarters. The best efforts of Archer, Deborah and

O'Carberry come to naught, however. In a diversion from Sandoz's novel, the Cheyenne unveil an arsenal of guns and rifles, many hidden among the swaddling clothes of their infants. Before the doctor can free them, the Cheyenne blast their way out of captivity, led by the hot-headed Red Shirt. The indiscriminate shooting that follows leaves women and children dead in the snow.

Having monumentalised the military in the opening titles of *Fort Apache*, the director in this case lauds the Native American, the credits rolling over a bronze statue of an Indian brave mounted atop his horse. This mirroring strategy continues in the narrative. The rivalry between Little Wolf and Dull Knife, that of hawk and dove, is reminiscent of that between Thursday and York in *Fort Apache*; while one party seeks only retribution and victory over the enemy, the other proposes compromise and a tentative hiatus in hostilities. Red Shirt (a flagrantly miscast Sal Mineo), the vengeful son of Dull Knife, is always the first to fire a shot in anger; this eagerness for battle is paralleled in Second Lieutenant Scott (Patrick Wayne). Neither Scott nor Red Shirt learns from events; Scott is wounded while Red Shirt dies in a duel with Little Wolf, ostensibly for attempting to seduce his chief's squaw, although one senses that what he is really being punished for is his recalcitrance.

Despite the honorable intentions of the script (or perhaps because of them, given the relentlessly haranguing tone), Ford's switching of allegiances from the cause of the whites to that of the Indian tribes seems somewhat clumsy. In a short but telling scene, we see a newspaper editor rush into his office and order his printers to change tack on the Indian question, deciding he will sell more papers by presenting the Cheyenne as noble savages. It is as if, in this vignette, Ford is confessing that he is trying to capture the zeitgeist rather than recounting this historical tale from the heart.

The film's central section exacerbates the feeling that the director was in two minds. The Dodge City sequence corrupts the general tone, descending into exaggerated scenes of Fordian ribaldry. James Stewart's Wyatt Earp, the town tamer of legend, is now a gambler and womaniser, abetted by Arthur Kennedy's equally cynical Doc Holliday, embodying the failings of this apathetic, vice-ridden anti-community. Challenged to a gunfight during a game of poker, Earp shoots his antagonist with a concealed Derringer. When the Cheyenne are reported to be descending on the town and stages and horses race to confront them, the tension is dissipated by the ill-fitting comedic approach. One particularly bawdy joke sums up the director's misjudgement of the situation: back in Dodge, a travelling good-time girl had been insisting that Earp knows her; in the melee, she becomes defrocked and

upended on his wagon – "By golly, I *did* know her in Wichita," realises the marshal as he looks down her petticoats, a gag befitting a *Carry On* film more than a sobering story of Native American suffering. Archer's voice-over sums up this silly sequence wryly – "Battle of Dodge City – casualties: one silk dress" – but the film would have been stronger without it.

Despite accusations to the contrary, the director often portrayed Indians as empowered, worthy of esteem. Here, their dejected bearing hinders rather than helps their cause, as does the absence of any dynamic individuals among them – they seem "more symbols of white exploitation than believable characters in their own right".[5] Ricardo Montalban and Roland are weighed down by stilted dialogue; Dolores del Rio fares marginally better as the intuitive Spanish Woman. (Ford's use of Latino principals was one of the compromises he was obliged to strike with Warner Bros. to get the project off the ground – he had wanted to cast Navajo non-actors in the principal Indian roles, although this would have earned him few plaudits among descendants of the Cheyenne.) Whereas Ford once carved his tribes from granite, his long shots here have a diminishing effect – the Cheyenne are like flotsam adrift in a hostile wilderness.

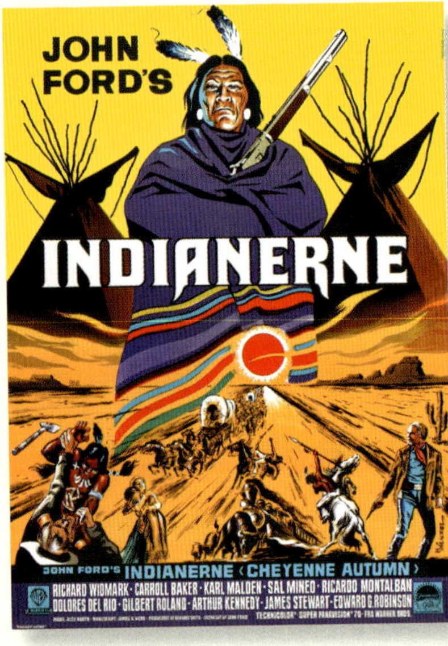

A feeling of weariness extends from the subjects to the production itself. Earlier, similarly intentioned films such as *Broken Arrow* and *Apache* were more strident in their attacks, more successful in their presentation of Indians as individuals; the following year's *Major Dundee* was more acute in its critique of the military mindset, sharper in discerning parallels between a divided command and a fractured nation. With its requisite shots of Monument Valley, gloriously rich colour palette and generally committed performances, *Cheyenne Autumn* could have been the summation of Ford's engagement with the western. Instead it feels like a discordant note in an otherwise rhapsodic career. **CH**

footnotes

1 Joseph McBride, *Searching for John Ford* (Faber and Faber, 2003).
2 *John Ford's Westerns* (McFarland, 2006).
3 Jim Kitses, *Horizons West* (BFI, 2004).
4 Ibid.
5 Michael Hilger, *From Savage to Nobleman: Images of Native Americans in Film* (Scarecrow Press, 1995).

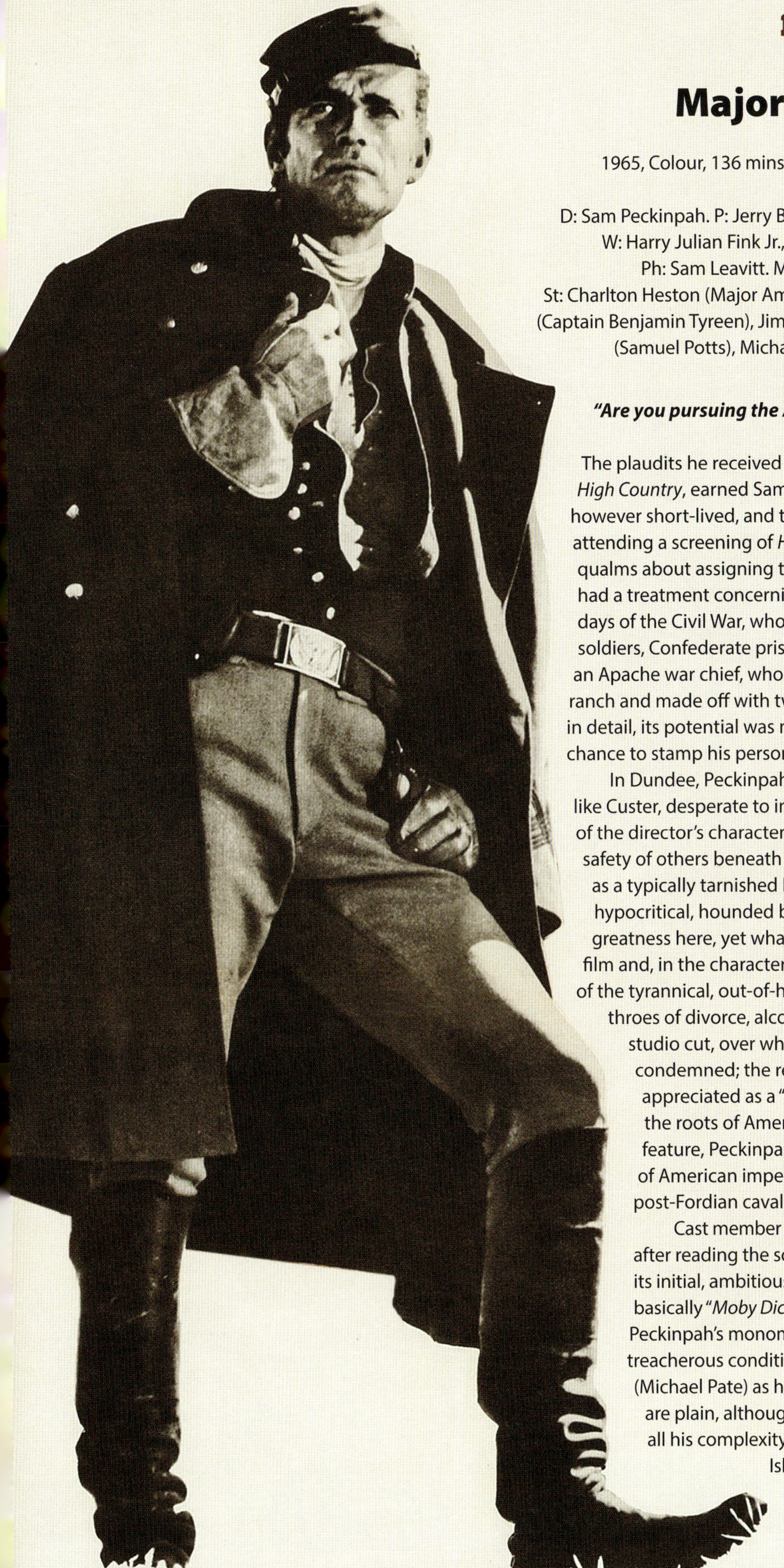

Major Dundee

1965, Colour, 136 mins. (original version 124 mins.)

D: Sam Peckinpah. P: Jerry Bresler (Jerry Bresler Productions).
W: Harry Julian Fink Jr., Oscar Saul, Sam Peckinpah.
Ph: Sam Leavitt. M: Daniele Amfitheatrof.
St: Charlton Heston (Major Amos Charles Dundee), Richard Harris (Captain Benjamin Tyreen), Jim Hutton (Lt. Graham), James Coburn (Samuel Potts), Michael Anderson Jr. (Tim Ryan)

"Are you pursuing the Apache, Major, or a promotion?"

The plaudits he received for his previous western, *Ride the High Country*, earned Sam Peckinpah the trust of studios, however short-lived, and the respect of Hollywood royalty. After attending a screening of *High Country*, Charlton Heston had no qualms about assigning the director to his latest project. He had a treatment concerning a Union jail keeper, in the twilight days of the Civil War, who assembles a ragtag platoon of Union soldiers, Confederate prisoners and criminal types to pursue an Apache war chief, whose braves have raided the Rostes ranch and made off with two children. Epic in scale yet intimate in detail, its potential was not lost on Peckinpah, who saw the chance to stamp his personal obsessions on the project.

In Dundee, Peckinpah saw not a righteous hero but a man, like Custer, desperate to imprint his mark on history. Like many of the director's characters, Dundee would put the liberty and safety of others beneath his need for validation. He emerges as a typically tarnished Peckinpah archetype – ruthless, hypocritical, hounded by demons. There was potential for greatness here, yet what we have is a profoundly disjointed film and, in the character of Dundee, a disturbing reflection of the tyrannical, out-of-his-depth film-maker, then in the throes of divorce, alcohol dependence and drug use. The studio cut, over which he had no control, was roundly condemned; the restored version, at least, can be appreciated as a "monumental attempt to lay bare the roots of America as a nation".[1] With his third feature, Peckinpah issued an unflinching indictment of American imperialism clothed in the sullied rags of a post-Fordian cavalry western.

Cast member R.G. Armstrong remarked to Peckinpah after reading the script, or at least after processing its initial, ambitious narrative, that *Major Dundee* was basically "*Moby Dick* on horseback". With Dundee as Peckinpah's monomaniacal Ahab, searching eternally in treacherous conditions for his foe, and Sierra Charriba (Michael Pate) as his enigmatic antagonist, the parallels are plain, although they don't capture the Major in all his complexity. (The story even has its own ersatz Ishmael in the person of Tim Ryan, the company bugler, who chronicles the increasingly complicated quest.)

Dundee is a Southern gent who has chosen to fight for the Union, reflecting his desire for social progression; a man who saw action at Gettysburg and doesn't feel he has received due recognition. Dundee's aims are, for the most part, transparent: glory and acclamation. For this, he is willing to sever ties with his own ancestry and exceed his authority, following the Apache into Mexico even after the children have been returned. (Here *Dundee* diverges from John Ford's similarly premised *Rio Grande*, in which John Wayne's Kirby Yorke breaches the border with the tacit permission of his superiors.) He talks of smiting the wicked; bubbling under, however, is frustration that he has been confined to the role of jailer in a miserable desert outpost. He is, as his second-in-command intuits, a man at war with everybody – including himself.

Equally fascinating is Tyreen, the idealistic Southern rebel and Dundee's mirror. An Irish immigrant, a settler in the North, he perhaps sensed, in the Southern cause, the rebel spirit of his motherland. He refuses at first to help Dundee in his mission: "It's not my country, Major. I damn its flag and I damn you." His ire is aggravated by a personal grudge: Dundee, his old friend, had voted to have Tyreen cashiered out of their regiment for an infraction, "to please the generals in Washington". However, the chance of a reprieve for his fellow Confederate POWs sways Tyreen's mind; unlike Dundee, he is altruistic rather than autocratic when it comes to his men.[2] Introduced in a dank cell, arms crossed and head bowed, almost messianic in appearance, he will eventually sacrifice himself for his comrades in an act of bravery that puts Dundee's glory hunting to shame.

Friends estranged by fateful decisions or force of circumstance can be found throughout Peckinpah's work; the theme of betrayal was one of his favourite refrains. By extension, the Civil War was a natural fit for this director. The spectre of the conflict stalks Dundee's brigade throughout, from the early scene in which Yanks and Rebs sing competing renditions of *The Battle Hymn of the Republic* and *Dixie*, to the racial friction that threatens to ignite when the redneck Jimmy Lee Benteen (John Davis Chandler) goads Aesop (Brock Peters), one of a small group of black volunteers. In scenes such as these, "the anomalies and divisions of early America are starkly evoked".[3] At the same time, the fragility of Dundee's command "acknowledges the racial and social divisions of the mid-Sixties while conjuring the hubris of the Great Society", as J. Hoberman put it retrospectively.[4] The pressure eases only when the men are reminded of the purpose of their mission: the pursuit of a mutually hated race – "Until the Apache are taken or destroyed." It is a mantra repeated throughout the two-hour running time, often employed to refocus both the troop and the sometimes meandering narrative.

Dundee's stubborn inflexibility only exaggerates the disunity among his command. When the Confederate absconder O.W. Hadley (Warren Oates) is captured by the Major's scouts, Dundee orders him shot. In this key scene, bristling with tension, it is Tyreen who takes responsibility, sparing his comrade the humiliation of being executed by his Union jailer. Both sides recognise the legality of the Major's order, but only Tyreen displays the kind of leadership skills that inspire confidence and loyalty. The schism thus deepens between both the officers and the Union and Confederate troops. There is no resemblance here to the romantic image of harmonious soldiery exemplified by John Ford's cavalry trilogy. Peckinpah's film questions both the legitimacy of

Hollywood's championing of the military, with an officer who has chosen to encroach upon foreign soil to fulfil his own ambition, and "the heroic and American values he embodies".[5] It is not difficult to draw comparisons between Dundee's mission, with its confused objectives, and contemporary misadventures in Korea and Indochina. (This is especially so given the vision of Indians – their only significant appearance in Peckinpah's canon, beyond a bizarre cameo in *The Deadly Companions* – as skilful guerrilla fighters, imbued with an almost ethereal spirit. In this, they anticipate their counterparts in the similarly unapologetic *Ulzana's Raid*.)

The closest Dundee's troop comes to performing as a cohesive unit, and in a heroic manner, is when they intervene in the chaotic social situation in Mexico. Renegade Apaches and interloping gringos are nothing compared with the occupying French forces. The colonial powers' treatment of peasant villagers – we see hanging corpses, starving children – "makes the Apaches look like missionaries", comments Potts, with a degree of overstatement. It is certainly unbecoming of a great, 'civilized' power, as Dundee recognises. Perhaps the Major's most outwardly noble act is to blast the French troops from their sanctuary, where they are hoarding the spoils of their occupation, and redistribute the stolen food among the villagers. The result is that as well as Charriba, Dundee's men acquire another enemy in Mexico. In their plumed uniforms, the French troops seem anachronistic, quasi-Napoleonic, Peckinpah introducing them to extend his critique of imperialism and to accentuate the undisciplined appearance of those from north of the border – there are distinct echoes of *Vera Cruz* amid the cannon fire.

Endearing himself and his soldiers to the Mexicans creates a diversion, however, that almost completely derails the plot. When the Major is injured by an Indian arrow while stealing a fleeting moment of intimacy with the widow Teresa, he is forced to recoup in Durango. It is here that the film begins to list, when the once all-powerful Dundee commences self-medicating with alcohol, "to obliterate his self-awareness" and blot out the stain on his standing and his reputation.[6] Tyreen becomes the director's mouthpiece, and could also be speaking for the audience when he asks: "Just what the bloody hell are you doing here in the first place, Amos?" For Dundee, Durango is a metaphorical sharp precipice, from which the hubristic major tumbles into a state of guilt-induced, inebriated self-loathing. Tyreen may be expected to enjoy the spectacle, but instead shows empathy: Dundee's conflicted identity is a reflection of his own; broaching a subject that was dear to Peckinpah's heart, he recognises the difficulty of being true to oneself, especially in time of war.

This is also the case of Riago, the company scout, who classes himself not as an Apache, like Charriba, but as a Christian Indian. He remains an isolated figure, peripheral to the narrative, trusted by nobody except the fiercely autonomous Samuel Potts, his fellow scout, a man of the wilderness who identifies with neither Union ideals nor Confederate. While Dundee's disposition, honed at West Point, crumbles amid the increasingly brutalising conditions, it is notable that the more 'primitive' Potts, who represents the assured individualism of the American male first celebrated in the Leatherstocking tales, never falters. The same is true of the ethnically diverse characters lower down the command chain – Riago, Aesop and Gomez, a naturalised American and expert tracker. This method of diminishing Dundee by unfavourable comparison with 'lesser' men was evidently part of Peckinpah's design, but it remains one of several loose threads in an imperfect tapestry.

For Peckinpah, *Major Dundee* became the harshest lesson in film-making he had yet experienced. The original cut, prepared by Columbia, was a contorted view of the director's vision. Even in its renovated state it does not achieve the eminence of *Ride the High Country* or *The Wild Bunch*. It is, in places, difficult to comprehend the director's purpose. Dundee's descent into drunkenness, for example, is such a shift in personality that it makes little sense. "I'm not sure that even if Peckinpah had been allowed to cut it in the way that he wanted to that *Dundee* could ever have been the picture he had in mind," commented Heston. "The studio tried to cut it into something simpler and more routine and I don't think they succeeded."[7]

Nonetheless, there is much to admire. Heston and Richard Harris are excellent; the cast brims with earthy Peckinpah regulars. The story's central themes resonate still, and much of the action carries a visceral charge: the opening scene depicting the aftermath of Sierra Charriba's attack is a macabre tapestry of hanging, bloodied corpses, plumes of smoke and desolation, while the final fight against the French is dynamically staged. Sam Leavitt's photography capitalises on the use of geographically disparate backdrops: broiling, sub-tropical desert badlands in the eerie light of dusk, stretching out into an infinite, forbidding plain of alien vegetation; the chaotic, purgatorial streets of Durango, which anticipate both Angel's village and Agua Verde in *The Wild Bunch*.[8]

Major Dundee may be a testament to failed ambition, but it was also a crucial evolutionary step for Peckinpah and American cinema. With *High Country* and this project, the director created what appeared to be traditional westerns, but a scratch at the surface reveals dismay and anger that the country he loved was being led astray from tradition, with greed and corruption dictating the pace and direction of change. He would soon vent that anger in the form of *The Wild Bunch*. **CH**

footnotes

1 Jim Kitses, *Horizons West (*BFI, 2007).

2 Later characters in Peckinpah's work would carry the psychological weight of betraying their principles, embodied by former comrades, and siding with corporate forces they covertly despise. Deke Thornton in *The Wild Bunch* and Pat Garrett in *Pat Garrett and Billy the Kid* are perhaps the best realised.

3 Jim Kitses, *Horizons West*.

4 'The Charge of the Peckinpah Brigade', *New York Times*, 3 April 2005.

5 Richard Slotkin, *Gunfighter Nation* (University of Oklahoma Press, 1998).

6 Michael Bliss, *Justified Lives: Morality & Narrative in the Films of Sam Peckinpah* (Southern Illinois University Press, 1993).

7 'It's All a Matter of Size', *Films and Filming*, April 1968.

8 Although Peckinpah wanted *High Country*'s cinematographer, Lucien Ballard, he was overruled by his executive producer, Jerry Bresler, whose decision to contract Leavitt proved to be fortuitous.

The Professionals

1966, Colour, 117 mins.

D: Richard Brooks. P: Richard Brooks (Pax Enterprises). W: Richard Brooks. Ph: Conrad Hall. M: Maurice Jarre. St: Burt Lancaster (Bill Dolworth), Lee Marvin (Henry Rico Fardan), Robert Ryan (Hans Ehrengard), Woody Strode (Jacob Sharp), Jack Palance (Jesus Raza)

"Maybe there's only been one revolution – the good guys against the bad guys. The question is, who are the good guys?"

Looking over its shoulder at Robert Aldrich's seminal *Vera Cruz*, Richard Brooks' popular, Latin-flavoured pulp western concerns the actions and mindsets of gold-hungry gringos seeking their fortunes in revolutionary Mexico. While Aldrich's narrative trailed two contrasting personalities – one amoral, one disillusioned – who offer their services to the highest bidder, Brooks's quartet are all more or less on the same page, having been employed by a wealthy American to retrieve a trophy wife, allegedly kidnapped and taken across the border by a guerrilla leader.

With gringos in the employ of oppressors, crises of loyalty and a perfunctory stab at Mexican social history, the film slotted into a sequence of major Hollywood productions in which a lusty Latin American atmosphere served as the set dressing for astute morality plays: *Vera Cruz* was the first; *The Magnificent Seven* (1960) the most illustrious; *The Wild Bunch* the final and most accomplished example. Brooks's film was the most straightforward, eschewing the internecine squabbling and antiheroic characterisations that marked the Aldrich and Peckinpah films, while retaining the altruism of the Seven and a fashionably cynical sense of humour, with some stinging barbs aimed at Yankee capitalism in particular.

Rancher Joe Grant (Ralph Bellamy) hires four 'specialists' – a weapons expert, Henry 'Rico' Fardan; explosives, Bill Dolworth; horses, Hans Ehrengard; tracker, Jake Sharp – for what he describes as a rescue mission.[1] Grant tells them that his wife, Maria (Claudia Cardinale), has been abducted by Jesus Raza – "Jesus – what a name for the bloodiest cut-throat in Mexico." (Grant, of course, fails to appreciate the symbolism of his enemy's full name, which paints him as the saviour of his people or *raza* – literally 'race'.) Raza's hacienda is surrounded by miles of scorching desert, a brutal landscape of salt flats tipped by a shimmering vanishing point. The heroes' arduous trek is punctuated by exchanges of firepower and macho repartee with assorted bandidos. They also witness Raza's small army storm a government supply train in a brilliantly staged guerrilla attack. To the disgust of Ehrengard, the government soldiers on board are all shot dead, but the war-hardened Dolworth explains that the executed men were Colorados – feared marksmen and experts at torture; Fardan's late wife was among their many victims.[2] Eventually, the hacienda is identified and the heroes assault the poorly fortified base camp, with Dolworth and his dynamite leading the way. Amid the flames and chaos, there is a factor they were not banking on – Raza and Maria locked in a passionate embrace. Ever the cynic, Dolworth turns to Fardan: "Amigo, we've been had. Let's get the hell out of here."

As in Peckinpah's turn-of-the-century westerns, the professionals' broadly honourable code proves to be out of step with the times, certainly on the American side of the border. On the other side, the revolution serves chiefly as a backdrop for a tale of conflicted allegiances and greed. The starkness of the desert locales creates an almost mythological atmosphere, with each man gifted a divine skill, giving them an advantage over mere mortals.

The film's grasp of the politics and social environment that foment civil war is tenuous. Indeed, an indigenous Mexican historian would baulk at most Hollywood interpretations of the conflict. Here, as elsewhere, there is little complexity in the delineation of good and bad, and no worthy roles for Latin actors. Fardan and Dolworth clearly respect Raza, but the man playing him, Jack Palance, is not Latino but the son of Ukrainian immigrants. Likewise, Maria is portrayed by an actress of Italian-Tunisian descent, with Cardinale dutifully spitfire-like as she espouses revolutionary ideology, slams her husband's depredations and questions her rescuers' scruples. Palance and Cardinale are suitably swarthy and exotic, but did Brooks miss an opportunity to tell the story using Mexican performers? The same accusations will always be levelled against westerns, particularly those with a strong focus on non-Caucasian characters. But box-office prospects usually dictate directorial choices, certainly in the case of major studio productions. *The Professionals* became the second-highest-grossing western of 1966 (after Henry Hathaway's *Nevada Smith*) and earned a trio of Academy Award nominations, so in that respect Brooks and Columbia were justified.

With a filmography that has dealt with social issues and human conflict, and liberal principles that brought him dangerously close to the Hollywood blacklist in the

The Dantean arena of Mexico (doubled by Death Valley and, more extensively, by Nevada's Valley of Fire) is a fittingly sweltering milieu for such a torrid tale. Conrad Hall's Oscar-nominated cinematography imbues the film with a singular starkness of vision, and he creates some of the most indelible vistas in a Sixties western.

The central figures do not quite have equal shares in the drama. Ehrengard shows the most compassion and humanity (as well as vulnerability – overcome by the desert heat, at one point he collapses from exhaustion). He is far less solipsistic than his associates and, therefore, can be read as a more "modern" man in sentiment and action; it is unfortunate that the character is sidelined in a number of key scenes. And Sharp is given little to do aside from displaying his athleticism, and spends much of the film moving sprite-like in and out of the action. It is significant that his colour is not an issue for any of his colleagues – only Grant crassly calls attention to it.[3]

Considerably greater importance is placed upon the characters played by the film's main attractions, Lee Marvin and Burt Lancaster. Old friends who had previously fought alongside Raza, Fardan and Dolworth complement each other. Fardan is serious and officious while Dolworth is cocksure and flippant. Dolworth's introduction in the opening credits, escaping from an adulterous clinch in his all-in-ones, is illustrative of his pervading attitude. He expresses cynicism about the legitimacy of the revolution (all insurrections for him are "a lost cause"), but also questions the veracity of Grant's claim that Raza has stooped to such underhanded deeds as kidnapping. Ultimately, however, Dolworth's is the most satisfying story arc. He moves from being a mistrustful but efficient soldier of fortune to displaying true sympathy with the insurgents' ideology, referred to by Raza as a wondrous love affair: "Without love, without a cause, we are nothing." Dolworth's moments comforting his dying former lover, Chiquita (Maria Gomez), are as poignant as they are symbolic. As the woman who embodied ideals he once held true is laid to rest, Dolworth resurrects the romantic spirit by reuniting a wounded Raza with Maria: "This'll come as a shock… I'm a born sucker for love." Grant's plan is thus scuppered.

Fifties – his only previous western, *The Last Hunt*, was a strident attack on white racism and environmental exploitation – the writer-director must have been acutely conscious of the radical increase in US troop deployment in Vietnam in the early Sixties. His film can certainly be read as an allegory for American involvement in wars being fought in exotic, alien lands, with Grant as a bullish Lyndon Johnson figure. In the end, though, the analogy falls just short, and Brooks's ideas are distilled into a terrific-looking action movie, a testament to individual expertise and collective solidarity. Speaking after the fact, the director expressed a certain amount of empathy with his protagonists: "I am fond of *The Professionals* because it's a lean job, and it has my code of honour in it without talking about it."[4]

Seen on its own terms, as a film about listening to one's heart and raising a symbolic middle finger to the powers that be, its message is eternal. As the satisfaction of executing his wife's lover is snatched away from him by the proud professionals he has attempted to hoodwink, Grant spits at Fardan, "You bastard." It leaves Lee Marvin to respond with one of the western's greatest put-downs: "In my case an accident of birth. But you, sir, you're a self-made man."[5] The professionals have made their point, but they also seem redundant, fighting for a moral cause that has long since been lost. For all its boisterousness, Brooks's film has the same plaintive undertone as many of its more openly pessimistic contemporaries: "[His characters] must remain true to a code of honour seen as untenable in a changing world," writes David Lusted. "The elegiac western calls into question not only the action of the hero, but also his function."[6] **CH**

above: Burt Lancaster with Claudia Cardinale and (*top left*) with Lee Marvin.

footnotes

1 Much like his character, Lee Marvin was something of an arms enthusiast; one of the Winchester shotguns featured in the film came from his own collection.

2 The Colorados were led by Pascual Orozco, a supporter of Francisco Madero who later joined the counter-insurgency under Victoriano Huerta. They were notorious for their brutality and had an especially bitter rivalry with the forces of Pancho Villa. Embedded with *Villistas* in the Revolution's second phase, John Reed wrote with vehemence of the Colorados in his powerfully vivid chronicle, *Insurgent Mexico*: "They were so called because their flag was red, and because their hands were red with slaughter, too. They swept through Northern Mexico, burning, pillaging and robbing the poor… I have seen a city of four thousand souls reduced to *five* after a visit by the *colorados*. When Villa took Torreon, there was no mercy for the *colorados*; they are always shot".

3 The role may not have stretched Woody Strode, but he saw it as a turning point in his film career: "Because of my mixed background I could play anyone from the Third World. I played natives in the old jungle pictures; I fought Tarzan to the death. They stuck a pigtail on me for *Genghis Khan*, and slanted my eyes to make me look Chinese in *7 Women*, and I could play all the Indians. I never played myself, a Negro-Indian breed, until I did *The Professionals* (Strode, *Goal Dust*; Madison Books, 1990).

4 Quoted in Patrick McGilligan, *Backstory 2: Interviews with Screenwriters of the 1940s and 1950s* (University of California Press, 1997).

5 Brooks agreed with Patrick McGilligan's suggestion that the character of Grant was a surrogate for a typical studio producer: "That's how I feel about those kind of people," he said, referring to Marvin's immortal rebuff (*Backstory 2*).

Ride in the Whirlwind

1966, Colour, 82 mins.

D. Monte Hellman. P: Monte Hellman, Jack Nicholson (Santa Clara Productions Inc, Proteus Films). W: Jack Nicholson. Ph: Gregory Sandor. M: Robert Drasnin. St: Cameron Mitchell (Vern), Jack Nicholson (Wes), Tom Filer (Otis), Millie Perkins (Abigail), Katherine Squire (Catherine)

"Strikes me peculiar, sitting here playing checkers while there's a bunch of men out there lookin' to string us up."

One of the most austere westerns made in America, *Ride in the Whirlwind* proved that scant resources and a tight schedule could be a spur rather than a hindrance. Provided with a pittance by producer Roger Corman, as was his wont, and a nuts-and-bolts script written by ambitious actor Jack Nicholson, Monte Hellman took a modest cast into the Utah badlands and scrimped on the escapism and glamour associated with the genre. At a time when most Hollywood westerns were bloated with stars and set pieces, designed to shore up the genre as a commercial proposition, this bleak, sparse film, which transposes the injustice theme of Vittorio De Seta's neo-neorealist *Bandits of Orgosolo* (1961) from rural Sardinia to the American West, offers little in the way of comfort or consolation for either characters or audience. In the process, "An American ideal is dismantled alongside the narrative codes that reinforce it, the target here being less heroism than the notion of 'justice for all' on which US democracy prides itself."[1]

In his fourth venture with Monte Hellman – following the adventure *Flight to Fury* and war film *Back Door to Hell* (both 1964), and immediately after *The Shooting* – Nicholson, who also co-produced, plays one of three cowboys who seek shelter with a gang of highwaymen and find themselves judged guilty by association. In a siege by vigilantes, one of the cowboys is killed while Wes and Vern flee the scene. They happen upon a remote homestead, briefly take the family hostage while they consider their options, but are forced to kill the man of the house and ride off when the vigilantes return. Vern is mortally wounded, and the film ends ambiguously, with the sound of Wes's horse beating a retreat into the mountains.

It is the kind of raw material that has been spun into a thousand tall tales, but the characters and the sequence of events are hardly the stuff of legend. And that, of course, is the point. There are no outsized personalities. The cowboys are plain folk pondering their employment prospects. (Nicholson researched the dialect and speech patterns of the period in frontier diaries.[2]) Wes and Vern are the heroes by default; fugitives by force of circumstance. The outlaws, led by a one-eyed Harry Dean Stanton, are hospitable rather than hostile. One of them complains about carbuncles. Another is a black man, but no attention is drawn to it. The self-styled 'Citizens Vigilance Committee' is an undifferentiated mob that hangs men summarily and unceremoniously. Wes and Vern never even consider pleading their case; they know if they surrender they will end up "trimmin' a tree". As Kent Jones puts it, "This is a new moral framework for westerns and, in this case, for American movies in general... Since Wes and Vern have been forced to behave like criminals, for all intents and purposes they have become criminals."[3]

The rural ideal is also undermined. The settlers eke out a dreary, hardscrabble existence, the ageing mother and father stern, their daughter (Millie Perkins) unsmiling. A conventional western would have manufactured a romance between Perkins and Nicholson's young buck, but this is never broached. As the father chops away at a stubborn tree stump in futility, memories of *Shane* (1953) fade as rapidly as they arise. It is no wonder Albert Camus' essay *The Myth of Sisyphus* has been cited as one of the inspirations for the film.

Hellman is not averse to 'action' scenes – the siege of the outlaws; horseback chases; a gunfight with the vigilantes – but he shoots them in a matter-of-fact manner, with minimal camera movement and cutting. The acting is understated (among the extras almost nonexistent); there is certainly no showboating from Nicholson, who bears a look of understandable bemusement, and it is the heavyset Cameron Mitchell, as his older, more fatalistic companion, who takes the laurels. Hellman grants him a rare display of dignity in this dystopian world, when he holds off the posse with his pistol, his life ebbing away through a bullet wound, determined to give his friend a fighting chance. Nicholson's flight is both desperate and directionless; the inconclusive fade to black echoes the enigmatic climax of *The Shooting*, which Hellman and co. wrapped a week or so before beginning *Whirlwind*, and prefigures the famous non-ending of the director's *Two-Lane Blacktop* (1971), which similarly disavows any sense of romanticism.[4] **KG**

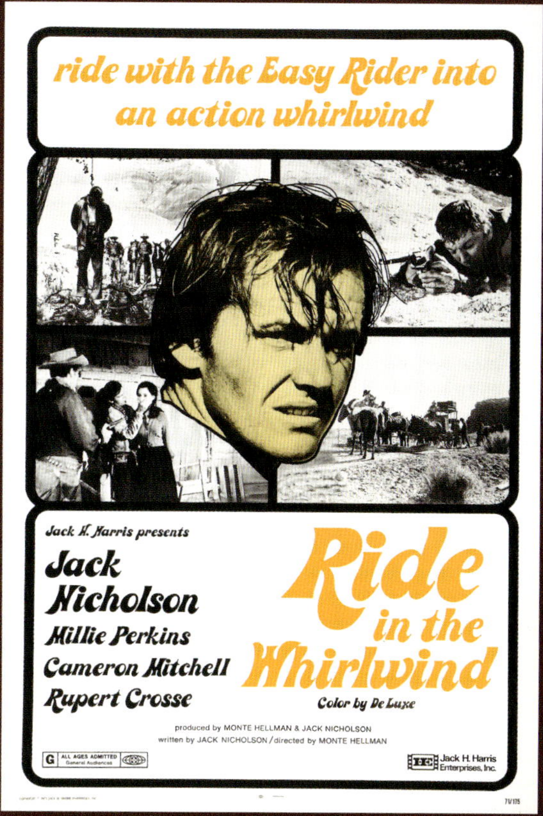

footnotes

[1] Brad Stevens, *Monte Hellman: His Life and Films* (McFarland, 2003).

[2] Brad Stevens names the source as *The Bandits [or Banditti] of the Plains*, A.S. Mercer's chronicle of the 1892 range war in Wyoming that was later the subject of *Heaven's Gate*.

[3] Kent Jones, "'The Cylinders Were Whispering My Name' – The Films of Monte Hellman', in *The Last Great American Picture Show: New Hollywood Cinema in the 1970s* (Thomas Elsaesser, Alexander Horwath, Noel King, eds., Amsterdam University Press, 2004).

[4] Neither *Ride in the Whirlwind* nor *The Shooting* – made for a combined total of $150,000 – gained a widespread theatrical release upon completion. *Ride...* screened at the San Francisco Film Festival in 1966, and both films played – to some acclaim – in France in 1969, but only in 1971 were they shown widely in American cinemas, when distributor Jack B. Harris decided to capitalise on Jack Nicholson's bankability. The tagline for *Whirlwind* – "Ride with the Easy Rider into an action whirlwind" – couldn't have been much more misleading.

The Shooting

1966, Colour, 81 mins.

D. Monte Hellman. P: Monte Hellman, Jack Nicholson (Santa Clara Productions Inc, Proteus Films). W: Adrien Joyce [Carole Eastman]. Ph: Gregory Sandor. M: Richard Markowitz. St: Warren Oates (Willet Gashade), Will Hutchins (Coley), Millie Perkins (Woman), Jack Nicholson (Billy Spear), Charles Eastman (Bearded man)

"I don't see no point to it."
"There isn't any."

A young woman employs two prospectors, one of them a former bounty hunter, the other a simple-minded naïf, to escort her across the desert; along the way, they pick up a menacing gunfighter. It develops into a manhunt. Tensions escalate; violence ensues. From this generic outline, which could have served as the basis for the kind of trek westerns directed by Budd Boetticher, or Sam Peckinpah's *The Deadly Companions*, Monte Hellman crafted one of American cinema's great conundrums.

Although several elements of a conventional western are in place, *The Shooting* is subversive for what Hellman and Carole Eastman choose to omit. It elides any sense of a redemptive purpose for its protagonists – the common feature of most genre films with an odyssey at their centre – or of a settled world beyond the barren desert setting, and eschews moral judgements. It is often labelled 'existential' (with no solid justification) or 'abstract'; oneiric is a more fitting epithet for a film that thrives on ambiguity, denying characters and spectators alike the ability to fully decipher its meaning: "The theme of the movie is the idea that, as observers of events, there are certain things which we can never know… [F]acts we don't have access to," said Hellman, who cited the killing of John F. Kennedy, and the unanswered questions surrounding it, as a key inspiration.[1] The director's biographer, Brad Stevens, recognised the influence of Samuel Beckett: "This sense of mystery which infects every frame… is less 'like life' [as Hellman liked to believe] than it is a metaphysical principle."[2]

A feeling that the complete picture is being withheld is engendered by the opening image, Hellman decapitating the familiar western establishing shot of rider and horse by focusing on the head of the horse alone. Following the lead of his scriptwriter, the actress Carole Eastman ("I think Carole deliberately wanted to be mysterious"[3]), Hellman keeps his notional heroes, Willet Gashade and Coley Boyard, off balance throughout. Pressed for details about the object of the journey, their employer is evasive, even deflecting requests for her name. It creates an atmosphere of uncertainty and mounting paranoia, exacerbated by non sequiturs (an encounter with a wounded bearded man in the desert – "Just a friend," says the woman, inscrutably) and peaking with the arrival of the woman's accomplice, the gunman Billy Spear.[4] Their relationship is unspecified, although Hellman implies a connection – familial, perhaps – by introducing Billy with the same kind of jarring close-up he had employed to bring the woman into the story, and having them dressed in similar attire.

The likeliest 'explanation' for the quest is revenge – Willet's brother, Coigne, is in flight following an episode in which he and another prospector, Leland Drum, "ran a man and a little person down" in a nearby town; Leland has already been killed before the film begins and, in the notoriously inconclusive ending, Coigne, also played by Warren Oates, is indeed revealed to be the object of the woman's hunt. But this hypothesis – and it is no more than that – in which the woman is an aggrieved mother (that was how Millie Perkins approached the role), can only be pieced together from narrative shards.

The characters' motivations, like their origins, are never established. Only the kind-hearted Coley, smitten with the woman, acts on a recognisably altruistic impulse; Willet, who could theoretically bail out of the expedition were it not for the likelihood of a bullet in the back from Billy, says simply, "It's just a feeling I got to see through." It sounds like an approximation of the old axiom, "A man's gotta do…", but is also a summation of the compulsive nature of Hellman's characters, not least those played by Oates in *Two-Lane Blacktop* and *Cockfighter* (1974).

Despite occupying the narrative space reserved for a Randolph Scott figure, with the obligation to resolve the situation, Willet never does; Oates' pensive performance suggests a man on a voyage of self-discovery, an idea underlined when he comes face to face with Coigne in the hallucinatory, slow-motion finale. Coigne appears to shoot his brother when returning the woman's fire – Hellman edits the scene in such a way that we cannot know for sure.

Although a number of shots emphasise the expanse of the Utah locations, which become increasingly inhospitable as the trek progresses, Hellman creates a paradoxical sense of confinement by grouping his characters in tight compositions, usually in medium shots, or framing them against or between rock forms. This technique supports one of the film's principal themes. Each of the main characters is constrained in some way: Willet by his compulsion to see the job through (he is also a hostage in a more literal sense, with Billy's gun a constant threat); Coley by a gallant nature that has no place in this unforgiving environment; the woman by her obsession and, perhaps, a psychological impairment, which could explain her neurotic behaviour and emotional frigidity – alerted to a "pretty little blue-jay bird" by Coley, she shoots it dead, and is entirely unfazed when her would-be suitor is later killed by Billy. The sneering, surly Billy, meanwhile, appears to be trapped in a dime novel of his own devising.

Roger Corman, Hellman's financier and silent partner, wasn't keen on the script (nor did he like that for *Ride in the Whirlwind*, the other Hellman-Nicholson western in the package), but having already fronted the money – a paltry $75,000 – gave the director all the latitude he needed. (This was on the condition that Hellman and Nicholson covered cost overruns.) Corman must have appreciated Hellman's ability to elevate routine material: the latter had made a trio of modest genre films for Corman's stable before this – *Beast from Haunted Cave* (1959), *Flight to Fury* and *Back Door to Hell* – all of them better than they needed to be. But Hellman truly arrived as a film-maker of singular vision with *The Shooting* and *Ride in the Whirlwind*. So singular was the vision, however, that they proved impossible to sell and lay undiscovered in America, like a seam of gold, until the early Seventies. **KG**

footnotes

1 Quoted in *Monte Hellman: His Life and Films* by Brad Stevens (McFarland, 2003).

2 Ibid.

3 Ibid.

4 Will Hutchins, although the least known of the actors today, was arguably the biggest draw at the time, having played the lead in the primetime TV western *Sugarfoot* from 1957-61. Oates and Nicholson – Hellman's friend since the early Sixties – clashed frequently on set, mirroring their tense relationship on screen. The opposite was true for Oates and Perkins: there is no love lost between their characters, but the actors had an affair during filming.

Hombre

1967, Colour, 111 mins.

D: Martin Ritt. P: Martin Ritt, Irving Ravetch (Hombre Productions). W: Irving Ravetch, Harriet Frank Jr. Ph: James Wong Howe. M: David Rose. St: Paul Newman (John Russell), Fredric March (Alexander Favor), Richard Boone (Grimes), Diane Cilento (Jessie Brown), Martin Balsam (Henry Mendez)

"Well now, just what do you think Hell is gonna look like?"

Hombre opens with John Russell, a white man raised by Apaches, supervising the capture of a magnificent black stallion and its herd of wild mares. The stallion is wily, but so is Russell, and the editing of the scene establishes a kinship between them. The horse is eventually fenced in, and the film follows Russell's efforts to maintain his own freedom and independence.

Russell is temporarily constrained when he is required to rejoin white society after his late adopted father bequeaths him a boarding house. Uninterested in property, he sets out by stagecoach to sell the deed in exchange for more horses. His fellow passengers view him mostly with suspicion or hostility; he responds with thinly veiled contempt. When bandits attack the stage and kidnap one of the passengers, they call on Russell to rescue her and lead them to safety, but he insists that attacking the villains – with a cunning and ruthlessness that shock his entourage – is the best means of defence.

Paul Newman's fifth film with director Martin Ritt continued the dismantling of genre archetypes they had begun in *Hud*. It is neither as forceful nor as compelling as that film, but Newman's antiheroic performance – cold, aloof, embittered – is emblematic of the changes forced on the western in the years since *Stagecoach*, to which *Hombre* could almost be considered a riposte. (Its release in 1967 put an anaemic 1966 remake of John Ford's first great western firmly in the shade.) Russell's role equates

roughly with that of John Wayne's Ringo Kid, as social outcast turned saviour, with the difference that Russell is an outcast by choice. His only real friend in the film is Martin Balsam's easygoing Mexican-American, who advises Russell to vault back over the racial barrier and join "the winning side" (an ironic term given that the town where he works is gasping its last breath, having been overlooked by the railroad companies). Russell's concession is to cut his Apache-style hair and wear 'white' clothes for the trip.

Where Ringo was friendly, big-hearted and courteous, Russell is inscrutable, sullen and predominantly impassive. He turns society's scorn for Ringo and Claire Trevor's Dallas on its head, maintaining an emotional and physical distance from his companions wherever possible. His dialogue, which has all the snap associated with Elmore Leonard, author of the source novel, is curt and caustic, coloured by his time with the Apaches.[1] He damns white America for its treatment of Indians, the way it has corralled them – like wild horses – onto reservations unsuited to their needs. Two of the travellers, an Indian agent (crooked, as such characters always seem to be) and his snooty wife, grumble about troublesome Apaches. "They live where they don't want to," explains Russell, where food is scarce and the conditions unforgiving. They deserve better. "But they eat dogs," she exclaims. "You ever been hungry lady? Not just ready for supper… You'd eat it – you'd fight for the bones, too."

Despite his affected indifference to their plight, Russell tries to educate his charges: not just to open their eyes to injustice, but to understand that the remit of 'civilisation' doesn't run to the badlands. He uses Apache guerrilla tactics to seek an advantage over his enemies, and thinks nothing of shooting the gang leader (the ever charismatic Richard Boone) from behind – something the Ringo Kid would surely never have countenanced. Russell's cold-blooded pragmatism is contrasted with the altruism of Jessie, the compassionate proprietress of Russell's unwanted boarding house, who spends much of the film chipping away at Russell's "hard bark". It is Jessie's gallant decision to take the money to the outlaws in exchange for the captive woman that seemingly prompts Russell to undertake the task himself – we must infer as much, otherwise his change of heart makes little sense, other than to force on him the kind of noble gesture he has shown no interest in performing hitherto. In the event, he sacrifices both his principles and his life, to the indifference of all the passengers bar Jessie.[2]

Intelligent and uncompromising, *Hombre* is a worthy successor to *Stagecoach*. It is a far more pessimistic, even cynical, proposition (Ritt's biographer calls it "the most hopeless of modern westerns"[3]), but it has a similarly ironic disdain for "the blessings of civilisation", updating the earlier film's attack on a "foul disease called social prejudice" for the civil rights era, in which Newman was an active participant – he had raised funds for, and attended, the 1963 march on Washington, scene of Martin Luther King's "I have a dream" speech. Newman's character shares common cause with the Indian or mixed-race protagonists who had forced their way into leading roles since the early Fifties like a rebellious tribe (Richard Widmark's Comanche Todd in *The Last Wagon* is a particularly close kinsman), adding race relations to the western's agenda and upending all kinds of preconceptions.[4] "His affinity for the land invests him with a mythic dimension, [but] his harsh response to the weakness and the sufferings of others makes him an uncomfortable and ambivalent hero."[5] It is a compelling performance, poker-faced and almost eerily phlegmatic – one of Newman's bravest. **KG**

footnotes

[1] The main difference between Leonard's novel and Irving Ravetch and Harriet Frank's adaptation is that in the film the perspective is fully that of Russell; the book is told in the first person by a young employee of the stage line – a minor character in the film.

[2] R. Philip Loy reads in Russell's demise a coded message on societal racism – one that was still relevant to an America riven along liberal/conservative lines on the issue of civil rights, among many other issues: "White society was not yet ready for a mixed-race [sic] White American Apache to live with it as an equal" (*Westerns in a Changing America*, McFarland, 2004).

[3] Gabriel Miller, *The Films of Martin Ritt: Fanfare for the Common Man* (University Press of Mississippi, 2014).

[4] Newman's character was inspired by Jimmy McKinn, an 11-year-old white boy – shown in a photograph during the closing credits – who was captured by Geronimo's Apaches in 1885. Known as Santiago, McKinn was returned to white society – against his will – when Geronimo surrendered in 1886. He later became a blacksmith and died in Phoenix in 1941. Another Elmore Leonard western that targets racial bigotry, *Valdez Is Coming*, was adapted for the screen in 1971, with Burt Lancaster, erstwhile Apache, playing an indefatigable Mexican lawman.

[5] Gabriel Miller, *The Films of Martin Ritt: Fanfare for the Common Man.*

Hour of the Gun

1967, Colour, 101 mins.

D: John Sturges. P: John Sturges (Kappa Corp, Mirisch Corp). W: Edward Anhalt. Ph: Lucien Ballard. M: Jerry Goldsmith. St: James Garner (Wyatt Earp), Jason Robards (Doc Holliday), Robert Ryan (Ike Clanton), Albert Salmi (Octavius Roy), Charles Aidman (Horace Sullivan)

"The whole thing is hypocrisy. The rules they tack on today that unless you're wearing that badge or a soldier's uniform, you can't kill. But they're the only rules there are. They are more important to you than you think. Play it that way, Wyatt, or you'll destroy yourself."

Although it functions broadly as a sequel to the director's *Gunfight at the O.K. Corral*, John Sturges' *Hour of the Gun* plays less like a star vehicle and more like a history lesson. If, as Voltaire said, "History is the lie commonly agreed upon," then the sequence of events depicted in the movie broadly corresponds to general historical consensus, making this one of the most accurate accounts of frontier legend to that point. Sturges is rarely ranked among the pantheon of western auteurs – Ford, Hawks, Mann, Peckinpah – but his unobtrusive style and superlative command of leading men has left a body of work that made a proud, even vital, contribution to the development of American cinema and its most enduring genre.

Many feel *Hour of the Gun* is his most accomplished western, but the emphasis on historical fact over contrived dramatic tension may be the reason it's not lauded as often as his most popular works: *Bad Day at Black Rock* (1955), *Gunfight at the O.K. Corral*, *Last Train from Gun Hill* (1959) and *The Magnificent Seven*. Gone are the lucid action sequences of the last-named film, replaced instead by a darker-hued melodrama, with introspective performances and a central theme of cathartic yet dehumanising retribution.

After gunning down Billy Clanton and Tom and Frank McLaury at the O.K. Corral, Wyatt Earp and Doc Holliday are tried for murder. When they are found not guilty, Ike Clanton embarks on a campaign to humiliate and discredit Earp and his brothers, beginning by paying for the bodies of the dead to be displayed in the undertaker's shop window. The Earps, meanwhile, concentrate on having Virgil elected as city marshal, while Doc spends his time in Tombstone's saloon, drinking and gambling. More blood is shed when Virgil is shot and maimed by a group of Clanton's employees, but again a trial comes to nothing. Morgan is the next target, killed with a scatter-gun while playing billiards in the saloon. Bereft, Wyatt takes the paralysed Virgil on a train to Tucson. En route, he is forced to shoot Frank Stillwell, one of Clanton's gunmen. Returning to Tombstone, Wyatt finds that the law is in Clanton's hands, and resolves to bring his murderous employees to justice – and avenge the violence perpetrated against his family. As Wyatt's revenge becomes colder, Doc, a self-proclaimed gambler and killer, tries in vain to make his friend observe the rules of his badge.

The ominous opening credits firmly establish the director's intentions. Each of the three major players in the drama is introduced in the tense moments before the O.K. Corral confrontation: James Garner strides to the front of the frame, Jason Robards loads his shotgun and Robert Ryan looks out to the deserted town street, waiting for the lawmen's approach. Each actor's name fills the screen in close-up, emblazoned against their edgy, intense faces. The sun-scorched Southwest locations are lensed with startling clarity by Lucien Ballard, two years away from his career-defining work on *The Wild Bunch*. Sturges squeezes maximum dramatic impact from the build-up to the gunfight as Holliday and the Earp brothers, with determined strides and fixed stares, walk the length of the town, halting within bullet range of the corral. Sam Peckinpah was said to have been so impressed with the "walk scene" that he sought to emulate it in the final reel of *The Wild Bunch*. What follows in *Hour of the Gun* is not a balletic apotheosis but a rudimentary exchange of gunfire less than one minute in duration. The real showdown lasted around 30 seconds – a brief moment in the history of the United States but one that has repeatedly informed its cultural heritage.

In the evolution of the western, *Hour of the Gun* bridges the divide between the psychological melodramas of Anthony Mann, with their damaged protagonists, on the one hand, and the morally ambiguous sunburnt worlds of Robert Aldrich's *Vera Cruz*, Richard Brooks' *The Professionals* and Peckinpah's *The Wild Bunch*. Sturges stresses the malleable nature of frontier morality. As the dust settles on the opening gunfight, Earp checks that Holliday had been sworn in as a deputy. "Well, wear your badge then," he orders, the tin star making a fraction of a difference between murderer and upholder of the peace. Earp treads this fine line. In the opinion of Old West scholar Allen Barra, Sturges' film offers "the least romantic Earp figure up to that time".[1] He begins the film as a relatively upstanding figure, given the threats against him and his family, but eventually succumbs to the ancient curse of vengeance. Garner handles the subtle metamorphosis deftly; it's a fine showcase for an actor who seldom received the praise (or the roles) he deserved. Earp is difficult to like but easy to empathise with, although one wonders if any of the men he is "forced" to kill could have been taken alive. There is an implication that Earp's morals are deteriorating in his thirst to settle the score; it is a sign that the genre was becoming more pragmatic, less rose-tinted, in the presentation of its protagonists.

The script's real coup is to position Doctor John "Doc" Holliday, ironically, as Earp's conscience. Killer, card player, alcoholic and consumptive, he taunts and goads Earp throughout the Vendetta Ride: "If you're gonna kill like me, you might as well drink like me." Afforded the most eloquent and insightful lines in Edward Anhalt's sagacious screenplay, Robards delivers in gruffly erudite style. Holliday was an intelligent but drink-damaged man, addicted to both the bottle and cards, employing his gun for survival. He hovers behind Earp's shoulders, moralising: "Those aren't warrants you got there, they're hunting licences." Knowing Earp is essentially a man of ethics, he tries to persuade him to work within the law, telling him bluntly, "You can't live like me." Despite these attempts to counsel Earp, Doc betrays his real nature after his friend shoots a Clanton man in a duel. "Boy, you sure gave him a chance. I would have killed him in his bed."

In contrast to Ford's celluloid poem to Earp and Holliday, *My Darling Clementine*, there are fewer flights of fancy here. Sturges prefers to shoot straight, structuring the Earp Vendetta Ride episodically, conflating certain characters and events to make the script digestible. Ford has Victor Mature's Doc killed at the O.K. Corral after a heroic gesture (some would say in punishment for his love of an ambiguously racialised heroine),[2] while Henry Fonda's Earp is relatively unchallenging to read. Garner endows this much-mythologised figure with greater complexity; he's a far more human, if not humane, character, and Garner's portrayal – a far cry from Fonda's frosty performance – does the actor huge credit.

Certainly one of the first westerns to burrow beneath the legend, *Hour of the Gun* is a bold departure from Earpian folklore. The abundance of characters and events sometimes threaten to muddy a taut screenplay, but as a study of man's conflict with his conscience it stands alongside great western melodramas such as *The Gunfighter* and *The Naked Spur*. While Holliday knows his body and soul are lost to disease and a murderous past, the only path he has to redemption is to save his friend. As the real Doc once said of his conscience to a newspaper reporter, "I coughed that up with my lungs two years ago." **CH**

footnotes

1 Allen Barra, *Inventing Wyatt Earp: His Life and Many Legends* (Carroll & Graf, 1998).

2 Holliday, in fact, died on 8 November, 1887, six years after the O.K. Corral gun battle. He was 36. To ease the symptoms of his tuberculosis, he had become increasingly dependent on alcohol and laudanum.

One bullet
can kill a town...
just like a man!
METRO-GOLDWYN-MAYER presents
HENRY FONDA
JANICE RULE
WELCOME TO HARD TIMES
Suggested For Mature Audiences
A YOUNGSTEIN AND KARR PRODUCTION
co-starring
KEENAN WYNN · JANIS PAIGE · JOHN ANDERSON · WARREN OATES · FAY SPAIN · EDGAR BUCHANAN
and ALDO RAY screen play by BURT KENNEDY directed by BURT KENNEDY produced by MAX E. YOUNGSTEIN and DAVID KARR
IN METROCOLOR
MGM

Welcome to Hard Times

1967, Colour, 103 mins. (cut version 78 mins.)

D: Burt Kennedy. P: Max E. Youngstein, David Karr (Metro-Goldwyn-Mayer). W: Burt Kennedy. Ph: Harry Stradling Jr. M: Harry Sukman. St: Henry Fonda (Will Blue), Janice Rule (Molly Riordan), Keenan Wynn (Zar), Janis Paige (Adah), John Anderson (Isaac and Ezra Maple)

"Not much of a country is it... If the drought or the blizzards don't get you, some devil with liquor in his soul and a gun in his claw will."

After his lean stories, witty dialogue and morally complex characters for the Ranown cycle had rejuvenated the classic western in the Fifties, Burt Kennedy directed a series of films in the following decade aimed at propping up the genre's myths. Roistering, light-hearted westerns such as *The Rounders* (1965), *The War Wagon* (1967), *Support Your Local Sheriff!* and *The Good Guys and the Bad Guys* (both 1969) ran parallel to – and counter to – the revisionist movement. Evoking latter-day Howard Hawks, all were predicated on the genial sparring of ageing icons (Henry Fonda, Glenn Ford, Robert Mitchum, John Wayne, Kirk Douglas), with a younger generation of actors (David Carradine, Bruce Dern) providing a dusting of Sixties cynicism, much as Randolph Scott had been offset by up-and-coming players in the films Kennedy wrote for Budd Boetticher. *Welcome to Hard Times* may feature Fonda and a host of grizzled actors associated with the genre, but in all other respects it is an aberration.

Kennedy's West was typically a haven for battered but defiant heroism. Ethical lines were blurred, but remained distinct. In *Welcome to Hard Times*, practically every character is infected with moral failings and physical cowardice, and the environment itself conspires against complacent frontier fantasies. The visitation of 'the Bad Man from Bodie' (Aldo Ray), not so much a character in his own right as what Kim Newman calls a "monstrous abstract",[1] a curse incarnate, occasions the material destruction and psychological deterioration of Hard Times, an isolated, one-street township.[2] With no dialogue, just peals of maniacal laughter, the stocky villain rapes, murders and burns his way through the opening sequence virtually unopposed, departing as suddenly as he arrived. For Hard Times, read Hadleyville – collective quavering in the face of an external threat is compounded here by the absence of a Will Kane figure; Henry Fonda's ineffectual, quasi-pacifist lawyer-cum-mayor is a sorry stand-in. The apocalyptic imagery that bookends the film, combined with the suggestion that the community deserves or in some sense *wills* its own devastation (a notion that comes over more strongly in the source novel), is as much a foretaste of *High Plains Drifter* as it is the acid reflux of *High Noon* and certain of its descendants, notably Richard Wilson's *Man with the Gun* and *Invitation to a Gunfighter*.[3]

The very absence of grit in Will Blue, Fonda's character, was the main reason that Kennedy adapted and directed E.L. Doctorow's novel in the first place: "In the first scene in the picture, the bad guy comes into the saloon, and the bartender says to Henry Fonda, 'You gotta get rid of him,' and Fonda says, 'If I go over there, he'll kill me.' I liked that – finally a guy who didn't strap on his guns and run to get the bad guy. He was honest, a realist, a complete anti-hero. The movie was way ahead of its time."[4] Of course, the anti-hero, as commonly understood, had made his mark in the American western in the preceding decade (one could argue as far back as the good-badman archetypes of the silent era) and was then running rampant in the European version.[5] What Kennedy is alluding to is something quite different. Blue is anti-heroic in a literal sense. He not only shies away from physically confronting the killer; he also persuades saloon-girl Molly to act as bait in a botched ambush, which results in her being raped and beaten in the course of the Man's unmotivated rampage.

Like Ransom Stoddard in *The Man Who Shot Liberty Valance* and James McKay in *The Big Country* (1958), Blue eschews conventional western machismo. Unlike those characters, he cannot muster sufficient conviction to deflect the scorn that comes his way. Here it is Molly, his would-be lover, who chides him throughout about his lack of "manliness", while he attempts to express his principles with platitudes. Only in the film's central section, when the focus switches from individual bravery to collective effort and endurance, does Blue come close to meeting Kennedy's requirement for heroism: "The leading man should be able to walk away at any point, but he chooses not to, and that's what makes him a hero."[6] Fonda rather wearily adopts his 'man of the people' persona in these scenes, as Blue refuses to abandon the smouldering remains of Hard Times and spearheads efforts to rebuild the town – and morale – among its few remaining inhabitants. These include young Jimmy (Michael Shea), orphaned in the opening sequence, a silent Indian medicine man (a sorely miscast Royal Dano) and a handful of newcomers: the blustery Zar and his retinue of prostitutes; Leo Jenks (Warren Oates), an easy-going drifter; and storekeeper Isaac.[7]

Even in this relatively optimistic passage, vicious winter winds rip through the community like portents, as if summoned up by Molly's predictions of the Man's return. Janice Rule's performance becomes increasingly histrionic as Molly attempts to mould Jimmy into the kind of man who will not hesitate to kill, buying him a shotgun and testing his mettle in a scene that puts Blue in the firing line. (Her role is clearly a conscious departure from the stereotypical function of the heroine, which is to deplore violence and defuse men's violent instincts.) For his part, Blue tries to free Jimmy from Molly's "spell" by instilling his own values in the boy. If Blue's argument – that violence achieves nothing – is intended as a bolster of liberal or pacifist views (widely associated with the actor playing the role, of course), it is not only anathema to the western genre (a conflict of interest that films like *Liberty Valance* and *The Big Country*, with stronger scripts and characters, have thrived upon), but ridiculous in context. Aldo Ray's malevolent villain is conceived, loosely, as a force of nature: "[Men like that] come with the land," says one character. "Nothing you can do about them any more than you can the wind or the cold or the dust." Clearly he cannot be appeased and, by standing back, the locals become culpable in their own crisis. Yet Molly's call to arms costs more lives, including her own, in a clumsy scene contrived to punish her for putting a gun in Jimmy's hand.

The finale invites contradictory readings: as a reaffirmation of the validity of retributive violence, and as a suggestion that "individual bravado with a gun is ultimately futile and self-destructive" (John H. Lenihan). Blue summons up the guts to face the Man, but his triumph is more opportunistic than heroic, since he can only kill his tormentor after the latter has run out of bullets, fatally undermining his own integrity. Kennedy – who retreated to safer ground with a string of self-deprecating westerns after this one was poorly received – cannot resolve the dilemma he creates, and the message of *Welcome to Hard Times* is finally as muddy as the rutted thoroughfare that bisects the town. As for Fonda, his one-paced performance suggests that the challenge of playing against type in his next westerns, *Firecreek* and, especially, *Once Upon a Time in the West* (both 1968), could not have come soon enough. **KG**

footnotes

1 *Wild West Movies* (Bloomsbury, 1990).

2 The villain's designation refers to a bogeyman invented in the late 1870s by journalist E.H. Clough, who wrote a humorous piece in the *San Francisco Argonaut* satirising the rowdy reputation of a California boom town called Bodie. The habitually violent 'Bad Man from Bodie' became the subject of many a tall tale, and was, for a short while, "a sort of a generic term for all the bad men in the State", as another publication put it.

3 Kennedy tips his hat to another classic western when the villain, in the course of his opening onslaught, blasts Elisha Cook's plucky undertaker into a muddy pothole, a flashback to the actor's famous demise in *Shane* (1953).

4 Interview with Burt Kennedy by Jeremy Arnold in *MovieMaker Magazine*, April 2000.

5 David Lusted detects the influence of the Italian western in *Hard Times'* bombastic set pieces and its demonic villain, but few of these had been released in America by the time this film was released in May 1967. This is not to say that Kennedy hadn't yet encountered the Euro-western: prior to beginning *Hard Times* in California, he had been in southern Spain shooting *Return of the Seven*. Perhaps he had the opportunity to see one or more examples while he was there. One Kennedy western that certainly was influenced by the European variety was the Raquel Welch vehicle *Hannie Caulder*, a revenge story of wildly varying moods.

6 Interview with Burt Kennedy by Jeremy Arnold in *MovieMaker Magazine*, April 2000.

7 Warren Oates had discovered E.L. Doctorow's novel in the early Sixties and hoped that his friend Sam Peckinpah would direct it, but it wound up in the unlikely hands of Kennedy, for whom Oates had just performed in *Return of the Seven*.

above: Henry Fonda and Janice Rule on a UK lobby card; the film was retitled and given an X certificate for its British release.

Will Penny

1967, Colour, 108 mins.

D: Tom Gries. P: Fred Engel, Walter Seltzer (Paramount). W: Tom Gries. Ph: Lucien Ballard. M: David Raksin.
St: Charlton Heston (Will Penny), Joan Hackett (Catherine Allen), Donald Pleasence (Preacher Quint), Lee Majors (Blue), Bruce Dern (Rafe Quint)

"It's just a case of too soon old and too late smart."

It is difficult to believe that the cowboy would have attained his pre-eminent position in frontier mythology had his lifestyle been related in as raw and unromantic a manner as it is in *Will Penny*. It was part of a sequence of westerns with stories and themes tailored for ageing actors, but there is nothing wistful about Tom Gries' film, which "discounted the premise of *The Misfits* and *Lonely Are the Brave* that the cowboy had ever been a happy, free individualist or had ever played a meaningful role in frontier progress".[1] Even embodied by Charlton Heston, portrayer of historical and legendary titans, Will is far from heroic material; admirable for his self-awareness, perhaps, but essentially ordinary. The film's focus on this humble protagonist prompted Roger Ebert to draw up a useful distinction between 'westerns' and 'cowboy movies', of which this is one of the most convincing and affecting early examples.

Weathered, illiterate and somewhat insular, Will is a pragmatist. Nearing 50, he knows he has few options left in life. His work is arduous, but it is all he knows. Paid off after a trail drive, he drifts around with two friends, gets into a pointless shoot-out with the crazed preacher Quint and his brood and lands a job on Ben Johnson's ranch as a line rider, "up in ridge country", patrolling the farthest reaches of the range. It is a solitary role for which he is ideally suited, but a complication arises when he encounters a woman, Catherine, and her son (Jon Gries, the director's boy) wintering, without permission, in a cabin on the edge of the spread. The trio develop a pseudo-familial relationship, with Will and the boy forging a *Shane*-like bond, and there is talk of buying a farm. But the return of the villains – coupled with Will's inability to imagine himself setting down roots and sowing seeds – forestalls any thought of this becoming a permanent arrangement.

Gries, directing a feature for the first time, spun out the script from a story he had written and directed for *The Westerner*, Sam Peckinpah's ground-breaking 1960 television series. Gries has a fine ear for dialogue and dialect and coaxes a vivid performance from Heston; it is regarded by many, including the actor, as the best he ever gave. There is no occasion for grandstanding, and Heston is all the better for it, eagerly playing against his larger-than-life star image, which had been the subject of subversion in his previous western, Peckinpah's *Major Dundee*. "It might be that it gives me a greater freedom," the actor mused of his public persona. "Since… whatever needs the audience has to have in its hero as a protagonist may… be satisfied with the chemistry that I bring to the camera to begin with, then I can safely wear the thirty-year-old torn hat, handlebar moustache, and the chaps which I stole from an earlier film… I don't have to wear a brand-new Stetson and a tightly cut cavalry twill cowboy suit."[2]

above: Joan Hackett and Jon Gries.

Will's reticence resonates, as does his weary resignation, and the stiffness that Heston was often accused of communicates his character's social maladjustment. Gries paces the film around his languid protagonist and his hesitant, awkward romance with the hardy Catherine – Joan Hackett is just as sincere as Heston in a role that calls for grit more than glamour. The only false note is struck by the intrusion of Donald Pleasence and his sons – or rather, by their presentation as pantomime grotesques, derivatives of Sam Peckinpah's peckerwoods or the maniacal villains in Euro-westerns. Their presence, while adding colour and conflict, feels like a concession to the decadent tone struck by many late-Sixties westerns, and jars in a film otherwise concerned more with mundanity – few frontier films depict their central character darning – than it is with melodrama.

Will Penny was received appreciatively – the *Monthly Film Bulletin* called it "the most intelligent western for some time" – with the reservation that it required a seasoned film-maker to smooth its rough edges. Yet if Gries' inexperience is evident, so too is the mastery of his DP, Lucien Ballard, who composes his images quite magnificently, not least when picking out Will against the Inyo Mountains of California in isolating long shots, putting the cowboy's lonely existence into perspective in more ways than one. Ultimately, the contrast between the freedom of the range – its abiding attraction for loners like Will – and the cluttered cabin, a shared space divided up in rudimentary fashion, redolent of domestic duties and responsibility to others, symbolises the internal dilemma that Will never manages to resolve. **KG**

footnotes

1 John H. Lenihan, *Showdown: Confronting Modern America in the Western Film.*

2 'It's All a Matter of Size', *Films and Filming*, April 1968.

Death of a Gunfighter

1969, Colour, 94 mins.

D: Allen Smithee [Don Siegel, Robert Totten]. P: Richard E. Lyons (Universal). W: Joseph Calvelli. Ph: Andrew Jackson. M: Oliver Nelson. St: Richard Widmark (Frank Patch), Lena Horne (Claire Quintana), John Saxon (Lou Trinidad), Carroll O'Connor (Lester Locke), David Opatoshu (Edward Rosenbloom)

"You see, gentlemen, what we're really deciding here is whether we move forward or backward. We either need to keep up with the times or we lose out."

A sour spin on *High Noon* for the cynical Sixties, *Death of a Gunfighter* takes to its grimly logical conclusion a breakdown in relations between a community angling for outside investment and an ageing marshal seen to hinder those aspirations. The decisive gunfight – really a gundown – even transpires on the lawman's wedding day after he has ignored admonitions to leave. Through his eyes, the film "critically examines the new politics of a modernising America and finds it wanting".[1]

The setting is Cottonwood Springs in Texas at the turn of the 20th century. The town councillors hope to lure "Eastern investors", but fear the presence of their truculent marshal, Frank Patch – who behaves and dresses, in their eyes, like a character from a dime novel – would hamper their efforts, not least because of Patch's reputation for ruthless efficiency. The film begins with him gunning down a drunken local in self-defence – the latest in a long line of confrontations that have earned him widespread enmity. (Rumours spread swiftly that Patch was sleeping with the dead man's wife. They are never confirmed, but their persistence reflects just as badly on the populace as on Patch himself.) "We don't want a man that *good* any more," says the mayor, alluding to the marshal's prowess with a gun, which suited the citizens' purposes in the past but jars against their vision of progress. But Patch is more than willing to stay where he's not wanted. Efforts to engineer his removal on legal grounds come to naught, even when one of his old deputies, now a county sheriff, is brought in to enforce a trumped-up arrest warrant, and a crisis looms as Patch is forced to meet more challenges the only way he knows how.

The script, adapted from Lewis B. Patten's "lusty, page-hammering" novel, is strong on turn of phrase and period detail, in portraying a town in transition (the sense of eras colliding is almost literal at one point, when the mayor's car careers through the streets, sending a horse skittering), but sketchy in other respects. We have only a general sense of what has caused the dispute – Patch is regarded as trigger-happy, and has been in the job for so long that he knows "every dirty, rotten, lowdown thing about everybody in this town" – but it is enough to create a poisonous atmosphere of mutual animosity, broken only now and again by some ill-fitting comedic business involving a local adolescent, one of Patch's few supporters. Several characters are poorly defined, their motivations obscure, leaving a number of subplots dangling: Lena Horne's role as Claire, town madam and Patch's woman, is insubstantial, her potential as a counterpart for *High Noon's* Helen Ramirez untapped; while Carroll O'Connor's sardonic saloon owner, the kind of acerbic smart aleck who says what others are thinking (voicing the town's racism towards John Saxon's mixed-race sheriff, for example), belatedly and implausibly backs up his cynicism with action, leading a sneak attack on the marshal that triggers the latter's final reckoning.

At 55, Richard Widmark looks every inch the veteran Westerner, and gives an immaculate performance as an ornery, uncompromising traditionalist, a man hard to like but equally difficult to judge. Clad in outmoded, sandy-hued frontier duds, contrasting with the city fathers in their metropolitan attire, he is contemptuous of his opponents, the kind of men who conspire in back rooms (anticipating gangsterism, as the *Monthly Film Bulletin* astutely observed) and lack the integrity that Patch, for all his faults, remains governed by. In a scene that calls to mind Barry Sullivan's bravado in *Forty Guns*, Patch demonstrates the kind of old-fashioned moral authority conspicuously absent elsewhere in Cottonwood Springs by brazenly walking into a would-be assassin's line of fire, gambling that his assailant will back down – which he does, turning the gun on himself and adding indirectly to Patch's grisly tally.

Widmark captures his character in all his complexity, a mixture of pride, professionalism, spite, bloody-mindedness and ultimately suicidal impulsiveness. To a man like this – cousin of the anachronistic gunfighters in Sam Peckinpah's *Ride the High Country* and *The Wild Bunch*, as well as the hounded outlaws of *Butch Cassidy and the Sundance Kid* – the only way to emerge from the crisis with any dignity, to stay true to himself, is to go down fighting. As events come to a head, Patch, like Will Kane towards the end of *High Noon*, has the air of a man putting his affairs in order; instead of drawing up his will, however, he hastily proposes to Claire and arranges a swift marriage ceremony, perhaps to make an "honest woman" of her, meaning that, as in *High Noon*, he faces his moment of truth with the ink on his marriage licence barely dry.

An overlooked addition to the cycle of elegiac, dying-frontier westerns, *Death of a Gunfighter* is remembered chiefly for being the directorial debut of the pseudonymous 'Alan [here Allen] Smithee'. Don Siegel completed the film at the behest of the producer after the man Siegel had suggested for the job, Robert Totten, fell out with Widmark. Totten, a graduate of TV westerns, shot the majority of footage, with Siegel stepping in towards the end of the schedule. The film is inconsistent as a result, chiefly in the preponderance of loose ends. According to Siegel, his primary contributions were what Totten called the "book-ends" – the haunting shots of Claire in mourning dress at the station, boarding a train along with Patch's coffin, that open and close the film. Totten, with some impetuosity, insisted his name be removed from the credits, and Siegel declined to claim the picture as his own, inventing the collective alias 'Smithee' that has been used intermittently in Hollywood ever since.

While this wasn't a personal project for Siegel, its principal theme resonates in some of his key works. Men out of place or out of pace with the times feature in *Madigan* (1968), in which Widmark played another no-nonsense law enforcer with antediluvian methods; the Clint Eastwood maverick cop movies *Coogan's Bluff* (1968) and *Dirty Harry* (1971); and, most pertinently, John Wayne's *The Shootist* (1976), likewise set at a turning point for the old West, with another imperious performance at its core. (Wayne had earlier declined the role of Frank Patch.) While not as poignant a film as Wayne's swan song, *Death of a Gunfighter* similarly plays like a valediction for a dying breed of individual and a fading brand of western. **KG**

footnotes

1 David Lusted, *The Western* (Pearson, 2003).

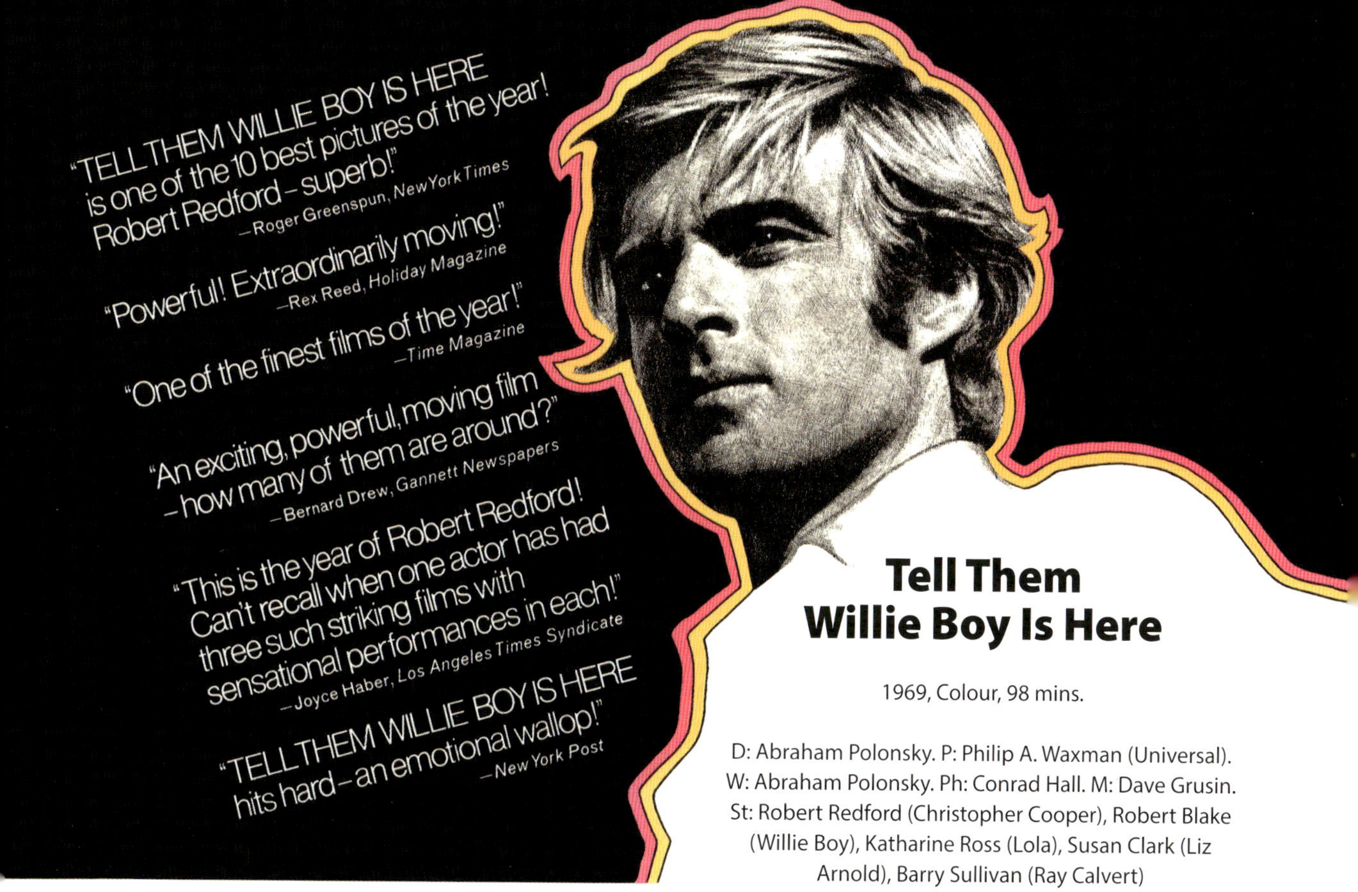

Tell Them Willie Boy Is Here

1969, Colour, 98 mins.

D: Abraham Polonsky. P: Philip A. Waxman (Universal). W: Abraham Polonsky. Ph: Conrad Hall. M: Dave Grusin. St: Robert Redford (Christopher Cooper), Robert Blake (Willie Boy), Katharine Ross (Lola), Susan Clark (Liz Arnold), Barry Sullivan (Ray Calvert)

"You can't win. You can't beat them, Willie, ever."
"Maybe. But they'll know I was here."

Issued as a kind of admonition to American youth, *Tell Them Willie Boy Is Here* recasts the eponymous Paiute Indian who in 1909 was the centre of 'the West's last famous manhunt' as a totem of dissentient individualism, "cool, unreconciled and angry… a one-man guerrilla insurrection".[1] Directed by Abraham Polonsky, a grandee of the Hollywood left and long-time blacklistee, it reflected its maker's own experience of exile and persecution while expressing contemporary cynicism about the 'imperialist' drift of domestic and foreign policy – a continuation, it was fashionable to assert, of the "genocide" (Polonsky's term) that accompanied the settling of the frontier.

This astringent western, based on a historical exposé by Harry Wilson Lawton, was Polonsky's return to directing after 21 years in the wilderness, and retains the provocative disposition of his best-known work: his script for Robert Rossen's boxing drama *Body and Soul* (1947) landed some telling blows against corruption and materialism; and his own directorial debut, *Force of Evil* (1948), employed a crooked lawyer as a bridge between big business and organised crime. (While blacklisted, he also wrote the blistering *Odds Against Tomorrow* [1959], a late film noir seething with racial tension.) The alienated anti-hero's bolt for freedom in *Willie Boy* struck the director as a metaphor for "a generation on the run",[2] and his script compresses the inexorable advance of Anglo-American civilisation into a pursuit narrative, with Willie's receding options as the chase intensifies mirroring those of his people.

Transpiring 20 years after Wounded Knee had effectively stamped out Native American resistance and independence, *Willie Boy* portrays Indians as a colonised people. The Paiutes' affairs are overseen by that rarest of species, a female reservation agent: the well-meaning, well-bred Easterner Dr. Elizabeth Arnold, for whom the moulding of "my Indians" into model Americans is a kind of social experiment, in line with the assimilation policies of the government's Indian Bureau. She believes she is helping her charges by educating them in the ways of the whites, but in reality she is stifling their cultural identity. (Significantly, Willie sheds his acquired Anglo trappings during his flight – he starts the film in shirt and slacks and ends it in a fringed buckskin jacket once worn by his father.) The Paiutes are an underclass even on their own reservation – tribal policemen have no power to act against whites illegally selling liquor – as well as outside it, where local rednecks rail against the right of Indians to enter a saloon as if they were white.

His tribe may have been pacified, but Willie – a study in controlled aggression and surly indignation by Robert Blake – is far from passive. He fights back against racism (with a pool cue, in the saloon scene) and is defiant of authority in any guise. He has served time in a "white man's prison" for previous infractions, and steals away his girlfriend, Lola, from her disapproving father, killing him in self-defence during a midnight altercation. Willie tries to reassure Lola that they'll not be followed – "Nobody gives a damn what Indians do" – while Lola's mother accepts the elopement as "marriage by capture", a valid tribal custom. But the event coincides with a planned visit to the region by President Taft,[3] and local deputy sheriff 'Coop' Cooper is obliged, against his better judgement, to put together a posse and follow the couple into a merciless desert drained of much of its colour by Conrad Hall's mesmerising photography.

While Polonsky's abhorrence of official attitudes towards the Indians is to be expected, he reserves sharp criticism for media scaremongering and misrepresentation. Newspapermen join the dots between Willie's evasion of the posse – who panic when Willie pins them down with rifle fire, convinced there must be more than one man out there – and the president's visit, and concoct wild stories about a mass uprising aimed at overthrowing the government. (At the time of production, comparably hysterical reporting was rife about the activities of the Black Panther Party. Willie Boy, however, is more of a lone wolf.) Polonsky uses the tension surrounding Taft's impending arrival as a comment on America's tradition of political violence: as sheriff Wilson (Charles McGraw, in a rare western role), overseeing security, remarks, "Anybody can kill a president," he is referring specifically to the assassination in 1901 of William McKinley, but Polonsky evidently had in mind Sixties audiences still reeling from the shooting of the Kennedy brothers.

The script establishes a duality between hunter and prey that makes a one-on-one reckoning inevitable. For John H. Lenihan, Coop "shares much of Willie Boy's contempt for society's false sense of respectability".[4] Robert Redford plays him more like Jeremiah Johnson than the Sundance Kid: disenchanted and cynical, you feel he would just as well let Willie abscond. (Pauline Kael, who hated the film, felt the use of 'Coop' as a nickname too obvious a signifier of scorn for the steadfast western heroes of old, typified by Gary Cooper.) Coop, whose father was a famed Indian hunter, discerns Willie's thinking and matches his cunning; when he finds Willie's handprint in the sand by a waterhole, his own hand fits perfectly.

Just as pointed, if rather more forced, are the contrasts Polonsky divines, cutting from the spontaneous love scenes between Willie and Lola, filmed in natural settings, to the loveless couplings of Coop and Elizabeth in darkened rooms. Despite Willie's occasional chauvinism, Lola is drawn to him both for what he means to her and for what his bolt for freedom represents for her people; her death, which occurs off screen, may even have been suicide, to speed Willie on his way. Coop and Elizabeth's relationship, on the other hand, is defined by mutual exploitation – they use each other to fulfil a physical need, but neither seems capable of forging an emotional connection.

As the chase becomes increasingly elemental – just two men, duelling in the rocks – the final distinction between the reluctant antagonists is the most significant: in choosing death to captivity, turning on Coop with

above: John Vernon (left) and Robert Lipton (right) as posse members on the trail of Willie Boy.

an empty rifle and forcing the lawman to kill him, Willie remains true to himself. Coop, as an authority figure, is denied this option. Nevertheless, he is conscientious enough to allow the ritual cremation of Willie's body by Paiute deputies, angrily dismissing Wilson's requests for proof of his quarry's death: "Tell them we're all out of souvenirs." Another conflicted lawman would echo these sentiments at the end of *Pat Garrett and Billy the Kid*.

Directed by a man forced for so long to sit on the sidelines, it is little surprise that in some ways *Willie Boy* was behind the times. Take its treatment of women: Lola, although played by Katharine Ross, "Hollywood's leading counterculture ingénue",[5] knows her place, and is certainly no Bonnie to Willie's Clyde; while Elizabeth, who has the superior air of the stereotyped Easterner, is made to seem hypocritical by her submission to rough sex with Coop, a man whose type she obviously despises. Yet to a remarkable degree, Polonsky, a refugee from old Hollywood, managed to keep pace with its firebrands, having helped set, in his Forties films, the liberal-progressive agenda the likes of Arthur Penn, Dennis Hopper and Peter Fonda were now following with their own tales of doomed outlaws caught in the crosshairs of modern America. **KG**

footnotes

1 J. Hoberman, *The Dream Life: Movies, Media, and the Mythology of the Sixties* (The New Press, 2005).

2 Paul Buhle and Dave Wagner, *A Very Dangerous Citizen: Abraham Lincoln Polonsky and the Hollywood Left* (University of California Press, 2001).

3 In 1911, President Taft was visited by a deputation of Cheyenne and Arapaho Indians. Among the items on their agenda was a film called *Curse of the Redman*, which they felt to be "racist and inflammatory". It was inspired by the manhunt for Willie Boy, which was still fresh in the popular memory at the time (Bob Herzberg, *Savages and Saints: The Changing Image of American Indians in Westerns*, McFarland, 2003).

4 *Showdown: Confronting Modern America in the Western Film* (University of Illinois Press, 1980).

5 J. Hoberman, *The Dream Life*.

The Wild Bunch

1969, 145 mins. (theatrical versions varied from 123-135 mins.)

D: Sam Peckinpah. P: Phil Feldman (Phil Feldman Productions Inc, Warner Bros.-Seven Arts).
W: Walon Green, Sam Peckinpah, Roy N. Sickner (story). Ph: Lucien Ballard. M: Jerry Fielding.
St: William Holden (Pike Bishop), Ernest Borgnine (Dutch Engstrom), Robert Ryan (Deke Thornton),
Edmond O'Brien (Sykes), Warren Oates (Lyle Gorch)

***"When you side with a man, you stay with him!
And if you can't do that, you're like some animal, you're finished!
We're finished! All of us!"***

"Those days are closing fast." Pike Bishop's observation reverberated beyond the narrative of this most epochal and personal of Sam Peckinpah's works. It signalled the closing of a chapter on the Hollywood western, blasting away the remnants of idealism that had lingered in the film's two most immediate antecedents: *The Magnificent Seven* and *The Professionals*. It lamented what the director called "the disintegration of a world" – the old West that formed the backdrop to his formative years and of which his renegade heroes were relics. Yet there was much ambiguity about the values this lost age was supposed to represent. Under subsequent analysis, *The Wild Bunch* also affirmed that an (illusory) era of innocence had passed; the positioning of children not just as spectators but as participants in the carnage symbolized the triumph of violence that Peckinpah saw around him, a victory that mass culture both recorded and perpetuated – with this film-maker cited in that process more than most.

Typically for Peckinpah, this bleak diagnosis is balanced by the value he finds in the camaraderie, however strained, of his rough-hewn protagonists, along with their adherence unto death to Polonius's maxim: "To thine own self be true." They appear archaic in a fast-mechanising world of equally rapid social change, of rampant, callous capitalism and, it would seem, receding virtue: "The society that represents the law," notes Richard Slotkin, "is one in which greed, force and mutual suspicion are the only binding ties."[1] Typical also that the director neither mitigates the Bunch's calling as killers – there are no hard-luck stories; they appear to have chosen this life – nor apologises for their ruthlessness, of which the first indication is Pike Bishop's instruction to his men regarding hostages: "If they move, kill 'em." (That William Holden, erstwhile Hollywood golden boy, utters these words amplifies the shock.)

Conventionally, they would be demonised. Peckinpah was never one for simple dichotomies, however. He sees strength in their unity of purpose, nobility in their recalcitrance, and he offers them up as heroes in a take-it-or-leave-it proposition that surely resonated with Americans for whom standard assumptions about good and evil were becoming unsustainable. *The Wild Bunch* was the most brutally forthright challenge to preconceptions and sensibilities that cinema – or at least the western – had yet mounted, and it remains a hard ride for anybody expecting moral transparency; here, it is opaque at best. Even before civilians begin dying in the streets of Starbuck, caught in the crossfire between the Bunch and the gutter-trash bounty hunters who "represent the law", "Manichaean morality," as Michael Coyne puts it, "is this film's first fatality."[2]

Peckinpah described his outlaw subjects as, "People who lived not only by violence, but for it." As Pike says, "I wouldn't have it any other way." Never has this idea been realised so forcibly, the outlaw mentality and lifestyle communicated with such candour and conviction – thanks in large part to Peckinpah's ability to forge hard-bitten, hard-living actors into a fighting unit. Here are players so thoroughly absorbed in their roles as to be indistinguishable from them. By the same token, there is greater depth to the characterisations – especially that of Pike and his alter ego, Deke Thornton, his partner in crime turned reluctant railroad lackey, with his own scuzzy 'bunch' in tow – and they display a wider range of emotions than movie outlaws of yore, building to a pitch of moral outrage rooted in remorse at their own past failings. This idea is focused on Pike as the leader of the outfit, the setter of standards – "When you side with a man, you stay with him" – he has too often failed to meet, most damagingly in Thornton's case. Pike's complacency led to Thornton's imprisonment and his current predicament; David Weddle calls him "a wild stallion, now broken, saddled and harnessed by the system", tethered to an agreement he can barely stomach but is forced to, not just by the threat of a return to prison, but also by the tarnished code of honour he shares with Pike.[3]

As outlaws, then, self-preservation dictates the Bunch's actions and reactions, but there is also the matter of self-determination, one of Peckinpah's principal refrains. Their stratagems amount to a rearguard action (almost, it might be said, on behalf of all the ageing, harried protagonists of twilight westerns) against "the great and fancy they" – the powerful corporate forces who have arrogated legal authority and are proving increasingly difficult for the Bunch to evade. Railroad executive Harrigan, his name almost homonymous with 'arrogant' (and nearly identical to that of the unseen rail baron, Harriman, in *Butch Cassidy and the Sundance Kid*), symbolises the indifference to suffering of monopolistic capital. He willingly puts unwitting citizens, for whom

resemble a quest for meaning and redemption, albeit in an abstract sense. But there is no immediate, Magnificent Seven-style awakening. The outlaws sympathise with the villagers, who have been raided recently by *federales* under General Mapache, but not enough to take an active role in their defence. Indeed, they have no compunction about riding into Agua Verde, Mapache's lair, to sell him first their excess horses, then their services in hijacking a US Army munitions train, the contents of which will make his raids deadlier still. Pike's response to Angel's protestations – "Ten thousand cuts an awful lot of family ties" – further erodes his credibility as a proponent of such endangered values as fidelity, "just like it used to be".

Contradictions of this kind affect all the major characters, increasing the film's emotional heft. Angel is the most romantic figure, yet his compassion is reserved for his people alone ("I didn't see no tears roll down your cheeks when you rode in from Starbuck," observes Sykes, the Bunch's elderly accomplice). His image as earnest idealist is obliterated when he shoots dead his sweetheart, Teresa, as she cavorts on Mapache's lap ("Puta!"), almost provoking a bloodbath; reading between the lines, Patrick McGee interprets Angel's action as a way of "reasserting patriarchal authority" and salving the honour of "the community it supports".[4] Dutch, along with Sykes, is the conscience of the Bunch, its resident moral relativist, sternly insisting that while they may be criminals, they are a world apart from the fascistic Mapache – "We don't *hang* nobody." Dutch's case is arguable, but ultimately no more than that, supporting Peckinpah's view that in a time of crisis and flux, fixed ethical positions become untenable. (Even the dissolute, despotic Mapache is shown to have inspiring leadership qualities, in a battle against Villistas that was cut for the film's initial release.[5])

The same is true of Pike's jaded sense of honour, which insists on the sanctity of a man's word irrespective of context – a reminder of Steve Judd, hero of Peckinpah's *Ride the High Country*, who also wished it were possible to see the world in black and white. Dutch counters that context is everything, that Thornton may as well have made a deal with the devil as with the railroad. Of course, the Bunch have essentially done the same thing by entering into a pact with Mapache, again with an element of constraint involved – financial necessity, in their case. But the train robbery, carried off with élan, at least allows them to restore their battered professional pride, something that is denied to Thornton, especially when he and his entourage are sent crashing into a river when the Bunch blow up a bridge from beneath them.

One of Pike's many compromises – agreeing to give one case of Mapache's rifles to Angel's revolutionary friends – marks an acceptance that doing the right thing can transcend the honouring of contracts, and lends weight to Dutch's assertion that the value of an oath is determined by its nature, as well as that of its recipient.

he clearly feels contempt, in harm's way to safeguard the railroad's interests. (The distinction – again, not a straightforward one – between the pragmatism of the Bunch, who also use human shields, and the malevolence of those they oppose, will assume compelling significance in the latter stages.) The Bunch could hardly be considered hip in a countercultural sense – what glamour these craggy men possess is invested almost entirely in William Holden's casting as Pike and is of the fading kind, not the vibrant allure of Butch and Sundance, Cool Hand Luke or the biker dropouts of *Easy Rider*. Nevertheless, it is not too great a stretch to see their flight from the constrictions imposed by big business and Temperance unions as springing from the same anti-Establishment urges ("We share very few sentiments with our government") – urges that perhaps spurred their criminal endeavours in the first place.

Following a pattern that was set in *Major Dundee* and would reappear in *Bring Me the Head of Alfredo Garcia* (1974), the breaching of moral boundaries – on the part of both filmmaker and protagonists – comes into sharpest focus once the action leaves the United States, as does the stern examination of character. Having lost half the gang in Starbuck, the Bunch seek repose in revolution-racked Mexico in the village of Angel (Jaime Sanchez), their youngest member. This sequence forms a bridge in the narrative, marking a subtle shift in the attitudes of men accustomed more to hostility than the hospitality and understanding they encounter here. Relaxing, they reveal other sides to their natures – even the boorish Gorch brothers (Warren Oates and Ben Johnson) relapse into a childlike state in the company of innocents. After this point, the Bunch's mission in Mexico begins to

(Mapache proves him right by attempting to take the cache of weapons without paying; his plan is thwarted by the Bunch's superior sangfroid.) This latest obligation makes them indirectly responsible for Angel's fate; when Teresa's mother delivers him up to Mapache, they are compelled to acquiesce in the act to cover their own complicity, compounding their demoralisation and distancing them further from the heroic ideal.[6] Pike, in theory the focal point for audience sympathy and identification, has been repeatedly forced to betray his code of loyalty to facilitate his own survival and escape. The price has been paid by comrades like Thornton, Crazy Lee (Bo Hopkins), an eager young simpleton left behind while his comrades fled Starbuck, and Sykes, whom the Bunch, pragmatists almost to the last, abandon when he is wounded in an ambush by Thornton's bounty hunters.

Surrendering Angel – to torture and the certainty of eventual execution – proves to be a dereliction too far. When Mapache rejects their offer to buy him back, the Bunch numb their senses with whisky and whores while the rest of Agua Verde enjoys a fiesta. Pike has reached what Aristotle termed the moment of recognition. He endures a long dark night of the soul, its effects inscribed on Holden's face as it registers self-loathing and remorse; not so much, one suspects, for his exploitation of the delicate-looking young prostitute, whose baby shares their squalid room, but for the accumulation of lapses and misjudgements that have brought him to this nadir. Holden's life had been blighted by alcoholism, and it is tempting to read this exquisitely introspective scene as an example of actor and character overlapping.

above: Emilio Fernandez (left) as the inebriated Mapache.
top right: Edmond O'Brien (left) and William Holden.

Then, "Let's go": Pike's call to arms signifies that remorse has turned to resolve, that the moral bind in which he finds himself has exerted all the pressure he can bear and demands a release. Dutch and the Gorches, for all the brothers' squabbling with Angel in the past, are of like mind, living up to their leader's mantra: "We started it together, we'll end it together." In marching so purposefully towards annihilation for the sake of a stricken comrade, they seem to have concluded that while there may be nothing worth living for, there is something worth dying for. Just as significantly, there is what Jim Kitses, speaking of Pike, calls a "reassertion of identity"[7], which applies equally to his colleagues and to all the director's key characters at moments of crisis and decision.

The concluding act of *The Wild Bunch* is an apotheosis for protagonists and Peckinpah alike. As with the opening shootout in Starbuck, the anticipation of violence is built up to an excruciating degree, reaching its apogee in the heavily pregnant pause that follows the Bunch's instinctive killing of Mapache, revenge for his butchering of Angel. The eventual eruption produces relief as much as shock. But, notes Richard Slotkin, "our experience of that 'relief' creates another kind of tension… [arising] from our realisation that the normal rules of genre and myth will not necessarily apply."[8] Pike breaks the silence, encouraged by a fiendishly grinning Dutch, by felling one of Mapache's German advisers. The 'Battle of Bloody Porch' that ensues outstripped any film before it in terms of visceral impact; it also fulfils the prophecy implicit in the opening scenes – of scorpions locked in futile combat with a teeming mass of ants, encaged in a makeshift arena. (The image of children poking the insects with sticks is paralleled when a boy soldier shoots Pike with a rifle.)

Peckinpah decried the sanitised violence of most Hollywood action films; he felt they shielded audiences from the horror of it. His own stylised approach – it was never intended to be 'realistic' as such – magnified and prolonged physical destruction so that it was impossible to disregard: "The point of the film is to take this facade

of movie violence and open it up… and then twist it so that it's not fun any more, just a wave of sickness in the gut." Of course, there is also grace in the slow-motion danse macabre, but the intercutting of shots at normal speed, instigated by the brilliant editor Lou Lombardo, disturbs any sense of 'pleasure' at the sight of bloodied, pirouetting bodies, conveying instead the disorientation, "the subjective distortion of time", induced by combat.[9] The deliriousness of the violence, exemplified by Warren Oates' frenzy as he fires Mapache's machine gun, may be considered distasteful, perhaps even counter-productive to Peckinpah's stated intent. What we are witnessing, however, is the exhilaration of warriors – "The savage pleasure taken by the killer in inflicting death."[10] These are men highly skilled in the art of killing, and Agua Verde is their masterpiece. The same is true for Peckinpah as a director fascinated by violence and its exponents, and concerned that society was in its thrall, or at least becoming numb to its effects.[11] He was determined that would not be the case here; that audiences would be forced to engage, to react.

At the same time, the Bunch's suicide mission registers resoundingly their rejection of any alternative mode of being. Indeed, a life "beyond [their] guns" has become almost impossible to imagine: "Back off to what?" Dutch asks rhetorically. Outlaws to the end, "not associated with anybody", their assault on Agua Verde marks what Terence Butler calls "a last defiant gesture of disaffiliation before they, like the rest of their breed, are wiped off the face of the earth".[12] Although Peckinpah's methods were radical, his message is consistent with the myth of the West. His protagonists are specialists, defined and segregated by their affinity with violence. This sets them apart from society and its regulations and yet, in a world seemingly of change for the worst – aggressive corporatism; technological advances loaded with intimations of closing eras and global conflict – imbues them with a perverse kind of purity. It was a typically provocative and ambiguous proposition.

If we share Peckinpah's assessment of the Bunch and what they represent, then they deserve the mantle of tragic heroes. As Bernard Dukore explains, "The action the tragic hero pursues, however painful or deadly it may be to himself or herself, has grandeur in it. Grandeur is what the final action of the Wild Bunch exemplifies."[13] Their elevated status is confirmed by the arrival of the posse members, portrayed pointedly as lower life forms. (As attentive as ever to symmetry and simile, Peckinpah has vultures surveying the scene from atop Agua Verde's viaduct to recall the bounty hunters perched on the rooftop in Starbuck, as well as heralding their appearance here.) While Coffer (Strother Martin) spots Pike and whispers his name in an awed tone, T.C. (L.Q. Jones) is merely insolent: "You ain't so damn much now, are you Mr. Pike?" A weary Thornton, who has repeatedly exalted the Bunch during the pursuit, takes Pike's handgun as a memento while his rapacious minions scavenge among the corpses. Thornton leaves them to their devices, smiling quietly at the sound of distant gunshots from the direction of their departure. Their deaths are confirmed by Sykes, who shows up with a guerrilla band and invites Thornton to join the rebel cause.

The closing shots preserve an idealised image of the Bunch. Ending the film on such an elegiac note struck some observers as a misjudgement: having framed his story around unrepentant killers, sullying the fantasy of the Old West, how could Peckinpah justify admitting them to the Elysium of heroic myth? But, as Paul Seydor has written, this is to misunderstand or ignore the question of perspective. Quite apart from the self-vindication it earns them – the highest attainment for a Peckinpah protagonist – their actions in Agua Verde – four men against the might of Mapache's forces – will surely become the stuff of legend in this part of Mexico. From the point of view of those fighting the *federales*, the gringos who liberated them from Mapache, whatever their motives may have been, will provide an inspiring example. In that context, the

above: Angel (Jaime Sanchez) at the mercy of Mapache's lieutenants (Jorge Russek, left, and Alfonso Arau, right).

reprise of their valedictory send-off from Angel's people is entirely 'justifiable'. Peckinpah's westerns transmuted their mythic material, rather than merely deconstructing it, expressing his own complex and contradictory personality. In this respect and many others, *The Wild Bunch* is his signature work. Its protagonists' demonstration of valour and prowess may not be for the selfless reasons we customarily ascribe to western heroes – whose time, the film conclusively announces, is past, if it ever existed at all – but, as Sykes' reasoning goes, it'll do. **KG**

footnotes

1 Richard Slotkin, *Gunfighter Nation: The Myth of the Frontier in Twentieth Century America* (University of Oklahoma Press, 1998).
2 *The Crowded Prairie: American National Identity in the Hollywood Western* (I.B. Tauris, 1998).
3 David Weddle, *If They Move, Kill 'Em: The Life and Times of Sam Peckinpah* (Grove Press, 2001).
4 *From Shane to Kill Bill: Rethinking the Western* (Wiley-Blackwell, 2006).
5 The excisions that hurt Peckinpah the most were those that caused the intricately woven thread of the story to fray – particularly the flashbacks that detail Pike's relationship with Thornton and the latter's suffering in prison.
6 This latest act of treachery by a woman, coming after Teresa's desertion of Angel, has led many to accuse the film and Peckinpah of 'typical' misogyny. So, too, his apparent obsession with prostitutes. But treachery is a hallmark of Peckinpah's West, practised by male and female characters alike, and the Bunch's enforced itinerant lifestyle would naturally make them reliant on prostitutes for female company; indeed, prostitution serves as a useful metaphor for the Bunch's solicitation of Mapache. The Gorches are probably content on that score, but Pike, for one, has longed for a more conventional relationship in the past. Flashbacks to his romance with the fiery but devoted Aurora, which ended when she was shot dead and Pike wounded by her estranged husband, remind us of the opportunities that he has let slip, or unwittingly sabotaged through lack of diligence. Aurora's fleeting appearance, and her importance to an understanding of Pike, nevertheless shows that Peckinpah had more dimensions than his detractors would suggest.
7 Jim Kitses, *Horizons West* (BFI, 2007).
8 *Gunfighter Nation.* Peckinpah described the interlude between Mapache's fall and the onset of battle as "a strange existentialist little number… they start to laugh… they know this is the end and they want it all".
9 *Gunfighter Nation.*
10 Peckinpah wanted to shake up his audience, not to repel them. Consequently, after some respondents reported disgust at early previews, he removed more gore than he was requested to by studio chiefs, trusting in the power of what remained.
11 *Crucified Heroes: the Films of Sam Peckinpah* (Gordon Fraser, 1979).
12 Ibid.
13 *Sam Peckinpah's Feature Films* (University of Illinois Press, 1999).

A Conversation with Crazy Lee

Bo Hopkins Interviewed

A character actor intimately associated with the western, South Carolina native Bo Hopkins announced himself spectacularly as a hostage-slaughtering gunman in *The Wild Bunch*. From his association with Sam Peckinpah to appearances in key revisionist films such as *The Culpepper Cattle Co.* and *Monte Walsh*, filmgoers came to know him as a new kind of performer – unselfconscious, naturalistic, impulsive – in a new breed of western.

What does the idea of the West mean to Americans? What is the continuing appeal?
The genre was all about bank robberies, train robberies, Jesse James… Things everybody would like to do, but we're scared to. In the true West, they shot you right there; they didn't go outside and count to three – that was added later in the movies, for dramatic purposes. This was a hard place to live in. It was hard for pioneers; it was hard for communities. They had to fight not only Indians – who had a basic right to be there in the first place – but also the weather, the dryness. They thought the land would produce crops, but it didn't… It was a time in life when you took a chance – to buy land, buy cattle.

I also think that people identify with good guys and bad guys. The cowboy was a hero in real life. They were a hard-working bunch, and when they did come into town, that's why they let off steam. The town wanted 'em in there, but they also wanted someone like Wild Bill Hickok or Wyatt Earp to calm 'em down after a while. It was an era where everybody had to look out for themselves and their neighbours. It wasn't how you see it in the movies. It was a tough time. It took a special breed of people. Sometimes a woman in the morning would have a baby on the wagon train, and that night she was cooking.

That's why the majority of Americans love that period, because it was a one-on-one situation. And there were great characters back then: Jesse James and Billy the Kid, Wild Bill Hickok and Wyatt Earp. I was in so many cowboy movies that once I was in my costume and on my horse, I felt like I was back there. It was a great time and also a tough time. America loves heroes – good and bad.

When you got your break in movies, what was the atmosphere like in Hollywood? Did you sense a changing of the guard?
Not right away. When I got *The Wild Bunch*, I think they tested 15 guys and they were tired of testing. Roy Sickner, the stuntman who helped write the movie, took a chance on me and told Peckinpah about me.

During the scene where I got shot, while I was on the ground shooting the three [bounty hunters], a piece of wood caught me above the eyelid. Sam was the first one to me. I just asked him, "Is my eye in?" And Sam said, "It's OK, let's wrap it up for today." But I said, "I'd just as soon finish it today." He said, "OK, what do you want to drink?" "Anything you got." He had some tequila, I took a shot and we redid the scene. And then all of a sudden Roy came up and hugged me. I got a big hand from the Mexican crew. I felt for the first time like I pleased somebody. They all invited me out to dinner; I had to wear a patch.

Afterwards, on the way to the house where I had to change out of my costume, I started cryin' in the cab. I couldn't stop. I'd been squibbed up 26 times; I'd never heard of a squib, so I was nervous about that. I was nervous about whether I would react to the shots; I didn't want to wear a T-shirt, because I wanted to feel it – big mistake, but that's OK. I was nervous about making it as real as possible. I think that's where it all came out, in that taxicab.

What sort of mood did Peckinpah create on the set of his movies?
It was a great atmosphere in the sense that, hell, we just about stayed in character, all of us. You'd go out at night with the stunt guys. I had to learn the hard way. You'd get drunk, sometimes get in a squabble or two. And they protected me, too. One time in Torreon, Bill Holden and Robert Ryan were sitting there, drinking beer, and I walked by. I was dating one of the Mexican stunt girls and they hollered out, "Hey, did you know that's one of [Mapache actor] Emilio Fernandez's ex-wives? Well, have a nice night." The rest of the night, I was looking over my shoulder.

Fernandez was a tough customer by all accounts…
He killed seven people; shot his leading man one day. He was a character…

What was it like to work with so many famous Hollywood veterans on your first movie?
Bill Holden was like a father to me. He helped get me my second movie, *The Bridge at Remagen*. The producer, David Wolper, wanted to interview me and I said, "I don't really know what to say." And [another *Wild Bunch* co-star] Robert Ryan said, "Let me do the talking." And he did the interview for me! Ben Johnson and I did some shows after that. They were all great friends and I was just a young kid, eager to learn. Strother Martin used to come to my daughter's birthday parties. Ernest Borgnine was also like a father to me, up until the time he died.

Peckinpah liked to tease me. He wanted me to shoot a shotgun to scare the horses. And I didn't know it had a full load. As soon as he pointed at me, I pulled the trigger and went flat on my butt. Everybody laughed; they were all in on it. That's what you get when you're a beginner.

That movie was a learning experience for me. In the scene where I'm marching around the office – "Yes, we shall gather at the river…" – when we did the first take, after I shot the hostages, Lucien Ballard told me to ad lib something. I said, "Ooh boy, those feathers flew like a turkey." He said, "That was great, kid, except you weren't on camera." He came over and he said, "Do you know what that is?" I looked up and said, "No sir." He said, "That's your key light." And he said, "Do you know what this is?" And I said, "Yes sir, that's my mark." And he said, "Well, you never hit your mark." I didn't know; I was just play-acting. Anyway, he taught me a lot; he took time with me.

Was Peckinpah a good teacher in that respect?
If you had rehearsed a scene and then you did it and he printed it, that meant it was good. He had to come up to me one time. There was this lady in the office scene. I would walk over to her and say, "Aww, just hush now." And she would go [softly], "Ohh." And Sam said to her, "Look, this guy's a killer. You've got to act scared." We did it again; it didn't work. And finally he said to me, "This time when you go up to her and she says to you, 'Filthy trash,' you lick her in the ear."

Sam was good to me. He got me into three pictures. We were great friends.

How would you summarise Peckinpah's impact on the western?

Sam was 20 years ahead of his time as far as westerns went. Look what he did with *Ride the High Country*; look what he did with [TV series] *The Westerner*. The hero got shot, the hero kicked his dog, the hero cussed – that's what a Western man was like.

Bill Holden told me *The Wild Bunch* was different from anything he'd ever done, with the squibs and the blood. I think Sam wanted to show what it was really like when a person was shot, in a moment of anger or in a war.

Sam could be cantankerous because, I realised later, the studios took away two movies from him. One was *Major Dundee* – even Charlton Heston said he'd buy it, to do it the way Sam wanted it done. He got screwed a lot, and he didn't trust anybody. That's why he liked to use the same actors, so he knew what he'd get. Like John Ford did, with John Wayne, Ben Johnson and others. And Sam had Strother Martin, R.G. Armstrong, L.Q. Jones… They understood each other. There were times when tempers flared, but there were times when it was called for. If I were a director, that's exactly what I would do – get my friends in.

With Crazy Lee, how much of the real Bo Hopkins was in that character?

Well, I was so nervous after I got the part, then I was nervous whether I could do the part, and then I was nervous when we started shooting. And I used that nervousness to play him – "I kill 'em now? I'll hold 'em till hell freezes over or you say different." It was being in a situation that was real to me, with the guns and the firing and the squibs. I mean, shit, you felt like you were in a real war.

Another time, when they were shooting the part where Bill Holden kicks the hostages out of the door and that starts the opening shoot-out, I was up by the camera with Ernest Borgnine, Ben Johnson and Warren Oates, and Sam gave us all rifles and told us to shoot at anything that moves, because he wanted the reaction – in that way, Bill Holden would have to play off the shooting, the same as us. And so as Bill kicked 'em out, and Dub [Taylor] was coming down the street with the marchers, all hell broke loose. We started firing those rifles – the damn shells were coming out and going down my shirt, and I got burnt again. And after he said cut, Sam said, "Well, I know why he's the real Crazy Lee. I was watching him and all he shot were kids and dogs." Bill Holden and all the rest of them got a kick out of that. That was a hell of a day of shooting.

Do you remember where you first saw the completed *Wild Bunch*? Was it at the famous premiere in the Bahamas, where it ignited such controversy?

No, I didn't see it there. I think the only guy who really liked it at that time was Roger Ebert. It was when the movie came out, and audiences saw it, that it really took off. I went with my girlfriend of the time to see it in Hollywood. The audience loved it, and that's what made the movie. A few other critics liked it, but the others were pissed off at Sam about all the blood and all the killings. Well, hell, that's what the movie is about – the end of an era. It was the first time it had been done.

Of course, they all copied Sam after that, with the slow motion and so on. It's the kind of western that can't be duplicated. There's been talk of making another *Wild Bunch* – there is no such thing. It would be like making another *Gone with the Wind*. That's like trying to rewrite a book in the way Mark Twain would write; it just wouldn't be the same.

Did you have the chance to make any more westerns with Peckinpah?

When Sam did *Pat Garrett and Billy the Kid*, I was up for the part of Billy, but Jim [MGM president James Aubrey] wanted big names. But the one who should have played Billy was Bob Dylan, because he looked like him. Of course, Sam didn't know who the hell Dylan was. If you want the looks to go with the part, I would definitely have had Bob Dylan do the role of Billy the Kid.

If you look back at some of the older westerns – like Robert Taylor as Billy the Kid, that's a laugh. But if you put Audie Murphy in the part [*The Kid from Texas*, 1950] – hell, everybody believes it, because he had that charisma about him.

The first time I was up for the role of Billy was in the John Wayne film *Chisum*; I couldn't do it because I was filming in Italy. I would love to have played that part, and to have worked with John Wayne.

Were you aware that you were making a new type of western – did they strike you as different from the classic westerns of the past?
I had that feeling when we were filming *Monte Walsh*. It was basically about a rancher and his cowhands, and what they go through to run a ranch. The reason I took that part was because I always wanted to work with Lee Marvin. I'm glad I did, because he became one of my dearest friends. The movie also had that "environmental" feel to it – that was something different. It was the same on *Culpepper*. Dick Richards wanted to wait for a certain part of the day to shoot us bringing cows to water – that might be a four-hour wait. He knew in his head what he wanted. We turned flies loose before we shot, we had cockroaches running across the tables – it felt like the real thing, and of course that gets you into the part a lot more.

above: Hopkins as Dixie Brick in *The Culpepper Cattle Co.*, with (from left) Billy 'Green' Bush (standing), Luke Askew, Geoffrey Lewis, Wayne Sutherlin (rear) and Gary Grimes.

Movies like *Culpepper* were targeted at a young audience; others like *Monte Walsh* and *Posse* were very critical of politicians and capitalism. Do you see them as part of a wider anti-establishment movement started by the likes of *Easy Rider*?
Yeah, I think so, because of the fact we were in a war that we either should have won or got out of. We were in a situation where students were being shot at Kent State. And we were in a situation where hippies were in. It was a time when people were beginning to think that the government was wrong in some of its dealings. When I did *Posse*, it was about a man running for senate. Well, it came out just after Nixon was kicked out of office. That didn't help the movie.

For me, when John Kennedy was assassinated, it killed me. I thought he was a great president – he was my first hero. He was the first one to get kids going overseas to help in other countries... That changed me. After that, I refused to vote and get into politics. Because what killed him was politicians – by that I mean, things like the mafia getting into politics. I think one day we'll find out what really happened. And then Bobby Kennedy came along. My first or second day of shooting in Czechoslovakia [on *Bridge at Remagen*], I found out he'd been shot. You were ashamed to be an American over in a Communist country.

Lately, I've come to understand that all politicians are full of shit. They all say they're going to do this and do that. They can't do a damn thing unless whatever party they're in votes for it. The Democrats and Republicans are like two eighth graders calling each other names. They try to make like they care. If they really cared, they'd find a way to get homeless people off the streets.

What's very striking in those Seventies westerns is your acting style. Your performances and those of your contemporaries, such as Matt Clark, Luke Askew and Geoffrey Lewis, are very different from those of actors from the classic Hollywood period...
We tried to make it as believable as possible – none of that, "I'll see you out in the street, count three and draw." I read a lot of books when I was doing *Culpepper* and my thinking was that if a guy got in a fight with you, you'd shoot him before he shot you. That calibre of westerns came along in the Seventies and the Eighties, and it was like a different genre.

Marlon Brando, Montgomery Clift and James Dean started a whole trend in Hollywood, with people trying to copy what they did. They were like good baseball players that come along only once in a while. They're special, they're different, and then everyone tries to copy them.

If you go back to the old actors like Bogart, Tracy, Tyrone Power, Henry Fonda, they were great actors because the studios took care of them. A lot of time they had to do parts in movies that maybe they didn't want to do, but they did them because they were professionals.

My favourite western performances were those of Gary Cooper in *The Westerner* – Cooper was my favourite western actor – and John Wayne in *Red River*. And I loved a lot of Joel McCrea's work.

***Red River* contains possibly Wayne's best performance...**
People didn't appreciate John Wayne till after he died. If you look back at *Red River*, he should have been nominated [for the Best Actor Oscar] for that.

Your style of acting was more naturalistic than the old guard. They're very physical performances, in that you're always doing things that real people would do, like scratching. It gives these films a more realistic edge.

By the time I got to *Culpepper*, I was more involved in the character and what he would do. I would swat a fly or step on a bug. Things like that are real life – you try to bring real life into the scene, using your ability as an actor, to create this character, and what he would do if he saw a fly. Like Jack Elam in *Once Upon a Time in the West*, when that fly landed on his nose – that was a great shot, and it was *real*. It's more of an unconscious effort to scratch when you think you have an itch…

We had a great time, Matt, Geoffrey, Luke Askew and I. And we'd talk about these characters, about what they would do. They were a great part of my life. We were all good friends, too, almost like family; there wasn't any friction between us.

There's a lovely moment in *Culpepper* after the shoot-out in the tavern when your character beats the table with his fists because he's so excited at having taken part – there's an almost childish joy there…

In that particular scene, as I was going to the table, because I knew that's where I'd want to shoot from, this old man was there. I poured a drink, gave him the bottle and motioned him to move. And that was like setting the dynamite, because you know something big's coming next. Lighting the fuse, I call it. I liked that little scene, because my character, Dixie Brick, didn't want to see the old man shot. It shows you he had a heart, even though he was fixing to blow people away.

I didn't want to do it all the time, but Dick Richards fell in love with the way I said, "Shit." [Hopkins has a distinctive South Carolina twang, which elongates the vowel.] I didn't want to do it in that scene, but I had to stay in character – I was shaking, I was nervous and happy. And that's the way I played Dixie Brick. He didn't want to die, but he wasn't scared to. He wasn't a hero, but he wasn't scared to back up what he thought was right. All four of them [Frank Culpepper's hired gunmen] were like that. There is a scene near the beginning of *Culpepper*, when you first meet us, after we leave the bar. Richards had me stop at a corner house, get off and go in. And this old lady comes out, an old Mexican lady, and a young girl, who I was dating. I kissed the old lady on the forehead, got on my horse and rode off. It was a great scene. I loved it; not a word was spoken. They couldn't use it because somehow or other they got a telephone wire in the shot. It told you what Dixie Brick was about – the good side and the bad side. I was sorry that particular scene was cut.

To what extent did the directors and the writers try to make their films look like authentic period pieces – how much research did they undertake?

They did a lot of research on *Culpepper*, and Sam and Roy Sickner did a lot of research on *The Wild Bunch*. I made a movie with Burt Reynolds called *The Man Who Loved Cat Dancing* and [director] Dick Sarafian took a lot of time for research in that. When an actor goes in and the director says to him, "What do you think you should wear? How do you feel about this?", it makes the actor a part of the creation, and it gives you a feeling of freedom – the director knows you're on the same page as him. You both want to make the most realistic movie that you possibly can.

Peckinpah's art direction on *The Wild Bunch* is extraordinary – it zaps you straight back to that period…

Sam had an idea of what the West was really like, and also the reality of being shot. He was trying to show what it was like. Bill Holden and Ernest Borgnine's characters knew they were coming to the end of an era. They couldn't rob banks any more; hell, law enforcement was too sophisticated. Then the motorcars come in, and they talk about planes. It was letting you see the end of a period in which cowboys had been free to do what they wanted to do.

The same theme occurs in *Monte Walsh*, of course – the dying of the days of the cowboy…

That's right. When Lee's character shot Shorty, that was the last time people could get away with doing that. The Tom Horns were being hanged. Again, it was the end of an era.

What can you tell us about working with Kirk Douglas on *Posse*?

He was a character. It was great working with him as a director, because he was also an actor. I actually turned it down at first, because I was doing a play with Stanley Kramer called *The Court Martial of Lieutenant William Calley*. And Kirk said to my agent, "Well, have him come see me," before rehearsals. I went to Kirk's house; a Swedish maid made me some coffee. Kirk started telling me about my character, Wesley. He did the whole damn movie for me almost. Hell, I couldn't turn him down then. I told my agent, "Go ahead and take it." Kirk even made my part bigger. One night I had dinner with him and Burt Lancaster and it was like sitting there with two icons.

It was a great experience working with Kirk. He was good to me and all the other actors. I watched him direct a lot of scenes; he'd be in his underwear on a horse, directing. Bruce Dern used to grab a megaphone and say, "Kirk, where are your pants? You don't have an ass!"

As a director, was Douglas a tough guy, or was he more easy-going?

He could be tough, yeah. When he's into it, he wants it done right. There was a scene where I got slammed against bars in the horse car by Bruce Dern; hell, that thing he wrapped around my neck was tight. But you don't go complaining about it, because Kirk would say, "Look, I got hurt in *The Vikings*, and I got hurt in *Spartacus*." He was a tough director, because he wanted it done right.

Unfortunately, that movie came out shortly after Nixon was forced to resign. Another story – when Sarah Miles and I were doing *Cat Dancing*, her husband, Robert Bolt, came over. She and I wanted to do [a remake of] *The Cowboy and the Lady*. We all wanted to do the movie, but it was right around the time that Nixon was forced to resign, and that killed the senator part in *The Cowboy and the Lady*. People don't want to see what happens in real life – you get enough of that every day. And then of course Kirk's movie was released a few months later, and that hurt the box office.

Moving into the late Seventies, early Eighties – why do you think the western went into a sharp decline?

One of the reasons was *Heaven's Gate*. They spent all that money – that movie was way, way over budget – and so people were scared to do a western in case they'd get caught in a similar situation. It didn't help in getting a movie off the ground. But you've got to remember, too, when I was growing up in South Carolina, I used to watch *Gunsmoke*, *Bonanza* and all those westerns on TV – there were three or four different westerns every night, and I think it got saturated. Also, it goes in cycles. The time of the western is coming around [again]; the only thing on television is reality shows, and I think people are ready for a good western to take their minds off of real life. And at that particular time, it was the closing of the cycle. I know in Europe, when I go over there, people clamour for westerns. I think you're going to see more, because I think that cycle – with westerns not being on the air and on screens – has run out.

After several years without appearing in a movie western, you had a major role in *The Ballad of Little Jo*. What attracted you to that particular role?

Well, it was something different. I finally got a chance to grow a beard – Maggie Greenwald wanted me to have one. Another reason the part was different from anything I had done prior to that was because I got to age along with the character. Maggie Greenwald did a lot of homework on that. Also, Suzy Amis did a hell of a job. She could be in ice-cold water and she never complained… She was a good actress.

It was a tough shoot. We shot it down in Montana. Sometimes the wind would blow so hard, I could hardly say my dialogue. It was done on a low budget, but they put more money into it once they saw how good the characters were. It was one of those little westerns that people might see late at night on television and wish they'd seen it when it came out.

Did it get much attention in the States when it was first released?

It came out during the latter part of [Oscar season], when all the Academy Awards movies started coming out. They like to release them just before Christmas, and unfortunately that's when they released this one. That was a bad move. If they'd waited until March, it would have got a lot more play. It got its share of notices, but all of a sudden you had all these movies being nominated for Academy Awards. The timing was bad.

Hopkins, grizzled and macho in *The Ballad of Little Jo.*

Little Big Man

1970, Colour, 139 mins.

D: Arthur Penn. P: Stuart Miller (Hiller Productions, Stockbridge Productions).
W: Calder Willingham. Ph: Harry Stradling Jr. M: John Hammond.
St: Dustin Hoffman (Jack Crabb), Faye Dunaway (Mrs Pendrake),
Martin Balsam (Allardyce T. Merriweather), Richard Mulligan (Custer),
Chief Dan George (Old Lodge Skins)

"There is an endless supply of white men, but there always has been a limited number of human beings. We won today. We won't win tomorrow."

A satire with a tragic undertow, *Little Big Man* was the most commercially successful and artistically rewarding western produced at the peak of the genre's expiatory phase. The likes of *Cheyenne Autumn*, *Hombre*, *Tell Them Willie Boy Is Here*, *A Man Called Horse* and *Soldier Blue* were historical re-enactments geared to contemporary sensibilities. Whether or not, as J. Hoberman opines, "Such movies were the equivalent of marching for peace beneath a Viet Cong banner"[1] – not an allusion *Cheyenne Autumn's* director, John Ford, would have appreciated, although it chimed with Arthur Penn's pronouncements – their value as vehicles for antiwar sentiment and what Penn called "the racial situation in the US at present" is transparent. All these films trumpeted respect for the Indians, but most forgot or neglected to include rounded indigenous characters. *Little Big Man*, adapted from Thomas Berger's picaresque novel, goes some way towards correcting this oversight. Although it, too, transmits its message via a white intermediary – Jack Crabb, who shuttles between Anglo and Indian societies and may well be a fantasist – its moral centre is located among the Cheyenne who take Jack under their wing.

The warmth of Jack's welcome radiates from the wise and witty Old Lodge Skins, deftly played by Chief Dan George with none of the stolidity borne by most of Hollywood's tribal elders.[2] The Cheyenne call themselves 'Human Beings'; individuality flourishes, and characters who would be mocked or belittled elsewhere, like Jack himself (renamed Little Big Man in tribute to his pluck[3]), are venerated – an effeminate tribesman, or *heemaneh*, is accorded particular esteem. All this classifies Cheyenne society as tolerant, altruistic and congenial – emblematic, in Douglas Pye's words, of "the commune dreams and alternative lifestyles of the Sixties".[4] It compares favourably with the hostility, corruption and venality of white America, where Jack is compelled to try out a number of roles without finding fulfilment – a very modern predicament.

There is at least a degree of idealisation about this view of Cheyenne life as what Michael Coyne terms a "countercultural idyll".[5] Calder Willingham's adaptation spares the Indians the barbs that Berger, to his credit, had aimed across the racial divide; it is notable that Pawnees kill Jack's family at the beginning of the film, whereas in the novel it is the Cheyenne themselves. This one-sidedness, while not as pronounced as it is in *Soldier Blue* or *Dances with Wolves*, which also utilises Pawnees as 'bad Indians', is the principal flaw in Willingham's elegantly woven fabric.

Nevertheless, this is not wholly, *pace* Penn, "a film about Indian culture". The panoramic sweep of Jack's recollections – from his 121-year-old vantage point – illustrates the digression of history into myth, the widening crevasse between ethics and actions in the forging of the nation. Attentive Americans could scarcely miss Penn's invitation to consider his critique of their forebears' hypocrisy, chicanery and moral degradation in relation to their own volatile times. Casting Dustin Hoffman – slight, Jewish – as the mock-heroic title character was not only a calculated rebuff to macho norms; it supports the sense of Jack as a Sixties misfit cast back in time. There is more than a touch of Benjamin Braddock about the bewilderment, disillusionment and moral uncertainty he displays as his innocence is progressively eroded by his experiences alongside a range of unworthy mentors: the sexually frustrated Mrs. Pendrake, a minister's wife who tries to seduce him, *à la* Mrs. Robinson, and later turns to prostitution; the huckster Allardyce T. Merriweather, who bemoans Jack's stubborn "streak of honesty"; the gunfighter Wild Bill Hickok, forever wary of assassins and eventually gunned down by a mere stripling; and the vainglorious General Custer, Penn's standard-bearer for imperialist military idiocy and brutality.

In between these vignettes, Jack returns to the Cheyenne, where he finds that his 'grandfather', Old Lodge Skins, has been blinded during a skirmish with soldiers, loses his white wife to Indian raiders, and his Indian bride and child to the Seventh Cavalry's bullets at Washita River – an episode that Penn related explicitly to current events: "Custer… gave the order to massacre the inhabitants of a village, just as we've been doing in Vietnam."[6] There is even a shot of a naked Cheyenne girl

engulfed by flames; it may as well have been napalm. Jack becomes despondent, sinking into drunkenness and near-suicidal despair, before he re-enters Custer's orbit and witnesses the general's demise – boots on, reason astray – at Little Bighorn.

The mood fluctuates but is broadly seriocomic, consistent with much of Penn's work. It demonstrates "almost a tone of absurdity", what Penn called "a certain sense that there is no single desperate line, but that the film is going to operate on a multiplicity of levels".[7] In this he is supported by Willingham's fidelity to Berger's novel, which mimics a 19th-century literary epic, with its everyman hero wedged among historical and fictional characters, actual and imagined events. For Penn, the film's parade of Dickensian eccentrics was intended to highlight "humankind's foibles and failures", from the dubious piety of Mrs. Pendrake – "We all must resist temptation," she purrs, while lustily scrubbing Jack in a bathtub – to the mendacity of Merriweather, who comes to resemble a pirate captain, complete with eye patch, hook and peg-leg, the more body parts he loses to vengeful victims of his swindles. Collectively they create an impression of warped values, of a society in a state of disequilibrium – the whites "do not know where

the centre of the Earth is", notes Old Lodge Skins, more in sympathy than anger. Jack only finds balance and openness with the Cheyenne, where the jesting has a gentler cast: a highly strung brave becomes a 'contrary', doing everything backwards; the free-love ethos of the Sixties is warmly satirised when a weary Jack is obliged to satisfy not only his wife (the fashionably monikered Sunshine), but her three sisters; Old Lodge Skins acknowledges a glitch in the Great Spirit's power with good-humoured grace: "Sometimes the magic works, sometimes it doesn't." (At other times, his faith appears to be rewarded: believing himself to be invisible, he wanders through the mayhem at Washita River with a beatific smile and emerges unscathed.)

Jack himself, as suggested by his appellation, represents the western hero in diminished form – a subsidiary figure in a grand narrative, dwarfed by events and buffeted by forces beyond his control. Hoffman keenly grasps the ridiculousness of his character's predicaments, the misjudgements, contradictions and shortcomings of a perennial square peg. He can be dogged, but also cowardly; when he kills a Pawnee to save a Cheyenne brave it is inadvertently, and he faints at the realisation. His nerve fails him at key moments, and his aptitude with a pistol – as the would-be gunfighter the Soda Pop Kid – is offset by squeamishness when he sees the damage guns can inflict on a human body, one of the few graphic images that Penn strategically employs. (This sequence exemplifies Penn's engagement with genre tropes for comic effect: Jack is trained in marksmanship not by an experienced gunman but by his sister, who is far more butch and capable than he is and who disowns him when he hangs up his guns to become a storekeeper.) For Hoffman, the part, with its gamut of emotions and physical demands, was a Method actor's dream. "[Penn] likes to show weak, even unattractive sides to a character that's basically sympathetic," the actor told Iain Johnstone, and Hoffman more than meets the challenge, even under the latex mask that transforms him into a centenarian.[8]

Jack makes an unlikely and unreliable conduit for the 'truth', as he sets himself up to be at the beginning of the film; this points towards the ethos of Berger's novel and its filmic adaptation – the seeming impossibility of disentangling fact from fable. "I don't mean to have this be representative of what I think of being historically accurate," said Penn, hoping to deflect gripes about ethnological oversights or his portrayal of Custer as a loose cannon, even a madman, rather than an instrument of government policy – a complaint also brought against *Soldier Blue*, with its eccentric Major Iverson. (If this does represent a conservative bias, it is the western's requirement for an individual villain. Dialogue in both films – diatribes in the case of *Soldier Blue* – combined with depictions of indiscriminate killing by white soldiers, expresses precisely the anti-imperialist sentiments detractors seemed to be demanding.) One can demolish myths, the film asserts, by giving another perspective on history – in some senses a counter-myth – but true objectivity on a matter that cuts to the heart of American national identity is likely to remain elusive. Jack comes to believe, like his counterparts in other pro-Indian westerns and like liberal sympathisers everywhere, that tribal societies occupied a higher moral plane and America has much to regret in the manner of their decimation, and much to learn from their system of values.

Little Big Man found no shortage of takers for its anti-Establishment message, its classification of the Indian Wars as "genocide" – a word used repeatedly by

both Penn and producer Stuart Millar during promotion. Indeed, Penn had been planning to make a film about the Holocaust until he was alerted to Berger's book and realised it addressed the same themes. His conclusions about this period in history were unequivocal: "If the whites destroyed Indian culture it wasn't for a geographical or economic imperative. It was for the sheer pleasure of conquest."[9] They were also indicative of the provocative disposition of New Hollywood cinema, a movement the director had fostered and inspired. **KG**

footnotes

1 J. Hoberman, *The Dream Life: Movies, Media and the Mythology of the Sixties* (The New Press, 2005).

2 The casting of Chief Dan George, of the Tsleil-Waututh Nation, was a masterstroke, but *Little Big Man* might have been less effective had one of Penn's other options for the role paid off. Laurence Olivier, Paul Scofield and Richard Boone were formidable talents, but none of them was right for the role of a droll, sagacious, Cheyenne elder. Despite Chief Dan George's winning performance, some commentators – Indian and otherwise – denounced his portrayal for lacking the martial air of a true war chief. For Michael Hilger, Old Lodge Skins' "acceptance of white superiority" was the hallmark of many a "noble", sympathetic Hollywood Indian, designed to make him agreeable to mainstream America. I prefer to see it as a sign of pragmatism on his part, not an admission of defeat.

3 The real Little Big Man was not a white man but an Oglala Sioux warrior, who served as Crazy Horse's envoy in negotiations with the Army, but was later instrumental in the latter's entrapment and murder (1877).

4 Douglas Pye, 'Ulzana's Raid', in *The Movie Book of The Western* (Ian Cameron, Douglas Pye, eds, Cassell, 1996).

5 Michael Coyne, *The Crowded Prairie: American National Identity in the Hollywood Western* (I.B. Tauris, 1997).

6 Interview with Arthur Penn by Jan Aghed and Bernard Cohn (1971), reprinted in *Arthur Penn: Interviews* (Michael Chaiken and Paul Cronin, eds, University Press of Mississippi, 2008).

7 Interview with Arthur Penn by Gordon Gow in *Films and Filming*, July 1971.

8 Iain Johnstone, *Dustin Hoffman* (Spellmount, 1984).

9 Interview with Arthur Penn by Jan Aghed and Bernard Cohn.

A Man Called Horse

1970, Colour, 114 mins.

D: Elliot Silverstein. P: Sandy Howard (Cinema Center Films, Sandy Howard Productions). W: Jack DeWitt. Ph: Robert Hauser. M: Leonard Rosenman. St: Richard Harris (Lord John Morgan), Judith Anderson (Buffalo Cow Head), Jean Gascon (Batise), Manu Tupou (Yellow Hand), Corinna Tsopei (Running Deer)

"I'm not an animal! I'm a man!"

Produced in the midst of a political and cultural reappraisal of Native American rights (and those of all racial minorities) and their place in the nation's history, *A Man Called Horse* illustrates the shortfall between noble intentions and what was evidently felt to be commercial necessity. As one film historian has it, the film "attempts to portray the Sioux as a distinctive culture with its own unique rituals, but ultimately fails because it lets the hero pre-empt the culture".[1] Hamstrung by Richard Harris's insistence that his character be the centre of attention, it is not so much a corrective to previous denigrating portrayals of Native peoples as a celebration of one (white) man's ability to endure, adapt and overcome adversity, and to lead others by implication less capable of surpassing obstacles themselves. While 1970's other major pro-Indian westerns, *Little Big Man* and *Soldier Blue*, were blatant anti-colonialist polemics, *A Man Called Horse* – given its pre-Civil War setting, the only one of these films not to feature murderous cavalrymen – could be taken as reassurance by Caucasian audiences about their inherent superiority over racial others.

Based on a gritty captivity narrative by Dorothy M. Johnson (*The Hanging Tree*, *The Man Who Shot Liberty Valance*), the script by Jack DeWitt combines masochistic fantasy with anthropological details, these aspects converging in the notorious Sun Vow tribal initiation sequence. This is the centrepiece of the film, when Harris's displaced English aristocrat, John Morgan, captured by Lakota Sioux while hunting birds, finally proves his worth to them after an untold period of humiliation and servitude in scenes reminiscent of *Planet of the Apes* (1968). It is not the inclusion per se of this hallowed ritual that has always excited controversy; nor is it the relative accuracy of its depiction, which seems to have been based, down to the lighting, on a painting and description by artist George Catlin, who is acknowledged as a source above the titles.[2] Rather, it is Morgan's motives for undertaking the ordeal that risk trivialising it.

Since his enslavement Morgan has been plotting his escape, confiding in the only other English speaker, the French-Flathead halfbreed Batise, another captive who has survived by playing the fool ("Crazy man no hunt, no work") and acts as an interpreter-cum-intermediary for both Morgan and the audience. Morgan concludes that his best chance to rejoin the outside world is to elevate his status among the Sioux until he is given command of his own war party, and thus the freedom to leave the village. He also has designs on chief Yellow Hand's sister, Running Deer, played by a Greek former beauty queen whose perfect features and light skin tone contrast markedly with those of the other women (many of them actual Sioux, from the Rosebud tribe). She thus follows in the footsteps of white 'Indian' actresses such as Debra Paget (*Broken Arrow*, *White Feather*) and Karin Dor (the German 'Winnetou' films).[3] It is to secure these ends that Morgan hazards the Sun Vow, which involves him being suspended by ropes attached to talons embedded in his naked chest – a harrowing image that featured heavily in the film's promotion and has been synonymous with it ever since.

The distortion of the ceremony's place in Sioux culture and that of many other Plains Indian tribes rankled with critics and Native activists alike. The motivation of any brave taking the Sun Vow, writes Jacquelyn Kilpatrick, "was to prompt a vision that would be of use to his entire tribe. Horse's motivations are purely personal."[4] As a kind of thanksgiving to the Great Spirit, it is hardly likely that any man – least of all a white man still technically considered a slave – would be permitted to commandeer this most sacred of ceremonies to bolster his macho credentials and bag himself a bride. Such is the skewed logic that gives the film-makers' professions of cultural and racial sensitivity a somewhat hollow ring.

The production hired Clyde Dollar, a white historian of the Sioux, as a consultant, but he was frustrated by the way in which tribal customs were misrepresented. The abandonment of a bereaved old woman who cannot fend for herself, for example, implies a callousness on the part of the Sioux ("Nobody protect her, nobody care," observes Batise) that is strongly disputed by Dollar and other experts, who insist that the elderly were and remain venerated in tribal societies. But Elliot Silverstein seemed more interested in the 'primitivism' of the Sioux – from their affinity with nature, captured in documentary-like montages, to self-mutilation and the scalping of slain enemies – than with creating a 'positive' image that would have appeased the pro-Indian lobby. Taking his cue from Dorothy M. Johnson's story, he believed the Sioux followed "the same law as the animals around them; that is, survival... The survival of the tribe seemed more important than the survival of any individual in the tribe."[5] To the chagrin of his adviser, the director considered his film's entertainment value of greater importance than its historical veracity.

Harris, taking on a role rejected by Robert Redford, evidently felt the same way. For all the respect shown to the Sioux in the film – they speak the Lakota language, unsubtitled; Silverstein neither condones nor condemns their more barbarous traits – it is Harris's character who is glorified. For much of the running time he flaunts his toned, half-naked physique, with the flowing locks and headband of a countercultural dropout. (In the opening scenes, Morgan explains to his hunting guides that in leaving England he relinquished "family titles, family property, family position", plus a military commission, implicitly in the search for a more spiritually fulfilling existence.) Morgan is seen to master Sioux techniques, gets the girl (although the script kills her off, implying the persistence of what Leslie A. Fiedler called "the bugaboo of miscegenation"[6]) and, in the climactic battle against Shoshone marauders, he demonstrates the kind of tactical nous – and deadly aim – that Hollywood has traditionally made the white man's preserve. It is Morgan's arrow that fells the enemy chief, and the battle turns on his commanding the disorganised Sioux braves to volley-fire their bows by rank, as if this were Rorke's Drift, not the middle of Dakota.

As *Film Quarterly* complained, in the final analysis *A Man Called Horse* "parades the standard myth that the white man can do everything better than the Indian". Like his counterparts in the like-minded *Run of the Arrow* and *Dances with Wolves*, Morgan learns to admire his adopted tribe, but it is from the exalted perspective of a saviour. The condescension continued in the first of two sequels, in which Morgan, having returned to England, decides to visit the Sioux again and is called upon to spearhead a revival of their fortunes against white trappers and rival Indians – once again, they cannot do it for themselves.[7] **KG**

footnotes

1 Michael Hilger, *From Savage to Nobleman: Images of Native Americans in Film* (Scarecrow Press, 1995).
2 *O-Kee Pa: A Religious Ceremony*, c. 1835.
3 Silverstein would no doubt have earned plaudits had his first choice for the role, Cree singer and activist Buffy Sainte-Marie, accepted his offer.
4 Jacquelyn Kilpatrick, *Celluloid Indians: Native Americans and Film* (University of Nebraska Press, 1999).
5 Interview with Elliot Silverstein by Angela Aleiss in *Making the White Man's Indian: Native Americans and Hollywood Movies* (Praeger, 2005).
6 *The Return of the Vanishing American* (Jonathan Cape, 1968).
7 *The Return of a Man Called Horse* (1976) was followed by *Triumphs of a Man Called Horse* (1983). Both films were executive produced by Sandy Howard, who also oversaw the semi-western *Man in the Wilderness* (1971), another vehicle for Harris as hardy survivalist and the precursor to the highly praised *The Revenant* (2015).

Beast of burden: Morgan (Richard Harris) is put to work by the Sioux.

The McMasters

1970, Colour, 90 mins.

D: Alf Kjellin. P: Monroe Sachson (JayJen Productions). W: Harold Jacob Smith. Ph: Lester Shorr. M: Coleridge-Taylor Perkinson. St: Brock Peters (Benjie), Burl Ives (Neal McMasters), David Carradine (White Feather), Nancy Kwan (Robin), Jack Palance (Kolby)

"We ain't gonna have no niggers owning land in Cullum County."

With its ethnic minority hero and a plot that melds racial antagonism with a dispute over land rights, *The McMasters* plays like an African-American variant of *Devil's Doorway*. Brock Peters' black Civil War veteran stands in for Robert Taylor's Shoshone chief – their military service counts for nought when they stake a claim to land coveted by, or considered the privilege of, their white neighbours. (And if Taylor's character could be considered a surrogate for non-white soldiers returning to a cold reception after the Second World War, the same might be said of Peters' Benjie, with Vietnam the frame of reference.) Exacerbating Benjie's situation is the fact that he fought for the Union but lives in the South. More pertinently, Alf Kjellin's film, a product of the civil rights era, was bound up with attempts in Hollywood to move racial issues to the foreground. Peters' presence, together with the politically sensitive Southern context, inevitably brings to mind his role as Tom Robinson in *To Kill a Mockingbird*, although the treatment of his persecution here and the caricatural rendering of the redneck villains is more sensationalistic, bordering on exploitation fare.

This derives largely from the atmosphere of barely controlled hysteria whipped up by Jack Palance as Kolby, a Confederate fanatic almost identical to the character he had played in the previous year's *The Desperados*. Chewing tobacco and scenery with equal relish, Palance leads local opposition when Benjie is gifted a half-share in his ranch by the beneficent Neal McMasters, his erstwhile employer and surrogate father. While Benjie forms a tentative alliance with White Feather's impoverished Indians, his opponents progress from poisoning his cattle to burning his property and raping his Indian bride. When Benjie kills two of his assailants, Kolby proclaims the slain men martyrs in a race war and leads a lynch mob of acolytes and weak-willed townsmen (with L.Q. Jones and R.G. Armstrong, Peters' co-stars from *Major Dundee*, prominent among them) against the McMasters ranch.

While Benjie's disdainful treatment by the locals is predictable – aside from McMasters he has just one supporter among the whites, a token liberal – his interactions with the Indians provide a more unusual angle on race relations and point up the irony of his situation. Although he saves three of them from Kolby's henchmen, gives them work and is repaid with Robin, the chief's sister, Benjie is just another landowner in their eyes, black skin notwithstanding. They criticise him for upholding "the white man's law", which has led to the carving up and fencing off of once-free terrain, and refuse his request for help in defending his property. (Given his background as a slave, Benjie's obsession with ownership is not difficult to understand.) The land "don't belong to nobody. We say, we belong to the land," says White Feather, articulating the same fashionably countercultural ethos espoused by most Native American tribes in westerns of this vintage.

Usually a supporting player, Peters is solid, if rather mannered, in the central role, but his efforts to give his character a dignified bearing are not always supported by the script. The most jarring scene occurs when Benjie reluctantly takes Robin as his squaw ("A slave for me?") and proceeds to rape her, in the open – a combination of repressed lust, perhaps, with the desire of a former slave to be the dominant party. There may be a point here about the brutalising effects of servitude, but it is never developed. Similarly, Robin's passivity and unswerving devotion are hard to fathom. They may be the result of her powerlessness as a squaw – she has no say in the matter when White Feather gives her to Benjie; as written, however, she is little more than an object to be passed around among men. It is a thankless role for the delicate and miscast Nancy Kwan, and it demonstrates the limits of the film's sensitivity towards traditionally marginalised characters.

These ambiguities and inconsistencies are typical of a script that is predictable in many respects, yet perceptive and wrong-footing in others. The finale encapsulates the point. After a nocturnal siege in which McMasters is killed, Benjie is on the point of being burnt alive when, despite their previous stance, the Indians ride to the rescue. This stock situation does not resolve matters, however. There is still occasion for White Feather to reiterate his disgust at Benjie's insistence on joining the landowning class. "You're like us," he tells him, as one racial outsider to another. "You ain't got no home." It is a disconcerting message, echoing the words of the local bigots that Benjie, emancipated or not, ought to know his place, and was perhaps intended to echo beyond the narrative. As with other westerns of the period, *The McMasters* seems to ask: is this really the land of freedom and equality, of opportunity for all? Kolby and his cronies may have been vanquished, but the fight against oppression, it is implied, goes on.[1] **KG**

footnotes

1 The uncertainty over the film-makers' intentions for the film can be measured by the fact that two versions were released – one in which the rednecks win, the other in which they are defeated.

Monte Walsh

1970, Colour, 99 mins.

D: William A. Fraker. P: Hal Landers, Bobby Roberts (Palladian Pictures, Cinema Center Films). W: Lukas Heller, David Z. Goodman. Ph: David M. Walsh. M: John Barry. St: Lee Marvin (Monte Walsh), Jeanne Moreau (Martine Bernard), Jack Palance (Chet Rollins), Mitch Ryan (Shorty Austin), Jim Davis (Cal Brennan)

"The kind of life you're talkin' about is dead."
"It ain't dead! As long as there's one cowboy taking care of one cow, it ain't dead."

As the western entered its own twilight years, its focus turned increasingly towards the fading of the light on the frontier. William A. Fraker's handsome film is a bittersweet contribution to the cycle, a compassionate character study of cowboys facing up to extinction. With "big Eastern money" buying up chunks of Montana and ranches closing down, ageing wranglers Monte Walsh and Chet Rollins consider their limited options.[1] Chet opts for storekeeping and domesticity, while Monte, maintaining the bruised dignity of a Steve Judd, Jack Burns or Will Penny, vacillates between his lover's boudoir and the illusory liberty of a way of life that is ebbing into history. When their friend Shorty falls in with criminals, rough-housing and rugged comedy make way for harsh economic reality and personal tragedy. The hardships mount up for Monte – Chet is killed by Shorty; Monte's woman, Martine, succumbs to tuberculosis – but the script, hewn from a novel by *Shane* author Jack Schaefer, preserves its hero for a cautiously optimistic ending.

With Mama Cass's sweet ballad, 'The Good Times Are Coming', establishing an ironic tone, Fraker juxtaposes nostalgia for hardy individualism with fashionably naturalistic details – outhouses, body odour, false teeth – and poignant vignettes. One of the older hands, Fightin' Joe (John McLiam), lives in a mnemonic haze, reminiscing about his glory days in the Civil War while stringing barbed wire on the range. "He talks like his life is over," observes Chet, and the demeaning chore eventually drives Joe over the edge, figuratively and literally, when he rides his horse in a suicidal charge down a ridge. Monte, too,

than sociopathic. The only real villain is capitalism, encroaching from the East like a faceless monster. In tracking down Shorty (their 'showdown', as such, is staged, anti-western style, in the shadowy confines of a slaughterhouse), Monte is satisfying his sense of honour more than a craving for vengeance. Yet this does not preclude ignoble actions: Monte shoots his erstwhile associate even though the latter has holstered his sidearm. As much as it pines for a mythical lost era of supposedly ironclad values, *Monte Walsh* was made at the end of the Sixties, and reflects the moral uncertainties of that most violent and divisive decade. Heroism simply cannot be taken for granted.

Flawed, likeable, flesh and blood characters fight through the director's somewhat rose-tinted perspective. Lee Marvin brings light and shade, charm and humour, to his portrayal of a man doggedly standing his ground even as it shifts beneath his feet. His scenes with Jeanne Moreau have an easy intimacy, the actress exuding warmth and sensuality in the clichéd role of golden-hearted whore; a scene in which Marvin proposes marriage, in a roundabout way, is beautifully understated.[3] Jack Palance, meanwhile, gives one of the most relaxed displays of his career, reining in the grandiloquence that marked his appearances in Euro-westerns of the period. He and Marvin convey the camaraderie of good old boys who have ridden together for untold years, making the point at which their characters' paths diverge especially moving.

dwells in the past, reciting anecdotes at random, insisting on the viability of cowboying even as more employees on the Slash Y ranch are laid off. When Chet gets married and Martine moves on in search of work (prostitution, like wrangling, is "a profession of diminishing returns"), Monte walks the streets of Harmony, the nearest town, in a wistful daze, stopping momentarily at Martine's deserted house. It is a keenly observed evocation of loneliness.

Such nuances make *Monte Walsh* atypical for a western. It is light on violent conflict, leisurely paced ("too slow", in Fraker's subsequent estimation) and largely eschews hyperbole.[2] Shorty and his accomplices (Matt Clark and Billy 'Green' Bush, both members of the subsequent *Culpepper Cattle Co.*, as was another co-star here, Bo Hopkins) are desperadoes in the truest sense. Stealing to stave off destitution, they are pathetic rather

Great care was taken to evoke 1890s Montana. The titles are superimposed on sketches by famed Old West artist Charles M. Russell; the costumes look stained and worn; period knick-knacks peer out from Martine's room. First-time DP David M. Walsh uses a dusky colour scheme for the open, empty plains and a soft, soothing glow for the interiors – it almost has the effect of preserving the characters in amber. (Fraker, best known as a cinematographer, could scarcely have bettered the results himself.) But a pall settles over the sets as the plot darkens, from the gloom of the saloon in Charleyville, where Monte locates an ailing Martine, to his silent vigil beside her deathbed and the confrontation with Shorty amid the shadows of the abattoir.

Another nocturnal sequence contains Monte's last hurrah. With the impending demise of his lifestyle preying on his mind, he spies a wild horse, sold by the Slash Y to a Wild West show, tied up in a corral in Charleyville. Even Shorty, a consummate bronco buster, could not tame this one, but Monte breaks it, after the horse has bucked wildly around the deserted street, crashing into a shop, knocking down signs and railings and toppling the town's water tower. It is a magnificent, impulsive and gleefully irresponsible display of skill and defiance. In this almost abstract setting – a private arena for man and horse; nobody comes running at the sounds of destruction – Monte asserts his self-worth; as with

A dying breed, from left: Tom Heaton, Jack Palance, G.D. Spradlin, Lee Marvin and Michael Conrad

Gregory Peck's unobserved conquest of the stallion Old Thunder in *The Big Country* (1958), it is the mark of a man not to seek attention for his accomplishments.

And it earns Monte his best shot at a steady job away from the range. The sole witness to his ride is Colonel Wilson (Eric Christmas), owner of the Wild West Roundup (and the horse), who offers Monte the role of 'Texas Jack Barrat', star cowboy in Wilson's outfit. (Monte will be replacing the original Texas Jack, now deceased: "He couldn't ride a horse worth a damn, but he put on a hell of a show.") Monte is tempted; he tries on a fringed buckskin jacket and listens to Wilson's patter, before pride takes hold and he issues one of the pithiest rejoinders in the western: "I ain't spittin' on my whole life." There is little doubt that Monte's financial prospects are bleak, but in remaining true to himself, he is triumphant. **KG**

footnotes

1 The characters' economic travails mirror those of contemporary labourers, whose own fortunes were at low tide at the time of *Monte Walsh's* release. In *Westerns in a Changing America 1955-2000* (McFarland, 2004), R. Philip Loy links wranglers and drovers with hard-pressed workers in the steel and automotive industries.

2 "Today, I would do it entirely differently," Fraker told Donald Zec in the Seventies. "The honesty would be there but it would have much more bezaz" (*Marvin: the Story of Lee Marvin*, New English Library, 1979).

3 Although Fraker feared that his hard-drinking star's legendary boorishness might send Moreau fleeing back to France, he was astonished at the change in Marvin's behaviour: "There was a softness, a tenderness that began to work in Lee that I'd never seen before. And Jeanne Moreau was the only one, it seemed, who could trigger it." Marvin was so struck by the actress that he even gave up alcohol for the duration of the shoot. Inevitably, rumours circulated that the pair were having an affair (*Marvin*).

Soldier Blue

1970, Colour, 115 mins.

D: Ralph Nelson. P: Gabriel Katzka, Harold Loeb (Katzka-Loeb Productions). W: John Gay. Ph: Robert Hauser. M: Roy Budd. St: Candice Bergen (Cresta Marybelle Lee), Peter Strauss (Honus Gant), Donald Pleasence (Isaac Q. Cumber), Bob Carraway (Lt. John McNair), Jorge Rivero (Spotted Wolf)

"Did you ever see an Indian camp after the Army has been there? Did you ever see the women and what was done to them before they were killed? Ever see the little boys and girls stuck on the long knives?"

Were it not for the devastating sucker punch with which is concludes, *Soldier Blue* – two parts light-hearted love story to one part antiwar philippic – would scarcely deserve the significance, or opprobrium, that has been attached to it. Channelling popular indignation directed towards Washington, the filmmakers' approach is about as subtle as one of their own metaphors: the sight of Old Glory being trampled into the dirt by those charged with defending its values. Few Hollywood films of the period went so far in trashing America's self-image, and none quite so baldly. John Gay and Ralph Nelson wield their arguments and allusions like blunt weapons, bludgeoning the historical reputation of the Army in the Indian Wars and joining the dots between Sand Creek and Vietnam, implicitly condemning military operations like that in My Lai on the fringes of the New Frontier.[1] In the process, as Paul A. Bartrop puts it, they "held up a mirror to US society and showed that genocidal massacre was not only possible but had already happened on US soil in the past."[2]

On 29 November, 1864, Colonel John Chivington, a former Methodist preacher, led a force of around 700 militiamen, complete with four howitzers, to an Indian village near Sand Creek, Colorado. The inhabitants had been told they were under the Army's protection, but Chivington, spoiling for a fight, gave the order to attack. When the smoke cleared, the butcher's bill amounted to almost 200 Cheyenne and Arapaho Indians; by many accounts, two thirds of them were women and children. The scale of the slaughter, combined with ghastly reports of sexual assault and other outrages ("Every one I saw dead was scalped… men, women, and children's privates cut out…"[3]), shocked even the authorities. Congress's Joint Committee on the Conduct of War concluded that Chivington's conduct fell well below that expected of a white man, although not that of an Indian: "[He] deliberately planned and executed a foul and dastardly massacre which would have disgraced the veriest savage among those who were the victims of his cruelty." Chivington was never punished for his actions.[4]

For Gay and Nelson, the injustice of the case (a petition for reparations by descendants of those killed continues to this day) demanded some kind of redress, while the myth that atrocities of this kind were the preserve of those "veriest savages" called for a rebuttal. The nation's involvement in a new conflict against a technologically disadvantaged racial Other had created a current of anti-imperialist, anti-militarist sentiment – and offered the filmmakers a ready-made analogy for their project.

Soldier Blue counters the impression expressed in the script of Native Americans as "bloody butchers", "godless barbarians". But it falls into the trap of replacing one ideological bias with another, reducing a complex issue to a black and white proposition. The "dark abominations" spoken of here in relation to the Cheyenne – an echo of the racist rhetoric of innumerable older westerns – are committed on the banks of Sand Creek by white soldiers: rape, the killing of children, (off-screen) mutilation. It culminates in a macabre mass jig of celebration, with cavalrymen waving aloft severed limbs and scalps like trophies. By contrast, Indian violence – the film opens with a Cheyenne raid on an Army paymaster's detail – is shown to be relatively 'clean', the Cheyenne themselves as defensive rather than aggressive, tolerant and trusting rather than breakers of treaties like the white man.

So far, so fashionable. Nelson's target audience was the New Left – counterculture theorists, civil rights campaigners, college students who had "embraced the Indian cause".[5] Hollywood liberalism was in the ascendant. Gay and Nelson were both antiwar; the former identified John Ford's apologetic *Cheyenne Autumn* as an inspiration for the tone of his script, while the director was energised by "the minority problem" in the US (his previous film, the Jim Brown vehicle *…tick…tick…tick…* [1969], dramatised contemporary race relations in the Deep South); the Cree folk singer Buffy Sainte-Marie, who performs the title song, was a darling of the peace movement; Candice

Bergen was a prominent supporter of the American Indian Movement (AIM) and the Black Panthers.

Yet the opportunity to present an indigenous perspective on Manifest Destiny – a cinematic equivalent of Dee Brown's *Bury My Heart at Wounded Knee*, published the same year – is passed up. *Soldier Blue* has more to say about white America's fractured psyche in the Vietnam years. The Cheyenne, notionally the subjects of the film, have very little screen time and no substantial roles. The bulk of the plot details the sparky yet increasingly affectionate relationship between displaced New Yorker Cresta Marybelle Lee and rookie trooper Honus Gant, sole survivors of the opening ambush, as they make their way cross-country to Fort Reunion, where she is due to meet her Army fiancé. Described by P.B. Hurst as "a sort of Wild West version of 'Hanoi Jane'", Cresta has spent time among the Cheyenne as a captive and, like the actress who plays her, become a spokesperson for Indian grievances, haranguing Honus about military brutality; he, meanwhile, blindly maintains patriotic pride in the uniform and faith in the moral justification of westward expansion.[6] It is like watching a freethinking Berkeley radical – or indeed a socially switched-on ingénue – clashing with an uptight West Point cadet.

Unfailingly straight, in the sixties sense of the word, Honus is appalled at Cresta's immodesty, her profanities, belching and cynicism – she mourns the loss of her hat more than the men killed in the paymaster sequence, whose corpses she plunders for supplies. In a film where western conventions are upended, however, it is inevitable that it is the gutsy, proto-feminist Cresta, not the rookie Honus, whose quick wits and survival skills guide them past danger – notably a run-in with Donald Pleasence's odious but comical trader – to the fort. When Cresta learns of the impending attack, she rides off to warn the Cheyenne, leaving Colonel Iverson (John Anderson), the film's stand-in for Chivington, to speak for the Establishment: "When I see young people today behaving like that... I can't help wondering what this goddamn country's coming to."

Many asked that question in relation to the film itself: was it regurgitating the cultural dissent and hijacking the cinematic trends of its era merely to profit from them? I see no reason to doubt or decry Nelson's intentions; he was upfront about wanting to "add fuel to the new militancy of Indian efforts to reach the mainstream of American life", and claimed that the visceral climax to his film accurately reflected eyewitness testimony from Sand Creek.[7] Yet he succoured those who accused him of opportunism by referencing Vietnam at every opportunity in promotional interviews (as did Candice Bergen), as if to drum up business among the antiwar lobby, and boasting, during production, that his film would be more "savage" than, for example, *The Wild Bunch*. (In one sense, Nelson was correct: his film features children as victims of violence rather than just spectators; he would use the same tactics to incite an emotional response in his subsequent, even more wayward semi-western, *The Wrath of God* [1972]. But there is far less on-screen bloodshed in *Soldier Blue* than its reputation suggests; its strong images are never held for more than a few frames, and there is greater emphasis on the frenzied troopers than on the destruction they are wreaking.[8])

More damaging to Nelson's case, and to the film's reputation, is the marginalization of the Cheyenne, who are reduced to little more than ciphers. As with many pro-Indian westerns before and since, this has invited a volley of (post-) revisionist criticism. "The employment of Indians' historical experiences as metaphor dilutes and distorts those experiences and threatens to trivialize their existence," contends Jacquelyn Kilpatrick.[9] One has to bear in mind the exigencies of commercial cinema – to disseminate a message widely, there has to be an audience to receive it; white actors, whether playing Anglo-American roles or interpreting Indian characters, will attract the widest number of paying customers. But *Soldier Blue* is more condescending than most, employing a feisty white woman to plead the Indians' cause while they are largely absent from the discourse.

Soldier Blue became, briefly, the *cause célèbre* that Nelson hoped it would be, but its thunder was stolen by Arthur Penn's similarly intentioned *Little Big Man*, which developed greater intimacy with its Indian characters and switched gears and moods much more smoothly. Nelson ended up making two films in one: a brutally frank exposé of military degeneracy; a fable of two young people – one disillusioned with her nation; the other conflicted – finding themselves, literally and figuratively, in the great outdoors. Common to both is the assertion that the Indians enjoyed a morally and spiritually purer way of life than that of their conquerors. Very much a product of its time, then, but its barbs against 'unjust' war – and the conduct thereof – are likely to retain their sting given America's commitments in new and evolving micro-conflicts. **KG**

footnotes

1 *Soldier Blue's* climax has often been called an allegory of the carnage at My Lai, inciting allegations that the filmmakers were cashing in on the controversy. Nelson admitted they had "Vietnam… in the back of our minds" during filming, but had already begun filming his massacre when news broke of Charlie Company's March 1968 assault on the Vietnamese village, in which as many as 500 civilians may have been murdered. (It had been covered up for a year and a half before journalist Seymour Hersh filed his first dispatch, on 12 November, 1969.) In his script, written before anybody outside the military had any knowledge of My Lai, John Gay included a detailed description of the butchery we see on screen, replacing the tame description in Theodore Victor Olsen's source novel: "The engagement had been short and swift." Nevertheless, parallels between the film's fictionalised version of historical events and then-current operations in Southeast Asia were inevitable. Nelson's western "resembles My Lai because Sand Creek and Wounded Knee resemble My Lai", concludes P.B. Hurst in his book-length study, *The Most Savage Film: Soldier Blue, Cinematic Violence and the Horrors of War* (McFarland, 2008).

2 'Massacre and the Movies', in *Film and Genocide* (Kristi Wilson and Tomás F. Crowder-Taraborrelli, eds, University of Wisconsin Press, 2012).

3 Eyewitness testimony quoted in US Congress report.

4 Many white Coloradans cheered Chivington's raid. Some years later, a town close to the site of the massacre was named in his honour.

5 Letter from Ralph Nelson to a friend, quoted in *The Most Savage Film.*

6 In contrast to most white women rescued from Indian captivity in westerns – see *The Searchers*, *Trooper Hook*, *Two Rode Together*, Nelson's own *Duel at Diablo* – Cresta seems unfazed by her experience and indifferent to the judgements of others.

7 The climax incorporates elements of the Wounded Knee encounter as well. The film's most glaring anachronism is Honus's statement that his father, also a soldier, was killed with Custer at Little Bighorn – an engagement that took place 12 years after the events depicted here. Presumably this was to provide Honus with motivation for taking up soldiering – a profession for which he seems temperamentally ill-suited.

8 Nelson toned down the content following preview screenings, although cuts were still requested by the ratings boards in the US and UK. It wasn't too difficult for *Soldier Blue's* distributors to snip out the more harrowing footage and rerelease it with a family-friendly PG rating in 1974; posters played up the romantic aspects of the story.

9 *Celluloid Indians: Native Americans and Film* (University of Nebraska Press, 1999).

Billy Jack

1971, Colour, 114 mins.

D: T.C. Frank [Tom Laughlin]. P: Mary Rose Solti [Tom Laughlin] (National Student Film Corporation). W: Frank Christina [Tom Laughlin], Teresa Christina [Delores Taylor]. Ph: Fred Koenekamp, John Stephens. M: Mundell Lowe. St: Tom Laughlin (Billy Jack), Delores Taylor (Jean Roberts), Clark Howat (Sheriff Cole), Bert Freed (Posner), David Roya (Bernard Posner)

"Being an Indian is not a matter of blood... it's a way of life."

More famous today for its creator's gall and tenacity – wresting distribution rights from Warner Bros. and circulating it himself, creating a hit of phenomenal proportions – *Billy Jack* is a film divided against itself, lauding pacifism and tolerance while glorifying violent resistance. Its most powerful scenes show the title character in a similarly conflicted state: whether to turn the other cheek or to smite it – in this case, with a well-placed kick. Specifically, whether to uphold the ideals of the staff and pupils at the multiracial Freedom School he is sworn to protect, or surrender to his violent instincts. These were honed in Vietnam and he unleashes them on a regular basis, often in admiring slow motion, against the local rednecks and power brokers who represent the kind of entrenched bigotry targeted by the new wave of westerns that *Billy Jack* – give or take its modern-day setting – was aligned with.

A white man with Cherokee blood, hapkido skills and anger issues, Billy Jack, played by director and co-writer Tom Laughlin, first appeared in a 1967 biker flick, *The Born Losers*, as a defender of the weak. Both the classic westerner – Richard Slotkin's 'man who knows Indians' – and the persecuted outsider in one stocky frame, in this film he embraces his heritage more deeply, swapping his white Stetson for a flat-brimmed, Jimi Hendrix-style banded 'Indian' hat, partaking in mystical rituals and proclaiming the spiritual and moral virtues of the Native American lifestyle. He has retreated from white society to a reservation in Arizona, which he patrols like an avenging angel, guarding it against white hunters who shoot wild mustangs for pet food (a nod to *The Misfits*), and arriving serendipitously – almost magically, the kids believe – whenever his charges at the school, effectively a hippy commune, are threatened.

Billy's contradictions – racial, cultural and temperamental – make him a fascinating protagonist, and Laughlin plays him with the intensity of a rattler poised to strike. His bloodline can be traced back to Robert Taylor's culturally dislocated Shoshone Union Army soldier in *Devil's Doorway*, via the mixed-race avengers in Euro-westerns and Paul Newman's antihero in *Hombre*. (Given Billy's proficiency in unarmed combat, perhaps a line can also be drawn to Spencer Tracy's karate-trained investigator in 1955's *Bad Day at Black Rock*, another film that exposes societal racism in the course of reconfiguring western motifs.) As a damaged war veteran with a particular animus towards injustice, Billy is also a forerunner of Travis Bickle, whose mohawk hairstyle signified his 'going native' (it was cribbed from US Army Special Forces soldiers in Vietnam), and John Rambo – scarcely darlings of the pacifist-humanist lobby. When he is off screen, however, we are left with a rudimentary plot about the cultural crevasse between the conservative establishment and nonconformist youth. Between scenes of badly acted pulp villains picking on Indians and "long-haired weirdos", there are extended interludes set in the school – semi-improvised footage of "psycho-drama", role-playing and music therapy ("Things the townspeople could never understand"). These sequences almost comprise a promotional film for the institution itself; they evidently meant a great deal to *Billy Jack's* creators, but they also stall the momentum of the wider plot.

The film never manages to resolve its internal tensions, its contradictory appeals eventually cancelling each other out. As the bad guys resort to rape and murder and Billy goes on the warpath, he is besieged in an old church, accompanied by a pregnant teenage runaway he has tried to shield and by his would-be girlfriend, Jean, the devoutly pacifist school principal (Delores Taylor, Laughlin's wife and co-author of the screenplay) who tries to talk him down: "So easy for you to die dramatically. It's a hell of a lot tougher for those of us who have to keep on trying." It is a compelling plea, more so because it was she who was raped and she is battling to keep her own anger in check. But Billy's point, expressed earlier in the film, is equally valid – liberal icons such as King and the Kennedys were killed (by "*your* people", he emphasises) because America as a whole, not just the West, continues to be ruled by the gun. "In what remote corner of this country – no, entire goddamn planet – is there a place where men really care about one another and really love each other?" Jean has no answer, but Billy's defiance – more in the spirit of Malcolm X than Martin Luther King – proves unsustainable and the film ends meekly, having ridden into the same *cul de sac* as countless other seemingly liberal exploitation films, albeit *Billy Jack's* intentions were unquestionably sincere.

Billy's surrender is his most heroic act in the circumstances. It spares the town further bloodshed and suggests perhaps that Jean's pacifism has had an effect after all. The outcome supports the view of *Billy Jack* as "a rebuttal of the traditional western", with Billy "refusing… the final shootout, the suicidal fighting to the end" associated with outlaw mythology.[1] Laughlin

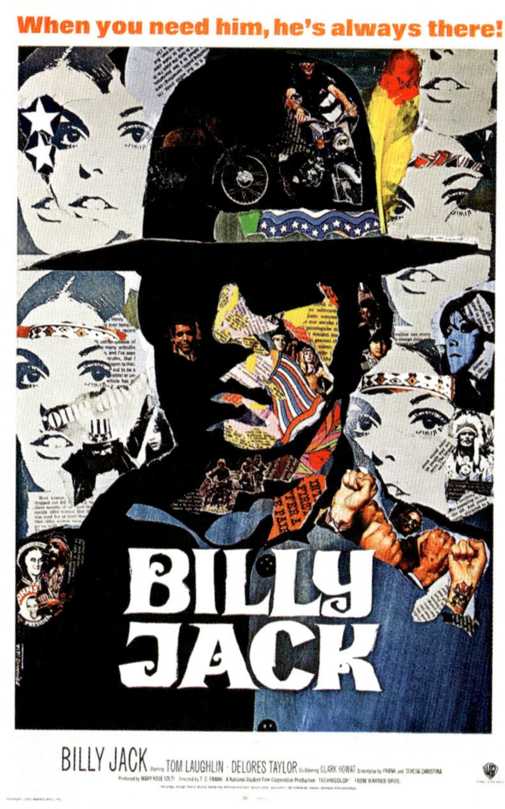

denies the character the martyrdom that sanctified the protagonists of *Easy Rider*, or his namesake in *Pat Garrett and Billy the Kid*. Billy Jack had further work to do: his trial was the focus of a sequel, and he continued his campaign in a third film, taking the fight to the Senate floor in Washington. (A fourth was long mooted before Laughlin's death in 2013; he and Taylor remained politically active well after their film careers had subsided.)

Billy Jack utilised aspects of the western myth to question both "the meaning of genre conventions, the value of which had previously lain in the easy orientation they offered viewers", and the validity of the "progress and civilization" for which former generations of western heroes had fought and sometimes died.[2] These criticisms found a receptive audience in 1971, yet the film is too muddled, too inconsistent, to be considered successful in an artistic or philosophical sense outside of that context. For that reason it must be considered a failure, but at least it is an honourable one. **KG**

footnotes

1 Maurice Yacowar, 'Private and Public Visions: *Zabriskie Point* and *Billy Jack*', in *The Journal of Popular Film*, summer 1972.

2 Eric Lichtenfeld, *Action Speaks Louder: Violence, Spectacle and the American Action Movie* (Wesleyan University Press, 2007).

FAYE DUNAWAY
STACY KEACH
HARRIS YULIN
DOC
(DOC HOLLIDAY)
UN FILM DE
FRANK PERRY
avec
MIKE WITNEY
SCENARIO : PETE HAMILL
MUSIQUE: JIMMY WEBB
REGIE & PROD.: FRANK PERRY
COULEURS
United Artists

Doc

1971, Colour, 96 mins.

D: Frank Perry. P: Frank Perry (FP Films Inc). W: Pete Hamill. Ph: Gerald Hirschfeld. M: Jimmy Webb.
St: Stacy Keach (John 'Doc' Holliday), Faye Dunaway (Kate Elder), Harris Yulin (Wyatt Earp),
Mike Witney (Ike Clanton), Denver John Collins (the Kid)

"I run the law, you run the gambling. We'll both end up rich."
"We sound like bad people, Wyatt."
"We are, John."

Its makers described *Doc* as an "Eastern western", alluding to the New York origins of its creative axis: writer Pete Hamill, a journalist by trade, and director Frank Perry. (The film's three leads, for their part, all cut their teeth on the New York stage.) The implication was that this was a genre film made by people with no emotional stake in its traditions and trappings, less susceptible to its mythic charms; people concerned more with contemporary relevance than historical accuracy. Hamill built his career chronicling the social upheavals of the Sixties, and these events, as well as the popular disillusionment they engendered, closely informed the tone of his script. (It's possible that Tombstone's sceptical newspaperman, played by Hamill's literary contemporary Dan Greenburg, was intended to be the screenwriter's mouthpiece.) The central characters, meanwhile, have an allegorical purpose over and above their place in national folklore. Hamill stated that his Machiavellian Wyatt Earp, for example, was modelled on Lyndon Johnson.

The tagline broadly sums up the approach: "For the past 90 years these three people [Doc Holliday, Wyatt Earp and, in deference to Faye Dunaway's prominent billing, Kate Elder] have been heroes – until now." Legend has it that Wyatt Earp was a straight-dealing, plain-speaking, virtuous law-bringer, with Doc Holliday his dark, debonair alter ego, a charismatic gambler/gunfighter and ruthless killer – "The nerviest, speediest, deadliest man with a six-gun I ever knew," according to Earp. Here, although Doc has not quite become a knight in Earp's stead, Wyatt has certainly been transformed into a knave. He is venal and corrupt, imbued with serpentine menace by character actor Harris Yulin, whose stocky frame and inscrutable features are almost the antithesis of the popular image of Earp embodied by Henry Fonda.[1] Stacy Keach's softly spoken Doc, meanwhile, is the more conscientious of the two, racked with remorse as much as by consumption. His relationship with Kate Elder, whom he forcefully "retires" from prostitution and takes as his common-law wife, and his shepherding of the Kid, the Clantons' impressionable young cousin, suggest a desire to settle down and save souls, even if he fears – as he drunkenly expresses to a noncomprehending and unsympathetic Earp – that it may be too late to rescue his own.

Given *Doc's* cultural context, Wyatt's machinations make him a surrogate for the detested political establishment, and the O.K. Corral confrontation, which he engineers, is seen as the culmination of his campaign for the sheriff's position in Tombstone. And that, he tells Doc, will mean control of the town's black economy. The Clantons are rough-hewn where Wyatt is slick; blue-collar rather than white shirt and suit. Read another way, they could be said to represent the counterculture – free-

living, longhaired, anti-authoritarian; either way, they make convenient scapegoats when their associate Johnny Ringo robs a stagecoach. As if the film-makers' sympathies were not plain enough, they have Wyatt soundly beaten in a fair fight by Ike Clanton – still boorish and belligerent, but not the black-hearted villain of earlier renditions of the tale. (Wyatt sets his bruised dignity aside to propose an underhanded deal with the Clantons, offering them the reward money for Ringo so long as Wyatt gets the credit – and the sheriff's badge.) Doc is somewhere in the middle of these factions, torn between loyalty to Wyatt, domestic bliss with Kate and dropping out entirely (he frequents Tombstone's opium den to recover from his coughing fits). Grasping after a deeper purpose, he resembles the nomads and misfits of the era's road movies: "Part of me wants the same things [as you]," he tells Kate, "part of me wants… something else."

For large parts of the film this vague longing centres on Kate, her prominence in the narrative helping earn *Doc* its unique place in the Tombstone canon. Played by Dunaway with ballsy exuberance, she is the most attractive of the central characters, uninhibited and adaptable. As if to emphasise the new westerns' determination to muddy the myths of the frontier, in her first scene Kate is smeared in grime, and seems indifferent to the fact. It signifies both her defiance of societal norms and her individuality. She enters into a relationship with Doc on equal terms – they playfully exchange insults in lieu of compliments – and later in the film she angrily rebuffs the scrupulously polite but smugly self-righteous entreaties of Wyatt's buttoned-up sister-in-law, who suggests Kate make plans to marry Doc in church. "When I'm on my knees, it ain't in prayer," she retorts. It is a 1971 attitude scoffing at 1881 moral rigidity.

Kate is sidelined, however, when Wyatt steers Doc towards the O.K. Corral, having goaded the Clantons into settling their feud once and for all. Perry's staging makes the encounter perhaps the most one-sided of all cinematic re-creations, as Doc and the Earp brothers, advancing abreast, open up on the terrified cowboys with shotguns. When it is over, Wyatt, standing over his slain brother Morgan, exploits the event to further impress his credentials as sheriff on the crowd.

This image of Earp may have been indigestible to those weaned on heroic myth, but the sourest note is struck by Doc's killing of the unarmed Kid. As with Burt Lancaster needlessly shooting a fleeing suspect in the back at the end of *Lawman*, the message is that behind the romantic façade these men were stone killers: brutalised, desensitised. The problem here is that throughout the film Keach has tried to rehabilitate Doc, to express his weariness of violence; consequently, the moment jars. With no credible motivation for his action ("He reminded me of too many things," he remarks enigmatically), it strikes as a cynically scripted sucker punch, especially since Doc had gone out of his way to help the youngster – even, in one scene, pulling a gun on Wyatt when it seemed as if the latter might rough the boy up. Hamill and Perry seem to have felt the need to underline their disdain for the classic western and its moral codes. But they also undermine one of the central premises of their film: that Doc is morally superior to Wyatt. Perhaps the shooting would not have been out of character for the real Holliday but, the way Keach plays him here, it makes little sense. **KG**

footnotes

1 *Doc's* debunking of Wyatt Earp had been anticipated to an extent by two of the western's major directors, John Ford and John Sturges. In Ford's *Cheyenne Autumn*, James Stewart played the marshal as a dandified gambler, clearly lacking in moral probity, two decades after Ford and Henry Fonda had practically canonized the character in *My Darling Clementine*. In Sturges' *Hour of the Gun*, meanwhile, Earp became a hard-nosed, obsessive avenger, played in scowling, surly fashion by James Garner.

In Bajo Rio, they pay to see a man kill a bull.

Today, they'll pay to see a man kill another man.

A Gunfight

1971, Colour, 89 mins.

D: Lamont Johnson.
P: Harold Jack Bloom, A. Ronald Lubin
(the Jicarilla Apache Tribe of American Indians,
Harvest-Thoroughbred-Joel Productions).
W: Harold Jack Bloom. Ph: David M. Walsh.
M: Laurence Rosenthal.
St: Kirk Douglas (Will Tenneray), Johnny Cash (Abe Cross),
Jane Alexander (Nora Tenneray), Karen Black (Jenny Simms),
Raf Vallone (Francisco Alvarez)

"There's nobody faster with a gun than me… There's nothing good or bad about it. It's certainly nothing brave or noble but… it's something I can do."

The first western to be financed by a Native American tribe does not, surprisingly, concern itself with indigenous issues. With investment from the Jicarilla Apaches, *A Gunfight* is instead a meditation on the fading image of the gunfighter as romantic hero, focusing on two famed pistoleros in their sunset years as they try to make sense of their notoriety. It treads the same ground as such films as *The Gunfighter*, *Death of a Gunfighter*, *The Shootist* and Peckinpah's best work, but never quite achieves their elegiac quality. Its intentions are similarly noble, even though its execution leaves something to be desired. Received with resounding critical indifference, it was also overlooked by the public as the genre was fast becoming unfashionable.

A lone rider crosses rugged desert plains while the granite voice of Johnny Cash laments the poverty and hunger of a transient way of life. After his horse is bitten by a snake, Abe Cross stops in an isolated border town. When he discloses his identity in the bank, ripples of anticipation rouse the slumbering community. Abe's reputation mirrors that of Will Tenneray, a local who entertains the saloon clientele with dextrous gun tricks. An excited, capacity crowd is drawn to the saloon, thirsting for blood, but the drinkers' excitement is dampened as the would-be rivals strike up a rapport.

As people gamble on the outcome of a showdown they think is inevitable, Will, dissatisfied with domestic life and his meagre income – "Making as much in a month as I used to spend in a day" – offers Abe a deal. Why don't they do it for real? Sell tickets to a gunfight, winner takes all? "This is your last chance. I'm talking about… big money." At first Abe is disgusted by the suggestion, but he needs to buy a new horse and, with his employment prospects limited, he agrees. A carnival atmosphere grips the town. Representing the commercialisation of violent spectacle is Alvarez, the store owner and promoter of bullring entertainment. Despite the pleas of the women in their lives, the two protagonists are compelled to fulfil their fateful contract: across the border, in a bullring, as every face in town looks on under the heat of the Mexican sun.

Abe Cross is a well-worn laconic outlaw in the Scott/McCrea mode. The film never tries to persuade us that he lives by any specific moral code, although he affirms to the inquisitive deputy marshal, "I got no reason to break your peace here." It's a finely judged performance by Cash, heavy with solitude and no little sadness. His advancing years are frequently addressed, as when he holds back from swigging the bourbon Will buys for him: "My belly ain't what it was." Conversations with Will focus on the degrading, back-breaking work he's had to do just to eat, his most humiliating gig being "trick-shooting in a medicine show. Besides me, they had a midget and a tattooed fella." Now, he's a wanderer, prospecting for gold here and there and reminiscing about past encounters with the likes of Wyatt Earp and Johnny Ringo.

Will's life is about as exciting. He has been tied down by marriage, but his apathetic character is revitalised by Abe's arrival. Matrimonial bliss with Nora masks the need for flight; the routine of civilisation has become stifling. There's a constant internal struggle between domesticity and machismo; a gentleness that turns to ugly rage when the frustration of compromise erupts into recrimination and low self-esteem. He imagines himself akin to a matador who is, simultaneously, promoting his own personal battle; it's a heavy-handed but effective metaphor that culminates in the corrida showdown. Through his reawakening as a gunfighter, Will's relationship with his son (played by Kirk Douglas's youngest son, Eric) is rekindled, his popularity increases and the possibility opens up of financial freedom.

The lead roles are tailored to the stars: Cash is stoical, his character bearing the psychological and physical burden of a gunfighter's lifestyle, while Douglas portrays another of his morally ambiguous antiheroes. It's disappointing that their female co-stars are given little to do. Nora's initially strong personality fades as she is reduced to desperate pleading with her husband. She becomes a woman waiting to mourn; at one point she tries to pre-empt fate by shooting at Abe in the street. As Abe's love interest, Karen Black's ditzy charm reminds us why she was one of the most engaging actresses of New Hollywood cinema, but she spends too much time fretting over a man who doesn't seem to care enough. The damage that the gunmen's terrible pact finally causes is, however, acutely realised: one woman, clad in black, is a husk of what she once had been; the other is repelled by what's taken place. This is a film where men have abandoned any compromises to the female world and the consequences are dire.

above: Johnny Cash with Kirk Douglas, and Robert J. Wilke as the marshal.

above: Johnny Cash with Karen Black.

Lamont Johnson was better known for his TV work than for cinema, and *A Gunfight* suffers from the kind of hasty, thrifty direction associated with the small screen. There are no outstanding set-pieces but, rather, a collection of memorable moments that strengthen the narrative. A scene in which Abe sees the townsfolk staring at him while he imagines their voiced opinions is a study in paranoia. A stovepipe in Will's one-room dwelling bisects the screen, creating a visual barrier as he argues with Nora. Close-ups of the baying crowd greet the two gunfighters as they enter the bullring, but those faces are stunned into silence when the duel is over. It is a masterclass in foiling audience expectations – Johnson placing us among the crowd, party to the killing.

It is the triumphant party's final vision that raises the film above some of its more pedestrian moments. We are invited to observe what would have happened had the outcome been reversed, and we see that his fate would, indeed, have been the same. Emerging from a dull, almost monastic existence to kill another man of equal stature would only foment the ambitions of wannabe gunslingers across the West. (In an earlier scene, Keith Carradine, making his feature debut, plays a young punk who pays with his life for challenging Will.) Like Gregory Peck in *The Gunfighter*, the surviving protagonist has to keep on riding and hiding, the cycle of violence once again set in motion.

A Gunfight presents the callous brutality of life in the West and the way in which it debases the people and communities it permeates. From the opening scenes of Abe stunning his poisoned horse with a pistol butt to the final unspectacular pay-per-view gunfight, via the image of a once virile *toro* being skinned and gutted, it is a considered and poignant film. Let down by low production values and an unenthusiastic publicity campaign, *A Gunfight* has become a footnote in genre history, but its left-field approach to the lore of the shootist merits attention, as does its sobering take on the selling of violence as spectacle. **CH**

WYNAJĘTY CZŁOWIEK
Reżyseria: PETER FONDA
BARWNY WESTERN AMERYKAŃSKI
W rolach głównych:
PETER FONDA,
WARREN COTES
VERNA BLOOM,
ROBERT PRATT
Produkcja: Pando Co

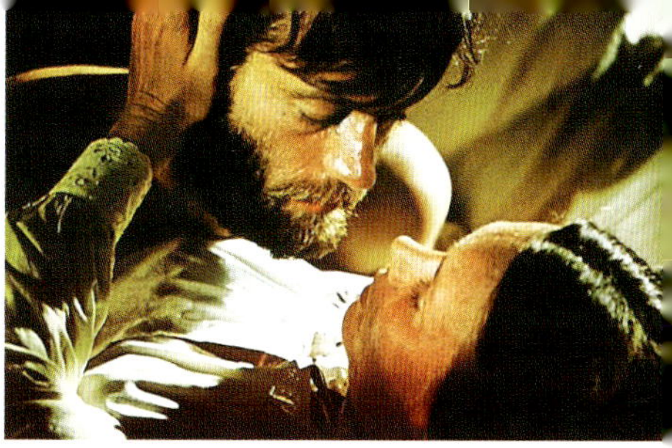

The Hired Hand

1971, Colour, 90 mins.

D: Peter Fonda. P: William Hayward (The Pando Company Inc, Universal). W: Alan Sharp. Ph: Vilmos Zsigmond. M: Bruce Langhorne. St: Peter Fonda (Harry Collings), Warren Oates (Arch Harris), Verna Bloom (Hannah Collings), Robert Pratt (Dan Griffin), Severn Darden (Sam McVey)

"The man who's in a woman's bed thinks he's her boss. And sooner or later they try to move their tackle out of the shed and in here and I didn't want that, cos I'd already had one man in here and I didn't want another."

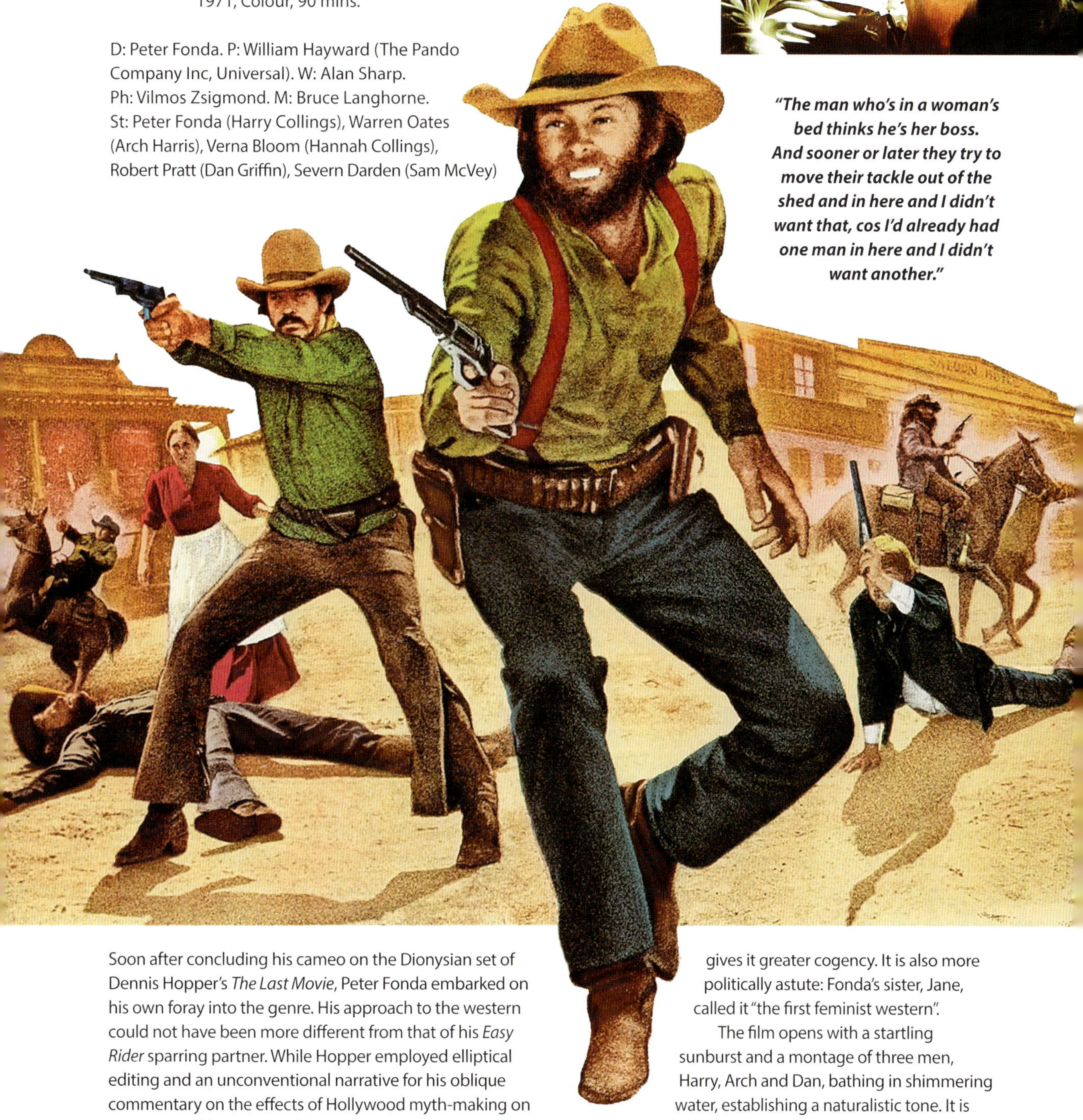

Soon after concluding his cameo on the Dionysian set of Dennis Hopper's *The Last Movie*, Peter Fonda embarked on his own foray into the genre. His approach to the western could not have been more different from that of his *Easy Rider* sparring partner. While Hopper employed elliptical editing and an unconventional narrative for his oblique commentary on the effects of Hollywood myth-making on a remote and impressionable Andean community, Fonda's film is rooted in more familiar territory. It is concerned with the asperity facing those who worked the land and pays tribute in particular to the fortitude of women on the frontier. *The Hired Hand* was as challenging stylistically and thematically as Hopper's vision, but its linear narrative gives it greater cogency. It is also more politically astute: Fonda's sister, Jane, called it "the first feminist western".

The film opens with a startling sunburst and a montage of three men, Harry, Arch and Dan, bathing in shimmering water, establishing a naturalistic tone. It is an idyllic image of a carefree existence, where the passing of time is marked by the elements, rather than the hands of a clock. As J. Hoberman commented enthusiastically, "This lazy desert mirage is a far-out cowboy paradise of surpassing tenderness – as though Captain America and Billy have died and gone to heaven."[1]

above: Warren Oates as Arch, right-hand man to Peter Fonda's Harry. *opposite top right:* Oates and Fonda were close friends in real life.

In his first major studio picture, Vilmos Zsigmond's pioneering techniques achieved a unique look. The dusky light was captured with an Arriflex: once the day's shooting had wrapped, Fonda and his cinematographer would venture out with the lightweight camera to record the evening footage that would be used to such visionary effect. Another vital aspect of the opening is Frank Mazzola's montage editing. (Ironically, Fonda had instructed him to avoid montages.) The outcome of these artistic innovations is the film's signature sequence – "multiple exposures, a combination of negative and positive elements, slow motion, repeated action, blue filters and optical reframing".[2] Light skips into the camera lens like a stone skimming across the water, until this Elysian vision is shattered when the men spy the corpse of a little girl, snagged on a piece of rope. Harry severs the rope, allowing the body to float away, as the glory of nature is rudely disturbed by the reality of mortality.[3]

The drifters had planned to go to California, but Harry has his heart set on returning home to his wife, whom he hasn't seen for seven years. Their journey takes them through the New Mexican outpost of Del Norte. Their arrival in this dust-blown settlement darkens the mood. With the Arriflex mounted atop a station wagon, a tracking shot studies the hostile atmosphere. Cowboys sitting on the saloon porch offer no greeting, their tone and posture intimidating. This uncordial air soon bleeds into violence. As Harry and Arch take respite in a saloon, Dan staggers in with a gunshot wound to the neck. Sam McVey, the town boss (a seedy turn by satirist and comedian Severn Darden), claims mendaciously that the young saddle tramp made advances towards his wife. Dan dies pathetically, calling for his mother, his body shuddering to an unnatural demise. There is no place in Fonda's conception of the West for showdowns conducted on equal terms. His own character bears no relation to the noble western heroes of yore, abandoning the code of fair play in the act of revenge. Aiming a gun through the open window of McVey's quarters, Harry wounds McVey in the soles of his feet before riding off with Arch into the wilderness.

Crimson sunsets, deserts that appear to be aglow with flame and a macro shot of a spider crawling across rippled sand – these transitory images mark time before the duo arrive at the Collings farm. Arch prods his friend with questions about his wife, but Harry doesn't recall her nature. (It's in scenes like this, where the two buddies pass the time of day, that we can see why Fonda entrusted the hardened but sensitive role of Arch to Warren Oates, whose easy rapport with his co-star – they were firm friends in real life – lends weight to the story's ultimate crisis.) Harry's hopes of resuming married life are dampened by his wife's position on the matter. Hannah has ensured that the farm has remained productive and has told their daughter that her father is dead. By showing that Harry cannot simply resume his status as man of the house, Hannah is presented not as embittered by the experience of being abandoned, but emancipated. In an attempt to win back her respect and love, Harry offers his and Arch's services as hired hands, and a tentative agreement is struck. Verna Bloom's manner in these scenes is understated, and her performance throughout all the more powerful for its lack of histrionics; once again, first-time director Fonda showed great instincts in casting an unglamorous co-star for a character-driven script.

Harry and Arch work the land on relatively harmonious terms with Hannah until they go to town to purchase provisions. In a saloon, Arch discovers that Hannah has not remained the virtuous wife in his friend's absence. "She's downright generous," says one of the drinkers. "Most men who work for the widow Collings get paid more than just cash and keep." Arch floors the obtuse drunk, but Harry has heard enough, and has to deal with this knowledge of Hannah's apparent sexual freedom.

Although there were sexually strong, even dominant, women in the genre before *The Hired Hand* – *Rancho Notorious* and *Johnny Guitar* being trailblazing examples – Hannah was among the first to fully retain her autonomy. On returning from town, Harry confronts her in a sombrely lit scene on the homestead. Offering no remorse, Hannah explains, "You were long gone before anybody got into my bed and don't you think I was hankering after you. That was as long as I could stand it." Instinctively, Harry understands he is in no position to argue about her choices. In a reversal of gender roles, Hannah rises to her feet to establish the new domestic hierarchy while her husband remains seated, his head bowed. In a later scene, she tells Arch frankly how previous employees have met her sexual needs: "Out in the field, on the hay, sometimes just down in the dirt. Wouldn't matter if it was you or him tonight." Her emotional detachment when recounting these liaisons is unusual in a female character in a western, but is attuned to the sexual mores of the era and enhances the film's feminist subtext. The scene is subtly eroticised when, transfixed, Arch begins to stroke Hannah's foot. Stolen moments like this, augmented by the nuanced performances of Bloom and Oates, provide a lyricism that was absent from most westerns of the period.

The comradeship between Harry and Arch is imperilled when Arch tells Harry that he's leaving for California, under pressure from Hannah, who will not accept Harry back as her husband unless Arch goes. With him around, she explains, it is like having a rival woman sleeping in the spare room. Arch and Harry have little choice but to acquiesce. Hannah thus welcomes Harry back into the marital bed, but it is on her terms. She demands autonomy, equality, and Fonda affords her a level of respect almost unseen in the genre hitherto. The hero's love for a strong, independently minded woman even comes close to usurping genre expectations of cowboy camaraderie, but the primacy of male inter-relationships is reasserted not long after Hannah and Harry have consummated their reunion.

When a McVey man turns up on the farm, Harry is faced with a conflict of loyalties. Arch has passed through Del Norte and been apprehended – his severed finger is proffered as proof; McVey will kill him unless Harry rides in for a showdown. From putting Hannah's needs first, Harry, and by extension Fonda, succumbs to the call of an endangered comrade and the lure of violence – the meat and drink of much western fiction. Once again, however, Fonda subverts genre conventions in the grubby gun battle that transpires. Arch takes part with bloody, bandaged hands, while Harry thinks nothing of shooting a man in the back. It is an anti-western climax, inelegant and ugly, a tableau of clumsy, survivalist violence in a film that has evolved from idyllic naturalism to coarse brutality.

Despite the power and beauty of its imagery, it is easy to see why Fonda's film was not appreciated by American cinemagoers, although critics were kinder.

(Britain's *Films and Filming* voted it the best film released in the UK in 1971.) It is in danger of being too experimental; at times, the human drama almost suffocates beneath layers of psychedelic visuals. But the premise of Alan Sharp's script remains strong: Harry has lost his wife emotionally and sexually and she will only accept him back under conditions that would have affronted any western protagonist to that point. And while criticisms usually focus on the colour-filtered imagery, (over)use of montage and languid pacing, in retrospect, those elements complement, rather than compromise, the major themes of the narrative. Zsigmond and Mazzola's combined efforts imbue the narrative with a beautifully realised elegiac quality. Writing of the film, and specifically of the opening sequence, Roger Greenspun proclaimed, "The film's glory is in the passing of the natural day, the coming of the evening light."[4]

Just as nature endures, indifferent to the actions of humans, so life goes on in the absence of the 'hero'. In the poignant final scene, Arch returns to the farm to tell Hannah of Harry's death. Respectful of her liberty, he takes his station in the shed, ready to replace Harry in his family home as both hired hand and, presumably, his wife's lover. **CH**

footnotes

1 J. Hoberman, *The Dream Life: Movies, Media, and the Mythology of the Sixties* (The New Press, 2005).

2 Norris Pope, *Chronicle of a Camera: The Arriflex 35 in North America, 1945-1972* (University Press of Mississippi, 2013).

3 Peter Fonda immersed his heart and soul in the making of the film. On the opening scene's thematic composition, he commented, "We used the four classical elements and signs of the zodiac – earth, air, fire and water, going from one to the other in slow motion, until finally, from the water – the water from which life first came – comes a man." Concluding the scene with the image of the dead girl would indicate that the scene symbolizes the cycle of life.

4 Roger Greenspun, *The New York Times*, 1971.

The Last Movie

1971, Colour, 108 mins.

D: Dennis Hopper. P: Paul Lewis (Alta-Light Inc). W: Stewart Stern, Dennis Hopper (story). Ph: Laszlo Kovacs. M: Kris Kristofferson, John Buck Wilkin, Chabuca Granda, Severn Darden, Villagers of Chinchero. St: Dennis Hopper (Kansas), Stella Garcia (Maria), Julie Adams (Mrs. Anderson), Don Gordon (Neville Robey), Tomas Milian (Priest)

"I hope that after this game is over, morality can be born again."

A western in inverted commas, *The Last Movie* set out to be the final word in cinematic deconstruction. Although, in its more lucid moments, it functions as a parable of colonialism, almost an adjunct of Third Cinema, Dennis Hopper's legendary folly is ultimately less than the sum of its influences, which range from the methodology of William S. Burroughs and Luigi Pirandello to the iconoclasm of Jean-Luc Godard and the avant-garde adventurism of Alejandro Jodorowsky. (Inspiration was also provided by intoxicants – the script was written in a haze of dope smoke, while alcohol and cocaine were consumed in heroic quantities on set. Hopper once summarised the shoot as "one long sex and drugs orgy".[1]) It beguiled judges at the Venice Film Festival, but alienated its financial backers and virtually every critic in America, was dumped by its Stateside distributor after barely a fortnight and put Hopper's directorial career on ice for the better part of a decade. Radical in form for a major studio production, it is a stinging critique of cultural imperialism and a self-reflexive dissection of myth- and film-making. At the same time, it is an indictment of New Hollywood hubris.

Hopper conceived this ill-starred experiment in meta-cinema while making *The Sons of Katie Elder* (1965) on location in Durango, Mexico: "I thought, my God, what's going to happen when the movie leaves and the natives are left living in these western sets?" Hopper didn't want to play the lead. He first thought of Montgomery Clift; Jason Robards and Jack Nicholson were also reputedly in the running. But Hopper had the right professional background. Before *Easy Rider* inflated his profile (and his ego) and made him a countercultural figurehead, his acting assignments had often found him strapping on six-guns, usually to play hotheads or mavericks at odds with authority (*Gunfight at the O.K. Corral*, *From Hell to Texas* [1958], *Hang 'Em High* [1968]). Engaging Stewart Stern (*Rebel Without a Cause*) to co-write the script (a "story about America and how it's destroying itself"[2]), Hopper briefly secured Phil Spector's financial support. When this fell through, the project was shelved until Universal, mindful of the profits accrued by *Easy Rider*, gave Hopper the green light, a fixed budget and, to its eventual regret, final cut. In a deliberate provocation masked as an artistic statement, or vice versa, Hopper delivered something that resembled more a rough cut.

Shooting took place in and around Chinchero, Peru, in 1970. Hopper staffed his film with friends and fellow cine-anarchists – Peter Fonda, Henry Jaglom, Dean Stockwell, Kris Kristofferson, John Phillip Law[3] – as well as Hollywood veterans Rod Cameron and Samuel Fuller.[4] Hopper spent 16 months cutting down some 40 hours of footage into a feature that blurs the boundaries between fantasy and reality. Flashing back and forth between narrative and quasi-documentary modes, it depicts the impact on Peruvian villagers of an American film crew (marshalled by Fuller, essentially playing himself) shooting a Billy the Kid western. ("I want balls when you die," Fuller demands of his leading man.) As an outcrop of the emergent 'Vietnam' western, with Peruvian Indians in place of the Cheyenne of *Little Big Man* and *Soldier Blue*, for example, its subject is also the corrosive effect on the country – any country – of American expansionism, the subjugation of one culture by a dominant other.

This jaundiced viewpoint – so characteristic of Hollywood's anti-establishment fifth columnists – is mediated through the figure of Kansas, a wrangler on the film who stays behind when the rest of the crew departs. Kansas/Hopper's perspective becomes increasingly occluded by drink, drugs and disillusionment. The film becomes a projection of his anguish, targeting materialism (Kansas's Peruvian lover [Stella Garcia] craves consumer goods and fur coats) and exploitation (ghastly "money's no object" American tourists pay for a tawdry, distinctly unerotic private sex show), sketching his tragicomic get-rich-quick scheme with a suicidal fellow expat (Don Gordon) and making Kansas the unwilling 'star' in the villagers' re-creation of the western.

The locals are not merely passive victims. Using cameras and booms fashioned from bamboo or wicker, they transform the fictional story – which, as Hopper would have it, they are incapable of distinguishing from reality – into something akin to a religious ritual. This is idolatry of a different order, with actual violence supplanting stunts. ("The movies have bring here violence," complains the village priest, played by Tomas Milian, fearing for the souls of his flock, although they don't seem to require much encouragement.) This is the real "last movie", announces the 'director'. In a delirious sequence, Kansas appears set to be their sacrificial victim – a scapegoat, perhaps, for anti-American resentment.

But to impose one particular 'meaning' on *The Last Movie* in preference to another is futile. Rather than submit to easy analysis, it subscribes to the Godardian belief that Hollywood-style narrative cinema forestalls the viewer's analytical process. The point of the enterprise, for Hopper, was to prevent firm conclusions from being reached. When they viewed the finished/unfinished product, sceptics thought the director had lost his senses (*The New York Times* labelled the film "an extravagant mess… [Hopper's] thoughts here have all of the impact of revelations written down during an acid trip"), but there was method in the madness. Hopper dismantled not only the more or less logical sequence of events (only the central section is relatively linear), but the modus operandi of mass communication.[5] Footage appears more than once, chronology is scrambled, and we jump – unprompted – back and forth between *The Last Movie*, 'Billy the Kid', the film being created by the Peruvians and, finally, what appears to be the making of *The Last Movie*, wherein Kansas/Hopper, dazed and confused, is assured by co-stars that it's all make-believe after all. Only when Hopper himself goofs for the camera and pulls a few modernist tricks out of his hat – "scene missing" flashes up on a white screen at one point – can the audience be certain. 'Sophisticated' filmgoers need signposts just as much as rural Peruvian villagers.

When he isn't tarnishing America's self-image or ripping up the film-making rulebook, Hopper turns his misanthropic gaze towards his own shortcomings. If *The Last Movie* was, in part, a vanity project, this is not reflected in his characterisation. In the early scenes Kansas seems a loner, distanced from the hedonism of the Hollywood smart set, but his vague hippy ideals (illustrated in travelogue-style inserts by Laszlo Kovacs) are undermined by equally vague plans to open film-making facilities of his own and to make a fortune from a gold mine. (In a film full of citations, Kansas's partner in this harebrained endeavour confesses that *The Treasure of the Sierra Madre* is his sole point of reference.) There are uncomfortable parallels between Kansas and Hopper: most obviously the character's eager consumption of alcohol, but also his cruelty towards his woman (Hopper had a history of spousal abuse). There are times when he is just as much an Ugly American as the heedless tourists he condemns.

Not quite the last movie he would make, nor the end of cinema in a Godardian sense, Hopper's *Heart of Darkness* nevertheless has an air of finality. Like the burning bike at the close of *Easy Rider*, it is a metaphor for the incineration of Sixties idealism, while Hopper's fall from grace foreshadowed the fates of other *enfants terrible*, from William Friedkin for *Sorcerer* (1977) to Francis Ford Coppola for *Apocalypse Now* (1979) and Michael Cimino for *Heaven's Gate*. Hopper's ambitions for *The Last Movie* lay in a different direction – that taken by Godard's own anti-western, *Wind from the East* (1970), for example, although Hopper's film has more passion. However muddled it may be, it does not play like an academic exercise. **KG**

footnotes

1 Interview with Dennis Hopper by Jon Wilde in *Uncut* magazine, February 2005.

2 Interview with Dennis Hopper in *Life* magazine, 19 June 1970.

3 "Peru was the cocaine capital of the world, and every cokehead in LA wanted to work on the picture in order to smuggle drugs back up north" Peter Biskind, *Easy Riders, Raging Bulls* (Bloomsbury, 1998).

4 Before shooting began, Hopper reportedly offered a role to John Wayne, his unlikely Hollywood patron, and wanted Henry Hathaway, with whom he had worked on three westerns, to play the director of the film within the film.

5 Legend has it that Hopper recut the material after Alejandro Jodorowsky – a big wheel on the counterculture circuit at the time thanks to his psychotropic semi-western *El Topo* (1970) – advised him his first version was too conservative.

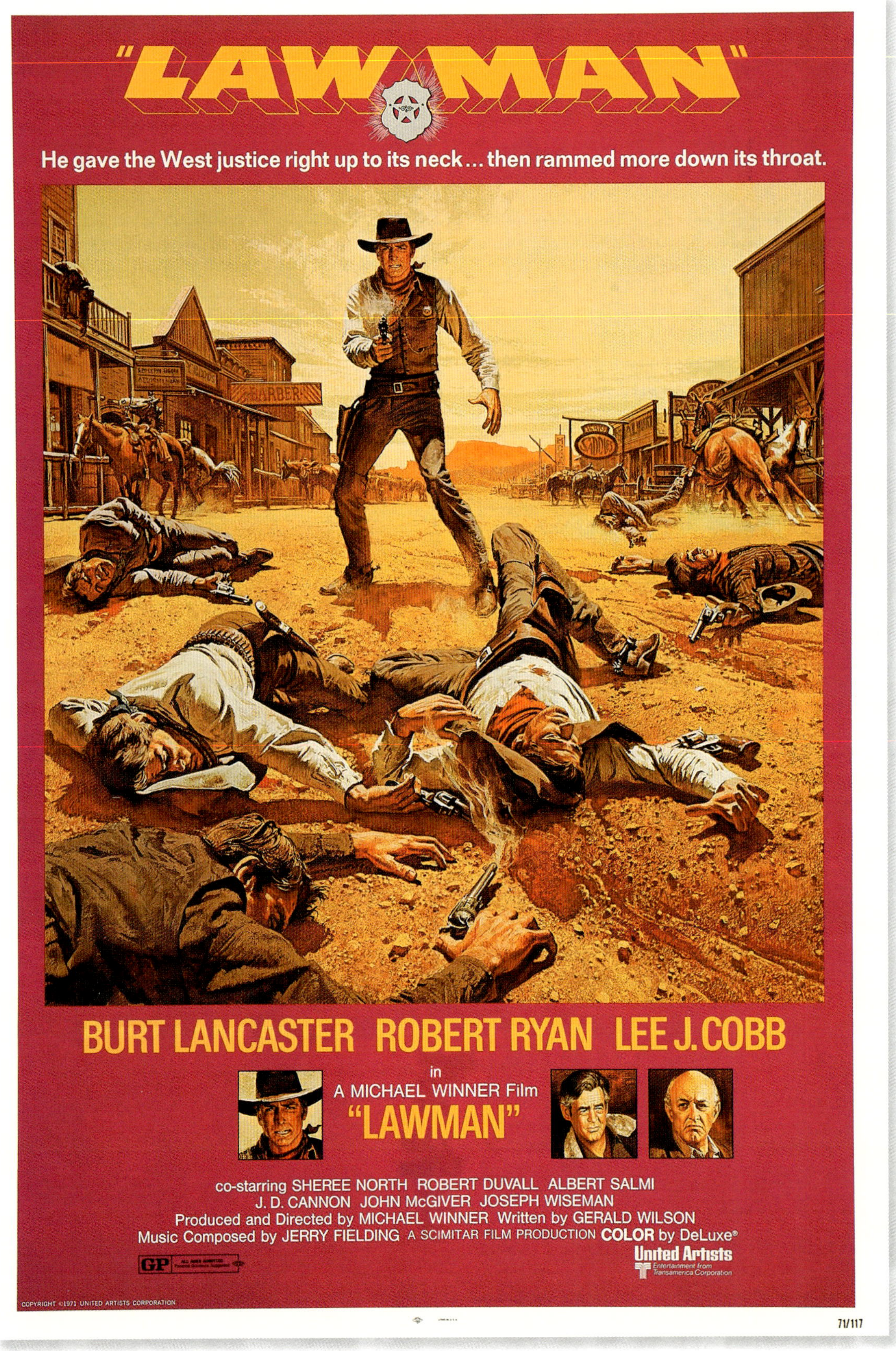
"LAWMAN"
He gave the West justice right up to its neck... then rammed more down its throat.
BARBER
BURT LANCASTER ROBERT RYAN LEE J. COBB
in
A MICHAEL WINNER Film
"LAWMAN"
co-starring SHEREE NORTH ROBERT DUVALL ALBERT SALMI
J. D. CANNON JOHN McGIVER JOSEPH WISEMAN
Produced and Directed by MICHAEL WINNER Written by GERALD WILSON
Music Composed by JERRY FIELDING A SCIMITAR FILM PRODUCTION COLOR by DeLuxe®
GP
United Artists
Entertainment from Transamerica Corporation
COPYRIGHT ©1971 UNITED ARTISTS CORPORATION
71/117

Lawman

1971, Colour, 99 mins.

D: Michael Winner. P: Michael Winner (Scimitar Films Inc.). W: Gerald Wilson. Ph: Robert Paynter. M: Jerry Fielding. St: Burt Lancaster (Jered Maddox), Robert Ryan (Cotton Ryan), Lee J. Cobb (Vincent Bronson), Robert Duvall (Vernon Adams), Sheree North (Laura Selby)

"Do you know what a lawman is, Crowe? He's a killer of men. That's what the job calls for. There are new ways to put it, but it reads the same."

Michael Winner's entrée into action-oriented cinema is often written off as a remake of the Robert Mitchum vehicle *Man with the Gun*. It isn't, but it belongs to the same sub-genre of morally problematic town-tamer/law-and-order westerns that originated with *High Noon* and became steadily more cynical as the decades passed and social mores progressed (many would argue the last point). Perceptive and bluntly efficient, it dabbles in one of the dominant themes of these films: what does society deem acceptable in the pursuit of justice, and what kind of man does it take to execute the task? Moreover, is society prepared to back him up?

The answers are neither reassuring nor definitive; they are not designed to be. As in the urban detective films of the period – really displaced westerns – the questions are intended to stimulate debate. Burt Lancaster's iron-willed marshal, Jered Maddox, is lauded for his unswerving devotion to duty, but his mindset makes bloodshed inevitable. His antagonists are not sympathetic in the conventional sense, but neither are they wicked; they are more reasonable in their way than Maddox in his. Drawing a line in the sand between hunter and prey becomes pointless. As ever, it is the hypocritical citizenry caught in the middle who receive the sharpest censure.

Lancaster plays Maddox as death incarnate, wringing almost all emotion from the role, his inflexibility manifest in his rigid body language. Despite his strict never-draw-first policy, Maddox has killed enough men to earn the sobriquet "widow-maker". He looks the part, in his charcoal-shaded attire, and his reputation precedes him when he arrives in the town of Sabbath ("Don't make an enemy of him," a local is warned. "Step wide of him") with warrants for seven men who shot up Maddox's town while drunk, inadvertently killing an old man. Maddox swiftly inspires fear and loathing in Sabbath, chiefly because his targets work for Vincent Bronson, another in the long line of western land barons who "built up this country" from nothing. Yet Bronson is no tyrant; learning of his men's actions, he intends to make amends, financially, if only Maddox will back down. But Sabbath's own marshal, the worn-down Cotton Ryan, warns Bronson that Maddox is not that kind: "Some men just go to things in a straight line… They don't bend and they don't trade." When Bronson's hot-headed foreman pays with his life for calling Maddox out, attitudes harden and pride takes hold on all sides. Neither Ryan nor Laura, Maddox's old flame, can dent the lawman's steely resolve, and a showdown moves inexorably closer.

above: Burt Lancaster as Maddox, the 'widow-maker' and lawman of the title.

Prior to *Lawman*, comedy was Winner's bailiwick, and he was as surprised as anybody when a Hollywood western came his way; "I've never been further West than Fulham," the London-born director remarked, nonplussed, when offered the script.[1] It is not such a shock that the director of *Death Wish* (1974) should engage with the issue of vigilantism. (Nor that there should be a character called Bronson – although *Lawman* was made before Winner and his totemic leading man began working together.) Organised, in the form of an informal citizens' committee, it is frowned upon, not least because its target is not the lawbreakers in the plot, but the lawman. "You want the law, but you want it to walk quiet – you don't want it to put a hole in your pocket," observes Maddox, echoing sentiments uttered with equal contempt by the protagonists of *High Noon*, *Warlock* and *Death of a Gunfighter*. Maddox is a different proposition. In the main, his killings are unavoidable and justifiable. Yet in the final reckoning, he shoots one of Bronson's minions in the back as he flees, unarmed. This man was Laura's lover, and thus in one sense a rival. In mitigation, the victim had threatened to trail Maddox but, in the circumstances, with Bronson dead by his own hand, the rest of his men gunned down by Maddox, it looks very much like homicide. Why the marshal breaks his own code, burying the chance of a peaceful retirement with Laura, who seems prepared to leave with him, is a matter of conjecture. It could be a ripple in the script's logic, a fashionable frisson of nihilism, or perhaps Maddox has simply accepted that killing is all he knows: "You can't change what you are. And if you try, something always calls you back."[2]

Gerald Wilson's script tips its hat to westerns of old – the love-hate relationship between lawman and layman, the distinction between quick draw and killer instinct, elegiac pining for past times. But the combination of an eager director new to the genre and an experienced cast keeps staleness at bay. The acting is uniformly strong. Sheree North and Joseph Wiseman (as a saloon-owner who has crossed Maddox's path before) add pathos and mordant wit, respectively, while Lee J. Cobb and Robert Ryan inject vitality into hackneyed roles, conviction into dialogue that often has an axiomatic ring. Ryan, in his 16th and final western, is especially fine as "*Lawman's* conscience and chief observer, cynically watching men walk down paths he has passed countless times before".[3] Ryan was ailing at the time – it transpired he had cancer of the lymph glands – and his haggard features stress physical and psychological fatigue. Cotton long ago cashed in the kind of principles that shackle Maddox and the Bronson bunch. He admits he's a puppet, a proxy – "I've been paid for... I sit there because Bronson says sit" (the image of a broken canine is reinforced when Bronson's foreman calls Cotton a "kick dog"), his once-glittering reputation reduced to "a bunch of yesterdays". It is a poignant performance, on a par with the actor's work in *The Wild Bunch*.

The film's reception was broadly positive, although there were derogatory comparisons with Italian westerns (the *Monthly Film Bulletin* patriotically suggested 'roast beef' as an alternative to 'spaghetti'). But Winner was no Leone, an inspired 'outsider' reviving a jaded genre, and *Lawman* doesn't testify to a bold new vision. Leone's second western, *For a Few Dollars More* (1965), was a tour de force; Winner's the tawdry *Chato's Land* (1972). But neither does *Lawman* feel like the work of a dilettante. Winner sought historians' advice when dressing his sets, and cinematographer Robert Paynter's copper-toned images are suitably evocative. (Winner's propensity for zooms is a conspicuous drawback, and he ought to have reined in Jerry Fielding's bombastic score.) The film is closer to the west of Peckinpah than Leone, both geographically (although set in the American West it was shot in Mexico, Peckinpah's spiritual home) and thematically. Maddox, like Cotton Ryan and Bronson, is a man out of his time, almost dehumanised by his capacity for violence. (He reveals his 'sensitive' side in a throwaway, frankly risible scene in which he plays a flute.) Ultimately, his 'triumph' in Sabbath, which scarcely even serves a civic function, seals his dislocation from society. **KG**

footnotes

1 Michael Winner, *Winner Takes All* (Robson Books, 2005).

2 It is a measure of Lancaster's professionalism that he didn't baulk at Maddox's ignoble action (he certainly had the power to order scripts rewritten), even though his director provided only a glib explanation of the character's motivation: "'Why do I shoot this man in the back?'" [Lancaster] asked. 'Because your character's a total arsehole, Burt', I said". *Winner Takes All.*

3 Franklin Jarlett, *Robert Ryan: A Biography and Critical Filmography* (McFarland, 1990).

追う！男が追う！
映画史上最も凄絶なラストの決闘にむかって
七人の男がなだれこむ……
LAWMAN
追跡者
〈テラックスカラー〉
バート・ランカスター
ロバート・ライアン／リー・J・コッブ
シェリー・ノース／ジョゼフ・ワイズマン
アルバート・サルミ／J・D・キャノン
製作・監督マイケル・ウィナー／撮影ボブ・ペインター
音楽ジェリー・フィールディング／ユナイト映画 United Artists
映倫 46175

McCabe & Mrs. Miller

1971, Colour, 121 mins.

D: Robert Altman. P: David Foster, Mitchell Brower (Lion's Head, David Foster Productions). W: Robert Altman, Brian McKay. Ph: Vilmos Zsigmond. M: Leonard Cohen. St: Warren Beatty (John McCabe), Julie Christie (Constance Miller), Rene Auberjonois (Sheehan), William Devane (the lawyer), John Schuck (Smalley)

"I guess if a man's fool enough to get in business with a woman, she ain't gonna think much of him."

The counterculture was in its full pomp by the early Seventies, and hip crowds demanded a new brand of hero. Knights of the frontier such as John Wayne and Randolph Scott were being overtaken by knights of the open road as personified by the amoral protagonists of *Easy Rider*, the film that proved decisively that subversive cinema, geared to a hip, youthful audience, could rake in huge profits. In this climate, where the dissenting sons of old Hollywood had taken over the studio machine, the western had to change course. A slew of so-called 'acid westerns' were produced, capitalising on a burgeoning box-office appetite for anything leftfield or psychedelic. From Mexico came Alejandro Jodorowsky's startling *El Topo*, a heady concoction of mysticism and violence that appropriated the stark imagery of the Italian western. Attempting to emulate Jodorowsky's style, *Easy Rider's* director, Dennis Hopper, was given free rein to direct *The Last Movie*, before disappearing for months to digest narcotics and edit an often incoherent ego trip. Then there was Robert Altman, one of New Hollywood's more assured hands. With Brian McKay, Altman had developed a script, from a novel by Edmund Naughton, that formed not only "a calculated and ironic response to the classic western", but also a major achievement in the genre's history.[1]

The Vietnam War was raging, as was domestic opposition to the USA's involvement. Symbolically, Altman – already a talisman among the anti-war lobby thanks to *M*A*S*H* (1970) – chose to shoot his film in British Columbia, augmenting his usual stock company with young North Americans who had fled to Canada to avoid the draft; tens of thousands had followed this course, taking advantage of the country's non-belligerent status. They helped build the sets and were used as extras, bolstering the sense of the nascent settlement of Presbyterian Church taking shape amid the cold, deeply forested wilds that doubled as the Pacific North-West of the United States. In this dislocated community, a titanic collision of egos was waged between the director and the film's star, Warren Beatty. However, in spite of Beatty's perfectionism and Altman's frustrations, both achieved career highs. An achingly melancholy soundtrack from Leonard Cohen and some of the genre's most exquisite cinematography supported the efforts of cast and crew to create a genre piece with an opiated languor. Pauline Kael, arbiter of cinematic taste at the time, would call it "a pipe-dream of a movie".

McCabe & Mrs. Miller is the singular story of a small businessman trying to nourish an independent enterprise in defiance of those "trusts and monopolies" that will stop at nothing in their voracious quest for profit. In common with many of the stateliest westerns from which it otherwise departs, it is also about town building. The *mise-en-scène* is richly detailed. With the church that gives the town its name being the only edifice that seems to be complete, we see stockpiles of timber strewn around, soon to become the shells of McCabe's saloon and the whorehouse he opens in partnership with the enigmatic Constance Miller. There is a bustling Chinese community, home to an opium den. Workers and prostitutes are transported by a steam-powered engine like pilgrims to McCabe's impious Mecca. A makeshift rope bridge connects two sides of the town, one occupied by Sheehan's saloon; once the focus of Presbyterian Church, it is in danger of losing that status to McCabe and Mrs. Miller's pleasure palaces. (The bridge will later come to be associated with death.)

above: McCabe (Warren Beatty) arrives in Presbyterian Church – the town was namechecked in the film's working title (top right).

Establishing a natural, organic atmosphere, Altman's camera roams freely, seeking out weathered faces and interactions between the characters. This style is prominent in the early scene when McCabe enters Sheehan's saloon and instigates a card game with the locals. As he holds court, the camera picks out reactions to his presence; joviality, curiosity, suspicion: is he the infamous John McCabe who shot and killed Bill Roundtree? It seems unlikely that this stuttering, clumsy but charming man is capable of dealing death with the deftness he does cards. Somewhat hamstrung by the muddied soundtrack that proved a bone of contention between director and soundman, it is still a well-scripted and important establishing scene, taking this western in a more modernist direction.[2]

This is offset by the archaic look of the piece, which owes much to the pioneering efforts of Hungarian cinematographer Vilmos Zsigmond. An exponent of the use of "flashing" or "pre-fogging" – whereby the negative is exposed to a controlled amount of light to give the

stock a muted palette – he achieves a visually rich design with a yellowish, almost sepia tint to some of the set-ups. (Zsigmond would later use this technique for 1980's *Heaven's Gate*, which offered a similar meditation on the use of violent action to propel the progress of corporate capitalism.) The dowdy, twilight world of the interiors – the saloons, the whorehouse – is matched by the muddy squalor of the town's streets, a result of almost permanent drizzle. Stan Dragoti may have taken cues from Altman's aesthetic when drafting ideas for the following year's *Dirty Little Billy*, a comparably gritty, squalid western with the same scent of random violence lurking in the mire.

In this town of coarse, grimy miners and labourers, women are represented almost exclusively by the tent-dwelling prostitutes brought in by McCabe to keep the workers happy. The first "chippies", as they are known in the vernacular-rich script, are an unattractive bunch, but this does little to repel the lusty townsmen. The only autonomous woman is Mrs. Miller, who stands apart, in Julie Christie's forthright performance, as one of the strongest female characters in the genre. A no-nonsense Cockney, she negotiates terms with the flabbergasted McCabe and persuades him to build a real brothel, with clean girls and proper hygiene, which will attract more custom and generate more dollars than his meagre canvas set-up. She undercuts his self-confidence and pomposity over their first dinner: "If you wanna make out you're such a fancy dude, you oughta wear something besides that cheap Jockey Club cologne." She is more ambitious than McCabe, shrewder, more grounded.

Thanks to her vigour, which masks a dependency on opium, they soon have the most lucrative business in town. McCabe is both intrigued and distracted by her.

In McCabe, Altman and Beatty created a western anti-hero who was almost antithetical to his forebears; charming yet bumbling, confident yet vulnerable, a man fatally out of step with his failings. The opening credits witness a fur-clad figure approach the isolated town, the camera tracking in unison with his steed. The lone rider entering a town and changing the course of its history is a common motif in the genre, yet the atmosphere here, underscored by Cohen's balladry, is doleful. Already there is a sense that greatness will not befall this man. He is clearly not from the same mould as the characters played by John Wayne or Gary Cooper. Not for them McCabe's naivety; by deriding the figure tendered by Harrison Shaughnessy's representatives for his holdings, he shows a lack of business savvy that distresses Mrs. Miller. Wiser to the ruthless ways of institutional capitalism, she knows too well the consequences of McCabe's refusal to sell: "You'd better hope they come back. They'd just as soon put a bullet in your back." When the company's agents depart, McCabe is forced to face its hired killers instead.

It's in this atmosphere of impending doom that the façade between McCabe and his business partner begins to crumble. Adopting an unusually masculine role in their relationship, she becomes increasingly fearful for McCabe, and he dependent on her. As the gunmen, led by the intimidating Butler (played with well-spoken menace by 6ft 7in Englishman Hugh Millais), station themselves in Sheehan's saloon and rebuff McCabe's conciliatory approach, a confrontation becomes unavoidable. The bell tolls ominously early in Presbyterian Church, with two instances of random violence that mark the settlement as being as savage as any other frontier town. These acts are sordid, without

above: Locals rush to save their church.

above: Warren Beatty with Julie Christie as Mrs Miller.

ceremony, less set pieces than senseless acts of murder. Miner Bart Coyle is beaten to death for defending the honour of his mail-order bride (Shelley Duvall), the sounds of laughter and drunkenness silenced as the camera picks out his corpse lying in the street. Later, a cocky cowboy (Keith Carradine), who drifts into town to sample the whorehouse, is goaded into reaching for his gun by Butler's bellicose young sidekick (Manfred Schulz, in a seemingly one-off screen appearance), who proceeds to blast the other man off the bridge.

This latter killing, and the seeming apathy of the town, sets the tone for the film's last act. Violence is shown dispassionately, almost documentary-like. Carradine's craven murder recalls the execution of Elisha Cook Jr. by Jack Palance in *Shane*. In the final, protracted gun battle, McCabe finds himself alone as heavy snow falls around him. Both hunter and hunted, he seeks sanctuary in the church only to be evicted by the priest; he, in turn, is shot by Butler, a stray bullet causing a fire from a broken oil lamp. As the church blazes, Altman cuts back and forth between the locals' efforts to save it – reflexive more than reverent – and McCabe's deadly cat and mouse game with three assassins: "The effect underscores the town's indifference to McCabe's plight and points out the insignificance of the outcome of his struggle."[3]

Although McCabe is an unorthodox hero in what Altman described as an "anti-western", he still exhibits nobility, resolving to face the consequences of his actions – "Someone's got to stand up for the little guy… someone's got to make a stand" – rather than yielding to Mrs. Miller's pleas to quit the town for somewhere "more civilised". Although the director was evidently disgusted by the strong-arm tactics of monopolies, Altman's politics were more likely anarchist than Marxist, not out of sync with the philosophy of the Founding Fathers. McCabe is an individual with an undisclosed source of capital who sets up a small, prosperous business; he is a pursuer of the American Dream, a pioneer in his own right. Beatty's full-bodied portrayal preserves the memory of those independent entrepreneurs who chose to follow the self-made route to success.

Altman's conclusion is bleak, however, surrendering to the fact that McCabe is but a minor cog in the capitalist machine, freezing on his image as he lies, fatally wounded, half-buried in the snow. "The final extended shot of McCabe's body represents not only his death, but also Altman's way of delineating the death of an ideal of moral action, as well as the death of a symbolic triumph over lawlessness and evil that the genre had heretofore invested in the western hero."[4] As her partner makes a desperate stand for the hard-working American everyman, Mrs. Miller seeks solace in an opium den, chasing away her pain behind a blue plume of smoke. Altman's camera zooms in on her eye and into her subconscious: "The idea was to diminish – just to take all that experience and put it inside her head so that it looked like you were looking at a planet from a spaceship."[5] **CH**

footnotes

[1] Deborah Knight and George McKnight, 'The Northwestern: *McCabe & Mrs. Miller*', in *The Philosophy of the Western* (Jennifer L. McMahon and B. Steve Csaki, eds, University Press of Kentucky, 2010).

[2] In Peter Biskind's *Easy Riders, Raging Bulls* (Bloomsbury, 1998), the author quotes Lou Lombardo, the film's editor, who claims he confronted Altman about the scene's murky live soundtrack only for Altman to storm off and shut himself in his bedroom. Lombardo states that editing the scene was "like trying to get an out of focus picture in focus". Altman countered that the soundtrack had been checked by his editor, commenting, "That bad soundtrack, on top of the design of the sound, really made it impossible to hear." Lombardo cut pictures for both Peckinpah and Altman and opined that Peckinpah "was a prick". His view of Altman was far less polite.

[3] Gary Engle, 'Robert Altman's Anti-Western', in *The Journal of Popular Film*, autumn 1972.

[4] Deborah Knight and George McKnight, 'The Northwestern: *McCabe & Mrs. Miller*'.

[5] Interview with Robert Altman by Harry Kloman and Lloyd Michaels with Virginia Wright Wexman in *Film Criticism*, Spring 1983, reprinted in *Robert Altman: Interviews* (David Sterritt, ed,

Wild Rovers

1971, Colour, 132 mins. (cut version 106 mins.)

D: Blake Edwards. P: Blake Edwards, Ken Wales (Geoffrey Productions Inc, Metro-Goldwyn-Mayer). W: Blake Edwards. Ph: Philip Lathrop. M: Jerry Goldsmith. St: William Holden (Ross Bodine), Ryan O'Neal (Frank Post), Karl Malden (Walter Buckman), Lynn Carlin (Sada Billings), Tom Skerritt (John Buckman)

"When it comes to something special... like judging a man, a man don't know shit."

Wild Rovers is not quite a film of two halves, but there is a discernible mood swing during its meandering midsection, away from roguish humour and rugged naturalism towards the savage irony of Peckinpah. It is a twilight western in the most literal sense, announcing itself with a sunrise-to-sunset montage, lovingly captured by Philip Lathrop; the paradox is that such lyricism holds the cold light of day in abeyance, somewhat at odds with the thrust of Blake Edwards' myth-deflating script.

Even films that refuted the genre's ideals more aggressively than this one found it difficult to resist the scenic values associated with an earlier generation of westerns. *Wild Rovers* goes so far as to carry its message into the hallowed environs of Monument Valley. As far as Edwards was concerned, lingering on the landscape was not pictorialism for its own sake: "It's very important to show the vastness, the loneliness, the boredom and natural beauty of the West of that period, because that loneliness and boredom are the main motivating factors that affect my principal characters."[1]

The characters in question are Ross Bodine and Frank Post, two amiable cowpunchers who decide to rob a bank, on a whim, to escape the physically and emotionally draining grind of life on the R-Bar ranch. Pursued by a half-hearted sheriff and, with more purpose, by the bickering sons of their overbearing employer, who takes their transgression as a personal affront, the duo drift towards Mexico with the aim of living it up before retiring to a ranch of their own.

Ryan O'Neal (*above*) and William Holden (*upper right*) in "a love story between two men".

Edwards agreed with *New York Times* critic Vincent Canby that his film was, at heart, "a 'love story' between two men", a theme that stretches back in the director's work at least as far as *Mister Cory* (1957), which starred Charles Bickford and Tony Curtis in roles occupied here by William Holden and Ryan O'Neal. (To be clear, their relationship is strictly platonic; MGM withdrew ads that showed the actors in an embrace, lest the public gain a false impression.) Neither man fits the heroic mould: Ross is nigh on 50 – considerably older, if not commensurately wiser, than his companion, with nothing to show for decades of back-breaking labour except chronic aches and the equally painful sense that life has passed him by; the puppyish Frank, paired appropriately with a whelp for part of the journey, has the impatience and recklessness of youth. They have none of the swagger or sangfroid of Butch Cassidy and the Sundance Kid, the stars of Hollywood's most enduring 'buddy western'; instead of glorifying his protagonists, Edwards humanizes them, subjecting them to ennui, frustration, fatigue, fear, crippling hangovers – even, in an earthy comic scene, to a shower of urine. Throughout, he plays up their vulnerability, and there is an inevitability about the fatalistic finale in which the duo meet lonely, meaningless deaths – the camera cranes back for a wide shot of majestic Monument Valley, reducing the players to insignificant specks, as if destiny is punishing them for attempting to alter its course.

Fickle fate makes its presence felt early on, with the random death of a fellow cowboy, thrown by a bucking horse, spurring the heroes' decision to take life by the horns. (The incident also offers them a penny for their thoughts, leaving us rather short-changed when the best they can muster is, "It just don't make no goddamn sense", and variations thereof.) The lack of urgency in their flight – the film is languorously, almost lazily, paced, the better for Lathrop's camera to feast on the scenery – demonstrates Edwards' play with genre conventions. The bank robbery is one of the most lackadaisical in cinema – Frank, holding the banker's family hostage, plays with their pet dog as if on a social call; Ross leaves the banker to bag up the money while he jaws in the saloon – while a shootout over a poker game is edited to convey panic and confusion rather than courage and composure. (A terrified Frank is wounded and a girl shot in the back, while Ross needlessly kills the bartender.) A sub-plot about a looming range war between the autocratic cattleman Buckman and an opportunistic sheepherder peters out, but not before a shocking scene in which Buckman's men slaughter his rival's flock; the death of the animals, in fact, is more jolting than the demise at this juncture of Buckman himself.

As Ross and Frank discover to their cost, the West that Edwards presents is not the mythical realm of adventure and opportunity. It is a place where lives wither, where people endure in gloomy, underlit interiors, yearning for a break (the banker's wife, tired of making ends meet, urges him to keep the $3,000 Ross leaves behind to pay the cowhands on the R-Bar). Nor is it an arena for champions. The one concession Edwards makes in this regard is a scene in a snowy mountain pass in which Ross, rolling back the years, tames a wild horse in graceful slow motion. Echoing a similar victory for the ageing hero of *Monte Walsh*, it is marred only by cutaways to Frank's childish cartwheels of delight, much as O'Neal's callowness as a performer is the film's Achilles' heel. Holden, however, is splendid, alternating loquacious charm with a quiet wistfulness, reminiscent of Pike Bishop in his interludes of self-reflection.

Part bleak fable, part picaresque adventure, *Wild Rovers* is, above all, a hymn to friendship, a worthy companion piece to *Butch Cassidy…* and *The Hired Hand*, from its own era, although not in the same league as *Lonesome Dove* (1989), the benchmark for the theme. The melding of elegiac tone, low comedy and slow-motion bloodletting proved a turn-off at the box office, but critics were generally kind, even if they didn't all share Edwards' view that this was his best film.[2] **KG**

footnotes

1 Quoted in Sam Wasson, *A Splurch in the Kisser: The Movies of Blake Edwards* (Wesleyan University Press, 2009).

2 Edwards changed his tune somewhat in the wake of cuts to the film ordered by MGM's ruthless then-president, James Aubrey, who removed around 30 minutes of footage. It has long since been available in a restored version.

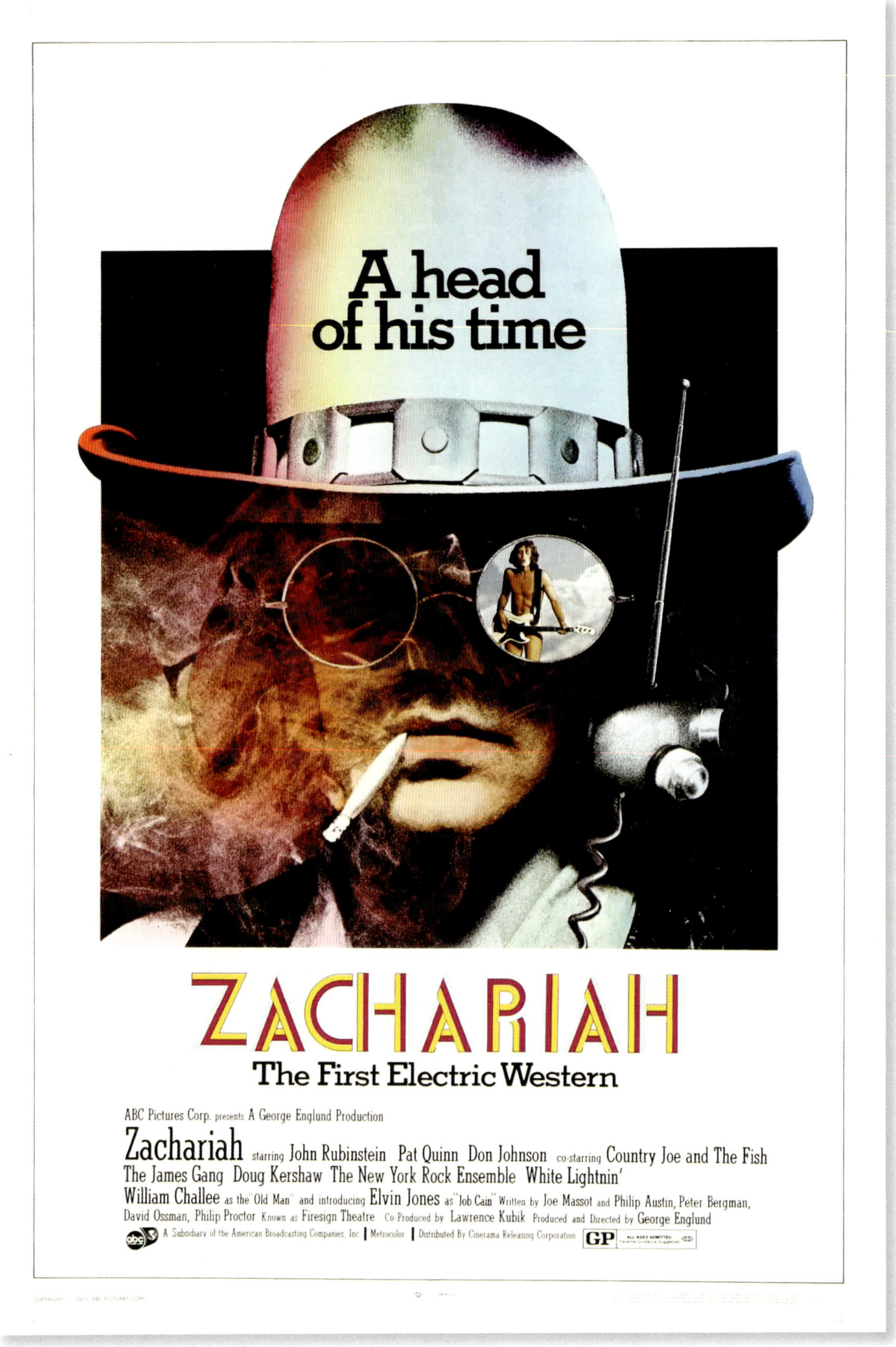
A head of his time
ZACHARIAH
The First Electric Western
ABC Pictures Corp. presents A George Englund Production
Zachariah starring John Rubinstein Pat Quinn Don Johnson co-starring Country Joe and The Fish
The James Gang Doug Kershaw The New York Rock Ensemble White Lightnin'
William Challee as the "Old Man" and introducing Elvin Jones as "Job Cain" Written by Joe Massot and Philip Austin, Peter Bergman,
David Ossman, Philip Proctor Known as Firesign Theatre Co-Produced by Lawrence Kubik Produced and Directed by George Englund
A Subsidiary of the American Broadcasting Companies, Inc. | Metrocolor | Distributed By Cinerama Releasing Corporation
GP
ALL AGES ADMITTED

Zachariah

1971, Colour, 93 mins.

D: George Englund. P: George Englund (George Englund Productions, ABC Pictures Corp). W: Joe Massot, Philip Austin, Peter Bergman, David Ossman, Philip Proctor. Ph: Jorge Stahl. M: Jimmie Haskell. St: John Rubinstein (Zachariah), Pat Quinn (Belle Starr), Don Johnson (Matthew), Elvin Jones (Job Cain), Country Joe and the Fish (the Crackers)

"Me and you are not on the same trip."

Opening with a nod to *2001* (1968), in the form of a monolithic amplifier standing incongruously in the desert, propping up a Lucite guitar – the first of many intentional anachronisms – this love child of Hermann Hesse and *Butch Cassidy and the Sundance Kid* riffs on numerous then-hip sources – *Head* (1968), the musical *Hair*, *Easy Rider*, mythographer Joseph Campbell, *Zabriskie Point* (1970) and *El Topo*, among others – as it sketches out a hippy fantasia about dropping out of society and finding oneself. It was famously proclaimed as the first "electric western", thanks to its supporting cast of psych-rock also-rans; its writers, a comedy troupe called the Firesign Theatre, were clearly switched on to countercultural concerns, but the film's grasp of genre dynamics is insecure at best.

Despite noble aims, it falls short either as parody (doubtless its almost openly gay heroes were intended to amplify the homoerotic undertones of traditional western partnerships; Andy Warhol had already been far more rigorous on the subject, and far less coy, in *Lonesome Cowboys* [1968]) or as polemic – the wayward tone, at times whimsical, at others crudely comedic, makes its intentions even fuzzier. The plot aspires to the universality and timelessness of myth, roping in Biblical allusions to little avail, but the film is tethered too tightly to its own time and place to resonate beyond them. *Zachariah's* failings are manifold: direction that ranges from clichéd to clumsy; the hollow ring of exhortatory dialogue; generally poor performances; sundry other distractions, chiefly the musical interludes and camp, discordant costume design.

Hesse's novel *Siddartha* was a countercultural touchstone in the Sixties, and the film copies the basic pattern, plotting a spiritual journey undertaken by Zachariah and Matthew, two fresh-faced young men, implicitly more than just close friends, who become the unlikeliest of outlaws, take divergent paths, but ultimately reunite and embrace a life of liberty. Zachariah – who scarcely deserves the mantle of prophet his name implies – is the focal point, flashing his alabaster teeth through a series of encounters familiar from the quest narratives of antiquity: he meets a wise Old Man, who educates him in the simple pleasure of getting back to nature (one of several sequences ruined by a combination of overacting and poor directorial judgement – here, superfluous slow motion); overcomes temptation (in the curvaceous form of Belle Starr, a frankly dreadful performance by *Alice's Restaurant* star Pat Quinn – the *New York Times* described it as an "untalented drag queen's ritual imitation of Mae West"); and crosses the wilderness/threshold, newly edified. With his wide-eyed, boyish looks and curly locks, John Rubinstein, dressed for much of the time in a fringed white outfit that would have shamed the Village People, evinces stoned befuddlement more than existential unrest. As his "disciple" who flirts with the dark side, Don Johnson, clad redundantly in black, displays an even narrower emotional range; his one memorable moment comes late on, when his petulance at Zachariah's filibustering during their inevitable showdown gives way to a tearful display of displaced sexual frustration.

Zachariah is occasionally championed as mind-expanding, surrealistic, the ultimate western trip. With nothing in the script to justify such claims – exclamations of "far out" aside – it could have been salvaged had director George Englund unleashed his imagination. He settles instead for standard scenic shots – sky, horizon, desert scrub, setting sun – with plentiful lens flares and fashionable zooms employed as psychedelic short cuts. But these stylistic inflections do not amount to a hallucinatory experience, let alone surrealism, while Englund's angles and compositions are similarly prosaic. Only the design of Belle Starr's town, a series of facades rising from the desert like gaudily coloured cacti, hints at what might have been.

Ultimately it is the novelty of contemporary musicians performing alongside the actors upon which *Zachariah's* modest reputation rests. Only a few are called upon to act: Country Joe and the Fish, remembered chiefly for their Vietnam War protest song *I-Feel-Like-I'm-Fixin'-to-Die Rag*, clown around like poor relations of the Monkees as goofy outlaws; jazz drummer Elvin Jones is fine, however, as a badass gunman, notwithstanding his glittery lamé vest. Although the music is diegetic, most of the songs have little bearing on the plot. It is not a traditional musical in that sense; once or twice they are employed as commentary, as when a fiddler offers advice to Zachariah, like the banjo-picking balladeers in *Cat Ballou* (1965). As a snapshot of Sixties idealism, complete with an (insinuated) open-minded attitude to homosexuality, it just about suffices; but in its attempts to "rock" the western – both musically and metaphorically – it hits all the wrong notes. **KG**

Bad Company

1972, Colour, 92 mins.

D: Robert Benton. P: Stanley R. Jaffe (Jaffilms Inc). W: David Newman, Robert Benton. Ph: Gordon Willis. M: Harvey Schmidt. St: Jeff Bridges (Jake Rumsey), Barry Brown (Drew Dixon), Jim Davis (Marshal), David Huddleston (Big Joe), John Savage (Loney)

"The worst goddamned idea in the world is to go West."

Rigorously deglamorised, yet with a countervailing romanticism, *Bad Company* is a film that tries to have it both ways, succeeding more often than it fails. It is a natural successor to Robert Benton and David Newman's best-known work, *Bonnie and Clyde* (1967), which they co-wrote. Historical conditions are again painstakingly re-created, with happy-go-lucky humour juxtaposed against jolting scenes of violence, and the central pairing have a sheen that sets them apart from the rest of the characters.

Given its wartime setting – 1863, in the wake of the Enrollment Act of that year, the first time national conscription had been employed in America – it is usually assumed that *Bad Company's* youthful cast of draft evaders are stand-ins for the "hell-no-I-won't-go" community refusing to fight in Vietnam. But while resistance to the draft dominates the opening scenes, with desperate young men rounded up by a Union recruiting party and thrown into wagons like prisoners, and is the trigger for young Drew Dixon to leave his sheltered life in Ohio and head West, it is his induction into aimless outlawry that swiftly becomes the focus of the plot. (Whether Benton and Newman intended their script as an allegory is not clear; perhaps not, since they have stressed their primary contribution to *Bonnie and Clyde* was its folkloric angle, ascribing its social content to director Arthur Penn. In any case, it is a moot point, since the parallels between 1863 and 1972 – the year of *Bad Company's* release – need no underlining.)

With his pacifism and his God-fearing upbringing employed as convenient metaphors for naivety, Drew comes from the same school of callow youngsters so brutally disabused in films such as *The Cowboys* (1972), *The Culpepper Cattle Co.* and *The Spikes Gang*. His classmates are a band of scruffy thieves led by the headstrong Jake Rumsey, who first robs Drew and then, impressed by his pluck, takes him under his wing. These "rough types", as Drew refers to them with ill-disguised snobbery, are less counterculture rebels than quasi-Dickensian ne'er-do-wells, drifting West with vague notions of striking it rich in the Promised Land. Theirs is a picaresque journey across a featureless landscape, punctuated by encounters with predatory outlaws, hostile farmers and disillusioned pioneers. (Benton and Newman named Mark Twain's *Roughing It* and *Life on the Mississippi* as primary influences.)

The gang's petty crimes are as unsuccessful as their attempts to live off the land (it takes a fusillade of bullets for them to kill a rabbit, and they are clearly nauseated by Jake's demonstration of skinning and gutting); worse, they have no more sense of loyalty than they do purpose, double crossing each other as opportunity dictates. *Bad Company* is not a tale of friendship forged in fire. Even Drew, for all his pretensions to probity ("I resolve never to do a dishonest act, or take part in any thieving, robbing or false undertaking"), is described with some justification as a "two-faced shit kicker", holding out on his partners with the money given to him by his parents and pretending to have robbed a hardware store to convince the gang of his worth.

Ranged against the superficial charm of the genteel Drew and the roguish Jake is a wealth of unflattering detail. Benton renders the environment and his characters in the acid tones of the contemporary ironist. As Philip French remarked, "Never have the West and its inhabitants appeared more uninviting." The scenery is bare, cold and damp. Gordon Willis's photography is leeched of vibrancy, modelled not on the romanticism of Frederic Remington but on what Benton and Newman called the "dark values" of Winslow Homer and Eastman Johnson, and the principals wear frowzy town clothes ("One of the virtues of working without stars is that you can make actors wear anything"[1]), the glamour of traditional western costuming conspicuous by its absence. (As are the hordes of Indians invoked like bogeymen by some of the gang members to scare their companions – we never see a Native American anywhere on the plains, a silent testament to the eradication or marginalisation of indigenous peoples.) Benton's myth-deflation often has a comic undertone. The gang meet a middle-aged couple returning from the West, driven back by tornados, bellicose cattlemen and bad soil. The man then offers his wife's services at $8 a head, which Jake views as a bargain, the desperation of the couple's plight lost in the bawdiness of the humour. Later, the boys barter for food at a farmhouse, where they are forced to eat at gunpoint by the wary farmer (a typical role for weasel-faced Charles Tyner). Even the bushwhackers who attack the gang prove to be incompetent; most of them are killed by Drew and Jake – driven on by youthful brio – in an encounter that is more like a farcical free-for-all than a traditional shootout. Benton relishes the sight of supposedly hardened criminals (played by such weathered roughnecks as Geoffrey Lewis, Ed Lauter and John Quade) fleeing like rabbits, while Drew's halo slips further when he shoots a man in the back.

Benton employs violence both as a shock tactic – a sobering reminder that the outlaw life was likely to be nasty, brutish and short – and for ironic effect, a characteristic inherited from European westerns and a

signature of the director's own brand of New American Cinema. The gang's relatively smooth progress is arrested when their youngest member, an 11-year-old, is shot in the head for stealing a pie from a window ledge; the horror is fleeting, the moment almost passed over. Similarly, when Jake and Drew come across the bodies of two of their erstwhile comrades who have been strung up for unstated offences, they react dispassionately. It makes the tragic waste of young lives seem mundane, immaterial. Death is never glorious in *Bad Company*. Rather, it is undignified, even ridiculous – a stricken Geoffrey Lewis, riddled with bullets, collapses into a sitting posture, legs splayed, head bowed towards the ground; Ed Lauter attempts to plug a smoking entry wound with his finger before taking another slug in the face. The lesson is lost on Jake, whose criminal career continues – after he has sapped Drew and robbed him yet again – until he is captured by a ruthless lynch mob led by a grizzled marshal, the lone remnant of conventional westerns.

It falls to Drew to set his untrustworthy associate free, resurrecting their on-off partnership for their first bank robbery. The frame freezes – whether this will be the birth of a legend in the manner of Butch and Sundance (or indeed Bonnie and Clyde), or merely hasten their appointment with the hangman, we can only speculate. Benton and Newman hedge their bets, but the odds are that they intended the former.[2] **KG**

footnotes

1 Interview with Robert Benton and David Newman by James Childs in *Film Comment*, March-April 1973.

2 According to the director, the freeze frame was "Benton's fuck-up": "It was the last shot to be made in the entire picture… [It] was supposed to stay on them and slowly fade to black… Suddenly I got so excited [at completing his first feature as director] that at the moment when they pull their guns out and say, 'Stick 'em up,' I said, 'Cut!' Somehow or other I didn't think I needed that time… So the freeze is there as a result of my hysteria." (*Film Comment*, March-April 1973).

Buck and the Preacher

1972, Colour, 103 mins.

D: Sidney Poitier.
P: Joel Glickman
(E & R Production Corp, Belafonte Enterprises Inc).
W: Ernest Kinoy, Drake Walker.
Ph: Alex Phillips Jr.
M: Benny Carter.
St: Sidney Poitier (Buck), Harry Belafonte (Preacher),
Ruby Dee (Ruth), Cameron Mitchell (Deshay), Denny Miller (Floyd)

"There's a whole way of life [in Louisiana] that's going down the drain. We don't aim to see it frittered away."

Isaac Hayes was not the only black artist to take on the mantle of Moses in 1971. While Hayes was recording his landmark album, Sidney Poitier was on location for his second western, guiding a group of "exodusters" – newly liberated slaves – out of the post-Civil War South and into the Promised Land of the West. Dedicated to "those men, women and children who lie in graves as unmarked as their place in history", *Buck and the Preacher* seeks to emancipate African-Americans from their peripheral status in the western film, and consequently in popular perceptions of the settling of the West.

Poitier's directorial debut was the most accomplished in a chain of black westerns from the period 1970-72 (*The McMasters*, *The Red, White and Black*, *Man and Boy, The Legend of Nigger Charley*) and the first to win the backing of a major studio.[1] (Marvin Miller, the producer of *Man and Boy*, claimed the majors had rejected him for "trespassing on the white man's domain by doing a western with black people".) The presence of Poitier and Harry Belafonte – black stars with proven crossover appeal, and co-producers here – was obviously key. Poitier, in particular, was a bona fide superstar, feted equally by the Academy and the film-going public. Yet in the context of radical black politics, he was derided in some quarters as Hollywood's 'house nigger', despite his advocacy of civil rights and the consistent addressing of racial themes in his films.[2]

Made partly in response to this sniping, *Buck* is wholly concerned with black history and racial struggle: "We wanted black people to see the film and be proud of themselves, be proud of their history," said Poitier. "As artists, we wanted to make a loving comment about the people we represent." However, it is a film very much in its maker's dignified image, and was not likely to appease critics who wanted Poitier to bare his teeth in the name of Black Power. An African-American *Wagon Master* (1950), with shades of *Butch Cassidy and the Sundance Kid* – it is the lot of genre films made by black artists to be measured against their mainstream equivalents – *Buck* is not radical in form or agenda like *Sweet Sweetback's Baadasssss Song* (1971). Nor does it possess the declamatory tone or overt stereotyping of the blaxploitation films that followed in *Sweetback's* wake. Instead, its racial twist on

Sidney Poitier (left) and Harry Belafonte (right) put a black spin on traditional western tropes.

western iconography – black actors as amiable outlaws, a wagon train of black settlers, white marauders and Indian rescuers – enlivens what is otherwise a rather ordinary genre film.

As Buck, guide and guardian angel to migrants from the plantations and cotton fields of the South, Poitier is unfailingly upright (give or take a little bank robbing); if it weren't for his ethnicity, Buck could be a throwback to western heroes of yore. For film historian Maria Pramaggiore, Buck is less a character in his own right than "a symbol for the African American community… its icon"[3], which is, of course, how many people continue to think of Poitier. Belafonte has greater leeway with his role as the phony Preacher, a fast-talking con artist whose Bible, predictably, conceals a pistol. Their relationship evolves via squabbling and one-upmanship into a partnership based on shared racial pride and a sense of duty. (Belafonte, always a more outspoken figure than Poitier, would have felt this no less keenly than his co-star, describing himself as "an activist who became an artist", rather than vice versa.) Their enemies in an uncluttered narrative are a band of 'nightriders', freelance thugs sent to round up black settlers and return them to Louisiana (the script establishes a geographical and moral divide between the racist South and the tolerant West). In an idealistic conclusion, reminiscent of *The McMasters*, Buck and the Preacher unite with an Indian tribe to rout the villains, proposing an alliance of racial minorities in the battle against oppression – although there is an important historical caveat, when the Indian chief with whom Buck parlays reminds him that buffalo soldiers fought against Indians in the white man's army. He could equally have been addressing black soldiers serving in the Vietnam War.[4]

The film's focus on its likeable heroes – who are augmented in the second half by Ruth, Buck's wife, imbued with wisdom and resolve by the great theatre actress Ruby Dee – comes at the expense of the settlers in their charge, who are, in narrative terms at least, largely left to their own devices. No individuals stand out among them, save for one old man who uses animal bones for divination, like a Zulu *sangoma*. This is not a detailed, gritty account of the black experience in the old West. The migrants are clearly impoverished and hard-pressed – although not to a greater degree than white settlers in traditional westerns – but the main threat to their survival comes not from local conditions (much less Indians, who are released from their usual antagonistic role in scenarios like this), but from the "labour recruiters" who represent the slave-owning classes in the South. The script, co-written by Ernest Kinoy, later an Emmy winner for *Roots*, delivers a mixed message on the extent of racism as a barrier to social integration. While a liberal sheriff asserts that black settlers are welcome in the West, Ruth suggests old attitudes are endemic even here: "I ain't gonna live in this land no more. The war ain't changed nothing and nobody. It's like a poison that's soaked into the ground."

Subtler than Fred Williamson's similarly themed *Nigger Charley* films, and intended for a broader audience base, *Buck* displaces contemporary racial tensions into a historical setting, implicitly calling previous westerns to account for the 'whitewashing' of frontier history. All-black westerns, aimed solely at African-American audiences, had been produced in significant numbers before the Second World War, but black actors remained conspicuously absent from major roles in mainstream westerns until the Sixties. Even then they were usually subordinate to white stars (Woody Strode to Jeffrey Hunter in *Sergeant Rutledge* and to Burt Lancaster, Lee Marvin and Robert Ryan in *The Professionals*; Poitier to James Garner in *Duel at Diablo*; Ossie Davis to Lancaster in *The Scalphunters*; Jim Brown to Raquel Welch in *100 Rifles*; Lou Gossett Jr. to Garner in *Skin Game*). *Buck* benefited from the surge in demand for black action films, a development the major studios were not slow to take advantage of. Ironically, however, Poitier's adherence to the codes and conventions of the classic western, albeit adapted to reflect an African-American perspective, hindered its chances of capturing audiences (of all races) hip to jazzier films such as *Shaft* (1971) and *Super Fly* (1972). Only with hindsight can its importance in black cinema history and as a vehicle for establishing a black presence in the western be appreciated. **KG**

footnotes

1 George Lipsitz, 'Genre Anxiety and Racial Representation in 1970s Cinema', in *Refiguring American Film Genres: History and Theory* (Nick Browne, ed, University of California Press, 1998). Poitier took over as director when he and Belafonte, as co-stars and producers, became dissatisfied with the work of their first choice, television specialist Joseph Sargent.

2 Harry Belafonte has always defended his friend's legacy: "He was the right person at the right place at the right time to be anointed as the first black force in American popular culture to break open a system that was so tightly closed to us," he told an interviewer in 2011 ('Belafonte's Activist Life', thedailybeast.com).

3 *Irish and African American Cinema: Identifying Others and Performing Identities, 1980-2000* (State University of New York, 2007).

4 Richard Slotkin extrapolates: "The 'black' western had to straddle the contradiction between identification with the Indians as another oppressed people of colour and the assertion of an African-American role in the 'heroic' actions that won the West – and dispossessed the Indians" (*Gunfighter Nation: The Myth of the Frontier in Twentieth-Century America*, University of Oklahoma Press, 1998).

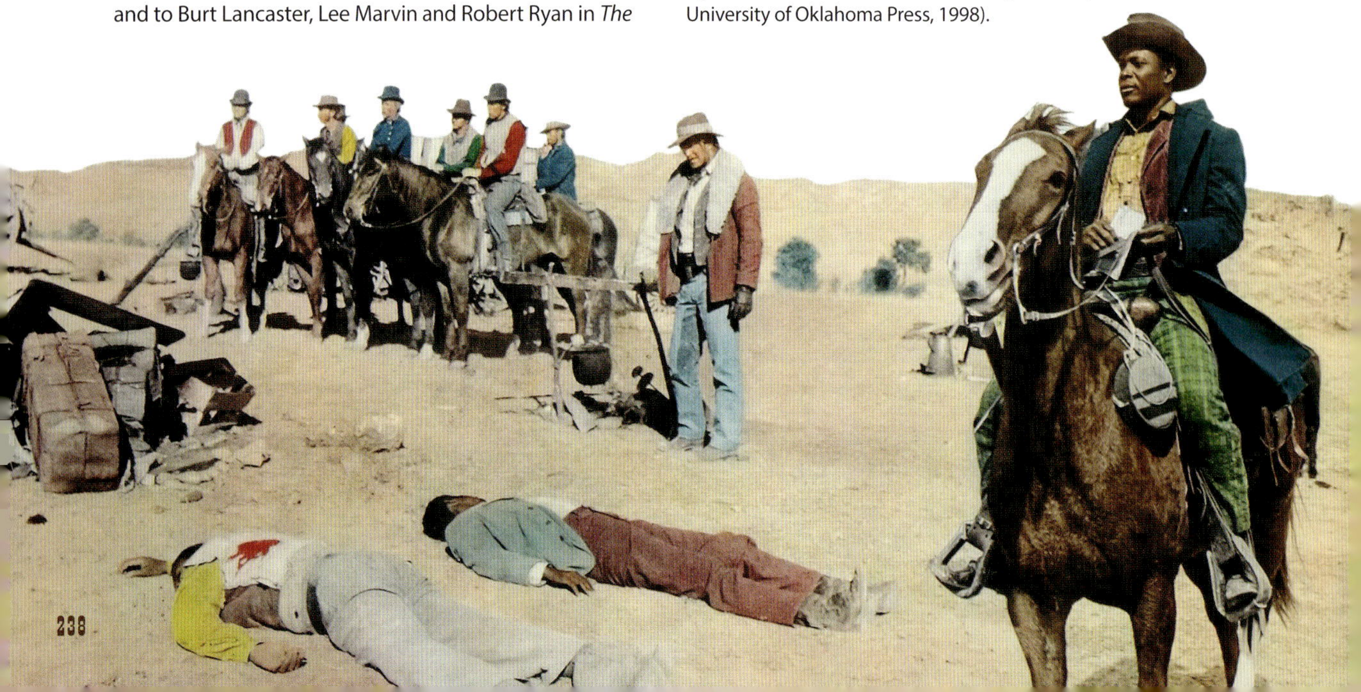

The Culpepper Cattle Co.

1972, Colour, 92 mins.

D: Dick Richards. P: Paul A. Helmick (Twentieth Century-Fox). W: Eric Bercovici, Gregory Prentiss, Dick Richards (story). Ph: Lawrence Edward Williams, Ralph Woolsey. M: Tom Scott, Jerry Goldsmith. St: Gary Grimes (Ben Mockridge), Billy 'Green' Bush (Frank Culpepper), Luke Askew (Luke), Geoffrey Lewis (Russ Caldwell), Bo Hopkins (Dixie Brick)

"Cowboyin's somethin' you do when you can't do nothin' else."

With these words, eager teenager Ben Mockridge is disabused of his idealistic notions when he signs on with the titular outfit in Dick Richards' directorial debut, a *bildungsroman* of the most sobering kind. The script, based on Richards' story, is structured as a series of learning curves, each steeper than the last, and contrives a climactic shootout, staged with post-*Wild Bunch* panache, involving a land baron and a quartet of gunfighters in which Ben's received wisdom that "there are some things more important to a man than cattle" is tested to the fullest. Exposed to the rigours of the trail, the violence and venality of frontier existence, Ben ends the film disillusioned but still noble of intention.[1]

Culpepper was not the first attempt to counter the cult of the cowboy. As early as 1903, Andy Adams' semi-autobiographical novel *The Log of a Cowboy* muddied the myths that had been circulated by dime novels and cemented by Owen Wister's phenomenal *The Virginian*. Closer to *Culpepper's* era, Delmer Daves, whose most famous western, *Broken Arrow*, was an exercise in challenging preconceptions, cast Jack Lemmon in *Cowboy* (1958) as a greenhorn who learns the ropes and loses his innocence under the tutelage of seasoned trail boss Glenn Ford. One of Ford's lessons dispels "all that hogwash about horses… No sensible man loves a horse. He tolerates the filthy animal only because riding is better than walking." His sentiments are echoed in *Culpepper*, when Ben asks the name of a gunfighter's horse and is told: "You don't have to put a name on something you might have to eat." Yet *Cowboy's* measured dose of realism failed to dislodge cherished conventions – or tarnish Lemmon's affable aura – completely.

Those conventions were trotted out again a year later on television, when the cast of *Rawhide* began their eight-season-long trek along the Sedalia Trail under the firm-but-fair stewardship of Eric Fleming's Gil Favor. For all their weekly tribulations and periodic squabbles, the series portrayed drovers as a relatively contented breed, almost a paradigm of unity and camaraderie. Whereas, in *Culpepper*, Pete (Matt Clark), the most sympathetic member of the company, is left to face an unwanted showdown with Geoffrey Lewis's pistolero alone, it is unthinkable that none of the *Rawhide* regulars would have pitched in to help him, or that Favor would not have done his best to prevent the confrontation from occurring in the first place. Frank Culpepper, steely and saturnine behind a thicket of beard, pointedly refuses to intervene.

Cowboying began to lose its lustre on the big screen in the late Sixties: the eponymous heroes of *Will Penny* and *Monte Walsh* are not so much agents of westward expansion or frontier knights as creaking emblems of encroaching obsolescence, their skills superseded by the industrial might of corporations with names such as 'Consolidated Cattle'. (Prior to this, in *Hud*, the decay of the contemporary cattle business had been portrayed as synonymous with the moral decline of the modern Westerner.) In the same year as *Culpepper*, an ostensibly similar film, *The Cowboys*, had John Wayne – revisiting *Red River* territory in more ways than one – training a scratch crew of youngsters for a cattle drive

that also becomes a painful rite of passage. As a vehicle for Wayne, however, it is primarily a tip of the Stetson to its star, by then well into his gruff paternal phase, and the boys' endeavours, which include avenging his death at the hands of psychotic longhair Bruce Dern, ultimately comprise a tribute to his memory.

By contrast, *Culpepper* never veers from Ben's eager gaze as he witnesses – and, in one instance, participates in – brutal acts of violence, experiences the limits of compassion and the alternating tedium and gut-punching ruthlessness of life on the plains, until the scales fall from his eyes. His enthusiasm for what he considers to be a great and noble adventure amuses the saddle-worn drovers he tries so desperately to impress, and it is strong enough to deflect the cynicism summed up in one drifter's credo: "Best part's getting into town, or getting out – in between's lousy." His determination to make up for mistakes earns him a stay of execution, but ultimately Culpepper is right to regret taking the youngster on board. Ben's inherent decency proves not merely to be out of place in this environment, but a liability as well. His chivalrous decision to defend a religious sect against the predatory rancher Thornton Pierce (John McLiam) convinces Culpepper's hired gunmen (Luke Askew, Bo Hopkins, Geoffrey Lewis and Wayne Sutherlin) to desert the drive and make a stand alongside him – less out of shame or a sense of duty, however, than because, having been humiliated by Pierce earlier, they are spoiling for a fight.

Culpepper's reception was respectful but muted. Much was made of its resemblance to period paintings and daguerreotypes: from the sepia-tinted title image of the collected company to the dusty haze that coats the exteriors; from the muted colour scheme (enlivened by sporadic eruptions of red) and shabby, soiled outfits to squalid, sparsely furnished interiors lit more or less naturally. (*The New York Times* damned its visual qualities with faint praise: here was an "overly handsome western… [with a] façade of atmospheric realism".) The casting of low-key character actors, many of them with strong western credentials, enhances its credibility: Royal Dano, playing a crafty cattle rustler, represents a link with the genre's past, while the quartet of Clark, Askew, Hopkins and Lewis – almost a repertory company in their own right – imbue their roles with grubby charm and a distinctly contemporary insouciance.

The final bloodbath and its coda seal Ben's graduation from a state of relative innocence to bitter experience. As the settlers prepare to abandon the land they had claimed in the name of God and which is now strewn with corpses, Ben has to force them at gunpoint to bury the bodies of his fallen comrades. The naïve man-child who began the drive becomes a surrogate for America's disaffected youth, post-Summer of Love (and post-*Summer of '42*, Gary Grimes's breakthrough film in his brief screen career). Authority figures are found wanting: Culpepper hard-nosed and humourless; Pierce power-crazed; Anthony James's religious leader hypocritical, interpreting "God's will" as he sees fit. Even Ben's mother, a blankly stoical figure glimpsed in a throwaway scene, seems unmoved by her son's departure. Only the free-spirited gunslingers radiate warmth to any degree, and they are stone killers. **KG**

footnotes

1 As harsh as it is, the conclusion eschews the mean-spiritedness of *The Spikes Gang*, another film in which Grimes, together with three other youngsters, learns to separate hard facts from romantic fantasy.

Dirty Little Billy

1972, Colour, 92 mins.

D: Stan Dragoti. P: Jack L. Warner (WGR/Dragoti Ltd, Jack L. Warner). W: Charles Moss, Stan Dragoti. Ph: Ralph Woolsey. M: Sascha Burland. St: Michael J. Pollard (Billy), Richard Evans (Goldie), Lee Purcell (Berle), Charles Aidman (Ben Antrim), Dran Hamilton (Billy's mother)

"Go ahead, blow my eyes out – kill me. You'd be doing me a favour."

Boots squelching in mud. A slate-grey sky. Crude buildings. A barren, featureless landscape. The Stars and Stripes fluttering in a damp breeze signals that we are in the American West; otherwise it could be medieval Europe. The opening images of Stan Dragoti's idiosyncratic back-story of Billy the Kid define the raw tone struck by many revisionist westerns in the Seventies. The characterisations follow suit, none more so than Michael J. Pollard's unique interpretation of Billy.

The screenplay, by Dragoti and his fellow Madison Avenue advertising executive Charles Moss, breaks with traditional fictional portraits of Billy as well as most historical descriptions of the outlaw. It depicts him as a slow-witted, indolent waster, utterly unsuited to life on the dusty, dilapidated farm that has drawn him from New York to Coffeyville, Kansas, with his mother and stepfather. His mother mollycoddles him; his stepfather berates and beats him. Soon Billy (given his probable original surname of McCarty) leaves for town, where he takes up with Goldie, a turbulent young gunman with a hair-trigger temper, and Berle, Goldie's much-abused but devoted prostitute lover.

Goldie's domain is the saloon. It is squalid, like every other part of town. The locals dare not enter – they refer to Goldie as the "poison" in their midst – and the stretch of boggy street outside is like a no man's land. Goldie is anti-authoritarian and Billy looks up to him, while Berle becomes his surrogate sister, albeit one who takes his virginity. The trio eke out a feckless, countercultural existence inside the saloon, subsisting on booze, provisions pilfered by Billy from local farms and whatever Berle can earn on her back. Dragoti demonstrates their enervating lifestyle via montage; just as the film itself

MUNDIAL FILMS.A.
SALOON
¡DISPARA, BILLY, DISPARA!!
CON MICHAEL J. POLLARD
LEE PURCELL • RICHARD EVANS • CHARLES AIDMAN • DRAN HAMILTON Y WILLARD SAGE
UNA PRODUCCION JACK L. WARNER Y WRG/DRAGOTI, INC. • ARGUMENTO Y GUION DE CHARLES MOSS Y STAN DRAGOTI • MUSICA DE SASCHA BURLAND
PRODUCIDA POR JACK L. WARNER • DIRIGIDA POR STAN DRAGOTI • COLOR

starts to get bogged down, the machinations of the would-be mayor, Ben Antrim, force a confrontation and a welcome change of pace. It also provides Billy with the opportunity to make his first kill.

Dragoti's commitment to realism in a general sense, as opposed to historical accuracy regarding the life of Billy the Kid, is nothing if not thorough. Costumes are ragged and stained. Faces are smeared with grime, interiors dank and smoky. The photography by Ralph Woolsey is overwhelmingly muggy and brown (he used similar hues in *The Culpepper Cattle Co.*), making the few instances of sunlight – the "famous sun showers" the locals joke about – all the more striking. The eruptions of violence are ugly and anxious, de-emphasising stunt choreography and dynamic staging. After some ineffective gunplay, a dispute between Goldie and a hunter in the saloon is resolved by a knife fight between Berle and the hunter's girlfriend, marginalising the men, who would ordinarily dominate this scenario. Even pistols are demythologised – Goldie damns his sidearm as "undependable" and "inaccurate", although he could just as easily be excusing his inability to hit a man from point-blank range. There are no clean kills, no glorification.

Everything about the film seems designed to antagonise purists, to puncture expectations and shatter myths, even if all it ultimately achieves is to replace them with new ones. With the exception of Berle, a performance of real substance by Lee Purcell, the characters are deliberately drained of warmth and colour. Coffeyville's citizens dream of attaining "third city status" for their drab little settlement, and with it federal funding and legitimacy, and are gleeful when wagonloads of newcomers – refugees from an epidemic that has ravaged the nearest community – straggle into town to swell their ranks. But their morality proves to be as shabby as much of the scenery when they ambush Goldie on his way out of town, reneging on a deal to allow their *bête noire* safe passage. It exposes the hypocrisy of Ben Antrim (named after the real Billy's stepfather – Antrim here has a flirtation with Billy's mother) as a representative of conservatism, while other authority figures, from Billy's bullying stepfather to the seasoned outlaws he and Goldie hope to join up with at the end, are painted as contemptible.

above: Michael J. Pollard, far from the romantic image of Billy the Kid, with Lee Purcell as his surrogate sister and seducer.

By contrast, Billy escapes moral censure, or even serious scrutiny. While the context – Billy exchanging one dysfunctional family unit, comprising his mother and stepfather, for another, in the form of Goldie and Berle – suggests a youngster floundering in search of acceptance and guidance, it doesn't suffice to explain Billy. But that doesn't seem to have been the point. We gain no insight into his motivation, but the absence of motivation is revealing in itself. This is a portrait of a psychopath in the making, a misfit led by the nose, slapped around and not taken seriously, who finds, in the gun, a way to assert himself. And he likes it. "Jesus, I *was* good," he reacts when he kills for the first time, with a nervous half-laugh and a victorious gleam in his eyes. The casting of Pollard was inspired. At 32, he doesn't look like a teenager; nor does he resemble contemporary descriptions of the Kid. But with his slight build, malleable features and childlike bearing, complemented by an imbecilic smirk, he conveys a young man emotionally and mentally adrift, lost in his own world, destined only to dole out violence and to suffer it in return.

Despite its best efforts, *Dirty Little Billy* did not prove to be "the end of [Billy the Kid's] legend", as its poster boasted. Old West myths are nothing if not resilient, and there was still scope for romanticising the character after this – Sam Peckinpah, Rudy Wurlitzer and Kris Kristofferson made him an anti-establishment symbol the very next year. But this is a fascinating alternative rendering of the tale, with a bleakness of vision the equal of any western in the 'mud and rags' school. **KG**

Greaser's Palace

1972, Colour, 91 mins.

D: Robert Downey. P: Cyma Rubin (Greaser's Palace Ltd). W: Robert Downey. Ph: Peter Powell. M: Jack Nitzsche. St: Allan Arbus (Jessy), Albert Henderson (Seaweedhead Greaser), Michael Sullivan (Lamy Greaser), Luana Anders (Cholera Greaser), Woody Chambliss (Father)

"Exactly six miles north of Skagg Mountain in the Valley of Pain, there lives an evil devil-monster. His name is Bingo Gas Station Motel Cheeseburger With A Side Of Aircraft Noise And You'll Be Gary Indiana. And he loves to hurt people."

It is probably fair to say that visions of the Second Coming have rarely featured Christ descending to Earth via parachute while dressed in a zoot suit. That is how he makes his entrance in Robert Downey Sr.'s cryptic, wilfully anachronistic ersatz western, an acid casualty of the experimental ethos of the era. Its import as a genre piece is negligible (*pace* Joel and Ethan Coen, who named it their third favourite western), but as a vehicle for biblical allusions it has numerous antecedents, from *Hell's Hinges* (1916), with its "Old Testament fury"[1], and the saccharine symbolism of *3 Godfathers* (1948), to the scores of Italian westerns that appropriated and subverted Catholic iconography. Downey's parade of images ('plot' implies structure – evidently too rigid a concept for Downey's purposes) amount to a satire of sorts on the marketing and reception of organised religion, although different meanings suggest themselves, and even the seemingly obvious ones may be wide of the mark – a rather neat analogy for religion itself. Ultimately, however, whatever point the writer-director had in mind is blunted by puerile humour and crass characterisations.

For Jesus, read Jessy, played by the softly spoken and solidly Jewish Allan Arbus. He is en route to Jerusalem "to be an actor-singer" when he enters the orbit of Vernon 'Seaweedhead' Greaser, an eccentric variant on the town-tyrant archetype who holds court in a multi-storey saloon that functions additionally as a place of worship. Jessy attracts a following through his

A martyr to his art: Jessy (Allan Arbus) meets the Holy Ghost (*top right*) and takes his Christ shtick to the extreme (*directly above*).

ability to resurrect the dead (beginning with Greaser's son, 'Lamy Homo', the equivalent of Lazarus), cure the lame ("If you feel, you heal") and walk – actually dance – on water. Pestered by his disciples for advice and direction, he delivers a pep talk (in the argot of a Sixties peacenik) that falls rather flat. Nor do the locals appreciate his big song-and-dance number on the stage in Greaser's Palace; it is only when he displays stigmata that the crowd erupts. This, it seems, is to be his shtick – the people want a showman as much as a saviour, and Jessy discusses career options with his agent, a sinister figure who tops off a red suit with a space helmet. (To succeed in show business, Downey may be implying, is to sell one's soul to the devil – or to William Morris, whomever you happen to encounter in the desert first.) There is still time for Jessy to succumb to temptation with Greaser's daughter, Cholera, before his destiny is decided by separate encounters. The first is with his father (the Father), an aloof and autocratic presence, indifferent to the wishes of his Son, and with the petulant Holy Ghost, who wears a white sheet and bowler hat and bemoans his lack of opportunities. The second is with a bereaved and persecuted settler woman, who mutates from being a stand-in for Job – and by extension the Jewish people – suffering terrible wounds at the hands of the capricious Almighty, into an unlikely surrogate for Judas.[2]

To outline *Greaser's Palace* in such a way is to bless it with a linearity that was plainly never the intention. It is not so much episodic as random, a series of surreal sketches in which recurring gags – such as Greaser repeatedly killing his son, for no clear reason, each time Jessy brings him back from the dead – form linchpins, providing a modicum of coherence. Some of the skits pertain, in the loosest of senses, to New Testament themes, with particular emphasis on Jessy's erratic powers: he 'heals' a crippled man, who discards his crutches only to collapse, proclaiming nonetheless, "I can crawl again"; and cures an Indian chief not with a miraculous touch but with physiotherapy. If that has the whiff of the Pythons, other jokes evoke the deadpan absurdity of Buñuel – as when the camera encounters, but does not acknowledge, a man holding a painting of the Last Supper – or 'work' by disassociation: anachronisms; a caged mariachi band; an Indian flailing himself with a boot. Much of the humour, however, is baldly juvenile, ranging from scatological – Greaser's frustrated efforts to clear his chronic constipation – to crude – sex acts described anecdotally in gynaecological detail; Jessy's painful encounter with a lascivious dwarf (Hervé Villechaize) and his bearded, foul-mouthed transvestite 'wife'. (Dwarfs were something of a trope for Downey – he employed two more in his most popular film, the ad-land satire *Putney Swope* [1969].)

As with *El Topo*, the original 'midnight movie', which had broadly similar aims but achieved more disturbing, oneiric results, *Greaser's Palace* is the kind of film for which extravagant claims are advanced, not least that it subverts the conventional western. This is reasonable up to a point, but really the settings and props are little more than signposts; genre staples – in particular a troupe of Indians, who are wasted in more ways than one – function merely as western window dressing. (It is perhaps unfortunate that Downey's film was released in 1972, the *annus mirabilis* of western revisionism, when other film-makers were more purposeful in their deconstructions.) Conflating the hero, the agent of change, with Christ, albeit in bastardised form, doesn't so much demystify the archetype – if that was indeed the aim; one can only second-guess – as take him in the opposite direction, setting him back along the mythological path he has been following since the quest legends of antiquity.

Despite the fatuous jokes and wanton silliness, one must assume that Downey, briefly the darling of the counterculture circuit, was sincere in his oblique criticism of the popular craving for salvation without personal sacrifice. When Jessy tells his audience, "I believe you can make this world a better place," they miss the point, entreating him to tell them of the afterlife, not what they ought to be doing in the here and now. And the director does succeed in creating a self-contained fantasy world that obeys its own peculiar brand of anti-logic. At one point, Greaser and one of his underlings regret that they're not "bizarre enough… Who is?" The implication is that there are no limits, or ought not to be. To that extent, at least, Downey's mission was accomplished. **KG**

footnotes

1 Scott Simmon, *The Invention of the Western Film* (Cambridge University Press, 2003).

2 The woman was played by director Downey's wife, her son by their own offspring, the future actor Robert Jr.

The Great Northfield Minnesota Raid

1972, Colour, 90 mins.

D: Philip Kaufman. P: Cliff Robertson, Philip Kaufman (Robertson & Associates, Universal). W: Philip Kaufman. Ph: Bruce Surtees. M: Dave Grusin. St: Cliff Robertson (Cole Younger), Robert Duvall (Jesse James), Luke Askew (Jim Younger), R.G. Armstrong (Clell Miller), Dana Elcar (Allen)

"I've searched back through the crannies of my mind. I can't think of one single honest man we ever robbed... Talk about givin' us amnesty. Hell, it's up to us to give amnesty to them."

Of the cluster of grimy revisionist westerns produced in 1972, Philip Kaufman's film is closest in spirit to *Bad Company*, if not as accomplished, and in intent to *Dirty Little Billy*, although not as astringent. Both self-aware and satirical, it examines how myths are made – not just individually, but on a national scale – at the same time as it debunks them. The quotation marks around the scene-setting narration are almost visible; the tone of delivery makes it clear we are not really expected to swallow its claims of authenticity, despite the documentary-like attention to period detail and fashionably muted palette.

Yet it is a faithful re-creation of the James-Younger gang's titular exploit, at least in outline, and probably the closest to an accurate depiction of Jesse James – certainly the least varnished one – as Hollywood has produced. As written by Kaufman and rendered by Robert Duvall, Jesse is less the social bandit of yore, except in his own imagination, than a delusional fanatic, who sees everywhere north of the Mason-Dixon line as enemy territory, even a decade after the end of the Civil War, and kills without conscience. "I thought it was important to do a more realistic portrait of Jesse James as a really scary, murderous guy who led certain members of his gang, like the Youngers, down the wrong path. It was the antithesis of the Tyrone Power version [directed by Henry King in 1939], which was very romanticised," the director has said.[1] Kaufman finds Cliff Robertson's laid-back, loquacious Cole Younger far more amenable, and shifts him to the centre of the narrative – no doubt encouraged by Robertson's position as co-producer.[2]

Cole is the whimsical brains of the outfit, given to regaling admirers with anecdotes, showing off his much-dented bullet-proof vest and expressing "wonderment" at the latest "contraptions" – a steam-powered tractor, velocipedes and the like. (He is almost unique in the modern western in embracing such technological advances.) But his plans, which he defines as 'visions', are usually appropriated by Jesse, who relates them with evangelical zeal, his delusions of grandeur reinforced by his unctuous brother Frank (John Pearce). Such is the case with the Northfield raid: shelved by Cole when an amnesty is in the offing; revived by Jesse when Cole is wounded by Pinkerton detectives, working for the railroad; revised by Cole when the amnesty motion is defeated – a result of Pinkerton bribing the speaker of the Missouri legislature. Posing as a cattle buyer, Cole inveigles bank president Wilcox (Robert H. Harris) into a scheme to replenish the bank's coffers – these are straitened times – by tricking Northfield's wary locals into depositing rather than hoarding their money. The stage is thus set for the gang's famously disastrous swansong on a rain-lashed, muddy Minnesota morning in September 1876.

Kaufman directs with an "amused detachment", as the *Los Angeles Times* put it, delighting in the escapades and eccentricities, both documented and imagined, of his characters and the era they lived in. Grounding his story in fact (he was a history major at university), but juggling the chronology and characters, his approach shores up the James-Younger legend – he dutifully paints the railroad as an agent of mass displacement, inciting an armed response that makes the gang folk heroes – while shearing away layers of myth. Jesse's introduction – squatting next to his brother in an outhouse – is only slightly less ignominious than his exit, fleeing

above: Cliff Robertson as Cole Younger, the amiable brains of the outfit.

above: R.G. Armstrong (left), a mainstay of westerns since the Fifties, as Clell Miller.

Minnesota dressed in the clothes of an elderly widow he has recently killed. (This is Kaufman's cynical coda to an oft-related incident in which the gang paid off the woman's debts to her landlord. In the film, Jesse justifies the murder of both the landlord and the widow as acts of guerrilla warfare.) With his 'wonderments', predilection for "light love" and drug-induced visions (herbal medicine and sexual stimulants will do that to a man, it seems), Cole, meanwhile, represents outlawry as a kind of alternative lifestyle. Robertson's performance is relaxed and disarming. Despite being culpable for the failure of the raid, which ultimately results in his capture, it is difficult to begrudge Cole the acclamation of Northfield: paraded through the streets in a prison wagon with his brothers (Seventies stalwarts Matt Clark and Luke Askew), he rises defiantly to his feet, vest riddled with yet more bullets, playing to the crowd unto the end.[3]

Manipulating history for his own ends, Kaufman makes Wilcox – in reality a book-keeper at the time of the robbery – the scapegoat for financial chicanery at the people's expense. By namechecking prominent robber barons Jay Gould and James Fisk, and even President Grant, Wilcox intimates that corruption is the American way; Cole is on the same wavelength – the gang have been bribed out of an amnesty, and he intends for them to bribe their way back in, using the proceeds from the raid. Equally populist is the portrayal of legendary detective Allan Pinkerton (Herbert Nelson) – who in appearance and bluster resembles Albert Dekker's odious railroad official in *The Wild Bunch* – and his men as tools of the establishment. Unlike the implacable pursuers of *Butch Cassidy and the Sundance Kid*, they are largely ineffectual, however, shunting up and down the tracks at each new report of the gang's whereabouts, finally arriving in Northfield in time to see their quarry under arrest. Nor are the townsfolk spared the lash. Having killed two of the gang and driven off the rest, they form a posse, but only succeed in hanging all the customers in the local whorehouse, just to be sure, and shooting it out with a posse from a different town. Philip French was justified when he summarised the film as a "Brechtian satire on capitalism and on American hypocrisy in which the vindictiveness, violence and self-justification of the outlaws is perfectly matched by those of the Pinkertons and the venal, vengeful civic leaders of Northfield".[4]

Directing his first major film with iconoclastic fervour, Kaufman swings wildly, like a wrecking ball, demolishing not just myths and assumptions – Jesse James has never seemed less like Robin Hood – but puncturing national pride. (As with the other *Zeitgeist* westerns of 1972, *The Great Northfield Minnesota Raid* seems more prescient in hindsight, released as it was in the year of Watergate.) Even baseball is fair game – as Cole witnesses a contest from the sidelines in Northfield, it frequently breaks down into brawling. Kaufman suggests America is a country in thrall to violence, underlined by Cole's riposte to a claim that baseball is now the national pastime: blasting the ball with his rifle, he says, "Our national sport is shooting, and always will be." **KG**

footnotes

1 Interview with Philip Kaufman by Alex Simon in *Venice Magazine*, December 2000.

2 This was not the first time that Cole had been promoted to starring status in the James-Younger saga. See also *Bad Men of Missouri* (1941), *The Younger Brothers* (1949) and *Cole Younger, Gunfighter* (1958). While Walter Hill's gritty-nostalgic restaging of the events leading up to and including the Northfield raid, *The Long Riders*, is really an ensemble piece, Cole, played by David Carradine, has a more pronounced role than his cohorts.

3 As the closing narration informs us, Cole and his brothers were sentenced to life imprisonment for their crimes. He lived for a further 40 years, 25 of them in prison, and died in 1916 in his home town of Lee's Summit, Missouri.

4 Philip French, *Westerns: Aspects of a Movie Genre* (Carcanet Press, 2005).

"Nobody knows whereabouts he come from and don't seem to matter much… Bought him a good horse, and traps, and other truck that went with being a mountain man, and said good-bye to whatever life was down there below."

Jeremiah Johnson

1972, Colour, 108 mins.

D: Sydney Pollack. P: Joe Wizan (Joe Wizan-Sanford Productions). W: John Milius, Edward Anhalt. Ph: Duke Callaghan. M: John Rubinstein, Tim McIntire. St: Robert Redford (Jeremiah Johnson), Will Geer (Bear Claw), Delle Bolton (Swan), Josh Albee (Caleb), Joaquin Martinez (Paints His Shirt Red)

The historical figure who inspired *Jeremiah Johnson* earned the sobriquet "liver-eating Johnson" for his habit of partly cannibalizing the bodies of slain Indian foes. Robert Redford may have admired the character and the lifestyle he represented, but he was not about to condone anthropophagy, not even for the sake of historical veracity. And so the script, like that by John Milius for *The Life and Times of Judge Roy Bean*, vacillates between humanising a man whose true nature and actions have been subsumed by myth, and perpetuating the legend for an audience tuned in to its implications.

The appeal of Redford's mountain man for the counterculture was broadly the same as that of other western 'dropouts': Dustin Hoffman in *Little Big Man*, for example, Richard Harris in *A Man Called Horse* or Tom Laughlin's Billy Jack. All sought a life away from the clutter, chaos and corruption of civilised society, spurning military careers (an important consideration in the Vietnam years) to engage in a search for self alongside the land's original inhabitants – even if, as here, race relations are not exactly cordial. Jeremiah is enigmatic almost to the point of abstraction; he is a perfect fit for Redford's nonchalance and a suitable vehicle for contemporary disaffection. (His relationship with nature chimed with the early flowering of modern eco politics – one of Redford's passions and a prime reason he has named *Jeremiah Johnson* as his favourite film.) We learn little about the character's background – the story, set sometime in the 1840s or early 1850s, was conflated from two literary sources, with much of the biographical detail and historical context excised[1] – such that his desire to live independently becomes his raison d'être. He is one of those men "planning to get from the mountain something that nature couldn't get him below", as one veteran trapper intuits, a throwback to the untamed, unwashed heroes of wilderness westerns such as *Across the Wide Missouri* (1951) and *The Big Sky* (1952). This sub-genre reappeared briefly in the late Sixties and early Seventies (Sydney Pollack's *The Scalphunters* [1968] was a taster), by which time "the matted beards and patchwork

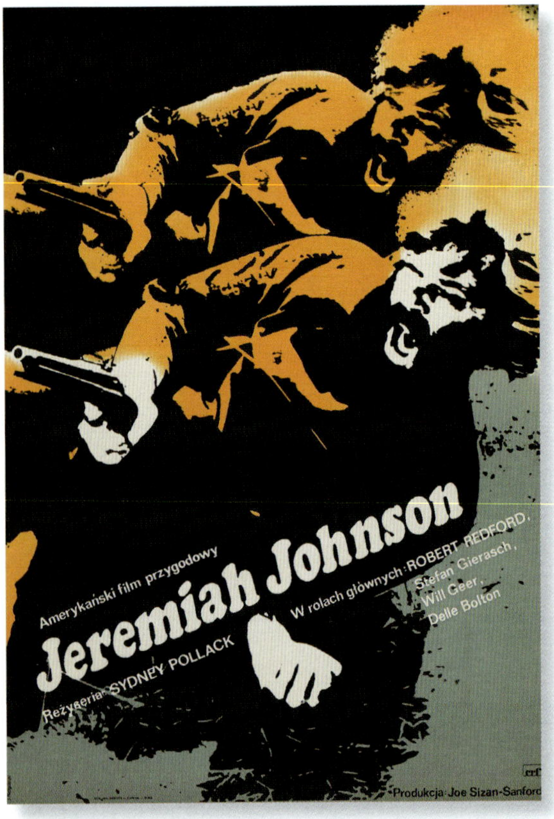

clothes… [had come] back into fashion", writes Kim Newman, along with a "resurgence of the distaste for civilization that must have driven the originals into the mountains in the first place".[2]

Jeremiah's initial efforts to live in harmony with nature, aided by the grizzled trapper Bear Claw, provide gentle comedy, as fish slip through his fingers in a stream and his mentor sets him the challenge of skinning a rampaging grizzly bear. There is an appreciation of the strangeness of mountain life, a matter-of-fact approach to grotesque or absurd situations that pays humorous dividends: Jeremiah discovering the frozen corpse of one 'Hatchet Jack', together with a note bequeathing his prized .50 calibre Hawken rifle ("it kilt the bear that kilt me") to whoever finds him; or encountering Del Gue (Stefan Gierasch), a fellow trapper, when the latter has been buried up to his neck: "Indians put you there?" "'Tweren't Mormons."

The character proves his mettle as the seasons change. Pollack tracks his progress via fashionable dissolves and montages, with long shots that emphasise the implacable majesty of the landscape and the challenge that Jeremiah has set himself. (The location was Utah – both Redford and Pollack were resident there.) The heart of the drama is the conflict between his yearning for solitude – human contact is limited to eccentric hermits such as Bear Claw and Del Gue, and the Indian tribes with whom they trade – and his inability to reject entirely his responsibility towards the world he has left behind. He takes pity on a settler woman driven mad by the murder of her family by Indians, taking her surviving son, mute with trauma, under his wing, and is compelled to accept the daughter of a Flathead chief as his bride after a friendly cultural misunderstanding. This leads to a surprisingly tender passage (involving yet another montage) in which the warmth of Delle Bolton's character counters some of Jeremiah's emotional austerity.

His fate turns on his agreement to escort a rescue party of soldiers towards a stranded wagon train through a Crow burial ground. When he returns to his cabin, he finds his surrogate family slaughtered, seemingly in retaliation for the sacrilege. From this point, the survivalist aspect of the plot yields to an increasingly far-fetched revenge scenario, during which Jeremiah acquires the nickname of 'Crow killer' and becomes the object of awe. As much as Redford embraced Jeremiah's flintiness – he was never one to accept blandly heroic roles – his transformation into cold-eyed assassin is a stretch too far.

Towards the end, the Crow construct a shrine of sorts to their nemesis, and the film follows suit. It never quite gets to grips with its protagonist, and settles for being a testament to the kind of legendary qualities endemic in the mythology of the West. Pollack wanted to puncture the legend – or preserve it – by having Jeremiah freeze to death, but Redford argued for an open ending in which he is seen heading vaguely in the direction of Canada. He warily acknowledges one of his Crow adversaries on the way – a parting plea, perhaps, for unity among outcasts, for peaceful coexistence in a nation seething with racial tension and social dissent. **KG**

footnotes

1 See *Crow Killer: The Saga of Liver-Eating Johnson* (1958), by Raymond W. Thorp and Robert Bunker, and Vardis Fisher's fictional *Mountain Man: A Novel of Male and Female in the Early American West* (1965).

2 *Wild West Movies* (Bloomsbury, 1990).

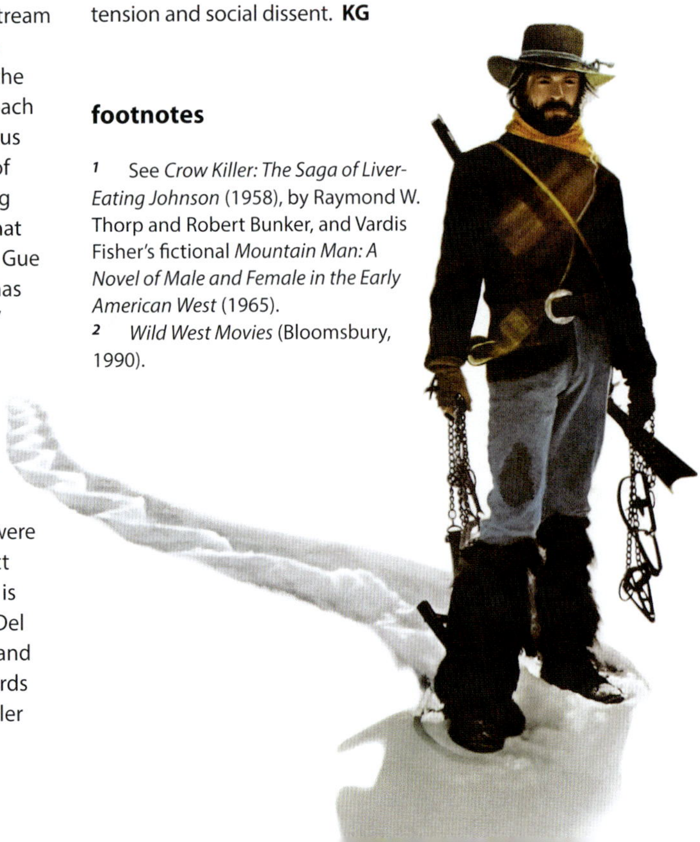

The Legend of Nigger Charley

1972, Colour, 98 mins.

D: Martin Goldman. P: Larry G. Spangler (Spangler & Sons Pictures Ltd). W: Martin Goldman, Larry G. Spangler, James Bellah (story). Ph: Peter Eco. M: Robert Banks, George Butcher. St: Fred Williamson (Charley), D'Urville Martin (Toby), Don Pedro Colley (Joshua), Thomas Anderson (Shadow), Jerry Gatlin (Sheriff Rhinehart)

The Soul of Nigger Charley

1973, Colour, 109 mins.

D: Larry G. Spangler. P: Larry G. Spangler (Spangler & Sons Pictures Ltd). W: Harold Stone, Larry G. Spangler (story). Ph: Richard C. Glouner. M: Don Costa. St: Fred Williamson (Charley), D'Urville Martin (Toby), Denise Nicholas (Elena), Pedro Armendariz Jr (Sandoval), Kirk Calloway (Marcellus)

"I ain't never gonna be a slave again for no man."

Produced cheaply and executed rudimentarily, the adventures of renegade slave 'Nigger' Charley reaped surprisingly rich rewards for Paramount and proved influential, decades later, on Quentin Tarantino's *Django Unchained*, which was not quite as ground-breaking in its employment of slavery as a context as its publicity and its director claimed.[1] Over the course of two films, writer/producer/director Larry G. Spangler and his star, the totemic Fred Williamson, attempted to carve out a place in western mythology for an authentic black superhero, tracing Charley's development from plantation slave to folk legend-cum-liberator. Whatever ambitions they may have had in this direction are reined in, however, by a reliance on blaxploitation clichés – crude racial stereotyping of both black and white characters; anachronistic soul and funk soundtracks – teamed with a superficial examination of the slavery issue and an inability to escape the trappings of the 'white-biased' western genre they purportedly seek to subvert.

The narrative arc is as perfunctory as the direction and characterisations. Granted freedom by his dying master, Charley is cheated out of his disenfranchisement by the plantation foreman, a caricatured white supremacist: "Only a man got a right to be free," he sneers, "and you ain't a man." Charley kills him in the course of escaping with his friends Toby and Joshua, the trio surviving random encounters with Indians, bounty hunters and a maniacal faux-preacher (Joe Santos), who seems to have strayed from the set of an Italian western and views blacks collectively as the incarnation of Satan. In the sequel, Charley and Toby, living legends by this stage, recruit like-minded freedmen to thwart an unregenerate Southern general's plan to establish a new Confederacy in Mexico by kidnapping blacks for servitude, a plotline that recalls both *Rio Conchos* and *Buck and the Preacher* and allows for the staging of more elaborate action sequences.

Would-be picaresque characters, such as the mixed-race adventurer, Shadow, and the Mexican bandit, Sandoval, make limited impressions, while Charley is provided with a romantic foil in the shape of Elena, whose experiences as a "house nigger" have given her a tough hide that nevertheless yields to Charley's masterful touch. Her role is an important one in such a macho-inflected treatment, a reminder that slavery was a burden borne by both sexes; Denise Nicholas communicates Elena's unbowed spirit with a minimum of fuss. Williamson, who stepped in after Woody Strode backed out, was still a tentative performer at this stage, outmuscled at the box office by heavyweight black

action stars like Jim Brown and Richard Roundtree. He does his best, however, to make Charley a more rounded character than he initially appears, running through a range of emotions, from surliness and resentment to remorse, compassion and magnanimity – befitting his stature, come the saga's conclusion, as a role model for the young and impressionable, like the boy orphaned at the beginning of *Soul...* by slavers.

Of all the black westerns of the period, the *Nigger Charley* films came closest to approximating the financial success of the urban thrillers that presented African-American characters trespassing on filmic terrain previously the preserve of white heroes. The formula – shaped by wider political and cultural factors, from civil rights to Black Power – was facile but effective, with the slicker examples – *Shaft* (1971) most famously – achieving considerable crossover appeal. Although *Legend...* in particular raked in a small fortune, critical hostility notwithstanding, it failed to cross colour lines; producer Spangler estimated that "ninety per cent of the take... has come from black patrons". The title alone would have been a turn-off for many audiences; not everybody shared Williamson's opinion that by wearing 'nigger' as a badge of pride he was neutralising it as a derogatory epithet, many years before hip-hop culture would brag about doing the same. Spangler was more pragmatic, or cynical, where the sensational title was concerned: "'Nigger' is box office."[2] It would stay that way until opposition from African-American pressure groups, combined with audience ennui, sapped blaxploitation of its strength as the Seventies wore on.

The kindest way to view these sloppily constructed works is to consider them as cousins of the pro-Indian westerns that aimed to overturn decades of negative Hollywood stereotyping; here, it is the image of the humble plantation black, content in servility, that is blasted aside by the aggressive, pro-active persona demanded by black audiences of the early Seventies. Charley's drive for self-determination, on behalf of his entire race, makes him more acceptable heroic material in hindsight than the pimps and hustlers usually associated with blaxploitation pictures. Williamson persevered with westerns, but failed to attain the same commercial heights: the routine *Boss Nigger* (1974), directed by the veteran Jack Arnold, was his best effort; the revenge-themed *Joshua* (1976), helmed by Spangler, by far the worst. **KG**

footnotes

1 Plantation life had been on the exploitation-film agenda before *Legend...* came along: in Herbert J. Biberman's melodramatic *Slaves* (1969) and the sensationalistic Italian 'mondo' movie *Goodbye Uncle Tom* (1971), for example. The most notorious film in this dubious cycle was Richard Fleischer's big-budget *Mandingo* (1975).

2 Spangler is quoted in the July and August 1972 editions of *Variety*.

The Life and Times of Judge Roy Bean

1972, Colour, 123 mins.

D: John Huston. P: John Foreman (First Artists, Coleytown Productions Inc). W: John Milius. Ph: Richard Moore. M: Maurice Jarre. St: Paul Newman (Judge Roy Bean), Roddy McDowall (Frank Gass), Victoria Principal (Marie Elena), Ned Beatty (Tector Crites), Jacqueline Bisset (Rose Bean)

"I know the law, and I have spent my entire life in its flagrant disregard."

John Huston and John Milius were wise to preface their disorderly tribute to one of the old West's more baroque personalities with the disclaimer, "Maybe this is not the way it was… It's the way it should have been." In one stroke they both summarise and satirise the role of the western in perpetuating myth at the expense of truth – "[elevating] the ideal over the authentic", in film historian Michael Coyne's words. They also acknowledge the near impossibility of separating historical fact from frontier fiction, especially with such a storied character at the centre.

The filmmakers' contribution to this process is pitched, unsteadily to say the least, between celebrating the dauntless pioneer spirit that brought law and order to the West (although Bean himself, played with almost maniacal intensity by Paul Newman, makes a mockery of due process) and embellishing Bean's legend with absurdities, all shot by Huston in a manner both comic and grotesque. More sincerely, they lament the advent of civilisation, which is viewed, typically for Milius, as an emasculating force and, typically for the genre, as hostile towards men like Bean who helped to pave its way. His intractability proves unpalatable to the new brooms of the new order, represented almost inevitably by a crooked capitalist, who leads the effort to eradicate Bean's memory ("Beanism") as the 20th century gets under way.

The film's contradictory nature does its erratic protagonist justice, however: a contemporary of Bean's, writing in the *San Antonio Weekly Express* in December 1882, described him as "a gambler, saloon keeper, Mexican

War veteran, Indian fighter, and bad man generally", but also as "generous, brave, courteous, and a keen lover of fun". Bean led a peripatetic life, surviving a number of scrapes with the law and run-ins with rivals; he was once almost hanged by vengeful friends of a man he'd killed. In 1882 he alighted on a site called Vinegarroon near the Pecos River in Texas, which is where Milius's script, flitting between fact and fantasy, takes up the tale: Bean is robbed and beaten by the denizens of a grungy saloon, but returns to wipe them out. He elects himself judge, becoming "the law West of the Pecos", and recruits five roving gunmen as his marshals, largely to drum up business by waylaying strangers and outlaws. He establishes a fiefdom, renaming the nascent town – and his saloon-cum-courthouse – in honour of Lillie Langtry, the actress he reveres and writes to, but is destined never to meet. (The real settlement of Langtry was about 15 miles to the West of Vinegarroon, its name inspired by the rather less glamorous figure of a railroad foreman.) Bean's regime is corrupt – there is much comic business made of his penchant for exacting arbitrary fines, even from a corpse at one point; another detail drawn from history. Nevertheless, he inspires loyalty among both his followers and the locals – although little is made of the real Bean's philanthropy – and the community begins to flourish.

The narrative fragments into vignettes, in which various characters cross Bean's path. Some of them have a bearing on the plot, notably Roddy McDowall's artful lawyer, Frank Gass, who subtly undermines Bean's authority and takes over the town when the judge resentfully rejects it, disappearing into the wilderness like another Milius character in a western made the same year, *Jeremiah Johnson*. Others are employed merely to put the judge's eccentricity into perspective: director Huston has a cameo as Grizzly Adams, who bequeaths Bean a beer-guzzling bear; Stacy Keach steals the film as Bad Bob ("Not Dirty Bad Bob from New Mexico, but the original Bad Bob"), an insane, raw-onion-eating albino who challenges Bean to a duel. This being a Seventies western, Bean has no compunction about shooting Bob through the back, with Huston aping Tex Avery by zooming in on a neat, gaping hole in his torso. "I don't abide giving killers a chance," says Bean. "He wants a chance, let him go someplace else."

This is a comic scene, but overall it is far from certain whether Huston and Milius are satirising Bean's cavalier brand of justice – an essential aspect of his character – or advocating it. The judge passionately defends public hanging as a deterrent while other, quieter characters set forth measured counter-arguments. The filmmakers'

muddled attitude towards their protagonist is the film's most problematic aspect, but should come as no surprise. It is safe to assume they were poles apart politically – Milius has consistently disdained liberalism, while Huston, less vocal on such matters, was among Hollywood's anti-HUAC elite in the Fifties – and they were allegedly at loggerheads throughout production over the tone of the film. (The director was also reportedly drunk for much of the time.) It doesn't help that Gass, whose respect for the law is more genuine than Bean's – he is aghast when the judge rips out a page from his statute book when it contravenes his opinion – is simultaneously depicted as a weasel, plotting his enemy's demise in the company of a gaggle of reformed prostitutes, who become Langtry's moral guardians. Laughing at Bean's hang-'em-high mindset, or the bad faith he demonstrates in the Bad Bob sequence, feels like an uncomfortable compromise. (The real Bean never deserved the ruthless reputation that has clung to him – biographer Jack Skiles found no evidence that he had ever hanged anybody; it is likely Bean became confused with Arkansas judge Isaac Parker, known to have strung up almost 90 men during his tenure.)

Writer and director expend most of their energy on lionising Bean, not so much deconstructing his legend as reconfiguring it, fashioning him into a symbol of what the character himself calls "moral fibre" – an ambiguous quality, redolent of ruthlessness and self-righteousness, that is implied to be lacking in the 20th-century world Bean ends up opposing. The judge himself fails to measure up to the heroic status he is afforded. Newman, who felt this was his best performance, immerses himself in the role, and it is entirely antiheroic: gruff, belligerent, often drunk and borderline callous (although Bean is no bigot: "I will hang a man for killing anyone, including Chinks, greasers, or niggers. I'm very advanced in my views"). Bearded and shambling, the star growls his way through the film – literally at one point, when face to face with his ursine companion. It is the most demented interpretation of Bean this side of Victor Jory's blazing-eyed portrayal in Budd Boetticher's *A Time for Dying* (1969). It is regrettable that Newman wasn't given more opportunities to portray the man behind the myth. This occurs only fleetingly, mainly in his scenes with his radiant young mistress, played by debutante Victoria Principal; one instance in particular stands out, when he outlines his vision for Langtry's future against a beautiful backdrop of setting desert sun.

That twilight is a metaphor for the decline of Bean and trailblazers of his ilk. The future of Langtry is not what he envisaged. In his absence – a period of 20 years – oil is discovered, derricks rise up, Gass becomes pre-eminent and gangsters exploit the opportunities provided by Prohibition (the voiceover narration blames this situation on the nefarious influence of newly emancipated women).

above: Paul Newman executes rough justice as the much-mythologised Roy Bean.

In a bravura yet ridiculous sequence, the judge returns, guns blazing, clearing up the town once again in the company of his dishevelled ex-marshals and his adult daughter, Rose, who has grown up in thrall to her father's legend. Better the individual eccentricities of a maverick like Bean, it seems, than the institutionalised corruption begat by oil and Gass. Only the Jersey Lily saloon survives the conflagration – a visual echo of the end of the silent western *Hell's Hinges*, in which William S. Hart's Blaze Tracy embodied the kind of "moral fibre" that Bean can only aspire to.

Bean's defiant stand against progress and modernity is the mark of a madman or a hero, or possibly both, depending on one's viewpoint. *The Life and Times…* is not a reliable guide – inevitable perhaps, given the uncertainty surrounding its creators' intentions. ("We departed from the… facts and made Bean more of a scalawag than he really was," admitted Huston, "but the film is, after all, more of a romance than a historical document."[1]) But the coda, in which Ava Gardner's Lillie Langtry finally pays a visit to Bean's saloon, now a monument to his memory as well as a shrine to the actress, certainly props up the legend, and sets a nostalgic seal on the story. The real Bean died in 1903 after a drinking binge prompted, it was said, by construction of a power plant nearby and a bout of melancholia that the world he knew was being transformed. Milius captures that feeling in his script, granting the judge a rare reflective moment: "The country's changing. The railroad's coming. People will pass by and look out the window and never know what it took to make all this… I guess it doesn't matter." Clearly, on this point at least, to Milius and Huston, despite their clashing perspectives, it mattered a great deal. **KG**

footnotes

1 Interview with John Huston by Gene D. Phillips (1973), reprinted in *John Huston: Interviews* (University Press of Mississippi, 2001).

Ulzana's Raid

1972, Colour, 103 mins.

D: Robert Aldrich. P: Carter DeHaven (Universal). W: Alan Sharp. Ph: Joseph Biroc. M: Frank De Vol.
St: Burt Lancaster (McIntosh), Bruce Davison (Lt. Garnett DeBuin), Jorge Luke (Ke-Ni-Tay),
Richard Jaeckel (Sergeant), Joaquín Martínez (Ulzana)

"Do you hate Apaches, Mr. McIntosh?"
"It would be like hating the desert because there ain't no water in it."

When a cavalry trooper, fleeing Apache braves, responds to a white woman's cry for help by shooting her in the head before doing the same to himself, it does more than graphically illustrate an old maxim of the Indian Wars. Putting a bullet in your brain, it was said, would be preferable to falling captive to an Indian – a fate worse than death, especially for a woman. This scene, shocking even in the wake of *The Wild Bunch* and *Soldier Blue*, demonstrates why one critic has called *Ulzana's Raid* a "post-liberal" western. This doesn't make it reactionary; its director, Robert Aldrich, was a lifelong liberal, as was the lead actor, Burt Lancaster; its writer, the Scottish novelist Alan Sharp, was a former shipyard worker who wrote films for some of New Hollywood's most notable leftists, from Peter Fonda (*The Hired Hand*) to Arthur Penn (1975's *Night Moves*). Rather, *Ulzana's Raid* offers a frank, unbiased reassessment of the Indian Wars as both a tragic clash of cultures and – somewhat inevitably, given its production context – a metaphor for racial discord in America and the conflict in Vietnam. Indeed, in purely narrative terms, with all its talk of tactics and strategy, this is as much a war film as it is a western.

Returning to a portrayal of Indians as inhuman savages, essentially unknowable, Aldrich's film contrasts

sharply with its revisionist forebears *Soldier Blue* and, especially, Penn's *Little Big Man*, while its pessimism concerning race relations is even more pronounced than in Aldrich's earlier *Apache*. The atrocities committed here are largely the responsibility of a band of Chiricahua Apaches, renegades from their reservation under the astute, ruthless leadership of Ulzana, played with inscrutable menace by Mexican actor Joaquín Martínez. They begin preying on isolated homesteaders, leaving mutilated corpses in their wake, including that of the suicidal soldier, and reinforcing the fear and hatred felt by the troopers sent to apprehend them.

The root of the trouble, as Aldrich and Sharp would have it, is incomprehension. Some of the soldiers, and their superiors, show no desire to understand why – and this is implicit, never baldly stated – Apaches imprisoned on what was once their land would behave this way; for the cavalry, it is about containing or eradicating an alien enemy. (More than one critic has compared the military's attitude and response here with that of Henry Fonda's command in *Fort Apache*, while the presentation of the rogue Indians is not dissimilar to that in *Major Dundee*.) But the key exchange in *Ulzana's Raid* involves the inexperienced lieutenant DeBuin, in charge of the pursuers, asking his Apache scout, Ke-Ni-Tay, why his people are so cruel: "It is how they are," he is told. "Each man that die, the man who kill him take his power. Man give up his power when he die. Like fire with heat. Fire that burn long time, many can have heat..." Ulzana, who is depicted as a force of nature, believes that torture, murder and desecration

above: Ulzana's Apaches revert to stereotype.

When in Southern California visit UNIVERSAL STUDIOS TOUR
AN MCA COMPANY
One man alone
understood the savagery
of the early American
west from both sides.
BURT
LANCASTER
In
ULZANA'S
RAID
co-starring
BRUCE DAVISON
RICHARD JAECKEL
Music by FRANK DeVOL · Written by ALAN SHARP · Directed by ROBERT ALDRICH · Produced by CARTER DeHAVEN
A CARTER DeHAVEN-ROBERT ALDRICH PRODUCTION · A UNIVERSAL PICTURE · TECHNICOLOR®

will restore the power he has lost while effectively in captivity; DeBuin that Christian fellowship will bring white and Apache together. The lieutenant's idealism crumbles along the trail, as he witnesses the barbarism of his own men ("Kind of confuses the issue, doesn't it?") and realises that the incompatibility of the races, and of their belief systems, will not be overcome so easily. The film "doesn't preach a policy of separate but equal, but it acknowledges that there is an irreducible difference".[1]

There is nothing facile about *Ulzana's Raid*; it neither vents its spleen nor fudges its conclusions. Script and direction are dispassionate, as are the characters who make the greatest impression: Ulzana himself, unmoved (on the outside at least) even by the death of his son; Ke-Ni-Tay, an Indian in Anglo service, is pragmatism personified; the veteran scout John McIntosh, whose hard-won wisdom – "Just sayin' my say – is ignored by an army brass portrayed as inflexible and unimaginative. (Had Aldrich had his way, the film would have focused on the education of DeBuin by Ke-Ni-Tay, but star power was required for financing and that led to Lancaster, returning to territory he and Aldrich had explored 18 years previously in *Apache*. The scout in that film was played by John McIntire; Lancaster's character here was named in his honour.[2])

The officers are indicative of what Douglas Pye has identified as a "failure of conviction" among the white colonists and their military guardians. There is an incongruity about their presence; the soldiers are first seen playing baseball against the backdrop of nature – its deceptive beauty captured superbly in Joseph Biroc's burnished images – and in the field they display little knowledge of or feeling for the land, whereas the Apaches seem to merge with the terrain. (Kevin Costner and Michael Blake would run further with this notion in *Dances with Wolves*.) Deferring to rank and rulebook, the troopers are frequently incompetent, not least in the final skirmish when they misread signals and mistime their attack. For all the soldiers' theoretical advantages in numbers and training, it takes the

above: Bruce Davison (left) and Burt Lancaster (right) as apprentice and veteran Indian trackers.

expertise of McIntosh and Ke-Ni-Tay to even the odds against versatile opponents skilled in guerrilla tactics. Fittingly, Ke-Ni-Tay has the honour of taking Ulzana's life – with McIntosh wounded, he is the only one able to match wits with the war chief and get close enough to make the kill. If DeBuin can ultimately report mission accomplished, it is a decidedly Pyrrhic victory.

"The film was saying at various levels that through ignorance of other peoples' cultures, behaviours, deities, customs, you do more damage to them than by intention," said Aldrich.[3] So it *is* a message movie of sorts, but one that requires, and rewards, careful scrutiny before the implications of its message can be properly understood. **KG**

footnotes

1 Edward Buscombe, *'Injuns!' Native Americans in the Movies* (Reaktion Books, 2006).

2 Director and star argued incessantly on the set: "The conflicts usually turned on the nuances of a given scene, how clearly the parallels were portrayed not only between the white men and the Indians but also with Vietnam," (Kate Buford, *Burt Lancaster: An American Life*, Aurum Press Ltd, 2000). Lancaster won the right to edit his own version of the film for European territories, rearranging a number of scenes, deleting some material and restoring footage not included in Aldrich's cut.

3 Interview with Robert Aldrich by Harry Ringel (1974), reprinted in *Robert Aldrich: Interviews* (University Press of Mississippi, 2004).

High Plains Drifter

1973, Colour, 105 mins.

D: Clint Eastwood. P: Robert Daley (Universal, Malpaso).
W: Ernest Tidyman, Dean Riesner [uncredited].
Ph: Bruce Surtees. M: Dee Barton.
St: Clint Eastwood (the stranger), Verna Bloom (Sarah Belding), Marianna Hill (Callie Travers), Mitchell Ryan (Dave Drake), Jack Ging (Morgan Allen)

"It couldn't be worse if the devil himself had ridden right into Lago."

Materialising out of a heat haze like an apparition, the title character of Clint Eastwood's sly allegorical western is the mysterious stranger *ne plus ultra*. Pertaining to the classical western while embodying the spirit of the new, he is both redeemer and ravager, a synthesis of Shane and the 'Bad Man from Bodie' from *Welcome to Hard Times*. He is also, of course, a reincarnation of Eastwood's enigmatic adventurer from the 'Dollars' films. Accompanied by synthesized whines and unearthly moans on the soundtrack, he descends from the mountains towards Lago, an isolated community perched vulnerably on the shores of a lake, and proceeds to puncture its veneer of bourgeois respectability, exposing its complicity in the fatal bullwhipping of its former marshal and devising a suitably fiendish punishment for the crime.

Riffing on *High Noon* and *Bad Day at Black Rock*, among other films, and with shades of the supernatural, the script was also a response to the Kitty Genovese incident of 1964, in which a young New Yorker was murdered while her neighbours allegedly looked on.[1] Lago is a "God-fearing town", but writer Ernest Tidyman finds little to admire in Middle American values. Far from being exemplars of the nation's noble self-image, "Each of the townsfolk seems to represent one of the seven deadly sins," as Christopher Frayling opined.[2] Like several prominent critics, Frayling interpreted the film as a "medieval morality play"; while Vincent Canby saw in Eastwood a personification of "pitiless Old Testament wrath".[3] The stranger targets the weaknesses of the townsfolk – their fear, greed, bigotry and mutual

animosity – with the same pinpoint accuracy with which he eliminates three heavies shortly after arriving ("Goddamnedest shooting I ever even heard of"). This prowess convinces the citizens to enlist his help against the trio of gunmen – played with lip-smacking relish by Geoffrey Lewis, Dan Vadis and Anthony James – whom they effectively abetted in the marshal's murder, only to sell them out to the law.

As a social critique, *High Plains Drifter* is often funny, but far from subtle. Lago is a crudely materialistic micro-society, "thoroughly corrupted by private economic interests".[4] The hotelier dismisses the marshal's murder as "the price of progress" – he had threatened to reveal that the local mine, the key to Lago's prosperity, is on federal land. So, given a free hand by the town burghers, the stranger hits them in the money belt, fleecing them of consumer goods and emptying the hotel for his sole use. (The preacher, outraged by this unchristian conduct, offers to put up

above: Clint Eastwood on set with Marianna Hill.

the expelled guests at the church – "And it won't cost you one cent more than regular hotel rates.") He preys on their prejudices, making the dwarf and dogsbody Mordecai (Billy Curtis) the town's new sheriff and mayor, and furnishing three "savages" – a harmless elderly Indian and two children – with supplies from the general store. (No other children are seen in town; clearly, this is not a healthy environment. Perhaps there is something in the water.) Compared with these moral failings, the film treats the stranger's indiscretions – raping Callie, the town hussy, to teach her "a lesson in manners" (for all her subsequent 'distress', she evidently enjoys the experience), and seducing the hotelier's frosty wife – as something of a tonic. Coming after *The Beguiled* and *Play Misty for Me* (both 1971), *Drifter* marked a step backwards for Eastwood's sexual politics, but this would be the last time, in his westerns at least, that he would allow his character's amorality to go unquestioned.[5]

Debate on the film usually focuses on the protagonist: is he man or ghost? As Eastwood recalls, the script identified his character as the late marshal Duncan's brother; there is enough of a likeness between the star and Buddy Van Horn, Eastwood's stunt double, who plays Duncan in flashbacks to his painful demise, to suggest a close familial relationship. But there is a mischievous ambiguity at play throughout. In the first flashback, Eastwood dissolves from a close-up of his face to that of the marshal, filmed at the same angle in similar low-light conditions, almost blurring their identities, while talk of Duncan's unmarked grave and restive spirit encourages the idea that the stranger is the lawman's vengeful spectre.[6] (And just how does he survive when Callie shoots at him in a bathtub from point-blank range?) Eastwood was keen to keep his audience guessing. "I thought about playing it a little bit like he was sort of an avenging angel," he told Richard Schickel; it is an early example of the star having fun with the image he had acquired, particularly from his Italian westerns, pushing his perceived invulnerability to near-parodic extremes. (Which may explain the miracle in the bathtub.) Allusions to the stranger's diabolical bearing, meanwhile, are given force by the bizarre sequence in which he instructs the inhabitants to paint the town red and renames it 'hell' – both a comment on their collective iniquity and, perhaps, a way for him to claim the place as his domain.

Not surprisingly, given this was Eastwood's first western as director, it bears the hallmarks of his mentors – "the abstract qualities of [Sergio] Leone and [Don] Siegel's commitment to genre conventions", as David Lusted has summarised.[7] But Eastwood, always his own man, finds a middle ground. The use of natural sound in the opening scene – hooves on soft sand, the squawking of gulls, the sudden crack of a whip – points to Leone's influence, as does the overt symbolism and mordant wit. (The baroque climax, when the stranger dispatches

above: Clint Eastwood (with Verna Bloom) plays a morbid joke on his mentors Don Siegel and Sergio Leone.

Duncan's murderers against a backdrop of flickering flames, would have graced the gothic Italian westerns centred on Django and Sartana.) But overall the style shows Siegel-esque restraint, reliant on Bruce Surtees' crisp, contrast-rich photography more than close-ups or extravagant angles. So too does the linearity of the storytelling (give or take the flashbacks that are shared between characters – a Leone lodestone) and the cynical perspective of a righteous outsider, *à la Dirty Harry* (1971). It is difficult to imagine Siegel, however, conjuring such an otherworldly atmosphere from the material. This has much to do with the way Eastwood maintains the protagonist's sinister mystique, but also his decision to locate the town of Lago on the edge of Mono Lake near Yosemite, an ancient oasis rich in alkaline deposits and ringed by volcanoes. It is an eerily isolated setting, trapping the characters in a world that is at once tangible (the timber-framed townscape, brilliantly designed by Henry Bumstead, was built from scratch) and dreamlike.

Eastwood was better placed than most American filmmakers to crossbreed ideas germinated in Europe with Hollywood western tropes: specifically themes rooted in *High Noon* and *Shane* – to which Eastwood would return in his *Drifter* rerun, *Pale Rider* (1985). John Wayne famously found *High Noon's* theme of cowardly citizenry un-American, an insult to the memory of the nation's pioneers. To nobody's surprise, he voiced the same complaint about *Drifter's* harsh lesson in civics. **KG**

footnotes

1 The incident occurred in Queens and gave rise to the so-called "bystander effect" or "Genovese syndrome", cited as a symptom of the callousness of contemporary urban life.

2 *Spaghetti Westerns: Cowboys and Europeans from Karl May to Sergio Leone* (Routledge & Kegan Paul, 1981).

3 *New York Times*, 20 April 1973.

4 John H. Lenihan, *Showdown: Confronting Modern America in the Western Film* (University of Illinois Press, 1980).

5 Older and wiser, although not necessarily abashed, Eastwood conceded to Richard Schickel in later years that the rape scene was probably a mistake: "I might do it differently if I were making it now. I might omit that" (Schickel, *Clint Eastwood*, Random House, 1996).

6 Students of the Italian western like to speculate that the 1969 film *Django il bastardo*, in which Brazilian actor Antonio de Teffè/'Anthony Steffen' played a gunman with a ghostly aura, may have influenced Eastwood and/or his writers. But that film was not distributed theatrically in America until 1974 – a limited run under the title *The Stranger's Gundown* – and the likelihood that Eastwood or Tidyman would have seen it (in Italy, perhaps) before beginning work on *High Plains Drifter* strikes me as extremely remote. A more likely antecedent would be the 1956 western *A Day of Fury*, in which Dale Robertson plays an unscrupulous gunfighter who contaminates a seemingly respectable town.

7 *The Western* (Longman, 2003). Although they are not visible in all prints, Eastwood had grave markers inscribed with Leone and Siegel's names planted in Lago's cemetery, as both an in-joke and an assertion of his independence as a film-maker.

Kid Blue

1973, Colour, 100 mins.

D: James Frawley. P: Marvin Schwartz (Marvin Schwartz Productions).
W: Edwin [Bud] Shrake. Ph: Billy Williams. M: Tim McIntire, John Rubinstein.
St: Dennis Hopper (Bickford Waner), Warren Oates (Reese Ford), Peter Boyle (Preacher Bob), Ben Johnson (Sheriff 'Mean John' Simpson), Lee Purcell (Molly Ford)

"You got no respect, boy."
"What am I supposed to have respect for?"

The architects of the counterculture were more likely to transmit their modish messages via contemporary cinematic forms such as the road movie or biker flick than the western. Nevertheless, a handful of westerns from this period were produced and staffed by the industry's merry pranksters, their protagonists advocating fashionable nonconformist ideals while undermining their message by recourse to the six-gun. These films were often misfires (see *Billy Jack*) or risible (*Zachariah*); *Kid Blue* is a case apart, although, from accounts of its chaotic production, it's a surprise that director James Frawley completed it at all. Co-star Lee Purcell recollects, "It was like being thrown into a Cirque du Soleil. People leaping out of second-storey windows; people with blood running down them. There was certainly acid and incredible amounts of drinking, incredible amounts of insanity. I'm surprised everybody didn't have a heart attack."[1] Yet from these hedonistic exploits there emerged a gentle meditation on social dislocation, the industrialisation of America at the turn of the 20th century and the nature of friendship.

above: Waner (Dennis Hopper) with his Indian allies

After bungling a train heist, outlaw Bickford Waner decides to go straight. In Dime Box, he finds an honest job as a barber's dogsbody but, due to his dishevelled appearance, soon finds himself under the scrutiny of Sheriff 'Mean John' Simpson. Staying in a boarding house, Waner is befriended by an open-minded Eastern couple, Reese and Molly Ford. After an altercation with one of the barber's customers, Waner gets work slaughtering chickens. He also ingratiates himself with a trio of displaced Indians, and spends philosophical moments with Preacher Bob, who is trying to build a pedal-powered "aerocycle". Unaware that Molly has seduced Waner, Reese finds his new friend a position in the Great American Ceramic Novelty Company. At a Thanksgiving Party given by its owner, Hendricks (Clifton James), the Fords discover Waner's real identity when an old consort of his, high-class whore Janet Conforto (Janice Rule), lets slip that he is in fact the notorious Kid Blue. As a rivalry grows between Janet and Molly, the outlaw is confronted by a heartbroken Reese, armed with a shotgun, and news of the affair reaches the townsfolk.

Rather than a nebulous notion of a moribund Wild West, Frawley and scriptwriter Bud Shrake place their story at a specific point in America's social history. The monolithic ceramics factory, by far the most prominent structure in Dime Box, represents the moment at which individuals, instead of being entrepreneurs or artisans serving their fledgling communities, began working, in their masses, for grand industrialists like Hendricks. New recruits load furnaces below ground while above them conveyor belts churn out homogenised items to be sold in the more developed cities of the East. Hendricks specialises in ashtrays – Waner is at first baffled to hear that, across the country, people smoke in their own homes. "You put yo' ashes on the ground," he says, the decorum of an evolving society beyond his comprehension.

What sets Waner apart from the town's suited drones is his long hair and casual demeanour. Outwardly naïve, his interactions with other townsfolk reveal him to

this page: Waner tries his luck with outlawry and modern modes of transport.

be streetwise, while his exchanges with the reactionary Drummer (Ralph Waite) crackle with generation-gap friction. Waner, all pin-head pupils and twitching energy, cannot share Drummer's pride in being a "working man" – although it is not for lack of trying – and dismays his antagonist with his ignorance of the Scriptures. (Drummer prescribes a dose of military discipline to teach the "boy" some respect – one can imagine the boos from the film's draft-dodging, antiestablishment demographic.) Waner's minor displays of rebellion enchant the Ford couple, and Warren Oates and Purcell delight as the proto-bohemian workers. Oates strikes a chord seldom heard with his fey, eccentric characterisation. More content with reading the classics than carrying a gun, and championing a society like that of the ancient Greeks where "men could love each other and they wouldn't be ashamed about it", Reese comes across as a man of fragile soul but enormous heart.

At 36, Dennis Hopper was a little weathered to play the "Kid", but he is far more endearing here than in the majority of his films. It's difficult to imagine him as a tough guy until we see his explosive attack, using a chair rather than his fists, on the loathsome barbershop customer who had earlier kicked him to the ground. The hostility he encounters expresses the film-makers' concerns about mainstream America's small-minded suspicion of misfits and outsiders. Why he has such a fearsome reputation is never satifactorily explained. He comes across more as a bumbler (in the opening scene, one of his fellow brigands literally bounces off a carriage roof during a train robbery), and the final demonstration of his alienation, when he joins the Indians to rob Hendricks' factory, is an anarchic mess, even if he does emerge victorious.

With Mean John, Drummer and Hendricks as traditionalist counterweights, the outlaw flits between a number of independent-minded characters. Peter Boyle dominates their scenes together as Preacher Bob.

Friends with benefits: Waner with Molly (Lee Purcell).

"God gave man the poppy and the coca plant for his benefit," he explains. "Also hemp and the peyote cactus." Although this amounts to a smug wink at the film's youthful target audience, the character has more substance. We find out that he has emigrated to the West because he lost his wife and children, the consequence of his weakness for beer and whiskey. The drug advocacy is less gratuitous than playful, particularly when Bob explains that eating peyote buds can bring a man closer to God. He's shown as a true believer rather than a charlatan, even willing to baptise the Native trio, in water shared by whites, despite Mean John's armed protestations.

Molly's character raises the issue of sexual politics, as it is she, rather than the more feral Waner, who kick-starts their affair. Her role eventually becomes that of a rejected, wounded lover, but she remains a stronger person than her husband. During his devastating confrontation with Waner, Reese tells his friend, "Can't you see that my insides are coming apart? You and her are the only people I have in the world." It's a desperately sad moment, anomalous in the context of the genre. Janet Conforto, meanwhile, is the more masculinised of the two women. Rather than just another whore, she is shown to be an equal to the bandit Kid, even assisting him in his return to his wayward life.

Touching on sexual politics, bigotry, social displacement and mass industrialisation, *Kid Blue* does not equal the sum of its parts. It is breezy and colourful, but there are too many elements to form a solid core. The counterculture western, which set down roots in Monte Hellman's *Ride in the Whirlwind* and *The Shooting*, was always going to be a tough proposition. How do you use the tropes of such a traditionally American genre to discuss seemingly radical themes? While the likes of Peter Fonda's *The Hired Hand* set about this more methodically, *Kid Blue* seems content to have fun with the proposition.[2] **CH**

footnotes

1 Quoted in Susan Compo, *Warren Oates: A Wild Life* (University Press of Kentucky, 2009). Purcell herself seemed to develop a temporary narcoleptic state and had to be supplied with oxygen between takes simply to stay awake.

2 It seems that *Kid Blue* was completed in 1972, but held back for distribution after Hopper's *The Last Movie* made his name mud in the film business. Even when it was released, its theatrical run lasted just four days and consequently it made no impression at the box office.

Pat Garrett and Billy the Kid

1973, Colour, 122 mins. (theatrical print 106 mins; 1988 restoration 115 mins.)

D: Sam Peckinpah. P: Gordon Carroll (Metro-Goldwyn-Mayer). W: Rudy Wurlitzer. Ph: John Coquillon. M: Bob Dylan. St: James Coburn (Pat Garrett), Kris Kristofferson (Billy), Bob Dylan (Alias), Richard Jaeckel (Kip McKinney), Katy Jurado (Mrs. Baker)

"So you finally found it out? When you gonna learn you can't trust anyone? Not even yourself."

A bona fide cinematic outlaw, Sam Peckinpah had, by the time of his final western, allowed his personal demons to devour much of his creative energy. Time-consuming, point-of-principle battles with studio executives hindered his ability to realise his ambitions. Clashes of personality resulted in him losing a war with MGM, declared in the middle of filming this eulogy to youth and the frontier spirit, and only a posthumous release of a preview print has allowed the scope of his ideas to be appreciated by modern audiences. Peckinpah would comment that he wanted to make films like Akira Kurosawa's, and *Pat Garrett and Billy the Kid* succeeds in achieving the epic intimacy of the great director's samurai pictures. Unlike the Boschian vision of *The Wild Bunch*, this film is, in Jim Kitses' words, "A languorous dirge, a drifting death-poem, a post-modern lament for an earlier America."[1] Moving in a dreamlike state towards an inescapable and tragic confrontation, Billy, embodying America's youth, is destroyed by the unholy alliance of capitalism and the state. Whereas *The Wild Bunch* alluded to the devastating effects of American foreign policy *à la* Vietnam, Peckinpah's genre swansong cried rage against the insidious corruption of Nixon-era politics.

Peckinpah was nothing if not an innovator and, in the film's justly lauded opening sequence, his editing expertise strengthens the bond between Billy and Garrett while elucidating the betrayal theme at the core of much of his work. While Rudy Wurlitzer's original script would not have the two men meeting until Billy's killing, Peckinpah sought to show the lawman as a victim of the same Santa Fe Ring that employed him to terminate Billy's reign as popular hero and scourge of big business. In his best cinematic sequence since the extraordinary gun battle at the close of *The Wild Bunch*, he crosscuts between sepia images of the elderly Garrett of 1909 being ambushed by minions of his erstwhile employers, and full-colour shots of Billy and his gang firing at chickens in Fort Sumner in 1881. Garrett joins in the grisly pastime, his rifle's report cutting back to his dying breath almost 30 years later. The implication is that Garrett's murder of Billy is also an act of suicide – the death of the older man's ideals as a true westerner. He meets his ignominious end as an accomplice, and finally an obstacle, to a dubious progress driven by the economic elite – "Chisum and every other goddamned landowner that's trying to put a fence around this country" – just as Billy in 1881 "has to be got out of the way" for rejecting "the collective reality".[2] The film's closing image segues back to Garrett's assassination, allowing the film to be read as the lawman's dying flashback.

In the first scene proper, in Fort Sumner's tavern, Garrett asks Billy to leave the territory; Billy elects to stay, despite knowing he'll have to challenge Garrett's authority as the new sheriff of Lincoln County. Garrett explains, somewhat mournfully, why he took up the badge: "It feels like… times have changed". Billy's retort, "Times maybe, not me," echoes the credo adopted by each of the director's romantic anti-heroes. It is what makes them admirable, yet makes their eradication a prerequisite for the evolution of America. Billy's gang are hostile towards Garrett, viewing him as a turncoat and a sellout; yet he is merely a pragmatist, who views their "stale" lifestyle – these are among the most

above: Friends disunited: Kris Kristofferson and James Coburn play out a theme dear to Sam Peckinpah's heart.

indolent, purposeless outlaws on film – with equal contempt. As Wurlitzer said, "Garrett represents the sort of compromise you had to make when the West began to get settled and big money came in."[3] It is little wonder that Peckinpah, a conflicted figure for much of his career, identified with Garrett so closely.

Constantly spinning yarns, forming legends, exaggerating – the characters give us a sense of a mythology germinating in the Western territories: "A vivid grassroots of the experience… a preoccupation with events and their audience."[4] Men are defined by past acts or, at the very least, by reputation. After an almost parodic gunfight in which both participants readily cheat, Billy shoots down Alamosa Bill (Jack Elam), a newly deputised former outlaw. "At least I'll be remembered," says Alamosa, satisfied that, in death, he will become part of Billy's legend. (His sentiments are echoed later by another of Garrett's reluctant helpers, Richard Jaeckel's Kip McKinney: "I hope they spell my name right in the papers.") Allusions to casualties of past skirmishes – an "old man they called US Christmas"; the historical lawman James Carlyle – precede killings in the present: a flock of bounty hunters who descend on Billy's hideout; the deputy J.W. Bell (Matt Clark), who makes the fatal mistake of turning his back on Billy during the latter's escape from Lincoln's jail.

Unlike *The Wild Bunch*, there is nothing ennobling or epic about violence in *Pat Garrett and Billy the Kid*; the grand scale is replaced by intimate encounters in squalid locales. In one such vignette, Garrett accosts three of Billy's cohorts in a ramshackle tavern. Garrett goads the increasingly inebriated Holly (Richard Bright) into reaching for his knife before shooting him, with no apparent compunction. There is no room for sentimentality in Peckinpah's West, any more than there is for fair play, as will be seen when Garrett finally tracks down Billy.

It is generally held by historians that Garrett and Billy were merely passing acquaintances, but dime-store and Hollywood mythologising has transformed this into a deeper, ultimately tragic, friendship. (Peckinpah based his first film script on this legend and it became, after much rewriting, *One-Eyed Jacks*, released in 1961.) The consensus is that Garrett did kill Billy at Fort Sumner and that his quarry was unarmed. In Peckinpah's film, the focus is upon this fictional alliance, the betrayal of friendship, old values and freedom, with Garrett the tool of Barry Sullivan's Chisum and other powerful landowners, Billy and his ragamuffin band idly rustling cattle or, in one zestful scene, wild turkeys. Ambiguity surrounds the central relationship. In the portentous opening exchanges in Fort Sumner's tavern, when Billy is asked why he doesn't simply kill Garrett, he replies, "He's my friend." (Billy's fidelity cannot be taken for granted, given he doesn't think twice about shooting or sacrificing other associates during the film.) There is also the question of Billy's means of escape from Lincoln. Who hid the gun in the outhouse, enabling Billy's flight? Could it have been Garrett himself, still unable to deliver his friend to the lop-sided justice of the ranchers?

Peckinpah augments the idea of intense male comradeship that had first surfaced in *Ride the High Country* and was laid bare in *The Wild Bunch*, culminating in something more akin to an ill-fated romance. A homosexual subtext may be too much of a stretch; Wurlitzer asserted, "What the film really is about is the love story of two men," but insisted this was not an interpretation that Peckinpah was comfortable with. Nevertheless, the protagonists' emotional proximity is far closer than any they share with their female counterparts. Garrett's marriage is fraught – his wife, whom he rarely sees, accuses him of being "dead inside" – and the romantic interludes Billy shares with women are fleeting and purely physical.

Herein lies the internal conflict of a director whose westerns were his most deeply personal works. The violence of his vision remains intact; if not, as intimated above, as spectacular as *The Wild Bunch*, it is still unrelentingly savage. During the Lincoln breakout, Billy peppers deputy Ollinger (another of R.G. Armstrong's demented religious zealots) with dimes from his own shotgun; the chicken shoot that adorns the title sequence is cruel and deservedly infamous; the torture of Paco and the rape of his daughter are graphic interludes; the brutal interrogation of a dotty old-timer by the odious Poe (John Beck), a Santa Fe Ring underling, is uncomfortable. However, more than any of his films, *Pat Garrett* is coloured by Peckinpah's essential romanticism, which lingers in the melancholy sunsets, the lament for lost liberty, the weary tallying of the true price of progress as a form of betrayal – "The systematic elimination of the youth and frontier spirit at the hands of its older generation, who are thus destroying themselves."[5] Perhaps the most fondly remembered scene is the death

PAT GARRETT E BILLY KID
METRO-GOLDWYN-MAYER PRESENTA PAT GARRETT E BILLY KID (PAT GARRETT AND BILLY THE KID)
CON JAMES COBURN · KRIS KRISTOFFERSON · BOB DYLAN E CON JASON ROBARDS
MUSICA DI BOB DYLAN
SCRITTO DA RUDOLPH WURLITZER
PRODOTTO DA GORDON CARROLL
DIRETTO DA SAM PECKINPAH
METROCOLOR · PANAVISION
LA COLONNA SONORA ORIGINALE DI BOB DYLAN E' INCISA SU DISCHI CBS

of Sheriff Baker (Slim Pickens), pressed into service by Garrett and mortally wounded in a shootout, his devoted wife (Katy Jurado) looking on as he staggers to the edge of a river to die, his dream of floating out of the territory in his unfinished boat dying with him.

No western of the Seventies amassed a greater array of acting talent, and the cameos and supporting players are vital to the sentiment of the project. Billy's gang are an idiosyncratic, eccentric bunch in whom "style has replaced substance". They are essentially "a cast of drifters, unhinged, heroes without a referent".[6] Among them are faces that gave Hollywood films of the era a new vitality. Kris Kristofferson had recently experienced the flush of fame, but it was beginning to dwindle. Paul Seydor commented that the director wanted "Kristofferson's persona as a self-destructive folk-rock star just beyond his peak years to infuse his performance as Billy", and it conveys the sense of a man snared in an existential crisis, unable to break from the shackles of his lifestyle, his stardom. Harry Dean Stanton, Richard Bright and Luke Askew bring rebel vigour to their roles as Billy's principal loyalists, while Kristofferson's bandmate, Donnie Fritts, firms up the periphery of the gang. Bob Dylan's Alias remains an enigma. Besotted with Billy, he throws away his printer's apron to join the gang and becomes an occasional confidant to his hero; there is a suggestion that he is an observer, a recorder of events, in line with Dylan's status as America's most feted balladeer.

The lawless lifestyle of this wild amalgam of new talent is threatened by some of the genre's most familiar character actors. James Coburn's gnarled elegance is perfect for a man whose ideals have been abandoned, while his increasingly reluctant deputies and accomplices bring with them the weight and experience of hundreds of westerns – Jack Elam, Richard Jaeckel, Slim Pickens, R.G. Armstrong, Katy Jurado, Barry Sullivan and Jason Robards, as the honourable Governor Wallace, all give fine performances as those who operate within the law, whether soiled by corruption or not.[7]

Like the faltering, shallow breaths of a dying man, the film draws towards its mournful close, and Peckinpah saves his final thoughts about the betrayal of principles and the demise of a pioneering era for his own character, the coffin-maker Will. Urging Garrett towards his ultimate treachery – and, by extension, his eventual fall from grace and favour with his paymasters – Will assails him with bilious but righteous anger, words that ought to cut deep in Garrett's heart. For Peckinpah, the surrogate patriarchs of *Ride the High Country* had succeeded in entering their houses justified despite the temptation of easy loot, and the Wild Bunch had earned redemption through camaraderie, blasting their way past the malevolent injustice of Mapache and into Valhalla. For the protagonists of this film, however, there appears that there is no hope. ("I'm a cynic now," Peckinpah said during shooting. "I don't think there's any more freedom left."[8]) They had been beaten by forces greater than a mere individual could challenge, and the director retired from westerns by inverting the famed final shot of *Shane*: Garrett rides away, a young boy pelting him with stones rather than pleading with him to stay, his own death sealed in the fate of his friend, lying on a veranda in New Mexico. **CH**

footnotes

1 *Horizons West: Directing the Western from John Ford to Clint Eastwood* (British Film Institute, 2004).
2 Rudy Wurlitzer to Jan Aghed, 'Pat Garrett & Billy the Kid', in *Sight & Sound*, spring 1973.
3 Ibid.
4 Jim Kitses, *Horizons West.*
5 *Horizons West.*
6 *Horizons West.*
7 Other actors considered for the role of Garrett included Charlton Heston, Rod Steiger, Paul Newman, Robert Mitchum and Henry Fonda. Had Fonda got the part, he could have faced off against his own son, Peter, who was in the running to play Billy.
8 Jan Aghed, 'Pat Garrett & Billy the Kid'.

top right: Kris Kristofferson with Bob Dylan as Alias, Billy's amanuensis.
bottom left: Billy's gang unload on a group of bounty hunters.

The Spikes Gang

1974, Colour, 96 mins.

D: Richard Fleischer. P: Walter Mirisch (The Mirisch Corporation, Duo Productions, Sanford Productions Inc). W: Irving Ravetch, Harriet Frank Jr. Ph: Brian West. M: Fred Karlin.
St: Lee Marvin (Harry Spikes), Gary Grimes (Will), Ron Howard (Les), Charlie Martin Smith (Tod), Arthur Hunnicutt (Kid White)

"I've left dying men behind me. What you do is shut your ears and close your eyes and run like hell... That's the only way to live."

The Spikes Gang capped a sequence of westerns that made it their business to educate young characters – as well as a film-going public weaned on romantic myths – in the unvarnished reality of life in the old West. In *The Cowboys*, *The Culpepper Cattle Co.* and *Jory* (1972), lessons were learnt on the trail drive; *Bad Company* portrayed its protagonists as fledgling outlaws. Richard Fleischer's entry combines elements of all these films, functioning almost as a coda to the last named as it apprentices its callow heroes to a grizzled criminal. As Tom Milne wrote, *Spikes* "might almost be said to unfreeze the last image of *Bad Company* to show what happens in that uncompleted tyro attempt at a bank robbery".[1] While Robert Benton's film preserved its heroes in an act of bravado, one could only infer that their prospects were bleak; *The Spikes Gang* confirms this likelihood with unsparing brutality.

The effect, if not always the object, of these coming-of-age tales was to harness the disillusionment of the 1968 generation with the social structures, regulations and mores associated with their parents. (Writers Irving Ravetch and Harriet Frank Jr. had previously sided with older characters against young upstarts, however, in the westerns *Run for Cover* [1955] and *Hud*, and took a lenient view of patriarchal authority in their John Wayne vehicle *The Cowboys*.) The trio of farm boys at the heart of this story rebel not just against the drudgery of frontier life, but against the inability of their elders to see beyond it. The youngsters are given a foretaste of the wider world when they rescue a wounded bank robber, Harry Spikes, who sees they are "old before [their] time", not to mention gullible, and paints for them an enticing portrait of his lifestyle. Will's father is a joyless disciplinarian with a Protestant work ethic, predestined to die working the land and seemingly intent that his son should follow suit. When he beats Will for abetting Spikes's recovery and giving him a horse, Will absconds with another mount and meets up with his friends, Tod and Les, for what they hope will be a great adventure: "The one thing we won't do is kiss any man's boot."

Inevitably, they encounter only hardship and hostility: subsisting on stolen communion wafers, shooed away by suspicious ranchers when they ask for work, ordered out of town by a surly sheriff. In desperation, and with Spikes's words ringing in their ears, they spontaneously rob a bank but, in the mêlée, Tod kills a man, they lose the money and flee into Mexico. The tone switches, not always smoothly, between dramatic and light-hearted modes as their ill fortune continues over the border, where they end up in prison after stealing from a shop and running straight into a police station. The fortuitous appearance of Spikes, like a smooth-tongued devil at a crossroads, marks the beginning of their criminal career in earnest. He bails them out, enlists them as his acolytes, buys them food and clothes (and spectacles for short-sighted Tod) and teaches them to shoot. These scenes are played genially, but they mask the tragic turn the boys' lives have taken and the true nature of the man they have adopted as their hero and leader.

Will has dreams in which he is rejected by the cold, judgemental figure of his father, and Spikes is positioned as a more attractive alternative – roguish, easy with his money and dedicated to the good life. Lee Marvin had charisma to burn, and it is easy to see how three impressionable youngsters would fall under Spikes's spell. But the menacing side of Marvin's persona, tied to his intimidating physicality, is never far from the surface, reminding us that Spikes is a seasoned criminal, with the hard-won cynicism accrued during a life spent on the lam and the instincts of a predator. Instead of honour among thieves, his credo is survival of the fittest. When a veteran bank robber (Arthur Hunnicutt) tries to convince Spikes that he still has what it takes, Spikes issues a savage rebuff – "Why don't you drag your ass up on a porch somewhere and eat your mush and let your grandchildren take care of you?" – and then watches dispassionately as the old man, desperate to prove his mettle, goads Tod and Will, who shoots him dead. The only way to stay alive in this business, he tells his pupils, is to shrug off dead weight and set aside compassion, and when Tod is badly wounded in a bank raid, Spikes orders him left to die: "He's a goner. Put a hat over his face." The disparity between the boys' camaraderie and their mentor's callousness ruptures their relationship. When Spikes, ever the opportunist, kills Les for the bounty on his head, Will tracks him down to a squalid hotel room for a shootout that claims both their lives.

The Spikes Gang is a modest film. Fleischer's direction generally lacks verve (he was being harsh, however, when he called the film "a disaster"[2]), sparking to life only intermittently – the initial, bungled bank robbery; the last, fatal meeting of Will and Spikes, the cramped setting almost dank with sweat and tension, their bodies slammed and smashed by bullets. As a tragedy of friends led astray by a combination of false hopes, merciless fate and diabolical design, its resonance derives from the unrelenting honesty of the script and from the central performances. Few young actors of the period communicated bruised ideals as sensitively as Gary Grimes, while Ron Howard and Charlie Martin Smith are likeable enough to make one forget that their characters are underwritten. But it is Marvin's film, his characterisation a rich stew of bonhomie, low cunning and steely impassivity. It is a convincing and candid portrayal of the ruthlessness without which an outlaw of advancing years would surely never have survived so long. **KG**

footnotes

1 *Monthly Film Bulletin*, July 1974.
2 Quoted in Donald Zec, *Marvin* (New English Library, 1979).

Posse

1975, Colour, 93 mins.

D: Kirk Douglas. P: Kirk Douglas (The Bryna Company). W: William Roberts, Christopher Knopf. Ph: Fred J. Koenekamp. M: Maurice Jarre. St: Kirk Douglas (Howard Nightingale), Bruce Dern (Jack Strawhorn), Bo Hopkins (Wesley), James Stacy (Hellman), Luke Askew (Krag)

"Where would this country be without ambition?"

Kirk Douglas's second accomplishment as a director reflects the influence of his liberal consciousness, and balances the traditions of the American western with the modish anti-Establishment vibe then pulsing through New Hollywood. A satirical critique of political manoeuvring in all its cynical, ugly glory, it is veiled by a violent cat-and-mouse plot in which lawman Howard Nightingale and law-breaker Jack Strawhorn are exposed as being more alike than either would care to think. "*Posse* made a significant statement," said Douglas. "It presents the two sides of a coin: how those who fight for the law can become twisted and become like the criminals they are pursuing. How easy it is to become the bad guy when you think you're doing good."[1] *Posse* is a flawed but thought-provoking example of what an intelligent and ambitious filmmaker can do by subtly subverting genre expectations.

Nightingale's objective is to be elected to the US Senate; for this to happen, he needs to ensure that notorious outlaw Strawhorn is captured and hanged. In a ballsy opening sequence, Strawhorn sees his men massacred and $40,000 in stolen money go up in smoke. He manages to escape, winding up in Tesota, Nightingale's power base, where he kills the turncoat who sold him out. The outlaw is then forced to shoot the town sheriff. Promising the citizens that justice will be done, Nightingale unleashes his quasi-militaristic posse on the scene. With their training and organisation they easily outclass the rag-tag "cucarachas" that replace Strawhorn's original gang and, after another bloody massacre, Strawhorn is finally captured.

As Nightingale gives a victorious speech to his potential constituents in Tesota, the outlaw looks on from his jail cell, amused by his opposite's silver-tongued oratory. Strawhorn then cunningly escapes from the prison car transporting him to his execution. While the posse members begin to realise that their employer plans to discard them, the outlaw takes the marshal hostage aboard his own private train – the symbol of his authority and overweening ambition. Returning to Tesota with his captive, Strawhorn books them both into the presidential suite of the hotel and, with the posse sorrounding the building, demands the return of his $40,000.

From Wyatt Earp to Will Kane, marshals and sheriffs have always been one of the bedrocks of American western mythology, bastions of the nation's noble self-image. Douglas's reimagining of this archetype is far less complimentary. Nightingale believes that the capture of Strawhorn is his golden ticket, a simple

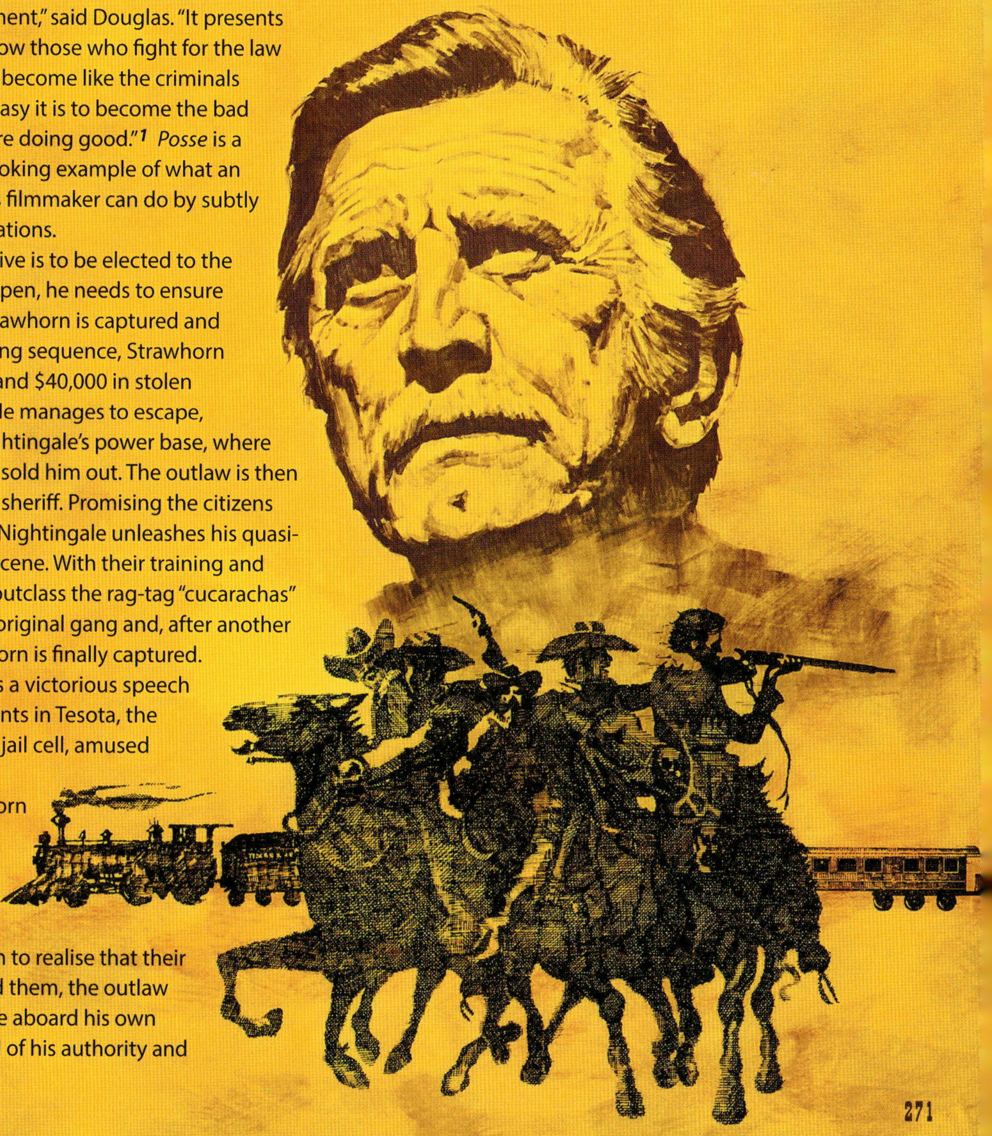

stepping stone to Congress: "If I don't get him, I don't get elected." His zealous pursuit of the bandit is clearly fuelled not by a calling to protect and serve, but to enhance his career. The twisted irony that a man's success can derive directly from the death of another is not lost on Nightingale's unruffled quarry: "Climbing over my dead body to get to the United States senate. That ain't honesty. That's horseshit." Even the local newspapermen have got the marshal's number. When confronted by the chief reporter, Nightingale brags that the country is built by ambitious men. "You're *too* ambitious," is the reporter's curt response.

Douglas plays Nightingale as a vainglorious monster, his lack of ideological conviction complemented by an unhealthy career lust. It is no fluke that this film was produced in 1975, not long after Americans were promised that, "There can be no whitewash at the White House." Any idealistic hopes had, by then, been snuffed out by violence, assassinations and evidence of corruption. The script captures the cynical zeitgeist and bludgeons it home with the central speech by Nightingale, immediately after he captures Strawhorn: "How do you reform a rattlesnake? With a shotgun." The boastful, swaggering lawman doesn't forget to laud his own achievements – "Every criminal I set out to capture is in jail or in his grave"– or those of his railroad paymasters, and finally capitalises on sentiment, uniting the people of Tesota in memory of their dead sheriff. As Nightingale presses palms and generally impresses, the members of his posse (among them the sterling character players Bo Hopkins and Luke Askew) enjoy the fruits of their association with the town's hero, screwing the wives and daughters of Tesota, causing rivulets of bad blood to flow through the community as the siege scenario plays out.

While Nightingale represents the venal political class, it is counterculture icon Bruce Dern's sardonic upstart who steals the show. This was astute casting. The B-movie veteran and Roger Corman protégé (*The Trip*; *The Wild Angels*) invades this western world like a serene street hipster. While not enjoying the more unpalatable aspects of banditry – he clearly doesn't want to shoot the sheriff of Tesota, giving him ample warning beforehand – Strawhorn garners a certain satisfaction from thwarting the marshal's plans. There are echoes of *3:10 to Yuma* (1957) in their jailhouse exchanges, although the language is savvier, updated for the Seventies, as marshal and bandit battle intellectually to achieve supremacy. Nightingale in particular betrays how deeply personal this contest has become: "I don't usually attend hangings; they make me sick to my stomach. But, in your case, I'll make an exception." The difference in the actors' styles adds resonance to the film's fashionable themes. Dern is a subtle player; asked to express emotion, he does so with a minimum of physical movement. In the presidential suite, Douglas is very rigid, maintaining his authoritarian posture while under duress, while Dern is so laid-back as to be almost somnambulistic.[2]

Dern's laconic characterisation, combined with the anti-Establishment themes, stark visual design and cynical denouement, align *Posse* with a brand of cinema, prevalent in the Sixties and Seventies, that sought to entertain while ridiculing traditional definitions of good and evil. It is fitting that Nightingale ends the film humiliated, deserted by the townsfolk and his own posse, who opt to side with Strawhorn. Without hitting all the right notes, the intelligent script, direction and performances document a time when disaffection was commonplace, when mistrusting The Man was *de rigueur*. As untrammelled as ever by notions of a 'star image', Douglas happily took on the mantle of antagonist while fashioning an outwardly conventional, yet quietly seditious, genre piece. **CH**

footnotes

1 Quoted in Douglas's autobiography, *The Ragman's Son* (Simon & Schuster, 1988). To further strengthen the film's political message, Douglas went on to say, "In our own government, people suddenly switch over and become agents, use their knowledge to work against us, like [Edwin] Wilson, the CIA agent who sold arms to Libya. Or the overzealous participants in Watergate. Now it's the Iran-Contra hearings. Ollie North captured part of the public with his boyish looks and endearing voice. They made him a hero. Or was he a villain who lied, altered and shredded documents, corrupted his secretary? He thought he was doing the right thing. That's a better movie than *Posse*".

2 Douglas was obviously impressed by his co-star, hoping that the film would establish Dern as a leading man. "I realised later that he would always be a character actor, because he thought of himself that way. In the scene that opens the picture, he comes out of a barn. Walks out, looks around. The first time he did it, he came out of the barn, looked around and squinted, his face all scrunched up. I said, 'Go back in the barn. Think that you're Gary Cooper and open the door. Walk right straight out and don't do anything. Just look around.' He looked handsome!" (*The Ragman's Son*).

Rancho Deluxe

1975, Colour, 94 mins.

D: Frank Perry. P: Elliott Kastner (EK Corporation). W: Thomas McGuane. Ph: William A. Fraker. M: Jimmy Buffett. St: Jeff Bridges (Jack McKee), Sam Waterston (Cecil Colson), Elizabeth Ashley (Cora Brown), Charlene Dallas (Laura Beige), Clifton James (John Brown)

"Filth and evil... is one subject I'm slow to tolerate."
"That's two subjects."
"Son, you are in a dangerous country."

This smart-mouthed, rather self-regarding semi-parody is significant as the first scripted effort by Thomas McGuane, subsequently a major literary figure. Charting the misadventures and musings of two shiftless modern-day rustlers (all of its major characters operate in pairs), it is like a wry rehearsal for McGuane's more fully realised western scripts: *The Missouri Breaks*, quirkier still, which transposed essentially the same plot and character types from contemporary Montana to a 'classical' western setting; and the more sober *Tom Horn*.

Frank Perry's matter-of-fact direction allows McGuane's misfits room to breathe, but doesn't provide them with much of a platform from which to develop. Jeff Bridges, as footloose and insolent as he was in *Bad Company* and *Thunderbolt and Lightfoot* (1974), has New American Cinema stamped right through him. Jack is carefree and cocksure. Like Bobby Dupea in *Five Easy Pieces* (1970), he is the scion of wealthy parents who has rejected his privileged background and played a losing hand at marriage. The film dispenses with these biographical details in a cursory

manner – one brief visit to his family home, including a terse reunion with his ex-wife, ends in recrimination and smashed crockery, but thereafter the matter is dropped. Jack's partner, played by Sam Waterston, is a sardonic mixed-race Native American, similarly alienated from tribal culture and similarly thinly sketched. It is Cecil who is the source of much of the film's offbeat observational humour. Looking around at the commercialised and semi-industrialised landscape of the modern West, he predicts that instead of *Cheyenne Autumn*, in 20 years Hollywood will be making *Aluminium Autumn*.

Shooting cattle and selling the beef, sometimes for rent money, sometimes for the hell of it, the protagonists refer to themselves, tongues in cheeks but not entirely inaccurately, given their resemblance to the casual drifters of numerous westerns of old, as "the last of the plainsmen". With no idea what to do with the money accrued from their schemes, one of which involves kidnapping and ransoming a prized white bull, they revel in the relative freedom their lifestyle affords them. Their one ambition, shared with their peers in other counterculture movies, is to defy their elders – positioned inevitably as the embodiment of a staid society.

More specifically, their mission, such as it is, is to poke their fingers through the hollow centre of Western and Middle American morality. Its guardians are typified by the middle-aged and starchy Wilbur Fargo (Bert Conway), whose daughters take up with Jack and Cecil. Bursting in on the quartet after a night of lovemaking, Wilbur makes a display of the "floozies and whoremongers" for his extended family: "Look what the world has come to," he growls before an audience of aunts, uncles and grandparents. (As representatives of an older age group, the latter rebuke Wilbur for this invasion of the youngsters' privacy.) It falls to Jack to defend the tarnished honour of the girls and, by extension, that of his generation. Pulling a gun, he forces Wilbur to apologise to his daughters. As a further rebuttal, he and Cecil steal Wilbur's beloved Lincoln Continental and riddle it with bullets. Taking a moral stand on the part of the Establishment in the present context merely makes a man look foolish.

This mocking tone colours McGuane's jaded contemplation of changing times and the fading of frontier values. For all his talk of upholding the code of the West, John Brown, the rancher who suffers most at the hands of the poachers (a suitably uptight turn from Clifton James) is a displaced Easterner, who patrols his spread in a helicopter. His ranch hands (Harry Dean Stanton and Richard Bright) are similarly inauthentic, not to mention incompetent; they even make common cause with Jack and Cecil in a plan to rob their employer. And the elderly stock detective Brown hires (a splendid role for Slim Pickens) is not only a former rustler but expends as little effort as possible in the course of his investigations. His interest is piqued only briefly when he discovers the cattle have been shot with a vintage Sharps buffalo rifle: "It's downright romantic!"

The glorious image of Pickens on horseback, six-gun in hand, confronting the anti-heroes in a trailer-rig on their way to meet their confederates, suggests that the old ways still have some relevance (and makes for an ironic reversal of the deflating climax of *Lonely Are the Brave*). Characteristically, however, it is a sham; the boys have been sold out and the ambush staged – for the benefit of picnicking locals – to rescue Pickens' reputation. Jack and Cecil check in to 'Rancho Deluxe' – the state prison farm – while the wily old Westerner, buttressed by his faux-naïf niece, proves he can hustle as well as any hipster. Perhaps, McGuane means to tell us, 'twas ever thus, a message his myth-deflating script for *The Missouri Breaks* was equally keen to impart. **KG**

above: Jeff Bridges (left) and Sam Waterston (right) as the rustlers/rebels bound for Rancho Deluxe.

Buffalo Bill and the Indians, or Sitting Bull's History Lesson

1976, Colour, 123 mins.

D: Robert Altman. P: Robert Altman (Mayflower Films, Dino De Laurentiis Corporation, Lion's Gate Films, Talent Associates-Norton Simon Inc). W: Alan Rudolph, Robert Altman. Ph: Paul Lohmann. M: Richard Baskin. St: Paul Newman (The Star, William 'Buffalo Bill' Cody), Joel Grey (The Producer, Nate Salisbury), Kevin McCarthy (The Publicist, Major John Burke), Harvey Keitel (The Relative, Ed Goodman), Geraldine Chaplin (The Sure Shot, Annie Oakley)

"History is nothing more than disrespect for the dead."

Heralded by a cavalry bugle and the bold colours of the Stars and Stripes, an assault on a homestead by Natives is repelled by the extraordinary bravery of New World pioneers. The camera's eye slowly draws back to divulge the deceitful nature of this tableau: it forms part of Buffalo Bill Cody's Wild West Show, a synecdoche for American mythology and the western genre itself. Staged for a paying audience and endorsing Manifest Destiny, Cody's travelling circus is exposed by Robert Altman as a repository of falsehood and legend-making. Off screen, in a nod towards the parallels between these shows and their cinematic counterparts, the master of ceremonies orders the action to cease. In a saloon, dime-novel bard Ned Buntline (Burt Lancaster) holds court, telling tales of "the scrawny-looking kid" he discovered and from whose exploits he created a legend. In Cody's shows, history was conflated with "mythology… [creating] a mythic space in which past and present, fiction and reality could co-exist."[1] In his film, Altman looks at the foundation of western mythology and marks, with both ire and heavy-handed irony, how historical fact has been largely ignored.

Earning his film-making spurs with TV westerns (*Maverick*, *Lawman*), Altman's immoderate directorial approach was firmly established for the big screen with the release of *M*A*S*H* (1970) and the western *McCabe & Mrs. Miller*. In *Buffalo Bill*, his style remains both innovative and frustrating – prowling camerawork, ensemble acting, overlapping dialogue. Quirkiness abounds: stuntmen career in and out of shot at inopportune times, as the film "constantly questions what reality is by declaring its own artifice as well as its own confusion."[2] Cody's chaotic troupe is full of oddball characters, from trick-shots to wranglers, while the involvement of Native peoples testifies to the taming of those feral elements for which men like Cody were responsible. So does the herd of bison that thunders into the arena, as imperious a symbol of the American West as the great Sitting Bull – Cody's biggest attraction (besides himself). The great chief's participation has been posited as "an ironic reversal of the captivity myth… with Sitting Bull, rather than the helpless white woman, held captive… [symbolising] the values imperilled by commercial mass culture."[3]

While *Buffalo Bill* does not declare itself as an accurate biopic of Cody and his achievements (or perhaps failures) in vintage entertainment, Altman nevertheless remains stolidly angry about the lies propagated by the Wild West and other spurious 're-enactments'. The oddball characters populating the film are spectres of the era, used figuratively as misrepresentatives of the past, emblematic of Altman's opinion of how his country has radically modified its bloody history. Cody was 11 when he lost his father – an anti-slavery activist – and had to support his family, eventually becoming one of the nation's most celebrated Indian fighters. He was a perplexing man: an army hero who once said that Indian outbreaks were always the result of "broken promises and broken treaties by the government"; a man who apparently had more empathy than most white men with a people in the process of being ethnically cleansed. However, this complex figure is portrayed here as a callous, preening braggart who oversees an operation in which casual racism is rife (there is segregation; black men are referred to as "darkies") and Indian folklore and spirituality are derided. Cody's bravery is undermined by Paul Newman's bombastic rendition of a whiskey-sodden, opera-loving, often impotent buffoon, his efforts to outsmart the implacable Sitting Bull and his interpreter, William Halsey (Will Sampson), constantly thwarted. In his attempt to hold the nation accountable for its misdeeds, Altman distorts the character of Cody to fit his agenda, citing him as an icon of Native American exploitation and historical falsification. As the foolish President Grover Cleveland (Pat McCormick) remarks of Cody in admiration, "It's a man like that who made the country what it is today."

Lancaster endows the small but intrinsic role of Ned Buntline with as much cynicism as the film itself "about the denial of history and justice in the promotion of the Wild West, both as myth and show."[4] Buntline's life, in which he associated with criminal gangs and escaped a lynching, was almost an adventure story in itself, but it was his associations with Cody and Wild Bill Hickok that would establish him as one of America's principal purveyors of myth. While the sycophants around Cody – typified by Harvey Keitel's naïve, idolatrous nephew – help to uphold the legends he tries to promote as gospel, it is Buntline who appears, with sagacious words, to ground Cody, his own literary creation, in reality: "Any youngster like yourself who figures to set the world on fire better not forget where he got the matches." Although the writer holds equal responsibility for the distorted history of the continental conquest, it seems that Buntline cannot reconcile Cody the Indian fighter with the showman before him. His presence is a cause of irritation for the star's fawning followers, leaving him to provide stinging commentary on a spectacle that even seems to mock the courage it took to conquer the frontier.

above: Paul Newman as Buffalo Bill (standing, 2nd left) with his troupe, including Kevin McCarthy (reclining) and Harvey Keitel (standing, 2nd right).

The ease with which mythology becomes accepted reality is the crux of Altman's argument. "My intention was just to take a more honest look – satirical or not – at some of our myths."[5] The timing was critical – the film's release during the Bicentennial was "a pie in the face, as it were, at the big patriotic party".[6] (If audiences were turned off by Altman's message, critics took umbrage more with his methods, firing out terms such as "puerile", "self-indulgent", "pretentious" and "smart-aleck".) For Altman, myths "become rigid. They don't move enough... They've all become imitated to the point where they become like granite, and they're not interesting."[7] Legends are constantly reinforced by the Show: Cody's marksmanship is made easier because his gun is loaded with buckshot; he expects the Indians to replay the Battle of the Little Bighorn as if it had been a sneak attack; when Sitting Bull tells him that to accurately re-create the skirmish he ought to show unarmed women and children being slaughtered by soldiers, Cody becomes apoplectic and threatens to fire his diminutive opponent. It is Annie Oakley, the only white character afforded Altman's sympathy, who forces him to back down; she functions as America's liberal conscience. Perhaps the most affecting scene, in a film difficult to engage with emotionally, occurs when news of Sitting Bull's death is relayed to the camp. While most remain unmoved, Annie is seen weeping, lamenting the mistreatment of such a noble warrior; the next image is that of an unmarked pauper's grave.

Was Altman vindicated in singling out Cody for pioneering what the director clearly saw as historical whitewashing? Certainly Cody's creation was one of the most celebrated Wild West pageants, even touring Europe; it greatly simplified frontier history for the curious, "clarified the ambiguities of the Old West... [and was] long on bombast and short on introspection".[8] According to Altman, "Buffalo Bill Cody was the first movie star, the first totally manufactured American hero."[9] Yet the Cody of fact conflicts with Newman's impersonation. Although Indian attacks on a settlers' cabin would often close the real Wild West Show, the re-enactment of Custer's Last Stand is apocryphal; its inclusion shows that Altman was following his own ideological programme. Cody and his entourage reflect a dismissive attitude towards the Indians – and consequently towards history – that seems to have provoked the director; it was an attitude that allowed the cleansing of the historical record and has shaped popular perceptions of the American West ever since. Redressing the balance was, in the director's eyes, the noble thing to do. In this sense it is not so much Sitting Bull's history lesson as it is Altman's. If he had framed his argument in a less didactic manner, the point may have been appreciated more readily than it was. **CH**

footnotes

1 Richard Slotkin, *Gunfighter Nation: The Myth of the Frontier in 20th-Century America* (University of Oklahoma Press, 1998).
2 William G. Simon and Louise Spence, 'Cowboy Wonderland, History and Myth', in *Westerns: Films Through History* (Routledge, 2001).
3 Ibid.
4 David Lusted, *The Western* (Longman, 2003).
5 Interview with Robert Altman by Bruce Williamson in *Playboy* (August 1976).
6 Shawn Levy, *Paul Newman: A Life* (Aurum, 2010).
7 Interview with Robert Altman by Graham Fuller in *Projections 2: A Forum for Filmmakers*, reprinted in *Robert Altman: Interviews* (David Sterritt, ed; University of Mississippi Press, 2000).
8 Thomas L. Altherr, 'Let 'Er Rip: Popular Culture Images of the American West in Wild West Shows, Rodeos and Rendezvous' in *Wanted Dead or Alive: The American West in Popular Culture* (University of Illinois Press, 1998).
9 Interview with Robert Altman by Bruce Williamson in *Playboy* (August 1976).

above: Tall in the saddle: fancy riding complements myth-making and pageantry.

The Missouri Breaks

1976, Colour, 126 mins.

D: Arthur Penn. P: Elliott Kastner, Robert M. Sherman (EK Corporation). W: Thomas McGuane. Ph: Michael Butler. M: John Williams. St: Marlon Brando (Robert E. Lee Clayton), Jack Nicholson (Tom Logan), Randy Quaid (Little Tod), Kathleen Lloyd (Jane Braxton), Frederic Forrest (Cary)

"Do you have anything to say to the court? Make it colourful, as life on the frontier can be pretty tedious."

A languid tale of a roguish horse thief clashing with an imperious land baron, *The Missouri Breaks* proved there was much about New Hollywood cinema that could leave audiences bored and confused, longing for simpler, more traditional fare. The presence of both Jack Nicholson and Marlon Brando should have guaranteed the film a better hearing, but such titanic names above the title didn't prevent theatre owners from breathing a collective sigh of relief when its brief run was over. Unlike the grizzled and embittered characters that populate the film, however, time has dealt a fairer hand to Arthur Penn's peculiar western drama.

David Braxton (John McLiam), an irascible landowner, whose stock is being depleted by a band of down-at-heel rustlers, hangs one of the miscreants without trial, and gang leader Tom Logan vows to even the score. He and his men kill Braxton's foreman and, to store their stolen horses, buy a small ranch close to Braxton's spread. All except Logan ride north of the border to steal horses from the Royal Canadian Mounted Police, leaving their boss to look after the property.

While the rustlers are conducting their mission, Braxton's daughter, Jane, whose viewpoint on hanging thieves is the opposite of her father's, takes a shine to Tom. Braxton, meanwhile, has hired Robert E. Lee Clayton, an eccentric and dandified regulator, to put a stop to the rustlers' activities. Armed with a deadly

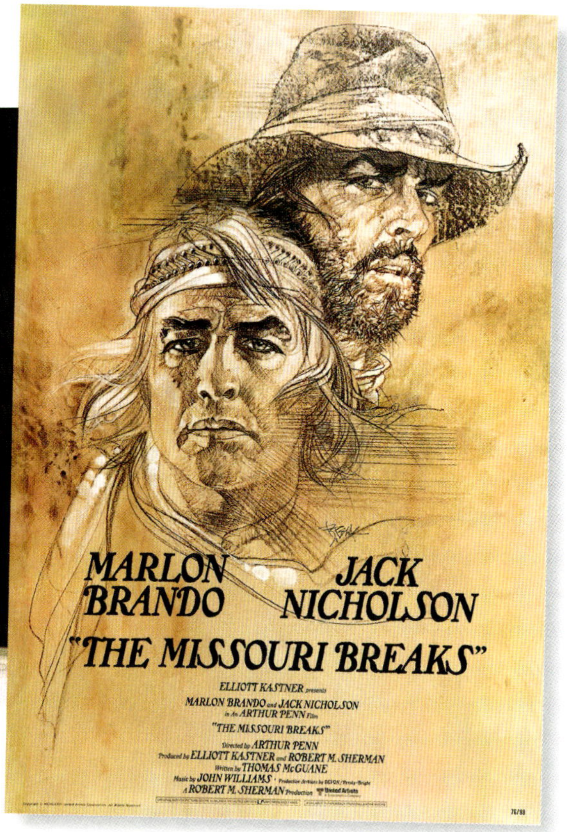

accurate 1859 Creedmoor Rifle and a makeshift throwing star, Clayton begins stalking his prey, taunting Logan and spying on his trysts with Jane. Too unpredictable and psychotic for Braxton, he is asked to leave, but the bounty killer, amused by the challenge, stays to eliminate the gang one by one – "I don't give a damn whether or not I get paid." Logan's blossoming relationship with Jane loses its significance as he is driven to kill both Clayton and Braxton to avenge the deaths of his comrades.

The unusual script sees the characters take unexpected directions, certainly unexpected for a western, and it may be the resulting idiosyncrasies that contributed to the film's poor reception. Logan, a career criminal, is at first reluctant to remain on the homestead while his partners are away, but is gently swayed by a less eventful but fulfilling way of life. Soon, stealing horses and robbing trains are replaced by irrigating crops and making tea for Jane, Nicholson's heavy beard failing to conceal his famously devilish charm.

As his opposite in the Romeo and Juliet subplot, Kathleen Lloyd gives her character an unusually robust presence, as well as an aura of sexual sophistication that renders Nicholson's Logan somewhat abashed. She is another of those resolute women one encounters in Seventies westerns who prove to be more insightful about frontier existence than their male counterparts. She is the perfect counterweight to her father, whose zealous pursuit of lowlifes clashes with her ideals. "Don't you believe in hungry thieves?" she asks, when Braxton asserts that all rustlers must be hanged. Hers is a liberal voice in a town of non-judicial execution and raucous kangaroo courts. Her father is fascistic in his condemnation of rustlers, equating criminality with ethnicity. One wonders if Braxton's goal is to cleanse the region of all non-Anglo-Saxon elements.

Upholding Braxton's version of law is Clayton. Marlon Brando's performance has been much derided; the passing of time has not lessened how downright bizarre he is here, or how mesmerising.[1] His arrival on the scene – hidden behind his steed, screaming in his Irish brogue at mourners attending the ramrod's wake – marks him immediately as a crackpot, but it's not until we see him operate alone that we realise that he is, in fact, a psychopath. Employing changes of accent and costume, Clayton dispatches his quarry from long distance with his Creedmoor. As Logan says, it's easier to kill a man if you "never have to look him in the eye". It is frustrating that the script didn't ring for more bouts between Brando and Nicholson, as their sparring is exceptional.[2]

Although this chameleonic killer adds flamboyancy to proceedings, his appearance conflicts with the muddy milieu and gnarled characters elsewhere, not least when he dons an unflattering dress and bonnet – another of Brando's whimsies. Logan's gang are as unromantic and dowdy a bunch of 'villains' as you're likely to see in a western. There are no displays of surliness or bravado, as we have grown accustomed to from screen outlaws. Nor do they seem epecially competent: the excursion to Canada ends farcically; during a train robbery, Logan almost loses the money on a trestle bridge – "You boys new at this?" wonders the train guard. The rustlers' decision to invest their plunder in property, rather than squander it, is also anomalous. Elsewhere, we see them crowded in shacks, arguing, laughing, darning socks by candlelight; on one occasion they visit a dismal-looking whorehouse. Braxton's lifestyle, in comparison, is one of luxury, complete with maids and a servant who is so submissive that he offers his life in exchange for his master's to placate the vengeful Logan.

The contemplative pace, typical for the period, is punctuated by moments of tender humour and contrastingly terrible violence. The killing of a rabbit (by Clayton's throwing star) may be the most jarring visual assault, and marks the film's shift in emphasis from conflicting principles to ruthless elimination, with each death occurring in squalid, ignominious circumstances: one rustler is killed mid-coitus; another shot while squatting in an outhouse, foreshadowing a similar incident in *Unforgiven*. It becomes a tale of men unable to change ancient ways, to the point that bloody conflict becomes inevitable. Only the classical narrative curve of retribution can follow.

Thomas McGuane also penned *Rancho Deluxe*, in which the contemporary setting made the process of demythologisation more conspicuous, and *Tom Horn*, in which corporatism was shown to trump the individualist ethos of the titular hero. *The Missouri Breaks* shares these concerns – "The abiding idea… was that this was the period when they were carving up Montana with as few owners as possible… There were enormous ranches owned by people who… were laws unto themselves," said Penn.[3] This notion obviously struck Penn as both abhorrent and absurd, as personified by Brando's regulator, who was based on the real Tom Horn but lacks even the slightest trace of nobility. While it is not as fulfilling as *The Left Handed Gun* or *Little Big Man*, *The Missouri Breaks* is a telling critique of both the western genre and the cult of violence in America. **CH**

footnotes

1 Thomas McGuane had written the role of Clayton with his friend Warren Oates in mind, who had recently co-starred in the author's adaptation of his novel *92 in the Shade*. McGuane was aghast at some of Brando's behaviour and demands – he had wanted to play the part as an Indian, inexplicably, and to have his pet wolf cast in the film. Brando was also said to have devoured a live frog on location, among other shenanigans.

2 Indeed, according to Penn, the original script included just one significant scene involving both Clayton and Logan, "but with actors like Brando and Nicholson we needed further confrontation between the two characters" (interview with Penn by Jean-Pierre Coursodon, 1977; reprinted in *Arthur Penn: Interviews*, University Press of Mississippi, 2008).

3 Interview with Penn by Richard Combs, 1981; reprinted in *Arthur Penn: Interviews*.

The Outlaw Josey Wales

1976, Colour, 135 mins.

D: Clint Eastwood. P: Robert Daley (Malpaso). W: Philip Kaufman, Sonia Chernus. Ph: Bruce Surtees. M: Jerry Fielding. St: Clint Eastwood (Josey Wales), Chief Dan George (Lone Watie), Sondra Locke (Laura Lee), Bill McKinney (Terrill), John Vernon (Fletcher)

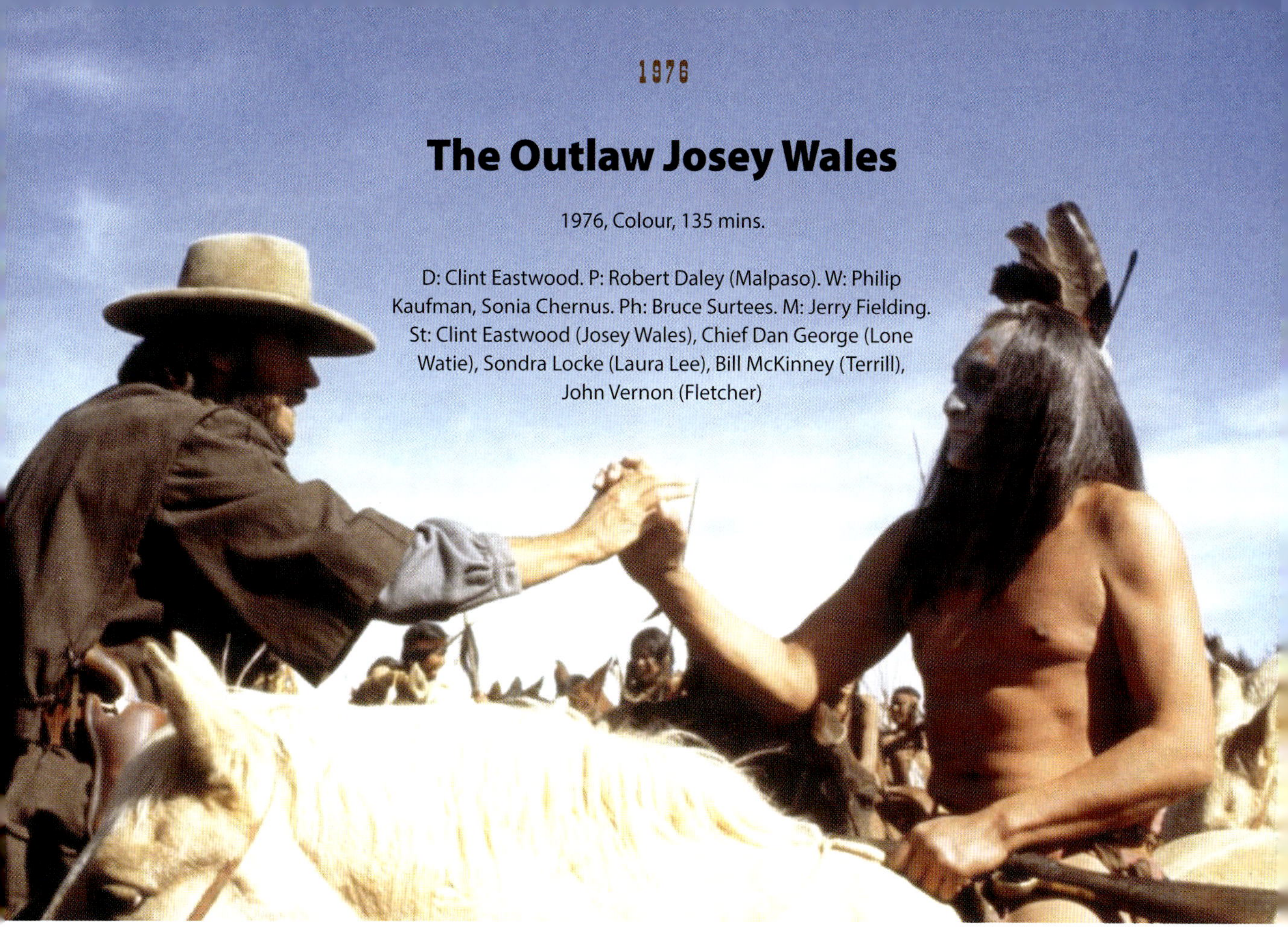

"I came here to die with you, or live with you. Dying ain't so hard for men like you and me; it's living that's hard."

The halfway point between *High Plains Drifter* and *Unforgiven*, Clint Eastwood's cautiously optimistic Bicentennial epic plots a course between territories mapped out in one direction by the genre's pioneers and in the other by its revisionists. Themes, characters and situations familiar from classic films by Ford, Mann, Henry King and George Stevens encounter motifs popularised by Leone, Peckinpah and Penn, coalescing around a vehicle for Eastwood's increasing self-assurance as a director and maturity as a performer. As the script addresses the rebirth of the nation following the great schism of the Civil War, with an inescapable message for Americans bitterly divided over Vietnam, the star reconsiders the position and status of the lone-hero archetype, as well as the Eastwood persona itself, in relation to the new society being forged.

"I'd done satiric westerns in the Italian-made films and there was an element of heroism in those, but I'd always wanted to do a more traditional classic western saga," Eastwood told Iain Johnstone.[1] The episodic plot, studded with acutely drawn minor characters, was derived from a 1973 novel (with a fascinating back story of its own[2]) that upholds the popular image of the outlaw as a thorn in the side of a discredited Establishment and defender of the oppressed. The title character is a farmer and family man who becomes a Civil War bushwhacker after his wife and child are murdered by fanatical Yankee Redlegs. When the conflict fizzles out and his fellow guerrillas accept a promise of amnesty, Josey sticks to his guns, and is proved right when his comrades are massacred on the orders of a state senator. Evading his pursuers, Josey drifts South, through beautifully photographed landscapes and seasons, grudgingly 'adopting' various dependents and rediscovering his humanity along the way.

Notwithstanding its literary origins, the film draws on a rich cinematic history. The pistolero as a combination of tarnished saviour and reluctant celebrity can be traced back to *The Gunfighter*, via *Shane* and numerous derivatives; Eastwood toyed with this 'fallen angel' motif in both *High Plains Drifter* and *Pale Rider*, and refined the notion in *Unforgiven*. As a member of Bloody Bill Anderson's guerrillas, affiliated to the notorious William Quantrill, Josey is a mixture of folk hero and bogeyman, preceded by tall tales of his murderous exploits – he is rumoured to have killed "50, 60 men", including his own allies.[3] He is a myth in the making, and Eastwood's action scenes do little to discourage such a legendary reading, as when Josey singlehandedly

annihilates Union soldiers who have killed his fellow fighters, or rides out of the sun like a desert wraith to wipe out a band of comancheros.

At various points, however, Josey's lone-wolf mentality – "I don't want nobody belongin' to me" – is undermined: supporting characters save his life on at least three occasions, and he only survives his final reckoning with the Redlegs with the aid of his surrogate family – the wily old Cherokee Lone Watie, garrulous squaw Little Moonlight, feisty Grandma Sarah and her willowy granddaughter, Laura Lee, with whom Josey enters into a hesitant romance. The denouement is both a mockery of Eastwood's self-reliant screen image and an emphatic demonstration of the Fordian community spirit that envelops his character over the course of

the film, subsuming the revenge aspect of the plot and bringing Josey full circle. He becomes paterfamilias at the ranch established by Laura Lee's late father – ironically a Redleg – as well as champion of the dormant town of Santa Rio, whose inhabitants pass the time reminiscing about the days when silver miners poured their money into its coffers.

Like most picaresque narratives, Josey's passage across country is simultaneously a voyage of self-discovery. Parallels can and have been drawn with the genre's most famous odyssey and redemption westerns – we could cite *Red River* and *The Searchers*, with Josey's nemesis, Captain Terrill, and his Redlegs standing in for Scar and his Comanche braves. But Josey is neither tyrannical like Tom Dunson nor borderline psychotic like Ethan Edwards. The characters played by James Stewart in Anthony Mann's *The Naked Spur* and, in particular, *Bend of the River*, in which Stewart's Glyn McLintock is, like Josey, a former Missouri border raider, are more pertinent predecessors – men similarly scarred, physically and mentally, by violent lifestyles and the ravages of war, compelled to accept assistance whether they like it or not.

Although Josey's mien for the most part remains that of the superhuman characters Eastwood played for Leone, with the same kind of sangfroid and mordant wit ("Buzzards gotta eat, same as worms," he remarks of one of many unburied corpses he leaves in his wake), there is also a palpable sense of psychic fatigue, an unspoken longing for redemption and repose, evident in the weariness with which he dispatches yet another bounty hunter late on: "Dyin' ain't much of a livin', boy." His transformation from man of peace to marauder is given a specific context, which sets him apart from the likes of Shane and the enigmatic figures Eastwood played in the 'Dollars' trilogy and *High Plains Drifter*. His journey back, meanwhile, begins with the resumption of responsibility for others: from an idealistic young comrade (Sam

Bottoms) wounded in the massacre, to the coterie that gathers around him in Texas. At the close of the film, his apparent forgiveness of Fletcher, the former comrade-in-arms who unwittingly led his men to the slaughter, signals that Josey may have found peace once again.

Eastwood referred to Vietnam and Watergate as examples of the kind of government betrayal executed near the beginning of the film, which manifests a general disillusionment with the political centre characteristic of both conservative and leftist sentiment in the early Seventies, albeit for different reasons. It is on this point that Josey, like many in the contemporary counterculture movement (not a constituency one would ordinarily associate with Eastwood), relates to Indians. Lone Watie explicitly calls out "the white man" for his chicanery. A wry and perspicacious relic of the Indian Wars, with Chief Dan George effectively reprising his quirkily sardonic performance in *Little Big Man*, Lone laments that he ever agreed to become "civilised" ("I didn't surrender… they took my horse and made him surrender"), so that now he has even lost the ability to sneak up on a white man – indeed, Josey first creeps up on *him*. His alliance with the outlaw rekindles Lone's insurrectionary spirit and he symbolically burns the Lincolnesque outfit he has worn since pacification: a first step towards reclaiming his cultural identity.

Equally dignified, although occupying a more traditional position in the narrative, is Ten Bears (Will Sampson), the feared Comanche chief with whom Josey barters for the safety of the ranch. In a scene famous for the unusual length of Eastwood's speech as much as for its pacifist tone, the duo bond over Josey's observation that, "With governments you don't always get a fair word or a fair fight." (Fletcher, an ambiguous character whose role is rather neglected, had earlier put it more colourfully when decoding the duplicitous senator's double-talk: "Don't piss down my back and tell me it's rainin'.") Eastwood was never one for denigrating Native Americans, and Ten Bears is portrayed as magnanimous and pragmatic, sharing Josey's desire for peaceful co-existence, his faith in the ability of straight-talking, square-dealing individuals to govern themselves.

In the final reckoning, *Josey Wales* is an appeal for national healing in the aftermath of tumultuous times. Philip French read it as "a binding up of the wounds caused by the Indo-Chinese War and the social divisions of the Sixties",[4] with Josey's closing statement to Fletcher – "I guess we all died a little in that damn war" – surely intended for a much wider audience. Josey's own recovery, at the centre of a new community, symbolises the "fervent belief in renewal" that Michael Coyne views as central to the American psyche.[5] In proposing an alternative destiny for the wandering gunfighter at the heart of western folklore, it frees the man from the prison of myth, just as Josey's companions chip away at his defensive exterior. For the first time in an Eastwood western, he acknowledges the limitations of the individualist ethos with which he had become synonymous; however inadvertently, the loner becomes a leader. **KG**

footnotes

1 Quoted in Iain Johnstone, *The Man with No Name* (Plexus, 1981).

2 *Gone to Texas* was the work of Forrest, really Asa, Carter, a campaigner against desegregation, organiser of a Ku Klux Klan splinter group (he'd chosen the alias 'Forrest' in honour of Nathan Bedford Forrest, an early leader of the KKK) and onetime speechwriter for Alabama's firebrand governor George Wallace. By the time of his literary career, Carter had covered his tracks to such an extent that his real identity wasn't uncovered until after the production of *Josey Wales*.

3 Although his career as a border raider is steeped in mythology, William Quantrill's most infamous exploit has been well documented: the massacre of around 150 male civilians in the abolitionist stronghold of Lawrence, Kansas, in 1863. Despite this, early dime novelists looked kindly on him as a freedom fighter. The belief that one of the most romanticised of all frontier figures, Jesse James, rode with Quantrill – or at least with his acolyte Bloody Bill Anderson – no doubt helped his cause. In his film career he has often been interpreted as a power-crazed would-be despot.

4 *Westerns: Aspects of a Movie Genre* (Carcanet Press, 2005).

5 *The Crowded Prairie: American National Identity in the Hollywood Western* (I.B. Tauris, 1997).

Heaven's Gate

1980, Colour, 217 mins. (original version 149 mins.)

D: Michael Cimino. P: Joann Carelli (Partisan Productions). W: Michael Cimino. Ph: Vilmos Zsigmond. M: David Mansfield.
St: Kris Kristofferson (Jim Averill), Christopher Walken (Nate Champion), John Hurt (Billy Irvine),
Isabelle Huppert (Ella Watson), Sam Waterston (Frank Canton)

"It's gettin' dangerous to be poor in this country." "It always was."

Michael Cimino's heretical vision of the expanding frontier describes the pioneer experience candidly, if crudely, as a collision between classes. In terms of budget and scale, painterly visuals and period detail, *Heaven's Gate* marks the apogee of the western as foundation myth, the logical culmination of such epic chronicles as *The Iron Horse* (1924) and *How the West Was Won* (1962). Cimino's quasi-Marxist thesis, however, moves it closer to *Once Upon a Time in the West* (1968), while the discouraging tone seems to have filtered through from the anti-westerns of the Seventies, as does the director's disparaging take on Manifest Destiny. As Patrick McGee writes, "Cimino chooses to shape the historical reality of the Johnson County War in order to dramatise a conflict between the social desires of the multitude, whom he identifies as the poor, and the desire of the dominant class for superfluous wealth."[1]

The script draws on the same historical material appropriated earlier – with opposing objectives – by two of the genre's key texts, *The Virginian* and *Shane*, and reshaped in myriad range-war plots over the decades. Cimino returns to the source but cherry-picks his details, blurring fact and fiction and radically altering the protagonists' social backgrounds.[2] Equally significant, for a western, is what Brian Woolland calls "the film's refusal to accept the primacy of individual action."[3] Kris Kristofferson's central character never fulfils his heroic obligations, due to a combination of his own procrastination and a plot that foregrounds collective organisation and resistance. Isolated acts of bravado occur, but they are futile gestures given Cimino's contention, supported by most accounts of the events he depicts, that justice is reserved for the rich.

The core issues – land and property rights, the rapacity of big ranchers, bankers and speculators – are as old as the genre itself. But when these figures appeared in dime novels and early B-westerns they tended to be rotten apples, and fairly easy to crush. By the early Seventies, when Cimino conceived *Heaven's Gate*,[4] this theme had been refined to implicate an entire capitalist ethos, usually associated with the East, as westerns increasingly adopted the anti-corporate animus identified with the counterculture and the New Left (viz. *Butch Cassidy and the Sundance Kid*, *Monte Walsh*, *McCabe & Mrs. Miller*, *The Life and Times of Judge Roy Bean*, *Pat Garrett and Billy the Kid*, *The Missouri Breaks*). Not that "refined" necessarily means "sophisticated": Cimino's villains are the stuff of the crudest melodrama. The odious Frank Canton (it's a wonder he never twirls his mustache), is the front man for the Wyoming Stock Growers' Association (WSGA), a cold-blooded cartel with solid government connections, a view of settlers as "paupers… thieves, anarchists and outlaws" and a firm belief that the cause of the cattle barons is tied to the fate of the nation itself: "If we fail, the flag of the United States will fail." The WSGA's brand of patriotism shades into a particularly vicious kind of nativism; to render their campaign more iniquitous still, Cimino gives it an explicitly xenophobic aspect by making the settlers on their "death list" foreigners, mostly from Central and Eastern Europe. While this deviates from most historians' research into the dispute, the multi-ethnic complexion of *Heaven's Gate's* frontier is nonetheless convincing.

The putative protagonist, Jim Averill, occupies a paradoxical position. A representative of the ruling classes, he nevertheless takes the side of the settlers, partly because of his romance with the prostitute and madam Ella Watson – whose name happens to be on the hit list – and partly to provide a parallel to Nate Champion, a WSGA gunman and rival for Ella's affections.[5] Champion, it is implied, is of immigrant stock

above: Rich man, poor excuse for a hero: Kris Kristofferson as Averill.
opposite top left: Christopher Walken with Isabelle Huppert.

himself (as elsewhere in Cimino's needlessly oblique screenplay, this seemingly significant detail is only fleetingly addressed) and thus a traitor to his class – the very accusation that Canton makes against Averill. As the latter points out, however, his own social standing (and, by implication, his moral stature) is greater than anything Canton can aspire to. A true patrician, Averill has been led West in pursuit of the high ideals urged on him and his Harvard classmates by the Reverend Doctor (Joseph Cotten) in the prologue, set 20 years earlier.[6]

But Averill, now a lawman, is evidently alone in his sense of responsibility. The wealthy elite, embodied by Canton and his cronies, see no need to change a world that is "on the whole, well arranged", as one of their number and Averill's old friend, the facetious Billy Irvine, had proclaimed in his valedictorian address at Harvard. Even Averill, although driven by altruism, "never questions the material foundation of the class system that privileges him".[7] Cimino wedges his ostensible hero between the opposing forces, *à la* Shane, only to subject him to a kind of existential paralysis, deliberately limiting his ability to act. Much given to brooding silences, Averill is too consumed by crises of loyalty and identity – "You're a rich man with a good name; you only pretend to be poor" – to be of much use to the increasingly militant settlers.

It is Champion who steals his laurels, however briefly, when he develops a conscience (Canton calls it "sentimentalism") and defects, at the cost of his life. Averill's denial of responsibility for Champion's death (it is suggested the two were once friends) sounds like an abdication of duty in a wider sense, and rather sums up his ineffectiveness as a protagonist. When Canton expedites his plan to unleash a 50-strong private army on the homesteaders, who respond by raising a posse and taking the fight to their oppressors, Averill rides to their aid with characteristic tardiness. When he leaves the field at the end of the clash, Vilmos Zsigmond's camera lingers on his slow departure: "This allusion to the ending of *Shane* could not make more emphatic the film's deconstruction of the western hero."[8] Averill is the only one of the three central characters to survive, but he lives to regret it. In the film's coda, set 13 years later aboard his luxury yacht off the coast of Newport, his bearing betrays a profound sense of loss and remorse; perhaps he is "still trapped between perception and action, still traumatised by his inability to act", as Christian Keathley suggests.[9]

For Cimino, American imperialism – the subtext of so many revisionist westerns – begins at home, with the maintenance of a top-down society and the

enforcement of an elitist monopoly on land ownership. Canton and his accomplices are stereotyped to an almost Eisensteinian degree, but their historical counterparts appear to have been every bit as disdainful of their enemies, just as cynical, arrogant (Canton's employment of manual labourers as mercenaries recalls the famous claim by railroad magnate Jay Gould: "I can hire one half of the working class to kill the other half") and ruthless in pressing home the advantage given them by their connections. The Johnson County War occurred against a backdrop of labour strikes – at Andrew Carnegie's Homestead Plant in Pennsylvania; among miners in Idaho – and concomitant middle-class anxiety. "Those needing government help to bolster their position were more likely to succeed if they used language that reflected middle-class ideals," says historian Heather Cox Richardson. This tactic served the WSGA well. When soldiers arrive to rescue Canton and his besieged vigilantes – at the end of a battle that is far costlier in human life than in fact it was – a disgusted Averill is reminded by the commanding officer that "it's the rules", compounding the sense of a conspiracy by the dominant order to protect its interests at the expense of the underclass. No member of the WSGA was prosecuted for his part in the 'invasion' of Johnson County; they were said to be suppressing an 'insurrection'. "By appealing to the idea that their opponents threatened middle-class order," continues Cox Richardson, "the Stock Growers won the support of the federal government and actually got away with murder."[10] With this in mind, Cimino can be accused of exaggerating the extent of the skirmish, but not the gravity of the injustice.

As what the French publication *Libération* called "the first socialist [American] western", *Heaven's Gate* appeared to be fatally out of step with the mood in Ronald Reagan's America: "When a new administration had come to office with a popular mandate to repeal half the services in this country that benefit the poor."[11] Rather than participating in what Christian Keathley calls "the cultural rebuilding of American ideological confidence", as might have been expected of a big-budget western, *Heaven's Gate* bucked the blockbuster trend by reverting to the sour mood of much Seventies cinema, bemoaning the betrayal of ideals that a majority of people still convinced themselves were valid. Philip French intuited "a general will in America in 1980, some expression of the collective unconscious, that *Heaven's Gate* should fail".[12] Critics excoriated it; audiences spurned it; studios moved to rein in their charges. In Kris Kristofferson's opinion, the controversy "was used by powers that be to stop a way of filmmaking where the author was the director and was in control of the money". Cimino is also routinely blamed for hastening the western's demise – a spurious claim given that the following year Universal released *The Legend of the Lone Ranger*, which also flopped but had none of *Heaven's Gate's* redeeming features. And within a decade, *Dances with Wolves*, which was just as reproachful as *Heaven's Gate* of America's failings, restored the genre to Oscar-winning respectability.

Beneath the hyperbole, *Heaven's Gate* reveals both formidable strengths and considerable defects. Cimino's legendary fastidiousness and Tambi Larsen's superb production design convey a vivid impression of a world in transition – the town of Casper, centre of the cattlemen's empire, teems with economic refugees while industrial smoke curls from chimneys. Beyond its borders, the environment is photographed reverently by Vilmos Zsigmond in similarly hazy tones to those he used for *McCabe & Mrs. Miller* and *The Hired Hand*, with special emphasis on dust clouds that blow through like the winds of change. Although Cimino's set pieces would all benefit from pruning, they are exquisitely choreographed, united stylistically by circular patterns: Harvard's class of 1870 mark their graduation with a waltz, its ritualistic pageantry later contrasted with an informal roller-skating sequence in

above: Momentary respite for Averill and Ella.
top left: Harvard's class of 1870 (Hurt and Kristofferson, front and centre).

the immigrants' dancehall (the titular Heaven's Gate). The frenzied climactic engagement, shrouded in yet more dust and gunsmoke, repeats the motif, with the posse of homesteaders riding around the outnumbered mercenaries in a parody of Indians besieging a wagon train, just as the soldiers' deliverance of the villains mocks another genre trope and forces us to reconsider the heroic fantasies of yesteryear as just that – fantasies.

Cimino had a novelist's eye for texture, but not the same attention to characters and their development. His interest in the immigrants is principally as a group entity. They are largely undifferentiated, not helped by sound design that makes the overlapping dialogue (in various dialects) difficult to discern; only Brad Dourif makes a notable impression as a civic dignitary cum political agitator.[13] Of the central triumvirate, Averill seems to have his mind elsewhere, probably on the world of wealth he has left behind, symbolised by a photograph he keeps of himself with an expensively attired woman. His aura of aristocratic detachment contrasts unfavourably with Champion's dynamism, although neither man's motives can be safely apprehended from Cimino's fuzzy writing. Champion and Ella, a performance of real *joie de vivre* by Isabelle Huppert, are engaging creations, and their violent deaths signify the brutal crushing of idealism that *Heaven's Gate* decries. The romantic triangle that ensnares this trio has little bearing on the main plot, however, and this failure to anchor seismic events in human drama detracts from the film's emotional impact. **KG**

footnotes

1 *From Shane to Kill Bill: Rethinking the Western* (Wiley-Blackwell, 2006).

2 Cimino was clearly interested in facts only so far as they supported his ideological position. The key characters are named after real people, but their roles have been altered. Neither Frank Canton nor Jim Averill was a member of the aristocracy: Canton was a former sheriff and outlaw, hired by the WSGA as Chief Range Inspector, while Averill was a justice of the peace and Ella Watson's business partner. She was a saloon owner said to be a prostitute by newspapers sympathetic to the Association and – as in the film – was accused of taking rustled cattle in exchange for sexual favours. She and Averill were hanged in 1889, three years before the events depicted in *Heaven's Gate*. Nate Champion was never on the WSGA's payroll; rather, he was on the other side of the conflict, and was later called "the king of cattle thieves, and the bravest man in Johnson County" by Sam Clover of the *Chicago Herald*, who witnessed the siege of Champion's cabin that resulted in his death. A ballad was subsequently composed in his honour.

3 'Class Frontiers: the View from *Heaven's Gate*', in *The Movie Book of the Western* (Studio Vista, 1996).

4 Cimino completed his first script, titled *The Johnson County War*, in 1971. Reputedly it is the most historically accurate version of the screenplay.

5 The casting of Huppert – at Cimino's insistence – implies that Ella may be of foreign extraction like the settlers. The script is not clear on this point.

6 The fictional Averill's breeding and bearing are unusual for a western protagonist, but pertain to some of the genre's earliest works: the same blue blood flowed through the veins of Edward S. Ellis's dime-novel hero Seth Jones [1860], while in *The Virginian*, Owen Wister styled his haughty title character as a member of the "true [Southern] aristocracy", the "best man" destined to bridge what Wister described as America's only class divide: "the quality and the equality".

7 Patrick McGee, *From Shane to Kill Bill*.

8 Ibid.

9 'Trapped in the Affection Image: Hollywood's Post-Traumatic Cycle (1970-1976)' in *The Last Great American Picture Show – New Hollywood in the 1970s* (Thomas Elsaesser, Alexander Horwath, Noel King, eds, Amsterdam University Press, 2005).

10 *West from Appomattox* (Yale University Press, 2007).

11 David Denby, 'The Second Time Around', *New York Magazine*, 11 May 1981.

12 *Westerns: Aspects of a Movie Genre* (Carcanet Press, 2005). The full story of the *Heaven's Gate* debacle was chronicled by Steven Bach, one of the United Artists executives who paid dearly for its failure: see *Final Cut: Art, Money and Ego in the Making of Heaven's Gate, the Film That Sank United Artists* (Newmarket Press, 1999).

13 One of Dourif's orations is based on a newspaper article written at the time by the real Jim Averill.

The Long Riders

1980, Colour, 99 mins.

D: Walter Hill. P: Tim Zinnemann (Huka Films). W: Bill Bryden, Steven Phillip Smith, Stacy Keach, James Keach. Ph: Ric Waite. M: Ry Cooder. St: David Carradine (Cole Younger), Keith Carradine (Jim Younger), Robert Carradine (Bob Younger), James Keach (Jesse James), Stacy Keach (Frank James)

"We played a rough game, and we lost."

Walter Hill refines the conventions of dime-store mythmaking with an earthier approach to the Jesse James legend. The director's first foray proper into a genre that has informed his entire career, *The Long Riders* was the centrepiece of a trilogy that focused on male fighting units, sandwiched between the urban fantasy *The Warriors* (1979) and the bayou nightmare *Southern Comfort* (1981). The James-Younger saga has been told often, but few productions have attempted such a rounded mix of realism and romance, or rendered so convincingly the outlaw spirit that bonded the protagonists – aided immensely, in the last respect, by the casting of real brothers, one of the film's key selling points. This is not the whole truth but, as a compromise between folklore and outright revisionism, it is a more considered work than most. As Hill says, "I wanted neither to celebrate nor to deny their importance… in the forging of [America's] national character post-Civil War."[1]

As in *The Wild Bunch*, this film's most obvious reference, the sound of gunfire jerks the viewer to attention in the opening scene as the James-Younger gang hold up a bank. When Ed Miller shoots dead a bank teller, it is the trigger for an exchange of close-range gunfire that leaves Jesse wounded. Ed is later banished from the gang and they return to their stronghold of Clay County. During their hiatus, the men occupy their time with gambling, whoring and, in the case of Frank and Jesse, juggling marital responsibilities with the demands of a violent lifestyle. They return to action by holding up a stage and a train carrying the Rock Island Payroll. The Pinkerton Detective Agency is hired to bring to justice or simply exterminate the rebel outlaws, who soon set their sights on the bank at Northfield, Minnesota…

Hill's disclaimer, "I was not trying to make an accurately historical film," applies principally to biographical detail. Great care was taken to re-create the post-Civil War era and the Midwestern milieu. Ric Waite's hazy photography conjures the same nostalgic ambience that pervades *McCabe & Mrs. Miller*, *Bad Company*, *Dirty Little Billy*, et al. The use of verdant backdrops – hills, trees, tall grass – rather than dusty or rocky terrain reinforces a sense of veracity, with Ry Cooder's twanging score augmenting the antiquated feel. Costumes, firearms and facial hair are largely period-specific, while a 19th-century world of murky gaslight and cigar smoke is brilliantly realised in the saloons and family homes. Only when they are working does the outlaws' world become brighter, starker, as if the gang are simply hibernating between heists.

The script, co-written by the Keach brothers, makes a valiant attempt to flesh out these legendary figures. Guerrilla fighters during the Civil War, the men are proud of their roots and enjoy considerable affection, even adulation, in 'Little Dixie'. A strong atmosphere of community prevails – Jesse's wedding is one of many impeccably staged group scenes, an extended hoedown attended by, it seems, "the whole county". It could almost be Hill's tribute to Ford's famous social gatherings. In this context, where the humiliation of being on the losing side continues to smart and Yankee encroachment is

deeply resented, the Pinkertons are viewed as intrusive, obtuse upstarts at best; murderers at worst. When agency deputies, searching the home of Frank and Jesse's mother (a gritty Fran Ryan), are introduced as Southerners, she is incredulous: "What are they chasing *my* boys for?" The incidents that helped seal the gang's reputation as righteous outlaws are economically plotted. The murder by Pinkertons of John Younger, an 18-year-old who never took part in raids, is trumped by the firebombing of the James family home and the death of their youngest brother.

The inspired casting enhances the emotional resonance. The Keaches, Carradines and Randy and Dennis Quaid, as the James, Younger and Miller brothers respectively, are entirely convincing as a working unit, veterans whose North-hating ideology is blurred by violence and greed.[2] The James boys appear stoical, hard working and family oriented; the Youngers full of charm, wit and guile; the Millers are rash, chosen for their guns rather than their cool. The Fords, meanwhile, portrayed unctuously by Christopher and Nicholas Guest, are the vipers in the nest, often posed in tight two-shots, like a double-headed serpent.[3]

Like Peckinpah, Hill believes in depicting violence in all its ambiguity – the detail is repulsive, yet the choreography of blasted bodies and spurting blood is undeniably graceful. It can be thrilling, too: the famous Northfield bank raid remains one of the finest action sequences in the genre. Time is stretched to emphasise the physical destruction caused by gunfire, complemented by the sonic assault of bullets slicing through air and smashing into flesh. Cole Younger's action in returning to the maelstrom to rescue younger brother Bob, blood spewing from his own bullet-riddled torso, is an inspiring sight, undermining Hill's assertion that, "It's a movie that doesn't have a hero."

David Carradine's charisma, allied to the character's composed demeanour, elevates Cole above the other members of the outlaw ensemble. Jesse James, by contrast, does not emerge with much credit. Unlike the elder Youngers or his own brother Frank, Jesse, coolly played by James Keach, never risks his life for another. Moreover, as their lifestyles become more hazardous, he becomes increasingly callous. This was the most damning depiction of Jesse since Robert Duvall's highly strung performance in *The Great Northfield Minnesota Raid*.

The unvarnished truth about the Jameses has yet to be told on film. Far from being a Robin Hood figure, James was a slave owner who once bragged that he would shoot any black in Missouri not fulfilling his role as a drudge, while during the Civil War both he and his brother are reported to have committed atrocities. As *The Long Riders* makes clear, there is no doubt that war shaped these men, but it could be argued that it doesn't go far enough in chronicling a reality that may be hard to stomach for those weaned on such legends. Whoever Jesse James and his gang were in reality, their position in US folklore was most eloquently summarised in a letter written by Oscar Wilde on a journey through Missouri: "Americans are certainly great hero worshippers, and always take their heroes from the criminal classes." **CH**

footnotes

1 Quoted in *Outlaw Brothers: the Making of The Long Riders* (2013).

2 The Carradines' father, John, played Bob Ford in Henry King's 1939 *Jesse James*.

3 Beau and Jeff Bridges were originally considered for the Ford brothers – in the event, Beau dropped out, while Jeff was busy making *Heaven's Gate*.

Tom Horn

1980, Colour, 97 mins.

D: William Wiard. P: Fred Weintraub (Solar Productions, First Artists). W: Thomas McGuane, Bud Shrake. Ph: John A. Alonzo. M: Ernest Gold. St: Steve McQueen (Tom Horn), Linda Evans (Glendolene Kimmel), Richard Farnsworth (John Coble), Billy 'Green' Bush (Joe Belle), Slim Pickens (Sam Creedmore)

"I'm afraid of losing my ability to be able to come and go as I please... lose my freedom... not being able to get back up in those hills again."

Much like *The Shootist*, this ode to an icon of the Old West – an actual historical figure in this case – derives its emotional impact, not to mention its elegiac quality, from the casting of an ailing, ageing screen legend in the title role. News of Steve McQueen's diagnosis with terminal lung cancer broke shortly before *Tom Horn*'s release, and while this knowledge did nothing to soften the critical blows it received, it cannot help today but colour one's approach to the story of a man past his prime (mirroring, additionally, McQueen's career trajectory) and consigned to die by people in "mail-order suits" who are unworthy of the inheritance they have reaped from troubleshooters of his ilk.

Comparisons with *The Shootist* extend no further than the broad outline (which, in both films, echoes *The Gunfighter*) and a turn-of-the-century setting that marginalises men like Horn and John Wayne's John Books, who made their mark in earlier, unsettled times. They could have gone further, however. Don Siegel, having directed *The Shootist*, was scheduled to do the same on *Tom Horn*, but left the project when McQueen, who was executive producer, began throwing his weight around, vetoing an initial script by Abraham Polonsky in favour of a gloomier scenario co-authored by new-wave western stylists Bud Shrake (*Kid Blue*) and Thomas McGuane (*Rancho Deluxe*; *The Missouri Breaks*). Curious, then, that the language lacks verve (rewrites cannot have helped), almost in sympathy with William Wiard's prosaic direction; he was brought in after other directors came and went, resulting in a film that lacks focus and consistency.[1] Drawing on Horn's memoirs, the script describes the character in high-flown terms as "a vestige of that heroic era we've just about lost". Horn himself, played by McQueen as the unassuming and plain-spoken fellow he reputedly was in real life, is quick to debunk romantic notions about his exploits and the "dirty and raggedy-assed Old West" in which he earned his spurs; grandly silhouetted against sunsets, however, he is never divested entirely of his romantic allure.

The picture takes pains to contrast the indignity of Horn's situation – a bona fide legend reduced to

Steve McQueen with Linda Evans, as the schoolmarm who softens Horn's heart.

sleeping in stables with his horse – with the stoicism with which he carries himself and eventually meets his fate. Rescued from ignominy by sympathetic rancher John Coble, Horn's reputation as a tracker convinces Coble's fellow cattlemen to hire him to eliminate rustlers. (Horn's career loosely inspired Marlon Brando's bounty hunter in *The Missouri Breaks*.) It is a hush-hush arrangement, and when Horn's ruthless efficiency begins to attract unwanted attention, the ranchers fear for their reputations. When an innocent teenage boy is shot dead on the range, Horn is accused, with the connivance of a politically ambitious marshal, and sentenced to hang at a show trial that serves as a crude indictment of the 'civilised' West.

Horn's curriculum vitae offers rich pickings for Hollywood myth-makers. As an army scout, he helped capture Geronimo (whose stature Tom praises above that of boastful boxer 'Gentleman' Jim Corbett in an apocryphal meeting in a bar, earning him a battering); he served as a sheriff and a Pinkerton agent; achieved notoriety as a range detective. (Among his clients was the Wyoming Stock Growers' Association, the nefarious organisation at the dark heart of another 1980 western, *Heaven's Gate*.) Yet this film and the 1979 TV mini-series *Mr. Horn*, with David Carradine in the title role, are

his only substantial screen biographies. Perhaps the murkiness surrounding the role of regulator and the killing of the child is the prime factor; Horn's conviction for the crime was based largely on a 'confession' he gave while drunk, and cannot safely be ruled just or otherwise, although it is clear enough in this version of events that he is the victim of a framing. The desire to render Horn a martyr probably explains the decision to concentrate on the last two years of his life.

Not that his reputation is whitewashed. The ambiguity inherent in Horn's position, and in his nature, illustrates one of the key themes of the postwar western: the essential incompatibility of the hunter, or hero figure in general, with the community that benefits from his exertions. In scenes of Horn shooting a would-be assassin in the back, on main street, or fatally bludgeoning another in front of the schoolteacher who has fallen for him, the reactions of the witnesses – mute, appalled, uncomprehending – register as powerfully as the violent deaths. Like the cattlemen who employ Horn to do their dirty work, society doesn't like to think about, let alone be faced with, the brutal necessities of 'social cleansing'. We can also gauge his measure, and the mindset of a frontiersman who related more easily to animals than he did to people, from the way he riddles a rustler with bullets, then torches his cabin, for killing Horn's horse.

Shot with an emphasis on seasons passing – Horn's arrest coincides with the onset of winter – this is a sombre, rather schematic portrait of a man in the autumn of his life. McQueen, rugged yet haggard, is the dignified centre; he seems fully engaged in the character's travails in a way that suggests at least a degree of identification. Horn recognises that his era has passed and, as David Lusted puts it, "appears to conspire in his own death" by offering no defence at his trial, repudiating the modern world by refusing to plead for clemency.[2] Horn's comment on the newfangled, 'user-operated' gallows that will end his life confirms that in the film-makers' minds he has become both symbol and spokesman for a vanishing breed: "It makes me feel like I'm committing suicide. Do you suppose that's what I've been doing all these years?" **KG**

footnotes

1 Siegel's departure set in motion a directorial merry-go-round, with *Cat Ballou's* Elliot Silverstein and *Electra Glide in Blue's* James William Guercio being attached to the project before TV director Wiard was hired to steady the ship. It has also been reported that McQueen took charge of much of the filming himself.

2 *The Western* (Pearson, 2003).

Dances with Wolves

1990, Colour, 181 mins. (director's cut 236 mins.)

D: Kevin Costner. P: Jim Wilson, Kevin Costner (TIG Productions, Majestic Films International). W: Michael Blake. Ph: Dean Semler. M: John Barry. St: Kevin Costner (Lt. John Dunbar), Mary McDonnell (Stands with a Fist), Graham Greene (Kicking Bird), Rodney A. Grant (Wind in His Hair), Floyd Red Crow Westerman (Ten Bears)

"When I heard my Sioux name being called over and over, I knew for the first time who I really was."

By embarking on such an ambitious project in an unfashionable genre, first-time director Kevin Costner made himself a tall target both during its troubled production (the phrase 'Kevin's Gate' was bandied around Hollywood) and on release, Oscars notwithstanding.[1] Although many Native Americans praised it – it won the top prizes at the American Indian Film Festival in San Francisco – others complained of a gap between Costner's earnest pronouncements and the supposedly condescending subtext of his film. For all the care it takes to construct a three-dimensional, sympathetic portrait of Native American life, its perspective remains that of its Caucasian hero. Moreover, it replays the literary trope of white man as champion/saviour of a 'primitive' people, albeit not as flagrantly as in earlier westerns such as *The Savage* (1952) and the *Man Called Horse* series. *Dances with Wolves* remains a landmark – up to a point – in commercial cinema's depiction of Native Americans. Yet it is ultimately John Dunbar's story, not that of the Lakota Sioux he comes to live among; those awaiting the mainstream film that allows Indians to narrate their own tale resented Costner's success.

Michael Blake's script, based on his novel, combines an odyssey with the 'going native' motif as it plots, figuratively, the death and resurrection of its disaffected protagonist, a man at odds with his own culture and who yearns to experience the frontier "before it's gone". The uncomplicated notion of rejecting the materialism and spiritual emptiness of modern life to reconnect with nature ("The trail of a true human being," to quote the medicine man, Kicking Bird) no doubt underpinned the film's immense appeal, together with its politically correct casting – all Natives are played by Indian actors, speaking authentic, subtitled dialogue – and environmentally friendly politics. But Dunbar's alienation and the film's caustic vision of white America and the military made it a throwback to the revisionist westerns that flourished first in the Fifties and then in the Vietnam era. If the latter was a divisive period, Costner and Blake show the nation tearing itself apart in a more literal sense, opening in 1863 on a Civil War battlefield where Dunbar has been badly wounded in the leg. Preferring death to amputation, he makes a suicidal horseback charge towards enemy lines,

arms outspread, in an act that is misinterpreted by both sides as heroic and illustrates the character's isolation from all strands of white society.

Rewarded with a posting of his choosing, Dunbar opts for remote Fort Sedgwick, "the furthermost outpost of the realm". The closer he gets to the frontier, the more white America seems stricken with mental derangement – the officer who sees Dunbar off is clearly insane – and the more anomalous the military presence. Dunbar's predecessors at Fort Sedgwick, a handful of ragged troops, appear to be utterly demoralised and bereft of purpose; their commander believes they have been abandoned by the army and sanctions their departure. Dunbar arrives to find the site deserted, polluted and disarranged – the antithesis of military orderliness; "I can make no sense of the clues left me here," he confides to his diary.[2] "The film's ideological point," contends Michael Walker, likening *Wolves* to *Apocalypse Now*, is that these unfortunate sentinels, "like the American soldiers in Vietnam... simply do not belong there".[3] *Wolves* thus continues a theme at the heart of *Little Big Man*, one of its closest ancestors, in which Manifest Destiny, entailing as it must the dislocation or elimination of native peoples (and, here, the desecration of the land), also seems symptomatic of collective madness on the part of whites.

Indeed, despite their film being greeted in some circles as a radical break with convention, most of the arguments Costner and Blake put forth are restated from prior liberal westerns, positing a white America inferior to Lakota society on every level the filmmakers choose to highlight. While the Sioux are in "harmony", with each other (if not with rival tribes) and with the environment, the whites are feuding among themselves and seem contemptuously wasteful of natural resources – from hunters leaving skinned buffalo corpses to rot on the plains, to Dunbar's guide, Timmons ("Quite possibly the foulest man I have ever met"), littering the trail with his trash. The fiery brave Wind in His Hair mocks whites for everything from their lack of fortitude and incompetence at working the land, to their poor personal hygiene (later, a Pawnee warrior recoils in disgust when he sniffs Timmons' blanket after the latter has been ambushed and killed). Dunbar, by turns childlike and mildly eccentric, is the only white character, apart from the adoptive Lakota Stands with a Fist, to demonstrate the same level of altruism and integrity as the Sioux, the same oneness with the natural world – his playful, if hesitant, relationship with the wolf, which symbolically ushers him into the Indian world, typifies the qualities that endear him to his tribal 'family'.

Similarly, *Wolves* stumbles into familiar pitfalls. Chief among these is the division of Indian tribes into noble – the Lakota – and savage – the Pawnee. While the flattering portrait of the Sioux puts preconceptions to flight – "Nothing I have been told about these people is correct," says Dunbar – our first impression of Indians could scarcely be more traditional, with shaven-headed, fiercely painted Pawnee braves, led by Wes Studi, bearing down on the hapless Timmons. It was Pawnee raiders who orphaned Stands with a Fist as a child – they are shown massacring her family in a flashback. And while we see the Lakota returning from a raid on their tribal enemies, we don't witness the raid itself; the opposite is true when the Pawnee come to attack the Sioux, Costner prefacing their arrival with a shot of advancing warriors silhouetted against a blood-red sky. For Robert Baird, "This strategy [of presenting viewers with both 'good' and 'bad' Indians] has the function of addressing white historical fear and guilt within the same narrative, providing a way in which a fiction can remain simultaneously true to contradictory emotional responses to history."[4]

'Contradictory responses' could also sum up the genre's historical treatment of miscegenation. One might have expected Costner to address the issue with greater maturity and bullishness than was deemed permissible by the majority of previous westerns, even revisionist ones. The script plays it safe, however, by making the object of Dunbar's affections a white woman, however deeply acculturated into Sioux life she may be. Yet Stands with a Fist, like the other leading women in the tribe, is no mere token presence. Played with acute sensitivity by Mary McDonnell, she is the principal character in her own micro-drama – a twist on the captivity narratives of old, in which she dreads the thought of being wrested from the tribe and returned to white society. Employed initially as a narrative convenience, facilitating Dunbar's entry into Lakota society, she becomes vital thematically, living proof – even before Dunbar's adoption – of a level of generosity, compassion and tolerance on the part of the Sioux that would be unthinkable were it an Indian seeking acceptance among whites. (The fate of the couple once they leave the tribe, fearful that Dunbar's presence – effectively as a deserter – will hasten military reprisals, remains ambiguous.[5])

It is this near-pious vision of the Lakota that encapsulates the tension between the film's progressive urges and its reliance on convention. Only once, when the naïve Dunbar is horrified to find his new friends celebrating the mutilation of white buffalo hunters, are we shown a darker side to the tribe, and even this brief scene is absent from the three-hour, Oscar-winning release print. By the time the Sioux rescue Dunbar from the clutches of thuggish soldiers, who have tortured him as a traitor, audiences have been conditioned to cheer every arrow

that finds a white target. The racial identity of heroes and villains has been reversed or even dissolved, although moral authority continues to rest in the white protagonist, as when Dunbar gently dissuades Wind in His Hair from scalping one of the bodies. While seeking to rectify racist portrayals of (select) Native Americans in westerns, *Dances with Wolves* feels the need to rehabilitate them. Another of its precursors, Samuel Fuller's *Run of the Arrow*, in which Rod Steiger sought refuge among the Sioux from Civil War-torn white America, had been considerably bolder, in accord with its director's personality.

Visually opulent, beautifully acted by its Indian cast, *Wolves* sweeps confidently from the epic – a buffalo hunt; lingering panoramas of the Great Plains – to the intimate, paying special attention to the intricacies of tribal customs, albeit as experienced by a white man. It would have been a significant achievement even for a veteran director, let alone a debutant, and Costner deserved the accolades that came his way. Yet naysayers raised salient points about generalisations, sentimentality, and a romanticism that sometimes verges on the cloying. There was also surprise at its popular reception. Richard Combs of the *Monthly Film Bulletin* concluded: "It's a Fifties western with inklings of the Seventies… in films like *Jeremiah Johnson* or *Little Big Man*. But where the Seventies had Vietnam to draw on for political or metaphorical meaning, *Dances with Wolves* has none." Now it seems clearer that Costner and Blake, with their vision of Lakota society as a prelapsarian haven from the madness and corruption of civilisation – a metaphor, perhaps, for Eighties excess – were bringing the western into the New Age. **KG**

footnotes

1 Costner was turned down by more than one studio while shopping around the script (Michael Blake had suffered the same frustration when pitching his novel to publishers); a three-hour western, much of it subtitled, with no major stars, was not considered good business. Eventually he secured financing from overseas, investing his own cash to keep the production afloat when overruns threatened to sink it.

2 Dunbar's bewilderment at this point was mirrored by a number of reviewers when the initial 181-minute cut of *Dances with Wolves* was released. What seemed like a plot hole – the fate of the soldiers at Fort Sedgwick – is filled in satisfactorily in the subsequent 'special edition', which runs around 50 minutes longer.

3 'Dances with Wolves', in *The Movie Book of the Western* (Cassell, 1996).

4 'Going Indian', in *Hollywood's Indian: The Portrayal of the Native American in Film* (Peter C. Rollins, John E. O'Connor, eds, University Press of Kentucky, 2003).

5 Michael Blake reprised the story in a second novel, *The Holy Road* (2001), in which the couple's happy family life is disrupted when Stands with a Fist and one of their children are kidnapped by white rangers.

above: Dunbar (Kevin Costner) and Stands with a Fist (Mary McDonnell) in a romantic interlude.

Unforgiven

1992, Colour, 130 mins.

D: Clint Eastwood. P: Clint Eastwood (Malpaso). W: David Webb Peoples. Ph: Jack N. Green. M: Lennie Niehaus. St: Clint Eastwood (William Munny), Gene Hackman (Little Bill Daggett), Morgan Freeman (Ned Logan), Richard Harris (English Bob), Jaimz Woolvett (the Schofield Kid)

"It's a hell of a thing, killin' a man. You take away all he's got, and all he's ever gonna have."

The story of a reformed gunman's relapse, *Unforgiven* traces its protagonist's harrowing journey into his past via the turbulent mindscape of film noir. It thrives on the tension between audience expectations and assumptions – of Clint Eastwood's star image, of the righteousness of western violence – and the revisionist impulses of David Webb Peoples' script.[1] Peoples' aversion to the intellectual justification of violence in traditional westerns, with their relatively clean ethical distinctions, was the key to his unorthodox approach to situations and character. He may have been surprised that the script found such favour with Eastwood, popularly associated as he was with might-is-right action films. Yet the blurring of moral lines in *Unforgiven* could scarcely have been tailored more sharply for the man whose own westerns had taken their lead on this matter from the 'Dollars' films. "I like it that the good guys aren't all good and the bad guys aren't all that bad," he said, a sentiment with which Sergio Leone, his first directorial mentor, would certainly have concurred.[2]

Eastwood was never one to bask in the romantic glow of the Old West; in *Unforgiven*, this quality proves to be as illusory as the fantasies peddled by dime novelist Beauchamp. Much of the film concerns the creation and destruction of myth. Characters act on hearsay and rumour; reminiscences are met by rebuttals; reputations brought low by cold reality. William Munny, widower, devoted father, bumbling farmer, is a dormant "assassin… killer of women and children"; Little Bill Daggett, Earp-like town tamer and hapless carpenter, is a bully and a sadist, yet not entirely unsympathetic; English Bob, the noble 'Duke of Death' of Beauchamp's apocryphal tome, shoots Chinamen for a living; the Schofield Kid, for all his Billy the Kid bravado, is a callow youth who can see barely 50 yards and has never drawn blood. It is entirely fitting that the event that unites these disparate characters – a vicious knife attack on an immature prostitute, for which her co-workers place a bounty on the cowboys responsible – becomes grotesquely exaggerated in the retelling: "They cut up her face, cut her eyes out, cut her fingers off, cut her teats… everything but her cunny, I suppose."

It falls to Munny and Little Bill to debunk the legends with which western historiography, as embodied

by Beauchamp, has become encrusted. When the supercilious English Bob arrives in Big Whiskey, the scene of the crime, Little Bill wastes little time in knocking him down to size – both physically and in terms of his credibility. (He will later extend the same welcome to a feverish Munny.) Bob's killing of Two-Gun Corcoran – so called "not because he was sportin' two pistols, but because he had a dick so big it was longer than the barrel on that Walker Colt he carried" – was not the fair fight depicted in Beauchamp's embroidered account, but the result of jealousy, drunkenness and opportunism on Bob's part. Beauchamp subsequently becomes Little Bill's pet, feasting on his colourful anecdotes; eventually he witnesses the truth of the sheriff's statement that speed on the draw is less important than a cool head, when Munny comes gunning for Little Bill at the end of the film. For his part, Munny's insights – "We've all got it comin'... Deserve's got nothin' to do with it" – establish a context in which considerations of innocence or guilt become moot, especially in the whirlwind generated by blood lust and bounty money. He becomes a conduit for Peoples' contention – hardly revolutionary, but not usually addressed in westerns – that violence has consequences; that it corrupts. Munny's perspective is skewed by shame and guilt at his own murderous legacy – the source, according to Richard Schickel, of the "soul sickness" that consumes him on the stormy journey to Big Whiskey.[3]

The moral is couched in such a rich vernacular, and borne by characters so fully realised, that any didacticism is muted. "Every killing in it has a repercussion. It really tears people up when they are violent," said Eastwood.[4] The point is illustrated most compellingly by the killing of the cowboys. Davey Boy, innocent of the attack but guilty by association, is mortally wounded by Munny, shooting from a ridge, when Munny's old partner, Ned Logan, finds he no longer has the stomach for murder. Davey's agonizingly protracted death militates against any sense of satisfaction on the bounty hunters' part, let alone that 'justice' has been served. The Schofield Kid is granted the 'honour' of dispatching the actual perpetrator, Big Mike, catching him off guard in an outhouse. Paradoxically, this sordid episode leads to the film's most optimistic scene, in which the once cocksure Kid, sickened by his actions, forswears violence and the riches he imagines it yields: "I guess I'd rather be blind and ragged than dead."

Stoicism in the face of conflict is a hallmark of westerns; it is not the case in *Unforgiven*. The Kid's trauma is paralleled by Munny's psychological torment, while Eastwood as director is just as concerned with the apprehension in the build-up to violence – what Janet Thumin calls the film's "articulation of fear"[5] – and the horror it provokes – hence the frequent reaction shots of wincing faces – as he is by the beatings and shootings themselves.

The only stage at which *Unforgiven* appears to bow to convention is during the climax, when Munny returns to Big Whiskey to avenge Ned's killing by Little Bill and his deputies. The backdrop of raging storm – a recurring motif at moments of tension – combined with Munny's wraith-like appearance and quasi-supernatural efficiency in the ensuing gunfight lend the scene a gothic air reminiscent of *High Plains Drifter*. Having being kept in check for much of the film, which subjects the director-star to indignities and anxieties that belie his invulnerable image, here is the Eastwood persona renascent, adding a layer of ambiguity that a number of critics have found troubling. Eastwood was savvy enough to realise that for all his efforts to address "the moral implications of violence", that it should not be used for entertainment, "The public may say, 'Yeah, I get the morality of it, but I like it better when you're just blowing people away.'"[6] In other words, Munny's slaying of his enemies "implicates the film in the violence it is critiquing".[7] The ending does indeed deliver the 'satisfaction' that Eastwood watchers may crave, but only if one overlooks the details – his killing of an unarmed man, shooting another in the back, executing the wounded Little Bill ("I don't deserve this..."), threatening the lives of innocent families – which seem to confirm that Munny really is the bloodthirsty madman his reputation suggests, and that, in the Nietzschean sense, he has acknowledged and accepted his "created essence".[8] In the context of Eastwood's westerns, it is as if the lies told about Josey Wales become the truth about William Munny – as far as truth can be ascertained in *Unforgiven*.

It was a mark of Eastwood's confidence in the material, and his ambitions for the film, that he cast other A-list actors alongside him – not often the case in his directed works. Gene Hackman, Morgan Freeman and Richard Harris transmit the residual glamour of ageing stars to roles evocative of the West's fabled past. Hackman's overbearing, moralistic lawman – Popeye Doyle meets Dirty Harry – represents the patriarchal conservatism that Peoples holds responsible for much of the bloodshed that ails the West and, by extension, America as a whole.[9] The fight for justice initiated by Frances Fisher's Strawberry Alice and her fellow prostitutes, outraged that Little Bill lets off the offending cowboys with a mere fine, was an attempt to challenge that dominance; perhaps even to open the door, however cautiously, to feminism. If the film does strike a blow for women's rights, however, it is the right to set in motion violent events with the same hot-bloodedness, the same scant regard for the consequences, as male characters always have done.

The limelight may be shared, but the focal point remains William Munny, as both a distorted reflection of the Eastwood persona, stripped here of his customary nonchalance, and a deconstruction of the gunfighter archetype, reduced to its psychopathic essence. Munny's tenure as a peaceful smallholder – glimpsed in the pastoral images that bracket the drama – proves as fragile as his grasp on reality, once he gets the smell of violence and the taste of whisky back in his system. David Webb Peoples recognised Munny's tragedy as his inability to be the 'normal' man he yearns to be. Joining the hunt for the cowboys purely, Munny claims, out of economic necessity, he also insists – principally, one suspects, to himself – that he has no intention of returning to the wild ways of which he'd supposedly been purged by his late wife. As a character with roots in the noir tradition, however, he ultimately has no choice. The confrontation in Big Whiskey's saloon represents not the character's apotheosis, therefore, but his nadir – his fragile new identity no match for the cold-blooded killer of old.

Light follows darkness: the closing script suggests that Munny took his children to San Francisco, "where it was rumoured he prospered in dry goods"; this says much about the enduring myth of the regenerative potential of the West, even for "a man of notoriously vicious and intemperate disposition". But *Unforgiven* shows that myths cannot bear scrutiny, and these tentatively optimistic words, imprinted on a golden sunset, fail to dispel the memory of Munny's terrifying reversion to type. **KG**

footnotes

1 Richard Schickel's term "re-revisionist" is actually more apt, given that the screenplay was written in the mid-Seventies, after the anti-western had overhauled some genre conventions while dispensing with others. Eastwood bought it in 1983, after Francis Ford Coppola had let his option lapse.
2 *Unforgiven* is dedicated jointly to Leone and Don Siegel, whose influence on Eastwood's career, as both actor and director, was equally profound.
3 Eastwood denied emphatically that he was somehow repenting for the lives his characters had taken with such indifference in many of his previous movies.
4 Interview with Clint Eastwood by Kenneth Turan in *The Movie Book of the Western* (Ian Cameron and Douglas Pye, eds, Cassell, 1996).
5 "'Maybe He's Tough But He Sure Ain't No Carpenter": Masculinity and In/competence in *Unforgiven*', in *The Western Reader* (Jim Kitses and Gregg Rickman, eds, Limelight Editions, 1999).
6 Interview with Clint Eastwood by Kenneth Turan in *The Movie Book of the Western.*
7 Jim Kitses, *Horizons West* (BFI, 2007).
8 Shai Biderman, 'Do Not Forsake Me, Oh My Darling', in *The Philosophy of the Western* (Jennifer L. McMahon and B. Steve Csaki, eds, University Press of Kentucky, 2010).
9 Eastwood wanted Hackman to pattern his portrayal of Little Bill after Daryl Gates, the long-serving, hardline Los Angeles Chief of Police who was in charge at the time of the Rodney King beating; invoking the King case, the director-star felt that *Unforgiven* was highlighting the same tendency to violence in American society.

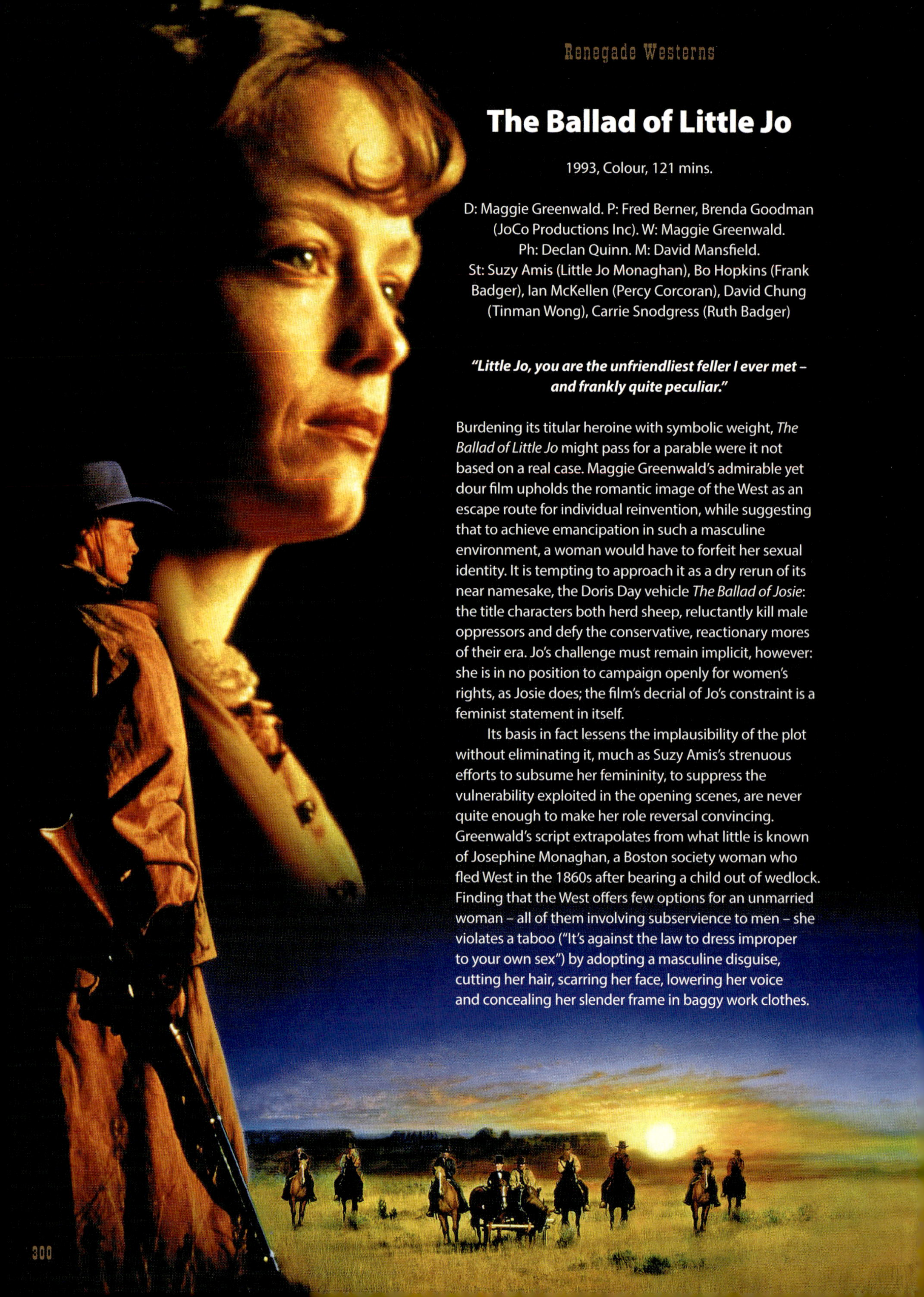

The Ballad of Little Jo

1993, Colour, 121 mins.

D: Maggie Greenwald. P: Fred Berner, Brenda Goodman (JoCo Productions Inc). W: Maggie Greenwald. Ph: Declan Quinn. M: David Mansfield. St: Suzy Amis (Little Jo Monaghan), Bo Hopkins (Frank Badger), Ian McKellen (Percy Corcoran), David Chung (Tinman Wong), Carrie Snodgress (Ruth Badger)

"Little Jo, you are the unfriendliest feller I ever met – and frankly quite peculiar."

Burdening its titular heroine with symbolic weight, *The Ballad of Little Jo* might pass for a parable were it not based on a real case. Maggie Greenwald's admirable yet dour film upholds the romantic image of the West as an escape route for individual reinvention, while suggesting that to achieve emancipation in such a masculine environment, a woman would have to forfeit her sexual identity. It is tempting to approach it as a dry rerun of its near namesake, the Doris Day vehicle *The Ballad of Josie*: the title characters both herd sheep, reluctantly kill male oppressors and defy the conservative, reactionary mores of their era. Jo's challenge must remain implicit, however: she is in no position to campaign openly for women's rights, as Josie does; the film's decrial of Jo's constraint is a feminist statement in itself.

Its basis in fact lessens the implausibility of the plot without eliminating it, much as Suzy Amis's strenuous efforts to subsume her femininity, to suppress the vulnerability exploited in the opening scenes, are never quite enough to make her role reversal convincing. Greenwald's script extrapolates from what little is known of Josephine Monaghan, a Boston society woman who fled West in the 1860s after bearing a child out of wedlock. Finding that the West offers few options for an unmarried woman – all of them involving subservience to men – she violates a taboo ("It's against the law to dress improper to your own sex") by adopting a masculine disguise, cutting her hair, scarring her face, lowering her voice and concealing her slender frame in baggy work clothes.

Arriving in the mining town of Ruby City, she tries to stay aloof from the uncouth miners and macho ranchers, chief among them the boorish Frank Badger, whose curiosity is nevertheless piqued by this insular, seemingly fragile yet quietly determined youngster, so unlike the gregarious locals: "I been trying to figure you out… Maybe you're one of those strange ones that can't stand company." He gives Jo a job, tending sheep over winter on the outskirts of his ranch, and Jo eventually earns enough to buy and maintain her own modest spread, relishing what Tania Modleski calls "the pleasures of solitude".[1]

All of this makes for a satisfyingly skewed perspective on the rituals associated with the western – panning for gold, learning to shoot and tend livestock, for example. But when Jo rescues Tinman Wong, an itinerant Chinaman, from the brutish attentions of Badger and his racist cronies, and then accepts him as her "houseboy" and, subsequently, lover, the film comes to resemble a rather strained metaphor for social prejudice and intolerance across gender and racial lines. "In our history and our popular culture, the same thing has been done to Asian men that's been done to women," said Greenwald. "They're extras, they're in the background, or they're in the kitchen… I felt the two would connect with each other through a similar experience of life."[2] The couple's life of blissful, gender-neutral domesticity – rendered in a series of unusually radiant, sensual scenes – is haunted by the knowledge that were they to be discovered, their neighbours would probably lynch them. The coda, set decades later, centres on the shock that courses through Ruby City when the recently deceased Jo's secret is exposed, rudely, on the mortician's table. Badger's fury at the deception only subsides when he finds a portrait of the young Josephine in her cabin.

For all its positive noises about individual forbearance, *Little Jo* comes dangerously close to being a sexist tract in reverse. Greenwald establishes early on that men cannot be trusted; they are predatory, duplicitous and bestial. Jo is seduced by a scoundrel, hawked like chattel by a shifty pedlar, assaulted and almost murdered by rogue soldiers. There is some irony, then, when Ian McKellen's clerk Percy Corcoran, the only other man in Ruby City to appreciate Jo's sense of "decency", is revealed to be the most misogynistic of all, a sexual sadist who inflicts an *Unforgiven*-style punishment on a prostitute because she "wouldn't put it in her mouth". The only fully sympathetic male character is Tinman, and it is noticeable that with his graceful movements, quiet manner and flowing locks, not to mention the domestic chores he undertakes, he occupies a space conventionally reserved for a woman. Hence a minor scene in which Jo, in "masculine" guise, gazes with voyeuristic pleasure as Tinman, coded as female in this scenario, bathes his glistening tresses in a creek, takes on a greater significance.

The film is at its most persuasive when depicting, à la *Heartland* (1979), both the rigours of frontier life and the satisfaction of working the land – scenes in which, paradoxically, Jo's gender seems irrelevant. (Although it is difficult to imagine the waif-like Amis successfully completing some of the more physically demanding activities.) "More than anything, I wanted the land to be a character in the film," said Greenwald. Declan Quinn's photography accentuates the ruggedness rather than the scenic properties of the Montana exteriors, employing relatively dull tones to neutralise their grandeur and utilising tighter compositions than most westerns, to emphasise the characters' intimacy with nature. Two scenes involving a family of Russian émigrés capture both the thrill of setting down roots in virgin wilderness and the onerous task it presents – five years after escorting these excited newcomers to their isolated plot, Jo pays a return visit; Greenwald's camera pans discreetly past a number of crosses that testify to the toll the land extracts from the weak and the vulnerable.

Greenwald is not averse to genre mainstays, embroiling her heroine in a confrontation with Eastern speculators that culminates in her shooting and killing two hired gunmen. In one sense this seems like a needless distraction, a foretaste of more commercial 'feminist' westerns such as *Bad Girls* and *The Quick and the Dead*; Greenwald does not even bother to follow the repercussions through. But the scene does serve a purpose: after Jo fells her assailants, the camera tracks round to reveal her distress; only a woman, it is implied, would be so affected by violence, compounding all her other travails, without becoming hardened. (We can only assume this of Jo – Amis maintains the character's camouflage so successfully that it is difficult to penetrate the façade to see the person within.) It is this sensitivity that Greenwald and the other main characters find attractive, even if, as in the case of Frank Badger, they don't really know why. **KG**

footnotes

1 Interview with Maggie Greenwald by Tania Modleski in *The Western Reader* (Jim Kitses and Gregg Rickman, eds, Limelight, 1998).
2 Ibid.

Geronimo: An American Legend

1993, Colour, 115 mins.

D: Walter Hill. P: Walter Hill, Neil Canton (Columbia). W: John Milius, Larry Gross. Ph: Lloyd Ahern. M: Ry Cooder. St: Jason Patric (Lt. Charles Gatewood), Gene Hackman (Brigadier General George Crook), Robert Duvall (Al Sieber), Wes Studi (Geronimo), Matt Damon (Lt. Britton Davis)

"With all this land, why is there no room for the Apache? Why does the White Eye want all land?"

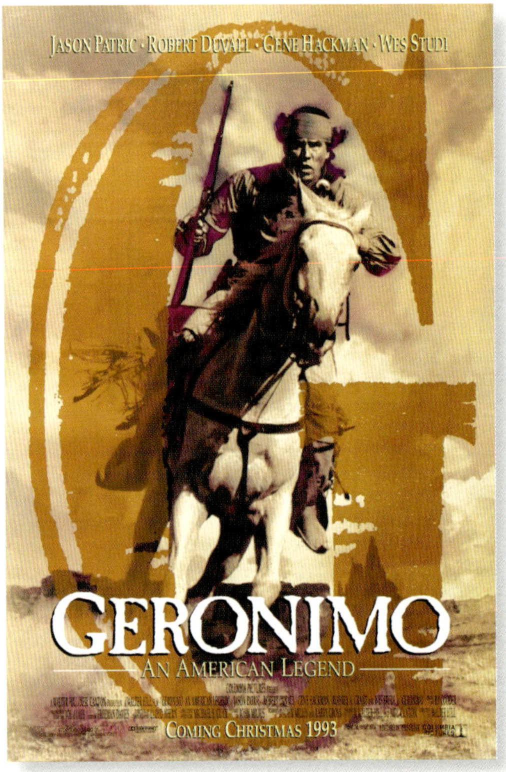

Although it was compromised by studio-mandated rewrites, Walter Hill's film is a commendable attempt to bring in from the cold one of the West's most vilified figures. Set in 1885-6, the dying days of the Indian Wars in the American Southwest, it follows the efforts of the US Army under the reformist General Crook to pacify the last of the Chiricahua Apache diehards. Almost inevitably, as a major Hollywood production, the point of view is that of white pursuers – principally the two junior officers, Charles Gatewood and narrator Britton Davis, most intimate with Geronimo. On the face of it this doesn't represent much progress from previous cycles of well-intentioned, pro-Indian westerns. Wes Studi, the imposing Cherokee actor and activist who gives a commanding performance as the chief, even felt the film's perspective contributed to its box-office failure: "People were disappointed… because it wasn't just about Geronimo, it was about interpretations of myth and stories."[1] The title, indeed, is something of a misnomer. In defending his film's even-handedness, however, Hill's reasoning was sound: "That came out of my reading of historical accounts, and realising that so much of what we think we know about the Indian campaigns is wrong. The Army is generally depicted as the enemy of the Apache, but in many cases, the people who were most sympathetic to their plight were those soldiers."[2]

Not for the first time, writer John Milius saw a project he intended as a hard-hitting history lesson – his Geronimo was less noble than savage – watered down into something more palatable for the masses (see 1972's *The Life and Times of Judge Roy Bean*). The finished script, reworked by Hill and Larry Gross (*48 Hrs.*), shows a keen interest in Apache customs and spiritual beliefs (as in *Run of the Arrow*, the Indians' religious system is equated roughly with Christianity as the film strives to collapse the distance between the races), gives the issue of territorial rights its due and decries injustice and governmental mendacity. But – and this is where Milius's disaffection comes in – it is comparatively coy regarding Geronimo. In his memoirs, Britton Davis balanced respect for the Apache's tenacity and leadership skills with caustic comments about his "vicious, intractable and treacherous" character. Hill doesn't shy away from detailing Geronimo's ruthlessness against his enemies – notably a scene in which his men massacre a band of unarmed miners – but there is none of the blunt brutality of Milius's original story, and nothing to suggest the title character was capable of callousness against his own people, such as the abandonment of women and children to facilitate his warriors' escape from an ambush.[3]

Nevertheless, there are traces of Milius's mythopoeic imprint. "At times it seemed we were chasing a spirit more than a man," says Davis, and many of Hill's shots endow the great warrior with an otherworldly aura. Studi's portrayal adds substance, however; his Geronimo is a man of flesh and blood, dynamic and resolute, bitter when recounting the litany of wrongs against his people, yet exhibiting sadness and flickers of dry humour (a quality sorely lacking elsewhere) behind the famous scowl. His complex take on the character is a welcome rejoinder to previous renderings, which ranged from straight-up villainy (*Geronimo* [1939]; *Broken Arrow*) to bland, square-jawed integrity (*Geronimo* [1962], with Chuck Connors in the title role).

The script is broadly faithful to the chronology of events: a sequence of Apache breakouts from the San Carlos reservation; a series of incursions into Mexico, the tribe's traditional hunting ground; hard bargaining between Geronimo and Gatewood; Crook's replacement by General Miles (Kevin Tighe), a hardliner from the old school ("I hate an idealist"); the final surrender and banishment of the Apaches – even the scouts who faithfully served the Army; Gatewood's own transfer to a remote post, "sentenced to obscurity" for criticising the government's forked tongue. The central characterisations also ring true. Gene Hackman brings a gruff, schoolmasterly quality to General Crook, whose sympathy for the Apaches is well documented: "[The Indian] is excusable in seeing no justice in a government which only punishes him, while it allows the white man to plunder him as he pleases," he once said.[4] Jason Patric is perhaps a shade too deliberate as the softly spoken Southerner Gatewood, whose empathy with the Apaches stems in part from his family's participation in an earlier lost cause, the Civil War; while Robert Duvall leavens the earnest tone as grizzled scout Al Sieber, a veteran Indian fighter who pinpoints the ambiguity in Gatewood's role: "You don't love who you're fighting for, and you don't hate who you're fighting against."

The major deviations from history include the retention of the narrator to the end of the campaign (Davis had, in fact, resigned his commission around the time of Crook's replacement by Miles, well before Geronimo's ultimate surrender) and the omission from the scenario of Captain Henry Ware Lawton, leader of the expedition that eventually brought the Apaches back from Mexico for good. That may be unfair on Lawton, but the filmmakers were justified in keeping the focus on Gatewood, whose crucial role in persuading Geronimo to turn himself in is not disputed by historians. Also absent is any sense of the chief's culpability in the events that led to Crook's enforced resignation, which followed Geronimo's alcohol-fuelled flight back to Mexico, reneging on a promise to capitulate.

Hill honours classic westerns, and their conventions, even as he reaches conclusions about the extirpation of the Apaches that many of his forebears would have ridden around. The Utah locations, rendered almost magical at times by cinematographer Lloyd Ahern's employment of colour filters, were once favoured by John Ford, while the narration by a callow cavalryman echoes *Major Dundee* and *Ulzana's Raid*. There are bad whites – a racist lawman, a pack of Peckinpah-esque scalp hunters – but not really any bad Indians. The iniquities of the reservation system and Washington's deception of its Indian charges come under fire, while the predicament of the Apache scouts, torn between blood ties and obedience to their Army employers, suggests an absorbing film could yet be made on the subject. Steve Reevis is especially impressive as the

diligent Chato – a character based on a Chiricahua chief who volunteered for the Geronimo campaign – who bears the scorn of his tribal peers (the Apaches converse with each other in their own language) and the injustice of his summary dismissal with silent dignity.

Where anger was once the dominant mode of pro-Indian westerns, here there is profound regret ("A way of life that endured a thousand years was gone" – a sentiment geared towards guilt-tripping white liberals rather than contemporary Apache, for whom "regret" is probably not apposite), as well as poignancy in the sight of Geronimo and his band bundled onto trains bound for exile in faraway Florida, where many of them would succumb to disease. "Once I moved about like the wind," the weary warrior says to his Army captors. "Now I surrender to you and that is all." **KG**

footnotes

1 Interview with Wes Studi by Walter Chaw, Film Freak Central. As Studi also points out, however, the film's chances were hit by the near-simultaneous airing of a rival biopic made for the TNT television network.

2 Interview with Walter Hill by Jon Zelazny, thehollywoodinterview.blogspot.com

3 Documented in Louis Kraft, *Gatewood & Geronimo* (UNM Press, 2000).

4 Quoted in Dee Brown, *Bury My Heart at Wounded Knee* (Holt, Rinehart & Winston, 1970).

"Once I moved about like the wind": Geronimo (Wes Studi) in captivity.

Posse

1993, Colour, 111 mins.

D: Mario Van Peebles. P: Preston Holmes, Jim Steele (Working Title). W: Sy Richardson, Dario Scardapane. Ph: Peter Menzies Jr. M: Michel Colombier. St: Mario Van Peebles (Jesse Lee), Stephen Baldwin (Jimmy J. 'Little J' Teeters), Charles Lane (Weezie), Tiny Lister (Obobo), Big Daddy Kane (Father Time)

"History is a funny thing… People forget their past, and they forget the truth."

Bookended by Woody Strode's Jack Crabbe-like retorts to the standard, Caucasian-centric history of frontier expansion, *Posse* proclaims the importance of African-Americans in the process by raiding cinema's stock of western motifs and restaging them from a black perspective. Sepia-toned photographs and seldom-quoted statistics – a third of all cowboys on the Chisolm Trail were black; freedmen established more than 20 African-American enclaves in Oklahoma alone towards the end of the 19th century – set the scene for Mario Van Peebles and his writers' rambunctious riff on plot elements familiar from innumerable older westerns.[1] "I have pocket watches with chimes and people crashing through windows in slow motion and gunfighters silhouetted against the sunset and golden bullets and good white guys and bad black guys and bad white guys and good black guys and lots of horses and dust and six-shooters. I don't think I missed much," said the director-star, trumpeting the qualities of pastiche that, combined with his gaudy direction, come close to smothering the message.[2]

An eclectic cast of veteran actors and swaggering hip-hop stars do their best to keep pace with the plot, which traces the flight West of Jesse Lee and a handful of renegade soldiers – the titular posse, in the urban slang sense. Stealing away from the

from left: Tiny Lister, Tone Loc, Stephen Baldwin, Mario Van Peebles, Big Daddy Kane, Charles Lane

Cuban-American War with a fortune in gold, evading their corrupt and eccentric commander (Billy Zane), they drift first to New Orleans for Mardi Gras, before following Jesse to the black settlement of Freedomville and a reckoning with his father's Ku Klux Klan assassins.

The cinematic references are copious, from plot points and costumes to directorial technique – Van Peebles cribs from Leone, Peckinpah and Eastwood (as both director and star), while a sojourn in Monument Valley serves no other purpose than to evoke the universe of John Ford. It is as if the western has been wrested from the ideological clutches of white artists, its racial hierarchy reordered to admit black heroes to the pantheon.[3] (In a sarcastic touch, Jesse Lee's band includes a token white, the irreverent Little J.) *Posse's* protagonists are amiable enough and solidly acted, but most of the roles are underwritten; more effort seems to have been expended on honing the jibes that ricochet among them. The performance styles, dialect and much of the soundtrack are deliberately anachronistic; together with the presence of Strode, one of the few black actors to boast a meaningful association with the western, and symbolic cameos by icons from the blaxploitation era – Isaac Hayes, Pam Grier, Robert Hooks, Van Peebles' father, maverick film-maker Melvin – they create a snapshot of black popular culture, past and present. Van Peebles extends the tribute to the screen's first black western star, inserting snippets of Thirties singing cowboy Herb Jeffries during the closing credits. (There is footage of Strode in *Once Upon a Time in the West*, to boot.)

All this might seem to flow from Strode's opening history lesson, which enjoins spectators to remember the racial minorities – Native American as well as black – extirpated from their lands and, in the case of blacks, from popular chronicles and fictional re-creations of the West. (We are expected to gauge the common lot of America's ethnic underclasses from a token scene in which Chinese immigrants, African- and Native Americans toil as railroad labourers.) But *Posse* does nothing to acknowledge the achievements of the many real-life African-American cowboys to whom it is ostensibly a panegyric. For that matter, a script based on the life of, say, Nat Love or Bose Ikard would have better served the purpose of reinstalling black pioneers to their rightful place in the history of the frontier.[4]

Whether such a film would have found studio backing and a willing audience is another matter. Van Peebles spoke of his frustration, while he was preparing *Posse*, that, "Nobody is interested in black period pieces. All black movies have to be set in the 'hood; that's the rule, or they fail." (This was two decades before *12 Years a Slave*.) His previous film was the inner-city crime thriller *New Jack City* (1991), with which *Posse* shares its brash modern style (one wag dubbed it 'New Dodge City') and salty, rapid-fire repartee, while the camaraderie of the outlaws and the coming together of the black community in self-defence has as much in common with the aforementioned "'hood" movies as it does with *The Magnificent Seven* et al. Considering the context, one can hardly blame Van Peebles for hewing closely to a successful formula. His own character, the studiedly laconic Jesse Lee, owes his demeanour to two further traditions: the Leone/Eastwood school of westerns and the narcissistic posturing of blaxploitation films.[5] Van Peebles' attempt to fuse these various influences results in what one critic called "sensory overload" – a ragbag of thematic odds and ends served up with a fussy, flashy visual style geared towards the attention-deficient MTV generation, with nods to the western's past masters.

Posse is unashamedly polemical; it ends with a denunciation of income inequality between races. This is not to say it is one-dimensional – not all its white characters are bad, not all blacks noble – but like other films that have challenged racial attitudes in the western, right up to *Django Unchained*, it falls back too readily on crude stereotyping. Its principal white villains are both portrayed as deranged: Richard Jordan gnashing his teeth as a white-supremacist sheriff; Billy Zane overstating his rogue cavalry officer's egocentricity. For a film with supposedly radical intentions, marketed as "the untold story of the Wild West", it remains fettered by convention. **KG**

footnotes

1 Co-writer Sy Richardson drew on the histories of his two grandfathers, one of whom had friends who claimed to have ridden with Jesse James.

2 Interview with Mario Van Peebles by Stephen Hunter in *The Baltimore Sun*, 9 May, 1993.

3 As Jim Kitses points out, *Posse* was one of a sequence of westerns that directed the spotlight away from white male protagonists – see also *Glory*, *Geronimo: An American Legend*, *The Ballad of Little Jo* and *The Quick and the Dead*.

4 Ikard, who rode on the famed Goodnight-Loving cattle trail, was the inspiration for the character Joshua Deets in Larry McMurtry's novel *Lonesome Dove*, played in the 1989 adaptation by Danny Glover.

5 Van Peebles replayed the role 10 years later for a cameo appearance in another black western, *Gang of Roses*, a distaff *Posse* that failed both artistically and commercially.

Dead Man

1995, B/W, 120 mins.

D: Jim Jarmusch. P: Demetra J. MacBride (12-Gauge Productions). W: Jim Jarmusch. Ph: Robby Muller. M: Neil Young. St: Johnny Depp (William Blake), Gary Farmer (Nobody), Lance Henriksen (Cole Wilson), Michael Wincott (Conway Twill), Robert Mitchum (John Dickinson)

"I've had it up to here with this Indian malarkey. I haven't understood a single word you've said."

Unpredictable and elegiac, beautiful and surreal, Jim Jarmusch's beguiling take on the genre distinguishes itself from other liberal westerns of the Nineties – Kevin Costner's *Dances with Wolves* being an important comparison – with its radical narrative and visual style and keen sense of irony, especially regarding its distinctly ineffective white protagonist. The odd-couple relationship between Johnny Depp's mortally wounded, slowly waning Cleveland accountant, William Blake, and his new-found friend, Nobody, an Indian of mixed blood, provides the platform for Jarmusch to explore a dystopian, decaying frontier. The deliberately uncommercial stylistic approach gives the director licence to push his agenda further than the more conventional Costner had dared. This skewed buddy movie is not just sympathetic to the historic plight of Native Americans; Jarmusch addressed his film to a nation "in denial of the fact that America is built on a genocide that far exceeded anything the Third Reich did".[1] Recalling the radicalism of earlier productions such as *The Wild Bunch, Little Big Man* and *Soldier Blue*, the film's bleak, black-and-white imagery and poetic allusions create a unique, hypnotic concoction; a eulogy for the plight of the downtrodden in a land whose indigenous inhabitants have been fenced in and vanquished.

Jarmusch also takes broad sideswipes at what he perceives as contemporary problems in the US. *Dead Man* has been described as "one of the most scathing critiques of modern American society in general".[2] The ugliness of unfettered capitalism is embodied by two individuals: John Dickinson, the metal-works owner in the town of Machine; and bounty hunter Cole Wilson. Introduced in an intimidating low-angle shot, Dickinson is every inch the rough individualist, with Robert Mitchum, in his final film performance, oozing that famed masculine menace. Truly without empathy, he refuses to listen to Blake's predicament after the man from the East turns up a month late for an accountancy job. His factory is a triumph of surreal set design, drawing from German Expressionism: the cantilevered platforms, hisses of steam and sweating, mute workers reflect a Langian nightmare.

Cole Wilson is a more explicit, primal version of the structured capitalism represented by Dickinson's empire. Paid to track Blake when the latter kills Dickinson's son, Charlie (Gabriel Byrne), in self-defence, Wilson is a man who will think nothing of slaying another to gain advantage. In one revolting moment he is seen eating human flesh, symbolically pushing to extremes the notion that in a ruthless, capitalist society, one man's gain can only mean another's loss. This grisly image also marks one of Jarmusch's most overt genre reversals: in a film in which Native Americans play a prominent role, it is a white man, a representative of the law, who is shown to be savage – a cannibal, no less – while the Indians, traditionally depicted in genre propaganda as a primitive race, are relatively benign.

Capitalism is not the only focus for Jarmusch's disdain. In one of the film's most oblique visual references, one of a pair of federal marshals – identically groomed and attired, they are named Lee and Marvin – has his head crushed under the weight of Wilson's boot. With his bald head and goatee, lying on a star-shaped pile of kindling, he is referred to as looking like a "goddam religious icon", but also bears an unmistakable resemblance to Lenin. This suggests that for Jarmusch, the political science of Marxism deserves no more respect than the rapacious industrialism of Machine – either that, or it indicates the utter contempt of capitalism for its rival creed. The most natural and balanced belief system in the film is that of the Indians, with their polytheistic lifestyle stemming from centuries living on land now being settled by whites.

Blake's friendship with Nobody, therefore, offers him the best opportunity for spiritual enlightenment, even if he is ultimately unable to perceive it. Nobody is first seen stooping over Blake while digging a knife into the white man's flesh, an image latent with menace, chosen by Jarmusch to upend another western trope: Nobody is not trying to end Blake's life, but to save it, by removing Charlie Dickinson's bullet. Nobody – in a standout performance by Gary Farmer, born in Canada into the Cayuga Nation – is neither a good nor a bad Indian, as indigenous people have been depicted in the majority of westerns. Instead, he is both complex and eccentric. He can be grumpy or witty, and doesn't suffer fools. When he is unable to remove "the white man's metal" from Blake's body, he asks him matter-of-factly if he has any tobacco, a question he poses to anyone they may meet on their subsequent journey together, and an important one given the film's elegiac closing moments.

It is the journey, and Blake's dawning discovery of the Indian way of life, rather than the flimsier outlaw-on-the-run plot, that is the film's central focus. The interaction between the two men provides much of the poetry and offbeat humour that make this film stand out in a decade of few truly challenging American films. Nobody explains how his father and mother came from different tribes, Blackfoot and Blood, how he was accepted by neither community and slowly learnt to cope with his outsider existence. Forcibly removed from tribal life by white settlers, he was enslaved and displayed to the people of Eastern cities before being shipped to England, where he was educated. There he discovered a passion for the verse of Romantic poet William Blake, and the revelation that the wounded man carries the same name convinces him that he is in the company of the poet's reincarnated soul.[3]

Nobody's biography grows gloomier when he explains how, on his return to America, he found settlements destroyed and many of his people dying – images of burnt-out Indian settlements pepper the film. Telling the tribe of his adventures in the East and across the Oceans, he was mockingly referred to as Exaybachay, meaning "He Who Talks Loud, Saying Nothing" – Jarmusch's reference to the James Brown song about liars and braggarts. 'Nobody' was another of Jarmusch's musical tributes, this time to country singer Conway Twitty, but the moniker also brings to mind the unorthodox Italian western *My Name Is Nobody* (1973), in which the title character similarly manipulates another man's destiny. It is also, of course, the 'name' Ulysses adopts in *The Odyssey* to escape from one of his most testing predicaments. Blake and Nobody are "both loners and... disoriented from their cultures", says Jarmusch, in many ways strangers to the land they were born in – a central theme in modern American independent cinema.

Two contrasting set pieces illustrate the differences between white and indigenous cultures, using point-of-view shots to introduce Blake's entrance into the town of Machine and, towards the end of the film, the riverside village of the Makah tribe. His arrival in Machine is an unnerving experience. (On the journey beforehand, the ominous train fireman, played by Crispin Glover, wondered why Blake was going to Hell to find a job. Glover's character has been identified with Charon, who ferried the dead to the underworld in Greek myth.[4]) There are drunks and gun-laden heavies. A prostitute services a client in a shadowy alleyway; he pulls a gun on the gawping Blake, who hastens away. Bones and skulls litter the pavement and streets, some proudly adorning buildings. The main street leads to Dickinson's factory, which belches black smoke – perhaps representative of Blake's dark Satanic mills. Nature has been rudely blighted by industrial progress. Towards the film's conclusion, the ailing Blake is carried through the Makah settlement. Jarmusch and DP Robby Muller substitute the hard, expressionistic style of the entrance to Machine with the fluid, documentary manner of neo-realism. The people here are poor and the streets grimy; totems indicate the importance of spirituality, in contrast to the factory that looms over Machine. The locals are mostly indifferent to the wounded white man; at any rate they are not hostile.

Scenes of destruction and discrimination against Native Americans appear throughout. Blake's mesmerising journey from East to West at the top of the film is disturbed by rifle fire from fur-clad hunters slaughtering buffalo from the train carriage as the engine slows – the result of a government decree, an attempt to cleanse the frontier by removing the Indians' chief source of subsistence. Later, telling the story of his return to the fledgling United States, Nobody recounts the nefarious methods used to eradicate the Indian; among them blankets, infected by tuberculosis and smallpox, given to them by tradesmen and missionaries. Christianity is treated as an invading theism, more destructive than the spiritual beliefs of Nobody and his people, supplying "the ideological justification for all manner of dishonesty, thievery, sexual rapacity, racism and murder".[5] In the act

above: Johnny Depp.
opposite top: Michael Wincott (left) and Lance Henriksen (right).

of befriending and escorting the dying man, Nobody has also encouraged Blake to be an avenging angel, "a scourge of God... a killer of white men". He tells Blake that now his "poetry will be written in blood". The cultural role reversal is apparent. This time it is a white man used by an Indian to do his bidding, not, as in many genre examples, an Indian – usually a cavalry scout – tamed by white civilisation to work against his own people.

With a bullet lodged in his chest and his life ebbing away, Blake has, although he never wholly understands it, undergone a transformation. For Nobody, he has become a spiritual being. While under the influence of peyote one night, the Indian envisages Blake's face as a skull, yet shows no fear at this omen. Unlike those who worship a Christian God, Nobody has no fear of what lies beyond death, viewing it merely as a passageway to "the next level of the world". Abandoned temporarily by Nobody as part of his initiation, Blake is subjected to his own visions. (To qualify as the hero that Nobody wants him to be, Blake must undergo this trial in the wilderness, this ancient rite of passage, by himself, just like his counterparts in the mythic narratives from which Jarmusch derives the structure of his story.) As Blake sleeps wild in a forest clearing, a tribe of Indians momentarily appears amid the foliage. Stumbling upon a dead fawn, Blake lies next to it in a foetal position, finding solace in nature. Eventually the friends are reunited. With Nobody securing a sea canoe from the Makah, into which he places a gift of tobacco, and Blake dressed in tribal clothes, the latter's journey enters its final phase. He remains bewildered, however, about the significance of his odyssey. Nobody tells him that he will be returning to the place whence he came. "You mean Cleveland?" asks Blake, his comic incomprehension undercutting the ritual preparation of the canoe and the sombre demeanour of his Indian friend.

With respect to the character's lack of understanding, Gregg Rickman calls *Dead Man*, "A comic deflation of the very notion of a spiritual quest."[6] Blake's trajectory from innocence to experience does not entail a simultaneous arrival at self-knowledge. His encounters with various grotesques along the seemingly meandering trail describe an almost infernal West ruled by greed, corruption and insanity. From Dickinson's ruthlessness, via the psychopathic bent of his hired hunter, to a bizarre episode involving three bickering trappers – tended to by a memorably befrocked Iggy Pop, playing mother – this is a place where freedom, like Blake himself, is already dying.

Nobody is both the hero's guide and ours. Neil Young's electric guitar, anachronistic to the period, is a sad chorus, echoing Blake's sense of being lost in a land where the customs and geography are alien to him. In the debate about the treatment of the Native American, Jarmusch, with an enigmatic style juxtaposed with moments of startling realism, directed a post-modern masterpiece; a key revisionist film about how the West was stolen, rather than won, an exposé of the nation's hidden history. **CH**

footnotes

1 Interview with Jim Jarmusch by Thomas Colbath and Steven Blush in *Seconds Magazine*, 1996.

2 Michael Valdez Moses, 'Savage Nations: Native Americans and the Western', in *The Philosophy of the Western* (Jennifer L. McMahon and B. Steve Csaki, eds, University Press of Kentucky, 2010).

3 This Blakeian subtext was a late addition, according to Jarmusch. "The character wasn't even named William Blake originally. I collected all my notes on the film and was about to write the script and I was reading all these books by American Indian people. Then I put all that stuff away and picked up William Blake, who I read a lot when I was younger... I was just struck by the connection in thought between a lot of the stuff I was reading and a lot of Blake's work. He just walked into the film on his own" (interview with Jim Jarmusch by Thomas Colbath and Steven Blush).

4 Gregg Rickman, 'Dead Man: the Western Under Erasure', in *The Western Reader* (Limelight Editions, 1998). Rickman also elucidates the many allusions in the film to the poetry of William Blake.

5 Valdez Moses, 'Savage Nations: Native Americans and the Western'.

6 Rickman, 'Dead Man: the Western Under Erasure'.

The Assassination of Jesse James by the Coward Robert Ford

2007, Colour, 160 mins.

D: Andrew Dominik. P: Brad Pitt, Dede Gardner, Ridley Scott, Jules Daly, David Valdes (JJ Pictures Inc). W: Andrew Dominik. Ph: Roger Deakins. M: Nick Cave, Warren Ellis. St: Casey Affleck (Robert Ford), Brad Pitt (Jesse James), Sam Shepard (Frank James), Mary-Louise Parker (Zee James), Paul Schneider (Dick Liddil)

"He was sorry about his cold-bloodedness, his dispassion, his inability to express what he now believed was the case – that he truly regretted killing Jesse, that he missed the man as much as anybody and wished his murder hadn't been necessary."

In the guise of a western, this is more accurately a psychological profile of two men who achieved notoriety, for different reasons, and were devoured by the cult of celebrity, which was almost as voracious then as it is now. The events and characters are familiar – the title alone indicates there will be no surprises here – but it locates their resonance for contemporary audiences in the way the deeds and personalities of these men, and men like them, were distorted, their options in life constrained, by the infamy that followed from their actions. Adapted from Roy Hansen's renowned novel, the script traces the last year of Jesse James's life, when his legend was intact ("Rooms seemed hotter when he was in them. Rains fell straighter. Clocks slowed. Sounds were amplified"), but his faculties and his hold over his men were beginning to fracture. The induction into his inner circle of 19-year-old Robert Ford, a sycophant with delusions of grandeur, accelerates Jesse's decline into terminal paranoia and brings to the fore what seems to be his death wish.

A dispassionate narrator imparts authorial gravitas to Andrew Dominik's sober analysis of sensationalised events. His elegant *mise en scène* is stylised almost to the point of distraction, in the early stages especially, by Roger Deakins' ostentatiously expressionistic photography. The settings tend towards austere, reflecting the desolation of the characters and the influence of the anti-westerns of the Seventies, while the colour palette, set to what has become the default desaturated mode, and the authentically drab costumes – suits, homburgs and bowler hats – reveal a drive for realism that is sometimes derailed by the self-consciously poetic imagery.

above: Jesse (Brad Pitt) keeps a wary eye on Bob Ford (Casey Affleck).

If there is something predictable about the look of the film, Dominik's take on the characters and the enduring mythology of the West is refreshing. As the marquee attraction, Jesse James/Brad Pitt often occupies the centre of the frame, or is silhouetted like a romantic hero, but it is the nonentity who worships him, Robert Ford, whose perspective predominates. (We might even imagine that the camera at these moments shows James as Ford has always imagined him.) There was a precedent for this seemingly radical step: in 1949, Samuel Fuller had focused on Ford, as played by John Ireland, in his snappy *I Shot Jesse James*, in which the killing of Jesse, who is portrayed in a kindly light, is dispensed with in the first reel. Dominik builds up to this event at leisure, recounting the story overall at almost twice the length of the earlier film, but this provides for a closer examination of the facts, so far as they are known (for Johnny D. Boggs, an authority on the James gang, *Assassination* is "the best movie about Jesse James in both historical accuracy and entertainment terms"[1]), and a much more detailed evocation of the era and the mindset of its inhabitants. It also gives Casey Affleck the platform to develop the role of Bob, whom he saw as "uncomfortable in his own skin… On one hand, this kid didn't know who he was, but he also felt like he was better than everyone else."[2] Affleck transmits the vulnerability of this self-regarding but socially inept young misfit, as well as the frustration of somebody convinced he is "destined for great things", but who is mocked and belittled by all around him. "The more you talk, the more you give me the willies," says Jesse's brother Frank, whose manner and dialogue are gratifyingly blunt in a film where characters are prone to obfuscation. ("You can hide things in vocabulary," notes one of the principals.)

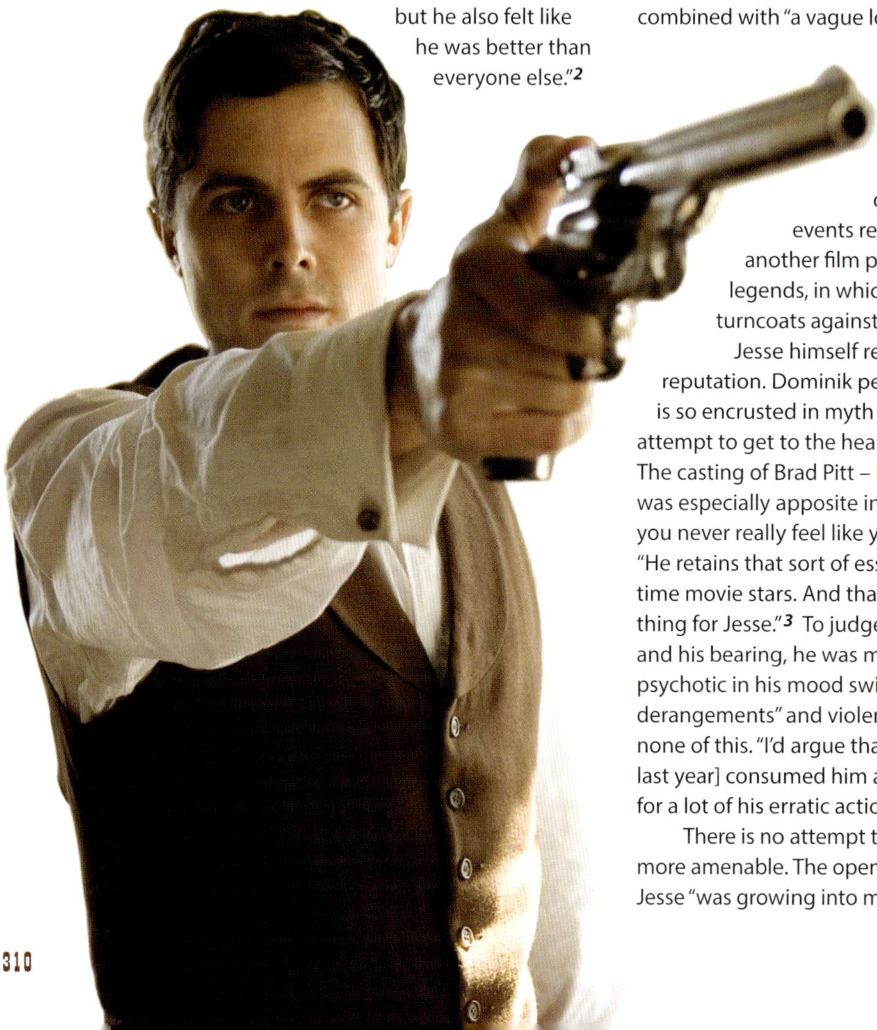

Almost spectrally pale, Bob haunts his scenes with Jesse like a harbinger of death, observing and scrutinising the charismatic outlaw with the fixity of a devotee. He keeps a shoebox full of dime novels dedicated to his idol and reads him romanticised newspaper clippings about his exploits; Jesse denies their veracity, but not too strongly. (Pitt calculates the character's vanity with the precision of a movie star accustomed to being flattered and fawned upon. Who better to understand how such admiration may corrupt the recipient?) Bob is like Moultrie from *The Left Handed Gun*, an obsessive fan who wants to believe the myth, even though he is subject to Jesse's mockery and witnesses his cruelty first-hand. Gradually, Bob, again like Moultrie, is disappointed to realise that his hero is "just a human being" – the last thing that Americans want their celebrities to be. This, combined with "a vague longing for glory", leads to his acceptance of what amounts to a commission from the state authorities to kill Jesse, thence to absorb the latter's lustre. (The Establishment's orchestration of these squalid events recalls *Pat Garrett and Billy the Kid*, another film predicated on the rewriting of legends, in which politicians pit outlaws and turncoats against their former allies.)

Jesse himself reflects the ambiguity of his reputation. Dominik perhaps realised that the outlaw is so encrusted in myth and spurious glamour that any attempt to get to the heart of the man would be folly. The casting of Brad Pitt – like Jesse, a native of Missouri – was especially apposite in this respect. "Brad is someone you never really feel like you know on screen," he said. "He retains that sort of essential mystery, like those old-time movie stars. And that seemed to be a really good thing for Jesse."[3] To judge the character by his actions and his bearing, he was manipulative, callous, almost psychotic in his mood swings, prone to "depressions and derangements" and violent outbursts. Pitt glosses over none of this. "I'd argue that [Jesse's] paranoia [during his last year] consumed him and certainly was responsible for a lot of his erratic action," the actor reasoned.[4]

There is no attempt to soften Jesse or make him more amenable. The opening lines inform us that in 1881 Jesse "was growing into middle age [he was 34], and was living then in a bungalow" with his wife and children. But this image of benign, pipe-smoking suburban anonymity is dispelled during the film's one conventional set piece, a nocturnal train robbery, brilliantly staged, in which Jesse brains a helpless guard with his pistol. Nor do his chroniclers play the Robin Hood card so often dealt by Jesse's apologists. He has the haggard look of a man physically and emotionally fatigued. (That he sleeps fitfully is confirmed in a late scene in which, sharing a room with Bob and his jittery brother, Charley [Sam Rockwell], Jesse is alive to Bob's furtive movements even though he appears to be slumbering. All the while, his hand is gripped tightly around his revolver.) By the end, Jesse seems to invite death, buying Bob the gun that will be used to kill him and, at the fateful moment, in the company of a clearly anxious Bob and Charley, deliberately disarming and turning his back. There is no evidence to support this interpretation of events; perhaps, though, cornered and weary, Jesse felt this was a way to control his legacy, perpetuate the myths that had already overtaken his reality. "He seems really indecisive about whether he wants to live or die, and the intention is that it's kind of a tale of assisted suicide," said Dominik.[5]

The film does not deny the popular view that Jesse was the victim of a betrayal – Ford's own testimony and his theatrical re-enactments of the event for public consumption allow for no misunderstanding – but it portrays outlawry in general as a web of treachery in which Jesse is caught as firmly as any of his men. Dominik presents it as a way of life that offers neither repose nor respite to its adherents. Jesse moves his family repeatedly, fearful of the Pinkertons; two of his henchmen, Wood Lite (Jeremy Renner) and Dick Liddil, likewise roam from one temporary refuge to another. Neither can these men relax in their own company. Jesse's minions are fearful of their leader's caprices; he, in turn, suspects their intentions, shooting the craven Ed Miller (Garret Dillahunt) in the back for sniffing after reward money. Wood and Dick also end up shooting each other; even at point-blank range, however, most of their bullets miss the mark, ridiculing the characters' nominal status as feared gunmen. It's in this scene that Bob is blooded: to spare Dick, he shoots Wood through the head, foreshadowing his killing of Jesse and visibly inflating his fragile self-esteem. Even this is not an example of camaraderie, however, since Bob later reveals Dick's whereabouts to the police.

above: Casey Affleck and Paul Schneider.
bottom left: Standing, from left: Garret Dillahunt, Paul Schneider, Jeremy Renner, Sam Rockwell, Casey Affleck. Seated, from left: Brad Pitt, Sam Shepard.

Dominik has been criticised for the languor of his pacing, but the coda, which condenses Ford's remaining 10 years after killing Jesse into 25 minutes, is a masterclass in economy. It is a compassionate account of Bob's relocation to New York and his increasing isolation from society. His unlikely stage career provides a means of both expiation and self-justification, but is also related to the grotesque commercialisation of Jesse's death that began with the exhibition of the outlaw's corpse immediately after the shooting. (There is a poignant section in which Charley, who plays Jesse in the re-enactments, becomes overwhelmed by guilt and takes his own life.) Wiping the smirk off Bob's face, Affleck ramps up his loneliness and bewilderment; having "expected applause" for killing Jesse, he meets only scorn. It is a brilliantly judged portrayal of an eternal outsider, a man who fatally misjudged the mercurial nature of popular acclaim, forced to accept the role of villain when he thought he'd become a hero. Fittingly, he meets his end in much the same way as Jesse – gunned down by a glory-hunter in his own saloon. **KG**

footnotes

1 *Jesse James and the Movies* (McFarland Press, 2011).
2 Interview with Casey Affleck in the *Chicago Sun Times*, 30 September, 2007.
3 Interview with Andrew Dominik by Paul Whittington in the *Irish Independent*, 30 November, 2007.
4 Interview with Brad Pitt in the *Chicago Sun Times*, 30 September, 2007.
5 Interview with Andrew Dominik by Paul Whittington in the *Irish Independent*, 30 November, 2007.

Bury My Heart at Wounded Knee

2007, Colour, 133 mins.

D: Yves Simoneau. P: Clara George (HBO). W: Daniel Giat, Dee Brown (book). Ph: David Franco. M: George S. Clinton. St: Adam Beach (Ohiyesa/Charles Eastman), August Schellenberg (Sitting Bull), Aidan Quinn (Senator Henry Dawes), Anna Paquin (Elaine Goodale), Fred Thompson (President Grant)

"They must adapt."
"Must they adapt, sir, to the point of their own extermination?"

Dee Brown's momentous chronicle of displacement, betrayal and broken treaties – "a narrative of the conquest of the American West as the victims experienced it" – was published a year after American Indian Movement activists occupied Alcatraz Island, the same year in which Vine Deloria Jr.'s *Custer Died for Your Sins* framed Indian demands as a political manifesto. Millions of Americans were agitating in favour of civil rights and against the Vietnam War. On screen, Brown's book had the incendiary *Little Big Man* and *Soldier Blue* for company, trumpeting the same causes. If one were to construct a backdrop for HBO's dramatisation – polite by comparison with its New Hollywood forebears – it would be the political and cultural divisions engendered by the occupation of Iraq. Moreover, the mutual incompatibility of Anglo-American and Sioux attitudes and lifestyles mirrors, presumably deliberately, the impasse between the major Western powers and the Islamic world.

The moral complexity that characterises HBO's flagship television series – *The Sopranos*, *The Wire*, *Deadwood* – is toned down drastically; the better, it seems, to further what has become a conventional ideological agenda. There is some attempt at balance, with flawed and bigoted characters on both sides. And Colonel Nelson Miles (Shaun Johnston) debunks the Sioux's 'divine right' to their ancestral lands: "No matter what your legends say, you didn't sprout from the plains like the spring grasses and you didn't coalesce out of the ether. You came out of the Minnesota woodlands armed to the teeth and set upon your fellow man… You conquered those tribes, lusting for their game and their lands, just as we have now conquered you for no less noble a cause."

In most respects, however, audience sympathies are directed dutifully and insistently towards the sad plight of the Indians, steered by plangent music, the gloomy pallor of the images – the colour drops out entirely when the Sioux's fortunes reach their nadir – and relentlessly dogmatic dialogue. Befitting a prestige, prime-time telefilm, the tone is one of apology rather than anger; this is western revisionism for the chattering classes rather than the counterculture.

Concentrating on the decline of the Sioux between their victory at Little Bighorn in 1876 and conquest at Wounded Knee 14 years later, and inserting white-educated Indian Charles Eastman into the narrative as an intermediary, the film is an adaptation of Brown's epic account only in the loosest sense. (Eastman, originally named Ohiyesa, is nowhere to be found in the book.) Its central theme, however, does elucidate the author's statement that "the entire Indian policy of the government… aimed to eradicate everything Indian among the tribes and make them over into white men". Charles, played earnestly by Adam Beach (*Flags of Our Fathers*), is deployed by the film-makers as a politically correct counterpart to those white characters (or Indians played by white actors) who used to straddle the racial and cultural divide in Fifties liberal westerns. He serves to focus the important theme of cultural estrangement: flaunted in Washington as a model of assimilation, he encounters resentment on the reservation and comes to despair at the dilution of his racial identity. This began at school, when he was compelled to adopt a Christian name, and continues under the aegis of his mentor, Senator Henry Dawes, who utilises Charles to further his plan to deracinate America's aboriginals and resettle them in homesteads.

Dawes, portrayed with a zealot's blinkered conviction, considers himself to be a champion of the Indian, but the choice he offers them is stark: "Assimilation or extinction." He is referring to their culture, should they reject the reservation system – and fail, therefore, to acknowledge the inevitability of the white man's ascendancy – but the more obvious implications of 'extinction' are realised at Wounded Knee. The major Sioux character is Sitting Bull, imbued with defiant dignity by the late Mohawk-Canadian actor August Schellenberg. The chief's trajectory, his authority slipping even as his celebrity increases, constitutes a micro-tragedy, vividly realised, that mirrors the general downfall of his tribe – whether they are being administered like prisoners on their own land, suffering from what Charles calls "an epidemic of hopelessness", or subsisting on boiled mice in self-imposed exile in Canada. The Ghost Dance movement, a revival of the mysticism that so alienates and unnerves their white antagonists, signals the re-ignition of Sioux resistance, but also precipitates their ultimate defeat.

Each of these biographical strands – Charles, Dawes, Sitting Bull – would have justified a film in its own right, but they are forced to compete for space in a cramped narrative. The good work of the actors ameliorates the feeling of potential unfulfilled. Similarly, a clutch of moving scenes, illustrating the privations and humiliation of the Sioux, compensates for the feeling that the tribe's story has been skewed to entice a wider audience – it is significant, for instance, that the Indians speak English rather than their own dialect. Perhaps not so unexpected, in light of this, is casualness regarding historical accuracy. The killing of Sitting Bull by a Lakota policeman resembles textbook accounts, and a frozen corpse on the killing ground of Wounded Knee is posed like Big Foot, the Minneconjou chief, in a famous photograph taken after the event. Yet there are also distortions – the representation of Red Cloud as effectively powerless; some aspects of Charles's biography were invented – and omissions – General George Crook, who led the crucial last-ditch negotiations with the Sioux in 1890, is given no role in the film. Strict fidelity to the facts has never been a hallmark of the western film; in this case, however, spun off from a landmark work of history, audiences surely had a right to expect more. **KG**

August Schellenberg as Sitting Bull.

Meek's Cutoff

2011, Colour, 102 mins.

D: Kelly Reichardt. P: Neil Kopp, Anish Savjani, Elizabeth Cuthrell, David Urrutia (Evenstar Films, Film Science, Primitive Nerd). W: Jonathan Raymond. Ph: Christopher Blauvelt. M: Jeff Grace. St: Michelle Williams (Emily Tetherow), Bruce Greenwood (Stephen Meek), Will Patton (Solomon Tetherow), Zoe Kazan (Millie Gately), Paul Dano (Thomas Gately)

"We're all just playin' our parts now. This was written long before we got here."

It is 1845. Three settler families are lost on the Oregon Trail. They are losing faith in their guide, the blustery frontiersman Stephen Meek, on whose assurance of a short cut they have broken away from the main wagon train. As water becomes scarce, they happen upon a solitary Cayuse Indian (Rod Rondeaux). Despite initial apprehension they press him into service, against Meek's judgement. Neither party can be sure of the other's intentions. Will the Indian lead them to water, or merely further astray?

One could almost dispense with the 'western' tag in appraising Kelly Reichardt's fourth independent feature. More reductionist than revisionist, it is a tale of endurance and encounter, based in fact but abstracted from the wider picture.[1] As in a fable, the events and characters (most of whom interpose only marginally on the narrative) could be transposed to an entirely different context and wear the same metaphysical complexion.

An uncompromising outlier among modern film-makers, Reichardt revokes the western's artistic licence, its reliance on spectacle and larger than life characters. The perspective is not that of the traditional authoritative male; rather it is predominantly objective. When the focus does narrow it rests on the stoical frame of Michelle Williams' Emily Tetherow – encased, like her female co-stars, in unflattering full-length frock and face-shrouding bonnet – rather than any of the menfolk. Certainly not on Meek himself who, with his matted beard and locks, greasy buckskins and reservoir of tall tales, merely sends himself up – and by extension the whole class of rugged individualist he is intended to represent.

Much as the wagoners discard extraneous possessions along the trail, the director jettisons most hallmarks of escapist entertainment. Narrative dynamism is one such sacrifice. Shots of characters in stasis, or navigating rivers, or undertaking mundane chores (Reichardt drilled her cast in 19th-century tasks for a week before filming commenced) are held well beyond standard duration. There are molasses-slow dissolves and plainly executed dialogue exchanges between figures in middle distance, with cutting kept to a minimum. Light sources are natural, such that detail in night scenes is difficult to discern, as it would have been in the pioneers' circumstances. There is one standoff at gunpoint, but the main drama in this western is wrung from other events: the discovery of a tree, for example, and with it the hope of water nearby (a visual echo, perhaps, of a passage from Genesis about the 'tree of life' recited earlier in the film).

Gone, too, is grandeur. There are no sweeping vistas or rich colours. *Meek's Cutoff* was shot in Academy ratio rather than widescreen, against a bland, barren backdrop in dullish, earthy hues, the better to ground existential drama in

Rod Rondeaux as the Cayuse.

this page: Michelle Williams as Emily, the film's most clear-sighted character.

stark physical reality.[2] The music, likewise, is quite unlike the bombastic scores with which the western is synonymous. The drones composed by Jeff Grace – an artist closely associated with the horror genre – have an unsettling rather than uplifting effect. In any case they are sparingly deployed – Reichardt emphasises instead diegetic sounds: rippling water, the flapping of canvas, the squeaking of wheel on axle.

At the same time, signifiers of genre – covered wagons and emigrants, frontiersman and Indian – are key to Reichardt and Jonathan Raymond's subversion of American mythology. The subtle foregrounding of Williams' character – the closest we have to a conventional protagonist – encourages a feminist reading of material usually centred on alpha males, with those roles putatively allotted to Meek and/or Emily's husband. Emily's attitude towards the Indian is not only more compassionate (a code for 'feminine'?) than that of Meek, who simply advocates killing the fellow, but likely to be more effective in the long run. Significantly, her concern for their captive's welfare – mending his shoe, fetching him food – is coloured by shrewdness: "I want him to owe me something."

For his part, the Indian comes to have a pivotal role, albeit inadvertently. He challenges, in a sense, Meek's notional position as potential saviour. The fear and suspicion projected at the Cayuse by the white majority, meanwhile, address racial and cultural tensions embedded like strata throughout North American history. Moreover, Meek's bloodcurdling tales of Indian atrocities, designed to foster hatred among his flock towards the savage in their midst and to justify a belligerent response, have their echoes in the worst excesses of 21st century political demagoguery (Reichardt had George W. Bush in mind as a referent during filming).

The process of paring back, of denying viewers familiar comforts, is the essence of Reichardt's approach, from the absence of a recognisably heroic focal point

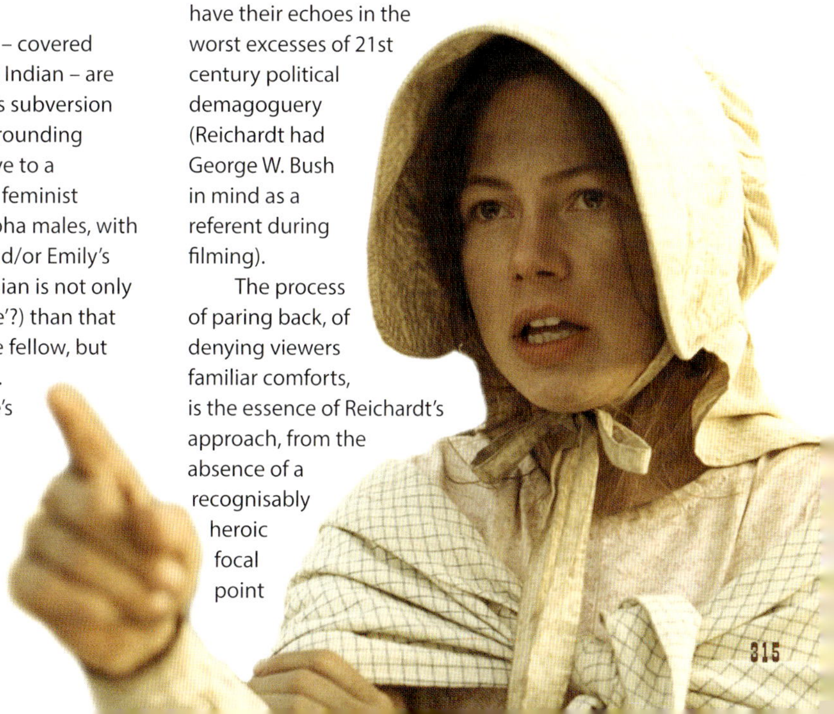

and the sparseness of the characterisations, to the paucity of knowledge we, like the settlers, are able to glean from the Indian – his dialogue is unsubtitled, Reichardt telling *Slate* magazine, "I didn't want to give the audience any information that the immigrants didn't have." Narrative closure itself is withheld, a consequence of the difficulty of discerning motive in a climate of ingrained mutual mistrust, of paranoia bordering on hysteria. There is anxiety, for example, about the symbols the Cayuse scratches into rocks along the journey – are they harmless religious doodlings, or signs enabling other 'hostiles' to track them? We are none the wiser come the conclusion. As Meek succumbs to fatalism, the people he has led to this impasse seem resigned to follow the Indian. Where that may lead is not the point of the story. **KG**

footnotes

1 The real Stephen Meek, a fur trapper by trade, led a breakaway group of around 200 wagons, carrying up to 1,000 settlers, on his ill-fated expedition across Oregon's high desert and central Cascade mountain range. By some accounts almost 30 people died along the way.

2 Reichardt felt the Academy ratio "gave you an idea of the closed view that the women have because of their bonnets"; "cutting out the peripheral" was a way of adding tension to the journey, giving the viewer "the idea that something could be there [on the prairie] that you don't know about" (*Fresh Air*, NPR, April 2011).

No direction home: Bruce Greenwood as Meek.

Django Unchained

2012, Colour, 165 mins.

D: Quentin Tarantino. P: Stacey Sher, Reginald Hudlin, Pilar Savone (The Weinstein Company, Columbia). W: Quentin Tarantino. Ph: Robert Richardson. M: Mary Ramos (supervisor), Robb Boyd (editor). St: Jamie Foxx (Django), Christoph Waltz (Dr. King Schultz), Leonardo DiCaprio (Calvin Candie), Kerry Washington (Broomhilda), Samuel L. Jackson (Stephen)

"Kill white people and get paid for it? What's not to like?"

Having skirted around the edges of the western in his previous films – a stylistic nod here, a borrowed musical cue there – Quentin Tarantino bit the bullet with this full-blooded pastiche. As with *The Hateful Eight*, he forms disparate material – Italian western machismo, plantation melodrama, blaxploitation swagger – into a pointed but misshapen critique of historical and contemporary racism.

This is not, as the director was quick to point out, "History with a capital H." The excoriation of slavery at the heart of the script coexists uneasily with pop-cultural references, comedic digressions and idiosyncratic flourishes. "I wasn't trying to do a *Schindler's List*… I wanted the film to be more entertaining than that," Tarantino said.[1] The approach is antithetical to Hollywood's traditionally sober rendering of problematic subject matter; indeed, …*Unchained's* release was sandwiched between *Lincoln* (2012) and *12 Years a Slave* (2013), both irreproachably straight-faced examinations of broadly similar events.

The middle film in Tarantino's 'revisionist history' trilogy (between its companion piece, 2009's *Inglourious Basterds*, and *The Hateful Eight*), …*Unchained* was announced as a 'southern' as much as a western, a story of 'life, liberty and the pursuit of vengeance'. It is another of the director's irreverent postmodern miscellanies. Onto a period setting and story elements ripped from *Mandingo* (1975) and *The Legend of Nigger Charley*, with a dash of *Boss Nigger*, he grafts close-ups, crash zooms and mordant cynicism derived from Sergio Leone and Sergio Corbucci. He pays dues to Mel Brooks, ridiculing Klan-like racists (and *The Birth of a Nation*) in a scene so incongruous it is almost dreamlike, while the splattery slow-motion gun violence honours Sam Peckinpah, Walter Hill and John Woo by way of anime. (The choice of name for the title character is merely another tip of the hat. Beyond gunfighting skills, the only connection between this Django and the one birthed by Corbucci and Franco Nero, the latter granted a cameo here, is a loathing of Klansmen.)

The plot proceeds along recognisable lines. The opening third, in which German bounty hunter-cum-dentist Dr. King Schultz liberates Django to help locate the valuable Brittle brothers, plays like the tutor/apprentice strain of spaghetti western, only without the chicanery.

Schultz's motives – a mixture of pragmatism, altruism and whimsicality – are put into perspective by those of Django. Having been granted his freedom, more or less, he is determined to do the same for his wife, improbably named Broomhilda, allowing Schultz to liken Django to Siegfried. Once slaves on the same estate – they are shown in grainy, desaturated flashbacks being whipped and branded after an escape attempt – they were sold separately, she to the Mississippi dandy Calvin Candie.

The journey from Texas to Mississippi via Tennessee is illustrated with evidence of ingrained racism. In Daughtrey, Texas, white townsfolk gaze in disbelief at the sight of "a nigger on a horse". (The abusive term is used throughout, in a variety of tones and contexts, by characters of all creeds.) Clearly, this is against the natural order. Further east, lines of miserable, dehumanised drudges shamble along in chains, muzzled like beasts. There are graphic 'mandingo' fights (gladiatorial combat among slaves, for the amusement of their masters), numerous whippings, the fatal mauling of a would-be runaway by dogs.

"A lot worse shit actually happened," said Tarantino, defending the content. Part of his mission statement was to render slavery in all its ugly reality (although the mandingo aspect is an invention), to confront modern America with a re-creation of events so horrifying they have been largely ignored in mainstream culture, along with their implications for continuing racial tensions in society. The moral clarity of Tarantino's argument dims, however, with the smashing together of tones and styles, the drift towards individual aggrandisement that alters and narrows the focus of the plot. This is where it diverges, quite deliberately, from the temper of more conventional slave dramas, such that exist: "They keep you at arm's length dramatically," Tarantino said. "There is this kind of level of good taste that they're trying to deal with."[2]

It is in 'Candieland' where Tarantino both sharpens his barbs and indulges his predilections. Leonardo DiCaprio's baroque impersonation of decadent, tyrannical Southern aristocracy, all impeccable manners and corrupted morals, effectively skewers the supremacist mind-set and sense of entitlement associated with those who profited from slavery. Holding forth on phrenology, smarmily convinced of the justness of subjugation, he is an extremely well-written caricature, matching the equally loquacious Schultz phrase for phrase in the most compelling of Tarantino's trademark sustained dialogue exchanges. Tension rises like steam all the while as Candie attempts to goad Django, posing as Schultz's partner in the slave trade.

True to its exploitation roots, *Django Unchained* has no time for subtlety in its delineation of bigoted stereotypes. Complicating the picture of white calumny, however, is Schultz – distanced somewhat by his foreign origins and the eccentric mannerisms that seem second nature to Waltz – and Stephen, Candie's obsequious retainer. Samuel L. Jackson's sinister twist on the Uncle Tom persona is the film's most audacious and priceless asset. A house slave, relatively privileged, pride long suppressed, he cannot abide it in other members of his race. Steeped in self-loathing, he turns this against any black with a vestige of dignity, a hint of an unbroken spirit, hence his hostility towards the "uppity" Django. Being of devious nature, he is sharp to signs of deceitfulness in others – it is he who intuits that Schultz and Django are not really interested in purchasing a mandingo fighter, as they claim, but in rescuing Broomhilda.

Notwithstanding the director's play with genre conventions, *Django Unchained* can be plotted on a continuum that began in the western proper in the Fifties and Sixties, when Native Americans were the beneficiaries of liberal historical revisionism. There are vestiges of those earlier films: a paternalistic relationship between the principals, with the white saviour guiding his black (read Native American) charge's destiny, before

above: The original Django, Franco Nero, makes the most of his cameo in the film's 'mandingo' sequence.

the sidekick supersedes his 'master' and becomes a self-determined hero – one might even say superhero, the "exceptional nigger" of Candie's imagining and solid blaxploitation lineage.

In the final 30 minutes, once Schultz has sacrificed himself to ideals it was not at all clear he possessed, the film becomes a full-blown, hip-hop-blaring revenge fantasy. Django carpets Candieland in corpses in bravura scenes of retributive violence. Jamie Foxx channels the character's indignation, his 'unchained' spirit, into an arrogance that plays as anachronistic, no doubt intentionally. As an embodiment of black power he is undeniably dynamic, yet he assumes no responsibility for his fellow slaves. His actions may benefit the remainder of the serfs in Candieland – we can't know; most likely other slavers will mop them up – but this is incidental. He is no Nigger Charley after all; nor is he like Jesse Lee from *Posse*, another character who appreciated the privileged status that goes with being 'exceptional'. Django's singlehanded destruction of the Candie estate and subsequent reunion with Broomhilda close the circle of revenge. Somehow that doesn't seem enough.

Nevertheless, with his customary brashness Tarantino began a dialogue about a subject on which Hollywood

had for too long been silent, or addressed with timidity. Timidity is not this film-maker's forte. "I felt no obligation to bow to any 21st century political correctness," he said, going on to reopen the debate, and the same festering wounds, in similar terms in *The Hateful Eight*.[3] **KG**

footnotes

1 Interview with Quentin Tarantino by Terry Gross, *Fresh Air* (NPR).

2 Ibid.

3 Interview with Tarantino by Kam Williams, aalbc.com

The Homesman

2014, Colour, 122 mins.

D: Tommy Lee Jones. P: Luc Besson, Peter Brant, Brian Kennedy (EuropaCorp, Ithaca, Javelina Film Company). W: Tommy Lee Jones, Kieran Fitzgerald, Wesley A. Oliver. Ph: Rodrigo Prieto. M: Marco Beltrami. St: Tommy Lee Jones (George Briggs), Hilary Swank (Mary Bee Cuddy), Grace Gummer (Arabella Sours), Miranda Otto (Theoline Belknap), Sonja Richter (Gro Svendsen)

"Mary Bee, you're as good a man as any man hereabouts."

As a testament to the suffering and endurance of women on the frontier, this compassionate adaptation of Glendon Swarthout's *The Homesman* comes close to being the feminist western Hilary Swank proclaimed it to be. The degree of sensitivity towards women is unusual yet despite this, and Swank's sterling work, the female lead eventually cedes the centre ground – and the narrative perspective – to a traditional, if eccentric, male individualist.

For Tommy Lee Jones, the film is not a 'western' at all. He sees it as a historical piece about the struggles of female homesteaders in 1850s Nebraska – specifically, three women traumatised by bereavement and austerity, as well as Swank's dutiful Mary Bee Cuddy, who escorts them (in a modified prison wagon) to a refuge in faraway Iowa when no man volunteers for the task. (The trajectory, West to East, signifies the film's departure from the western's thematic terrain.) Along the way, she recruits George Briggs, a grizzled claim-jumper and army deserter whose life she saves and whose services she purchases for $300.

The Homesman is also, in Jones's view, a "consideration of American imperialism", although this doesn't stretch much further than a few pointed reminders from Briggs that white settlers were not the first occupants of the Western lands. Not that Jones is one for political correctness: the one encounter with Natives, a Pawnee raiding party, passes off peacefully, but these are still 'savages'; "They'll probably eat her," Briggs says of Mary Bee's beloved horse, which he trades for safe passage. He also urges her to shoot the women, and then herself, should he be overcome. Jones told an audience at Cannes he was not "ashamed of the fact [the Indians] were considered by our characters potentially to be homicidal. We're not bending the truth, or stereotyping anybody." It is unfortunate, then, that some of his dialogue in this scene has the ring of a dime novel, where most of the western's clichés – not least the 'save the last bullet' dictum – were forged.

Briggs's role is somewhat tutorial throughout – leading by pragmatic example where Mary Bee's moral rigour fears to tread. He is an irreverent foil for her unbending piety,

a seasoned Rooster Cogburn to her guileless Mattie Ross. Actions that to her appear abhorrent – Briggs stealing a buffalo hide from a dead Indian for cold nights – are geared towards survival. Jones's character embodies a ruthless logic, derived from hard-won experience, that is inconsistent with Mary Bee's Christian values. The lesson is driven home when she insists on "tidying" a child's desecrated grave on the prairie (Indians have raided it "for the clothes", mirroring Briggs's example). Briggs, long drained of sentimentality, drives on, leaving her to wander for hours at night in the unforgiving outback, subsisting on grass before she eventually finds the wagon again, altruistic urges intact but exposed as folly in the circumstances.

The loneliness of life on the Great Plains is accentuated by daunting wide shots of isolated figures against the flat expanse. On a more intimate level, Swank's nuanced performance offers a moving insight into the sadness of an ostensibly fiercely independent, yet desperately reluctant, spinster. Twice Mary Bee practically begs male acquaintances to marry her – even the gruff Briggs, of whom she largely disapproves – only to be rejected for her bossiness and plain looks. With Briggs she gambles her dignity, and finds the psychological toll too exacting. Her tragic fate is consistent with the film's starkness of vision (self-harm; filicide; depression – scarcely the stuff of conventional frontier sagas), but her presence is sorely missed once Briggs takes her place as protagonist.

At that point, *The Homesman* becomes a vehicle for its director-star's well-oiled roguery – and a less challenging proposition. With the action keyed to his character's idiosyncrasies, the plight of women – the film's 'feminist' agenda – recedes. The new direction is encapsulated in a bravura sequence in which Briggs and his charges roll up to the spick-and-span Fairfield Hotel, a blue anomaly on the bare brown horizon, where they are refused food and shelter by James Spader's impeccably mannered, implacably businesslike Irish proprietor. Briggs's response – torching the place and wounding Spader – exudes both moral outrage and maverick bravado. The fact he also pilfers food for his "cuckoo clocks" is secondary but not insignificant.

Crossing the Missouri River and delivering the damaged women to the care of Meryl Streep's minister's wife seems to set Briggs on the road to redemption – deeply furrowed as it is by the passage of countless antiheroes before him. Mary Bee's example has avowedly created an impression; he takes pity on an impoverished young waitress (*True Grit's* Hailee Steinfeld), even mooting the possibility of marriage. Yet he ends the film – crossing back over the waterway, which serves as a symbolic frontier in its own right – very much as he began it: as a law unto himself. **KG**

The Hateful Eight

2015, Colour, 168 mins.

D: Quentin Tarantino. P: Richard N. Gladstein, Shannon McIntosh, Stacey Sher (Double Feature Films, FilmColony). W: Quentin Tarantino. Ph: Robert Richardson. M: Ennio Morricone. St: Samuel L. Jackson (Major Marquis Warren), Kurt Russell (John Ruth), Jennifer Jason Leigh (Daisy Domergue), Walter Goggins (Sheriff Chris Mannix), Demián Bichir (Bob)

"I strongly suggest we do not re-create the Battle of Baton Rouge, in a blizzard, in the middle of Millie's Haberdashery."

Released on a wave of heightened anticipation – the first film in decades to use the ultra-wide 70mm Cinerama format; the first Ennio Morricone western score since 1981 – and controversy – calls for a boycott after Quentin Tarantino's comments about police brutality – *The Hateful Eight* manages to titillate and frustrate in equal doses.[1] The director riffs at length on his pet subjects, the result being a kind of epic potboiler in which his obnoxious characters, not all of whom are who they claim to be, are cloistered in an intimidating atmosphere meant to represent postbellum America and all its festering tensions. Gallant attempts are made to draw parallels with contemporary racial frictions, which the director perceives as a sign of regression in a culture he so clearly adores.

While audience reactions were divided, the initial reviews, focusing generally on Robert Richardson's stunning cinematography and Tarantino's command of space, were largely glowing. In the opening third, the panoramic format captures the snowy expanse of Wyoming in all its foreboding glory. Morricone's portentous score swells. A flock of birds disperse. An unearthly pink sky is glimpsed through a cloud break. The camera crawls around a carved Christ figure, revealing the last stage to Red Rock.

From this breathtaking scene-setting the film segues uneasily into separate phases in confined areas – the stagecoach journey to Red Rock by the principals; their arrival at their overnight stopover, Millie's Haberdashery, where the ingrained prejudices of its denizens are played out. Then comes a protracted mystery element that forsakes western conventions. More Agatha Christie than Budd Boetticher, it culminates in sanguinary scenes reminiscent of Grand Guignol, with stylistic nods to Peckinpah carried over from *Django Unchained*.

As a grizzled bounty hunter, Kurt Russell devours the décor inside Millie's as he holds rancid outlaw Daisy Domergue in his charge. Recognising they'll be stranded there during a fierce blizzard, it's not long before he intuits that one of the customers is in league with Domergue. He excuses one straggler picked up on the way, Major Marquis Warren, a black Union officer turned fellow bounty hunter.[2] Ruth's faith in Warren hasn't stopped him from subjecting the latter to a barrage of racial insults in the first 10 minutes or from cuffing him for the journey to Millie's, the allusion to slavery blunt – another refrain from *Django Unchained*.

Despite winning the war for emancipation, Warren's race is still treated as inferior. To emphasise this state of disharmony Tarantino introduces an ex-Confederate raider, Chris Mannix, who claims to be incumbent sheriff of Red Rock. Mannix is portrayed as pure Southern trash ("I'll be double dog damned") and is full of exultant stories about his father's gang of guerrillas, responsible for terrorising black communities. Warren counters by telling him he joined the war "to kill Southern crackers" and by pressing a gun to Mannix's temple.

The occupants of Millie's are a rum bunch: doddery Southern general Sanford Smithers (Bruce Dern); Oswaldo Mobray (Tim Roth), English gent and card-carrying hangman; cowpoke Joe Gage (Michael Madsen); the irascible Señor Bob, a Mexican left in charge of Millie's in her absence.

Kurt Russell and Jennifer Jason Leigh.

While Mannix gushes over Smithers, Warren is bitter, accusing the general of killing a troop of black POWs rather than taking them to prison. "We didn't have the time, nor the food, nor the inclination," spits Smithers. Mobray suggests a way of easing the tension by dividing the room in half, "the Southern side and the Northern side", enlarging the cabin's restrictive environment so that it becomes a geographical and ideological microcosm of the United States.

During a hiatus, Mannix challenges the authenticity of a letter Warren carries, allegedly written to him by Abraham Lincoln. Admitting it is a fake, Warren earnestly describes, in a speech crafted as subtly as a shotgun blast, how his people are still constrained by white autocracy and violence, despite the outcome of the Civil War. For him the letter is a passport to equal treatment: "The only time black folks is safe is when white folks is disarmed … and that letter disarms white folks." As he explains to Ruth, "It got me on that stagecoach."

The subtlety of this stratagem is not pursued. As in *Django Unchained*, Tarantino proffers a vision of black empowerment painted in the lurid tones of blaxploitation. Fastening his attention on Smithers, Warren initiates a power play based on the racist's worst nightmare: an autonomous black man. With each man symbolically seated either side of a chessboard, Warren moves his first psychological pawn, the camera positioned at a low angle to show his ascendency in the battle of nerves. Smithers is en route to Red Rock to build a shrine to his son, who died in Wyoming while trying "to make his fortune". Warren contradicts him: Smithers junior, one of many Southern bounty hunters to have tailed the major, really died on "the day he met me", after an oral rape recounted in gloating, salacious detail. This is likely to be another of the tall tales that seem to be second nature to the characters, but it serves its purpose, provoking Smithers into pulling a pistol and justifying Warren's fatal retort.

The film's change from drama to mystery – who poisoned the coffee? – sees Warren shed his *Nigger Charley* mantel to become a Poirot-like investigator. The issue of race, which dominates the first half of the film, is largely forgotten and the mephitic presence of Domergue comes to the fore. Many commentators have found the treatment of the film's main female character repugnant – she is punched, elbowed, slapped – but Tarantino is nothing if not egalitarian. Why shouldn't a female be as malevolent a frontier outlaw as any the genre has seen? She is mendacious and ruthless, and can take as much

punishment as the toughest of western villains. When she is struck in the face by Ruth, she reacts by winking discomfortingly at Warren while black blood runs down her temple. As Stephanie Zacharek opines, "The more she gets hit, the more she grins and cackles, as though she were drawing banshee strength from the abuse."[3] Once her accomplices are revealed, it's clear she is the dominant force in this outlaw 'family'.

Tarantino has never been shy of revising history; he assassinates Hitler in *Inglourious Basterds* and exterminates slavers in *Django Unchained*. Here, however, he emits a plea, coated in stage blood, to acknowledge and redress the crimes of the past in the hope of progressing more peacefully into the future. After the gunfire has stopped and Domergue, her face covered in blood and grey matter, fails to enlist Mannix into killing Warren, there is a sense the director believes that co-operation is possible even among the unlikeliest of allies – the only way to heal the rift between America's races.

The subversion of genre tropes is not fully realised, the message submerged in gore. As usual in a Tarantino film, thematic points are suborned to style and the flaunting of influences, from *Day of the Outlaw* and Japanese drama *Incident at Blood Pass* to the Italian westerns *The Great Silence* and *Shoot the Living and Pray for the Dead* (both of which Tarantino has named among his 20 favourite films from that genre). Nevertheless, like other maverick directors, Tarantino's engagement with the western can be seen as part of an evolutionary process, wherein the confines of the genre, like its supposedly ironbound politics, are expanded beyond expectations. **CH**

footnotes

1 Morricone's prior western score was for the Italian Bud Spencer vehicle *Buddy Goes West*. The last film shot on 70mm was *Song of Norway*, a musical released in 1970. Addressing the Rise Up October Rally in New York, a protest against police shootings of unarmed black people, Tarantino's statement – "When I see murders, I do not stand by ... I have to call the murderers the murderers" – drew flak from police organisations, including the Patrolman's Benevolent Association.

2 Warren would have been one of a select few. Of nearly 186,000 black soldiers who fought for the Union, there were fewer than 100 officers (Isaac Hampton, *The Black Officer Corps: A History of Black Military Advancement from Integration Through Vietnam*, Routledge, 2012).

3 *Quentin Tarantino's Hateful Eight Revels in Snow, Not So Much in People*, Time online, 22 December 2015.

Slow West

2015, Colour, 84 mins.

D: John Maclean. P: Iain Canning, Rachel Gardner, Conor McCaughan, Emile Sherman (See Saw Films, DMC Film, Film4, New Zealand Film Commission). W: John Maclean. Ph: Robbie Ryan. M: Jed Kurzel. St: Kodi Smit-McPhee (Jay Cavendish), Michael Fassbender (Silas Selleck), Ben Mendelsohn (Payne), Caren Pistorius (Rose Ross), Rory McCann (John Ross)

"One day… they'll build a railroad… to the moon. And when we get there, first thing we'll do is hunt the natives down."

Beginning with its backdrop of prairies, woodland, brooks and plains, so redolent of the American frontier but actually located in New Zealand, the filmic environment of *Slow West* is both familiar and alien. Scottish director John Maclean, while clearly conversant with the trappings and clichés of the movie western, carries none of the cultural baggage borne by Hollywood directors; his vision, consequently, is uncoloured by chauvinism. As a stranger in a strange land, his perspective complements that of his immigrant protagonists for a fresh, funny, often disturbingly frank evaluation of a historical moment swathed in myth.

Maclean felt the immigrant experience in the Old West was under-represented on film. "When I travelled around America everyone said to me, 'Oh, my grandfather was Scottish,' or, 'My great-grandfather was Irish.' In one or two westerns there are nods to that, but I just thought it would be quite nice to fill a film with that, because it hadn't been done before."[1] His story draws similar conclusions to *Heaven's Gate*, in that both natives and newcomers to the Western territories are stigmatised and victimised by vested interests. *Slow West* is more intimate, however, not to mention half the length. It is also more pointed as a critique of Manifest Destiny than another recent western, *The Salvation* (2014), which likewise moved immigrant characters from the margins of events to the centre.

Slow West plays like a skewed fairy tale, set "once upon a time" in a West described as both a land of dreams and a den of wolves, Robbie Ryan's colour scheme woozily lush, the scenery inducing what *Variety* called "a surreal, almost subliminal sense of dislocation". Young Scotsman Jay, a wide-eyed man-child in a too-big suit, has come to Colorado to find Rose, the girl he loved back home. Hopelessly out of his depth – riding through the woods, as vulnerable as Red Riding Hood, he almost falls victim to some murderous soldiers – he accepts the aid of Silas, a brusque Irish gunfighter, who sells him his services as a guide. Silas has an ulterior motive – Rose and her father have a bounty on their heads, having fled Scotland in the wake of a fatal altercation with Jay's uncle. For all Michael Fassbender's Eastwoodian nonchalance (he is rarely seen without a cigar clamped in his teeth), Silas is not merely a cynical mercenary. He refers contemptuously to the soldiers as "Indian slayers", and adopts a protective posture towards the younger man even while planning to profit from his innocence – to which end, he tries to shrug off rival bounty hunters led by Payne, a former confederate.

The meandering quest narrative could scarcely be more venerable. Nor could the central motifs – physical journey as rite of passage; characters in a subtly shifting mentor/disciple relationship. This is the lumber from which countless westerns have been fashioned, including the best of the past decade: the Coens' *True Grit* and Tommy Lee Jones's *The Homesman*. Like those filmmakers, Maclean – a musician by trade, with just two shorts to his name before this – is not trying to break new ground. He knows there is more than one way to reach a destination, however, and the signposts on his chosen route point to some decidedly idiosyncratic places. Valid comparisons can be made with the oneiric texture of *Dead Man*, the hazy languor of *The Hired Hand*

above: Ben Mendelsohn and Michael Fassbender.

and *McCabe & Mrs. Miller* (a further nod is the fur coat worn by Ben Mendelsohn as the outlaw Payne), while the deadpan humour is reminiscent of Robert Benton's *Bad Company* and, especially, the Coen brothers. Maclean's penchant for absurdist twists and incongruous imagery call to mind Werner Herzog – surely the name of Werner, the anthropologist Jay encounters in the middle of a parched plain and is subsequently fleeced by, was not chosen by accident.

This vignette is typical of how the film imparts its messages indirectly. The displaced Werner is studying the decline of the Native American, and predicts the devastated tribes will one day be mythologised and romanticised – anticipating the development of western fiction on page and screen. Maclean employs the same method to puncture the hype of the American Dream, when a Swedish couple, driven to desperation, try to hold up a general store, killing the proprietor before being blasted themselves. (Jay, despite the good-natured naïveté that flows so naturally from the fragile Codi Smit-McPhee, shoots the wife in the back without apparent compunction.) Jay and Silas venture outside to find the couple's two young children awaiting their return – the most bleakly ironic of Maclean's visual punch lines.

The director has a keen eye for discomposing details of the kind that commonly go unremarked in the traditional western. Seemingly tangential images and events portray the West as heterogeneous – European settlers, a dreamlike encounter with three Congolese singers – and illustrate, in a typically unconventional fashion, the myriad dangers of frontier existence – Jay

and Silas waking in the middle of a flash flood, or looking down with wry amusement at a fallen tree trunk, beneath which lie two skeletal arms outstretched, axe in one hand. The abrupt cut from the duo riding in long shot to standing in medium close-up makes this moment especially disorienting.

The acts of violence have a blackly comic undertow – not to make light of them, but to point up the futility and indignity entailed. A run-in with hostile natives in a forest ends with Jay's hand skewered on an arrow and two Indians sprawled on their backsides, thrown from the horses they are trying to steal. When the bounty hunters converge on the Rosses' cabin, a dead man's trousers snag on a nail, exposing his buttocks. And in a richly bathetic moment, Jay's romantic longing for Rose – who in flashbacks treats him more like a brother than a lover – is stopped short by a bullet: defending herself manfully, as it were, Rose shoots him unwittingly when he enters the besieged house unannounced. Maclean literally rubs salt in the wound, the contents of an open bag spilling down on the hapless hero.

No fairy-tale ending for Jay, then, but the joke is on him only briefly. In another of the tonal shifts that Maclean pulls off so adeptly, he cuts from this bravura exhibition of carnage to sobering shots of the corpses left in the characters' wake – a tally that not many directors would be considerate enough to record. Silas, for his part, absorbs a related lesson from his pupil – "There is more to life than survival." Maclean's coda suggests the law of the gun can be circumvented even in the killing fields of the Old West, a point surely intended for modern audiences to ponder. **KG**

footnotes

1 Interview with John Maclean by Ann Lee, June 2015 (bfi.org.uk).

Hostiles

2017, Colour, 133 mins.

D: Scott Cooper. P: Scott Cooper, Ken Kao, John Lesher (Le Grisbi Productions, Waypoint Entertainment). W: Scott Cooper, Donald E. Stewart (manuscript). Ph: Masanobu Takayanagi. M: Max Richter. St: Christian Bale (Captain Joseph Blocker), Rosamund Pike (Rosalie Quaid), Wes Studi (Chief Yellow Hawk), Rory Cochrane (Master Sgt. Thomas Metz), Adam Beach (Black Hawk)

"When we lay our heads down out here, we're all prisoners."

In many ways a summation of arguments propounded by westerns since the Fifties, *Hostiles* confirms that revisionism is the new traditionalism. This is evident in both a general sense – the blurring of moral contrasts between enemies, the insistence that the Indian Wars were tantamount to genocide, the subliminal appeal for racial harmony – and in the reference points one can check off on the way. Echoes of *Broken Arrow*, *The Searchers*, *Run of the Arrow*, *Ulzana's Raid*, *Dances with Wolves* and *Unforgiven*, among other major westerns, linger like the low notes in Max Richter's sombre score or the clouds that periodically blanket the magnificently photographed horizons. The characters suffer as much from psychological scars as physical wounds, while also testifying to other truisms of the liberal western: that to make peace with oneself it is first necessary to reconcile with adversaries, to recognise the human beneath the war paint or the uniform. And almost 70 years after *Broken Arrow*, it remains the case that the narrative perspective is biased towards a white man, with his indigenous counterpart accorded plenty of screen time but little more than symbolic value.

Thus our fulcrum is Christian Bale's tightly wound cavalry captain who is ordered, under threat of court martial, to escort an old nemesis, the cancer-stricken Cheyenne chief Yellow Hawk, and his family from prison in New Mexico to their ancestral lands in Montana's Valley of the Bears. It is 1892, two years after Wounded Knee, and this is a compassionate gesture the government can afford, entrusted to a man with a reputation for ruthlessness. Yet Blocker's visceral loathing of "savages" diminishes inexorably as his proximity to Yellow Hawk forces the realisation that they are essentially alike, and that the myth of racial supremacy that has justified his bloody deeds (he is said to have taken "more scalps than Sitting Bull") can no longer be sustained. The path to Blocker's enlightenment – it is customary by now that the journey is as much figurative as physical – is smoothed by the more self-aware of his subordinates, particularly Sergeant Metz, who even apologises to the chief for the treatment of his people, and by Rosalie, the lone survivor of a Comanche raid that claims her husband and children in the first scene. (True to form, the film differentiates between those Indians worthy of sympathy and those who merit the slur of "savage". Even Yellow Hawk demonises the Comanches – they are "rattlesnake people… the worst kind".)

It might be expected in a western geared to 21st-century sensibilities that a woman would manage her trauma, if not overcome it, more readily than Blocker, who wears his terse masculine angst like body armour. (It need hardly be said that the role moulds itself to Bale's simmering persona.) Scott Cooper wanted his female lead to represent "the indomitable strength of the human spirit", and Rosamund Pike adeptly navigates the raw emotions and harrowing circumstances to which Rosalie is subjected. Yet one of the surprising features of *Hostiles*, and again this is a mark of its contemporary provenance, is the time it allots to male characters venting their feelings, whether in private – Blocker's anguished howls in the night – or among themselves. The captain fights back tears when parting from a wounded comrade; other soldiers huddle in confessionals like veterans at a PTSD meeting. There is a welcome maturity to dialogue exchanges about the taking of life (if rather too close to *Unforgiven* in places; "I've killed everything that's walked or crawled," says Blocker at one point), as when experienced troopers assure a rookie that he will grow accustomed to killing. "That's what I'm afraid of," he responds, intuiting a theme that runs throughout the film: the tenuous hold that all of the 'hostiles' – and the term encompasses all the principal characters, irrespective of race or gender – have on their humanity.

Less commendable is the familiar marginalisation of Native American characters, especially given Cooper's espousal of racial equality and the moral equivalence he draws between both sides in the conflict. Hence the opening two scenes show Indian cruelty and military brutality side by side, and the Comanche raid on Rosalie's homestead is matched near the end by a shootout provoked by racist white land-grabbers. Yet the script keeps Yellow Hawk at arm's length; he occupies that figurehead capacity so often reserved for characters of his stature. Imbued with unflappable dignity by Wes Studi, in his most prominent role since 1993's *Geronimo*, he and his family members are barely developed beyond their basic function as vessels for white guilt. Blocker speaks of the chief as a fearsome opponent, yet the latter never addresses his personal history of violence in the way that the captain confronts his conscience. (Students of the western can fill in the gap by flashing back to Studi's portrayals of Indians both noble – *Geronimo* – and savage – *The Last of the Mohicans*, *Dances with Wolves*.) Cooper could conceivably have cut back on Blocker's brooding silences or the troopers' fireside reflections in order to afford Yellow Hawk comparable emotional complexity. With the emphasis squarely on Blocker's redemption, however, the film squanders its good intentions towards his Native opposite number in a manner further evocative of *Dances with Wolves*.

As redemptive fables go, however, this is an intelligent and forceful example. Richard Slotkin wrote of the settlement of the American frontier as a process of regeneration through violence. A great many revisionist westerns have focused this theme on their protagonists, from James Stewart's roles for Anthony Mann to Clint Eastwood's William Munny in *Unforgiven*. Blocker is but the latest to undergo the rite, a painful cleansing process that reveals underlying anxieties, even psychotic drives, to which heroes of yore appeared to be immune; certainly, the western rarely if ever explored these areas in its 'classic' form. Bale's troubled Indian-slayer is a worthy ancestor for all those morally compromised outsiders with similarly blood-stained souls – and a spokesman, perhaps, for damaged veterans of the War on Terror. He has no time for civilians who sneer from the sidelines without having witnessed, let alone participated in, the kind of unconscionable violence that occasionally quickens the movie's measured pace. Early on Blocker unleashes his resentment on a smug liberal journalist who wafts words like "butcher" far too casually for the captain's liking. A later scene at an army fort, where the wife of the commanding officer holds forth on the crimes committed against the red man, has none of the same bristling tension, partly because Blocker's rigid viewpoint has already begun to abate.

His learning process recalls that of Tom Jeffords in *Broken Arrow*, another 'hostile' who was surprised to discover that his adversaries were not the barbarians of government propaganda (at least not all of them), but real people with whom one could empathise. That lesson was directed at a wider audience and the same is true of *Hostiles*. "The racial divide in our country is widening," said Cooper. "We're living in polarised times, and I wanted to speak to this notion that we need to better understand one another and to reconcile." All the more surprising, then, that he should neglect his Native characters. There is also on Blocker's part a dawning self-awareness about just how extensively violence has distorted his perspective. (This, too, addresses the nation at large and its turbulent heritage. Cooper's choice of epigraph – D.H. Lawrence's observation that "the essential American soul is hard, isolate, stoic and a killer. It has never yet melted" – could hardly be more pointed.) A new character is introduced midway, an unrepentant rogue soldier (Ben Foster) under arrest for slaughtering an indigenous family. Now it is Blocker's turn to be told "judge not, that ye be not judged" – without the sanction of the uniform, it is pointed out, it could easily be the captain in chains, given his own record of exterminating Indian women and children; of being, in Cooper's words, "a cylinder of the engine of genocide". Blocker's refrain, "I was just doing my job," lacks any kind of conviction, which is very much the point.

The theme of transformation is externalised in the diversity of terrain – rocky slopes, green valleys, sweeping grassland – through which the party rides in knowingly Fordian formations, their numbers dwindling steadily until the surviving handful reach Montana, where the chief receives the burial on tribal land he so longed for. After a final bloody skirmish straight out of *The Culpepper Cattle Co.*, Blocker's regeneration culminates in what has widely been seen as an inversion of *The Searchers'* famous ending. Where one door closed on Ethan Edwards, Blocker opens another – his conversion to the Indian cause, embodied by Yellow Hawk, has sufficiently purged the captain of his demons to merit him a place in society. That is the filmmakers' verdict. Whether the countless Native Americans the character has helped to subjugate would see it that way is another matter. **KG**

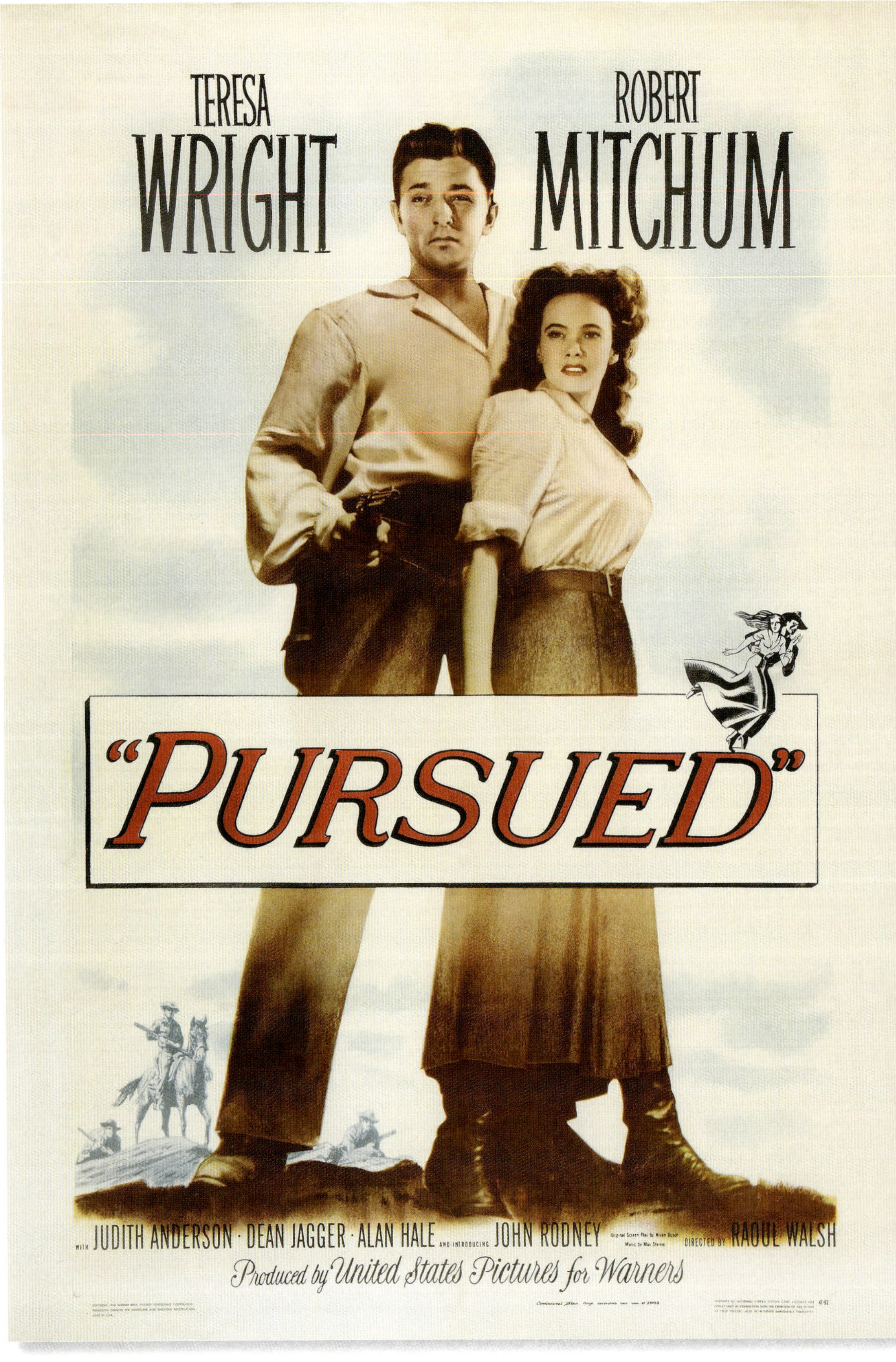
TERESA
WRIGHT
ROBERT
MITCHUM
"PURSUED"
WITH JUDITH ANDERSON · DEAN JAGGER · ALAN HALE AND INTRODUCING JOHN RODNEY
DIRECTED BY RAOUL WALSH
Produced by United States Pictures for Warners

Shadows West

Noir Westerns

As a hybrid film style, 'western noir' sounds like a contradiction in terms. The pessimism and moral ambiguity that characterised Hollywood's dark thrillers, not to mention their dank urban settings, seem too far removed from the Manichaeism and open-air idealism associated with traditional American westerns. There is surely no home on the range for expressionistic film-making and murky interiors.

The essence of noir was not confined to a particular genre or setting, however, any more than the western was limited to white hats and black hats (or cowboys and Indians). Noir's spirit, if not the extent of its tropes, was apparent as early as 1943's *The Ox-Bow Incident*, but it really began seeping into the western after the Second World War. Its preoccupations were evident particularly in the psychological instability and increasing vulnerability of formerly self-assured heroes, a new emphasis on shadows and night scenes, and a *mise-en-scène* that gave prominence to visual snares. The magnificence of rocky buttes, mountains and cliffs took on a threatening cast when shot from low angles.

Many major westerns of the late Forties and Fifties have strong connections to noir – thematically, stylistically and in terms of their personnel: most films by Anthony Mann; *High Noon*; *Johnny Guitar*; *Forty Guns*, to name but a few. In this section, we have isolated other examples, from A-features such as the ground-breaking *Pursued*, to largely forgotten, cheaper productions such as the bleak *Jack Slade*, where the noir elements are almost as prominent as they were in those big-city thrillers with which the term remains synonymous.

Pursued

1947, B/W, 101 mins.

D: Raoul Walsh. P: Milton Sperling (United States Pictures, Inc). W: Niven Busch. Ph: James Wong Howe. M: Max Steiner. St: Teresa Wright (Thor Callum), Robert Mitchum (Jeb Rand), Judith Anderson (Mrs. Callum), Dean Jagger (Grant Callum), Alan Hale (Jake Dingle)

"There was a black dog riding my back..."

A kind of sagebrush *Spellbound*, *Pursued* was the first western to harness Hollywood's postwar fascination with psychoanalysis and remains a textbook example, stylistically and thematically, of film noir's infiltration of other genres.[1] In Jeb Rand, it has the equivalent of a key noir archetype: a man oppressed by a childhood trauma he cannot decipher. It manipulates his destiny, estranging him from his adoptive family, poisoning his relationship with Thor, who is both his foster-sister and lover, and twice forces him to kill assailants, including Thor's brother. A veteran of conflict, he also fits Foster Hirsch's description of "the returning soldier [who] has the disconnectedness of an ex-con; he seems both amnesiac and somnambulist"[2] – the perfect template, in other words, for Robert Mitchum's fatalistic outsiders: the physique and swagger of a champion offset by the mien of an eternal loser.

Mitchum's victim-hero is one among several iconographic features of noir: flashbacks to a formative event that frustrate both narrative linearity and the protagonist's trajectory; a near-fatal attraction; expressionistic settings, from the looming buttes that symbolise "the inescapable repressiveness of which the characters are simultaneously embodiments and victims",[3] to the claustrophobic, low-ceilinged courthouse that bears down on Jeb like the weight of his misfortune. There are ambushes in dark alleys that demonstrate James Wong Howe's masterly manipulation of shadows. Above all, there is the brooding aura of what Alain Silver and Elizabeth Ward identify as noir's true antagonist – "an unseen force… a relentless, deterministic abstraction" that has hounded Jeb throughout his life: "I always have a feeling something's after me…".[4]

This 'something' resolves into the authoritarian Grant Callum, who orchestrated the massacre of Jeb's family when the latter was a boy as punishment for an adulterous affair between Grant's sister-in-law and Jeb's father. Niven Busch's tortuous script eventually allows the truth to shine through, as Ma Callum kills Grant to prevent him from completing his revenge against the Rands by lynching Jeb – the "signifier of [her] guilt".[5] Nevertheless, the formless 'something' lingers around the Rands' ruined ranch-house like fate itself, overshadowing Jeb and Thor's prospects like the vertiginous rocks that tower over the landscape.

Raoul Walsh's handling of such volatile material is assured and occasionally inspired, but *Pursued's* darkly melodramatic bearing marks it as Busch's property. As in *Duel in the Sun* (1946), also centred on a quasi-incestuous sexual obsession, and Busch's novel *The Furies*, filmed in the blackest tones by Anthony Mann, there is a sickness at the heart of a western family that can only be cured by breaking its facade. The courtship of Jeb and Thor is marked by the mutual awareness that she intends to avenge her brother, while Ma Callum represents family as both a repository of damaging secrets and a repressive agency. "What you don't remember doesn't matter," she counsels Jeb. "Don't ask questions about the past." Of course, nothing of the sort could be expected of a noir hero; Jeb's disregard for his foster mother's warning may not lead to his destruction, as it would Mitchum's character in *Out of the Past* (1947), but it does destroy "the western family ideal" that Grant has already corrupted and yet remains, for many, one of the cornerstones of the genre itself.[6] **KG**

footnotes

1 The title, *Pursued*, connotes the same mood of abstract threat, alienation and dread as other stark noir appellations: *Caged*, *Caught*, *Cornered*, *Desperate*, *Fear*, *The Hunted*, *No Way Out*, *Trapped*, and so on.
2 *Film Noir: The Dark Side of the Screen* (Da Capo, 1981).
3 Andrew Britton, 'Notes on *Pursued*', in *The Movie Book of the Western* (Ian Cameron and Douglas Pye, eds, Studio Vista, 1996).
4 *Film Noir* (The Overlook press, 1992).
5 Britton, 'Notes on *Pursued*'.
6 David Lusted, *The Western* (Pearson, 2003).

Ramrod

1947, B/W, 94 mins.

D: Andre de Toth. P: Harry Sherman (Enterprise Productions, Inc).
W: Jack Moffitt, Graham Baker, Cecile Kramer, Luke Short (story).
Ph: Russell Harlan. M: Adolph Deutsch.
St: Joel McCrea (Dave Nash), Veronica Lake (Connie Dickason), Don DeFore (Bill Schell), Donald Crisp (Jim Crew), Preston Foster (Frank Ivey)

"From now on, I'm going to make a life of my own. And, being a woman, I won't have to use guns."

Driven by an impassioned performance by the usually laid-back Veronica Lake, Andre de Toth's first western is a potent fusion of genre motifs, mixing a range-war plot with the shadowy *mise en scène* and psychological preoccupations of noir. In Joel McCrea's Dave Nash it has a prototype of the tortured protagonist who came to prominence in the Fifties: an ex-drunkard, mired in guilt for the death of his son in a house fire, he has an uncommonly anguished aspect for a western hero of this vintage. He is hardly the resolute figure one associates with the genre, and this allows Lake's purposeful Connie Dickason to dictate proceedings.[1]

Sexually alluring and unscrupulous, Connie is painted in the same grey tones as other femmes fatales. As a neophyte landowner who plans to raise sheep, her feud with the cattle baron Frank Ivey masks a desire to challenge in general male dominance (as well as patriarchy – Ivey's staunchest crony is Connie's own father). "Men are so easy," crowed the posters. "A little lace, a pair of lips, a touch, and they kill for you." She manipulates the men around her: putting her fiancé in harm's way; persuading a hired hand to stampede her own stock to implicate her enemies; beguiling both Dave and his best friend to help achieve her ends. The violence she unleashes – protracted beatings, shotgun killings – is rendered in a realistic manner associated more with noir than with westerns of the period.

Typically for the time, and for noir, the enlightened decision to grant a woman such a dynamic role cannot disguise distaste for her methods and a conservative bias: the script contrasts Connie with homely dressmaker Rose (Arleen Whelan), who condemns the other's "greed and ambition", implying that, like Rose, she ought to know her place. Ultimately, Connie's plan succeeds, in that Dave kills Ivey, but she doesn't get everything she wants: Dave opts for Rose, a more conventionally redemptive figure, instead. "So you don't want [power] alone. I guess that squares everything," Dave tells Connie when it is clear, from Lake's astute portrayal, that for all her gains she is crushed to have lost him. It is a vindictive conclusion given that the character retains an appealing vulnerability in spite of her wiles. **KG**

footnotes

1 It is perhaps not so surprising that de Toth should have accepted a property that afforded Lake so much prominence, since he was married to her at the time. Then again, the role is profoundly morally ambiguous and not necessarily glamorous – the actress's trademark 'peekaboo' hairstyle is conspicuous by its absence and she spends much of her time wearing masculine riding gear, not chic frocks.

Blood on the Moon

1948, B/W, 88 mins.

D: Robert Wise. P: Theron Warth (RKO). W: Lillie Hayward, Harold Shumate, Luke Short (novel). Ph: Nicholas Musuraca. M: Roy Webb. St: Robert Mitchum (Jim Garry), Barbara Bel Geddes (Amy Lufton), Robert Preston (Tate Riling), Walter Brennan (Kris Barden), Phyllis Thaxter (Carol Lufton)

"I've been mixed up in a lot of things, Tate, but up to now I've never been hired for my guns."
"Can you afford to be so particular?"

Visually the blackest of all Forties westerns, *Blood on the Moon's* traditional plot is less the point of interest than the manner of its execution and the increasing self-awareness of Robert Mitchum's hangdog antihero. As a drifter in a moral quandary, Hammett-esque aloofness segueing into righteous support for the homesteaders he has been hired to oppress, he shows greater range than he had in *Pursued* in a role that fits him equally snugly – far more comfortably than his shabby trail outfit, which is among the most convincing of the era.[1]

The memorable opening, with Mitchum on horseback, cresting a hill during a nocturnal downpour, establishes a brooding quality that remains throughout, even when motivations are clarified and the narrative sewn up with a too-neat flourish. Robert Wise was a versatile director, but he rarely ventured West; this excursion finds him either shooting at night or shrouding events in dense shadows, the ambiguity of tone and sense of unease, however illusory, imported from his breakthrough films for Val Lewton. Nicholas Musuraca was RKO's in-house cinematographer and, with his expressionist-influenced work on *Stranger on the Third Floor* (1940), Wise's *The Curse of the Cat People* (1944) and the exemplary *Out of the Past*, arguably did as much as anybody to define the densely textured look later identified with noir. Here he enriches the world of the western with shafts of moonlight through branches, faces glowing ethereally in lamplight, figures isolated in the blackness by campfires. Even routine rough stuff is imbued with greater depth and drama by Musuraca's signature low-key lighting – the blistering bar-room brawl between Mitchum and Robert Preston and climactic siege of Walter Brennan's ranch are outstanding set-pieces even by Wise and Musuraca's standards.

The style compensates for a plot that runs out of steam once Mitchum, aided by the besotted Barbara Bel Geddes, resolves the crisis of conscience that pits his battered integrity against loyalty to old friend Preston, now a ruthless swindler. In making the best of a bad deal and rejecting Preston ("I've seen dogs that wouldn't claim you for a son"), he earns redemption – something not always available to Mitchum's characters in noir. **KG**

footnotes

1 Western stalwart and Old West enthusiast Walter Brennan remarked to Robert Wise during filming, "That is the goddamnedest realest cowboy I've ever seen," when he saw Mitchum in his costume (quoted in Lee Server, *Baby, I Don't Care*, Faber & Faber, 2001).

above: from left: Robert Mitchum, Barbara Bel Geddes and Tom Tully.

The Man from Colorado

1948, Colour, 99 mins.

D: Henry Levin. P: Jules Schermer (Columbia). W: Robert Hardy Andrews, Ben Maddow, Borden Chase (story). Ph: William Snyder. M: George Duning. St: Glenn Ford (Col. Owen Devereaux), William Holden (Capt. Del Stewart), Ellen Drew (Caroline Emmett), Ray Collins (Big Ed Carter), Edgar Buchanan (Doc Merriam)

"Could the war get a man, a decent man like Owen, so sick he can't stop killing?"

Film noir is given a lush, Technicolor veneer in this psychological western. Post-war trauma was examined in many thrillers of the period – *Crossfire* (1947), *Dead Reckoning* (1947), *Act of Violence* (1949) – but here it's the Civil War that is the root of the protagonist's sociopathic behaviour and paranoia. "Whatever the war, its destructive effects are the same… where killing is presented as morally and socially accepted."[1]

Glenn Ford's Devereaux is an army officer who, in the dying days of the conflict, orders his Union troops to fire on a ragtag bunch of vanquished Confederates. His friend and fellow officer, Del Stewart, remains silent out of loyalty. Returning to their hometown, Devereaux is gifted the position of federal judge while Stewart is sworn in as marshal. However, when Devereaux's methods of protecting the status quo for local business interests become increasingly draconian, Stewart sides with an outlaw gang to bring an end to his terror.

Devereaux is no pedestrian protagonist. His wartime diary entries spell out his torment. He wants to stop the killing, and questions whether the end of the war will repair his fragile mind. Noir style and atmosphere accentuate the mood, with muted, candlelit close-ups betraying his anguish. Ford gives the character a smouldering, brooding demeanour. He is unable to engage emotionally and socially with those he loves, and his aggression towards his wife, Caroline, sees her turn to Stewart for solace.

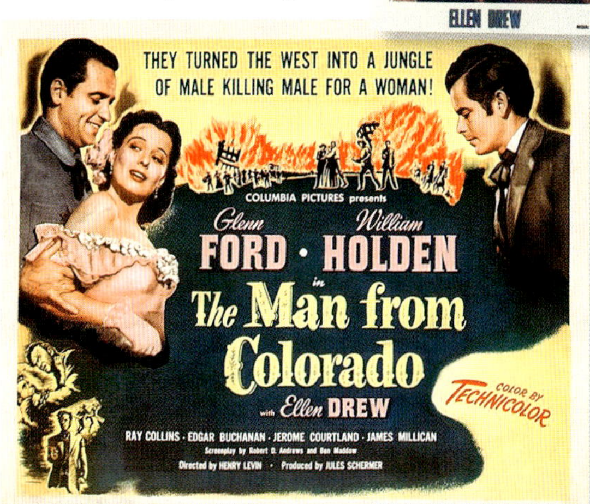

Devereaux is, in many ways, "a continuation of the unstable character [Ford] played in *Gilda* (1946)".[2] His compulsion to kill is too great for the love of a good woman to dispel, and his final solution is to set the town ablaze to smoke out his enemies. Inevitably, events conspire to consume Devereaux instead. The climax is overly tidy, sparing Stewart the necessity of dispatching his former friend, but the latter retains the taint of noir even in death. **CH**

footnotes

1 Geoff Mayer and Brian McDonnell, *The Encyclopedia of Film Noir* (Greenwood Press, 2000).

2 Ibid.

Station West

1948, B/W, 92 mins.

D: Sidney Lanfield. P: Robert Sparks (RKO). W: Frank Fenton, Winston Miller. Ph: Harry J. Wild. M: Heinz Roemheld.
St: Dick Powell (Lt. Haven), Jane Greer (Charlie), Agnes Moorehead (Mrs. Caslon), Burl Ives (hotel clerk), Tom Powers (Captain Iles)

***"I believe every man has his price…
Every woman knows it."***

Keyed to Dick Powell's sardonic noir persona, and with Jane Greer as enigmatically alluring as she had been in the previous year's *Out of the Past*, this modest RKO western possesses a hard-boiled undertow buttressed by pithy dialogue and a corrupt small-town setting that evokes Dashiell Hammett.[1] Powell's army investigator – effectively a private detective – is sent to a remote frontier town to flush out a murderous band of gold robbers, and finds Greer's elegant saloon owner pulling the strings in a foretaste of female-centric Fifties westerns such as *The Oklahoma Woman* and *Forty Guns*. They circle each other warily, with barely subdued romantic longing, until her karmic demise in a contrived but affecting finale.

Powell wears his Marlowe-like manner lightly, cutting down Greer's minions with wit while not lacking in brawn – his victory against the far burlier Guinn 'Big Boy' Williams in a show-stopping bare-knuckle brawl earns Greer's respect and allows him to infiltrate her organisation. The script, adapted from Luke Short's novel, is flush with sharp verbal sparring and shady personalities: Greer's dandified right-hand man; Raymond Burr's craven lawyer, cowed by Greer over his gambling debts in a scene that would be forgettable if not for her ability to switch between sedate charm and Medusa-like menace. Agnes Moorehead's wily Mrs. Caslon, another woman who takes no nonsense from men, makes it an even stronger showcase for female roles.

Harry J. Wild's chiaroscuro technique – seen to excellent effect in the Powell thrillers *Farewell My Lovely* (1944), *Cornered* (1945) and *Pitfall* (1948) – is employed sparingly; not often enough to sustain an air of mystery that dissipates once Greer and her rotten entourage are introduced. But Powell's cynical tough guy and Greer's jaded entrepreneur, who finds that fate is the one thing she can't control, impart the authentic flavour of noir as fatally attracted fellow travellers. **KG**

top right: from left:
Gordon Oliver, Guinn 'Big Boy' Williams and Dick Powell.

footnotes

1 Greer's presence and performance are central to the film's success on an emotional level, yet director Sidney Lanfield lobbied strongly for Marlene Dietrich to play the part. So much so, he apparently made Greer's life a misery on set. Dietrich would have her chance to dominate a western four years later, in Fritz Lang's *Rancho Notorious*.

Yellow Sky

1948, B/W, 98 mins.

D: William A. Wellman. P: Lamar Trotti (Twentieth Century-Fox). W: Lamar Trotti, W.R. Burnett (novel). Ph: Joseph MacDonald. M: Alfred Newman. St: Gregory Peck (James 'Stretch' Dawson), Anne Baxter (Constance Mae, 'Mike'), Richard Widmark (Dude), Robert Arthur (Bull Run), John Russell (Lengthy)

"I guess the war has upset a lot of those boys... and set them off on the wrong foot."

Visually reminiscent of *My Darling Clementine* (also shot by Joseph MacDonald) and William A. Wellman's *The Ox-Bow Incident*, *Yellow Sky*, with its story of greed, dissension and redemption, is pitched somewhere between a traditional outlaw western and the heist variant of film noir.[1] In Gregory Peck's Stretch Dawson it has an antihero at odds with himself, while Anne Baxter's macho heroine targets (literally, with a Winchester) postwar male anxiety in a manner both noir-esque and predictive of Fifties western trends (see *Johnny Guitar* and *Forty Guns*, which borrows one of this film's most arresting images – a figure framed through a rifle barrel).

Stretch leads a gang of bank robbers across the baking salt flats of Death Valley, after which they stumble into the ghost town of Yellow Sky, inhabited only by Mike and her grandfather. Stretch's leadership is tested when the men – nicely differentiated by a stalwart cast – lust after both Mike and her grandfather's gold. Initially boorish, not unlike Peck's Lewt in *Duel in the Sun* (1946), Stretch is gradually moulded into a nobler figure – chiefly under Mike's influence, although the script is unconvincing in this respect – who fights his own gang rather than let them take the gold.

While the plot alludes broadly to *The Tempest*, it is fairly run of the mill for a western, as are the settings. Characters ruing wrong turns and misfortune, however, signal a departure, showing the influence of noir trickling in (Richard Widmark's cynical performance is another marker), much as the harsh glare of the desert gives way to semi-darkness for most of the action in Yellow Sky. Wellman's compositional sense and MacDonald's mastery of high-contrast lighting and deep-focus photography, meanwhile, invest the derelict buildings and the imposing rocks that surround them with claustrophobic menace. The closing three-way shootout, coated in thick shadows, exploits darkness particularly effectively: from outside the unlit saloon, the camera catches flashes from the gunfire within as Stretch, Dude and Lengthy settle their differences.

Having veered towards noir, *Yellow Sky* abruptly changes course: Stretch, rehabilitated by Mike, convinces his remaining acolytes not only to renounce the gold, but to help him return the money they had stolen at the outset. It is a peculiar coda, which may have appeased the Production Code, but impairs the narrative's integrity. **KG**

footnotes

1 The opening scene refers directly to *Ox-Bow*, when Stretch and his men amble into a saloon and gaze lustily at an erotically charged painting behind the bar.

Colorado Territory

1949, B/W, 94 mins.

D: Raoul Walsh. P: Anthony Veiller (Warner Bros). W: John Twist, Edmund H. North. Ph: Sid Hickox. M: David Buttolph. St: Joel McCrea (Wes McQueen), Virginia Mayo (Colorado Carson), Dorothy Malone (Julie Ann Winslow), Henry Hull (Fred Winslow), John Archer (Reno Blake)

"You can bust out of jail, maybe, or mud holes like I was in, but you can't bust out of what you are."

Raoul Walsh's remake of his own *High Sierra* (1941) blends the moral stringency of the classic western (and the post-Code Hollywood gangster film) with the sense of entrapment that permeates the noir universe and conspired against many of Walsh's characters: Eddie Bartlett in *The Roaring Twenties* (1939); the trucker brothers in *They Drive By Night* (1940); John Wesley Hardin in *The Lawless Breed* (1952); Jeb Rand in *Pursued*. Joel McCrea's Wes McQueen is a man who, as his predecessor in *High Sierra*, Roy Earle, expressed it, yearns to "crash out" of the outlaw lifestyle but is compelled to take part in "one last job", which proves as fateful for him as it has for screen criminals *ad infinitum*.

McQueen's desire for normality fuels his attraction to rancher's daughter Julie Ann, who symbolises the purity and decency just beyond his grasp; even she is corrupted by the curse of noir, however, when she lusts after Wes's reward money. He meets a more suitable match in half-Indian dance-hall girl Colorado, a fellow outcast with similar longings but fewer illusions. Virginia Mayo puts heart and soul into the most clichéd of roles.

Working from a tough-minded script, Walsh adroitly transposes the staples of the urban crime film – backstabbing cohorts, double-dealing middlemen – into a western milieu, and the plot's pitch into the blackness of noir is expertly paced. The climax is especially fine. Whereas Roy Earle's death atop a mountain at the end of *High Sierra* was interpreted as an escape from his torment, the site itself as a kind of Valhalla, there are no such illusions here. The cliffs in the "canyon of death" where McQueen and Colorado meet their end under a posse's fusillade have the same function as the buttes in *Pursued* – as an impassable barrier, a literal dead end, scattered with the bleached bones of long-deceased Indians. The lovers' dying clasp is another link in the chain of doomed fugitive couples in postwar westerns and noirs, from *Duel in the Sun* (1946) and *Criss Cross* (1949) to *Gun Crazy* (1950). **KG**

From left: James Mitchell, John Archer, Joel McCrea and Virginia Mayo

Lust for Gold

1949, B/W, 90 mins.

D: S. Sylvan Simon. P: S. Sylvan Simon (Columbia). W: Ted Sherdeman, Richard English. Ph: Archie Stout. M: George Duning.
St: Ida Lupino (Julia Thomas), Glenn Ford (Jacob Walz), Gig Young (Pete Thomas), William Prince (Barry Storm), Edgar Buchanan (Wiser)

"It's simple to get to, the mountain… but inside, it's like Satan's private art gallery."

The black cloud of noir hovers over this flawed but fascinating western, with its vipers' nest of wretched chancers bound together by betrayal, greed, obsession and cruelty. A treasure hunt-cum-murder mystery, set in the Forties, brackets the more engaging backstory of the fabled Lost Dutchman's gold mine in the inhospitable Superstition Mountains of Arizona. Running with the legend – the mine was sealed up, its Spanish discoverers massacred, by Apaches angered at this desecration of sacred land – the script embellishes the rumours surrounding German expat Jacob Walz, who locates the gold and determines to keep it to himself, resorting to murder on more than one occasion.

Opinions diverged about the real Walz; here, he is unambiguously "a mean and wicked man". His scowl departs only when the opportunistic Julia Thomas dupes him into thinking that she loves him, and not just for the riches that have made him a source of both envy and unwanted advances. This passage initially fails to convince – Walz doesn't seem the type to be taken in – but it works because of Ida Lupino's fatale charm and that sympathetic, boyish quality that Glenn Ford could never quite banish. In any case, Walz's mistrustful nature reasserts itself, literally with a vengeance, when he lures Julia and her no-account husband to the mine and traps them on a narrow ledge, the gold within their grasp but of no use as they wilt under the cruel sun and Walz's remorseless vigil. Husband and wife turn on each other in an unseemly display of recrimination and desperation, before fate, the ultimate arbiter in noir, intervenes spectacularly.

The unpitying mountain is a fitting backdrop for such a severe examination of character; where this is typical of the western, the use of visual metaphors and expressionistic effects – Julia's dual nature suggested by a mirror shot; Walz's eyes illuminated in close-up when he sees the light about his lover's double game – betray the influence of psychological melodrama, as noir was widely classified before the term gained currency. This central section, driven by the powerful playing of Ford and the intelligence of Lupino, who conveys Julia's internal conflict as well as her avarice, outweighs the flimsy framing story. Told in a semi-documentary manner, this tracks Walz's grandson as he searches for the mine at the same time as a murderer seeks to kill off competition.[1] The moral of both stories is the debasing effect of fortune-hunting, hinting at the debt owed by this film to *The Treasure of the Sierra Madre* (1948). **KG**

footnotes

1 The lead character in the contemporary scenes, Barry Storm, is named after the author of the (nonfiction) book that inspired *Lust for Gold*. The real Storm – actually a non de plume – took offence at the portrayal and sued Columbia for libel, later settling out of court.

Raton Pass

1951, B/W, 84 mins.

D: Edwin L. Marin. P: Saul Elkins (Warner Bros). W: Tom W. Blackburn, James R. Webb. Ph: Wilfrid M. Cline. M: Max Steiner. St: Dennis Morgan (Marc Challon), Patricia Neal (Ann Challon), Steve Cochran (Cy Van Cleave), Scott Forbes (Prentice), Dorothy Hart (Lena Casamajor)

"Because of that woman you're like a child who's burnt his hand on the stove. Because of that woman men are going to die."

In this obscure fusion of genres, a ranchero's grasping new wife thrusts her hand in the hornet's nest of a range war. Patricia Neal, an unlikely succubus, attempts the kind of emasculating role perfected by the more convincingly ruthless Barbara Stanwyck. At first glance a well-heeled society lady, Ann's sexual attraction to men of a baser kind is revealed when she caresses outlaw Van Cleave's pistol. He is swiftly abandoned, however, when Ann sees him bested in a fistfight by cattle baron Marc Challon, to whom she turns her attention.

An arch manipulator, she observes what makes men tick and works her education to her advantage. Gazing at a portrait of Challon's mother, Ann attempts to emulate her in the affections of both Marc and his father, but this is just a veil for her own ambition. After seducing Prentice, a railroad director, she buys out Challon, only to find herself deserted by his loyal crew. Isolated, she calls on Van Cleave for help.

Neal is suitably glacial, if rather one note. To provide a sense of balance, a 'pure' polar opposite of the femme fatale emerges – here literally from the shadows – in the angelic vision of Lena, who will facilitate Challon's figurative resurrection.

While there is little distinctive aesthetically, nocturnal scenes prevail in the latter scenes, shot on stages in low-lit conditions, suggesting the noirish shadow Ann's scheming has cast over familiar range-war proceedings. Steve Cochran bristles with hoodlum charm as the only man low enough to see through Ann: "I'm your kind. You wouldn't have to pose with me." Whether shooting men in the back or beating women, his character has been dredged up from the gutters of noir. He is also granted the film's most striking visual beat: a ranching family hide in the darkness of their homestead when they hear Van Cleave approach, only for his moonlit shadow to appear in the doorway, heralding the man, guns blazing. **CH**

Rawhide

1951, B/W, 86 mins.

D: Henry Hathaway. P: Samuel G. Engel (Twentieth Century-Fox). W: Dudley Nichols. Ph: Milton Krasner. M: Sol Kaplan. St: Tyrone Power (Tom Owens), Susan Hayward (Vinnie Holt), Hugh Marlowe (Rafe Zimmerman), Dean Jagger (Yancy), Edgar Buchanan (Sam Todd)

"Sure, I let 'em walk all over me. Why? Cos I was scared stiff… I want to live just as long as I can."

Based on the 1935 gangster film *Show Them No Mercy!*, *Rawhide* transposes the contemporary anxiety of hostage dramas such as *The Dark Past* (1948), *Dial 1119* (1950) and *The Desperate Hours* (1955) to the old West. A sense of entrapment is established by the remoteness of the location – the stagecoach relay station at Rawhide Pass – and exacerbated by much of the plot unfolding within the claustrophobic confines of the station itself, where four outlaws imprison Tom Owens, who works there, and Vinnie Holt, a woman travelling with her infant niece, while they plan their attack on a gold shipment.

In his landmark *Panorama du film noir Américain* (1955), Raymond Borde identified *Rawhide* as one of the "neo-westerns" caught in noir's shadow, in which the dynamics of the western are downgraded from the spectacular to the intimate, its tropes thwarted like the plans hatched by noir's ill-fated malefactors. A stagecoach robbery is in the offing, but "the main thrust of the film [is] to show why the attack fails, by analysing the internal tensions that cause the band of outlaws to disintegrate" – specifically, a battle of wills between gang boss Rafe Zimmerman and his psychotic lieutenant, Tevis (Jack Elam), whose idea of fun is to take potshots at the baby.

Rawhide has more in common with Henry Hathaway's Forties thrillers than with the grand westerns of his later career. He mines suspense from Vinnie and Tom's escape attempts, and repeatedly frames characters in visual traps, from doorways and corridors to a hole dug through a wall. Susan Hayward's forceful heroine and Tyrone Power's reluctant hero, who betrays the genre's code by readily confessing his fears, are likewise more noir than western in lineage. The order of their relationship is decreed when she takes his pistol from his holster in a blatant emasculation metaphor; she even denies him the traditionally male privilege of dispatching Tevis at the climax. It was a mark of both noir and the "neo-western" to present ordinary people as unlikely or unwilling protagonists in situations they struggle – and often fail – to overcome.

When this same 'ordinariness' describes the antagonist, however, it can leave a void. Hugh Marlowe, an everyman type, lacks the menace and vitality of his henchmen, notably the leering, jittery Jack Elam. *Rawhide* cries out for a villain as well written and subtly played as those faced by Randolph Scott in the Ranown cycle, in particular Richard Boone's affable Frank Usher in *The Tall T* (1957) – structurally, the most similar of those films to this one. **KG**

above: Tyrone Power with Susan Hayward.

The Secret of Convict Lake

1951, B/W, 83 mins.

D: Michael Gordon. P: Frank P. Rosenberg (Twentieth Century-Fox). W: Oscar Saul, Anna Hunger (story), Jack Pollexfen (story). Ph: Leo Tover. M: Sol Kaplan. St: Glenn Ford (Jim Canfield), Gene Tierney (Marcia Stoddard), Ethel Barrymore (Granny), Zachary Scott (Johnny Greer), Ann Dvorak (Rachel Schaeffer)

"I hope you're not too much in love with Rudy Schaeffer… I have to kill him."

Five escaped prisoners descend from the mountains towards an isolated settlement, seeking refuge from a blizzard. There are only women in residence, their menfolk absent on a mining expedition. While the women, marshalled by Ethel Barrymore's formidable matriarch and Ann Dvorak's neurotic spinster, grant their guests food and shelter, sexual tension, mutual mistrust and vengeful desire keep the plot simmering.

The Secret of Convict Lake, based loosely on fact,[1] centres on two characters – and performers – strongly associated with film noir. As the most sympathetic of the felons, Glenn Ford essays another of his victimised outsiders – hard shell encasing a basically decent core, bitterness at an unjust charge of murder (he killed in self-defence) driving his pursuit of the man who framed him. As the culprit's fiancée, Gene Tierney's pristine beauty is another disguise of sorts, masking profound sorrow (the actress herself was prone to depression) and self-loathing for a life spent "kicking around in gambling halls and saloons", following the deaths of her father and brother in a feud. It is their shared experience of twists of fate and social ostracism – evident in Ford's imprisonment; implicit in Tierney's bid for a fresh start in the wilderness with a man she doesn't really care for – as much as the mechanics of genre and plot that brings them together and paints them as refugees from noir.

The wintry backdrop serves to confine the characters in much the same way, although not as thoroughly, as it would in *Track of the Cat* (1954) and *Day of the Outlaw* (1959). The use of studio sets for the lakeside community is also constraining, in a noir sense, with an emphasis on dark interiors, lit by lanterns or flames, and night scenes in general. Finally, however, the film emerges into light, bowing to convention by allowing Ford his revenge – again, his hand is forced – and the promise of exoneration and fulfilment with Tierney. **KG**

footnotes

[1] In 1871, a group of prisoners broke out of a prison in Carson City and were tracked to Monte Diablo Creek, in California's Sierra Nevada, by a posse. The subsequent shootout led to the lake being renamed in the convicts' honour.

The Outcasts of Poker Flat

1952, B/W, 81 mins.

D: Joseph M. Newman. P: Julian Blaustein (Twentieth Century-Fox). W: Edmund H. North, Bret Harte (story). Ph: Joseph LaShelle. M: Hugo Friedhofer. St: Anne Baxter (Cal), Dale Robertson (John Oakhurst), Miriam Hopkins (Mrs. Shipton aka 'The Duchess'), Cameron Mitchell (Ryker), Craig Hill (Tom Dakin)

"You can't scare us. We're finished anyway. So are you."

In Bret Harte's wistful source story he writes that the town of Poker Flat was "experiencing a spasm of virtuous reaction" after the theft of "several thousand dollars", which sees four undesirables cast out by the town's new moral order.[1] Joseph M. Newman's adaptation broadens the story to concentrate on the tribulations of the refugees, levering in a siege plot that, as in *Rawhide*, combines with an intense, sombre aesthetic borrowed from the noir tradition.

In the nocturnal opening sequence, noir veteran Joseph LaShelle's camera stalks Ryker, a desperado bereft of emotion, as he ducks in and out of shadows, into alleys and through the mud-sodden streets of Poker Flat.[2] This murky ambience continues as Ryker enters the bank, sidekicks in tow, and blows the safe to steal its contents, unmoved as he guns down two townsmen.

As in Harte's tragedy, four scapegoats – a gambler, a drunk, a saloon madam and another woman, the enigmatic Cal – are ejected from Poker Flat the next morning. Seeking refuge in a mountainside cabin along with a young couple, they are soon stranded by a snowdrift. Cal is actually Ryker's wife; she is in possession of the stolen money when Ryker arrives to claim it.

Ryker is a malevolent creation, dominating the cramped, ramshackle cabin, physically incarcerating the unwanted souls of Poker Flat just as he has psychologically shackled Cal. When a tense, clammy game of poker with the nerveless Oakhurst reveals that some of the loot is missing, Ryker berates his wife about her feelings towards the gambler, his insecurities spilling over in an off-screen violation.

Histrionics aside, it is the dynamics of noir – mind games, paranoia, hopelessness, violent retribution – that hold sway in the final reel. Cal turns on Ryker; by declaring her admiration for Oakhurst, she verbally cuckolds her husband as venomously as the cruellest femmes fatales. Tensions explode in a savage showdown in the snow but, as in many westerns of the era, there is a romantic coda that contrasts detrimentally with the preceding night of torment. **CH**

footnotes

1 The essence of Harte's story has proved very attractive to western filmmakers. It had already been adapted in 1937 by Christy Cabanne and, at the tail end of the spaghetti-western boom, Lucio Fulci drew upon Harte's *Outcasts* and *The Luck of Roaring Camp* for his more lurid, metaphysical adaptation, *The Four of the Apocalypse* (1975).

2 Among his credits, LaShelle provided the chiaroscuro cinematography for *Laura* (1944), *Fallen Angel* (1945) and *Road House* (1948).

above: from left: Cameron Mitchell, Anne Baxter, Dale Robertson, Barbara Bates, Miriam Hopkins.

Jack Slade

1953, B/W, 90 mins.

D: Harold Schuster. P: Lindsley Parsons (Allied Artists, Monogram Pictures). W: Warren Douglas. Ph: William Sickner. M: Paul Dunlap.
St: Mark Stevens (Joey 'Jack' Slade), Dorothy Malone (Virginia Dale), Barton MacLane (Jules Reni), John Litel (Judge Davison)

"I guess we're all alone… Nobody knows what's inside of us, what makes us the way we are."

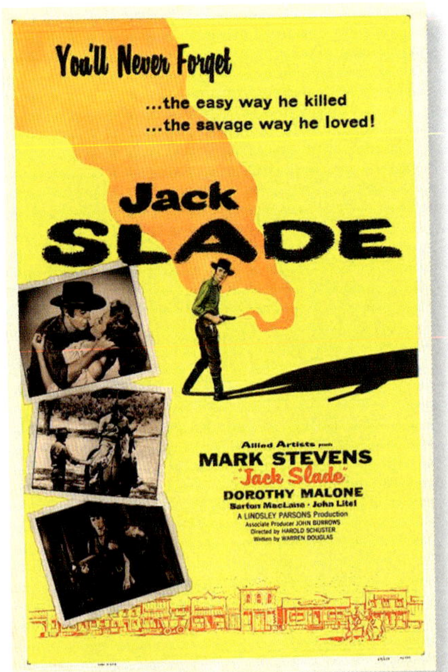

A bare-bones biopic of a second-string gunfighter, this is one of the most pessimistic westerns of the Fifties. Slade was marked by death at an early age. He killed his first man, inadvertently, when just 13, and – at least in this iteration of his story – saw his father shot down by highwaymen shortly afterwards. The script rattles through his career as a freight-line enforcer, his marriage to the doughty Virginia, his increasing reliance on alcohol and his deadly feud with the outlaw Jules Reni, but skimps on historical detail.

Slade's proficiency antagonises the community, in a foretaste of *Warlock et al*, and makes him a target for aspiring gunmen ("I draw trouble like a dead horse draws flies"), but this angle is less pronounced than the character's deeply noir predicament as a plaything of fate.

Mark Stevens, like Slade, was not quite top-of-the-range material. Reputedly volatile and prone to anguish, his intensity compensated for a lack of charisma. He was temperamentally suited to noir, summing up the plight of its victim-heroes in *The Dark Corner* (1946): "I'm backed into a dark corner and I don't know who's hitting me."[1] His relentlessly focused performance as Slade – a man who "lives inside himself" – is a study in extreme alienation. His dialogue expresses self-loathing and guilt; he speaks of being hounded by the past – a basic tenet of noir – and cursed by his violent nature. The curse extends to innocent parties, as when Slade is tricked into killing his surrogate father, and cripples a young girl while drunk.

The low budget produces a raw, spare look that fits the mood. Harold Schuster's direction is routine; occasionally he reveals an eye for the grotesque, as when a hanged man's swaying legs strum the strings on the guitar at his feet. Among Stevens' co-stars, Dorothy Malone impresses as a woman who doesn't merely stand by her man, but fires at his enemies. Eventually, even she realises he is beyond salvation, when he shoots through a bystander on his way to killing Jules. Slade finally engineers the violent death he has prophesied for so long, leaving us with an unsparing, if highly distorted, portrait of "a man of violence… a builder of the empire of the West" who "destroyed his own soul" in fulfilling his duties.[2] **KG**

footnotes

1 Stevens directed and starred in a pair of taut Poverty Row noirs in the mid-Fifties: *Cry Vengeance* (1954) and *Time Table* (1956).

2 The real Slade was more of a rowdy than a gunfighter. His reputation was embroidered by newspaper reports and by Mark Twain's *Roughing It* (1872), in which he recalls meeting this legendary "ogre" and being surprised by his affability. Slade fell victim to vigilante justice when locals in Montana brought his belligerent reign to an end via the noose. (Schuster directed an entirely fictitious sequel to this film, centring on Slade's son, in 1955.)

Three Hours to Kill

1954, Colour, 77 mins.

D: Alfred Werker. P: Harry Joe Brown (Columbia). W: Richard Alan Simmons, Roy Huggins, Alex Gottlieb (story). Ph: Charles Lawton Jr. M: Paul Sawtell. St: Dana Andrews (Jim Guthrie), Donna Reed (Laurie Mastin), Dianne Foster (Chris Plummer), Stephen Elliot (Sheriff Ben East), Richard Coogan (Niles Hendricks)

"I want to see them beg; I want to see them sick with fright..."

With Dana Andrews cast as the victim of a lynch mob, albeit a survivor this time, comparisons between Alfred Werker's characteristically abrasive western and *The Ox-Bow Incident* are inescapable. The plot, which finds Andrews, wrongly accused of murder, returning to the town that almost executed him to expose the real killer, also evokes the social consciousness of Fritz Lang's *Fury* (1936) and presents a jaundiced vision of provincial sanctimoniousness and moral cowardice familiar from *High Noon*.

At the same time, the fateful shift in fortunes that transforms stagecoach guard Jim Guthrie from everyman to desperate fugitive is very much the stuff of noir, as is the obsessiveness with which he pursues his vendetta. Feared and despised as the embodiment of the town's collective guilt, traumatised by the revelation that his fiancée has married another man and taken their son with her, the scapegoat hero embraces his fate with a grim determination peculiarly suited to the man that plays him. "They killed the Jim I knew," observes compassionate saloon girl Chris. "That's right, they did," he replies tersely.

As in his other town-based westerns, Werker envisions a community gripped by fear and paranoia, the consequences of its own malfeasance. People watch anxiously from windows; friends turn against friends; the sheriff's request for posse volunteers is met with the retort, "Why should we do your job?" It is no great surprise, given the influences on the film and the director at the helm, that the sheriff himself, the only man to have treated Jim sympathetically since his return, should be unveiled as the murderer. When the chastened citizens ask Jim to stay – chiefly, one suspects, to salve their consciences – he spurns their advances: "Knowledge of what the town is really like has killed both his desire to belong and his willingness to overlook moral evil."[1] As in *High Noon*, the betrayal of an individual by his peers represents a betrayal of sanctified American community values in a wider sense. **KG**

footnotes

1 John H. Lenihan, *Showdown: Confronting Modern America in the Western Film* (University of Illinois Press, 1980).

Backlash

1956, Colour, 84 mins.

D: John Sturges. P: Aaron Rosenberg (Universal). W: Borden Chase. Ph: Irving Glassberg. M: Herman Stein.
St: Richard Widmark (Jim Slater), Donna Reed (Karyl Orton), William Campbell (Johnny Cool),
John McIntire (Jim Bonniwell), Barton MacLane (Sgt. Lake)

"I've spent six months looking for a killer. What do you do when he turns out to be your father?"

With key Borden Chase themes in place – a hero divided against himself; the shadow of a powerful father figure – this muscular John Sturges western is firmly in the Anthony Mann mould. It also fits the pattern, albeit loosely, of the Freudian strain of film noir. As in *Pursued*, the *Urtext* of Freudian westerns, Jim Slater's quest for knowledge – about a crime; about the origin of his own violent urges – leads to a crisis of identity and conscience.

Slater is hunting an unknown man who betrayed five partners – among them Slater's father, or so he believes – to the Apaches, making off with $60,000 in ill-gotten gains. As well as familiar western hazards – Indian raids, vengeful outlaws, a trigger-happy young hotspur – he encounters the fatale-like Karyl Orton, whose husband was among those killed. Freely employing feminine wiles, she both helps and hinders Slater's investigation.

Sturges directs with his customary formal restraint – there is none of Mann's manic urgency, although the potential is there; John McIntire's exuberant villain comes closest to realising it. The role of Slater, latent with psychological torment, was seemingly tailored to the totemic James Stewart, but builds effectively on Richard Widmark's legacy of noir victim-heroes. The character becomes more tortured, and the star's performance more stirring, the closer he gets to the truth: that his estranged father is the guilty party. Cursing the blood that flows in his veins, his patricidal urges appear to be driving him towards one of those purgative acts so typical of Chase and Mann (*Winchester '73*; *Bend of the River*; *Man of the West*). The script spares him the need: his ire is deflected by a stray bullet, which fells his father before he can.

The one false note is struck by the presence of Donna Reed, who seems a shade too proper to play with conviction a worldly, morally compromised widow. Her sparring with Widmark lacks the erotic spark that may really have set *Backlash* alight. **KG**

above: Son of a gun: Richard Widmark (left) confronts John McIntire.

Black Patch

1957, B/W, 83 mins.

D: Allen H. Miner. P: Allen H. Miner (George Montgomery Productions Inc). W: Leo Gordon. Ph: Edward Colman. M: Jerry Goldsmith. St: George Montgomery (Marshal Clay Morgan), Dianne Brewster (Helen Danner), Tom Pittman (Carl, 'Flytrap'), Leo Gordon (Hank Danner), Sebastian Cabot (Frenchy DeVere)

"I'm different, Helen... I've seen too much war and killing."

A latecomer to noir that got lost among a slew of adult-oriented westerns, *Black Patch* has drifted into relative obscurity. War veteran Marshal Morgan's respect for the law is tested when his old friend Hank Danner arrives in town with his new bride, Helen – Morgan's old flame. Reluctantly, Morgan has to jail Hank when county lawmen accuse him of robbing a bank. DeVere, the saloon owner, offers to help Hank escape in exchange for half of the loot, but instead sets him up to be shot.

In one of his first screenplays, Leo Gordon recounts the story through richly drawn characters. Hank, part villain, part loving husband, is described with gruff sensitivity. George Montgomery's serious-minded lawman suppresses the mental wounds that are manifest in a damaged eye, which he covers with the titular patch, while the gangster-like DeVere is a study in decadent sleaze. Acting is solid throughout, with Tom Pittman revelatory as Carl, a parentless adolescent who hero-worships Hank and is manipulated by DeVere.[1]

Nocturnal chiaroscuro compositions complement the script's psychological leanings, which are augmented further by Jerry Goldsmith's portentous soundtrack (his first). Isolated in the jail, back to the camera, Morgan lifts his patch to bathe his eye – symbolically, one feels, cleansing his disturbed soul. Helen spies his shadow pacing back and forth through the bars of the jail, his true nature caged by the demands of his vocation.

above: Morgan (George Montgomery) faces an unwanted showdown

Carl's own inner rage turns on Morgan, whom he blames for killing Hank. It points towards a potential tragedy, but the tension between them is resolved when DeVere's guilt is revealed. The marshal deputises Carl, assuming the paternal role that had seemed earmarked for Hank.

It is an enlightened conclusion to an absorbing story, but Gordon's typecasting as a B-movie heavy was, he felt, the reason he was never taken seriously as a writer. Based on this evidence, that was Hollywood's loss. **CH**

footnotes

1 Pittman died too soon, at the age of 26 in 1958; he crashed his car in Benedict Canyon, Los Angeles. Like his idol James Dean, he was driving a Porsche Spyder.

The Fiend Who Walked the West

1958, B/W, 101 mins.

D: Gordon Douglas. P: Herbert B. Swope Jr. (Twentieth Century-Fox). W: Harry Brown, Philip Yordan, [Ben Hecht, Charles Lederer – original screenplay], [Eleazar Lipsky – story]. Ph: Joseph MacDonald. M: Leon Klatzkin (music supervision). St: Hugh O'Brian (Daniel Slade Hardy), Robert Evans (Felix Griffin), Dolores Michaels (May), Linda Cristal (Elena Hardy), Stephen McNally (Marshal Frank Emmett)

"You might say he died hard – like I think you will someday."

Saddled with a B-horror title and ushered in on eerie musical cues, Gordon Douglas's western/thriller hybrid purloins ideas from the noir classic *Kiss of Death* (1947) without matching that film's power.[1] However, the marriage of styles is largely harmonious and makes for a refreshing take on commonplace material.

Convicted bank robber Hardy says too much to his disquieting cellmate, Griffin, about the likely whereabouts of the loot. When Griffin is released he embarks on a spree of murder and sexual intimidation in pursuit of the money. Hardy escapes – with the connivance of the law – with the aim of bringing Griffin down.

The film's unusual dynamic is generated by the creative conflict between Douglas's affinity with western clichés and Joseph MacDonald's expressionistic tableaux. In the prison wagon, shadows cloak Hardy's anguish as his wife is illuminated, angelically, from outside; in their cell, low angles of Hardy and Griffin, with Griffin foregrounded, suggest the latter's dominance in their relationship.

The sordid noir ambience is capped by Robert Evans' skin-crawling performance as Griffin. From feeding glass to a rival inmate to shooting an elderly lady with an arrow, his is a wholly despicable villain, an arrested adolescent with an implied history of bullying underlying his own sadistic impulses. However, where Richard Widmark's showboating as the cackling Tommy Udo in *Kiss of Death* imparted genuine menace, Evans's sub-James Dean mumbling, greased quiff and socially obtuse posturing seem too contemporary for a western. (Evans felt the film's gaudy title – earlier options included *Quick Draw* and *The Hell Bent Kid* – demeaned the final product. "I'll become Fatty Arbuckle," he complained, largely blaming his acting career's decline on this decision.[2])

The other performances are sturdier, especially from the female leads. Linda Cristal is sensual and sympathetic as Hardy's ailing wife, revolted by Griffin's creepy advances, while Dolores Michaels brings a pathetic quality to May, the villain's physically and emotionally abused girlfriend, who turns on her craven abuser with a ferocious and cathartic rope-whipping.

It is Evans's film, however, erratic acting notwithstanding. He conveys palpable contempt for humanity; with his dying breath, he spits in the face of the latest weak-willed female to have fallen under his spell. **CH**

footnotes

1 The scripts for *Kiss of Death* and *Fiend...* were derived from the same story by Eleazar Lipsky. The music in question was borrowed – without authorisation – from Bernard Herrmann's score for *The Day the Earth Stood Still* (1951).

2 Robert Evans, *The Kid Stays in the Picture* (New Millennium Press, 2006).

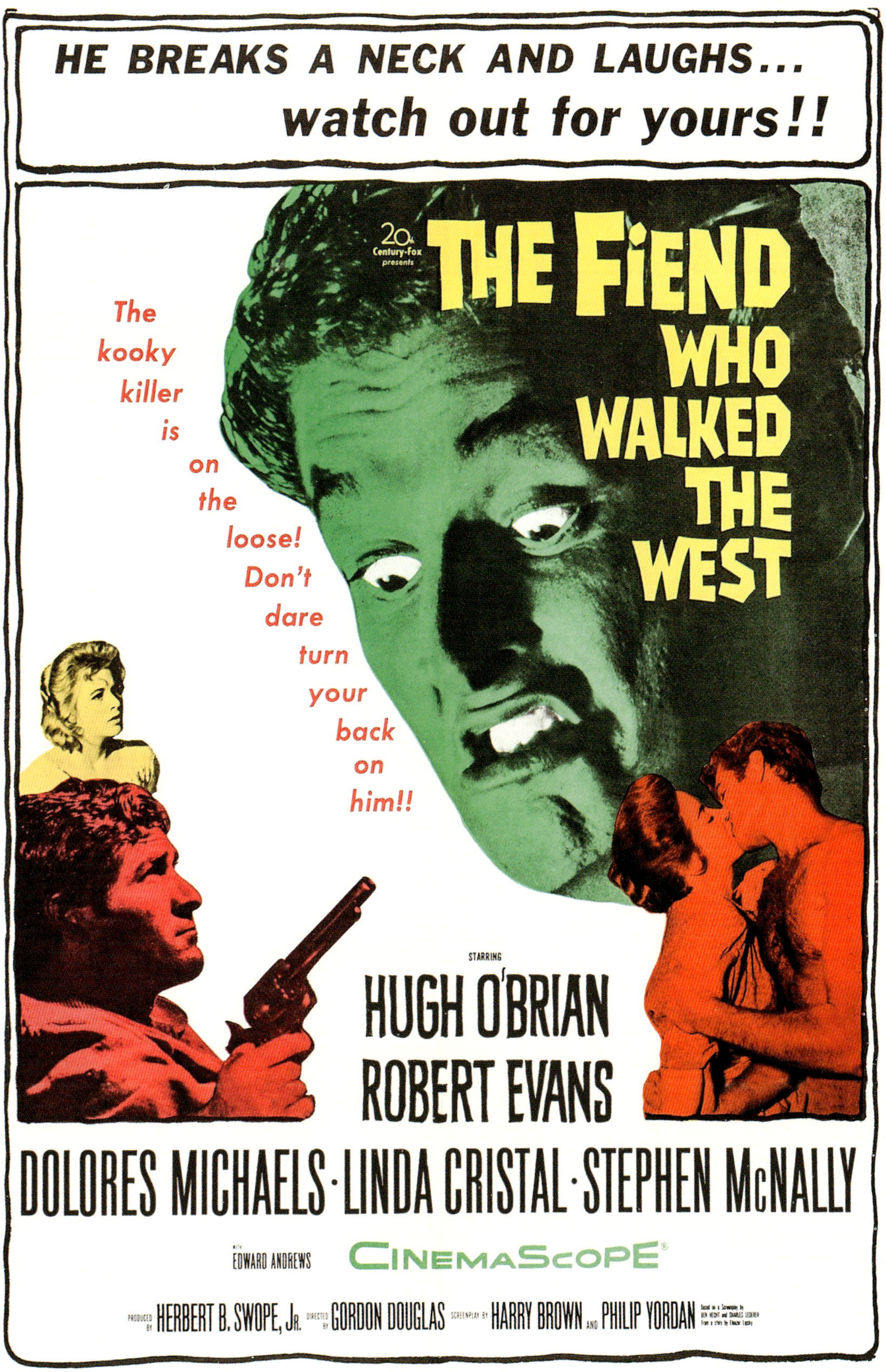
HE BREAKS A NECK AND LAUGHS...
watch out for yours!!
20th Century-Fox presents
THE FIEND WHO WALKED THE WEST
The kooky killer is on the loose! Don't dare turn your back on him!!
STARRING
HUGH O'BRIAN
ROBERT EVANS
DOLORES MICHAELS · LINDA CRISTAL · STEPHEN McNALLY
WITH EDWARD ANDREWS
CINEMASCOPE
PRODUCED BY HERBERT B. SWOPE, JR. DIRECTED BY GORDON DOUGLAS SCREENPLAY BY HARRY BROWN AND PHILIP YORDAN
Based on a Screenplay by BEN HECHT and CHARLES LEDERER
From a story by Eleazar Lipsky

BAD
GIRLS

Gunning for Peggy Castle

Women Take the Reins

The most masculine and chauvinistic of American film genres, the western, much like its male protagonists, has generally looked upon women as objects rather than subjects in their own right. They tend to be rigidly categorised: the little woman, holding the fort, metaphorically, on the homestead; the blowsy saloon girl, often destined to take a bullet, either for her sins or for the hero she has waylaid; the Indian maiden, symbolic of nature; the schoolteacher, exemplified by Cathy Downs' Clementine Carter; the sharp-tongued Puritan, a favourite target of John Ford.

Of course, these are generalisations, and good actresses could invest even stereotypical roles with vitality, even where the films retained a male focus (see Marlene Dietrich in *Destry Rides Again*; Joanne Dru in *Red River*; Katy Jurado in *High Noon*; Jean Arthur in *Shane*; Angie Dickinson in *Rio Bravo*, *ad nauseam*). The pattern became distorted in the postwar years, amid moves to challenge gender roles in society – after effects of the 'Rosie the Riveter' campaign, which saw greater numbers of women enter the labour market than ever before.

According to conventional wisdom, women's growing sense of empowerment as a result of their wartime experiences, and the threat this posed to male hegemony, helped give rise to the femme fatale in film noir – again, in a general sense. To this we can add a raft of more proactive, if not always positive, roles for women in westerns. Formidable performers such as Barbara Stanwyck and Joan Crawford and, further down the Hollywood pecking order, Peggy Castle and Beverly Garland, stamped their personality on familiar material that had been given a diverting, distaff twist. In many cases, they overshadowed male co-stars in the process. There were films about female outlaws and gunfighters, cattle baronesses and gambling queens, most of them richer in novelty value than in plausibility – an impression more recent examples such as *The Quick and the Dead* and *Bad Girls* have done little to dispel.

above: Sharon Stone draws a bead on sexist aggression in *The Quick and the Dead*.

Belle Starr

1941, Colour, 87 mins.

D: Irving Cummings. P: Kenneth Macgowan (Twentieth Century-Fox). W: Lamar Trotti, Niven Busch (story), Cameron Rogers (story). Ph: Ernest Palmer, Ray Rennahan. M: Alfred Newman. St: Randolph Scott (Sam Starr), Gene Tierney (Belle Starr), Dana Andrews (Major Thomas Crail), John Shepperd [Shepperd Strudwick] (Ed Shirley), Elizabeth Patterson (Sarah)

"You're so full of the devil, Miss Belle."

Myra Maybelle Shirley, privately educated daughter of a prosperous entrepreneur, teen bride and mother, alleged lover of Cole Younger, common-law wife of Cherokee rustler Sam Starr, overseer of a refuge for outlaws on the Canadian River, convicted felon, rumoured 'bandit queen'. Filtered through dime novels, Belle's life story became that of a freedom fighter-cum-female Robin Hood. This glossy production dispenses with the sordid details and alters key facts – Belle is now a virginal Southern aristocrat, Sam Starr a gentlemanly guerrilla of pure white stock. (The same fate befalls Blue Duck: in reality a fearsome Cherokee outlaw and rumoured lover of Belle; here Starr's comical Caucasian lieutenant.)

Very much in line with Fox's populist *Jesse James* (1939), the script portrays Belle as a diehard patriot resisting Yankee encroachment; her Southern pride is complemented by a sense of moral probity that eventually rubs off on Starr, who renounces his outlaw ways after Belle is shot dead by a cowardly horse thief. (Belle's real murderer was never identified. The most scurrilous rumour pointed towards her own son, said to have been abused by her.)

Then a raw ingénue, Gene Tierney was by no means an obvious choice for the lead, but tackles Belle's graduation from coquettish Scarlett O'Hara type to hard-riding rebel with gusto, quite unlike the coolness that characterised her later turns in film noir.[1] As a romanticised and largely falsified biopic, the film is framed around the central character and the narrow social vision she shares with her entourage. Background detail is limited. Director Irving Cummings doesn't dwell on the ironies that arise from Belle and Starr's battle cry of freedom on the one hand and their support for slavery on the other; Belle is clearly disturbed at the sight of newly emancipated blacks, preferring the devotion of her maid, the caricatured Mammy Lou (Louise Beavers), while Starr's language exposes his own deep-rooted racism.

Belle has never received her due on screen. In 1941, her true exploits, as far as they can be ascertained, would have been both too racy and, paradoxically, too mundane; she is not known to have participated in major crimes personally. Cummings' idealised portrait, combined with Tierney's spirited performance, wraps her in legend's warm embrace.[2] **KG**

above: Belle (Gene Tierney) stands her ground against the Yankees.

footnotes

1 Tierney saw off intense competition from more established actresses for the title role. Also tested were the likes of Ida Lupino, Barbara Stanwyck and Carole Landis.

2 The closest approximation of the real Belle Starr, in terms of multifaceted personality and relaxed moral standards, is reckoned to be Elizabeth Montgomery's portrayal in the 1980 TV movie *Belle Starr*.

Outlaw Women

1952, Colour, 75 mins.

D: Sam Newfield, Ron Ormond. P: Ron Ormond (Howco Productions Inc). W: Orville H. Hampton. Ph: Ellis W. Carter, Harry C. Neumann. M: Walter Greene. St: Marie Windsor (Iron Mae McLeod), Richard Rober (Woody Callaway), Carla Balenda (Beth Larabee), Jackie Coogan (Piute Bill), Allan Nixon (Dr. Bob Ridgeway)

"It may be a man's world outside, but it stops at Las Mujeres city limits."

A fantasy of female empowerment with an exploitative undertow (viz, a catfight in a saloon), this Howco quickie sends a mixed message, endorsing women's liberation from male supremacy while seemingly reinforcing that hierarchy at the end. Thus its unusual premise – a gambling town run by women, with men in their employ – peters out with the pairing of its female leads with condescending suitors.

Before then, B-movie queen Marie Windsor reigns over lawless Las Mujeres as Iron Mae McLeod, with a retinue of female toughs and card sharps based in the Paradise saloon.[1] Mae's mission – to beat men at their own crooked games – encounters difficulties when she crosses swords with the Bass-Slater gang and tries to fend off the advances, romantic and entrepreneurial, of her old flame, the gambler Woody Callaway. The set-up becomes a battle of the sexes between reluctant confederates on the one hand and criminal rivals on the other, leading to a shootout in which Mae and her girls more than hold their own. "Kings and queens are a pretty strong combination," observes Callaway approvingly, sealing the deal by marrying Mae.

The notion of a female fiefdom in the macho old West, coupled with references to women's lack of suffrage stacking the deck against Mae's plans, suggests ambitions beyond those of the average programme filler. Writing and direction fail to meet the challenge, however. In a rushed-looking production, musical numbers and comic interludes dilute whatever serious intent there may have been; even Iron Mae takes her dethronement in a good-natured fashion. Together with the conquest by the suave Dr. Ridgeway of the tomboyish Beth, who takes her more glamorous sister's advice and dons a frock to catch his eye, this seems to presage a male victory. It is not conclusive, however: it is clear from Mae's manner that Callaway won't be the only one wearing the trousers in their marriage. **KG**

footnotes

1 Windsor had some pedigree as a female western lead. She gave a purposeful performance as a quick-witted avenger in 1949's *Hellfire*, and played a counterfeiter who tangles with Tom Horn in 1950's *Dakota Lil*.

Rose of Cimarron

1952, Colour, 74 mins.

D: Harry Keller. P: Edward L. Alperson (Alco Pictures Corp). W: Maurice Geraghty. Ph: Karl Struss. M: Raul Kraushaar, Edward L. Alperson Jr.
St: Jack Buetel (Marshal Hollister), Mala Powers (Rose of Cimarron), Bill Williams (George Newcomb), Jim Davis (Willie Whitewater), Dick Curtis (Clem Dawley)

"Cherokee? I coulda sworn you was a white girl."

Orphaned after an Indian attack, a baby girl is rescued and brought up by Cherokees, who name her Rose of Cimarron. When horse thieves murder her adoptive parents, Rose, now a flame-haired young woman, vows revenge. A largely second-string production benefits greatly from its commanding female lead who, in keeping with evolving attitudes, bears comparison with the protagonists of *The Savage* (1952) and *Run of the Arrow* by renouncing the trappings of Europeanised frontier society and embracing indigenous culture, crossing what had seemed an impassable racial divide.

The refreshing marriage of feminism and multiculturalism is derailed briefly by Rose's dalliance with Marshal Hollister, to whom she turns for assistance in tracking her parents' killers. He, in turn, attempts to 'civilise' her by introducing her to the town matriarchs, whose snide remarks – "It must be wonderful to be rescued from a life of savagery" – provide the impetus for Rose to discard her ridiculous but flattering corset and hit the vengeance trail once more.

Mala Powers cuts a striking figure in her buckskin duds, the Natural Color process accentuating her scarlet hair. Rose conjures an aura of machismo to rival that of any cowboy and, when confronting two of the bandit-killers, her two-gun draw is both true and lethal. Jailed for the killing, she finds herself part of a prison break orchestrated by the boorish outlaw Newcomb. As a fugitive, she demonstrates her toughness and resourcefulness on the trail without, as was the norm in many Fifties B-westerns, sacrificing her sexual integrity.

The fortitude of Powers' performance is, sadly, unmatched by the script, and the final reel unfolds like a cheap TV serial, padded out with horse pursuits, until Hollister and his lawmen catch up with Newcomb's gang. When Rose learns that Newcomb was the third killer of her parents, a final confrontation ensues, along with the promise of romance between Rose and Hollister. It is an asinine ending given that "Cherokee girl" seems too much a force of nature to be a homemaker. **CH**

Woman They Almost Lynched

1953, B/W, 90 mins.

D: Allan Dwan. P: Allan Dwan (Republic Pictures Corp). W: Steve Fisher. Ph: Reggie Lanning. M: Stanley Wilson. St: John Lund (Lance Horton), Brian Donlevy (Quantrill), Audrey Totter (Kate Quantrill/Kitty McCoy), Joan Leslie (Sally Maris), Ben Cooper (Jesse James)

"Why don't you try acting like a woman… look at you, a bloodthirsty female, a disgrace to all women."

Amid a sandstorm of pedestrian B-westerns, Republic jazzed up this example with a proto-feminist subtext. When Quantrill's Raiders massacre Sally Maris's Union Army escort, the guerrillas guide her to neutral Border City for a reunion with her brother, Bill. This proves short-lived when Bill is gunned down after drunkenly drawing on Quantrill and his woman – Bill's ex-fiancée. Hence the seeds of conflict are sown between Sally and the acidic Kate Quantrill.

With Audrey Totter's fatale-like performance and her recurring clashes with Joan Leslie's tough-natured good girl, Allan Dwan's film builds a bridge between *Rancho Notorious*, with its masculinised den mother, and the campier aspects of *Johnny Guitar.*[1] The female leads are buttressed by Nina Varela as the town's formidable mayor, a larger-than-life harridan who dangles justice from the end of a rope and surrounds herself with bonnet-wearing minions.

The stars are evenly matched. While Totter smoulders with self-confidence, firing off acerbic retorts, Leslie develops into her equal with both sass and a pistol. The surrounding story, concerning Quantrill's efforts to pilfer from a local lead mine, is banal; the women call the shots, rejecting macho assumptions that a "big, strong man" should do their fighting for them. As well as a one-on-one brawl in a saloon, remarkable for its brutality, the leads partake in a well staged gunfight – Leslie demure but strident in billowing skirt and petticoat, Totter sensual in leather, strutting towards her enemy.

The more traditionally feminine Sally displays both mettle and mercy, sparing the wounded Kate's life. After this, Kate's ire dissipates. The women's sisterhood is sealed when Kate rescues Sally from a lynch mob; Sally's dalliance with Horton, a dashing Confederate spy, has aroused local ire. When the Raiders retreat from Union troops, Kate becomes unshackled from her psychological bondage, swapping trousers for ribbons and lace, the hallmarks of her former life as a saloon singer. Sally, meanwhile, settles down with Horton. Despite the heroines' attempts to redress the gender balance, harmony is achieved only when they return to the roles society has prescribed for them. **CH**

footnotes

1 Cineaste Peter Bogdanovich said of the director's approach, "Dwan resorted to his own brand of subtle satire... consciously and only to amuse himself, Dwan was creating camp twenty years ahead of its time" (*Savage Detours: The Life and Work of Ann Savage*, McFarland, 2009). Savage herself plays the spunky Glenda, the head of Sally's saloon girls.

Cattle Queen of Montana

1954, Colour, 88 mins.

D: Allan Dwan. P: Benedict Bogeaus (Filmcrest Productions Inc). W: Robert Blees, Howard Estabrook, Thomas Blackburn (story). Ph: John Alton. M: Louis Forbes. St: Barbara Stanwyck (Sierra Nevada Jones), Ronald Reagan (Farrell), Gene Evans (Tom McCord), Lance Fuller (Colorados), Anthony Caruso (Natchakoa)

"Jonesy, you're quite a gal."

The title of Allan Dwan's handsome but haphazard western jumps the gun: as the headstrong daughter of a pioneer murdered in an Indian raid, Barbara Stanwyck is not yet the regal rancher she would portray in *Forty Guns* or the TV series *The Big Valley*. Her role here is clearly a precursor, however, with the same strong will and dauntless spirit that made Stanwyck such a dynamic screen presence – even in the Fifties, theoretically her 'waning' years. With characteristic tenacity, plus the aid of Ronald Reagan's army agent and Lance Fuller's peace-loving chieftain, she pursues her father's claim and exposes the landowner guilty of inciting Blackfoot renegades.[1]

So vigorous is Stanwyck's performance, one feels her mission could almost have been accomplished alone; certainly, the film suffers when she is off-screen, given the stolidity of the supporting actors and the blandness of their roles. All the characters are poorly served by stilted dialogue, which comprises stock phrases and platitudes about prejudice, ignorance and misunderstanding – the stuff of numerous Fifties westerns that proposed simplistic answers to the 'Indian question'. Neither this theme nor that of disputed land rights is addressed with anything like originality.

Bright and sprightly, Stanwyck's Sierra Jones is accustomed to living among men and refuses to be subservient. She rides, shoots and kills alongside the male heroes, almost dissolving the distinction between genders; Reagan refers to her informally as "Jonesy", as he might a male accomplice.[2] Stanwyck's characters resisted easy categorisation, however, and Sierra is not strictly a tomboy, although the one time she wears a dress it is to appease the villain, who, predictably, falls for her ruse.

Dwan's rapid-fire action scenes and John Alton's radiant colour scheme deserve praise, but this remains the weakest of Stanwyck's Fifties westerns, her presence excepted.[3] It also falls some way short of other Indian-friendly films that similarly declaimed the manipulation and exploitation of native peoples. **KG**

footnotes

1 Stanwyck was given an honorary title, Princess Mary Victories III, by the Blackfoot Indians who worked on the film, in respect of her physical stamina during production.

2 Robert Mitchum was offered the male lead, but took exception to the script.

3 Stanwyck wrote off *Cattle Queen* as one of those films where, "You get taken in by what seems like a basically good idea and a sort of rough screenplay, and you sign on to do the picture without ever having seen a completed script… You do the best you can – and you privately hope that nobody goes to see it." Quoted in *Barbara Stanwyck*, by Al DiOrio (Coward-McCann Inc, 1983).

Two-Gun Lady

1955, B/W, 70 mins.

D: Richard H. Bartlett. P: Richard H. Bartlett (Associated Film Releasing Corp., L&B Productions Inc). W: Norman Jolley. Ph: Guy Rowe. M: Leon Klatzkin. St: Peggy Castle (Kate Masters), William Talman (Dan Corbin), Marie Windsor (Bess), Earle Lyon (Ben Ivers), Robert Lowery (Big Mike Dougherty)

"She's got more guts than any man in this town."

Famed trick-shot artist Kate Masters arrives in a sleepy town, where she has a run of performances booked and, more urgently, a score to settle against powerful rancher Jud Ivers and his volatile son, Ben. The script nods towards a number of Fifties motifs: the gunfighter burdened by his – or her – reputation ("A fast gun is always challenged, even when it's in the hands of a lady"); strained relations between a father and son; the collective cravenness of a frontier community. But this is too much for the B-movie budget and second-feature running time to bear, and it settles for being a minor, albeit feminocentric, revenge film.

Former femme fatale Peggy Castle's first western as star posits her as a cross between Belle Starr and the Sharon Stone character in *The Quick and the Dead*, alternating flattering frocks and figure-hugging slacks. She is adequate in the role, but toughness was not really her forte; that was the coolness she displayed so effectively as a film noir vamp. Her mission here is complicated by the machinations of fellow noir mainstays Marie Windsor, as a two-timing saloon girl, and William Talman, cast against type as a lawman who intuits that Kate is not a killer at heart (the film would have been a stronger proposition had she been so) and tries to block her path to the villains. When it seems as if Kate will be marginalised in favour of Talman's marshal, the plot turns back in a distaff direction, throwing up a showdown with Ben Ivers in which he is wounded by Kate and finished off by his simple-minded sister.

Budgetary limitations account in part for Richard H. Bartlett's one-paced direction, with its static set-ups; he made a stronger showing with more money behind him when he moved to Universal. In any case, the script is too formulaic, and Castle too reserved, to give Kate's story the emotional heft it required and the character deserved. **KG**

above: Kate Masters (Peggy Castle) gets the drop on rancher Ivers (Ian MacDonald).

Gunslinger

1956, Colour, 75 mins.

D: Roger Corman. P: Roger Corman (Roger Corman Productions). W: Charles B. Griffith, Mark Hanna. Ph: Frederick E. West. M: Ronald Stein. St: John Ireland (Cane Miro), Beverly Garland (Marshal Rose Hood), Allison Hayes (Erica Page), Martin Kingsley (Mayor Gideon Polk), Jonathan Haze (Jake)

"Why don't ya get out of those pants and find yourself a man?"

A mainly mediocre western, this is nevertheless of interest for its occasionally successful stabs at varying the formula. Keen to devise novel angles for his low-budget oaters, Roger Corman struck upon the idea of a female gunfighter – the wife of a murdered marshal who pins on his star.

Shot in six rainy days, which may account for the glum texture of the outdoor scenes ("This picture should have been retitled *Mudslinger*," wrote Corman[1]), the film tracks Rose's vendetta against her husband's killers. She soon crosses Erica Page, the town's grasping saloon owner, and her hired gunman Cane Miro, who skulks around the sodden set like a refugee from film noir. Despite Miro's black nature, Rose falls for him; in a tempestuous climax – very much a ricochet from the ending of *Duel in the Sun* – the pair exchange rifle fire, the sexual symbolism unmistakable.

Simmering, sometimes Sadean sensuality prevails: a catfight between Rose and Erica; Rose bound to a tree by three scantily clad saloon girls. At another point, she strokes the barrel of a rifle as Cane offers her a little "night-time company". The western cliché of the doting, piteous female is given a male makeover in the form of the jealous Jake (Corman regular Jonathan Haze), who's driven to histrionic fits of jealousy by Erica's flirtations with Cane. When Corman voiced the fear that there may be too much lurid content in the movie, he was told by his veteran Texas distributor that "there was no such thing as a movie with too much violence and passion", a mantra that would guide the young director over the course of his cinematic journey.[2]

Beverly Garland made a career out of tough-talking, fast-acting women, and her gunslinger is a persuasive siren. However, it was de rigueur in the genre for the male antihero to be a more complex and therefore more engaging character. Afforded a surprisingly moving soliloquy about the effects of his Civil War experiences, and shifting easily from disdain to heartfelt desire, John Ireland adds polish to a creaky production. **CH**

footnotes

1 Roger Corman, *How I Made a Hundred Movies in Hollywood and Never Lost a Dime* (Da Capo Press, 1998).

2 Constantine Nasr, *Roger Corman: Interviews* (University of Mississippi Press, 2011).

The Maverick Queen

1956, Colour, 90 mins.

D: Joe Kane. P: Herbert J. Yates (Republic). W: Kenneth Gamet, DeVallon Scott. Ph: Jack Marta. M: Victor Young. St: Barbara Stanwyck (Kit Banion), Barry Sullivan (Jeff Young, 'Jeff Younger'), Scott Brady (Sundance), Mary Murphy (Lucy Lee), Howard Petrie (Butch Cassidy)

"Most dangerous woman the West's ever seen."

This Zane Grey adaptation was a neat fit for Barbara Stanwyck, and not only because her off-screen nickname was 'the Queen'. She plays a good-time girl turned cattle baroness who earned her status by manipulating and discarding powerful men, including outlaw the Sundance Kid. This is Stanwyck at her brazen best: contemptuous of societal opprobrium; uncowed by Sundance's jealous threats; strong in the saddle.

Even a Stanwyck vehicle from the heyday of 'enlightened' Fifties westerns, however, had to abide by certain genre rules. Having set up Kit as an emblem of autonomous womanhood – a maverick, indeed – the script begins to reel her in, setting her on the path to redemption by aiding Barry Sullivan's Pinkerton detective in his fight against Butch Cassidy's Wild Bunch, her partners in crime.

Stanwyck connotes both Kit's flintiness and her veiled anguish with more assurance than the clichéd script deserves ("You can't turn back the clock"). In dramatic terms, however, the character steadily loses ground to the rival scheming of Sullivan's agent, who poses as a member of the Younger clan, and Sundance, played by Scott Brady as a malicious lout – the antithesis of the easygoing rogue immortalised by Robert Redford. (Sundance, in real life of European ancestry, is here given Indian blood, presumably to accentuate his 'wildness'.) Mary Murphy provides spirited support as a small rancher – as fearless and self-reliant as Kit, but civic-minded and, therefore, a more suitable romantic prospect for Sullivan.

References abound to key Fifties westerns, notably *Rancho Notorious* and *Johnny Guitar*, with their powerful female leads (another similarity with the present film is the employment of ballads as commentary), but these only highlight Joe Kane's routine handling of comparable pulp material. (The photography is far sharper, showcasing Republic's Naturama widescreen system.) The film is best appreciated in the context of Stanwyck's other westerns, especially the authoritative persona she established in *The Great Man's Lady* (1942) and displayed so majestically in *Forty Guns*, in which she resumed her onscreen relationship with the dour Barry Sullivan. **KG**

The Oklahoma Woman

1956, B/W, 73 mins.

D: Roger Corman. P: Roger Corman (Sunset Productions). W: Lou Rusoff. Ph: Fred [Frederick E.] West. M: Ronald Stein. St: Richard Denning (Steve Ward), Peggy Castle (Marie 'Oklahoma' Saunders), Cathy Downs (Susan Grant), Touch [Mike] Connors (Tom Blake)

"This'll be my town before I'm finished."

Partly out of sympathy with feminism, partly at the behest of his studio, Roger Corman pushed strong women to the forefront in a number of his early directed works, including three of the four westerns he made in a two-year burst in the mid-Fifties. Not as feverish as *Gunslinger* but livelier than *Apache Woman* (1955), this largely pedestrian effort was tailored to the cool, calculating persona of Peggy Castle, whose saloon-owner-cum power broker, Marie 'Oklahoma' Saunders, spends her time bullying smallholders and manipulating elections when she isn't (literally) whipping bad losers at her card table. If one inserted a man in her place it would make little difference to the outcome, with Castle attired for much of the film in a black dress in lieu of a black hat.

While this was hardly a unique scenario – there were similar characters in *Johnny Guitar*, *Man Without a Star* (1955), *The Maverick Queen* and others – it represented sound business sense: to imbue saddle-sore material with enough curiosity value to give it an edge in the marketplace, not to mention a whiff of decadence. (As tame as Corman's film seems today, it was singled out as an example of the genre's moral decline by historians George N. Fenin and William K. Everson.[1])

Castle's sensuous presence lifts an otherwise perfunctory affair. The same cannot be said for Richard Denning, the nominal lead, who sleepwalks through the typical role of a gunfighter trying to live down his past. An old flame of Marie, Denning's Steve Ward is drawn to her polar opposite, a rancher's daughter played, in a significant bit of casting, by Cathy Downs; her character represents the idea of woman as civilising force, much as Downs had done a decade earlier in *My Darling Clementine*.

Castle relishes the spotlight, all cold smiles and seductive glances, playing off current and former lovers against each other and fending off a mud-slinging lynch mob at gunpoint, until plot mechanics intervene and she is bested by Downs far too easily in a bar fight. A case of a villain receiving her customary deserts (Marie's male partner-in-crime is similarly defeated by Ward), or a rebuke to self-sufficient women in general – a victory for homemakers over harpies? It remains a matter for debate. **KG**

footnotes

1 *The Western: From Silents to the Seventies* (Penguin, 1979).

The Dalton Girls

1957, B/W, 71 mins.

D: Reginald LeBorg. P: Howard W. Koch (Bel-Air Productions Inc, Clark Productions Inc). W: Maurice Tombragel. Ph: Carl E. Guthrie. M: Les Baxter. St: Merry Anders (Holly Dalton), Lisa Davis (Rose Dalton), Penny Edwards (Columbine Dalton), Sue George (Marigold Dalton), John Russell (W.T. 'Illinois' Grey)

from left: Merry Anders, Lisa Davis, Penny Edwards.

"You can't trust a man... A man is a cheater... A gun's always faithful, a gun never strays."

The outlaw western often functioned as a form of displaced social criticism; this otherwise routine example applies a fanciful but earnest feminist twist. The lawbreakers driven to desperate measures by social injustice are, in this case, the hypothetical sisters of the notorious Dalton brothers, the last of whom are gunned down by a posse in the opening scene.[1] Tarred with their siblings' reputation, the women reason they may as well carry on the family tradition by robbing banks and stages to make ends meet. Holly, a pragmatist, does most of the planning; trigger-happy Rose is the angriest; Columbine the most conscientious; Marigold the most naïve. Verisimilitude was evidently not a priority – neatly coiffed and fully made up, the sisters are hardly the picture of destitution – but the lead performances are ardent and the plot pursues a ruthless logic, leading to a final shootout that is no respecter of gender.

The Dalton Girls was both forward-looking for its time and outmoded, locating its protagonists' tribulations in societal prejudice, a special concern of the prewar western, rather than the individual neuroses that fascinated film-makers of the Fifties. Inevitably, given the production company was operating at the exploitation end of the market, there is a degree of eroticisation in the way Reginald LeBorg presents his heroines. (Not that they use sex as a weapon, despite promotional hyperbole: "With hot guns or warm lips, they dared the men of the West to come and get it!") There is also a fashionable play on gender roles, as when Holly and Rose slip out of prim frocks to reveal tight-fitting jeans and shirts.

Men make a generally poor impression, from the undertaker who displays the brothers' bodies for money before forcing himself on Holly, to the romantic lead, the smug gambler W.T. Grey, who has designs on Columbine. Significantly, it is the latter, the only sister to contemplate surrender, who fares best at the finale, carried away by Grey with the promise of a settled life. **KG**

footnotes

1 There were indeed Dalton sisters, but they had different names and are recorded as being homemakers, milliners and dressmakers, not criminals.

The Ballad of Josie

1967, Colour, 102 mins.

D: Andrew V. McLaglen. P: Norman MacDonnell (Universal). W: Harold Swanton. Ph: Milton Krasner. M: [Frank] De Vol. St: Doris Day (Josie Minick), Peter Graves (Jason Meredith), George Kennedy (Arch Ogden), Andy Devine (Judge Tatum), William Talman (Charlie Lord)

"A pretty girl, a sturdy girl, made of solid timber."

The Fifties saw advancements in the representation of women in westerns, but in most cases gender order was restored in male favour by the end. (Not least in Doris Day's *Calamity Jane*.) In this film from the tail end of the Sixties little has changed, even though by that stage modern feminism was in full flow.

Day plays the widow of a brutish rancher whose bid for financial independence shakes up the sexual politics of a patriarchal town. The story challenges, none too seriously, various forms of gender bias, from the legal position on domestic violence ("You can't fault a man for jostling his woman around a little bit… There's a principle involved") and equality in the labour market (applying for 'men's' jobs, Josie is told, "Remember your place"), to the fight for women's suffrage.

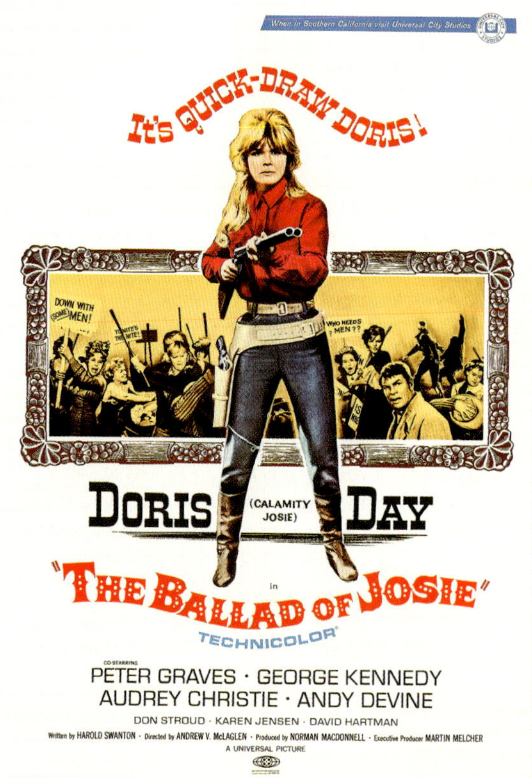

Day restrains her customary exuberance, but the dignity of the character, even in the face of male mockery, is regularly undermined by comic business – demonstrating her ineptness at waitressing, for example, the only job for which a woman is deemed suitable. Andrew V. McLaglen, an alpha-male director, didn't have the sensitivity for this kind of material. When Josie's campaign for equal rights is taken up by the townswomen, it is the occasion for a knockabout brawl. It is only when Josie, blackballed from entering the cattle business, instead takes up sheepherding – anathema to red-blooded ranchers – that the menfolk, rallied by the domineering Arch Ogden, stop laughing and start threatening. An old antagonism – livestock rivalry – is reworked as a battle of the sexes.

In a rushed conclusion both sides are forced to compromise, but it is Josie, hitherto so obdurate, who proves most pliable. Her 'true' function in the community, it seems, will be that of housewife and homemaker, not the ruler of her own roost. That role will fall to Jase, Josie's patronising suitor. "You don't want to get too independent," she reasons. It is significant that she marks the moment by burning her mannish work clothes, not her brassiere. **KG**

Hannie Caulder

1971, Colour, 85 mins.

D: Burt Kennedy. P: Patrick Curtis (Tigon British Film Productions Ltd, Curtwel Productions). W: 'Z.X. Jones' [Burt Kennedy, David Haft], Peter Cooper (story). Ph: Edward Scaife. M: Ken Thorne. St: Raquel Welch (Hannie Caulder), Robert Culp (Thomas Luther Price), Ernest Borgnine (Emmett Clemens), Jack Elam (Frank Clemens), Strother Martin (Rufus Clemens)

"You're a hard woman, Hannie Caulder."
"There aren't any hard women, only soft men."

A repudiation of women's allotted status in revenge westerns as something to be raped, discarded and avenged by proxy, this atypical star vehicle describes its heroine's attainment of self-determination after she is violated and her husband murdered by three boorish brothers.

Hannie's tutoring in triggernometry by the bounty hunter Price is juxtaposed with the comedic bickering of the Clemens boys. Hannie's resolve and growing competence show up the bungling and bluster of her macho assailants and earn the grudging admiration of Price, whose gruffness inevitably softens over time. Belittle me if you dare, is Hannie's message to a patriarchal society in which sexual assault is mere sport, where it is acceptable for a sheriff to pat your behind (not even Hannie seems to mind) and where the notion of a female gunfighter is subject to ridicule.

The director's predilection for earthy comedy repeatedly stalls the heroine's progress. When Hannie kills her first man, Burt Kennedy tarnishes this purportedly significant event by showing the body crashing through a window to land on a prostitute taking the air. It is a crass punchline, indicative of misplaced priorities. And the villains are played with such blustering gusto by a trio of western stalwarts – Kennedy's kind of people – that Raquel Welch's subtle injections of sensitivity can go unnoticed.

There are other distractions. The impact of Sam Peckinpah may account for the splashy violence, which was anomalous for Kennedy, and the influence of the European western stretches beyond the gritty Spanish exteriors and the serape worn by Welch (often with little else underneath) – Stephen Boyd's mysterious man-in-black, for example, who aids Hannie at the death but remains an abstraction. Somehow the star maintains the protagonist's integrity as well as her femininity, despite Price saying that Hannie "wants to be a man", meaning that gunning for vengeance is a male prerogative. The film pitches a feminist counter-argument but, with so many scenes given over to comic exaggeration, the original intention is difficult to discern. **KG**

Bad Girls

1994, Colour, 100 mins.

D: Jonathan Kaplan. P: Albert S. Ruddy, Andre E. Morgan, Charles Finch (Twentieth Century Fox). W: Ken Friedman, Yolande Finch, [Albert S. Ruddy, Charles Finch, Gray Frederickson – story]. Ph: Ralf Bode. M: Jerry Goldsmith. St: Madeleine Stowe (Cody Zamora), Mary Stuart Masterson (Anita Crown), Andie MacDowell (Eileen Spenser), Drew Barrymore (Lilly Laronette), James Russo (Kid Jarrett)

"I was worthless until I married. So now, I guess I'm worthless as a widow. Funny, I had some value as a whore."

Bad Girls lays its liberal intentions on the table, or rather the saloon bar, in the opening scene, the camera panning across black faces as well as white ones in a welcome gesture of inclusivity. It is in this spirit that four prostitutes are liberated from subservience – in both narrative and social terms – when one of them kills a violent patron and they become fugitives, narrowly escaping a lynch mob led by a fire-and-brimstone preacher. The implied criticism of the patriarchal structure of society suggests a feminist parable along the lines of *Thelma & Louise*; what we get resembles more a crude variation of *Young Guns* in female garb.

The actresses, marshalled by a steely Madeleine Stowe, do what they can with such threadbare material, but they are too well-groomed and healthy-looking to convince as frontier prostitutes, always filmed in the most flattering of light and from the most becoming of angles. The script is platitudinous rather than politically astute, and largely eschews psychological insight or realism as the heroines are thrust into hazardous scenarios drawn from the well of western clichés. The plot has them planning to pool their resources and start afresh in business, but when Stowe's old flame (James Russo) steals their money, it descends into a series of rote confrontations, hostage-taking and credulity-straining shootouts, from which the women emerge unscathed.

The tone is neither sufficiently gritty nor self-aware to distract from the blandness of Johnathan Kaplan's direction and the flimsiness of the characters. Men are generally oafish; the exceptions being James Le Gros' young rancher, who falls for Andie MacDowell's faux Southern belle, and Dermot Mulroney as an avenging cowboy who catches Stowe's eye. Both actors have noticeably softer features than the other men in the cast.

If the opening nods towards *Unforgiven*, with its proactive prostitutes, the finale apes *The Wild Bunch*, with Russo's gnarly Kid Jarrett pretending to free the captive Mulroney but then, like a two-bit Mapache, killing him before his rescuers can react. Director Kaplan throws in a machine gun and slow-motion photography, but these allusions to past masters do *Bad Girls* no favours. **KG**

above: Andie MacDowell, Mary Stuart Masterson, Madeleine Stowe, Drew Barrymore

The Quick and the Dead

1995, Colour, 108 mins.

D: Sam Raimi. P: Joshua Donen, Patrick Markey, Allen Shapiro (TriStar Pictures). W: Simon Moore. Ph: Dante Spinotti. M: Alan Silvestri. St: Sharon Stone (Ellen), Gene Hackman (Herod), Russell Crowe (Cort), Leonardo DiCaprio (Kid), Tobin Bell (Dog Kelly)

"There's no rule against ladies. It's just that women can't shoot for shit."

Ellen, a female gunfighter, rides into Redemption, where an unbridled atmosphere prevails for its annual quick-draw tournament. Herod, outlaw turned despot, is the man to beat. Although there is a substantial pot of money for the winner, Ellen's vengeful aim is focused on Herod himself, who was responsible for her father's death years before.

Sam Raimi pays blatant homage to Sergio Leone. Close-ups and deep focus are liberally employed; time is stretched during the gunfights to manufacture tension; the use of flashbacks, which gradually reveal Ellen's motive, also recalls Leone's oeuvre. Raimi's emulation of the Italian aesthetic feels sincere, but he falls short in terms of dramatic punch. Ellen's grudge against Herod, for instance, is too easy to second-guess, rendering its final revelation somewhat redundant.

Momentum is maintained by the interplay among a well-chosen cast of rising stars and seasoned veterans. The cocky yet affable Leonardo DiCaprio plays Herod's illegitimate son, determined to win the respect of a father lacking in empathy. Gene Hackman displays the same monomaniacal energy as he had in *Unforgiven*, while Russell Crowe sensibly underplays the part of Cort, an ex-acolyte of Herod's, now a preacher, forced to participate in the contest against his will. Sharon Stone, for her part, apes the beady-eyed stare and inscrutable mien of Clint Eastwood, although she is not above using feminine wiles. This is the film's vision of empowerment: Stone/Ellen de-emphasises her femininity for the gunfight scenes, but plays it up elsewhere to advance her cause.

Ellen's violation of gender rules invites mockery at first. The barkeep tells her to go next door with the other whores, only to find his stool kicked out from under him. Apart from a subdued attraction to Cort, she is, to all intents and purposes, just another shootist, albeit one who shows compassion for her victims. Only the zeal with which she cuts down Herod's filthiest henchman, who has sexually abused an adolescent girl, can perhaps be read in terms of gender politics.

Although there are perfunctory asides about the role of women in the West – and the western – little is done to flesh out the historical/cultural context. Raimi's film feels less like the culmination of the feminist struggle of the '70s and '80s than it does a glib fantasy; in his western world the female is, indeed, more deadly than the male. **CH**

Ellen (Sharon Stone) proves her mettle in a man's world.

Jane Got a Gun

2016, Colour, 98 mins.

D: Gavin O'Connor. P: Terry Dougas, Aleen Keshishian, Scott LaStaiti, Natalie Portman, Mary Regency Boies, Zack Schiller, Scott Steindorff (1821 Pictures, Boies/Schiller Film Group, Scott Pictures, Straight Up Films, Unanimous Pictures, Handsomecharlie Films, WeatherVane Productions). W: Brian Duffield, Anthony Tambakis, Joel Edgerton, Brian Duffield (story). Ph: Mandy Walker. M: Marcello De Francisci, Lisa Gerrard. St: Natalie Portman (Jane Hammond), Joel Edgerton (Dan Frost), Ewan McGregor (John Bishop), Noah Emmerich (Bill Hammond), Boyd Holbrook (Vic Owen)

"Whatever happens, I'm going to put my face to it."

Nurtured by Natalie Portman through sundry vicissitudes (changes of personnel, script revisions, release delays), this story of hardship and revenge is perhaps something she should have nurtured for even longer, into middle age, the better to render the ravages to which her character has been subjected. While Portman evinces raw trauma and maternal anguish forcefully enough, steeliness rests uneasily on her slender frame; austerity scarcely scours those porcelain-perfect features.

When her husband returns wounded from an encounter with the Bishop gang, Jane deposits their child with a neighbour and solicits the assistance of her old flame, Dan Frost, to defend the ranch against the pursuers. Amid mutual recriminations and the gradual clearing of emotional debris, they prepare for the invaders (led by a black-mustached Ewan McGregor, relishing his villainous duties). Dan makes an embittered and somewhat reluctant Shane; Jane seemingly keen to demonstrate that a woman can be the equal of a man.

To the extent that the film allows her to, that is. For all her resourcefulness she remains tethered to familiar gender roles – forlorn prostitute (coerced into that profession by Bishop); homemaker; object of dispute between competing males.

Moreover, she is reliant upon men for her deliverance, such that claims advanced by some observers that the film is a feminist critique fall wide of the mark.

A straightforward, even slight, story is given an ungainly structure, with a number of expository flashbacks disrupting narrative flow. These mainly concern Jane and Dan's pre-Civil War romance – painted in glowing tones as a kind of prelapsarian idyll. Especially during the latter stages, when the duo wait in the dark for the Bishops' assault, the perspective wavers between them, both diluting tension and diverting dramatic emphasis from Jane. It makes this as much a story of male redemptive violence – in other words, just another western – as it is a testament to female resolve. One can sympathise with Jane's point that "other people's tales", not just those of men, deserve to be heard.

Unfortunately her story, much changed from the first treatment, simply isn't very interesting, and does little to correct the genre's traditional gender imbalance. Perhaps if original director Lynne Ramsay had stayed on board, the potential for a feminist vision of a woman fighting her own battles would have been realised. **KG**

Index

Page references in **bold** refer exclusively to illustrations, though pages referenced as text entries may also feature relevant illustrations.

Index

ALSO AVAILABLE FROM FAB PRESS...

ANY GUN CAN PLAY
THE ESSENTIAL GUIDE TO EURO-WESTERNS

Written by Kevin Grant, with a foreword by Franco Nero.

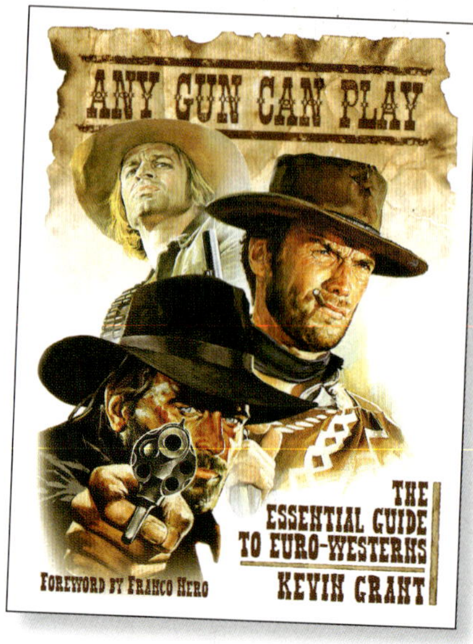

The worldwide success of Sergio Leone's 'Dollars' trilogy in the '60s sparked a gold rush, as a legion of European filmmakers – many of whom shared the get-rich-quick mentality of Leone's mercenary anti-heroes – followed the master's lead to create some of the wildest westerns ever made.

Cynical and stylish, bloody and baroque, Euro-westerns replaced straight-shooting sheriffs and courageous cowboys with amoral adventurers, whose murderous methods would shock the heroes of Hollywood westerns. These films became box-office sensations around the world, and their influence can still be felt today.

Any Gun Can Play puts the phenomenon into perspective, exploring the films' wider reaches, their recurrent themes, characters, quirks and motifs. It examines Euro-westerns in relation to their American ancestors and the mechanics of the Italian popular film industry, and spotlights the unsung actors, directors and other artists who subverted the 'code' of the western and dragged it into the modern age.

Based on years of research backed up by interviews with many of the genre's leading lights, including actors **Franco Nero**, **Giuliano Gemma** and **Gianni Garko**, writer **Sergio Donati**, and directors **Sergio Sollima** and **Giuliano Carnimeo**, ***Any Gun Can Play*** will satisfy both connoisseurs and the curious.

Complete with a foreword by Euro-western legend Franco Nero, this stunningly illustrated reference guide takes aim at the lingering notion that the genre has little to offer beyond the 'Dollars' films and a fistful of others, exposing the full, vibrant history of the Euro-western.

- **WHO'S WHO IN EURO-WESTERNS**
  A biographical A-Z of the most important and prolific actors, directors, composers, etc.
- **EURO-WESTERN FILMOGRAPHY**
  A chronological listing of European westerns.
- **FOREWORD BY FRANCO NERO**
  The star of many great Euro-westerns, including **Django**, **Keoma**, **Compañeros**, **Texas Adios**, **Massacre Time** and more.
- **64 PAGES IN FULL COLOUR**
  A spectacular selection of Euro-western posters, film stills and lobby cards.

www.fabpress.com

FAB PRESS

Quality Books for Cult Connoisseurs